NATIVE PEOPLES

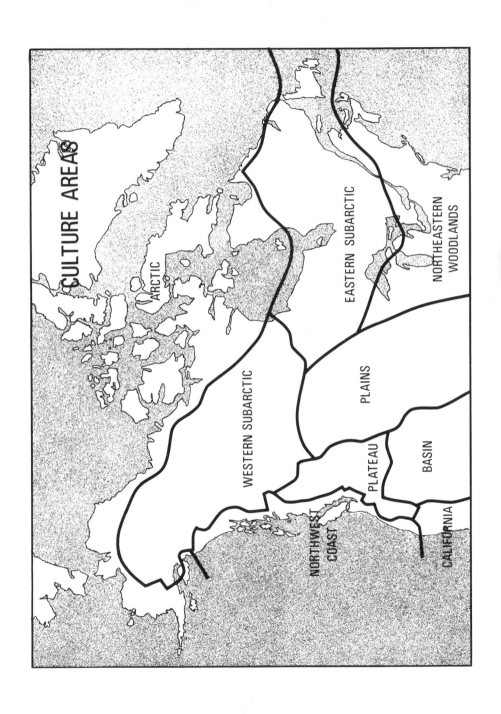

CULTURE AREAS

ARCTIC

WESTERN SUBARCTIC

EASTERN SUBARCTIC

NORTHEASTERN WOODLANDS

PLAINS

PLATEAU

BASIN

NORTHWEST COAST

CALIFORNIA

NATIVE PEOPLES:

The Canadian Experience

Second Edition

Edited by

R. Bruce Morrison

and

C. Roderick Wilson

With love and gratitude to our parents –
who put up with a lot!

Robert N. Morrison
Gladys E. Morrison
J. Charles Wilson
A. Marie Wilson

Canadian Cataloguing in Publication Data

Main entry under title:
Native peoples: the Canadian experience
2nd ed.

Includes bibliographical references and index.
ISBN 0-7710-6511-6

1. Indians of North America – Canada. 2. Inuit – Canada.
I. Morrison, R. Bruce. II. Wilson, C. Roderick.

E78.C2N389 1995   971′.00497   C94-932019-6

Maps drawn by Sharon Abbott and Carl O. Grichen
Printed and bound in Canada

McClelland & Stewart Inc.
The Canadian Publishers
481 University Avenue
Toronto, Ontario
M5G 2E9

1 2 3 4 5   99 98 97 96 95

CONTENTS

ACKNOWLEDGEMENTS

A scholarly effort reaches completion only with the dedication and co-operation of more people than could possibly be mentioned. So while we mention only a few, our appreciation extends to all who contributed in myriad ways.

The contributors to this volume have endured a great deal of editorial constraint and comment from us. Yet they still managed to produce manuscripts of exceptional quality. We thank them.

The excellent maps in this book were produced by Sharon Abbott and Carl O. Grichen of Edmonton.

This book could never have come to fruition without the generous institutional support provided by Athabasca University and the University of Alberta.

The excellent editorial advice and encouragement offered by the staff of McClelland & Stewart throughout the preparation and revision of the second edition are much appreciated. We also appreciate our publisher's patience! Thanks also to Richard Tallman for his thoughtful and thorough copy editing. His excellent work significantly enhanced the book.

Our agent, Joanne Kellock, also deserves a vote of thanks for her support and encouragement.

Our wives, Joyce Morrison and Keithal Wilson, were always there when we really needed them, and that's not always easy.

The many Native persons and groups whose co-operation made these chapters possible are gratefully acknowledged.

CONTRIBUTORS

Margaret Seguin Anderson (Ph.D., Michigan) is the Chair of the program in First Nations Studies at the University of Northern British Columbia, as well as the Regional Coordinator for the university's northwest region. Among her publications are an edited book, *The Tsimshian: Images of the Past, Views for the Present* (1984) and a monograph describing Tsimshian feasts, *Interpretive Contexts for Traditional and Current Coast Tsimshian Feasts* (1985). She is continuing to do research with Tsimshian people, focusing currently on the names that are central in the feast system.

Michael Asch (Ph.D., Columbia) is Professor of Anthropology at the University of Alberta. He was adviser to the Dene during the Berger Inquiry. Among his publications are a contribution to *Handbook of North American Indians* (vol. 6), a book, *Home and Native Land* (1988), and a monograph, *Kinship and the Drum Dance in a Northern Dene Community* (1988).

Mary Druke Becker (Ph.D., Chicago) is Research Associate at the Iroquois Indian Museum in Howes Cave, New York. Her research activities have focused on Iroquoian culture, particularly its ethnohistory. She is author of a number of articles and was associate editor of *The History and Culture of Iroquois Diplomacy: An Interdisciplinary Guide to the Treaties of the Six Nations and Their League* (1985). She is presently writing a book about mid-eighteenth-century Mohawk and Oneida leadership.

Jennifer S.H. Brown (Ph.D., Chicago) is Professor of History at the University of Winnipeg. As an anthropologist specializing in ethnohistory her work has focused on the Canadian fur trade. *Strangers in Blood* (1980) dealt with the significance of Native families in the fur trade. More recently she co-edited, with Jacqueline Peterson, *The New Peoples: Being and Becoming Metis in North America* (1985).

Ernest S. Burch, Jr. (Ph.D., Chicago) is Research Associate, Department of Anthropology, Smithsonian Institution. For the past thirty years he has pursued his interest in the macrosociology of foraging peoples through ethnographic and historical studies of early historic Eskimo

9

populations. He is author of *The Eskimos* (1988), in addition to many technical studies based on his research.

Sarah A. Carter (Ph.D., Manitoba) is Associate Professor of History at the University of Calgary. Her publications include *Lost Harvests: Prairie Indian Reserve Farmers and Government Policy* (1990). Her present research interests focus on the interplay of gender, race, ethnicity, and the colonization of the Canadian West.

Julie Cruikshank (Ph.D., British Columbia) is Associate Professor of Anthropology at the University of British Columbia. For more than a decade she lived in the Yukon Territory, where she worked with the Yukon Native Language Centre recording oral histories and life stories with Tlingit and Athapaskan elders. Her books include *Life Lived like a Story* (1990) and *Dan Dha Ts' edenintth'e / Reading Voices* (1991).

Hugh A. Dempsey (LL.D., Calgary) retired in 1991 as Associate Director of the Glenbow Museum in Calgary after thirty years with the organization. He is the author and editor of several books relating to Indians and western Canadian history, including *Crowfoot, Chief of the Blackfeet* (1972); *Red Crow, Warrior Chief* (1980); and *Big Bear, The End of Freedom* (1984). In recognition of his work with Native people, he was awarded the Order of Canada and an honorary doctorate from the University of Calgary. He is an honorary chief of the Blood tribe.

Harvey A. Feit (Ph.D., McGill) is Professor of Anthropology at McMaster University. He has written on the historical and contemporary culture and economy of the James Bay Cree of Quebec, and on their social and political efforts to resist domination by the state. Recent publications include "The Construction of Algonquian Hunting Territories" (1991) and "The Enduring Pursuit" (1994). Since 1972 he has served as an adviser to the James Bay Cree and other indigenous organizations on issues related to self-governance, land claims, and subsistence hunting.

John E. Foster (Ph.D., Alberta) is Professor of History at the University of Alberta. His research interests focus upon the pre-1870 Canadian West with an emphasis on the history of Metis peoples. He is the author of numerous scholarly articles.

Elizabeth Furniss is a Ph.D. candidate at the University of British Columbia. She has conducted ethnographic and ethnohistoric research on the Shuswap and Carrier Indians, and her scholarly interests include theories of knowledge, social and cultural change, and Indian–non-Native relations in Canada. She is the author of *Victims of Benevolence: Discipline and Death at the Williams Lake Residential School* (1992), as well as two high school textbooks on Carrier culture and history.

Douglas Hudson (Ph.D., Alberta) is Assistant Professor of Anthropology at Fraser Valley Community College in British Columbia. He has worked as an adviser for the Carrier, Okanagan, and the Nisga'a Indians of British Columbia.

Eleanor Leacock (Ph.D., Columbia) was Professor of Anthropology at the City College, City University of New York before her recent death. In addition to her research on the Montagnais-Naskapi, her scholarly interests focused on issues in urban anthropology, applied anthropology, and the cross-cultural study of women. Among her significant publications she co-edited, with Nancy Lurie, *North American Indians in Historical Perspective* (1971).

Peter Macnair (B.A., British Columbia) is Curator of Ethnology, British Columbia Provincial Museum. As curator, Mr. Macnair has been actively involved with Native communities both in doing ethnographic research and in the establishment of community museums. In addition, he has prepared a number of exhibits, including "The Legacy" (Edinburgh Festival, 1980). His scholarly publications have focused on Northwest Coast material culture, art, and artisans. He has also written about the Kwakwa̲ ka̲'wakw winter dances.

John S. Matthiasson (Ph.D., Cornell) is Professor of Anthropology at the University of Manitoba. His own primary fieldwork has been among the Inuit of northern Baffin Island, but he has directed extensive work by students among First Nations and settler populations in the northern prairie provinces. He is presently conducting research with the Icelandic Canadian communities of Manitoba. Topical interests are cultural/social change and applied anthropology. He is the author of *Living on the Land: Change among the Inuit of Baffin Island* (1992).

Virginia P. Miller (Ph.D., California) is Associate Professor in the Department of Sociology and Anthropology at Dalhousie University. She is presently preparing an ethnohistorical monograph on the Yuki people of northern California and is working toward a monograph on the Micmac people of the Maritime provinces.

R. Bruce Morrison (Ph.D., Alberta) is Adjunct Professor of Anthropology at the University of Alberta. His applied and scholarly interests have taken him to the Caribbean, Southeast Asia, South Asia, and Canada. Most recently he has conducted applied, ethnohistorical, and ethnographic research in Nepal. In 1994 he retired from Athabasca University to write and do development consulting for groups concerned with indigenous knowledge and social forestry. He is also finishing a book on the Expedition Sherpas of Nepal.

Robin Ridington (Ph.D., Harvard) is Professor of Anthropology at the University of British Columbia. He has done fieldwork with the Dunne-za since 1964. Among his publications on them are *Trail to Heaven: Knowledge and Narrative in a Northern Native Community* (1988) and *Little Bit Know Something: Stories in a Language of Anthropology* (1991).

C. Roderick Wilson (Ph.D., Colorado) is Associate Professor at the University of Alberta. He has done anthropological research among the Navajo and Papago of the American Southwest, the Cree and Metis of Alberta, and Waorani of Ecuador. His theoretical interests are related to questions of cultural change.

Carl Urion (Ph.D., Alberta) is Professor of Anthropology at the University of Alberta. His research interests have focused on the study of Algonquian languages. He is co-editor of the *Canadian Journal of Native Education.*

PART I
Introduction

CHAPTER 1
On the Study of Native Peoples

R. Bruce Morrison and C. Roderick Wilson

National attention has in recent years frequently been given to such issues as Aboriginal claims, unfulfilled treaty promises, and the constitutional status of Natives. As a result one often hears questions such as: "Just what do Native people want?" or, "Why don't we simply get rid of the reserves?"

Such questions reveal that most Canadians have some interest in Indians, but they share stereotypes that are not well founded, show little appreciation for the role of Native peoples in our history, and do not understand the basis for Native claims. Canadians are not necessarily ill-disposed toward Natives, but there is currently little basis for real understanding.

Many Canadians revel in a national self-image as a mosaic – each ethnic group maintaining its distinctive character while still being essential to the whole. The image has some validity, but it seriously underplays pressures toward cultural conformity, especially at the regional level. How many immigrant children have been ridiculed because they spoke

French or English with an accent? How many of us learned more British history in school than Canadian? Being Ukrainian is marvellous, if it is limited to matters primarily aesthetic: grandmothers dyeing Easter eggs, teenagers folk-dancing, and so on. At this level, being Native is fully acceptable, if rather quaint: totem poles and Inuit prints are widely recognized as striking art forms and a few chiefs in Plains-style regalia dress up a parade. Unlike other groups, Natives are not content simply to be Canadians or even to be hyphenated Canadians. They generally recognize that they are in Canada and are necessarily Canadians, but they also insist that they are first of all Indian – or Inuit, or Metis. In so doing they place themselves beyond the experience and understanding of most Canadians.

The Book's Approach

This book is based on three assertions. First, an understanding of Native peoples must start from an appreciation of Aboriginal society as it existed and as it continues, in its own terms and not as an appendage to that larger conglomeration of peoples and provinces that we call Canada. It is a fundamental anthropological premise that cultures are best understood, that behaviour is meaningful, within their own frameworks. One cannot comprehend, far less evaluate or judge, behaviour grounded in one cultural system by the standards of another. Much that follows is therefore an attempt to understand Canadian Native societies as, first of all, *Native* societies.

Second, any explication of either the objective conditions of contemporary Canadian Native peoples or the perceptions they have of themselves and of their place in the larger Canadian society must also take into account the history of relationships between Indians and Canadian society – particularly in its governmental aspects. Native societies have not existed within the last century simply as Native societies, but to greater or lesser extents as parts of Canadian society: Natives have become tribal peoples encapsulated within a colonial state. That the life of Canadian Indians is defined by the Indian Act – legislation enacted by the federal government without consultation, amendable and enforceable without Indian consent – unambiguously indicates that the subjects of the legislation have literally been created by government. From this point of view, status Indians are Canadian in a way that none of the rest of us are. Ironically, the life of non-Inuit Native people declared by the Indian Act not to be Indians (the Metis and non-status Indians) has largely come to be defined by the absence of that legislation. This

PLATE 1.1. Dr. C.M. Barbeau, Quebec's first university-trained anthropologist, transcribing Native folksongs. Courtesy of the Canadian Museum of Civilization.

equally speaks of their embeddedness within Canadian society, of inextricable links and connections.

Third, the scholars who here present their views of Native society and history are not simply recording devices mechanically reproducing data to which they have been exposed. They are people – who happen to be scientists, who find themselves in interactive situations with other people who happen to be Indians. The resulting analysis is in this sense not an objective reality but a product shaped by shared experiences. This interaction is influenced by the nature of the Native community and also by the anthropologist's background. Most immediately, that background includes a particular kind of professional training and an interest in specific kinds of theoretical problems. It also includes a personal, social, and cultural background. All these affect research in numerous and subtle ways. Ultimately, anthropological analysis is a creative act. By emphasizing the human elements in the research process we are not suggesting whimsy or speculation. The point, rather, is that critical rigour is obtained not by mechanizing the fieldwork process but by openly recognizing its interactive nature: greater knowledge of the "subjective" factors tends to increase a study's validity and reliability.

This work is not encyclopedic, but it does discuss representative groups from each region of Canada. Not all that is known about each society is presented; each chapter most completely presents that aspect of the culture of particular interest to the author. Cumulatively, this allows the reader some sense of the richness and complexity of Native life. Finally, each author examines Native life from one particular theoretical perspective. Cumulatively, the reader acquires a sense of the current state of Canadian anthropology.

It goes almost without saying that the authors believe that efforts to further the public understanding and awareness of the ways of life of the Native peoples, of the history of relationships between autochthonous and immigrant peoples in Canada, and something of how various anthropological pictures of Aboriginal people are constructed, are all worthwhile goals in themselves. At a very practical level, the future of Canada for both Indians and non-Indians alike may well hinge on how well we have learned the lessons of our past.

Anthropological Concepts

This book is written for the general reader; it does not assume extensive knowledge either of Indians or of anthropology. Most concepts are explained as they arise, but some general comments may help. This book uses the notion of culture area as a general organizing principle – and the reader will note that each of the culture areas represented by Parts II to VIII begins with a brief overview chapter. Canada is a very large country, possessing diverse environments, and the Native population exhibits great variety. Nevertheless, within this spectrum of variability are regional similarities, and neighbouring groups tend to have features in common. This regional patterning of Aboriginal societies results from two major factors. First, primary food resources are regionally distributed: salmon is the prime resource in some areas, buffalo or moose in others, and so on. Since each is taken by techniques that have different social as well as technological requirements – some require communal activity, while others reward individual effort – regional patterns of subsistence developed. The second factor is that neighbouring groups, especially ones that inhabit essentially the same kind of environment, tend to influence each other. As ideas and techniques spread from one group to another the regional patterns tend to become intensified: while each group remained unique, areal patterns of life emerged that persisted for millennia.

Regional patterns were not, however, simply the automatic response of people adjusting to a specific environment. New World prehistory was dynamic: populations moved from one region to another; major environmental changes occurred, as did technological and social innovation. Throughout, regional patterns developed, persisted, and changed.

Although European colonization disrupted Aboriginal patterns, the disruptions themselves were patterned areally. Various regions were contacted at different times, in differing ways, and by varying groups. The first sustained contacts for most Inuit were whalers, while on the west coast they were traders seeking sea otter pelts and on the east coast they were fishermen. Each group had different economic interests that strongly affected relationships with local Natives. Furthermore, the interests of all three contrasted strongly with those of Europeans who penetrated the interior of the continent in a fur trade that required major inputs of labour and material goods by the indigenous population. Although colonialism in whatever guise tends to produce parallel patterns of events, and although Canada's recent past has featured numerous national events that affected all Native people, much Native-European interaction has had a decidedly regional quality.

Having argued that it is sensible to think of Indians in regional terms, it is necessary to warn against taking the concept of culture area too literally. "Culture area" is only a generalization, an indication of central tendency: each group also possesses unique practices. Arguments about boundaries (are the Micmac really Eastern Woodland or Eastern Subarctic Indians?) are essentially spurious, giving to a line on the map a specificity that is not present in reality. This particular boundary could with equal logic be drawn north or south of the Micmac; we have chosen to run the line through them! A further danger of the culture-area concept is that it tends to shape our thinking, leading us to ignore other possibilities.

Culture areas are a set of mental boxes. Some boxes are necessary to do anthropology, to attempt to explain human behaviour, or to talk about anything. We cannot forget, however, that we ourselves have created the mental boxes: another set of such organizing categories would likely put things in a different perspective.

It is fairly clear that culture areas are mental constructs, not visible in the natural world. It is less obvious for seemingly more concrete realities, such as "tribe." At a nineteenth-century Blackfoot Sun Dance, for instance, one could have encountered virtually the entire tribe. Other groups that never gathered together or acted as political units, however, are also customarily spoken of as tribes. Further, as Leacock points out, the Montagnais and Naskapi are virtually identical except that the latter hunt caribou. Because of other equally restricted differences, separate tribes have been created. The concept of tribe is thus quite loose: it can refer to people who think of themselves as a clearly identified political unit and to people who do not; it can refer merely to people designated a tribe by ethnographers on the basis of common language and generally similar behaviour.

Even with this flexible understanding, it is tempting to think of tribes too narrowly. Partly this stems from the European heritage – a Europe of nation-states and fixed boundaries – of those writing about Natives. Tribal boundaries often were permeable, with joint-use areas between more central zones, and fluid, as tribal fortunes changed. Maps of Indian societies usually are not dated, implying a timeless fixity to the boundaries; chapters on the Iroquois, Cree, and Blackfoot indicate otherwise.

In conclusion, the argument here is not that anthropological concepts are deficient. Rather, the world is a complex place where human behaviour does not come prepackaged. In attempting to explain behaviour, anthropologists have devised various concepts, some of which have proven to be useful, all of which are limited, and none of which provides final answers.

On Doing Anthropology: Agreements and Disagreements

This is a book about Native people; it is necessarily also a book about Canada. Further, it is a book about anthropology, or at least about how some anthropologists work and think, and the analytic frameworks are anthropological. As such, they differ from ones used by sociologists, political scientists, or economists. One should *not* think of one of these disciplines as right and the others wrong. Rather, they present complementary perspectives, different windows into the complex reality of human life. Similarly, anthropologists have diverse perspectives. Some anthropologists focus on the words that people use, others on how they make a living, still others on the rise or fall of their numbers. All are potentially useful topics of investigation that add to our knowledge of how societies and cultures survive.

A more troublesome matter arises. At times Native people are in profound disagreement with what has been written about them. Sometimes this is not a matter of differing perspectives but of the researcher's being wrong. There are a number of ways in which this can occur: a linguist analysing an unwritten language once spent hundreds of hours working with an informant who had a speech impediment. The resultant analysis was correct – but only for that informant. This is a case of sampling error, in principle a simple matter to avoid. But since anthropologists may well have good reasons for working intensively with very few people in a community, it is a recurrent problem. (In a village of 100 people, how many can speak personally of events that took place sixty years ago?) Or what if the anthropologist is the victim of a practical joke but never discovers it? What if (s)he simply misunderstands what happens? The anthropologist should validate all information – but errors can occur.

Error may be difficult to determine. The earliest substantial sources of information on the Chipewyan, for instance, are the journals of the fur trader Samuel Hearne. In numerous ways he pictures their women as drudges, the victims of abusive and domineering men. Since this seems not to fit what is known of more recent Chipewyan society or of other boreal forest people at the time of first contact, what should be made of his account? Was he misinterpreting what he saw because of his European background and his unfamiliarity with the semi-nomadic hunting and trapping life? Or was his account essentially correct, but he happened to be with a small band that, in taking up a fur-trading life, had dropped much of traditional Chipewyan values and was now composed of social deviants? Or was Hearne describing behaviour typical for the Chipewyan of that time? Contemporary Chipewyan, women in particular, may well take umbrage at anthropologists and historians who accept Hearne's account, but the question is not capable of definitive resolution.

In other instances where Natives object to anthropological interpretations, it seems parallel to the disagreement between two scholars. A classic case would be those who object to archaeological accounts, particularly to the notion that Amerindians ultimately derive from Siberian populations or that there have been relatively recent shifts of Aboriginal peoples from one region to another. These accounts are seen to be in opposition to the traditions of the elders, to the view that they have occupied this land from the time of creation. At a time when Indians are increasingly turning to the elders for leadership, an apparent challenge from archaeologists cannot be tolerated. The position taken here is that the two kinds of accounts regarding the past do not confront each other because they cannot. They are different kinds of truth and both can have relevance to contemporary Native people.

A related feature of anthropological writing that Native peoples (and others) frequently find unsettling is that truth seems to change through time. It seems self-evident that truth, particularly scientific truth, should be immutable. However, new data continuously arise, making necessary the re-evaluation of previous conclusions. Second, conclusions are always tentative because they are interpretive. Folk explanations, of course, also change, but not so visibly, nor are the contradictions sudden.

Indians have criticized some anthropology as irrelevant to their needs. Mandelbaum's *The Plains Cree*, the standard work on that group, presents their life during the buffalo-hunting days of the late nineteenth century, as remembered by elderly people in the 1930s. Nowhere does it mention the trauma of everyday life on the reserves of that period. For some, a political and economic analysis of reserve life would seem more to the point. In Mandelbaum's defence it must be noted that his fieldwork could not have been duplicated at a later date and that one's sense of relevance can change. Many contemporary Cree have found the book to be a treasure house. As Hudson points out, he was recently hired by an Okanagan band to collect precisely this kind of material. One cannot be sure which book would have been more relevant, the one he wrote or the one his critics wanted.

A final criticism is that some ideas propounded by anthropologists have actively harmed Native people, a charge made both by Indians and by anthropologists. The most obvious examples involve acculturation theory. The general argument is that in focusing so exclusively on how Indian culture changes to accommodate to Euro-Canadian culture, anthropologists have unwittingly supported the ideas that such change is inevitable and that ultimately Indians will be totally assimilated. The issues are complex, but some preliminary comments may be helpful. First, whatever the merits or faults of acculturation theory, its practitioners as a group were actively involved in working with and for Native peoples. Second, neither scholars nor Natives can afford tests of orthodoxy. The issue should not be whether a conclusion is "politically correct" but whether the analysis is sound. Interestingly, good analysis seems to lead to anti-assimilationist conclusions. Third, anthropologists, like nuclear physicists, cannot guarantee that their work will not be misused.

One means of minimizing the misuse of anthropology is to increase the involvement of the Native community in the process of doing anthropology. Several chapters touch on this, but Macnair's is most explicit in speaking of training Native people in anthropology. Macnair makes it clear, however, that not all community members saw this as relevant to their interests. Increasingly, though, it has been seen as important to the community in terms of its own internal dynamics; it is particularly important to the process of reviving pride in being Indian.

Attention has been given recently to the relevance of anthropology in the external relations of Native communities. Other chapters mention this, but Feit provides most detail. When threatened by proposed development, the James Bay Cree turned to him to provide expert witness in court. They were able to do so because they had an understanding of this research. It was not that the Cree acquired his academic, ecological understanding of their life, but that his acquisition of their understanding of hunting necessarily involved communicating to them in their terms something of what he was doing.

This discussion has focused on the anthropologist-Indian relationship. The anthropological audience also includes other anthropologists, students, the general public, and, at times, client agencies. The concerns expressed here have also had an impact, in somewhat different forms, on these audiences: the issues are not merely specific to Native peoples; they are general.

In summary, anthropologists have always been concerned with accuracy, or more technically, reliability and validity. This has been one of the factors in the search for new methods and new ideas and in the introspective analysis of past problems. Our current understandings are hopefully neither a defence nor a rejection of the past, but a building upon successful parts of the past. Anthropology started in the belief that it was possible to comprehend other cultures if one sought an insider's understanding and that this was possible through objectively recording material obtained by the technique of participant-observation. The insider's viewpoint remains a valid ideal, but we are now more aware of its unattainability. Participant-observation is still a basic technique, but we no longer assume that our presence does not alter what happens. The community being studied is not simply there as an object, but actively and purposively interacts with the researcher. Writing of one's field experiences, including emotional responses to the very demanding task of fieldwork, demands both courage and personal insight, but it creates a more human ethnography and allows the reader to judge more fully its merit.

This volume, then, is both a discussion of some current perspectives on Canadian Native peoples and a comment on the scholarly enterprise itself.

CHAPTER 2

First Nations Prehistory and Canadian History

C. Roderick Wilson and Carl Urion

Beginnings

If we were to peer through the mists of time to the Age of the Ancestors, the First Americans, what would we see? Probably we would see a small group of people, about fifteen or twenty. At times they might be joined by people from other bands, but usually that was about the right number of people to live together. Mostly they lived near the sea. They might follow streams to places where it was easy to spear salmon or go inland to hunt deer or bear, or to gather berries on hillsides, but they were seldom far from water. They had spears and baskets, warm clothing and sleeping robes, and, especially in the winter, shelter from the Subarctic storms. But they moved frequently and did not have much else by way of physical possessions. [1]

What they mostly had was not things, but knowledge, the knowledge to find what was needed, that which was provided. Anthropologists for the most part would say that they had environmental knowledge (what do the land and sea provide and how can they be used?) and social knowledge (how do members of the group relate to each other in order to get things done?). Anthropologists might also state that the Ancestors themselves (to judge from their descendants) would have given primacy not to environmental knowledge or to social knowledge but to religious knowledge as being more fundamental.

In our view, however, the Ancestors (again inferring from their descendants' views) would have put it still differently. They would not have thought of hunting or gathering or even of knowledge as things unto themselves. They would not have thought of hunting as a specialized skill to be learned so much as an expression of the hunter's spirituality.

In sum, we are suggesting that: (1) just as contemporary Native people are the biological descendants of the Ancestors, and hence we can infer that the Ancestors had straight black hair, skin that tanned easily, and so on, so can we look to the traditional ways of thinking of Native people across the New World to get some sense of what their world view was; (2) the Ancestors were real people in time and space about whom we will never know many things but about whom some matters of importance and interest may be said; and (3) Native peoples and anthropologists frequently see things differently and speak about things with different vocabularies, but dialogue on these matters is both possible and important.

Native peoples have their own ways of speaking of beginnings. Tsimshian groups, for instance, consider that they are descended from an ancestress who was carried away and married by one or another supernatural (for example, grizzly or killer whale) in the form of a man, but who eventually returned to her homeland with her children. Such stories, among other things, define the nature of reality and (spiritual) power, the basis for relationships within the group, and the nature of relationships with external groups.

Just as we noted in the first chapter that one should not think of one academic discipline as right and the others wrong, so one should not think of one origin story as right and another wrong. For one thing, each story is told in its own vocabulary; the resulting conflicts in view are more apparent than real. For instance, Native elders commonly assert that the First Nations have been here forever, since the creation of the world. This view is seen as being in conflict with those of the archaeologists, some of whom place the original peopling of the New World as recently as 12,000 years ago. How does one relate the archaeological discourse of hypothetical carbon-dated years to the discourse of Aboriginal origin myths? One approach is to ask what even 12,000 years means, not in the scientific language of radiometric dating (where it seems almost as yesterday), but in the language of culture. What does 12,000 years mean in terms of the history of Western culture, the cultural frame for most of us? Two meaningful comparisons, of the many possible, would be to point out that the Judeo-Christian-Islamic tradition is usually seen to begin with Abraham, only some 4,000 years ago, or to point out that the proto-Indo-Europeans, the small horticultural group ancestral to speakers of modern languages ranging from Hindi and Russian in the East to Icelandic and Portuguese in Western Europe, began their migrations, as best as we can now reconstruct, some 8,000 years ago. In other words, the most recent suggested date for the inhabiting of North America is far more distant than most ancestral events in Western culture for which there is any glimmering of cultural memory. Thus, the Native elder and the archaeologist, in their different ways, seem to be saying much the same thing: 12,000 years ago is, in almost any sense, at the beginning of the world.

In the following sections we will discuss, without making exclusive truth-claims, first, what various kinds of anthropologists have to say about the original settling of the continent and about how Native societies developed in the millennia prior to European discovery, and second, some general issues from the history of Native–Euro-Canadian relationships that will help the reader form a context for the following chapters.

The Settling of the Continent

Viewpoints from Physical Anthropology

All humans are related, forming one species. But some of us are more alike and some are less alike. It is in this perspective that we use the term "Amerindian." It suggests that in general the Aboriginal inhabitants of North and South America are more like each other than they are like people deriving from elsewhere on the globe. This in turn implies that Amerindians have been here for a long time, long enough to become somewhat distinct from other peoples.

The perspective of relatedness also suggests, however, that Amerindians are more like people from eastern Asia than anywhere else. This does not prove that the long-distant ancestors of Native peoples came here from Asia, but it does suggest it as a strong possibility.

Even to a casual observer, Amerindians and people from eastern Asia share features that link them together and separate them from the rest of the world. People from both areas tend to have straight black hair, a lack of male-pattern baldness, and little facial or body hair; they have skin that tans easily, rarely have blue eyes, and may have epicanthic eye folds. Less visible traits linking these peoples include the Inca bone (the occipital bone at the back of the skull is divided in two, the smaller, upper portion being referred to as the Inca bone, in commemoration of its first being noticed by archaeologists working in Peru), and the Mongolian spot, a purplish spot about the size of a dollar coin on the skin at the base of the spine. Such a list could be expanded at some length. It is not that everyone in these populations has all these characteristics, but these heritable traits are found more or less frequently among these people and are not found among other peoples.

While the relative biological affinity of New World and East Asian peoples is visible to the layperson, we are not limited to the approach of simply listing points of genetic connectedness. For instance, large numbers of heritable traits, including non-visible characteristics such as blood proteins, can be treated mathematically to create an index of genetic similarity. While the specific numbers generated in such an approach depend on exactly which characteristics are included, such studies generally attempt to be broadly inclusive and typically conclude both that there are interesting variations within New World peoples and that they are linked more closely to eastern Asia than elsewhere. In fact, the people of the far northwestern part of North America are genetically closer to the people of Siberia than they are to the people of South America.

Ultimately, the question of New World origins must be placed in the context of human evolution generally. The present evidence is that North and South America, like Oceania and Australia, have been inhabited only by fully modern human beings. That is, the evolution of human beings took place primarily in Africa, secondarily in Asia and Europe, and not at all in the rest of the world. While this line of thought categorically concludes that the ancestors of Amerindians must have come here from somewhere, with respect to time it is vague; almost any time within the last 200,000 years or so would do.

Teeth have played a special role in the study of evolution (human and non-human alike) for two reasons. First, they tend more often than other parts of animal anatomy to be preserved. Second, they are evolutionarily conservative, that is, they tend to vary less within populations and to change more slowly over long periods of time than many other anatomical features.

This becomes relevant for us in a comparative study of tooth morphology by Christy Turner. He studied the shape of fossil teeth in museum collections around the world and also contemporary teeth. He found a small number of major types, including what he called the sinodont pattern, encompassing the prehistoric and contemporary peoples of China, northeastern Asia generally, and the New World. Within the sinodont pattern, he distinguished a number of sub-types. New World peoples divide into three sub-types: the Eskimoan peoples, the Athapaskans, and all other Aboriginal New World peoples. Each of these sub-types in turn is most closely associated with fossil populations coming from distinct areas of northeast Asia. The implication is that there were three separate migratory streams into the New World from that area, with the Eskimoans being the most recent, preceded by the Athapaskans, in turn preceded by the original stream.

In summing up the evidence from the sub-discipline of physical anthropology that relates to the question of the settling of the New World, one can firmly state that the ancestral populations came here from eastern Asia in what seems to any living person a very long time ago but in evolutionarily modern times. It can further be stated, though with less certainty, that they probably came over long periods of time in three separate streams of migration.

Viewpoints from Linguistic Anthropology

LANGUAGE CLASSIFICATION SYSTEMS
It has always been clear to people that some languages are closely related. A shared or similar vocabulary leads easily to the conclusion that there must be a shared past. The widespread existence of dialects suggests that contemporary languages might over time evolve into separate languages; the widespread existence of families of related languages suggests that processes of linguistic fission have been going on for a long time.

As early as 1786 Sir William Jones, a British colonial official in India, reported structural similarities between some European languages (by then common knowledge) and the Asian languages Sanskrit and Persian (at the time quite surprising). The idea that peoples who looked quite different and who had very different cultures might nevertheless share, at least in part, a common linguistic ancestry was electrifying.

In North America the first comprehensive attempt at classifying Aboriginal languages was made in 1891 by John Wesley Powell of the Bureau of American Ethnology. He classified the Aboriginal languages of North America into fifty-eight (later revised to fifty-one) different stocks. We can now see that his classification was very much a product of the times: there was virtually no information on some of the languages; he assumed that all Amerindian languages represented a single stage of evolutionary development and therefore ignored grammar as a factor in determining relationships; and, because the primary purpose of making the classification was to provide a basis for the placement of tribes on specific reservations, there was no particular interest in the degree of relationship but only in the fact of a relationship. In spite of these rather severe defects it is still regarded as a foundational, if conservative, statement. In the context of this particular discussion, it is a minimalist statement about the past.

In 1921 Edward Sapir constructed a classification that dramatically reduced the number of stocks to six. Although much linguistic work had been done in the intervening thirty years, and Sapir himself had by then worked on seventeen Native languages, the difference between the two classifications lies less in the quality of analysis than in the fact that Powell was a "splitter" and Sapir was by inclination a "lumper" who was willing to go beyond the hard evidence and who had an eye on the grand sweep of historical processes. For instance, he classified Beothuk, an extinct language, as Algonquian; it may well have been, but we will never know this. He attempted to link the Na-Dene phylum to Indo-Chinese. He even suggested that Hokan-Siouan was the basic North American Indian language and implied that an ancestral proto-language might at some point be reconstructed.

This is not to suggest that Sapir was indifferent to the question of to what extent the suggested connections between various languages had been demonstrated. The 1929 version of his classification contains two separate lists. The first is the six-unit radical classification; the second is a more conservative grouping into twenty-three units. The premise for the second list was that by this date linguistic analysis had proceeded to the point where even the most conservative would now accept some linking of units listed separately by Powell; twelve of the twenty-three represent this kind of well-substantiated clumping.

Until recently the lists of Sapir and Powell more or less defined the parameters of the classificatory discussion. In 1986, Darnell noted that to an unfortunate extent linguists generally chose one list or another but that the field was now generally conservative in that there was growing insistence on thoroughly demonstrating relationships. Table 2.2 lists her sense of established linguistic groupings for Canadian languages.

This all changed in 1987 with Joseph H. Greenberg's radical proposal that there are three basic groupings in the New World: Eskimo-Aleut stretching across the Arctic rim from eastern Siberia to Greenland, Na-Dene running from central Alaska to Hudson Bay with outliers as far south as Arizona, and Amerind covering all the rest of North and South America.

C. Roderick Wilson and Carl Urion

Table 2.1
North American Linguistic Classifications

Sapir 1929-A	Sapir-B	Powell 1891
I. Eskimo-Aleut	Eskimo	Eskimo
II. Algonquian-Ritwan	*Algonquian-Ritwan	Algonquian, Beothukan, Wiyot, Yurok
	*Mosan	Wakashan, Chemakuan, Salish
	Kutenai	Kutenai
III. Na-Dene	*Tlingit-Athapaskan	Haida, Tlingit, Athapaskan
	Haida	
IV. Penutian	*California Penutian	Miwok, Costanoan, Yokuts, Maidu, Wintun
	*Oregon Penutian	Takelma, Coos (-Siuslaw), Yakonan, Kalapuya
	*Plateau Penutian	Waiilatpuan, Lutuamian, Sahaptin
	Chinook	Chinook
	Tsimshian	Tsimshian
	(Mexican Pen.)	—
V. Hokan-Siouan	*Hokan	Karok, Chimariko, Salinan, Yana, Pomo, Washo, Esselen, Yuman, Chumash
	*Coahuiltecan	Tonkawa, Karankawa, Coahuiltecan,
	*Tunican	Tunica, Atakapa, Chitimacha
	*Iroquois-Caddoan	Iroquois, Caddoan
	Yuki	Yuki
	Keres	Keres
	Timucua	Timucua
	Muskhogean	Muskhogean
	Siouan	Siouan, Yuchi
VI. Aztec-Tanoan	*Uto-Aztecan	Nahuatl, Pima, Shoshonean
	*Tanoan-Kiowan	Tanoan, Kiowa
	Zuni	Zuni

* Twelve units that Sapir considered to be accepted by most of his colleagues. The reduction of Powell's fifty-five units to twenty-three reflected the work of a generation of linguists, largely trained by Franz Boas. The further reduction to six units Sapir considered to be his own work.

Table 2.2
Languages and Language Families of Canada

Family	Language	In Canada	Outside Canada
		Number of Speakers	
Algonquian			
Eastern Branch	Abenaki	10	5
	Delaware	5–10	100
	Potawatomi	100	1,000
	Malecite	1,200	300
	Micmac	3–5,000	few
Cree	Cree	55,000	few
	Montagnais-Naskapi	5,000	none
Ojibway	Ojibway	30,000	10–20,000
	Odawa		
	Algonkin		
	Saulteaux		
Blackfoot	Blackfoot	4,000	1,000
Athapaskan	Tagish	5	none
	Sarcee	10	none
	Han	few	few
	Sekani	1–500	none
	Kaska	2–500	none
	Beaver	300	none
	Hare	600	none
	Dogrib	800	none
	Chilcotin	1,000	none
	Tahltan	100–1,000	none
	Tutchone	1,000	none
	Slave	1–2,000	none
	Kutchin	500	700
	Carrier	5,000	none
	Chipewyan	5,000	none
	Yellowknife	4–600	none
Eskimo-Aleut	Inupik	16,000	47,000
Haida	Haida	225	100
Tlingit	Tlingit	500	1,500

Table 2.2 continued:
Languages and Language Families of Canada

Family	Language	Number of Speakers In Canada	Outside Canada
Iroquoian	Onandaga	50–100	50
	Oneida	200	50
	Cayuga	360	10
	Seneca	25	400
	Mohawk	2,000	1,000
	Tuscarora	7	40
Kutenai	Kutenai	200	25
Salishan			
Interior	Lillooet	1,000	none
	Okanagan	1,000	none
	Thompson	1,000	none
	Shuswap	1–2,000	none
Coastal	Sechelt	10	none
	Squamish	12	none
	Straits	30	30
	Bella Coola	200	none
	Comox	400	none
	Halkomelem	500	none
	Songish	few	none
	Semiahmo	few	none
	Cowichan	500	none
	Pentlatch	?	none
Siouan	Dakota	5,000	15,000
	Assiniboine (Stoney)	1,000	none
Tsimshian	Southern Tsimshian	5	none
	Nass-Gitksan, Coastal Tsimshian	3,500	200
Wakashan			
Northern Branch	Haisla	100–1,000	none
	Heiltsuk	300	none
	Kwakwala	1,000	none
Southern Branch	Nitinat	60	none
	Nootka	1–2,000	none

The first two groupings are not new and are fairly conventional; the proposal of an Amerind macrofamily is startling (as is including Eskimo-Aleut in another macrofamily, Eurasiatic, which also includes stocks as diverse as Chukchi-Kamchatkan, Altaic, Uralic, and Indo-European).

Table 2.3
Amerind Linguistic Relationships

Language Family	Language	Form	Meaning
Afro-Asiatic	Proto-Afro-Asiatic	*mig	"to suck, breast, udder"
Indo-European	Proto-Indo-Euro.	*meig-	"to milk"
Uralic	Proto-Finno-Ugric	*malke	"breast"
Dravidian	Tamil	melku	"to chew"
Eskimo-Aleut	Central Yupik	melug-	"to suck"
Amerind	Proto-Amerind	*maliq'a	"to swallow, throat"
Almosan	Halkomelem	melqw	"throat"
	Kwakwala	m'IXw-'id	"to chew food for baby"
	Kutenai	u'mqolh	"to swallow'
Penutian	Chinook	miqw-tan	"cheek"
	Takelma	mulk'	"to swallow"
	Tfaltik	milq	"to swallow"
	Mixe	amu'ul	"to suck"
Hokan	Mohave	malyage	"throat"
	Walapei	malqi	"throat, neck"
	Akwa'ala	milqi	"neck"
Chibchan	Cuna	murki-	"to swallow"
Andean	Quechua	malq'a	"throat"
	Aymara	malyq'a	"to swallow, throat"
Macro-Tucanoan	Iranshe	moke'i	"neck"
Equatorial	Guamo	mirko	"to drink"
Macro-Carib	Surinam	e'moki	"to swallow"
	Faai	mekeli	"nape of the neck"
	Kaliana	imukulali	"throat"

This etymology illustrates connections between eight of eleven Amerind sub-families and ties to the Eurasiatic/Nostratic grouping. Adapted from Greenberg and Ruhlen (1992) and used with the permission of *Scientific American*.

Greenberg's macrofamilies are startling for at least two reasons. One is that they link geographically distant peoples whose separation would have taken place well over 20,000 years ago. The other reason is methodological: instead of a painstaking point-by-point analysis of the sound, word, and grammatical sub-systems, comparing two languages at a time, repeating the process for possibly numerous diads, and eventually reconstructing a hypothesized proto-language, Greenberg looks at words only and does so for large numbers of languages at the same time. Table 2.3 provides an illustration of the kind of relationships he posits. His work is controversial; it also points to a far horizon.

IMPLICATIONS OF TYPOLOGICAL AND DISTRIBUTIONAL DATA

In considering the implications for us of the various classification systems and the distribution of language families across the New World map, let us start with some of the points that linguists agree on.

One such point is that the map of Canada is virtually covered by only three language families. Most Canadian Natives, and the vast majority in southern Canada east of the Rockies, are members of the Algonquian family. Cree and Ojibway are very closely related, implying very recent separation; Blackfoot is more distantly related, implying a somewhat earlier independent history. Much of northwestern Canada and Alaska is occupied by Athapaskan speakers. Like the Algonquians, their general lack of diversity implies relatively recent occupation of much of their range. Their greatest linguistic diversity is found on the southeast coast of Alaska; an implication is that they spread from there into the Alaskan interior and thence eastward across northern Canada and that subsequently some groups moved southward, with some (ancestral to the Navajos and Apaches) reaching the American Southwest. The third family is Eskimo-Aleut, represented in Canada by Inupik (Inuktitut). It is an extreme case, a single language spread from northern Alaska across to eastern Greenland. Apart from any archaeological evidence, this is a strong indication of relatively recent occupation of the region.

The British Columbia coast stands out as the one region of Canada characterized by linguistic diversity. On principle, then, one would expect that the B.C. and Alaskan coasts were inhabited earlier than the other parts of Canada. This is entirely likely when one considers that parts of the coast were virtually the only regions in the country to escape glaciation, *if the continent generally was inhabited prior to the last Ice Age* (the Pleistocene). At this point we have moved to the controversial.

It should be noted that the controversy here is not really linguistic. It arises because the dominant archaeological model has the New World settled very quickly and very late (post-Pleistocene). Since for the most part linguists are more concerned with establishing relationships than with establishing how old the relationships are, this issue is not often considered.

We have already noted that on grounds relating to where the most linguistic diversity is to be found within their language family, the Eskimo-Aleut generally are thought to have reached their present distribution from points of origin on the Alaska coast. This is both orthodox linguistics and consistent with the standard archaeological view; it should also be noted that both groups are thought to be relatively late arrivals on the continent and that the point of origin of both would have been on the Beringian side of the Ice Age glaciers.

The point here is that the pattern of inferred historic dispersal presented by the Eskimo-Aleut and the Athapaskans is not exceptional but is very much the general pattern. In plotting the distribution of the likely centres of major Amerindian language phyla and language isolates, Gruhn (1988) notes that forty-two of forty-seven such centres are to be found in coastal regions, virtually all of them on the Pacific coast or on the Caribbean coast. In other words, the distributional evidence is that the original settlement of the Americas was along the coastal areas, with interior areas being settled later. The linguistic evidence does not support the notion of people funnelling into an empty North American continent from a northern corridor between mountains of ice, but of people moving eastward from the Pacific and northward from the Caribbean.

Gruhn also argues that the 12,000 years of the standard archaeological model is not sufficient to generate the degree of linguistic diversity found in many of the major language families of the continent. It is at this point that the work of Greenberg becomes critical for this discussion. If 12,000 years is thought to be inadequate to generate the linguistic diversity found within the Hokan or Penutian groups, for instance, what does one make of 12,000 years as the time frame within which the entire Amerind macrofamily – all of the diverse languages and language families south of the Athapaskans – must have developed?

Viewpoints from Archaeological Anthropology

Archaeologists all agree that people have lived in the New World for at least 12,000 years. That general time frame was established in 1927 when a magnificently crafted stone spear point, to be named Folsom, was found still embedded in the ribs of an extinct form of bison, itself lying in a datable geological formation. That direct association of a human artifact with a datable object in an undisturbed context forever silenced the then dominant conservative view that people had been here for only some 3,000 years. Since then other Folsom sites have been found across the High Plains, dated from about 11,000 to 10,000 years B.P. (before the present), along with numerous other "Early Man" sites of undisputed authenticity across virtually the entire continent, so that an entry date of 12,000 B.P. has now become the conservative position. The Early Man debate is now centred on the question of whether there is really good evidence for an earlier date. Part of this question, naturally, is also the question of what constitutes good evidence.

The conservative view is that there is no shortage of sites for which claims have been made for earlier dates, but that a careful examination of these sites raises questions that have not been fully answered. Old Crow in the northern Yukon is an example. The most famous Old Crow artifact is a hide flesher made from a caribou leg bone. Originally dated at 27,000 B.P., improved technical knowledge has led to it being reassessed at only 1350 B.P. Numerous other bones from the area showing unmistakable evidence of having been worked on or made into tools are dated from 45,000 to 25,000 B.P. The problem for the conservatives is that these artifacts have been washed out of their original context by the Old Crow River (to which one is forced to ask, "Is not a tool out of context still a tool?"). Lastly, modified bones have been found in contexts reliably dated at 80,000 B.P. and earlier, but there is not universal agreement that the cuts were made by humans.

The radical view is that although it is true that in the past some unsubstantiated claims for extreme antiquity were made in a few cases, and although some sites like Old Crow are less than perfect in some regards, there is an ever growing list of sites from much of North and South America that have been reliably dated as being older than 12,000 B.P.

One of the most interesting of these sites is Monte Verde, in southern Chile. The main site is exceptionally well preserved because of its waterlogged condition and includes a series of wooden houses with numerous wooden artifacts and even some food remains in wooden bowls. It is dated at 13,000 B.P. Given its far southern location, not just in terms of distance, but in terms of a sequence of major environmental adjustments that people must have made as they made their way south, one can only speculate at what a reasonable starting time would have been. But below this site is an earlier occupation floor with simple stone artifacts that have been dated at 33,000 B.P. The implications of such an early date this far south are staggering.

Two sites recently excavated near Calgary, Alberta, may shift opinion more solidly to the radical perspective. Both sites contain an assemblage of flaked artifacts reminiscent of northeast Asian materials. The key point is that, although there was no directly datable material at the sites, they are found underneath debris associated with the advance of the Laurentian glacier, or prior to 21,000 B.P. In other words, the area along the eastern slopes of the Rockies, recognized in the conservative view as the most likely route for colonizing that part of the Americas south of the glaciers, was inhabited early, was abandoned due to glacial advance, and subsequently was recolonized much later.

One other factor in this controversy must be mentioned, even in such a brief summary. The lifestyle of the oldest "Early Americans" about which archaeologists generally agree, in western North America from about 11,500 to 7500 B.P., is often referred to as big-game hunting. The sites giving rise to this designation are characterized by the remains of large animals and the tools to kill and process them. These killing tools are fluted, lanceolate spear points, the earliest being termed Clovis (in use from 11,500 to 11,000 B.P.). The radical view is that the conservatives simply project this lifestyle into the older past and assume that the very first Amerinds must also have been big-game hunters and must also have been using the same type of stone hunting tools. There are alternatives, including bone tools, fire-hardened wood tools, and other types of stone tools. The argument is that the conservatives are not finding pre-Clovis sites because they are not looking for the right kinds of things.

It is entirely appropriate to end this discussion of the settling of the New World on this note because we need to remind ourselves that the past is not there simply to be dug up; rather, anthropologists are actively reconstructing the past. The patterns upon which reconstructions are based are not only in the data but in the minds of those doing the reconstruction. If the radicals and conservatives can resolve their differences, perhaps we can start paying more attention to the mental patterns of those who originally constructed the data.

The Time before History or Canada

The view taken here is that the first people came to this continent from what is now Siberia earlier than conventionally thought, via a land bridge known as Beringia that existed intermittently from 70,000 to 12,000 B.P., and first spread down the Pacific coast and then into the continent's interior. Most of what is now Canada was either abandoned

MAP 2.1. Vegetation Zones and Archaeological Sites of Canada

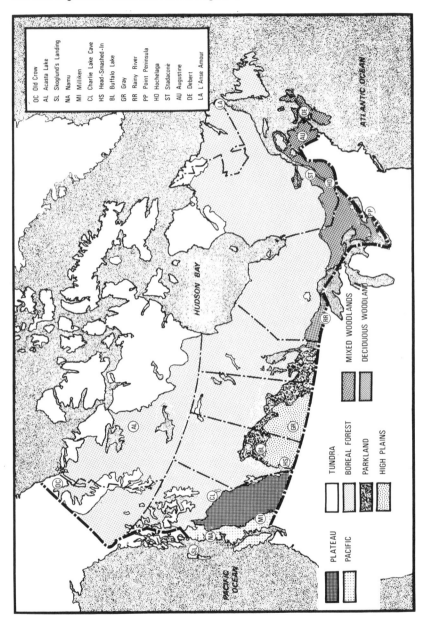

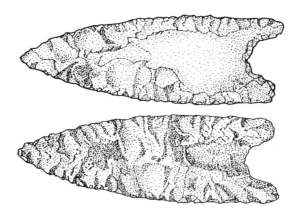

PLATE 2.1. Fluted projectile point from the Debert site in Nova Scotia. Given what we know of the ecological context, these particular points most likely were used to hunt caribou. Courtesy of the Canadian Museum of Civilization.

when the glaciers came or was not settled at all until they melted. At that point ancestors of the people now known as Kutenai and Salish could move into the B.C. interior from the west coast, the Algonquians and then the Siouans and Iroquoians into central and eastern Canada from the south, and the Athapaskans into the interior northwest from the coast. Still later, the Eskimoans moved across the Arctic in a series of west-to-east migrations.

The Paleo-Indian Stage (11,500 to 7500 B.P.)

These are the earliest people about whom there is relative agreement, both because there is more evidence and because they produced "diagnostic" forms. We have already mentioned two of these, Folsom and Clovis. They are both bifacially flaked projectile points, a style found widely across the continent. Fluted points have been dated in Canada from the Debert site in central Nova Scotia (10,600 B.P.), Sibbald Creek near Calgary, Alberta (9570 B.P.), and Charlie Lake Cave north of Fort St. John, B.C. (10,500 B.P.). The Debert site included 140 artifacts, including spear points, drills, knives, wedges, and scrapers, providing a fuller view of the range of activities and skills of these people than most sites. The distribution of fluted points extends to the Yukon and Alaska, but is most extensive in the U.S.

PLATE 2.2. Plano artifacts: a) projectile points; b) scrapers used to work various materials such as hide, wood, and bone; c) knives; d) a roughly shaped "preform," an early step in making projectile points, knives, and other tools; e) a tool used for slotting bone and wood; f) hammerstone, core, and flakes (typical of quarry sites where tools were "mass-produced").Courtesy of the Canadian Museum of Civilization.

Microblades, very small, unifacial, parallel-sided blades that presumably were often inset into bone or wood tools, are found in Alaska and the Yukon before 11,000 B.P. Part of their interest is that they appear in Siberia from 35,000 to 11,000 B.P., and hence they quite directly link peoples on the two continents. They are also of interest because their use persists so long, on the B.C. coast and interior until after 4000 B.P. and in the Arctic (where they are associated with people called Paleo-Eskimos, or the Arctic Small Tool tradition) until about 2800 B.P.

About 10,000 B.P. fluted points were replaced on the Plains by stemmed points that are quite thick in cross-section. Collectively called Plano points, they were developed in the U.S. Great Basin around 12,000 B.P. They were then used on the Plains, on the northern barren grounds by 8000 B.P., and as far east as the Gaspé Peninsula. While they generally seem not to have been used after about 7500 B.P., their use persisted in northern Ontario until as recently as 5000 B.P. One needs to be cautious in assuming that their persistence in the Subarctic has to do with cultural isolation; Plano style points at Acasta Lake in the Keewatin District dated at 6900 B.P. have side notches, presumably showing an awareness of a new hafting style developed on the Plains.

Paleo-Indians east of the Rockies concentrated on hunting big game. In the Far West a more diversified economy developed, although from quite early times salmon constituted the primary resource. The productivity of specific locations has led to spectacular archaeological sequences. The Milliken site near Hell's Gate, the narrowest part of the Fraser River and a natural location for fishing, provides an almost continuous record of occupation dating from 9000 B.P. Further north, the Namu site provides the longest essentially continuous record of occupation, dating from 9700 B.P. The deepest level provides the earliest microblades on the coast. The 6000 B.P. level has a wide array of animal and fish bones, including the bones of sea mammals, indicating the use of seaworthy craft. Skoglund's Landing, on the Queen Charlotte Islands, may be 10,000 years old, which would make it the oldest site on the B.C. coast.

After the Paleo-Indians: Western Canada

Not only are the sequences on the west coast the oldest in Canada, they link at early stages to the area's contemporary residents. That the Haida are a linguistic isolate living on unglaciated islands and that sites such as Skoglund's Landing show a growing cultural complexity without significant intrusions suggest that the Haida have occupied the islands for at least the last 10,000 years. The sequence in Prince Rupert harbour begins about 5000 B.P. and leads directly to the Tsimshian. Because the site was waterlogged, there is remarkable preservation of perishables after 2000 B.P., including whole houses and canoes. Further south on the coast,

Wakashan history can be inferred to extend to at least 4500 B.P. and Salish to 3500 B.P. That is not to say, of course, that these people did not exist earlier as distinct groups.

The interior Plateau of B.C. is less well known, partly because people tended to live in the same places as earlier people did, and making a new semi-subterranean pit house often meant digging up an old one. In any case, small villages appear by about 4000 B.P., located near good fishing sites. Houses of much the same style were still used in the last century.

The Plains were relatively depopulated from about 7500 to 5000 B.P., due to the effects of the hotter and drier period known as the Altithermal. In a sense, this was merely an extreme example of the standard Plains adaptational pattern: both the buffalo and those who lived off them moved from the Plains to the adjacent mountains and parkland during times of stress, including the average winter. Head-Smashed-In, a buffalo jump in southern Alberta, was in use from at least 5700 B.P. Such sites, where massive quantities of meat were processed repeatedly, leave an interesting chronology, but of only one aspect of life.

Pottery appeared on the Canadian Plains somewhat before arrowheads. It is found as far northwest as central Alberta, and like burial mounds (found as far northwest as southeastern Saskatchewan) and farming (as far northwest as North Dakota), was derived from the Woodland culture of southern Ontario and the Mississippi Valley and ultimately from the cultures of Mexico.

Eastern Canada: Archaic Period (9500-3000 B.P.)

"Archaic" is an unfortunate term, but it is thoroughly embedded in the literature. It generally refers to people who have a broadly based foraging lifestyle of hunting, fishing, and gathering.

L'Anse Amour is the earliest known burial mound in North America (7500 B.P.). Located in southern Labrador, it is associated with the Maritime Archaic culture. It contains the body of a young teenager and numerous grave goods, including points, knives, needles, a flute, and a toggle carved from an antler. Key interpretations are that the grave goods indicate not only a belief system including an afterlife, but: (1) a productive maritime hunting economy (a toggle harpoon head pivots inside the hide of a speared animal after the attached line is pulled, allowing the offshore hunting of sea mammals), and (2) the subsequent development of some degree of social differentiation. By 5000 B.P.

Maritime Archaic people had expanded to Newfoundland, indicating they had seaworthy craft.

The Laurentian Archaic developed in southern Ontario and Quebec, later expanding to New Brunswick and Maine. Few campsites have been found (they moved a lot), but about 6000 B.P. they started placing grave goods in burial sites. These goods indicate an extensive trade network, including conch shells from the Gulf of Mexico, copper work from west of Lake Superior, and ground slate points from Maritime Archaic people.

Eastern Canada: Woodland Period (3300 B.P.-Historic Era)

Woodland culture is primarily a culture of the eastern U.S., extending into the southern part of eastern Canada. It is a northern extension of a settled, agricultural way of life originating in Mexico but achieving a regional cultural focus in the central Mississippi Valley. The archaeological convention is to refer to people as Woodland if they made pottery even if they were not actually agriculturalists.

About 3300 B.P. Laurentian Archaic people started making ceramic beakers with pointed bottoms and cord-marked walls. This marks the beginning of Woodland culture in Canada, although the people continued to be nomadic hunters.

The Point Peninsula phase began about 2750 B.P. The pottery marking this phase clearly was strongly influenced by the Adena culture of the Ohio Valley; it also demonstrates local affinities (like cord marking) and influences from northern Ontario ("toothed" markings). As time goes on, the extensive trade in regionally identifiable goods indicates complex and continuing connections spanning half the continent.

Canadian Woodland culture clearly developed in part out of local antecedents generally thought to be associated with the Algonquian language family. Just as clearly, southern Ontario has also been inhabited for some time by Iroquoian speakers. Although there are reasons to think that Iroquoians may have reached the area as early as 3500 B.P., only by 1100 B.P. are there corn farming palisaded villages and large ossuaries clearly identifiable as Iroquoian. About 700 years ago these people experienced a significant geographic expansion from a southern Ontario base leading to their historically known territories.

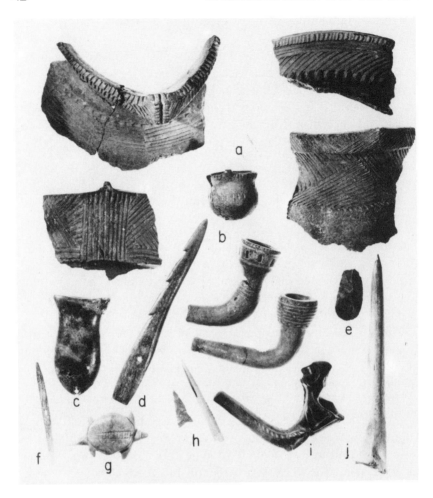

PLATE 2.3. Iroquoian (Huron-Petun) artifacts: a) rim fragments from pots; b) pot, probably made by a small girl; c) stone pipe bowl; d) antler harpoon; e) scraper; f) netting
needle; g)turtle amulet made of stone; h) stone and bone arrowheads; i) clay pipes;
j) dagger made from human bone. Courtesy of the Canadian Museum of Civilization.

Boreal Forest and Subarctic Tundra

From earliest times this has been a region of hunters living in small bands
that moved frequently. It is also a region of acidic soils that quickly destroy most of the things that humans leave behind. It is not surprising,
then, that we know relatively little about the area.

PLATE 2.4. These are examples of the kinds of stone tools made by people in Alaska early in the post-glacial period. At lower left is a microblade core from which sharp, parallel-sided microblades (lower right) were removed. Microblades could be used as knife blades or further modified to form small points on weapons. Above these artifacts are a larger stone core and a spear point. Few other artifacts have been preserved from this time period. Courtesy of the Canadian Museum of Civilization.

As noted earlier, Paleo-Indians moved into the region as the glaciers melted. The lanceolate points characteristic of them continue after the side-notched points that archaeologists use to define the Shield Archaic (6000 B.P. to historic times) were introduced. About 2200 B.P. Shield Archaic people living in eastern Manitoba and the adjacent Rainy River region of northern Ontario started making Laurel pottery. The Rainy River region is also known for burial mounds with especially rich grave goods. This is most unusual for boreal forest hunters, but perhaps the point is more that the area is relatively close both to the Great Lakes and to the Plains and so to people living different lifestyles. About A.D. 700 other types of pottery originating in southern Ontario came into use.

The Arctic

The Arctic is the most recently inhabited part of Canada. Only 4,000 years ago did people spread eastward from what is now Alaska, moving quite rapidly across the High Arctic islands to northern Greenland. These first inhabitants of Canada's Arctic are known as Independence I people, from the Greenlandic fiord where they were first identified. They were part of a cultural tradition known both as Paleo-Eskimo and as the Arctic Small Tool tradition, from their use of microblades as tool components. The use of microblades and a complex of other features link the Paleo-Eskimo both to earlier Alaskan cultures and ultimately to the Djuktai culture of northeastern Siberia, dated to 35,000 B.P.

The rapid movement of the first Paleo-Eskimos across previously uninhabited areas seems to require some explanation. One possible factor may be that, although people had been living in the North for some time, their annual cycle had them oscillating between forest and shore; only now had they learned to live throughout the year near the Arctic shoreline. Another factor may be that the shore region was now habitable for the first time since the glacial age due to a stabilized sea level and increasing (although still low) stocks of maritime resources. This may be reflected in the apparently greater reliance of the Independence I people on land resources like caribou and muskoxen than on seals and walrus. Since the number of land animals living on islands is limited and since these land animals reproduce slowly, an explanation for why the people kept moving from island to island and why they disappeared shortly after reaching the eastern end of the High Arctic island chain may be that they simply ran out of food and in the end literally had nowhere to go.

Only 300 years later, however, a second wave of Paleo-Eskimos, known as Pre-Dorset people, moved eastward out of Alaska. Perhaps because they had a more balanced reliance on land and sea resources, their colonization of the Arctic was successful. In any case, for about 1,000 years small, mobile groups of these people occupied the Far North.

This is not to say they occupied all the territory all the time. Richer areas seem to have been used continuously; other areas were moved into or abandoned as local conditions warranted. The cultural variability one would expect under these conditions did in fact arise. In general, we can say that these people lived in skin tents for much of the year. They also used snow houses (they may have invented them) and heated them with oil lamps. They may have used skin-covered boats. They had dogs, but not dog sleds. They used sinew-backed bows much like more modern ones.

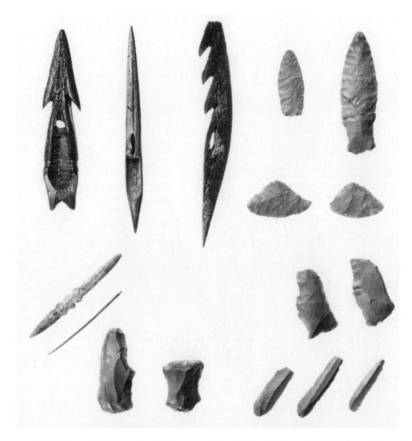

PLATE 2.5. These Pre-Dorset artifacts are quite similar to those of the Independence I culture, except for some stylistic features and the two harpoon heads (upper left). Proceeding clockwise, the other items are: what is probably a broken fish spear head, two harpoon or spear points, side blades for insetting into the sides of weapon heads, two burins for working bone or antler, microblades, two scrapers, a bone needle, and a bone pin. Courtesy of the Canadian Museum of Civilization.

Life in the Arctic is never easy, but life for the Pre-Dorset became harder as the decades went by because their entry into the Arctic coincided with a long-term cooling trend. With game becoming scarcer, even good hunters may go hungry. By 3000 B.P. the Pre-Dorset range seems to have become restricted to Foxe Basin and Hudson Strait.

Given these circumstances, we are not surprised to find that people turned increasingly to hunting sea mammals, particularly those, such as seals and walrus, that are "ice-loving" and hence fairly accessible. With this orientation there is a concomitant decline in the number of dogs, bows and arrows are abandoned, the snow knife is invented, oil lamps are

PLATE 2.6. These are examples of the more "sophisticated" technology of the Dorset people. Clockwise from the upper left, we see: two harpoon heads, a large lance head, a knife utilizing a microblade, a ground burin-like implement with its handle, two flaked stone and one ground stone points, a fish arrow or spear head, a bone needle, and an ivory ice-creeper. Courtesy of the Canadian Museum of Civilization.

used more, stone cooking pots are used, ice creepers (to strap on the feet while walking on ice) are found, and the kayak is definitely used.

By 2500 B.P. the cumulative effect of these changes had become transformative; the new society is referred to as Dorset. Dorset culture flourished and recolonized the sea margins of the North from Labrador to Greenland and westward toward Alaska.

While our narrative is focused on the Canadian Arctic, we must now turn to Alaska. The archaeology of Alaska is complex, in part because it was a meeting ground between North Pacific and Arctic peoples. A criti-

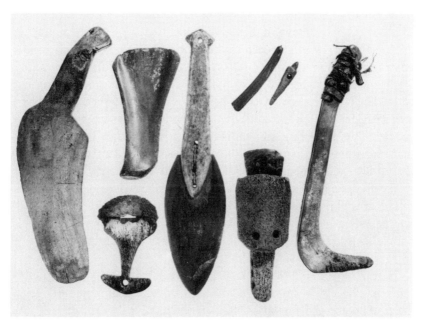

PLATE 2.7. Illustrating the great difference between Thule and the earlier Paleoeskimo technology, we see clockwise from the right: an adze handle, an adze head with a ground stone blade, a man's knife with a ground stone blade, a woman's knife (ulu) with an iron blade, a whalebone snow knife, a bone scraper for skin working, an engraving tool with an iron point, and a drill bit with a ground stone point. Courtesy of the Canadian Museum of Civilization.

cal event was the adaptation in the ninth century by northwestern Alaskan peoples of a Japanese innovation, making large floats out of animal skins. By acting as a drag and a marker, the device greatly improved the efficiency of walrus and whale hunting. As a result the population expanded greatly and society became more complex. The resultant cultural tradition is referred to by archaeologists as Thule culture. For a variety of reasons, but certainly in part because it was effective both economically and socially, Thule culture spread into southwestern Alaska, into the interior of Alaska, and eastward across Canada to Greenland.

The bearers of Thule culture into Canada were Inupik speakers, ancestral to the modern Inuit. While it is clear that their sweep across the Arctic was rapid, we know very little about the nature of their relationship with the Dorset populations already there. It is easy to envision hostile encounters between bands of armed hunters, but there is no direct evidence of such conflict. Perhaps the Dorset simply retreated. Or, as Hickey (1986) thinks more likely, the Thule incorporated significant numbers of Dorset people.

In Hickey's scenario, it would be advantageous to the immigrant Thule to take advantage of the detailed local environmental knowledge of Dorset men. Dorset women would be valued as domestic and procreative assets, but more importantly as a medium for social alliances. Such a process would leave little archaeological evidence. An intriguing line of evidence in favour of Dorset people being incorporated into Thule society is the continued tradition of women in the eastern Arctic making special "dress-up" clothing that is much more complex in construction than are utilitarian garments. This seems more consistent with the ornate Dorset artistic aesthetic than with the generally austere Thule taste. In this view, Dorset women in Thule households would generally have raised their children as Thule, but might well also pass on special skills and aesthetic judgements that they valued highly. In any case, Thule people prospered and for roughly 1,000 years evolved into the several historic Inuit societies.

In sum, North and South America were inhabited an unimaginably long time ago by at least three waves of migrants coming out of Asia. They, of course, did not think of their experiences in those terms, for their frames of reference were different. Nevertheless, they created a series of diverse and successful adaptations to the entire range of environments to be found. And here, in turn, they were "found" by another kind of migrant.

A Millennium of European Immigration

European immigration began with at least one aborted attempt at settlement by the Norse almost a thousand years ago. There is scant but tantalizing evidence for contact between Europeans and indigenous Americans over the next 500 years. European and African immigration to the territory that is now Canada began building in the sixteenth century, accelerated dramatically in the seventeenth century, increased even more dramatically in the eighteenth century, and became overwhelming in the nineteenth century. The human migration from Europe between the early 1600s and 1930 was probably the largest ever, and it changed the face of the Americas. The history of the First Nations of Canada in the face of that massive immigration of Europeans is one of survival. It is first of all a history of physical survival, given the effects that European diseases had on indigenous populations. An aspect of history that is resonant with our own era has to do with another kind of survival: the history of the relations between indigenous Canadians and the Europeans, Africans, and Asians who migrated here after 1600 is one of the struggle for survival of indigenous community autonomy and integrity. The current discussions about indigenous peoples' inherent right to self-government is a twentieth-century manifestation of that struggle.

It has been customary to think of the last decade of the fifteenth century as a decade of European discovery of the Americas and to divide American history into pre-contact and post-contact eras. It is more nearly accurate to describe that decade as one in which the sure knowledge of the existence of the Americas entered the popular European imagination; there is simply too much evidence that contact between Aboriginal Americans and people in other areas of the world had been going on for a very long time. There are no records to confirm it, but comparisons of culture traits indicate that the Pacific Northwest was part of a huge Pacific Rim maritime culture area. There are tantalizing indications of contact between maritime Indians of the far Northeast and Scandinavia. The nature, duration, and effect of American contact with Asia, Europe, and Oceania may never be known, and the arguments about it are based mostly on apparent evidence for transoceanic diffusion of plants such as cotton and maize, and on cultural traits that appear to be similar. The clearest indisputable and documentable evidence of contact is the establishment of a small colony of Greenlandic Norse, along with their Celtic slaves, in Newfoundland in A.D. 1004. It is well established that there was contact between the Norse colonies in Greenland and Dorset people and Inuit in what is now Canada, and Norse sagas include mention of lands that must be Labrador and Newfoundland.

The sustained contact between Europeans, Africans, and Aboriginal Americans that began in the 1490s, however, fundamentally altered migration patterns of humans and the balance of political power in the world. The contact of the 1490s set the stage for European technological domination of the rest of the world.

At the time of the first sustained contact, Europeans found a continent inhabited by hundreds of very diverse groups. It is an irony that the European cosmology that justified imperialism has so informed the concepts we use to describe contact that we are in many ways blinded to the similarities and differences between Europeans and indigenous Americans at that time of contact. For example, agriculture was very widely practised in North America. It was based on maize and its cultivation did not require the tilling of the soil or the use of draft animals. Because Indians did not farm like Europeans, Europeans did not recognize it as "true" agriculture.

European claims to American land were based on "discovery" of land held by "non-Christian" or pagan peoples, which as such had no claim to sovereignty within a European Christian conception of land rights. The paradox was that during the first century of sustained contact, it was obvious that Europeans stayed on at the sufferance of their hosts and trading partners. While explorers could claim a territory for a European crown, the reality of control over the territory was not always coincident with the claim. Recognition of the reality of Amerindian control made it necessary to purchase land from Indians or for Europeans to ally themselves with Indians for trade and warfare.

European claims were sometimes made by right of purchase of land. They professed dual postures to their Indian allies, trading with them, even adopting indigenous forms of negotiation and trade protocols, but claiming European sovereignty in law. Thus, more than a century and a half after the beginning of sustained contact, the French could claim to the English that French presence in Acadia was by right of Indian invitation to be there, yet in negotiating the Treaty of Utrecht in 1713 they completely ignored consideration of Micmac or Malecite interest or opinion in the French relinquishment of Acadia to the English.

In the European conception of things, America was a wilderness and Natives were part of that wilderness. That idea could be maintained despite all the evidence: the obvious concentration of indigenous populations, the obvious control and management of unfenced pasture areas in which many Native people harvested mammals for food, the practice of agriculture, the military power and skills of indigenous groups, and the extensive trade networks. The country was no wilderness, and given the evidence it is a wonder that Europeans could see it as one.

The period of sustained contact began in Canada in Newfoundland and the Maritimes, followed shortly thereafter by Gaspé and the immediate St. Lawrence watershed. During the sixteenth century European settlement in North America was focused on the subtropical regions, but Europeans had become familiar with the North Atlantic coast through the activity of the Atlantic fishery. Portuguese, Basque, and English exploitation of the Newfoundland fishery accelerated during the 1500s, until every summer saw around 17,000 European males along the northeast coast. Though occasionally some crew members wintered over, there was no really permanent settlement. Trade in furs, at first an adjunct to exploration, began in earnest during this time, with French and English voyages of trade and exploration along the coast and up the St. Lawrence River.

The first and lasting effect of sustained contact was disease. No one knows the extent of the first great smallpox epidemic in 1520-24. It began in the West Indies and Mexico and spread northward to affect most of

North America. It was followed by a devastating epidemic of measles just seven years later. An epidemic caused by an unknown pathogen afflicted people of the St. Lawrence Valley in 1535, and smallpox struck again in the eastern Great Lakes region in the early 1590s. European diseases took a crushing toll: smallpox, for example, seemed to hit every other generation, as each generation that had gained some immunity was replaced by a new, susceptible one.

The number of people who died or who were permanently disabled by disease is a matter of speculation. Estimates of the population of North America north of the cities of Mexico in the early sixteenth century vary from 4.5 million to as high as 18 million, and one of the difficulties in making the estimate is the incalculably devastating effects of the early epidemics. The cost in human life has been very great: susceptibility to European disease was a major factor in the decline of the indigenous population until the 1920s, to the extent that by the last part of the nineteenth century the indigenous population of the United States and Canada dropped to around 300,000. Epidemics of smallpox, measles, influenza, and bubonic plague were the greatest killers, and diphtheria, cholera, typhus, scarlet fever, and typhoid also caused high mortality. The early epidemics preceded initial European settlement in the Northeast, so when that settlement began in earnest in the early 1600s it was among an indigenous population already seriously affected by European diseases.

Alliances in Trade and Warfare

Acceleration of the trade in furs was coincident with the first sustained European settlement in the early seventeenth century in the areas that now comprise Canada and the United States. European immigration began building in the 1630s, with French, English, Dutch, and Swedish establishment of fur-trading posts and with experiments in agricultural settlement by the French and English. Trade relationships begun during the sixteenth century formed the basis for the initial pattern of European settlement, with the various European nations establishing colonies in territory controlled by the indigenous nations with which each European nation had regularly allied itself in trade.

We tend to look at those alliances nowadays in terms of their lasting significance rather than in terms of what motivated them at the time. Perhaps we lend too much relevance to those alliances that seem to have endured and to have changed history because of the eventual balance of power between European nations. The seventeenth century was a time of huge increase in trade between Europeans and Amerindians as well as

European encroachment on Indian land. Our discussions cloud a very complex period of competition among the European groups themselves for control of land for expansion and of competition among indigenous nations, both in economic terms and for favourable terms of survival given the European onslaught.

The alliances built on, exploited, and irrevocably disrupted ancient trade patterns between indigenous nations. Indigenous trade patterns had been predominantly north and south, but the French inroad had been east to west, from Acadia to Gaspé, the St. Lawrence Valley, and then the Great Lakes and south through the Ohio and Mississippi River systems. The French were allied initially in the Maritimes with the Micmac and Malecite, then with factions of those groups' occasional enemies, the Eastern Abenaki. Their allies north of the St. Lawrence were the Montagnais and, in the interior, the Algonquians and a major group of Huron nations. The Dutch were initially allied with the Algonquian groups around the Hudson River, but sought alliance with the group that became known as the Five Nations Iroquois. England's beachhead was first in New England and then in its settlements south of Chesapeake Bay.

The Iroquois of the Five Nations gained tremendous political power by challenging the French and their allies to control trade on the St. Lawrence and then by allying themselves with the British. As the English took over Indian land in New England and along the Hudson River, groups displaced by British encroachment moved westward and some former enemies of the Five Nations put themselves under the protection of their erstwhile foes. Five Nations ascendancy was clearly realized when they destroyed the strongest interior trading partners to the north, the Huron allies of the French, during the mid-1600s.

Disease was a continuing major factor in the European expansion of the 1600s, with epidemics of bubonic plague in New England during the years 1612-19, measles in 1633-34 throughout the whole Northeast, and again in 1658-59, scarlet fever in 1637, among the Hurons, diphtheria in 1659 in New England and eastern Canada, and smallpox, which racked the entire Northeast at least once during each decade from the 1630s to the 1690s. Military action against Indians was usually along lines consistent with the pattern of European alliance, but in New England there was military action against Indians for control of land. The military action, from the European colonizers' standpoint, was probably not as effective as disease. The effects of disease on Native populations were so obvious that English colonists could interpret the devastation brought by epidemics as divine sanction for European possession and repopulation of the land.

Control over territory and trade was clearly the cause of war. France and England were at war during much of the seventeenth century. The Five Nations Iroquois fought the French for nearly the entire century, the Abenaki fought the English for control of northern New England, and New England Algonquians went to war to attempt to remove the English from their territory.

European Expansion into the Interior during the Eighteenth Century

The eighteenth century was a time of continued conflict between European powers and conflict between England and her American colonies. A significant part of that conflict was played out in America. The Five Nations Iroquois established peace with French colonists in 1701, but their allies the Fox, in the area that is now Wisconsin, continued hostile action against the French and their Dakota allies. The French sought to maintain a continental sphere of influence through the Great Lakes to the Mississippi, and fought with the English over control of trade in Hudson Bay. During the early part of the eighteenth century French interests were well served by Micmac military conflict with the English in the Maritimes.

If the focus is on European conflict, the history of relationships between European colonists and the different Indian nations during the seventeenth and eighteenth centuries is one of shifting alliances and unclear national boundaries: for example, during the last era of formal conflict between the French and the Five Nations Iroquois, many Christianized Iroquois settled in villages near Montreal. That illustrates two aspects of Amerindian-European relationship: (1) missionization had become important as a policy of control and pacification; (2) Amerindian political organization was markedly different from that of Europeans. Indian military strategy, patterns of alliance, social movement, and migration are more clearly explicable if the focus is not on European spheres of influence and power balances but on Amerindian groups' own attempts to control trade and land on their own terms, to adapt to the presence of Europeans, and above all to retain a land base for themselves that they might control. In other words, Indian political alliance was not a matter of less powerful nations aligning with more powerful European partners, but was instead a series of strategic partnerships, negotiations, diplomatic ventures, and armed hostility, all oriented toward maximizing each Amerindian group's interests.

Relationships among Indian nations were oriented to the same end, maximization of the specific national interest of the individual nation.

The nations of New England and the American Atlantic seaboard, displaced and decimated by European disease and finding refuge with other groups, were among the first to couch the struggles of the seventeenth and eighteenth centuries in terms of a conflict of a duality, Indians against Europeans. Groups such as the Delaware, formed as a collectivity from Algonquian survivors of groups north of Chesapeake Bay, first moved west to put themselves under the protection of their former antagonists, the Five Nations Iroquois, and then further west to the continental interior and to Upper Canada. Some of their leaders were influential in attempts to bring Indian nations together to fight in common cause against European colonists.

The English Royal Proclamation of 1763, requiring that any alienation of Indian land be negotiated and that the crown be the sole European agency in negotiation, was a strategy to ally Indian nations with Britain. When English domination was established in Quebec and the Maritimes during the last half of the eighteenth century, the possibility for Indian nations to play off one power against the other was removed, but during the war between England and the thirteen American colonies Indian nations were fighting on both sides, and they continued to face other Indian nations in battle in alliances with Europeans until the cessation of hostilities between Canada and the United States in 1814.

Patterns of European migration changed as well. Until the establishment of the United States, around two-thirds of the immigrants other than slaves had been indentured labourers. After the American Revolution, European immigration to North America was predominantly by free persons, and there was a large one-time immigration of British loyalists from the United States to Canada.

The last part of the eighteenth century saw increased direct trade between Europeans and Indians in the interior, building on primarily east-west trade routes that had been established in the fur trade among Indian groups. That trade was extended through the watersheds that led to Hudson Bay.

Trade with the Pacific Northwest began during the last part of the eighteenth century. It was joined by the Russians, who established permanent trading and missionary ventures with their claim to Alaska. English and American trading in the Northwest was initially by ship, and the commodities bought from Indians were primarily maritime products, such as sea otter pelts. By 1821 the trade was based primarily on land mammals and was conducted in trading posts, the Hudson's Bay Company having extended its domain to the coast. The decade of the 1830s saw the beginning of European settlement in the area that is now British

Columbia. Though conflict between west coast Indians and individual traders could be bloody, the pattern of alliances and warfare of the east coast was not repeated in the West, except for the battles fought between Tlingits and Russians.

Before any appreciable contact, around 1770, the first of the great smallpox epidemics hit the Northwest Coast. It may have reduced the total population by 30 per cent. Before the introduction of European disease, the area had been the most highly populated of any non-agricultural area in the world, with as many as 180,000 inhabitants. Losses from a single epidemic would claim as much as two-thirds of the population of a single community, and as each succeeding epidemic claimed lives the Native population was reduced to just over 30,000 by the late 1800s.

The eighteenth century was also a time of displacement and migration. In the West, some nations whose way of life and habitation had been primarily in woodlands and parklands saw some of their people move onto the Plains. In the south, adoption of the horse as a central part of the culture facilitated that movement. Some groups whose livelihood had been in agriculture and the harvest of land mammals abandoned agriculture to hunt with horses and to trade for agriculture products and European goods with indigenous agriculturalists in the river valleys. In the northern Plains, the move was facilitated by a growing market to provision the fur trade with food and other supplies.

A Tide of Immigration and the Beginning of the Reserve Era

The nineteenth century, by contrast to the preceding 200 years, was a period of relative peace between European powers and a period of wholesale change in the Americas. The United States and Canada had used Aboriginal groups as buffers along their common border. When the possibility of war between the two countries diminished after the signing of a formal treaty in 1817, the importance of Indians as military allies decreased and a period of oppressive attempts to control them began. The United States began relocating Indians westward, including groups who had lived near the eastern international border with Canada, and by the 1820s the strategic importance of Indian nations in that area, as military allies of Canada, was diminished.

The intensification of industrialization in Europe displaced many of its own people and created a world demand for agricultural land and agricultural products. Between 1814 and the First World War around 50 million people migrated from Europe to the "new Europes" of the Americas and Australasia. Two-thirds of them came to the United States and 4 million of them to Canada, where the largest tide of immigration was to the West after the 1890s.

The policies of both the United States and Canada were westward expansion and the alienation of ever more Indian land to provide a place for Europeans to farm. Populations of Amerindians continued to decline in the face of repeated epidemics, but the birth rate of new immigrants was one of the highest ever recorded, especially among Caucasians. The African-American population increased as well, through natural increase and the importation of slaves, so that their population in North America went from 1 million in 1800 to around 12 million by 1930.

Policies that became pre-eminent in the early 1800s seem to have driven Canadian government interaction with indigenous nations for the next two centuries. It appeared to most non-Native observers that indigenous groups were dying out. The continuing dramatic toll of disease in Native populations appeared to make their eventual demise inevitable. Social philosophy as it developed during the nineteenth century saw all human groups as developing through inevitably sequenced stages, and Native cultures were thought to be in a stage of "savagery." In that conception of things, Euro-Canadian culture was an aspect of Western Europe's pre-eminent development to "civilization." During the last half of the nineteenth century the concept of social Darwinism expanded on the assumption that Indian cultures represented less progress and less cultural development than European cultures, and it was assumed that "civilized" cultures were "fittest" to survive in any context of cultural conflict over resources.

Native people became objects of altruism: European social philosophers saw them as being in need of "advancement" to participate in "civilization." Christians who promoted a new practice of the social gospel of the Christianity of the early 1800s saw Natives as needy in economic, social, moral, and spiritual terms. Indians needed to be protected and, eventually, assimilated. Churches and philanthropic organizations, primarily in Britain but also in the United States, focused on Canadian indigenous nations as subjects of concerted missionary activity. The British organizations were a powerful lobby in the British Parliament for reorienting colonial policy toward the philanthropic end of Christianizing and civilizing Indians and Eskimos.

Since the Royal Proclamation of 1763, the management of the relationship between Indians and the government had been the responsibility of the British government rather than any colonial government. An imperial policy of "civilization" of Indians as communities began in 1830. It marked the beginning of the reserve period in Canada. Indians were to congregate on land reserved for them, apart from the rest of Canadian society, and, as communities, to adapt to Canada's changing social order by learning to farm. Missionary activity was encouraged, and the nineteenth-century debate over which came first, civilization or Christianization, seems to have had its popular origins in this period.

The policy had its greatest impact east of Lake Superior. Rupert's Land was still the domain of the Hudson's Bay Company and the indigenous nations there were autonomous and relatively self-sufficient through participation in the fur trade and through harvest of natural food. They effectively controlled the Plains, the western and northern woodlands and parklands, and the Arctic. European settlement began to increase in British Columbia in the 1840s, and the first reserves in that colony were established during this early period of increased government control of Indians.

Toward the end of the 1850s the policy changed from one of assimilation by community to one of outright assimilation as individuals: the policy of establishing isolated reserves changed, and it was thought that reserves should be close enough to non-Native communities for individuals to have an incentive to become "enfranchised," that is, to have the same legal status as individuals as non-Native Canadians. Though provision was made for individual enfranchisement, the number of people who opted for it was minuscule.

When Canada took over control of Indian affairs at the time of Confederation, indigenous nations became internal colonies. Until then, Indian groups had had control over their land, financial arrangements, membership, business dealings with outsiders, and internal governance. The first legislation about Indians in Canada effectively removed their control in all those areas and imposed systems of band governance that allowed the federal government exclusive control over Indian national leadership, land, membership, and money. Another challenge to internal band authority and First Nations community integrity was the policy's manifest orientation toward individual enfranchisement. Canada had no effective control over those matters in the North and West, so at first the policies applied only to those bands east of the Lakehead.

The issue for all indigenous nations in Canada where they were in contact with Europeans became one of maintaining the integrity of their individual communities. During the last part of the 1860s, Native community integrity was at the heart of the conflict surrounding the admission of Manitoba as a province, and it was most surely the issue in the 1885 Rebellion. In the case of Manitoba, an attempt was made to resolve the issue by negotiating terms for the admission of the province that appeared favourable to the retention of Metis community structures. The almost immediate failure of those provisions was one of the origins of the tension that resulted in the 1885 uprising.

During the 1870s pressure to alienate Indian lands in western Ontario and in Manitoba motivated the federal government to enter into treaties and to attempt to extinguish Metis claims. The self-sufficiency of the nations of the prairies and western parklands was threatened during the decade after Confederation because of the dramatic decrease, then absence, of the great buffalo herds upon which they depended. During the 1870s the Plains nations joined treaty negotiations as an alternative to starvation, though some groups of Cree, Assiniboine, and Saulteaux attempted to maintain autonomy through coalition by congregating in the Cypress Hills.

In the early 1870s British Columbia entered Confederation with the federal government assuming responsibility for the administration of Indian affairs, but with a proviso for provincial involvement in any Indian land settlements. (Except for a few early treaties on Vancouver Island and the extension of Treaty No. 8 into the northeastern part of the province, the alienation of Indian land in B.C. has not involved treaties.)

Thus the establishment of reserves and the policy of wardship of Indians during an anticipated period of assimilation were cornerstones of the policies governing indigenous nations within Confederation. The policies that characterize the reserve period were begun in the 1830s, were modified in the 1850s and again in the late 1860s, and then were implemented as each area of the country was alienated from effective Native control. A most interesting aspect of the policies was the uniformity with which they were applied. The policies directed governmental relations with groups such as the Micmac and Iroquois, who had been trading with and fighting alongside Europeans for almost 300 years; with groups such as the Cree and Blackfoot, who had had completely different trading relationships with Europeans; and with groups in the Mackenzie watershed and northern B.C., some of whom were entering their first sustained relationships with Europeans.

If we focus on the government's rationale for the institution of such policies, it is possible to accept Tobias's (1991) interpretation that the policies were directed by a concern for the "protection, civilization, and assimilation" of indigenous people. If, instead, we look at the legislation itself, the way policies were operationalized, and the effect of the policies "on the ground," the idea of protection is not an acceptable interpretation. The reserve era was one of control and containment of Indians, primarily under authority provided by the Indian Act. Characteristics of the era are:

- duplicity in the alienation of even more land, including land previously reserved for Indians;
- heavy-handedness and arbitrary judgement in the definition of who was an Indian, both through the Indian Act itself and most particularly in the way recognition as being Indian was effected in individual cases;
- control over internal governance of bands, the election and recognition of leadership, and the definition of band responsibilities;
- corruption in the provision of goods and services to bands;
- legal sanctions against the practice of indigenous religion and spirituality;
- the establishment of industrial schools, then residential schools operated by churches, in which Indian custom was denigrated and in which an attempt was made to wipe out the use of indigenous languages;
- the institutionalization and structuring of schooling, generally, that made academic success and achievement extremely difficult;
- control over persons and individual movement and mobility, with the institution of "passes" for leaving reserves;
- control over the finances of individuals and bands;
- the institution of policies that made early Indian successes at farming impossible to maintain; and
- legal sanctions against meeting and organizing.

Though the reserve era is characterized by the Indian Act, federal administration of reserves, and oppressive policies, it is in fact simply a name that characterizes oppression over a period of time, whether or not the people affected were resident on reserves. Reserves were not established in the North for either Inuit or northern Dene, and some bands whose treaties provide for reserves have still to see them established, but the Indian Act has applied to all people recognized as Indian under the Act, and the constraint and regulation of the reserve era have been as oppressive to off-reserve Indians as to those who live on reserves. Exclusion from identification as Indian, under the Act, had the effect of socially defining a significant number of "non-status Indians" as "Metis." During the early part of the century, Inuit were specifically excluded from definition as Indian but nonetheless had their affairs administered by the same department as Indians. The Metis, the large community of mixed-ancestry people who had begun forming indigenous communities west of the Great Lakes as early as the late 1600s, did not have reserves, as their rights to land were supposed to have been recognized by the issuance to individuals of "scrip," which was to be exchanged for land.

Resistance

The record of First Nations resistance to the measures of the reserve era is a long and detailed one. From the very beginning of the reserve era, individual leaders approached the government with complaints, protests, and constructive suggestions. The kind of control exerted by government agencies over the lives of Indians and whatever Inuit were in the orbit of government influence militated against either economic development or individual achievement. The era between the two world wars was one of particular economic hardship for many Canadians, and particularly so for the many First Nations people whose traditional subsistence base of agriculture and resource harvest had been destroyed.

Pan-Canadian organization of Indians began in 1919 with the efforts of F.O. Loft, a Mohawk army officer who was an organizer of the League of Indians of Canada (Cuthand, 1991). Regional coalitions of First Nations groups began organizing in the 1920s and 1930s, one of which in Alberta was responsible for eventual government establishment of Metis settlements in the only province to set such land aside.

After World War Two it became increasingly clear to government that the inequities perpetuated in the name of wardship had to change, but change was slow and often apparently in the wrong direction. As after World War One, returning Indian veterans were in the vanguard of organization and protest. For the first time since sustained contact, the rate of increase in the indigenous population was accelerating but post-war economic development largely excluded Indians, so the economic distinctions between Euro-Canadians and Indians became more marked. The middle part of the century brought the last relatively isolated groups of indigenous people into sustained contact with government agencies, and yet another revision of the Indian Act in 1951 reinformed policies of control. The concept of wardship was still firmly entrenched in its provisions. A major change came in 1960 when registered and treaty Indians – quite abruptly and with negligible consultation – were recognized as citizens of Canada. The federal government took over administration of Indian and territorial schools from the missionary groups who had operated them since at least the 1850s, and many of the residential schools were phased out. The courts took on more importance as contentious issues were increasingly being settled there.

In 1969 a major change in governance was proposed in a government White Paper: the Indian Act and reserves were to be phased out and provinces would take over administration of Indian affairs. Echoing the policy changes of the 1850s, indigenous people were to be dealt with individually by government, not as groups. The government professed the changes to be a movement toward equality and justice.

A very strong indigenous protest, particularly from the National Indian Brotherhood, came in response: the message was that injustice had indeed been perpetuated but that government had not got the main point about the nature of the injustice. Rather than an equality in law as assimilated individuals, indigenous people – as groups and not as individuals – had rights that derived from their status as indigenous people. There were rights to land that had never been ceded, rights that derived from treaty, rights that inhered in the nature of indigenous peoples' relationship with land, and rights to govern themselves. Those rights had not been granted by the government and could not be removed by government: treaty rights had been negotiated and could not be unilaterally changed; other rights were inherent in Aboriginal status in Canada.

In the 1970s, two important court decisions in Canada about land, one brought by the Nisga'a in B.C. and the other by Cree and Inuit in northern Quebec, made First Nations' claims about land and rights credible to the federal government. For the first time since Confederation there was a government willingness to discuss a remedy for the negative consequences of the policies of the reserve era. The federal government instituted processes whereby claims for compensation and land could be heard, and those claims were to be distinguished as either comprehensive or specific. Comprehensive claims were primarily those where rights to Euro-Canadian use of land had not been negotiated and specific claims were for cases in which specific obligations had not been met by the government. The claims process continues, but the system set up to deal with claims has been overwhelmed by the several hundred claims brought to it, and should it continue to work at its present pace, claims will not be resolved for centuries.

The policy foundation for a return to First Nations self-government was established in the 1970s, though it was laid piecemeal. The substantive foundation was the persistent will of First Nations leaders and grassroots people to demonstrate that the right and responsibility for self-governance had never been relinquished. One of the first government policy objectives was to mandate control of First Nations schools by First Nations peoples. A corollary was the provision of funding for legal treaty

research in connection with claims processes, as well as the federal provision of funding for national and regional First Nations organizations to
represent indigenous interests to government.

As a result of those measures, the nature of schooling has changed
dramatically since the 1960s. Most schools on reserves, for example, are
now run under the authority of band councils; access to post-secondary
schooling, while still a problem, has improved dramatically; and there
has been a movement to make curriculum consistent with First Nations
interests and cultures. Another result of those measures is that Aboriginal
organizations have become key players in constitutional issues.

First Nations issues were front and centre in negotiations to patriate
the Canadian constitution in the early 1980s, not because of a priority
placed on those issues by government but because of very strong First
Nations representation to the Canadian public and to the Parliament of
the U.K., which was required to pass the measure as a last vestigial act of
Canadian colonialism. The constitutional conferences of the mid-1980s
between federal, provincial, and territorial governments and First
Nations leadership came to no formal definition of the "existing rights"
of indigenous people – rights that had been codified in the new constitution – but media attention to those conferences brought the concept of
First Nations self-government to public awareness. One of the lasting
consequences of those debates is that Aboriginal self-government is now
a putative objective of the Department of Indian Affairs.

It is a rocky road. A good example of the complexities of establishing
First Nations self-government within Canadian Confederation is the
debate over reinstatement of Indians who had been forced to enfranchise
at marriage. Bill C-31 was passed in 1985 as a measure that recognized
gender equality: Indian women who had married non-Indians had been
forced to enfranchise, while Indian men who married non-Indians
brought legal recognition as Indian to the spouse. The complex question
was whether or not the principle of gender equality was paramount over
the principle that First Nations, as all nations, have the right to determine
membership and affiliation. Parliament imposed a resolution by passing
legislation reinstating large groups of people as Indian and requiring
bands to establish clear membership criteria.

When the Meech Lake Accord of 1987 sought to bring Quebec to
agreement on constitutional issues, it was couched in terms of recognition of Canada's having been created by "two founding nations," British
and French. First Nations response was to recall a long history of alliance, trade, negotiation, and participation in the establishment of the
current Canadian polity. It was more than symbolic that a treaty Indian

member of the Manitoba legislature was able in 1990 to delay – and thus obviate – passage of the Accord and its acceptance by the rest of Canada.

The subsequent attempt through the Charlottetown Accord of 1992 to reconcile differences between Quebec and the rest of Canada, an effort that included a national referendum, saw First Nations people vote with the majority for rejection, even though national First Nations leadership had been instrumental in fashioning the Accord, and even though it included measures that were supposed to lead to self-government.

It was not a defeat for the concept of self-government. The federal bureaucracy remains committed to the concept, as does national First Nations leadership. Any such movement will obviously not be formulaic but will be effected with local and regional sensitivity to particular First Nations histories and situations. Given the diversity of First Nations, that is as it should be. As comprehensive land claims are resolved regionally, as courts bring down decisions that redefine the playing field, and as new governmental arrangements develop, such as the establishment of the new territory of Nunavut, self-government will be realized differently in each area.

That makes an important point: self-government is not a right that can be granted by any other government. Thus it is not something for which any formula or policy can apply across the board. It is instead a principle. The long history of First Nations on this part of the continent and the important place that self-directed First Nations have had in the creation of Canada are evidence of the principle that the rights and responsibilities of self-government are inherent and have never been compromised. Except for the most oppressive period of the reserve era, between the 1870s and 1970s, First Nations have in fact been self-governing. In the 1990s and into the next century, individual First Nations will reaffirm self-government in a modern Canadian social context.

In the past 100 years the effects of Europe's diseases have been diminished. Physical survival is no longer in question. Survival in terms of community integrity is a continuing struggle, even in the face of federal government commitment to a move to First Nations self-government. Survival as nations honours the Ancestors who established those nations thousands of years ago, and those who have struggled to maintain the integrity and autonomy of First Nations communities.

Note

1. The first edition of *Native Peoples* had three chapters at this point, one on Canadian Native languages by Regna Darnell, one on the prehistory of

Canadian Indians by Alan Bryan, and one on the archaeology of Arctic Canada by Cliff Hickey. The reader wishing a survey of these topics is directed to them; they are thorough and still very relevant. We chose to drop them for this edition because we realized that the average reader did not require this detailed background. At the same time, we also felt that we had to provide readers with an overview of key issues in Canadian history as they relate to Natives generally before taking up the stories of specific peoples.

Many Natives, it should be noted, object to the term "prehistory" on the assumption that it implies that First Nations have no past worth talking about. We have chosen to use the term on the grounds that its use emphasizes that European migrations represent a sharp break in traditions, that this discussion takes place within a particular tradition, and especially that within the anthropological tradition First Nations peoples have a very substantial past, but one that is not knowable by the same methods as the recent past.

Recommended Readings

Bryan, Alan Lyle
  1986   "The Prehistory of Canadian Indians," in R. Bruce Morrison and C. Roderick
          Wilson, eds., *Native Peoples: The Canadian Experience*. Toronto:
          McClelland & Stewart.
              One of the very few brief national synopses on the topic. Written from an
          early entry, hemispheric perspective.
Darnell, Regna
  1986   "A Linguistic Classification of Canadian Native Peoples: Issues, Problems,
          and Theoretical Implications," in R. Bruce Morrison and C. Roderick Wilson,
          eds., *Native Peoples: The Canadian Experience*. Toronto: McClelland &
          Stewart.
              A theoretically and historically focused survey. Written prior to
          Greenburg, it takes a moderately conservative view.
Dickason, Olive Patricia
  1992   *Canada's First Nations: A History of Founding Peoples*. Toronto:
          McClelland & Stewart.
              Dickason's account is authoritative and comprehensive and is becoming
          the standard reference for Canadian First Nations history.
Dobyns, Henry F., and William R. Swagerty
  1983   *Their Number Become Thinned: Native American Population Dynamics in
          Eastern North America*. Native American Historic Demography Series.
          Knoxville: University of Tennessee Press in co-operation with the Newberry
          Library Center for the History of the American Indian.

Dobyns has become known for his relatively high estimates of Aboriginal North American population before contact. This work details the effects of European diseases on the population of the eastern part of North America.

Foster, Michael K.

1982 "Canada's First Languages," *Language and Society*, 7. Languages of Canada Series. Office of the Commissioner of Official Languages, Ottawa.

An enumeration of Canada's Aboriginal language families, including data on the number of speakers for each.

Francis, Daniel

1992 *The Imaginary Indian: The Image of the Indian in Canadian Culture.* Vancouver: Arsenal Pulp Press.

This history of popular and scholarly Euro-Canadian perceptions of First Nations peoples provides a valuable background for contemporary studies of First Nations history.

Greenberg, Joseph H.

1987 *Language in the Americas.* Stanford, Calif.: Stanford University Press.

A revolutionary re-examination of linguistic affinities in the Western Hemisphere.

Gruhn, Ruth

1988 "Linguistic evidence in support of the coastal route of earliest entry into the New World," *Man*, 23: 22-100.

Exactly what the title says it is. Gruhn has become the leading spokesperson for this perspective.

Hickey, Clifford G.

1986 "The Archaeology of Arctic Canada," in R. Bruce Morrison and C. Roderick Wilson, eds., *Native Peoples: The Canadian Experience*. Toronto: McClelland & Stewart.

Presents both a cultural history of the region and a regionally focused perspective on the work of archaeology.

McGhee, Robert

1978 *Canadian Arctic Prehistory*. Toronto: Von Nostrand Reinhold.

Now somewhat dated, this is nevertheless the standard survey of its topic. Especially useful for the non-expert.

Miller, J.R., ed.

1991 *Sweet Promises: A Reader on Indian-White Relations in Canada*. Toronto: University of Toronto Press.

A collection of essays by noteworthy Canadian scholars oriented toward explaining government policies in changing social and political contexts. The periods covered range from earliest European settlement to the present.

Trigger, Bruce C.

1985 *Natives and Newcomers: Canada's "Heroic Age" Reconsidered.* Montreal
and Kingston: McGill-Queen's University Press.

A ground-breaking account of Canadian history giving attention to its
Native aspects.

Washburn, Wilcomb E., ed.

1988 *History of Indian-White Relations. Handbook of North American Indians,*
Vol. 4. Washington, D.C.: Smithsonian Institution.

Almost half the articles in this large collection are of direct relevance to a
discussion of contact between Canadian First Nations and other peoples.
More specific local, regional, and areal information about Canadian First
Nations culture, language, and contact with Europeans is in the volumes of
the *Handbook* edited by David Damas, *Arctic* (Vol. 5, 1984); June Helm,
Subarctic (Vol. 6, 1981); Wayne Suttles, *Northwest Coast* (Vol. 7, 1990); and
Bruce Trigger, *Northeast* (Vol. 15, 1978).

Additional References Cited

Cuthand, Stan

1991 "The Native Peoples of the Prairie Provinces in the 1920s and 1930s," in J.R.
Miller, ed., *Sweet Promises: A Reader on Indian-White Relations in Canada.*
Toronto: University of Toronto Press.

Greenberg, Joseph H., and Merritt Ruhlen

1992 "Linguistic Origins of Native Americans," *Scientific American,* 267, 5:
94-99.

Powell, John Wesley

1891 *Linguistic Families of America North of Mexico.* Bureau of Ethnology
Annual Report for 1885-86: 7-139.

Sapir, Edward

1929 "Central and North American Languages," *Encyclopaedia Britannica,* 14th
edition, 5: 138-41.

Tobias, John L.

1991 "Protection, Civilization, Assimilation: An Outline History of Canada's
Indian Policy," in J.R. Miller, ed., *Sweet Promises: A Reader on Indian-White
Relations in Canada.* Toronto: University of Toronto Press.

PART II
The Arctic

CHAPTER 3
The Eskaleuts: A Regional Overview

Ernest S. Burch, Jr.

An Aboriginal population, known to science as the "Eskaleuts," extended from the western tip of the Aleutian Islands and the Asiatic coast of the Bering Sea around the western portion of Alaska, across northern Canada to the Atlantic Ocean, and further still to the shores of Greenland. This immense region, some 20,000 km (12,000 miles) long, was inhabited in the eighteenth century by about 81,000 people speaking at least seven related, but different, languages.

The diversity of Eskaleut peoples in the eighteenth century was much greater than most people realize, but it is not really surprising given their extensive geographic distribution. "Eskaleut," of course, is an artificial word derived from the names of the two major linguistic divisions of the general population, Eskimos and Aleuts.

Aleuts

The Aleuts occupied the Aleutian Islands and a portion of the adjacent Alaska Peninsula. Their country is characterized by a maritime climate noted for its perpetual strong winds, overcast skies, frequent fog, and violent storms. Although the area receives a fair amount of snow in winter, the ocean remains ice-free year round. Aleutian waters are home to a rich and diverse marine fauna. Whales, sea lions, seals, sea otters, walrus, several varieties of fish and shellfish, sea birds, and seaweed provided a reliable resource base for a relatively dense human population. Aleut hunting technology was admirably developed to harvest these resources.

The estimated 14,000 Aleuts of the mid-eighteenth century were divided into three major groups: Eastern Aleuts, numbering some 9,000 people; Central Aleuts, numbering perhaps 4,000; and Western Aleuts, numbering about 1,000.

Rather little is known about the traditional life of the Central and Western Aleuts. The Eastern Aleuts, who have been more thoroughly described, were organized in terms of relatively large-scale (for hunters) societies of up to some 2,000 people, and these societies generally were more complex in structure than any Eskimo society. They were divided into a series of hereditary, ranked classes consisting of chiefs, nobles, commoners, and slaves. Aleut societies were apparently divided into matrilineal lineages whose major orientation was toward child-rearing and marriage practices. Girls were raised in their mother's household, but boys were brought up by their mother's brother. Residence was matri-patrilocal; newly married spouses lived with the wife's parents until a child was born, at which point they joined the household of the husband's parents. Aleut societies were also divided into patrilineal lineages, whose major function was to own land. Ritual, folklore, and art (particularly work with grass) were highly developed among the Aleuts. Inter-societal relations, too, were relatively complex, and included an extensive network of trade, a framework of relatively formal political alliances, and a complementary pattern of active warfare.

Eskimos

The second major branch of the Eskaleut language family is Eskimo. Eskimo-speaking peoples inhabit by far the largest portion of the Eskaleut area and are divided into several language groups. The most fundamental division within Eskimo is between Yup'ik and Inuit. Yup'ik Eskimos live in south-central and southwestern Alaska, and on portions

MAP 3.1. The Canadian Arctic

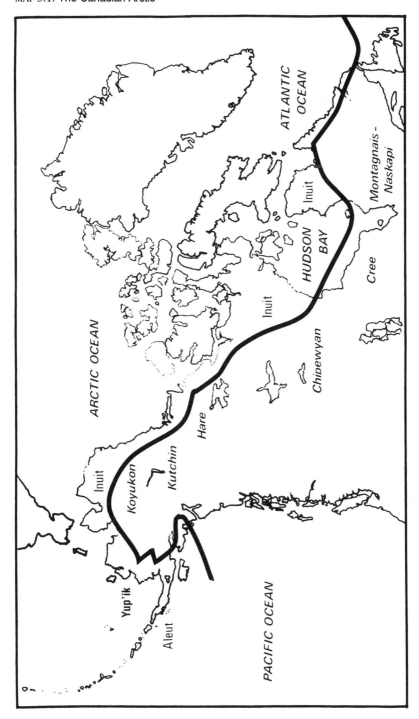

of the Asiatic shore of the Bering Sea and Bering Strait. Inuit Eskimos are distributed the whole way across North America, from Bering Strait to Greenland and Labrador.

Linguistic variation is much greater among the Yup'ik Eskimos than among their Inuit cousins. The Inuit Eskimo language is divided into a number of dialects, but all of them can be comprehended, at least after a brief period of familiarization, by a native speaker of the language. Yup'ik Eskimo, on the other hand, is divided into at least five totally different languages: Pacific, Central Alaskan, Naukanski, Chaplinski, and Sirenikski.

Pacific Yup'ik was spoken in south-central Alaska by perhaps as many as 10,000 people in the mid-eighteenth century. There were two groups of dialects: Chugach and Koniag. Like the Aleuts, Pacific Yup'ik societies had economies oriented to the harvest of marine mammals, although fish were also important. Their societies also were characterized by a system of ranked classes, by relatively elaborate art and ritual, and by complex inter-societal relations. Unlike the Aleuts, they apparently lacked any sort of lineage system.

A second Yup'ik language, Central Alaskan Yup'ik, was spoken in southwest Alaska, along the Bering Sea coast, and for a considerable distance inland along the major river systems. The region has ranges of hills and mountains scattered here and there, but most of it consists of an immense delta.

The Central Alaskan Yup'ik population of some 14,000 people in the mid-eighteenth century was concentrated along the rivers and along portions of the Bering Sea coast. There were three major dialect areas, Bristol Bay, Kuskokwim, and Yukon, and a number of small, local dialect areas. The relatively dense human population was sustained by salmon and several other types of fish, by caribou, by sea mammals along the coast, and by a variety of plant and other animal foods. Unlike the Aleuts and Pacific Yup'ik peoples, the Central Alaskan Yup'ik Eskimos did not have a system of hereditary, ranked classes, and, in most respects, their social system was less complex than that of their southern relatives.

The other three Yup'ik languages are often lumped together under the heading of "Asiatic Yup'ik," although that is strictly a geographic designation, not a linguistic one: the three languages were quite distinct from one another, and Sirenikski was the most divergent of all Eskimo languages.

The northernmost of the three Asiatic Yup'ik languages was Naukanski Yup'ik. In the mid-eighteenth century it was spoken by perhaps 1,000 people living on or near East Cape (on the west side of the strait), and

MAP 3.2. Eskaleut Peoples

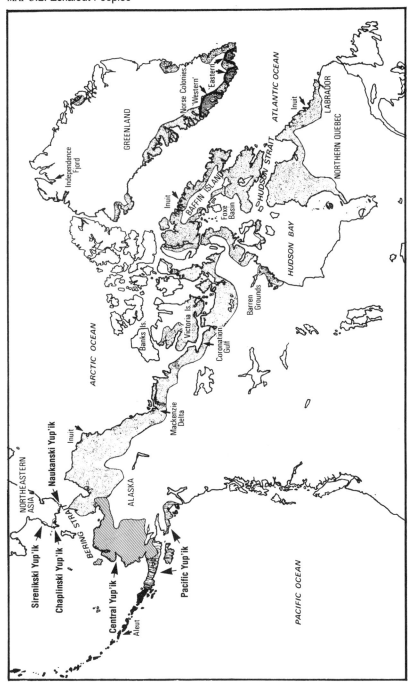

possibly at scattered points along the coast for another fifty km or so on either side of the cape area. Chaplinski Yup'ik was spoken by perhaps 6,000 people who lived on St. Lawrence Island and on the adjacent Asiatic mainland. Sirenikski was spoken by only 150 to 200 people who lived along the southern shore of the Chukchi Peninsula, just west of the Chaplinski language area. This language is now extinct.

All three Asiatic Yup'ik-speaking groups occupied rugged, barren coastal regions, and their economies were nearly as marine-oriented as those of Aleut societies. They had little access to fish resources, and they acquired virtually all of their reindeer (Eurasian caribou) skins and meat through trade with neighbouring Chukchi. Asiatic Yup'ik societies are distinguished from all other Eskimo societies in that most of them were organized in terms of exogamous, patrilineal clans.

All other Eskimos, some 35,000 people, spoke the Inuit language, which also has been referred to as Inupik and as Eastern Eskimo. Inuit speakers were spread the whole way across the top of the continent, many portions of the Canadian Archipelago, and most of coastal Greenland. They were organized into several dozen societies, which anthropologists have lumped together for descriptive convenience into geographic groups, which are listed in Table 3.1.

Inuit Eskimos generally have been thought of as maritime peoples. In fact, few Inuit were as dependent on marine resources as the Aleuts, the Pacific Yup'ik, or the Asiatic Yup'ik Eskimos. Almost all Inuit relied to a significant extent on caribou as a source of raw materials, and anadromous fish were very important in some regions. A few Inuit groups – in northwest Alaska, in the region just west of Hudson Bay, and in northern Quebec – had economies oriented more toward terrestrial than toward maritime resources. The precise combination of animal and plant species available to Inuit populations varied considerably from one section of their vast territory to another, as did the climate and the topography. With few exceptions, Inuit economies, yearly cycles of movement, and lifestyles were precisely adjusted to deal with both the assets and the liabilities each local environment had to offer.

Inuit Eskimo culture, in general, was less complex than that of either the Aleuts or the Yup'ik Eskimos. Inuit societies were not divided into ranked classes of any kind, and neither clan nor lineage organizations have been reported for any Inuit group. Art and ritual also were not as well developed among the Inuit as among their Aleut and Yup'ik relatives. On the other hand, Inuit culture was more complex in some areas than most Westerners generally realize, particularly in northwest Alaska and in the Mackenzie Delta region of Canada.

Table 3.1
Major Divisions of Inuit Eskimos, circa 1750

Group	General Location	Approximate Numbers
Northwest Alaska	Bering Strait to the mouth of the Colville River, Alaska	10,000
Mackenzie Delta	Herschel Island to the Baillie Islands	2,000
Copper	Cape Parry to Queen Maude Gulf, including much of Victoria Island	1,300
Netsilik	Adelaide Peninsula, King William Island, Boothia Peninsula, and Pelly Bay	650
Caribou	West central coast of Hudson Bay	400
Satlirmiut	Southern portion of Southampton Island	200
Iglulik	Wager Bay, Repulse Bay, west side of Foxe Basin, and northern Baffin Island	700
Baffin Island	East, south, and west coasts of Baffin Island	2,750
Labrador Peninsula	Coastal area from Great Whale River, on west, to Sandwich Bay on east, including Ungava Peninsula	4,200
Polar	Extreme northwestern Greenland	200
Southwest Greenland	West coast of Greenland south of Baffin Bay	12,000
East Greenland	Southeast coast of Greenland	1,100
	Total	35,500

Contact with Europeans

The first definite encounters between Europeans and Eskaleuts took place about 800 years ago, when Norse settlers encountered Inuit in Greenland – although encounters may have taken place somewhat earlier, when Norse explorers first visited Greenland, Baffin Island, Labrador, and Newfoundland.

The second period of Eskaleut-European contact also occurred in the

PLATE 3.1. Ahiarmiut caribou hunters in their kayaks on the upper Kazan River, 1894. They are taking a break from spearing caribou crossing the river. The man in the foreground is smoking a pipe, a habit the Inuit acquired very early in the historic period. By permission of the J.B. Tyrrell Papers, Thomas Fisher Rare Book Library, University of Toronto.

East. In the late 1400s, Portuguese and Basque fishermen and whalers began to frequent the waters of the western North Atlantic. They were followed by explorers, and in 1501 Gaspar Corte-Real's expedition encountered Inuit in Labrador and captured several dozen of them to take back to Europe. Other explorers and increasing numbers of whalers and fishermen from several European countries followed. They encountered Inuit in Greenland, Baffin Island, and Labrador with increasing frequency over the course of the fifteenth and sixteenth centuries.

The eighteenth century saw a new phase of Eskaleut-European contacts when permanent European outposts began to be built in Native territory. In the eastern Arctic these outposts were established by missionaries and traders, for the most part, and their relations with the Inuit were usually peaceful, if not always friendly. In the West, outposts were first established in the 1740s, when Russians began to move into Alaska. The Russians were bent on conquest and plunder, and the Aleuts, Pacific Yup'ik Eskimos, and the Tlingit Indians mounted a formidable armed resistance to them. Ultimately the Russians prevailed, and missionaries and traders were able to begin working in the area well before the end of the eighteenth century.

Over the course of the eighteenth and nineteenth centuries, explorers, missionaries, traders, and occasional other people of European descent gradually pushed forward into Eskimo territory, proceeding from both the East and West toward the centre. Despite their generally good intentions toward the Natives, they spread disaster in their wake in the form of diseases for which the Natives had neither immunity nor cure. Smallpox, measles, mumps, and many others wrought terrible havoc, particularly in the more densely populated areas of Alaska and the Atlantic coast. By the beginning of the twentieth century, the overall Eskaleut population may have been reduced to only half its size of 1750.

By about 1920, outposts of non-Natives had been established at key points over the entire length and breadth of Eskaleut country. With few exceptions, each of these tiny settlements included one or two missionaries and traders, and, in the Canadian North, a detachment of the Royal Canadian Mounted Police. In some areas there were schools as well, typically run by missionaries. In most cases there was also a small resident population of Natives, but the great majority still spent most of the year living in small, widely dispersed camps; they made periodic visits to the mission/trading post settlements during the winter, but came in for a month or two in the summer. This general pattern prevailed, particularly in Canadian Inuit territory, until the end of World War Two.

World War Two and the Cold War that followed it heightened U.S. and Canadian interest in northern regions, leading to the construction of military bases and radar sites all across northern North America. The labour requirements of this work led to the hiring of hundreds of Natives for varying periods of time and to contacts with outsiders of a type and on a scale never before seen in the North. The resulting changes, combined with increasing concern for Native health and welfare and a growing sense of obligation on the part of governments to provide better schooling for Native children, led to still greater government involvement in Native affairs in the 1950s. However, it was impossible to deliver the necessary services to people living in widely dispersed camps, so a systematic effort was made to encourage the Natives to abandon their camps for the administrative centres. This campaign had been largely successful by the late 1960s.

In 1990 there were approximately 1,700 Yup'ik Eskimos and 700 Aleuts living in Russia; 3,000 Aleuts, 24,500 Yup'ik, and 12,000 Inuit Eskimos in Alaska; 30,500 Inuit Eskimos in Canada; and 44,000 Inuit Eskimos in Greenland. The great majority of these people lived in small, widely dispersed communities in or near their traditional homelands.

Although geographically isolated, most villages were connected with the outside world by radio, television, telephone, and fax, and they were easily reached by scheduled air service. Virtually all of them had electricity, but plumbing was less widespread due to the extreme climate and harsh terrain. A mixed subsistence-market economy had replaced the traditional subsistence economy. Despite the importance of cash in modern Eskaleut life, hunting and fishing continued to be a major affirmation of cultural identity as well as an important source of food.

The two most significant issues in the Arctic over the last twenty years have been animal rights and land claims. In what began as a well-intentioned effort to curb certain excesses in harvesting wildlife and in dealing with animals generally, many animal rights activists have advocated programs that, if taken to their logical conclusion, will stop wildlife harvest altogether. So far they have not achieved that goal, but they have been successful enough to cause considerable hardship among people who must hunt and trap to earn a living, particularly in northern Canada.

The land claims movement in the Arctic has been part of the efforts of indigenous peoples in North America generally to regain ownership, or at least some control, over their homelands. The first major landmark in the North was the Alaska Native Claims Settlement Act of 1971, under which Eskimos and Aleuts, along with other Alaska Natives, could select nearly 18 million hectares of land and receive $962.5 million in cash. The second was the Home Rule Act of 1978, under which the Danish Parliament granted a high level of local autonomy to Greenlanders to run their own affairs. The third landmark was the 1984 settlement between the Inuvialuit of the western Canadian Arctic and the government of Canada. This and related developments in Canada are discussed in greater detail by John Matthiasson in Chapter 4 of this volume. In Russia, the Eskimos and Aleuts have not recovered sufficiently from the harsh treatment they received under the Soviet regime even to begin an effective land claims campaign.

Recommended Readings

Burch, Ernest S., Jr.
  1988   *The Eskimos*, with photographs by Werner Forman. Norman, Oklahoma: University of Oklahoma Press.
        A lavishly illustrated, comprehensive description of Eskaleut ways of life during the early 1800s. Intended for a general audience.

Damas, David, ed.

1984   *Handbook of North American Indians*. Vol. 5, *Arctic*. Washington, D.C.:
        Smithsonian Institution.
        An encyclopedic source of information on Eskaleut peoples.

Wenzel, George

1991   *Animal Rights, Human Rights: Ecology, Economy and Ideology in the
        Canadian Arctic*. Toronto: University of Toronto Press.
        An excellent analysis of the impact of the animal rights movement on the
        Inuit of the eastern Canadian Arctic.

CHAPTER 4
The Maritime Inuit: Life on the Edge

John Stephen Matthiasson

Introduction

Kaj Birket-Smith, one of the legendary early Arctic anthropologists, stated that the Inuit live on the edge of the inhabited and the brink of the uninhabitable. The depiction is compelling and accurate. Today it takes on a new meaning, as the Inuit prepare to take charge of the most northerly territory in Canada – Nunavut.

Surely no human population has ever engaged in a more demanding adaptation than have the Inuit, as over centuries they have eked out a living from, and created a rich culture within, one of the harshest environments on our planet. Other populations have adjusted to the hardships of desert life; the Inuit also exist in a desert, one that serves up bone-chilling temperatures.

At the time of European contact, most Inuit living in what is now Canada had developed a maritime culture. Although the land provided some resources for them, their lives were directed toward the sea. The Caribou Inuit were an exception, but they are discussed elsewhere.

In most respects the social arrangements and cultural patterns of the Inuit at the time of European intrusion were relatively identical from northern Alaska across the northern rim of the continent to eastern Baffin Island and Greenland and down into Labrador. I will treat them as homogeneous here, while warning the reader that regional variations are being glossed over.

The Inuit, then, have made remarkably successful adaptations to the vicissitudes of life on the fringe. Over time, there have been dramatic changes in those patterns of adaptation. Two important points are that these changes were primarily evolutionary and that they were the creations of the Inuit themselves.

It was the last stage, characterized as Thule culture, that Europeans encountered. Those encounters forced the Inuit to make a new form of adaptation. Suddenly, they were no longer the only ones interested in the Arctic regions of North America. Now, they had to adjust to the presence of aliens who brought with them a vastly different culture and a force for change as difficult to avoid as that of a juggernaut. To a large extent the Inuit drew on the resources of their own traditions to cope with these outsiders, and they did so successfully.

This chapter will consist of two main parts. In the first, I will describe Inuit culture and society as they existed in pre-contact times. Second, I will trace Inuit responses to outsiders from the earliest contacts up to the present, when they prepare for Nunavut and a new millennium.

Anthropological Representations of Inuit

Virtually everyone who has become aware of the Inuit has been fascinated by them, and anthropologists have not been different. Franz Boas, later to be known as the father of North American anthropology, provided the first comprehensive ethnographic depiction of them in his *The Central Eskimo* (1888). When he did his fieldwork Boas was still a geographer, but the anthropologist who was to emerge is evident in this classic work. It was typical of its time and reads almost like a trait list, with broad categories filled with minute details. Boas claimed to have lived with the people he studied, but there is some suggestion that he had a manservant along with him, who would surely have acted as a buffer between the young geographer and the real hardships of Inuit life.

Vilhjalmur Stefansson, an anthropologist and explorer who began life in Manitoba, provided ethnographic materials on the Inuit in the early years of this century, but his accounts have been criticized for their tendencies to romanticization as well as his attempts to prove Nordic influences on Thule culture. Of Icelandic heritage himself, it is perhaps understandable that Stefansson would look for some genetic and cultural blending of the medieval Icelandic settlers in Greenland with the Inuit.

Certainly the richest material on traditional Inuit life is found in the reports of Knud Rasmussen and his colleagues on the Fifth Thule Expedition in the early 1920s. Of mixed Danish-Inuit parentage, Rasmussen led the expedition of scientists on a monumental voyage from Greenland to Alaska. The reports stand alongside the *Jesuit Relations* as the most encyclopedic of any documents on Aboriginal peoples of North America.

Stefansson and Rasmussen brought with them young ethnographers who were to become the leading interpreters of Inuit society and culture. Diamond Jenness, who had previously done fieldwork in Oceania before accompanying Stefansson to the western Arctic, became the ethnographer of the Copper Eskimo and later the interpreter of Inuit experiences with colonial powers. Kaj Birket-Smith wrote about the Caribou Inuit after returning from the Fifth Thule Expedition and later produced a major synthesis of traditional Inuit culture.

Other anthropologists, as well as novelists and adventurers, have portrayed the Inuit, but these early explorer-ethnographers were the ones of whom a younger generation stood in awe. They were figures of legendary proportions. In more recent times, a new generation has attempted to reconstruct aspects of traditional Inuit society and culture. Names like Burch, Wenzel, Briggs, Damas, and Balicki come immediately to mind, but most of these have been far more problem-oriented than their predecessors, and their representations have been less comprehensive.

During the last several decades, anthropological observers of the Inuit have directed their greatest attention to the consequences of change rather than the reconstruction of tradition. In this genre are writings by Frank Vallee, John and Irma Honigmann, and Robert Williamson, among many others, which focus on interactions between Inuit and outsiders – whether European or Canadian.

It is primarily from these anthropologists that I will draw the generalized portrait of the pre-contact time as well as the time of adaptations to outside presences. I will also use my own fieldwork experiences among the Inuit as a sounding board for their observations and interpretations.

Like Jenness, my own earliest anthropological interests were in more temperate environments – in my case, India. I applied to graduate schools – originally in sociology – with specialists in India studies and was admitted to one. Later, I transferred for doctoral work in anthropology to

MAP 4.1. Iglulingmiut and Tununirmiut Territories, Late Nineteenth Century

Reprinted from the *Handbook of North American Indians* (Washington, D.C.: Smithsonian Institution Press), vol. 5, page 432, reprinted by permission of the publisher.

Cornell University, which had strong programs in both Asia and South Asia. However, lingering on the back-burner of my imagination was a fascination with the people of the Far North. What product of a Canadian school system could avoid it?

At Cornell I became interested in the anthropology of law, and through the influence of Pertti Pelto, my area interest changed to the circumpolar regions. I had also been seduced, while still in an M.A. program, by the newly popular paradigm of neo-evolution, which was replacing the static structural-functional model. Before long I had decided to try to find funds for a study of the consequences of contact between the legal or social control systems of societies placed at the two extreme ends of the evolutionary continuum – hunters and gatherers and industrialized societies. I hoped to examine the ways in which Inuit coped with the presence of Royal Canadian Mounted Police (RCMP) and the enforcement of Canadian laws.

The region I selected was that surrounding Pond Inlet, a small settlement located on the northern tip of Baffin Island. A search of the literature revealed that nothing had been done there by socio-cultural anthropologists, although Therkel Matthiessen had made some excavations of Thule sites in the area while with the Fifth Thule Expedition, and the archaeologist-missionary Father Guy-Marie Rousseliere had done so more recently. It was probably the dream of every anthropologist of my generation to find a setting for research that had not been studied before, and Pond Inlet seemed to provide me with such an opportunity.

Fortunately, I was awarded a grant for the study, and in the summer of 1963 I arrived in Pond Inlet with a tent and plans to set it up somewhere in the settlement and use it as a base for carrying out formal interviews. I had been told in Ottawa that there would be no difficulty in locating a local interpreter.

It turned out that the majority of the local Inuit, who called themselves Tununirmiut, lived in small hunting camps located out on the land and there was no one in the settlement who could act as an interpreter. I soon found myself residing with a family in their own tent in a camp some distance from Pond Inlet. There were five households in the camp.

For the next nine months I lived with the family of Jimmy Muckpah, and later spent time in other camps. During that period I often forgot about my study of what I called legal acculturation and instead immersed myself in day-to-day camp life. I hunted with the men and lived on the spoils of our hunts. In anthropological terms, I became much more a participant than an observer.

Ten years later I returned to Pond Inlet and spent an extended period of time studying the effects on the Tununirmiut of having abandoned their camps and moved into the settlements. In the interim and later I taught a field training course in Rankin Inlet, Northwest Territories, and conducted research in Yellowknife, the territorial capital, as well as in several communities in the northern parts of the western provinces.

The "Ethnographic Present" as a Form of Representation

Social and cultural anthropologists have traditionally written their descriptive accounts of the lifestyles of the people they have studied in the so-called "ethnographic present." That is, they have used the present tense, and their accounts read as if the peoples still lived as they had before encountering colonialism. In some ways, there is nothing seriously wrong with this practice, yet, it has come under attack in the past decade or so. One reason for the criticism is that readers may forget that the ethnographic present being represented is a life that is no longer lived. In addition, it is a construction created by the anthropologist, who has attempted to depict a society and culture but has to do this in a language and with descriptive and analytic categories that may not be real for the people being represented.

Use of the ethnographic present also may lead the reader to assume that the people lived in some sort of isolation from other human societies, with real socio-cultural markers setting them off. Few human societies have lived in such isolation. Also, anthropologists are beginning to ask whether the very ideas of "culture" and "society" do not imply some artificial boundaries that aid in representation but do not fit with social reality.

Finally, use of the ethnographic present may imply that the anthropologist was the first outsider to have encountered the people. Although earlier generations of anthropologists liked to think of themselves as adventurers who went off into lands where others feared to tread, it is realized today that in most cases someone else preceded them. In the case of the Inuit, it was explorers, whalers, missionaries, and traders. So the societies and cultures represented in the ethnographic present were always both constructions and reconstructions. I will avoid its use here, although the authors whose work I will draw upon often did employ it.

The Maritime Inuit before the Europeans

The Inuit culture first encountered by Europeans was primarily oriented toward life on the coastline. The people who practised it were able to harvest from the sea everything from fish to large mammals such as walruses and whales. Their technology was geared toward the exploitation of sea resources, and the animals captured provided for many of their needs, from clothing to materials for house construction.

The populations of Inuit who inhabit the northern fringes of the continent have been classified into several groupings that represent some internal cultural similarities as well as regional distribution, but are not political entities. They are more meaningful for the anthropologist, perhaps, than for the Inuit themselves. Still, there are some differences between the several Canadian Inuit categories, which are, from the West, the Mackenzie or Inuvialuit, Copper, Netsilik, Iglulik, Baffinland, and Labrador or Ungava Inuit. (To the south of the Netsilik Inuit are the inland Caribou Inuit.) Prior to the 1980s, they are all referred to as Eskimo, as in Copper Eskimo. Today that term has been replaced by the indigenous one, "Inuit" (singular: "Inuk"). The most common explanation for the word "Eskimo" is that it is a Chipewyan expression for "eaters of raw meat." Canadian Inuit today find it to be obnoxious and unacceptable.

Subsistence Activities and Technology

Anthropologists classify Inuit among hunters and gatherers – a subsistence pattern found in varied forms in most areas of the world. In recent years, there has been considerable criticism of what has been termed "the hunting hypothesis," which has placed major importance for food procurement on hunting activities in societies that practise both hunting and gathering. Ecological studies have demonstrated that in many such societies, where women do the gathering of wild plant life while men hunt, most of the food that nurtures the population is provided by the women's activities (Lee and DeVore, 1968). For the Inuit, however, there is no question. While during the brief summers women and children might collect arctic moss for their soapstone lamps and some berries, these were negligible contributions – they were dependent on hunting and fishing.

The Inuit were nomadic peoples and would move about over the Arctic landscape in yearly rounds, which were determined largely by the migration patterns of the species hunted. In spring and summer, camps

MAP 4.2. **Thule, Norse, and Historic Inuit Populations**

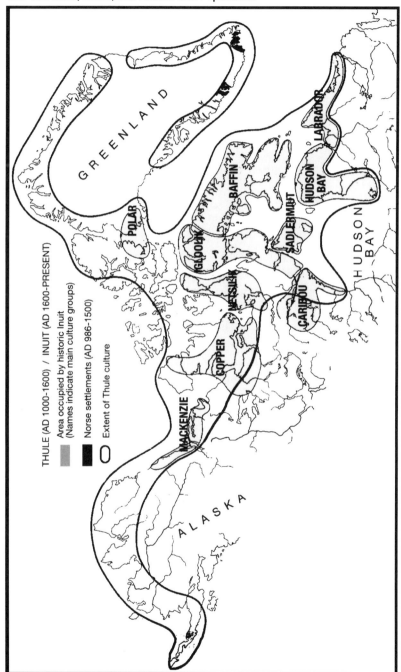

R. Cole Harris and Geoffrey J. Matthews, *Historical Atlas of Canada* (vol. 1),
plate 11. Copyright University of Toronto Press Incorporated (1987). Reprinted
by permission of the publisher.

might be established near where the seal mothers and their young congregated. Hunters would creep up on these pairs as they lay on the ice basking in the spring sun. During those seasons birds were an important source of food as well. Spears, bows and arrows, and bolas were used to kill them, and individuals would also climb cliffs and steal eggs from nests. Some birds, such as the raven and seagulls, were not considered proper food, but most others were.

The caribou was the most important land animal. Even the coastal peoples hunted it when herds were nearby, for its meat was considered a delicacy, its horns provided material for tools, and its hide made the warmest clothing. Each hair of the caribou is tubular and so provides excellent insulation. Caribou hides were also used as mattresses and bedding in houses and tents. Men usually hunted them during the summer months at points on the migration routes where they would be most densely massed.

Even though caribou meat was valued because of its taste, Inuit preferred sea mammals and fish – in part because of their higher fat content. Muskoxen were another source of land food, but their numbers in the High Arctic have been so small that they have probably never been important. Polar bears might have been killed on occasion, but quite rarely. They were never about in large numbers, and they are extremely dangerous animals to hunt, even now with rifles.

Fishing was done year-round, and it was a task in which everyone could participate. The most common technique was to use the three-pronged fish spear. In winter, holes would be made in the ice for fishing, and in fall, open cracks could be used. Hooks, sometimes with lures attached, provided another method.

The Inuit developed two types of skin-covered boats, the *kayak* and the *umiak*, that enabled them to hunt sea mammals during the summer months of open water. The *kayak* was basically a one-man vessel, although in the classic film documentary, *Nanook of the North*, there is a scene in which Nanook the hunter pulls close to shore and steps out of his *kayak*, followed by his wives, children, and a dog. Many anthropologists have criticized the film because it presents some stereotyped images of the Inuit, but I have always found the disembarkment scene appealing, and I think it would draw laughs if it were shown to an Inuit audience. *Kayaks* could be used to hunt caribou at crossing points along rivers, but more crucially, for seal hunting at sea. The *umiak* has often been termed the women's boat. Larger and more bulky than the *kayak*, it allowed several men together to go in pursuit of whales.

PLATE 4.1. Tununirmiut hunters in search of sea mammals (ca.1923). Courtesy of the Canadian Museum of Civilization, 61068.

Inuit technology was extensive and elaborate – far too much so to go into it in detail. Tools were made from available materials, such as stone, bone, antler, and driftwood. There was an inventory of tools for each gender, and the women's fully equalled that of the men. Graburn has suggested that a dualistic distinction existed between the worlds of male and female, and that it is evident in the tool assemblages (1973: 151). Later I will discuss relationships between the sexes, but I want to say here that his explicitly Freudian symbolism used to characterize the two domains is too sharp and exclusive. Nevertheless, the images of the long, pointed harpoon, which was exclusively a male tool, and the half-moon-shaped *ulu*, or woman's knife, are suggestive. To push that symbolism too far, though, could lead one to miss the interwoven nature of the two domains.

Housing

Inuit are probably known best for the remarkable way in which they used the almost ubiquitous snow as the main material for a type of dwelling perfectly suited for a nomadic people. Schoolbooks usually refer to the famous snow house as an *iglu*, but actually that word applies to any kind of residence. More properly, the snow house is, in the Inuit language, Inuktitut, an *igluviga*. In it, the seal-oil burning soapstone lamp, or *kudlik*, and human body warmth provided the only heating, but snow provides excellent insulation, and Inuit would often walk about comfortably with no clothing above the waist, and laughing, naked infants would be passed from one adult to another. The snow house was highly efficient for mobile hunters, who could make one in an hour or two after a day of hunting.

The snow house was used throughout the winter by the central Inuit, but in the western and eastern regions it was used primarily by hunting parties. The main winter residence in those areas was the *karmat*, which was a relatively permanent semi-subterranean building made of whale bone, stone, and sod. The *karmat* is what has often been called the Thule house, and remnants of them have provided a source of aged whale bone for carvers.

Neither type of dwelling was very large, and usually entry was gained by crawling through a cold trap, which was dug into the snow lower than the main portion of the floor and trapped warm air in the house. A platform at the rear, which was sometimes raised, and small benches on either side of it provided the only furniture, and family members would sleep side by side on the platform on caribou hides, with their heads pointing toward the entrance. At times, though, snow houses could be quite roomy, with smaller rooms attached for individual family units. A snow porch would often be attached to either type of house, which might be a place to store meat or to keep the dogs. It was also not uncommon to build larger buildings, whether of sod and bone or snow, which would be used for ceremonials and other group functions.

In the summer months skin tents were used. These were the times of well-planned nomadic wanderings, and the easily collapsed and transportable tents were ideal for this. The internal arrangement was the same in tents as in houses, with the sleeping area at the rear.

Social Organization

The Canadian Inuit did not have formal political systems, and they cannot be regarded as having had tribal organizations. That is, they did not have well-defined territories over which there was a sense of ownership, some internal social stratification, or gradings, and hereditary leadership positions. Still, this does not mean that the societies they created were devoid of political attributes.

The social organization of the Inuit can be compared in some respects with the layers of skin of an onion. Each one encompasses another one.

The layers of organization for the Inuit were found in the "*-miut*" groups. For example, a population would have a certain identification with a geographical area. This area might be quite small, but it would be given a name. On a larger scale, the people might identify with other peoples in adjoining areas, and another term would apply to all of them. On top of that, there may be some sense of identification with an even broader range of other Inuit, and a name would apply there as well. Each name would have the *-miut* suffix.

To give an example, I live in the west end of Winnipeg, so I am a westender, but when travelling to Brandon, I identify myself as a Winnipeger. On a trip to Ontario, though, I will say that I am a Manitoban, and if I visit Europe, I am a Canadian. These are my own *-miut* groups. Mobility was always possible from one *-miut* group to another at the lower levels, so I might move from the west end of Winnipeg to the north end. I would still be a Winnipeger, a Manitoban, and a Canadian. The identification I would be unlikely to change would be the last, or the most embrasive – Canadian. Similarly, there seem to have been very broad categories of *-miut* groups that involved a kind of ethnicity or nationality, and to some extent these corresponded to the classifications of Inuit used by anthropologists. When I did fieldwork among the people of northern Baffin Island in the early 1960s, I lived in the camp of the Allativikmiut, who were part of the broader category of Tununirmiut, which included the people of Pond Inlet as well as all other nearby camps. On a broader level, they were Iglulingmiut and shared an identity with other Inuit, such as those of the Iglulik area.

The band probably was the level of social organization that had the most real structure in a political sense. It was also the smallest and the most unstable in terms of membership. People would congregate together at certain times of the year and then split into smaller groupings at others. Borrowing terms from physics, anthropologists call this a pattern of fission and fusion. The units that went off together at times of splitting might be as small as individual nuclear families. The groupings that came together were never very large, but might include as many as twenty or even thirty people. The decisions to congregate and to separate were determined by the migratory habits of the animals upon which they were dependent and by the weather. In winter, for example, when breathing-hole hunting was good, several families might congregate together. During the days the men would go off to hunt while the women and children performed chores, practised crafts, and played games.

These bands, each with its own name, with a *-miut* suffix attached to it, constituted the main form of socio-political organization for the Inuit.

PLATE 4.2. Tununirmiut families, Pond Inlet (ca. 1923). Courtesy of the Canadian Museum of Civilization, 61077.

Membership in the bands was not stable. Individuals and families were free to move from one to another at will, so long as they were accepted in the new setting. This pattern was continued when Inuit moved close to the trading posts and established fairly permanent camps. Movement from one camp to another was common and acceptable. Membership in bands, therefore, was extremely flexible.

Each band had its own leader, but that person had very little real authority, and virtually no power, if we will accept as a definition of power the ability to coerce others. The Inuktitut word most commonly used to describe such leaders is *isumataq*, "the one who thinks." The person holding the position was usually one of the older males, who was probably also well placed within the kinship network. The ideal band leader was a wise decision-maker, a good hunter, and an exemplar of Inuit values, and must have demonstrated all three qualities over time. He might be asked for advice on where men should hunt, or may decide when it was time for the band to separate. Although a skilled hunter, he would be sure to share his kills with members of his band and to loan his hunting equipment to other men when not using it himself. Sharing meat and sharing tools were both ways to show a commitment to basic cultural values.

Members of a band would take direction from an *isumataq* so long as it was sound advice, but they were not bound to do so, for at any time they were free to pack up their belongings and move to a different band. They might even ignore his counsel and stay around, for he could not coerce anyone to follow his will. To be an incumbent meant validating one's position continually, so it might be said that the status rested in the display of the attributes rather than the person.

As a corollary to this, the position was not hereditary. My impression has been that sons of leaders tended to succeed their fathers, but to do so they also had to show the proper qualities of personhood and behaviour.

Essentially, then, there was minimal social stratification among the Canadian maritime Inuit. Leaders were like everyone else in most ways, or even more so, for they were expected to be paragons of virtue. There were stories about leaders who were authoritarian, but the fact that this was tolerated was more a reflection of individual personalities. Also, there were limits to what would be tolerated.

However, because of this lack of formal social stratification, Inuit society has usually been characterized as being egalitarian. On the basis of my fieldwork among the Tununirmiut, I suggest that there was an accepted "ideology of egalitarianism," but there was also considerable manoeuvring for political position. This was very subtle, and had to be conducted within the context of, while also giving recognition to, that ideology. This interpretation provides an explanation of why Canadian Inuit have been able to move into the different levels of the Canadian political context so successfully. They have been drawing on traditional models of political behaviour.

Thus, there were limited roles among the Inuit. Basically, other than those of *isumataq* and *angakuk*, or shaman, the roles were limited to either hunter or spouse of hunter. Individuals did not differ from one another in terms of material wealth, for all had basically the same skills as all others of the same gender, and there were explicit expectations that hunters would share their spoils with others. There were differences between individuals, and many observers have commented on the individuality of the Inuit, but there was also a high degree of conformity and considerable levelling.

The second specialized position was that of the shaman. Most discussions of shamanism begin with the societies of central Siberia, partly because the word "shaman" is from the Tungus language, but a more basic form is surely that of the Inuit. The position of shaman in Inuit society was open to both males and females, although there were probably more of the former. Reasons as to why individuals would choose the role have never been adequately addressed in the anthropological literature, and a variety of conflicting explanations have been put forward. Some observers have claimed that the role was sought by persons who were psychotic, that it allowed them some freedom to act out their illness. Personally, I find this suggestion difficult to accept, for the activities of shamans were far too complex to be carried out by persons suffering from serious personality disorders.

A less extreme hypothesis has been that individuals who had mild problems in interpersonal relationships were attracted to the role, that behaving as a shaman had a therapeutic value for them. This has been termed the "healed healer" explanation, for the shamans were indeed healers. It may have some validity, for the question must be asked as to why, in a society with two primary roles – those of males and females – an individual would want to take on a role that put him or herself into a position separate from the rest. For the average person, conformity would likely have been more appealing. It could be suggested that, for a male, at least, by becoming a shaman one did not have to engage in the risks and dangers associated with hunting, but that does not hold up because among the Inuit the shaman was not removed from the hunt. Services might be paid for, but they would not have provided complete support for the individual shaman.

A third explanation, which I find appealing myself, is that the men and women who were attracted to the shaman role were the more creative members of their society. In a different setting, they might have become philosophers or artists. The role of the shaman may have given them greater freedom for personal expression.

The role itself was multifaceted and the person playing it had considerable influence, but all of the scripts acted out by the person-qua-shaman were contingent on what most observers claim to be the essential characteristic of shamanism. That is, the individual had to have – or at least believe that he or she had, and be able to convince others of that – spirit helpers who would assist in performing the proper functions. I pose the possession of personal spirit helpers as the minimal definition of a shaman.

Healing was perhaps the primary task, and through healing the shamans gained credibility. The spirit helpers took the shaman off to another world or plane of existence to discover the cause of the illness, which often was believed to be soul-loss, and to find a possible cure. The use of trance states is common to shamans around the world, and whether induced by hallucinogenic drugs, chanting, meditation, or whatever, shamans would typically enter such a state to communicate with their helpers. Inuit shamans did not use mind-altering substances, perhaps because none were available.

Shamans were legal functionaries as well, and acting in this capacity might be intrinsic to healing. For example, if someone was ill, the shaman might call other members of the band together and, in full view of them, begin to ask the patient a number of questions about possible taboo violations. This was somewhat like a reading of the laws, in that a series of offences might be mentioned, which the shaman knew had not been committed by the patient. Then, when the correct one had been mentioned, and the patient-qua-defendant had pleaded guilty, a remedy would be sought. A punishment might be ordered, such as having sexual relations with the shaman or observing sexual abstinence with the spouse for a defined period of time. The shaman could not coerce the person to follow his or her order, but the members of the band would believe in the power of the spirit helpers and the shaman's connection with other spirits, both benevolent and malevolent. In this procedure, members of the band would be reminded of several possible taboo violations, which I suggest are analogous to laws, the patient would, hopefully, be healed, and the world would be returned to a steady state.

The shamans were also entertainers, and their public performances, such as acts of healing, were theatrical events that entertained as well as reinforced commitment to common beliefs and values, and shamans were not averse to manipulating their audiences. As examples, the shaman might employ tricks of ventriloquism, using different voices to represent his or her spirits, or be tied up before the event, only to appear from behind a hide screen unbound at its conclusion.

Much more needs to be learned about shamans, and we can only hope that it is not too late. Shamans jealously hold on to their secrets, for mystery is the basis of their influence. There are not many traditional Inuit shamans left alive today, and those keep their persona as shamans hidden – perhaps because missionaries have often labelled them as "agents of the devil."

I have been discussing social organization among the Canadian Inuit, and have done so largely in terms of role theory. It is important to remember that underlying all other relationships among Inuit were the patterns of kinship. People saw themselves as related to others through blood and marriage, and principles were used in sorting out these relationships. Many of the ethnographers who studied Inuit society during the post-World War Two period focused on kinship. In large part, this was because of a traditional emphasis in anthropology – in most societies entered by anthropologists, kinship rules were the basic principles of social organization. In such societies one's identity came not from achieved statuses but rather from place within a kin network. In Inuit society, kinship was important, but less so than in many other societies. In fact, it has been claimed that the Inuit system is almost identical to that used in mainstream North American society, where kinship has a place, but often one that is secondary to other forms of relationship. In the last several decades anthropologists have increasingly turned their attention to the non-kin relationships people employ to relate to and work with one another, and these were important among the Inuit. Nevertheless, kin relations did have considerable meaning for the Inuit.

Kinship groupings among the Inuit were not real groups at all, and this is a significant point, for in societies organized largely around kinship principles the descent groups were the primary social units. In these societies, individuals traced their identity through either the mother's or the father's line. These are unilineal or one-sided patterns of kinship reckoning. Among the Inuit, as in Canadian society, the system was bilateral. Descent was traced on both sides, and an individual was a member of two families, the father's and the mother's. There would be groups, but they existed only for the individual, for members of them did not necessarily see themselves as being related to one another, even though they recognized a relationship with the individual. So, for example, I am related to my mother's family and my father's family, but neither side regards itself as being related to the other. This arrangement results in a kind of quasi-kinship group termed a "kindred." Kindreds were the relatives, to use the English expression, of the individual. Both the kinship system, which gave the individual some sense of continuity over generations, and the kindred, which provided a large network of relatives for the individual, were sources of social support.

This fact of bilaterality is a prime example of why kinship was not that central to Inuit society, and is another instance of the flexible nature of their social arrangements. As with the band, individuals were not bound to the dictates of particular kin groupings. Bilaterality meant that newly married couples could affiliate with either the husband's family or the wife's, although there was a tendency toward patrilocality in residence. This preference for patrilineality was also reflected in kin terminology, with terms for the male side being more differentiated than those for the female.

Marriage itself was not highly ritualized; in fact, none of what anthropologists term the life crises – such as puberty – were much dramatized. The young couple would decide to form a union, and usually that was all

PLATE 4.3. Tununirmiut woman and children (ca. 1923). Courtesy of the Canadian Museum of Civilization, 61063.

that was required for the marriage to be recognized. However, infant betrothals were not uncommon and were expected to be honoured. Monogamy was the usual pattern, but polygynous marriages, in which there was more than one wife, were occasionally found. It was difficult for a hunter to support more than one wife. Marriage break-up was a regular occurrence and divorce was easily achieved. Men competed with one another for women, and in spite of the well-known wife exchanges, the jealousy engendered by such competitions often led to serious consequences, such as murder.

Within many family units there was considerable harmony, with a fairly well-defined division of labour between the sexes and with young children accepting family responsibilities at early ages. Young girls, for example, would be expected to share in caring for younger siblings.

Children were highly valued among the Inuit, and they were treated with great indulgence by their parents, but male offspring tended to be preferred. In difficult times infanticide was practised, but it was probably fairly uncommon. A cultural explanation for the practice is that infants did not become real persons until they were named, but it is difficult to envisage Inuit parents leaving an unnamed female baby outside to freeze without having some real sense of sorrow, given the love that was expended on named children. Circumstances forced the choice to be made, and the culture provided a rationalization for it, but that probably did not totally mitigate the pain of loss. Early accounts implied that infanticide was fairly common, but later studies have shown it to be less so. Possibly the first observers made much of infanticide simply because of a tendency to dramatize what seemed to be unusual.

Non-Kin Associations

Formal relationships between individuals seem to have been more common among males than females, and the most typical were partnerships. A partnership was a ritualized connection between two males who may or may not be kin. Often this was expressed in hunting co-operation, but other partnerships involved wife exchanges – usually with the consent of the wives – and joking relationships, in which partners could say things about one another that in other instances would be cause for a fight. Not all such associations were related to the food quest, but all seemed to have some social value. Joking partnerships, for example, might be mechanisms for release of tensions between hunters that otherwise could erupt into violence.

Social Control

A long-standing debate among anthropologists has been over how societies such as the Inuit, without any centralized forms of authority and institutions such as police, were able to avoid anarchy. Certainly it was necessary to maintain good relations between individuals in a setting where so much depended on co-operation with others. Individualistic though the Inuit may have been, they were dependent on one another. Yet, no one had recognized power over anyone else – no one could force others to behave in a manner supportive of the well-being of the community. Small populations of people in regular face-to-face contact with one another could not afford open conflicts between individuals, but the Inuit managed to do that without any overriding political structures.

One technique employed games of strength. Two men might stand together in a small space and, placing their powerful fingers into the other's mouth, pull at the sides. Eventually one would concede defeat and both participants would break up in laughter. Or they would stand facing one another and take turns punching the other on the shoulder. Painful games, but also, I suggest, effective ways to relieve tension and interpersonal hostilities, and far better than free-for-all fights.

The institution of the drum duel – sometimes called the song duel – was a more elaborate version of the games just described, and was saved for more serious disputes. Two men who, as an example, were competing for the same woman would each compose songs about his adversary. Then, in a public contest with other members of the band as an audience, they would perform their songs of derision, recalling real and invented sins while accompanying themselves on their drums. Alternately, each would have his opportunity, until eventually one would reluctantly admit defeat. The duel may last for weeks, and during it others in the band would respond to the songs by showing support for one or the other of the antagonists. Knud Rasmussen collected a large number of song duel compositions during the Fifth Thule Expedition, and these often reveal a high level of poetic elegance.

As discussed earlier, the shaman often acted as a judge when healing and would make adjudications that were supported by the band and usually accepted by the patient-qua-defendant. If the behaviour of an individual was so disruptive that the community itself was threatened and he or she refused to accept any socially acceptable resolution, members of the band might simply pick up and leave. Ostracism was a serious penalty in the Arctic. Should the person choose to follow the band and continue to be a social threat, individuals might decide to put him or her to death. Such an extreme act would be considered a socially permissible execution, as it would restore the social order.

In the absence of courts and police, then, the Inuit were able to maintain social control using mechanisms provided by their culture.

The Supernatural World

Many of the religious beliefs of the Inuit were lost after contact with missionaries, which is unfortunate, for they reveal a rich cosmology and mythology and were central to their culture. Most of the information on Inuit religion was collected by the early Arctic anthropologists, such as Boas and Rasmussen, but a major attempt at synthesis has recently been provided by Merkur (1991).

Inuit religion has often been called animistic. Animism was first defined in the last century by Edward Tylor, who claimed that it was the elemental form from which all religions developed – a belief in spirit entities. In Inuit religious belief humans had souls, the world was populated by animals who had spiritual qualities, and certain places, such as hills, also had spiritual attributes. Those spirits found in nature were much like humans, with emotions and intelligence, and could be offended if not treated properly. Along with beliefs in spirits are rituals. Thus, when an Inuk killed an animal, he would perform rites to assuage its spirit. An example is of a hunter giving a drink of water to a slaughtered seal and removing and eating its liver at the place of the kill in order to please its spirit, which would then return in a new form to be hunted again.

The world of the Canadian Inuit, then, was filled with spirits, and associated with them were a host of taboos. An Inuk had to be careful at all times to avoid insulting the spirits. One might ask why, in a very uncertain natural world, additional risks of a supernatural nature would be added. A functionalist interpretation would be that there is really no paradox at all, for the belief in following proper acts of commission and omission gave the people a sense of control over the world. By observing the rules, the hunt would be less uncertain and perhaps adversities such as illness would be averted. The individual most in touch with spirits was the *angakuk*, and he or she was the repository of knowledge about the appropriate ways of dealing with them.

The supernatural world of the Inuit was not limited to spirits attached to animals and places in the landscape, though, for there were larger and more powerful spirits that had dominion over lesser ones. The more mundane spirits were known as *tornat*, and they "owned" the objects or bodies to which they were attached. Merkur refers to the other class as *inua*, "indwellers" who organize the forces of nature and are responsible for the *tornat* and indeed all of life (1991: 1). Stories about the *inua* were embedded within myths passed on from one generation to the next. These myths often explained the origins of animals and of the Inuit themselves.

An intriguing fact about the indwellers is that they were often female. The best known of these beings is described in the Sedna myth, found in varying forms from Greenland across to northern Alaska. She was the sea mother, or the mother of the sea animals, who dwelt in the bottom of the ocean.

The most common version of the Sedna myth tells of a young woman who was betrothed by her father to a denizen of the deep to whom she was not attracted. Her father was fearful of her suitor and so took her out in a boat and threw her overboard. As she attempted to climb back onboard, he first cut off her fingers, which became fish, and then, on each successive effort by his daughter, other parts of her arms. The last ones to be severed became the large sea mammals, such as whales. The sea animals harvested by the hunters, then, were originally from Sedna's own body, and she controlled them. The paying of respect to the soul of a killed seal, therefore, was also a sign of respect for Sedna and her power. Periodically, shamans were expected to go on a voyage to the bottom of the sea with their spirit helpers to comb the hair of Sedna.

A lesser spirit, who had ominous qualities, was also a female. This was the woman with the hood, the *amaut*, on her back. (The *amautik* was the woman's parka, which had a hood used to carry infants.) As with Sedna, belief in her was widespread, but in some regions the spirit had, instead of a hood, a large hole in her back. There was also variation in terms of where she lived – a rock, the bottom of the sea, or the underworld – but there was general agreement that she was a large woman who would steal away children who did not behave in her parka or the hole in her back. Stories about the woman with the *amaut* were used to keep children in line, and mention of her name was apparently enough to do just that.

Sedna ruled the sea and provided its largesse to the Inuit, but it was the indweller of the earth, the "earth mother," who gave form to the land and all that grew upon it. It was she who gave the hunters and their families the animals of the land, such as caribou and muskoxen, although the caribou also had their own protector in some regions – the caribou mother. It seems that the earth mother was less important to the maritime Inuit, who were primarily oriented to the sea, than was Sedna, but both were venerated and described in legends. Each had her own domain and was jealous about maintaining its boundaries. A serious violation of taboo was to eat land and sea food together, for to do so would insult both indwellers.

There were also male indwellers, the most important of which was the "moon man," although some ethnographers have suggested that he was a fairly recent addition to the pantheon. Still, like the earth mother, moon man was extolled in myths from Greenland to Alaska. He was the protector of game, and would send animals only to hunters who observed the proper respect for them. It seems that the two major goddesses were responsible for the animals in the first place, but moon man had the task of ensuring their reincarnation, so there may have been a complementarity between their domains.

The Inuit placed little importance in organized ritual activities, and the seances of the shamans were the main opportunities for group religious observances. On the other hand, individual observation of rituals, which showed the proper respect for the specific spirits as well as the indwellers, was mandatory.

Their cosmology incorporated ideas of different levels of existence, with an upper world and a lower one surrounding the everyday plane. The *angakuk* might voyage with his or her spirit helpers to either in search of the lost soul of someone who was ill. Reincarnation occurred with human souls as well as those of animals, and the souls of the dead waited in the upper world for their rebirth. This usually took place when a child was given the name of a deceased relative, for the name and the soul were one and the same. Thus, a child became a human when it was named, for that act also transformed it into more than simply a body. The Inuit practised senilicide, and the aged and infirm would often request that they be put to death because they felt they were no longer able to contribute to society, but they did so with the firm cultural knowledge that they would be reborn.

The religious life of the maritime Inuit was far more complex, and included many more supernatural entities, than this brief description has covered. It seems important to place emphasis on the female deities, for their importance in the pantheon of spirits reflects the traditional relationships between males and females in Inuit society. Families preferred male offspring and might put a female infant to death, and the work of hunters may have been more valued than that of females, but at the same time there was relative equality between the sexes. The importance of the goddesses in the supernatural spheres was a strong indication of the fairly equal position of women in the natural world. My own observations supported this conclusion. The women I knew were strong personalities who held their own with their male counterparts.

The traditional life of the maritime Inuit, then, was one of nomadism over one of the most challenging areas of the globe. That they survived and created a rich set of cultural traditions is testimony to their adaptability and the powerful resources their culture provided for them. But eventually they were discovered by outsiders, and they had to turn their coping strategies to new challenges.

The Arrival of Europeans

Charles Hughes once wrote that the Inuit were the first North Americans to come into contact with Europeans. He was referring to their encounters with the early Icelandic settlements in Greenland, described in *The Greenland Saga* and *The Saga of Eric the Red*. In the latter part of the tenth century an Icelandic chieftain, Eric Thorvaldsson, known as Eric the Red because of his flame-coloured hair, was banished from Iceland for three years for murder. Under certain weather conditions it is possible to sight Greenland from Iceland, even though the curvature of the earth should preclude this. Whether or not Eric made this same sighting, along with his family and followers he set off for a distant island, until then unsettled by Europeans, to spend his period of exile. He hoped to attract others to join him in the new settlement, and in what was possibly the first example of false advertising, he named the island Greenland.

Greenland is a beautiful, yet forbidding, place, most of it covered by an ice cap. Nevertheless, the Norse settlements flourished for some time, and from there his son, Leif Ericsson, made the first recorded European voyage to the shores of Canada. The Icelandic sagas, as well as archaeological evidence, show that the relocated Icelanders had extensive contact with Natives, whom they called Skraelings. In time, for reasons still mired in some mystery, the settlements ceased to exist. But during their existence, for the first time Europeans and North American Aboriginal peoples interacted with one another.

However, this narrative is about what is now Canada, and it was some centuries before contact was re-established there. That region of the world now known as the Canadian Arctic has not until fairly recently had any more than a cursory interest for anyone other than the Inuit.

The quest for the Northwest Passage, a way through the Arctic to the fabled riches of the East, first motivated Europeans to attempt to explore the Arctic regions of North America. The first accounts of Arctic exploration are the journals of Martin Frobisher, who gave his name to some of its territories. On his first journey, in 1576, Frobisher made several encounters with Inuit and recorded the first descriptions of Canadian Inuit. In spite of the image of Inuit as a peaceable people, not all of Frobisher's meetings with them on this and subsequent voyages were amicable, and on one encounter Frobisher himself was shot in the buttocks by an Inuit arrow.

Others followed Froisher in search of the Passage, and in time European explorers came who were interested in mapping the Arctic itself. All of these expeditions undoubtedly met Inuit, and many of these meetings were indeed peaceful. Some trading probably ensued, as sailors and officers gathered souvenirs and in return gave trinkets. The journals of the captains and the chroniclers they brought with them all have depictions of the Inuit. Most are highly stereotypic, while others have real ethnographic value. However, for the most part encounters between Inuit and Europeans during the age of exploration had little long-range impact on the Inuit, and they continued to live as their ancestors had done.

The Comings and Goings of Whalers

The first exploitable Arctic resource for Europeans was the whale population, and by the 1800s whaling ships from Scotland and the United States could be found scattered over all regions of the Canadian Arctic. The whale's oil was a valuable resource, its bones were used in the bodices of women's dresses, and virtually all parts of its body had some commercial utility.

Whalers made the first major impression on the Canadian Inuit. Many of them wintered over, and so had prolonged contact. Inuit men were hired as guides and hunters, and assisted in the butchering of carcasses. During the long winter months, crew members had shore leave, and many left behind offspring. Ship physicians offered medical aid to the Inuit and captains invited them aboard ship to attend religious services and festivities such as Christmas celebrations.

The whaling period peaked during the latter part of the nineteenth century, as alternatives were found for whale products, and eventually died – fortunately, before the whale populations had been totally decimated. Before it disappeared in the early part of this century the Inuit had been irrevocably influenced. They had experienced outsiders at an intimate level, and their impressions, as well as trade goods to which they had become accustomed, were to stay with them.

An important point is that the whalers were transients who came and left, but they were followed by other intruders who set up fairly permanent residence. These were the traders, the missionaries, the Royal Canadian Mounted Police (RCMP), and, prior to 1920, the North-West Mounted Police. Before that, the new nation-state of Canada had laid claim to the High Arctic regions, and the Inuit had become Canadian citizens, but that change in status probably meant little to them as they continued to move back and forth across the land. With the arrival of representatives of the three arms of what has been termed "the Arctic troika," the Inuit became locked into participation in Canadian society, and their lifestyles began to change in often dramatic ways.

The first to arrive were traders who established posts at places to which supply ships would have good access. Independent men, they often showed a high degree of respect for the Inuit, although not always. In one instance a trader was executed by local Inuit in the vicinity of what was later the settlement of Pond Inlet because he had made serious threats to their well-being when they refused to follow his demands. In time, the monopolistic power of the Hudson's Bay Company (HBC) became more than the independent traders could cope with, and they were replaced by company managers.

The Inuit have always been quick to accept new technological artifacts if they seemed superior to what they already had, and it did not take long before they were dependent on traders for rifles and ammunition, kerosene for primus stoves, foodstuffs such as sugar and tea, materials for clothing and tents, and other trade goods. In return they gave seal and fox skins. One major consequence of this new dependency was a change in residential patterns, as people established camps near the trading posts and hunters restricted their activities to travel within limited parameters.

Soon the traders were followed by missionaries. In parts of Labrador, Moravians established missions where they also maintained their own trading posts, but it was Anglican ministers largely recruited from rural areas of England, and Roman Catholic priests from France and Belgium, who brought a new form of religion to most Canadian Inuit. They based their missions adjacent to trading posts, and so the nuclei of settlements began to take shape.

At first, the Inuit must have been puzzled by these evangelists in their midst, for although they claimed to proclaim one God, they often pitted themselves against one another. In some cases, a missionary of one faith would claim openly that his counterpart was a representative of the devil. Eventually, one or the other would win, and each settlement became predominantly either Anglican or Catholic.

Christianity was accepted without serious opposition by most Inuit, and even some shamans were converted, although they often continued to maintain their shamanistic beliefs and practices. The missionaries railed against the shamans, and in many areas they went "underground" for a period of time, but even today a few older ones still follow their ancient calling. Actually, Christianity was not that radically different from the traditional religion in some respects, in that the minister or priest could communicate through prayer with the powerful spirit of Jesus just as the shamans could talk with their spirit helpers. A syncretic blending of the traditional with Christianity was practised by many Inuit.

In time, the RCMP set up detachments in many settlements. They brought with them the right to enforce Canadian law but found little crime among the Inuit, a few highly publicized cases notwithstanding. Mounties were trained as paramedical practitioners, and they often provided medical care for the ill and injured as well as acting as midwives in difficult obstetric cases. They maintained records of vital statistics for the federal government and kept the peace, but usually criminal matters were limited to ensuring that hunters from the camps kept their dogs tied when visiting a settlement. RCMP officers also kept the ubiquitous "disc lists." Because the Inuit did not have family names, each Inuk was given a number identifying him or her as an individual as well as the region of residence. While it assisted in record-keeping, it also had a depersonalizing aspect.

With all three arms of the troika present, the Inuit were in year-round contact with outsiders who had considerable power over them in economic, religious, and legal terms, yet they continued to live in most respects as their ancestors had done. Individual hunters or entire families would visit the nearest settlement periodically to trade, but then would return to the land. This has been called the contact-traditional period, and the term is self-descriptive. It was in the best interests of the three agencies not to change those circumstances too radically and so a symbiotic relationship was formed between Inuit families in camps and southerners living in the settlements. (A few Inuit might reside in settlements while working for one of the agencies. For example, police and missionaries would keep dog teams, and they hired men to hunt for dog food, and HBC managers hired women to keep house for them.)

One major impact on the Inuit during this period involved health. More than one in every thousand Inuit developed tuberculosis – a rate more than twenty times that for the general Canadian population. Many having the disease were taken south to hospitals, where they were out of contact with families for lengthy periods of time, and on release they often were returned to the wrong settlement areas. If they died while in hospital, bodies were rarely returned to their families for burial, and in some instances individuals were mistakenly identified as Indians and interred in reserve cemeteries. The Inuit also suffered from other diseases, such as measles, for which they had no natural immunity and so for them these were often fatal.

During the contact-traditional time the Inuit language, Inuktitut, was used in communications between members of the troika and the Inuit.

Missionaries, traders, and police usually had relatively lengthy stays and learned the language. Also, during that period the Inuit acquired a medium for writing in Inuktitut. A system of syllabic writing, which had been developed by Reverend Peck, an Anglican missionary, for the Cree language, had been modified to suit that of the Inuit. Signs such as triangles were used to represent what the missionary, who had not been a linguist, thought were the syllables of a language. Once they had accepted the syllabic system, Inuit passed it along themselves from region to region. The original intention of Peck had been to make the Bible accessible to Aboriginal peoples in their own languages, but the Inuit used it for a variety of purposes – for example, sending messages on any available scrap of paper, such as the back of a soup can label or a cigarette package, between relatives or friends in outlying camps.

An important feature of the contact-traditional period was that the Inuit were left relatively alone, to continue to manage on their own resources, and this made for a very different recent history from that of most Canadian Aboriginal peoples. Mounties made periodic tours to the camps, but other than those visits, so long as there were no serious crimes they left the people to themselves. In those camps, men were still full-time hunters, although some did carving as a way of supplementing household income, and the language spoken in the homes and on the trail was Inuktitut. To a large extent, then, the Inuit had control of their own decision-making and were quite autonomous, and this was to continue until only a few decades ago.

In short, they had not been placed on small reserves and forced to submit to the authoritarian demands of Indian agents. Among many southern Aboriginal populations there has been a need to "bring back" the cultures of their ancestors, which had become highly fragmented as a result of years of forced dependence on the whims of a federal Department of Indian Affairs, and as they have become politicized this has taken place, but much healing is needed in the process. The Inuit – in part because until recently the Canadian federal government was little interested in its Arctic regions – never lost touch with their own culture. They have not had to face a long hiatus of what might be called "cultural abuse." Their culture and society had been modified as a result of contact with outsiders, but they had to a large extent been able to manage that change.

Movement Off the Land and Into Settlements

Suddenly, in the 1950s, events took place that profoundly affected the Inuit and sorely tested their ability to handle outside intrusions. The political and industrial powers in the south had long known that the Arctic had rich resources, but it had never seemed practical to exploit them. The popularly held negative image of the North had, in this instance, worked for the good of the Inuit. But in the post-World War Two environment these mineral deposits became increasingly attractive, and new technologies provided ways to bring them from the frozen earth and down to the southern markets. Also, other northern nation-states were looking at the Canadian North with envy. (During World War Two the United States had maintained several air bases in the Canadian Arctic.) This was the time of the Cold War, and the U.S.S.R. lay one jump away across Alaska and immediately adjacent over the North Pole. Suddenly the Canadian federal government took an interest in its Arctic territories and became concerned with finding ways, under international law, to protect its sovereignty.

A consequence of this new southern interest in the Arctic was the establishment in 1954 of the federal Department of Northern Affairs and National Resources (DNANR). The new agency was given a massive budget, and its primary activity was the implementation of a program of community development. Thus was ushered in the "period of relocation," during which Inuit families across the Canadian Arctic were wooed into settlement living and the hunting camps were abandoned. Each settlement had its own Ottawa-appointed administrator who became the senior civil servant in the area and usurped many of the duties of the RCMP.

Housing projects were initiated, schools and nursing stations were built, and attempts were made to find new employment opportunities in the settlements. Each settlement had its own community council, composed primarily of Inuit, but any decisions made by them were subject to the authority of the administrators, who were not Inuit, and they in turn could make few decisions without approval from their own seniors in regional centres or Ottawa. Monolingual Inuktitut-speaking children were enrolled in school, where their non-Inuit teachers, who were monolingual English speakers, spent most of their time in language instruction using teaching materials designed for southern schools and largely irrelevant in an Inuit cultural context. The experience must have been one of extreme boredom for the pupils – a far change from traditional learning, in which boys learned the excitement of the hunt and girls acquired the many skills of their mothers. Their fathers found employment providing services such as supplying water and emptying toilet tanks for the new residents from the south – during the 1950s and

1960s most skilled positions were reserved for southerners, even in cases where local Inuit had the appropriate skills and training.

With fathers no longer hunting, families increasingly were reliant on food purchased at the HBC post, or, in time, as the co-operative movement grew in the North, from the local consumer co-operative. The way of life of the Inuit had changed dramatically. Nurses in residence provided a new level of health care, but there was greater need for such services as diets changed, foreign diseases were introduced, and a more sedentary existence was established. Tuberculosis began to disappear, but cancer and diabetes rates rose dramatically, and both had been unknown to the Inuit in traditional times. Sexually transmitted diseases began to take their toll, and young girls entered into sexual liaisons with the single *Qallunat* (non-Inuit) males found in every settlement. Children of a people who in the past had few dental problems suffered from dental caries, and in adolescence their faces erupted in acne as a consequence of the increased intake of sugar. As well, for the first time, a population that had never had any indigenous alcohol or mind-altering drugs began to reap some of the negative effects of the introduction of both, as aircraft brought in alcohol and, in time, both soft and hard drugs.

For the first decade or so after the movement off the land the Inuit maintained a "wait and see" posture, and many outside observers predicted a demise of their culture and sense of identity. Eventually, they began to take control of their lives once again. Community councils demanded more autonomy, and many requested a change of status for their communities from settlements to hamlets. As hamlets, they could do away with the administrators or, as many did, hire them to work for the councils. Local associations were formed to teach young people traditional skills while other committees took control of the allocation of housing and other matters. Community-organized referenda were held to decide whether communities should have access to satellite television and if alcohol should be permitted. (Several have gone "dry," while in others alcohol consumption is illegal for Inuit but legal for *Qallunat.*) The process of reclamation of control had begun.

Children had attended schools, and most had become fluent in English, although only a small number progressed through the grades to high school completion. A major reason for the high dropout rates was simply students' boredom with a curriculum that was not culturally relevant. High schools were not built in most of the settlements, and students had to go to residential schools in regional centres such as Iqaluit for a high school education. Separation from their families for the winter months and life in alien, dormitory-like environments were traumatic for many and left psychological scars. Nevertheless, in spite of the youth's proficiency in English, Inuktitut continued to be the language spoken in the homes. In those same homes, stories told during the winter nights were the same ones recounted in the snow and sod houses a generation before, even if rock or country and western music created a background for their telling. In time, men returned to hunting when they had the time, and eventually whole families would go off on camping trips to live on the land. Virtually every adult male who could afford it had purchased a snowmobile, but some began to keep dogs again, feeding them whale meat and fish. They were a symbolic way of retaining ties with the past. Some even went back to camp living on a full-time basis, but these were isolated cases.

The Inuit were committed to a new way of life and the advantages it seemed to offer, but they were also cognizant of the need to preserve some aspects of the way of life and human values of their ancestors. Whereas the latter had taken their Inuit culture for granted, these town dwellers began to look at it, and its retention, in a self-conscious manner. Real efforts were made to ensure that their culture would not disappear. They had been temporarily seduced into following another way by the development of the DNANR and its policies, and there had been many casualties, but most survived, and the time for taking stock of their situation was over as they sought more ways to regain control of their own lives. In many respects, the Inuit began to behave much as immigrant populations in southern Canada did – as an ethnic group that self-consciously selected parts of the old and the new.

Creating a Place for Themselves in a Nation-State

After centuries of making their own social and cultural changes, the Inuit of Canada had, in a single century, been forced to cope with changes imposed by outsiders. First, the whalers, followed by the agencies of the troika, and finally the strength of the DNANR had brought them out of their long isolation. In the settlements and hamlets of the Northwest Territories the Inuit had truly come to grips with these intrusions. On the local level, community councils and other organizations were successfully experimenting with autonomous ways of bridging the gap between two worlds – that of their ancestors and that of the new nation of Canada of which they were now a part. In many respects, theirs was a quasi-colonial situation, but they refused to be treated like a colonized people.

In the past few decades a new political process began to emerge that was to sweep across the Canadian Arctic and link the isolated communities. This was a period in which pan-Indian movements had appeared among Aboriginal peoples in southern Canada and the United States. In Canada, one major impetus was the publication in 1969 by the Department of Indian Affairs and Northern Development of a White Paper outlining a plan to terminate the Department of Indian Affairs and integrate Aboriginal peoples into the larger society. Native peoples were outraged by it, and soon regional and national organizations were formed across the country to counter this proposal. It is not clear as to what extent these and other developments influenced the Inuit, but they surely had an impact.

Initially, Inuit concerns were more with the provision of culturally relevant curricula in schools and the discovery of better economic opportunities for men and women. It must be remembered that the Inuit had no treaties with the federal government and were not subject to the Indian Act, so the White Paper as such had little immediate significance for them. Their neighbours in the Yukon and non-Inuit Aboriginal peoples in the Northwest Territories had become increasingly concerned about issues over land claims and Aboriginal rights, and associations had been formed by both populations in the late sixties and early seventies, such as the Council of Yukon Indians and the Indian Brotherhood of the Northwest Territories. Out of these grew the concept of the Dene Nation. Soon, regionally based Inuit associations began to be formed in the Northwest Territories, such as the Committee for Original Peoples Entitlement (COPE) in the west and the Keewatin Inuit Association and the Baffin Region Association in the central and eastern sections. However, at a meeting held in Coppermine in July, 1970, attended by Inuit from across the Arctic, the idea of a pan-Inuit association was conceived.

A year later, at an historic meeting held at Carleton University in Ottawa, the Inuit Tapirisat of Canada (ITC) was formed. (The name is usually loosely translated as Inuit brotherhood.) A committee formed there, consisting largely of young Inuit from across Canada, declared its mandate of speaking out on issues of education, northern development, and the preservation of Inuit culture. With an organization that, symbolically, had an Inuktitut name, their goal was to "control our own future."

As mentioned earlier, their first concerns were with education and maintenance of cultural heritage – the creation of the Inuit Cultural Institute in Arviat (formerly Eskimo Point) was an early effort in this direction – but before long their goals became far more comprehensive. Soon, several of the regional Inuit associations amalgamated with the ITC. The Inuit of the Northwest Territories now had their own territory-wide organization. It was led by young men and women, most of whom had received formal education but who in all cases wanted to define the future of their own people in Inuit terms.

With the emergence of the ITC, the concept of Nunavut was also conceived. In 1976, the ITC presented a document to then Prime Minister Trudeau and his cabinet that became the basis for Nunavut. The term means "our land" and the ITC used it to refer to a large section of the Northwest Territories that, the early planners hoped, would in time become an Inuit-dominated territory of Canada. Once conceived and publicly declared as a goal, the concept was to take on a life of its own. However, the trail to Nunavut was not without its hurdles.

Originally, COPE had joined forces with the ITC, but before long its leaders began to be uncomfortable with that alliance, in large part because they regarded land claims as the most important issue. The ITC first had to build a network linking the many isolated communities of the eastern Arctic and considered education and heightened cultural awareness as means to achieve this. Also, the people of the western Arctic, whose populations were larger and settlements not so dispersed, were beginning to see themselves as a separate entity. For instance, instead of Inuit, they used the term "Inuvialuit" for themselves. The finding of large oil and gas deposits in the Beaufort Sea area created a sense of immediacy, as they saw the possibility of losing all claim to their lands, and so, after withdrawing from the ITC, COPE set forth its own claim, which was presented to the federal government in 1977.

Ottawa responded fairly quickly, signing an agreement-in-principle in 1978 and a final agreement in 1984. The Inuvialuit settlement was the first significant land claim case under a new federal land claims policy established in 1973. The settlement has been debated, in that the people had to make some major concessions, but they did receive claim to between one-third and one-half of the lands they had traditionally occupied, as well as mineral rights to one-seventh of that. In addition, they received substantial financial compensation, which is being paid gradually over time.

COPE was eventually replaced by the Inuvialuit Regional Corporation, which is controlled by the six communities in the Mackenzie Delta-Beaufort Sea area ceded by the federal government, and it administers the terms of the settlement. However, there is no provision for local government, and the agreement states that federal and territorial laws are to prevail in the settlement area. Whether or not the Inuvialuit will eventually move toward the establishment of a western version of Nunavut, only time will tell.

In the meantime, the ITC began to focus its concerns more and more on the issue of land claims. It is interesting to note that the ITC – indeed, this is true of all Inuit organizations – has never been confrontational in its dealing with Ottawa or Yellowknife. Instead, its case has been built up slowly and methodically. Applied anthropologists, geographers, biologists, and other specialists have been hired as consultants to research and document long-term Inuit habitation on and use of the land, and university law professors have helped build the legal arguments. The Inuit, for example, never maintained individual hunting territories or regarded land as property, so anthropologists interviewed the elders about long-term hunting activities over generations. The process has been painstaking and thorough, but that meticulousness has finally paid off.

In Iqaluit, on May 25, 1993, the Canadian government signed an agreement with the Tungavik Federation of Nunavut (TFN), an outgrowth of the ITC, for the establishment of a new territory in the Canadian Arctic. It constituted the largest land claims settlement in Canadian history and involved the 17,500 Inuit of the central and eastern Canadian Arctic. When Nunavut is formally established in 1999, it will likely incorporate all of the present Northwest Territories north of the treeline and comprise approximately one-fifth of the land mass of Canada. It will become the largest territory, and in time, perhaps, the largest province. The majority of its inhabitants will be Inuit, and so it will be the first ethnically dominated territory in the nation.

Nunavut will be an Inuit-dominated region in more than mere demographics. It will have three official languages: English, French, and Inuktitut, with Inuktitut being the one used in government. Some southern migrants to the North have learned Inuktitut, but they still are the minority, so key positions in the new civil service will of necessity be largely filled by Inuit. Inuit will retain the right to hunt, fish, and trap in Nunavut, and if they do so to obtain the basic necessities, no licences will be required. There may in time be some judicial recognition of customary Inuit law – something that successive chief justices of the Northwest Territories going back to the legendary Justice Jack Sissons have sought to achieve. (As early as 1961, decisions by Justice Sissons recognized customary rules in adoption and marriage, although these were not easily accepted by the Ottawa mandarins.) On more than 36,000 square kilometres of the land deeded to them, Inuit will own subsurface rights to oil, gas, and minerals. What will finally transpire in terms of mechanisms instituted to protect Inuit culture remains to be seen, and that will probably take place after April 1, 1999, when Nunavut finally becomes a reality.

There are still problems to be worked out. One is a dispute between the Inuit and the Dene of northern Manitoba and Saskatchewan, who claim they have traditionally hunted in lands at the southern fringe of Nunavut. (There is also archaeological evidence to support their ethnographic claim.) Further, some Inuit voted against the referendum on Nunavut, charging that the accord was not inclusive enough of their demands. Others did so because they felt their people were not yet "ready for it" (personal communications). Canadians in the south may be appalled at the cost of setting up the new structures necessary for creating and maintaining the territory, which will be paid by the federal government, but no organized backlash has occurred.

Some observers point to the low educational level of most residents of the Northwest Territories. Few Inuit have graduated from high school, and even fewer from universities, and so these critics question the ability of the Inuit to manage such a large territory. An appropriate response might be that the territorial government, which until now has been run on a basis of consensus rather than through party politics, has, according to many of its non-Inuit members, done so effectively largely because of the politically adroit mediation of its Inuit members – some fear that the consensual approach will become impossible to maintain without the Inuit present to act in that mediatory role. Other critics refer to the many social problems that beset northerners, such as unemployment, substance abuse, and domestic friction. Inuit I have spoken with tell me that they did not have these problems before southerners came into their land and wrested control from the Inuit, and that they can address them if they are once again in charge. For what it is worth, I agree.

The dawning of the territory of Nunavut will soon stand as dramatic testimony to Inuit ability to cope, both with a forbidding landscape and with intrusive social and cultural forms. It may become the first place in Canada where truly innovative ways are created for a multicultural society to exist.

Recommended Readings

Balikci, Asen
   1970   *The Netsilik Eskimo.* Prospect Heights, Ill.: Waveland Press.
            A rich ethnographic account which has stood the test of time. An excellent
      film series from the National Film Board is available to accompany it.

Brody, Hugh
    1987 *Living Arctic: Hunters of the Canadian North.* Vancouver: Douglas &
    McIntyre.
          A popular account, with no references, but widely quoted as a source in
    journalistic writings. Deals with non-Inuit Canadian Aboriginals as well as
    Inuit.
Coates, Kenneth, and Judith Powell
    1989 *The Modern North: People, Politics and the Rejection of Colonialism.*
    Toronto: James Lorimer and Co.
          Written by historians, this is a detailed account of political developments
    leading to the creation of Nunavut.
Duffy, R. Quinn
    1988 *The Road to Nunavut: the Progress of the Eastern Arctic Since the Second
    World War.* Montreal and Kingston: McGill-Queen's University Press.
          Very readable account of recent developments. A good accompaniment to
    Coates and Powell.
Matthiasson, John S.
    1992 *Living on the Land: Change Among the Inuit of Baffin Island.* Peterborough,
    Ont.: Broadview Press.
          A highly personalized longitudinal case study of the Tununirmiut Inuit as
    they lived in camps during the contact-traditional period and later in the
    settlement of Pond Inlet.
Merkur, Daniel
    1991 *Powers Which We Do Not Know: The Gods and Spirits of the Inuit.* Moscow,
    Idaho: University of Idaho Press.
          Possibly the best synthesis of the literature of Inuit religion available.
Oswalt, Wendell H.
    1979 *Eskimos and Explorers.* Novato, Calif.: Chandler and Sharp.
          Probably the best treatment of the early contacts between Aboriginal
    peoples of Greenland, Canada, and Alaska with Europeans. Excellent
    scholarship and very readable.
Purich, Donald
    1992 *The Inuit and Their Land: The Story of Nunavut.* Toronto: James Lorimer and
    Co.
          Some good material on recent political and economic developments, but
    very journalistic.
Swinton, George
    1972 *Sculpture of the Eskimo.* Greenwich, Conn.: New York Graphic Society.
          Possibly the definitive work on a topic not covered in this chapter –
    Inuit art.

Williamson, Robert G.

    1974 *Eskimos Underground: Socio-Cultural Change in the Canadian Central Arctic*. Uppsala: Almqvist and Wiksell.

        A sound survey and analysis by a writer who has had long first-hand experience of the Canadian Inuit and their land.

CHAPTER 5
The Caribou Inuit

Ernest S. Burch, Jr.

The Caribou Inuit live on the southern edge of the barren lands west of Hudson Bay, in the area that is now the southern portion of the District of Keewatin, Northwest Territories. They were first mentioned in the anthropological literature by Franz Boas, in 1888. They were not the subject of much interest, however, until the members of the Fifth Thule Expedition visited them in the spring of 1922. Two members of that expedition, Kaj Birket-Smith and Knud Rasmussen, published comprehensive monographs that became the original basis of our knowledge of the Caribou Inuit way of life.

Field and archival research conducted during the last twenty-five years has significantly enhanced our understanding of Caribou Inuit history, ecology, and social organization.[1] While the work of Birket-Smith and Rasmussen will always be an essential part of the foundation of our knowledge of the Caribou Inuit, we now realize that those authors overlooked several important features of Caribou Inuit life. They also failed entirely to appreciate the particular historical context in which their observations were made.

The foundations of my own interest in these people were laid forty years ago when, as a teenager, I spent a summer as a junior assistant on a scientific expedition to Labrador, Greenland, and northern Baffin Island. When I left I wanted to become a biologist, although my specific interests were still undefined; when I returned three months later I wanted to become an anthropologist, do research in the Arctic, and study the Inuit way of life.

My introduction to the Caribou Inuit specifically did not come until much later. I was seeking an Inuit group that was different enough from the northwest Alaskans with whom I was familiar to provide me with instructive contrasts. On more practical grounds, I had just joined the Anthropology Department at the University of Manitoba and, as a condition of getting the job, had agreed to do research among Canadian Inuit.

A literature survey indicated that the Caribou Inuit might provide me with the contrasts I was looking for. That view was confirmed by a new colleague at Manitoba, Thomas C. Correll. Correll had spent several years among the Caribou Inuit as a missionary-linguist before entering anthropology, and everything he told me about them suggested that their way of life was very different from the one I had studied in northwest Alaska. Correll and I joined forces and, between 1968 and 1971, we carried out a total of some fourteen months of fieldwork in both northwest Alaska and southern Keewatin. As a part of this endeavour I re-read the ethnographic literature on the Caribou Inuit, finding a number of important discrepancies between what it said and what Correll and I had learned from Native sources.

When I extended the literature review to historical sources, I discovered one anomaly after another. The more I learned the less I understood, and what began as a relatively straightforward exercise in ethnography quickly became a very complicated project in ethnohistory. Instead of one year it has taken substantial portions of twenty, and it is still not finished. During this time my original interest in the structure of Caribou Inuit societies expanded to include an equal, if not greater, fascination with the history of those societies. Both of those concerns are reflected in the following account.

The Country

The Caribou Inuit region is located about halfway down the west side of Hudson Bay, between approximately 60° and 65° N. It extends roughly 600 kilometres from north to south and 500 kilometres inland from the coast, for an approximate total area of some 300,000 square kilometres.

The country is an undulating plain of generally low relief that rises gradually from the shallow waters of Hudson Bay toward the west and south, where it reaches a maximum elevation of some 500 metres above sea level. A heavily glaciated portion of the Canadian Shield, the region is characterized by a variety of post-glacial land forms, such as eskers and rocky outcrops, and countless rivers, lakes, streams, and ponds.

The tree line angles irregularly across southern Keewatin from southeast to northwest (see Map 5.1). North of this line, the country is covered by barren or lichen- and moss-covered outcrops and boulders interspersed with grass and sedge meadows, and copses of dwarf trees and shrubs that seldom exceed one metre in height. Here and there in the southern and western portions, in a sheltered valley or hollow, is an island of spruce, which remained behind when the forest retreated southward during the bitter weather of the Little Ice Age, some 400 years ago. Below the tree line, spruce fill the valleys and hollows, and grow progressively farther up the hillsides as one proceeds from northeast to southwest.

Plant growth in southern Keewatin is severely restricted by the harsh climate. Frost occurs on an average of more than 260 days per year, and the average temperature, reckoned for a twelve-month period, ranges from about –5°C in the southwest to –16°C in the north. Precipitation, which fluctuates considerably from year to year, is at near-desert levels most of the time, averaging between about twenty centimetres and thirty centimetres a year: 60 per cent of this usually falls as rain between early June and early October. The dominant feature of the weather, however, is the wind; it blows incessantly across the land, day and night, all year long.

The harsh climate and lack of vegetation mean that relatively few species of animals are to be found in Caribou Inuit territory. Historically, barren-ground caribou and muskoxen have been the dominant terrestrial species. Both have experienced dramatic fluctuations in numbers over the past 300 years, ranging between extreme abundance and virtual extinction. Several varieties of fish – most notably char, lake trout, and whitefish – are to be found in the lakes and rivers. The shallow coastal waters of Hudson Bay are home to several kinds of sea mammal.

MAP 5.1. Caribou Inuit Societal Territories, 1890

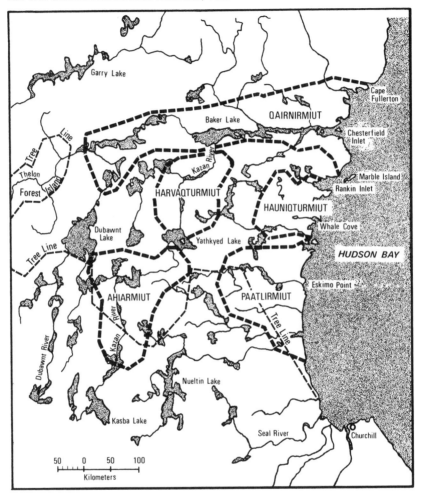

The most common is the small ringed seal, but the much larger bearded seal is also present in some numbers. Walrus formerly were numerous in the central and northern sections of the coast, and belukha were abundant in some areas in early summer. Bowhead whales frequented the waters off the mouth of Chesterfield Inlet before they were nearly exterminated by American whalers in the nineteenth century. Arctic fox, wolverines, wolves, polar bears, and several varieties of birds – particularly ptarmigan, ducks, and geese – constitute the remaining faunal resources of the area.

Origins and Early History[2]

Precisely when and how the Caribou Inuit originated as a distinct population has been the subject of debate for more than half a century. Birket-Smith maintained that they were living representatives of the earliest Eskimos, and that they were still living in the original homeland of all Eskimo-speaking peoples. This conclusion, which was based on a comparative analysis of the material culture of various historic Eskimo groups, is both logically invalid and empirically untenable. A contrary view, based on the study of archaeological evidence, was developed by Birket-Smith's colleague, Therkel Mathiassen; he argued that all historic Inuit peoples were descended from prehistoric migrants bearing the Thule culture eastward from Alaska. Subsequent archaeological research has shown that Mathiassen was correct.

The Caribou Inuit are definitely the biological and cultural descendants of Thule people, but just how and when they reached the west coast of Hudson Bay is still being debated. Regardless of when they arrived or how they got there, the Caribou Inuit were firmly ensconced in the central portion of the west Hudson Bay coast in the summer of 1719, where they were encountered by Hudson's Bay Company traders Henry Kelsey and John Hancock.

The Founder Society

The eighteenth-century Inuit population of southern Keewatin seems to have ranged between about 250 and 450 people, as good times alternated with bad to keep their numbers in a state of flux. Their territory extended along the coast from Eskimo Point to Rankin Inlet, and probably inland for several tens of kilometres; a few families also wintered periodically on or near Baker Lake. The greatest concentration of people was in the vicinity of Whale Cove, in the richest sector of the southern Keewatin coast. Observations made over several decades by Hudson's Bay Company traders of the location and movements of specific individuals and families indicate that all of the eighteenth-century Inuit inhabitants of southern Keewatin were members of a single social system. Lacking information on the Inuit name for this system, and in the absence of a suitable alternative, I call it the "Founder Society" of Caribou Inuit.

The way of life of the members of the Founder Society was an adaptation to local conditions of the one they brought with them from the north. Their winter houses, which were made of stone chinked with moss and dirt and covered with snow, were situated on the mainland coast. In the spring, they moved out to islands and points of land, where they lived in conical, skin-covered tents. There they hunted seals, walrus, belukha, and an occasional bowhead whale, and fished for char. They dried the meat and fish in the sun, and stored it, along with blubber, in sealskin bags. The supplies they accumulated between May and early August formed the bulk of their food during the following winter. In mid- to late August they walked inland to hunt caribou, acquiring skins for clothing and meat and fat for food. They returned to their winter dwellings near the coast with the hides and dried meat some time in the fall. After the ocean froze, they retrieved from the islands the supplies stored there in early summer. During the winter they hunted caribou and seals, as conditions permitted. Overland transportation must have been by foot, since there is not a single reference to dogs in any of the observations made of their camps by explorers and traders over the course of the eighteenth century. On water, they travelled by *kayak*, frequently lashing together several such craft to form a raft when carrying bulk goods or large numbers of people.

The members of the Founder Society apparently were rather isolated from other Inuit populations. However, they were in intermittent contact with Chipewyan Indians, hundreds of whom ventured onto the tundra each summer to hunt caribou. Relations between the Chipewyan and Inuit during this period usually are depicted as being invariably hostile, often violently so. The Hudson's Bay Company factors later took credit for establishing peace between the two groups. A careful examination of the archival sources indicates that, while Chipewyan-Inuit relations did indeed sometimes result in bloodshed, they were peaceful more often than not. If anything, the Hudson's Bay Company made things worse because members of the two groups began to compete with one another for the traders' attention. After a smallpox epidemic decimated the Chipewyan population in the early 1780s, contacts became less frequent, and overt hostility between Chipewyan and Inuit pretty well disappeared.

The early trade between the Caribou Inuit and the Hudson's Bay Company was conducted from sloops sent north from Churchill during the summer. The trade was so meagre that one has to wonder why the Company pursued it. The only furs southern Keewatin has in quantity are arctic fox, with some wolf and wolverine, and the market for these was very weak during the eighteenth century. The bulk of the trade was in caribou skins and sea-mammal products, primarily blubber, with some baleen and walrus ivory. In exchange, the Inuit received knives, hatchets, fish hooks, files, beads, and tobacco. After about 1770, guns, powder, and shot were also traded. The balance of trade was much to the advantage of the Inuit, a fact realized early on by the Company men at Churchill but overlooked or ignored by their superiors in London. It was not concluded until 1790, after which the Inuit had to make the long trek to Churchill if they desired goods of European manufacture.

Expansion

The conclusion of the coastal trade, which apparently occurred during a period of increasing population, led the Caribou Inuit to expand their geographic horizons. For much of the eighteenth century, and especially after 1750, they had moved to the coast each spring to hunt seals, and the Hudson's Bay Company had kindly delivered a boatload of trade goods to their very door. The Inuit had not become dependent on this trade, for, if the trading vessel was late, no one waited for it after caribou hunting season arrived. However, it had been a very comfortable arrangement for them.

The people whose winter houses were situated in the northern sector of Caribou Inuit territory were understandably loath to make the 700- to 800-km round trip to Churchill to acquire trade goods after 1790. Such goods were nice to have, but they were by no means crucial to survival. When the coastal trade was broken off, the inhabitants of this sector began to spend more time hunting, fishing, and exploring in the Chesterfield Inlet and Baker Lake area than they had previously, and they probably also travelled more extensively toward the north along the Hudson Bay coast.

About the same time that the Caribou Inuit were expanding the scope and frequency of their journeys toward the north, the Aivilik branch of the Iglulik Inuit was expanding toward the south from Foxe Basin. Apparently, members of the two populations came into contact for the first time around 1800. This was a major event for the Caribou Inuit because, from the Aivilik, they evidently learned the art of making a snow house, a vastly more suitable winter habitation than a rock house for life on the barrens. They may also have acquired their first dogs from the Aivilik. Conversely, the Aivilik gained their first access to iron tools, which they could purchase from the Caribou Inuit.

While the northern segment of the Founder Society was gradually reorienting its activities toward Chesterfield Inlet and Baker Lake, the southern segment was beginning to focus its attention on Churchill, 250 to 300 km to the south. On June 9, 1791, twenty Caribou Inuit arrived in Churchill, bringing fifty caribou skins, six fox skins, and a wolf skin to trade. They were hired by the Company to hunt seals until the ice left the coast, and they subsequently hunted belukha whales for the company for a week or so before returning to their own country. When they departed, the chief factor told them that, henceforth, all trade would be done at Churchill, and he asked them to tell that to their friends. They did so, and another group of Inuit arrived at Churchill on August 22 of that same summer. These two visits initiated a trend that was to persist, with occasional modifications, for more than 130 years.

By 1810 the members of the northern and southern segments of the Founder Society were not getting along, and by the mid-1820s they had split. Company people at Churchill referred to them as the "Distant Esquimaux" and the "Homeguard Esquimaux," respectively. The former spent the winter in the interior, near Baker Lake, and the summer along the shores of Chesterfield Inlet and on Marble Island. A few made the long trip to Churchill each year, but they headed back north in time for caribou hunting season. The "Homeguards" probably spent the winter along the Lower Maguse River and the spring on the islands near Eskimo Point. Several of them visited Churchill each spring, then hunted belukha for the Company during the summer. The area around Whale Cove, the geographic centre of the Founder Society, became relatively uninhabited.

The Caribou Inuit population grew rapidly, albeit with occasional setbacks, over the next century or so. It reached a total of perhaps 1,100 in 1881, and some 1,500 in 1915. As the population grew in size, it also expanded in space, particularly toward the interior.

Several developments, in addition to simple population growth, contributed to the westward expansion of the Caribou Inuit. Chipewyan had dominated the interior, at least in summer, until the smallpox epidemic of 1781 and until the lure of the fur trade led many of them toward the southwest. Their decline created a population vacuum in the interior of southern Keewatin, although groups of Chipewyan continued to make annual trips as far north as Dubawnt Lake at least into the 1870s.

The second important development was the adoption of the snow house as a winter dwelling. As noted above, this apparently occurred between 1790 and 1810. Much warmer in the winter wind and cold than a tent, but equally suited to a nomadic way of life, snow houses were a vast improvement over stone houses. In 1750, people had had to stay fairly close to their (stone) houses whether there was any food there or not, or else live in tents all winter long. By 1820, if food was running short, they could go anywhere they wished.

The third development was a crisis, in the form of a caribou decline along the coast. Lasting for most of the 1840s, this decline led to considerable hardship, particularly among the Homeguard Esquimaux. In an effort to locate caribou, several families apparently moved west to the middle Kazan River, where they discovered an abundance of muskoxen, enough to sustain them through the crisis. Finding the country to their liking, they simply stayed there after the caribou population recovered.

As the Caribou Inuit population grew numerically and expanded geographically, it also became further divided socially. The two societies of 1850 had become five only thirty years later. It was these five that were in operation during the Classic Period of Caribou Inuit history.

The Classic Period

Caribou Inuit culture, as a distinctive way of life, was marked by a general emphasis on terrestrial, as opposed to marine resources, and by an overwhelming reliance on caribou as *the* specific resource with which all material needs could be satisfied. The European recognition of these characteristics in the descriptive label "Caribou Inuit" was closely paralleled in the Inuit term "Nunamiut," or "Inland People," which other Inuit populations used to designate even those Caribou Inuit groups who spent much of the year on the coast.

The economic orientation of the late nineteenth-century Caribou Inuit was markedly different from the one prevailing in the same population in the mid-eighteenth century. In the 1750s, Hudson's Bay Company traders literally had to beg the Inuit to give up even a small portion of their precious supply of seal oil. A century later the Inuit still killed hundreds of seals and belukha each summer, but they sold virtually their entire production to the Company and relied almost entirely on caribou, muskoxen, and fish for their own sustenance. Just why this change occurred, and particularly why it took such an extreme form, remains a mystery.

The change from a diversified economy to a specialized one based largely on caribou occurred gradually during the demographic and geographic expansion of the first half of the nineteenth century, but definitely had been completed by 1880. That year, therefore, may be designated as the beginning of the Classic Period. The end of that period may be designated, much less arbitrarily, as 1915, the first year of the Great Famine.

The period 1880-1915 has a number of features that commend it for special treatment. During those years the Caribou Inuit population in general was high and still growing, the extent of their territory was

Ernest S. Burch, Jr.

Table 5.1
Caribou Inuit Societies, circa 1890

Inuit Name	Established	H.B.Co. Name	Est. Population	General Location
Paatlirmiut	by 1825	Homeguard Esquimaux	450	Maguse River and nearby coast
Qairnirmiut	by 1825	Distant Esquimaux	200	Thelon River, Baker Lake, and Chesterfield Inlet
Ahiarmiut	by 1858	Inland Esquimaux	350	Middle Kazan River
Hauniqturmiut	by 1871	Middle Esquimaux	175	Wilson River and nearby coast
Harvaqturmiut	by 1890	None	200	Lower Kazan River
Estimated total population, 1890			1,375	

greater than at any other time, before or since, and, despite more than a century and a half of contact, the people, in general, remained extraordinarily uninfluenced by Euro-Canadian culture. Finally, this is the earliest period for which traders' and explorers' accounts have been enriched by information obtained directly from Caribou Inuit sources.

Societies

During most of the Classic Period the Caribou Inuit were organized in five societies, the Ahiarmiut, Harvaqturmiut, Hauniqturmiut, Paatlirmiut, and Qairnirmiut (see Table 5.1). A sixth group, the Tahiuyarmiut, may have become a society before 1915, but too little is known to establish that as a fact; it was all but wiped out by famine almost as soon as it emerged.

All five societies had developed out of the Founder Society, but they had become separate social systems by 1880 – the hunter-gatherer equivalent of five different countries. Each society was a relatively (although not absolutely) discrete network of families connected to one another by marriage, descent, and partnership ties. In addition to occupying separate territories (see Map 5.1), each was characterized by a distinctive subdialect of the Caribou Inuit dialect, slightly contrasting clothing styles, a general ideology of uniqueness, and a sense of superiority over other peoples.

Families

The organizational core of a Caribou Inuit society was the extended family. Children were betrothed very early in life. Girls, and often boys, were frequently betrothed while still infants. The arrangements were made by the parents of the prospective spouses, and the principals had no say in the matter. According to Caribou Inuit belief, the best marriages were those of first cousins, and the very best arrangement of all was a brother-sister exchange (*akigiik*) between two sets of cousins; thus, a brother and sister of one family would marry a sister and brother of another, the two sibling pairs being cousins to begin with. When a cousin marriage occurred, people who started life as siblings, cousins, nieces, and nephews suddenly would become spouses and in-laws of various kinds as well, thus building one layer of kin relations upon another. The condition in which a small number of individuals became related to one another in several different ways simultaneously was known as *tamalrutit*, and was regarded as a highly desirable state of affairs.

If Caribou Inuit ideology was carried to its logical conclusion, all the members of an entire society would live together in one place, intermarrying, having children, and generally operating as one huge family. Tight limitations on the food supply and the inevitable personality conflicts prevented them from even remotely approaching this condition, however. Actual families ranged in size from simple conjugal units comprised of just a married couple (or sometimes a man and two wives) and their non-adult children to relatively complex extended families of two or three dozen people. The Caribou Inuit did not have any ideological preference for either the male or female line, and extended families took a variety of forms: a group of adult male and/or female siblings, their spouses and children; or, two adult brothers, their widowed mother, spouses and children; or, an aged couple, an adult offspring (of either sex), an adult nephew or niece, and their spouses and children – and many other variations along these general lines.

The members of a small family could easily live in a single dwelling. The larger the family, the greater its need to have two or more dwellings, since there are fairly narrow limits on the size of a snow house and tent. The average family involved nineteen people living in three tents, in summer and fall, or two snow houses, in winter and spring.

PLATE 5.1. A Paatlirmiut woman carrying her baby on her back, inside her parka, not as commonly supposed, in her hood. By permission of the National Museum of Denmark, Department of Ethnography.

Most settlements were occupied by the members of only one extended family. In times of hunger even these might split up, the constituent households spreading out over the country in the hope of finding game. In late spring or summer, though, when food supplies were greater, two or more related families often joined forces. Aggregations of more than seventy-five people sometimes occurred, but they were unusual and temporary, generally associated with the arrival of a Hudson's Bay Company trading vessel, a whaling ship, or an unusually large caribou kill.

A Caribou Inuit society was entirely lacking in politically, economically, or other specialized institutions, such as governments, businesses, churches, or schools. Almost all of the functions required to sustain life were performed within the extended family context. Indeed, to a degree that most Canadians could scarcely comprehend, the life of a Caribou Inuit revolved around the family – from the moment a person was born until the time one died.

Other Social Bonds

Family ties, as Canadians would understand them, were supplemented in the Caribou Inuit social system by only two other types of social bond. One consisted of a series of special family relationships created through a co-marriage; the other was a dancing partnership.

A co-marriage was established when two married couples agreed to exchange sexual partners for a night or two. This was not the casual, lustful affair implied by the common phrase "wife trading," because it really was a form of marriage. The arrangement created a number of relationships in addition to the original husband-wife ties. *All* of these relationships were imbued with rights and obligations of mutual support and assistance, and these rights and obligations were considered binding for the rest of the lives of the individuals involved.

A dancing partnership was established in a rather elaborate way. After agreeing to become partners, two friends would ritually hit each other on the face and shoulders as hard as they could, often raising large welts. Eventually one would give up, at which point they would exchange gifts. The third and final stage was to dance together, beating drums, while the onlookers sang. By the time exhaustion finally overcame them, they had become *mumiqatigiik*, dancing partners.

Dancing partners normally lived in different settlements, but they visited each other from time to time. When they met after a prolonged absence, they would repeat the initiation ceremony with only slight modification. At first sight they hit each other and tried to knock each other down. Later they danced and exchanged gifts. In addition to the ceremonial features, a dancing partnership was imbued with a great deal of joking and horseplay, each member trying to outdo the other in, say, an exchange of jibes or in a shoving match. *Mumiqatigiik* were very fond of each other and eagerly looked forward to their meetings.

The Political Process

Politically, each family was a hierarchical system based primarily on generation and relative age, and, to some extent, on gender differences. In general, people in higher generations had authority over people in lower ones, older individuals had authority over younger ones, and, within a given generation or relative age category, males had authority over females. At the pinnacle of each of these tiny hierarchies was an *ihumataq*, or "chief."

An *ihumataq* was a mature adult, usually a middle-aged or older man – someone who had lived long enough to have experienced life, acquired wisdom, and demonstrated in practice that he was qualified for the responsibilities of leadership. An *ihumataq* was also a very close kinsman of most people over whom he wielded authority. He was related to them as husband, father, older brother, older cousin, uncle, grandfather, and senior in-law. In short, the *ihumataq* typically was a person who wielded authority automatically by virtue of the fact that he filled a superior position in a whole series of hierarchical kin relationships. But the role always carried greater authority than would be conveyed by age, generation, and gender considerations alone, and it could be filled by any man whose extraordinary ability overrode those considerations. In a family large enough for there to be more than one candidate for the position, the actual *ihumataq* was likely to be a physically powerful individual, an excellent hunter, an understanding counsellor, an expert at human relations, and often a shaman as well. He would have more wives, more living children, better clothing, and generally more and better of everything than anyone else in the group.

An *ihumataq* led by a combination of demonstrated wisdom and ability. Where he was lacking those qualities, he might try to wield authority by brute strength, but a family headed by such a person would not stay intact for long. Individuals or conjugal family subunits could leave at any time. But where could they go? They either had to set out on their own or join another family identical in structure. This possibility acted as a check on the abuse of power by an *ihumataq*, while at the same time helping to concentrate people around the most effective leaders.

An *ihumataq* had no institutionalized authority over anyone outside of his own family. At the *inter*-family level, therefore, power and responsibility were allocated in a very haphazard manner. Families whose members could not get along very well together either had to fight or separate. Most of the time they chose the latter course.

Subsistence

The animals that formed the basis of the Caribou Inuit economy are remarkable creatures. Caribou skins can provide satisfactory raw material for clothing, foot gear, tents, boat covers, sleeping bags, mattresses, insulating materials, house covers, blankets, and bags. Excellent thread can be made from their back sinew, and components of tools, weapons, and utensils can be manufactured from their antlers and bones. People who consume all of the meat, viscera, stomach contents (rich in vitamin C), and fat of caribou are able to satisfy all of their nutritional requirements. If caribou are available in sufficient numbers at appropriate times of year, and if they are fully utilized, they can provide for the *total* subsistence requirements of a human population.

Given the real benefits that an adequate harvest of caribou can bestow, it is not surprising that hunting peoples living on or near the boreal forest-tundra border all the way around the world had economies based heavily on this species (which includes the Eurasian form, the reindeer). But barren-ground caribou are highly migratory animals, travelling hundreds or even thousands of kilometres each year. The only predictable feature of these movements is that the animals move onto the tundra for the calving season in early summer and return to the boreal forest for the winter. Even that is far from certain. Hunters have three alternatives: (1) try to follow the caribou over immense distances; (2) harvest caribou in great quantities when they are present and store enough food to last for the rest of the year; or (3) harvest other species when caribou are not available. The Caribou Inuit followed a combination of the second and third strategies.

The main caribou hunt was from late August to October, when the hides are in prime condition and the animals are normally fat. Hunters waited at places where caribou were likely to cross rivers or lakes, then speared the swimming animals from *kayaks*. While women processed the meat and hides, men hunted, killing as many animals as they could. Meat, bones, and viscera not required for immediate use were wrapped in skins and cached under rocks. If the meat putrefied a bit before frost halted the process, that only enhanced the taste. The success or failure of this late summer hunt generally determined how life would be during the winter.

Caribou hunting for most of the rest of the year was erratic. Whenever caribou were present they were hunted – with bow and arrow, with pitfalls dug in deep banks of snow, and occasionally with old-style muzzle-loading guns. Sometimes thousands of animals remained on the tundra all winter, sometimes there were none at all. When there were not enough caribou, the Inuit turned to muskoxen.

Muskoxen generally live in small herds of perhaps twelve to twenty-four animals. These herds, which travel only short distances, were widely distributed across southern Keewatin at the beginning of the nineteenth century. They were not heavily hunted by the Chipewyan. But when the Inuit moved inland in mid-century, they killed muskoxen whenever they ran out of caribou. This happened in mid- to late winter almost every year. During the Classic Period they are known to have killed more than 3,000 muskoxen, and the real number must have been much higher. In the process, they effectively exterminated their most important source of emergency food.

Fish also played a part in the Caribou Inuit diet, particularly in spring, when char run out to sea, and again in August and September when they return to the rivers and lakes. Char were caught with stone weirs, leisters, and with hook and line. But fish were needed most in late winter, when caribou meat was often exhausted. Although southern Keewatin lakes contain large populations of whitefish and other species, none of the Caribou Inuit techniques were very effective for winter fishing. Fish are simply too difficult to locate in large, deep, frozen lakes. Gill nets, set under the ice, would have been relatively effective on lakes, and very effective on rivers. Yet almost every March would find people chopping holes through the thick ice and jigging with hook and line. Sometimes they found fish, but often they did not.

The Caribou Inuit had been exposed to the use of gill nets since 1720. They had been shown how to use them, and nets were available to them in trade. But it was not until the 1930s that gill nets were widely adopted. Why? Birket-Smith provided an answer, which has three parts. First, they had a powerful taboo against eating fish taken dead from the water – and fish often drown in gill nets unless removed very quickly. Such prompt removal is very difficult in winter. Second, it is just about impossible to dry and mend nets in a snow house where the temperature is below or near freezing most of the time. Finally, nets are heavy, bulky items to carry around, and Caribou Inuit moved quite often. For all of these reasons, but particularly the first, nets were simply out of the question.

The Ahiarmiut and Harvaqturmiut, who remained inland year-round, lived almost exclusively on caribou, muskoxen, and fish, supplemented by ptarmigan in early spring, other birds in summer, fur-bearing animals such as foxes and wolves, and such other small game as they might encounter – right down to and including mice in extreme situations. Most members of the other three societies moved to the coast each spring. There they fished for char and hunted seals and belukha – unless caribou or other game were available.

It is worth repeating that throughout the Classic Period Qairnirmiut, Hauniqturmiut, and Paatlirmiut men remained active and competent sea-mammal hunters. But most of their harvest was sold to the Hudson's Bay Company in Churchill or to whalers farther north. They regarded sea-mammal meat as suitable for dogs, but as little more than emergency food for themselves. Even the blubber was hardly used. This is surprising because the meat of northern mammals is much leaner than beef, and people must have fat in their diet. Blubber is also an efficient fuel for lamps and an excellent medium in which to store dried meat and fish for prolonged periods. For fatty food they relied on fish and caribou – or went without; for fuel they depended on dwarf willows – or went without; and for a food preservative they relied primarily on the cold weather. And whenever caribou, fish, or, say, geese appeared on the scene, sea mammals were all but forgotten. It is this utter disdain for sea-mammal blubber, not the obsession with caribou as such, that made the Caribou Inuit unique in the Eskaleut world.

Yearly Cycle

Caribou Inuit societies manifested two forms of yearly cycle. One, followed by most Ahiarmiut and Harvaqturmiut, involved year-round residence in the interior of the country. The other, followed by most Qairnirmiut, Hauniqturmiut, and Paatlirmiut, involved residence in the interior from late summer to early spring and settlement on the coast in spring and early summer. This second pattern obviously required extensive travel between the two areas. Beyond that, the similarities among the five societies were much more numerous than the differences; the similarities receive treatment here.

In summer the Caribou Inuit lived in conical tents consisting of a frame of poles over which a cover made from several caribou skins was

PLATE 5.2. Moving camp near Yathkyed Lake, early July, 1922. The women and children move out first to be followed by the men and dogs. By permission of the National Museum of Denmark, Department of Ethnography.

stretched. Cooking was done outside on a fire made of dwarf trees and shrubs. The smoke also helped drive away some of the billions of mosquitoes that infest the country each summer. Light was provided by the sun. Although southern Keewatin is well south of the Arctic Circle, it is still far enough north to have relatively little darkness during the late spring and early summer months.

Children amused themselves or helped their parents, women tended to their babysitting, sewing, or butchering chores, and men roamed the country searching for game. Individuals ate whenever they were hungry, although a cooked meal was usually prepared for the entire family each evening. When food was abundant and there were no pressing matters to attend to, the members of the tiny community often came together in the largest tent, or perhaps in two tents linked together, and danced, sang, told stories, and generally enjoyed themselves.

People usually stayed in one place as long as the hunting or fishing was good, although hunters often covered a tremendous area in their excursions around the camp. If a large kill was made at some distance from the tents, or if the hunting appeared to be better somewhere else, camp was moved.

Movement in summer was primarily on foot. People and dogs had to carry literally everything; what they could not carry, they cached under rocks. Each man carried his *kayak* upside down on his shoulders, his head inserted into the cockpit. When the group reached a river or small lake, they ferried themselves and their equipment across by making repeated trips. If two or more *kayaks* were available, they were rafted together. By alternately walking and camping, moving slowly but steadily across the country, an entire family, including infants and old people, could cover hundreds of kilometres in just a few weeks. Caribou Inuit were marvellous walkers.

The people lived in their unheated tents until snowdrifts of the right depth and quality formed on the downwind side of the countless eskers and ridges. Usually the right snow conditions did not develop until November or even December. The snow houses that they could then build were of the general central Canadian Inuit type – dome-shaped structures perhaps four to five metres across at the base, made by stacking progressively smaller rows of snow blocks on top of one another until they converged at the top. To the basic house was added a long entrance tunnel, off which were built one alcove for cooking and perhaps one or two others for storage. Often the two or more houses occupied by a single family were linked by tunnels.

Unlike all other snow-house dwellers, and, indeed, unlike most other Eskaleuts, Caribou Inuit did not normally heat or light their winter houses. A few people used seal-oil lamps, but they usually ran out of fuel by early winter. Light generally was provided by sunlight, which came directly through the translucent snow walls and through a window of clear ice placed in the roof. But during the short days of early winter the Caribou Inuit spent most of their inside hours in total darkness. They did without heat altogether, except for that provided by the bodies of the house's occupants. Any cooking was done over a fire of dwarf willows built in the alcove. At most there was one cooked meal (of boiled meat or fish) a day, but during the winter months most food was consumed raw and frozen. During daylight hours people occupied themselves much as they did in the summer, but during the long hours of darkness they lay in their warm sleeping bags and chatted, told stories, sang songs, or just slept.

When people moved they hauled their baggage on long (c. 750 cm), low (10 cm), narrow (42 cm) sleds, which looked more like ladders than sleds capable of hauling 500 kilograms. In the morning, people loaded the sleds and, pushing and hauling along with the dogs, moved out slowly. When travelling downwind they erected sails and let the wind do much of the work. When darkness began to fall, they built new snow houses and created a new settlement within an hour or two.

PLATE 5.3. A Paatlirmiut woman bringing a sled of dwarf willows into camp at Eskimo Point, in the spring of 1923. She has gone several miles inland to collect this fuel despite the fact that seal blubber, a more efficient fuel, was available in great quantities in camp. By permission of the National Museum of Denmark, Department of Ethnography.

Religion

The Caribou Inuit believed that a spirit called Hila constituted the supreme force underlying all phenomena. This general force also had a special female form, Pinga, which dwelt somewhere in space. It was Pinga who made it possible for people to live in the world, who kept a close watch on human activities, and who intervened from time to time in people's affairs. Hila determined which acts were good and which were bad, but Pinga was the spirit who monitored people's behaviour. The soul of a person who had lived according to the rules laid down by Hila was believed to ascend at death to Pinga. That spirit would receive it in space and subsequently return it to earth in the body of an animal, human, or otherwise. The souls of people who had not lived properly, on the other hand, were condemned to eternal misery somewhere outside the earthly domain.

Caribou Inuit did not pretend to know much about the spirit world. What knowledge they did have was acquired by their shamans, or *anga-qut* (plural). The primary duty of a shaman was to act as intermediary between the human and spiritual worlds. By communicating with Hila, a shaman could determine the cause of a problem and ascertain its solution. The latter invariably involved adherence to one or more taboos stipulated by the spirit. In addition, a shaman could perform magic of various kinds and make certain kinds of predictions about the future.

Caribou Inuit religion, while ostensibly quite otherworldly in nature, had a considerable immediacy about it. One did not spend one's time worshipping an intangible and dimly perceived God or attempting to attain a satisfactory reincarnation in the next life. Rather, one tried to sustain oneself in *this* difficult life by conforming to an extensive set of rules governing quite specific acts. Practically every act was governed by some taboo: the technique, timing, and location of the hunt, the technique and timing of butchering, birth and death, menstruation, eating – these and more were governed by taboos so numerous that no one could remember them all.

The taboos were laid down by Hila, and obedience to them helped maintain a balance of amicable relations with that power. If people disobeyed them, on the other hand, Hila would subject them to hunger, sickness, bad weather, or other calamity. Observance of the rules was basically an individual matter, but a transgression by one person often resulted in punishment being visited upon an entire settlement. It was therefore in everyone's best interest not only to watch one's own behaviour but also to monitor that of one's neighbours.

Misfortune was usually interpreted as a sign that a taboo had been broken. In order to determine what was involved, a shaman would go into a trance to contact Hila, who would specify who had committed what particular offence and stipulate the procedures necessary to rectify the situation (and perhaps also to prevent its recurrence). It was through this repeated sequence that the extensive body of taboos governing Caribou Inuit life gradually developed. Since Hila would not entertain general questions, the shamans were forever denied the kind of comprehensive revelation that has led to the development of more complex religions in other parts of the world.

Concluding Remarks

This brief summary of the structure of Caribou Inuit societies during the Classic Period depicts a system that was thoroughly non-European, not only in its basic structure but in almost every detail. The Caribou Inuit were still very much in control of their own affairs. Despite the fact that their land was one of the least hospitable areas in the world, and despite nearly two centuries of contact with Europeans and the attendant lure of the fur trade toward the south, they remained in their own country, dealt with life's problems in traditional ways, and generally remained aloof from the wider world of whose existence they had long been aware.

Denouement

Europeans had had very little interest in Caribou Inuit territory and in the people who occupied it ever since Luke Foxe sailed down the west coast of Hudson Bay in the summer of 1631. A few had come to explore, and others had come to hunt whales or to trade for furs, but all remained for just a little while and then left.

This geographic isolation began to be broken when the North-West (later, Royal Canadian) Mounted Police established a post at Cape Fullerton, on the northeastern corner of Caribou Inuit territory, in the summer of 1903. The police established the post partly to keep an eye on American whalers, and partly – probably primarily – to establish an official Canadian presence in a land whose ownership was not yet established in international law.

In the summer of 1912 both the Roman Catholic Church and the Hudson's Bay Company established permanent posts on the south side of Chesterfield Inlet right in Caribou Inuit country. Over the next two decades tiny Euro-Canadian settlements sprang up at several widely scattered points across southern Keewatin. The largest ones contained an RCMP post, a Hudson's Bay Company trading post, sometimes a competing trader or two, and two missions, one Anglican, the other Roman Catholic. The missionaries often ran schools, in addition to trying to convert the Inuit to Christianity.

Traders, police, and missionaries all set out to influence the Inuit in one way or another, and they competed in attempting to achieve a dominant position. During the early years, however, the Inuit remained almost as aloof as ever.

The event that did more than anything else to terminate Caribou Inuit societies was the "Great Famine," which began in 1915. Snow alternating with rain, and frost alternating with thaw, produced a thick crust that the caribou could not penetrate to reach their food. Consequently, they fled the country. The muskoxen, which had played a crucial role in the original inland expansion of the Caribou Inuit, had been all but wiped out by 1900.

The people turned to fish, but they had only hook and line. Weakened by hunger, they chopped holes through the thick ice in the lakes and jigged their lures, but with little success. Eventually they slaughtered their dogs and even ate boiled pieces of skin clothing. During the winter of 1915-16 the famine struck the Hauniqturmiut the hardest, cutting their numbers from nearly 200 to less than 100 in that year alone.

The unstable weather continued for several winters, always with devastating effect. Famine struck all five Caribou Inuit societies, in most cases for several winters in a row. It was not until the fall of 1924 that caribou returned to the Qairnirmiut, and not until the summer of 1925 that they reached Ahiarmiut country again.

Altogether the Great Famine lasted a full decade. The precise figures remain debatable, but in 1915 there were probably some 1,500 Caribou Inuit. By 1925 only about 500 survivors remained. (It is one of the great ironies of Arctic ethnography that Kaj Birket-Smith and Knud Rasmussen should visit southern Keewatin during the latter stages of this catastrophe and, either not understanding or deliberately ignoring its effects, proceed to write the most comprehensive account we have of *the* Caribou Inuit way of life. What they actually saw were people on the verge of extinction.) In desperation, the Inuit turned to outsiders for help. Police, missionaries, and traders tried to assist them, but there was little they could do. The Inuit starved and died in their isolated camps as they had lived, on their own.

The Great Famine led the Caribou Inuit to become trappers. They had believed that, despite periodic fluctuations, caribou would never abandon them for long. And if they ran out of caribou meat for a while, they could always turn to muskoxen, which did not travel far, were easily killed, and whose general whereabouts were well known. By 1915, however, the muskoxen were gone, and by 1920 the Inuit realized that total reliance on caribou was fatal. By historic standards, the price of white-fox pelts was quite high in 1920, so the people turned to trapping and trading as the only realistic way to survive.

Somehow they did survive. All five societies emerged from the Great Famine intact. However, a sixth, the Tahiuyarmiut, which was in the process of splitting off from the Paatlirmiut when the famine began, was reduced to only a few individuals. And, although their will remained unbroken, Inuit ability to maintain independence and to assert ownership of the land had been effectively destroyed.

During the period from 1915 to 1945, several additional developments contributed to the erosion of Caribou Inuit autonomy. One, noted previously, was the gradual expansion of police, missionary, and trading operations all across Caribou Inuit territory. Another was the migration of members of other Inuit groups to the northern fringe of Caribou Inuit country. Some of them came from the northern Hudson Bay and Foxe Basin coasts. These were members of the Aivilik branch of the Igluling-miut Inuit and descendants of Netsilik Inuit who previously had migrated eastward to the Hudson Bay coast, attracted there by American whalers. Both groups began to be drawn southward by the post at Cape Fullerton, and later at Chesterfield. Somewhat later, other Netsilik, this time from the Back River, also began to move south, attracted by the timber along the Thelon River and by the opportunities for trade at Baker Lake.

While these incursions were taking place in the extreme northeastern and northwestern sectors of southern Keewatin, the Caribou Inuit continued to suffer periodic famine farther south. None was as geographically extensive or as prolonged as that in 1915-25, but each society was struck by more than one period of extreme hunger. The Qairnirmiut, and particularly the Hauniqturmiut, began to fragment under the pressure, and the surviving families began to disperse in an effort to find game. Epidemics took an even greater toll. The nadir was reached in 1948, when a combination of tuberculosis, influenza, and infantile paralysis reached such an extreme state that all of southern Keewatin was placed under quarantine for almost two years by the federal government. Seriously ill people could not hunt, and epidemics were invariably accompanied by famine.

Genuine concern on the part of missionaries, police, and public health officials, and a storm of public outrage stimulated by the writings of Farley Mowat and Richard Harrington, led the government to take a more active interest in the early 1950s. Administrative centres were set up in the old settlements of Baker Lake, Chesterfield Inlet, and Eskimo Point, and new settlements were established at Whale Cove and Rankin Inlet, the latter in conjunction with a mining operation.

The government was faced with a dilemma. The combination of genuine concern and political pressure dictated that something be done to help the starving Inuit. On the other hand, Canadian taxpayers did not want to foot much of a bill for whatever action was taken. Given the dispersion of the Inuit population in southern Keewatin, regular monitoring of conditions in the camps and the provision of adequate medical and other assistance would have been extraordinarily expensive. Consequently, the decision was made to centralize both the Caribou Inuit and the nearby Netsilik and Aivilik groups in the five administrative centres.

To a considerable extent, centralization of the Caribou Inuit population was voluntary. Conditions on the land had been desperately difficult for two generations. Between 1956 and 1960 most came in on their own. A few diehards were brought in later by force.

By 1968 the centralization process was complete. Of the five settlements, only Arviat (formerly Eskimo Point) was inhabited primarily by people of Caribou Inuit extraction. Baker Lake and Whale Cove each contained, in addition to Caribou Inuit, significant numbers of Netsilik, Aivilik, and other Inuit immigrants. Rankin Inlet was largely Aivilik, and Chesterfield Inlet was primarily Netsilik.

Vastly improved medical care and other government services have helped the Inuit population of southern Keewatin rise dramatically over the last three decades. In 1990, more than 3,600 Inuit lived in the five administrative centres, along with some 550 non-Inuit. Thirty years of living together and of intermarriage between the different Inuit groups, which was virtually unthinkable in 1915, had blurred the ancient boundaries. Although the elders had not forgotten their roots, people generally have come to be identified more by the settlement in which they now live than by the society to which they, or their ancestors, had once belonged.

The centralization of the population and intermarriage terminated the geographic and demographic foundations on which the traditional societies rested. At the same time, the work of government administrators, teachers, missionaries, police, and many other outsiders destroyed the economic, political, cognitive, and motivational bases on which the self-sufficiency of the traditional societies depended. Caribou Inuit still survive in their ancient homeland, but their distinctive way of life is gone forever.

The biggest problem facing the Caribou Inuit today is how to make a living without leaving their traditional homeland. Although Inuit can still meet much of their food needs by hunting and fishing, they must have a cash income to acquire the equipment and fuel required to hunt and fish, not to mention clothe and house themselves. Trapping can provide some cash, but not enough to live on. The country is rich in minerals, but at current price levels no one can afford to extract them and take them to market. Located far from population centres, industries of even modest size are unlikely to locate here at any time in the foreseeable future. The rivers and lakes can provide excitement for a few adventuresome canoeists and fishermen as well as income for the outfitters who look after them, but the landscape is too bleak and homogeneous to attract large numbers of tourists. The production of carvings and other forms of art is one possibility – and, indeed, some of the finest artists in Canada live in southern Keewatin – but this can never support more than a small percentage of the population.

The only steady employment is for support and maintenance staff of schools and other public services, and for government employees.

Income from these sources has no local foundation but is based on the general tax revenues of the government of Canada. There are local businesses of various kinds, but most of them depend ultimately on the cash generated by trapping, jobs funded by the government, and welfare. The Caribou Inuit, like many of their Inuit relatives, approach the end of the twentieth century in difficult circumstances. On the one hand, they have been forced by hard times and a rapidly changing social environment to abandon their traditional way of life. On the other hand, because of their geographic isolation, they cannot participate as constructively as they would like in the modern Canadian way of life. The obvious alternative, leaving their homeland for the cities in the south, does not offer much promise either. Only slightly prepared by training and experience for urban life, confronted by blatant discrimination on all sides, and isolated from family and friends, the urban Native often has an even harder time than his rural counterpart. Most people living in northern settlements have heard about these difficulties and are reluctant to try city life themselves. Even a happy ending with the establishment of their own territory, Nunavut, will not resolve these problems.

Notes

1. From 1968 to 1974 the research on which this chapter is based was supported by the Canada Council (now the Social Sciences and Humanities Research Council of Canada). The historically oriented research, most of which was carried out after 1974, proved to be vastly more productive, but also much more time consuming, than I was prepared for. That and a growing number and variety of other demands on my time have prevented me from publishing more than a fraction of the material I collected. This brief summary is therefore the first comprehensive account of Caribou Inuit social history to appear in print.

2. It is inappropriate here to cite the specific sources on which this historical account is based. Since I have never published the material, however, it is appropriate to indicate at least the general nature of the sources. In addition to the surprisingly sizable published literature available on the Caribou Inuit area, my sources included the following: (a) Hudson's Bay Company Archives: Churchill post journals, sloop and ship logs, correspondence, accounts of trade, and miscellaneous other records, from 1717 to the early twentieth century; (b) National Archives of Canada: Record Group 18, Records of the RCMP ; Record Group 85, Records of the Northern Administration Branch; (c) original field journals and other data collected by J. Burr Tyrrell in 1893 and 1894, housed in the National Archives of Canada,

Record Group 45, Records of the Geological Survey of Canada, and in Manuscript Collection No. 26, in the Thomas Fisher Rare Book Library, John P. Robarts Research Library Complex, University of Toronto.

Recommended Readings

Arima, Eugene Y.

1975   *A Contextual Study of the Caribou Eskimo Kayak.* Ottawa: National Museum of Man, Canadian Ethnology Service Paper No. 25.

Arima begins with a rather technical account of the form and construction details of *kayaks*, broadens the discussion to a consideration of how Caribou Inuit *kayaks* were used, and goes on to Caribou Inuit history and economy. It is a useful supplement to more comprehensive works.

Birket-Smith, Kaj

1929   *The Caribou Eskimos: Material and Social Life and Their Cultural Position. Descriptive Part.* Copenhagen: Report of the Fifth Thule Expedition 1921-24, Vol. V, pts. I and II.

Part I of this substantial work, together with Rasmussen's 1930 volume, is *the* basic ethnography of the Caribou Inuit. It focuses primarily on economic and technological matters. Part II, a reconstruction of Inuit history and prehistory, is an extraordinary example of outmoded reasoning.

Burch, Ernest S., Jr.

1978   "Caribou Eskimo Origins: An Old Problem Reconsidered," *Arctic Anthropology*, 15, 1: 1-35.

A comprehensive review of the literature dealing with Caribou Inuit origins. The conclusions differ from those reached by Clark (1977). The historical sequence outlined in the present chapter begins where this article ends.

Clark, Brenda L.

1977   *The Development of Caribou Eskimo Culture.* Ottawa: National Museum of Man. (Archaeological Survey of Canada Paper No. 59.).

Primarily an analysis of archaeological sites in the Caribou Inuit region, this monograph also draws on information in published historical sources to develop a particular view of Caribou Inuit history from prehistoric to recent times.

Rasmussen, Knud

1930   *Observations on the Intellectual Culture of the Caribou Eskimos.* Copenhagen: Report of the Fifth Thule Expedition 1921-24, Vol. VII, pt. 2.

This monograph is companion to Birket-Smith (1929, pt. I), and the two stand together as the major ethnographic account of Caribou Inuit culture. Rasmussen, like Birket-Smith, was a poor historian, but he had as much

insight into traditional Inuit thought processes as anyone who ever wrote
on the subject.

Smith, James G.E., and Ernest S. Burch, Jr.

1979 "Chipewyan and Inuit in the Central Canadian Subarctic, 1613-1977," *Arctic Anthropology*, 16, 2: 76-101.

The Chipewyan and Caribou Inuit are invariably described as having been in a state of perpetual armed conflict. This comprehensive survey concludes that Chipewyan-Caribou Inuit relations were much more peaceful than earlier thought.

Vallee, Frank G.

1967 *Kabloona and Eskimo in the Central Keewatin.* Ottawa: The Canadian Research Centre for Anthropology, St. Paul University.

This excellent book is the most comprehensive account of the Caribou Inuit in the late 1950s: it is arguably one of the best monographs on any Inuit group from that era. Its major geographic focus is on the northern part of Caribou Inuit territory.

VanStone, James W., and Wendell Oswalt

1959 *The Caribou Eskimos of Eskimo Point.* Ottawa: Department of Northern Affairs and National Resources, Northern Co-ordination and Research Centre (NCRC-59-2).

This short monograph describes Caribou Inuit life in or near Eskimo Point in the middle and late 1950s. It is a good summary of the southern sector of the Caribou Inuit region, and a useful supplement to Vallee's book.

PART III
The Eastern Subarctic

CHAPTER 6
The Northern Algonquians:
A Regional Overview

Jennifer S.H. Brown and C. Roderick Wilson

The Eastern Subarctic is sometimes referred to as the Northern Algonquian culture area because the entire region is occupied by a branch of the widespread Algonquian-speaking peoples. The surviving languages form two series of closely related dialects that can be grouped into two languages, Cree and Ojibway. Our usual terminology does not reflect this understanding very well: terms like Naskapi and Montagnais imply the status of being separate languages, rather than being two of the nine dialects of Cree. In any case, Cree and Ojibway seem to have developed independently from Proto-Algonquian, possibly separating about 3,000 years ago. The relationship between the dialects of these languages is quite complex, in part because in historic times (and earlier?) whole groups of people have shifted from one dialect to another.

The inhabitants of any region must come to terms with their environment. The Eastern Subarctic is characterized by long winters, short summers, and a continental climate. The generally cold climate is also related to the jet streams which, passing from west to east, tend to draw arctic high-pressure air masses to the southeast. In spring and summer, intensified sunlight decreases the dominance of arctic air, so seasonal contrasts are strong. Minimum/maximum daily mean temperatures in the Severn River drainage in northern Ontario, for example, range from between −29° and −19°C in January to between 11° and 21°C in July. But even hot summer days may soon be followed by frost, and variations from the average can be considerable in either direction.

Precipitation in much of the area is relatively light. Total annual precipitation in northern Ontario averages only about 60 cm, most of it coming in summer thunderstorms. However, the climate east of James Bay is much affected by Hudson Bay. Air currents in fall and early winter pick up moisture from Hudson Bay to dump it along the eastern shores and inland. From midwinter to early summer, the Bay remains ice-covered, depressing temperatures and delaying the coming of spring in lands to the east. As a consequence, this area experiences very heavy snowfall and cold temperatures.

The presence of such extreme climatic conditions in these latitudes was difficult for Europeans to accept. When in 1749 the Hudson's Bay Company faced a parliamentary inquiry into its conduct, critics complained that it had not established agriculture and colonies around Hudson Bay and asserted that company representatives must be lying about the climate; after all, York Fort was on the same latitude as Stockholm, Sweden, and Bergen, Norway; and the Severn River was on a level with Edinburgh, Copenhagen, and Moscow. The critics' ignorance was pardonable, however. Fuller understandings of the effects of large-scale and even global weather patterns on the region have only recently been developed. Current research, in fact, is drawing on Hudson's Bay Company journals from the 1700s and 1800s to trace the regional weather patterns.

Northern Algonquians have therefore long been adapting, with a success that startled their early, ill-equipped European visitors, not only to cold, but to unpredictable and extreme climatic conditions. A late spring, for instance, would mean late breakup of lakes and rivers for travel, and late arrival of migrating geese and other birds important as food. Less moisture than usual meant, among other things, less snow cover, meaning in turn less shelter and lowered survival rates for some basic food sources such as ptarmigan, hare, and other ground-dwelling animals. Drying of streams is a serious impediment when the movements of people to different seasonally used food resources (between winter hunting camps and summer fishing spots, for example) depend on canoe

MAP 6.1. The Eastern Subarctic

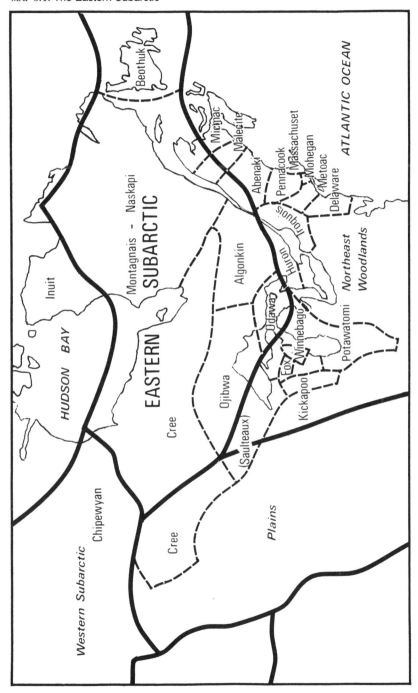

PLATE 6.1. Hudson's Bay Company post at Moose Factory on James Bay, 1934. Courtesy of the Hudson's Bay Company.

transport. Excess precipitation would bring floods, mud-filled portages, and swollen rapids dangerous to small vessels.

The land forms, rocks, and soils of the Algonquian Subarctic support many forms of life, but they, too, pose challenges and constraints. The Canadian Shield is the single topographic feature that has most influenced the shape of Northern Algonquian life. Even a casual traveller sees how this rough rock base, polished clean in places by glaciers and overlain in other places by glacial clays, sand, and gravel, provides the contours for countless lakes, streams, and swamps – ideal habitat for beaver, muskrat, and other animal species long important for food and furs. The French who reached Ontario in the 1600s found that the Hurons valued the trade furs and leather they received from the Algonkin, Nipissing, Ottawa, Ojibway, and others who made their home in the Shield region. And these Algonquian groups in turn valued their trade with the Hurons, prizing in particular Huron cornmeal.

The Shield country in central Ontario and Quebec is transitional between temperate and Subarctic. The observant traveller notices, going north, that the mixed deciduous trees of the south yield increasingly to evergreens – white and red pines mingled with spruce – then to a predominance of black spruce. Continuing northward the landscape changes again. The rocks of the Canadian Shield mostly disappear. The Hudson Bay lowland – a spruce-dominated forest on poorly drained, clayey soil – covers a vast area west and south of the Bay. The growing season is short and intense throughout the Algonquian Subarctic. People intensify their activities, taking advantage of the open waters, the fisheries and waterfowl, and such plants as blueberries, which can only be harvested for a few short weeks.

The landscape presents limits of various kinds to its occupants, and anthropologists and other Western scientists are only now beginning to appreciate the extent to which Aboriginal peoples interacted with the environment. Europeans, for example, have always described the forests they found in America as "virgin," "primeval," "wilderness," and so on. In contrast, the forests were not only occupied, but their productivity was actively managed and maintained. We have long been aware that one could manage game directly by varying the intensity of hunting; it is now clear that Native peoples also managed game levels indirectly by manipulating the environment, primarily through the selective use of fire.

Small, carefully located and timed fires were extensively used to hasten new growth in the spring, which would attract desired animals and birds, foster desired plants such as blueberries and raspberries, create a more varied habitat that would support larger numbers of animals, and open up areas for travel and hunting. Some species that benefited from controlled burning were moose, deer, beaver, muskrat, bear, and ducks. Other species, notably caribou, require the mosses and lichens of mature, "climax" forests. Where caribou was the preferred basic resource, as it was in the northerly parts of the region, the use of fire was lessened. The choice was not simply a matter of food preferences but ultimately one of social organization, since the strategies for hunting solitary and herd animals vary substantially. In either case, the forest was not something simply provided by nature.

Changing patterns of human activity have also been major determinants of Northern Algonquian life. Because the following chapters are strongly historic in orientation, the historic context for the region will be limited to two generalizations. First, despite the fact that large numbers of its contemporary inhabitants pursue lifeways that are seen as strongly "traditional," this region had an extremely long period of contact with Europeans. Almost certainly its southeastern reaches along the St. Lawrence River were visited by Bretons before 1500, and by 1670 the

Hudson's Bay Company had initiated trade in the more northerly Hudson drainage. First European contact for the Cree in the northwestern corner of the Eastern Subarctic was only a few years prior to the first direct contacts for their closest neighbours in the Western Subarctic, the Chipewyan. As a whole, contact in the east of the region was substantially earlier – in some cases more than 350 years earlier.

Partly because of the length of the cultural contact, people's lives over the years have changed substantially. Again, this is most true of the south and of the coast, but it also places the Eastern Subarctic as a region in contrast to the Western Subarctic. This region saw very early missionizing of its people, early exposure to new diseases, and generally a greater involvement in the fur trade than similar zones further west. As an extreme example, by the end of the era of competitive fur exploitation between the Hudson's Bay Company and its Montreal rivals (1763-1821), in some areas the dominant resource bases, caribou and moose, had been virtually exterminated. A consequence of this longer and more intense period of cultural contact in the Eastern Subarctic than in the West is that we are less sure of what the eastern Aboriginal life patterns and beliefs were. On the other hand, in the East there is substantial historic (European) documentation of events dating from the early seventeenth century, for which there is no parallel in the Western Subarctic.

There follow three final points of general relevance. First, there is always the problem of sources – which voices have spoken to us and why. Native voices are rarely heard from the documentary record, and, when they are, they are often reported at second or third hand.

A second matter is that of homogeneity versus local variability. A superficial observer sees a great sameness: Algonquian hunters inhabiting a vast, cold, mainly spruce-covered region. In fact, local variations – the shape of a lake, the slope of the land, pockets of soil – produce a considerable range of micro-environments. Local food resources, particularly game, are not evenly distributed. People have reacted in even more complex fashion. Furthermore, their lives have never been solely subsistence-oriented. They evolved distinctive social traditions, world views, and cultural and religious patterns that had their own dynamics of variability and conformity.

Superficial generalization is accordingly to be avoided. The challenge is to get beyond the simple traditional stereotype of hunters in wigwams or the more modern one of isolated northern villages, to begin to know the Northern Algonquians as complex, diverse human beings whose lives have their own historic richness and vitality. We close with a series of contemporary facts that have implications worth pondering. Cree children who first learn to read in Cree, reading stories produced in their home community, later learn to read English better than their older siblings did. Some families ensure that some children learn the old bush skills and send others to university. The Grand Council of the Crees is rooted in tradition; it is also a contemporary political innovation of the first order.

CHAPTER 7

The Montagnais-Naskapi of the Labrador Peninsula

Eleanor Leacock

The Montagnais-Naskapi in Anthropological Theory

The Montagnais-Naskapi people of the Labrador Peninsula have figured importantly in the history of anthropological theory. This follows from the significant part they played in the early history of Canada, and from the fact that this history was relatively well recorded by missionaries, political figures, merchants, and travellers long before anthropologists arrived on the scene.

The early growth of Canada as a nation-state was based on the fur trade. The people who summered on the St. Lawrence coast, called Montagnais by the French although they called themselves by many local names, were trading furs with Europeans even before Cartier first sailed up the river. Competition among French and English merchant ships was intense during the sixteenth century, and the Montagnais became drawn into rivalry with the Iroquois over access to furs. In 1609, seeking to engage Champlain in war against the Iroquois, the Montagnais and their Algonquian allies led him in the expedition on which he "discovered" the lake that now bears his name. The Montagnais-Naskapi were also the subject of concerted missionary efforts by Jesuits in the seventeenth century and other orders in that and succeeding centuries. Thus, the history of close relations between Montagnais-Naskapi and Euro-Canadians spans almost a half-millennium. The changes in economic and social life that the Montagnais-Naskapi made during this time have figured in lively anthropological debates.

In the early decades of this century, when the formal study of Montagnais-Naskapi culture was well under way, the "historical particularism" associated with Franz Boas in the United States and the functionalism associated with A.R. Radcliffe-Brown and Bronislaw Malinowski in England were coming to the fore. In differing ways, adherents to both schools of thought were countering the evolutionary propositions formulated by Lewis Henry Morgan in *Ancient Society*, and refined and applied by Friedrich Engels in *The Origin of the Family, Private Property and the State in the Light of the Researches of Lewis H. Morgan*. A major evolutionary proposition was that egalitarian socio-economic relations and communal ownership of basic resources had preceded the emergence of economic and political stratification in the course of human history. Correlated with this proposition is the theoretical assumption that the way people organize the production, distribution, exchange, and consumption of their basic subsistence goods (in Marxist terms, their "relations of production") in combination with productive technologies, knowledge, and skills ("forces of production") exerts a profound influence on the way they organize the rest of their lives and determines certain directions of socio-cultural elaboration and change. According to this view, a limited number of "modes of production" underlie the myriad cultures of the world. To understand this makes it possible to analyse basic historical processes that are often masked by culture's bewildering variations.

Since the middle of this century, evolutionary propositions have been re-examined and refined in the light of the challenges raised by historical particularism and ecological studies and by the massive amounts of data being collected on non-urban cultures. At the time of my own undergraduate years, however (1939-43), evolutionary theory was generally either ignored in the classroom or ridiculed as thoroughly outdated. Marxist theory as elaborated in Engels's book was seldom, if ever, mentioned.

Antagonism toward evolutionary theory had a significant effect on the concept of culture that was emerging as central to the relatively new field of anthropology. Anthropology was making a most important contribution by stressing the role of culture as a socially learned set of relations, norms, and attitudes, thereby contradicting racist arguments that inborn behavioural disabilities were responsible for racial and national inequality and oppression. It was necessary, too, to divest evolutionary thought of ethnocentric biases, and of any implication that cultures could be valued as "lower" or "higher" according to the extent that they approximated Western norms. "Cultural relativism" was insisted upon by the Boasian school as an essential corrective to racism and ethnocentrism. However, the refusal to place culture in context as part of evolutionary historical process enabled ethnocentric and racist attitudes to creep in the back door.

Culture was conceived of as a trait list: in the words of Robert Lowie, Boas's most prolific student, cultures were "things of shreds and patches" (1920: 441), random assortments of characteristics that societies had acquired in the course of their contacts and in their adaptation to their environments. The dynamics of integration and change were seen in largely psychological terms, that is, in terms of the values and attitudes that caused a society to take on some traits rather than others. The term "acculturation" was used with reference to the results of "contacts" between Europe-based and other cultures. The implications of the term, as exemplified by Ralph Linton's edited *Acculturation in Seven American Indian Tribes*, were that "contact" meant that a people would simply lose "traditional" traits and take on "modern" ones as it "adapted" to Western culture. The realities of colonization and the fundamental economic changes that it brought about were dealt with superficially if at all in analyses such as Linton's; instead, colonized peoples were treated as passive victims whose problems were seen as primarily psycho-cultural problems of "adjustment."

By contrast, an evolutionary historical approach makes it possible to define the egalitarian economic and social relations that characterized most (not all) Native North American cultures, and it makes it possible to pinpoint the nature of basic changes brought about when European merchants and planters introduced market relations (in most of what became Canada) and wage and/or slave labour (in parts of what became the United States), and when Native access to lands and resources became increasingly restricted. Close analyses of these changes make clear that Native North Americans were not, and are not, simply submitting to pressures toward "assimilation" or failing to do so because of inability to cope. Instead, they have always been actively involved making choices, trying to take advantage of new potentials, and attempting to deal with new problems. Natives have been constantly changing their cultural practices, although in ways specifically theirs, as they build on traditions born of their past history. Further, in the face of exploitation and oppression, they fight to maintain access to their lands and as much independence as possible.

When the anthropologists Frank Speck and John Cooper interviewed the Montagnais-Naskapi of the southern Labrador Peninsula in the 1910s and 1920s, they found people who ranged widely over their lands, hunting, trapping, fishing, and gathering wild vegetable foods; who spoke their own language; and who observed many ritual and other traditional cultural practices. To Speck and Cooper, therefore, the trapping of furs to trade had merely changed traits of material culture – food, tools and equipment, clothing, and tent and canoe covering. The tradings of furs, as they saw it, had not required changes in socio-economic or political forms, and Speck and Cooper did not consider the loss of political independence or the greatly reduced access to lands.

Speck and Cooper inquired about land rights. The Montagnais assured them that hunters owned individual lands, which had belonged to their fathers, which would be passed down to their sons, and which were protected against trespass by witchcraft. (Since their lands were being constantly encroached upon by white Canadians, any other answer would have been folly.) Neither Speck nor Cooper inquired about practices of land *use*. Instead, Speck wrote that the various band territories of the Montagnais were "subdivided into tracts owned from time immemorial by the same families and handed down from generation to generation in the male line" (1926: 327), a position with which Cooper concurred (1939). Lowie cited their data in support of his position that a mode of production based on communally owned property had never existed in human history, and Speck and Eiseley wrote that the existence of privately owned hunting territories among the Montagnais must be "troubling" to those who saw the culture of hunters "as representing a stage prior to the development of the institution of individualized property" (Speck and Eiseley, 1942: 238). Thus, anthropologists tried to do by fiat what the Jesuits had tried and failed to do in the seventeenth century: transform the Montagnais from a people who honoured collective rights to lands into individualized property-holding families.

Further Research on the Montagnais-Naskapi

Foremost among the opponents of Speck and Cooper's position on individual land ownership among the Montagnais were Diamond Jenness and Julian Steward. Jenness (1935: 4-11) had worked among the Ojibway of Parry Island, where he found that hunting grounds, fishing places, and maple groves had in the past been jointly owned by the band as a whole. At certain seasons the entire band would come together; at other times the exigencies of the food quest required that the band separate into groups of four or five families, and sometimes even fewer. Jenness wrote that family rights to territories developed as a consequence of colonization, the restriction of lands, and the reduction of game, as well as of the establishment of trading posts and their emphasis on small fur-bearing animals. Interestingly enough, at the time of Jenness's writing in 1935, although trapping territories were held by individual families, maple groves remained communally owned. Jenness (1937: 44) found that parallel changes had occurred among the Athapaskan Sekani, and Steward (1941: 501) reported similar developments among the Carrier.

As a graduate student at Columbia University in the 1940s, I was interested in Marxist theory and in the Morgan/Engels hypothesis that communal ownership had predated the emergence of private property in human history. I questioned the insistence of Lowie and others that communal ownership was not characteristic of most hunting and gathering economies. I was lucky to have as one of my professors William Duncan Strong, who had been to northern Labrador and had spent part of the winter of 1928 with the Davis Inlet band. Strong documented the fact that the northern peoples, called "Naskapi" by people to the south, owned their lands jointly, and that bands were generous about sharing the use of lands with others. Speck was aware of this, but argued on ecological grounds that communal ownership was practical, even necessary, in the northern Labrador Peninsula where people depended on the migratory caribou, but that to the south dependence on the more sedentary woodland caribou and on beaver called for delimitation of territories and conservation of game. He argued that in this respect the Naskapi and the Montagnais were different, although in other respects they shared the same culture. In support of his argument, he tried to prove that evidence of private land-holding predated the establishment of fur trading as important in Native economy.

I decided to undertake as my doctoral research the whole issue of land use among the Montagnais-Naskapi. After a year of archival work I spent the summers of 1950 and 1951 at Natashquan on the north shore of the St. Lawrence River and at Northwest River, respectively. I looked into the early history of the fur trade and combed through the *Jesuit Relations* and other later accounts of the Montagnais-Naskapi. In the field, I collected genealogies, hunting histories, and anecdotal accounts of hunting and trapping trips as well as general cultural and observational materials. With respect to the "family hunting territory" issue, I found the following (Leacock, 1954).

(1) The hunting territory system as practised by the Montagnais did not involve ownership of land as such, but the usufruct right to lay traplines on it. Products of the land – game, fish, berries, birchbark – were available to all band members; the sole exception was fur-bearing animals. However, the meat of a trapped fur bearer could be eaten by someone in need as long as the fur was returned to the owner. This pattern of ownership shows a clear relation to the fur trade. Meanwhile, generally co-operative traditions remained strong; indeed, they influenced the lifestyle of white trappers (Lips, 1937; Speck, 1933).

(2) Semi-permanent traplines and associated usufruct rights were first established near centres of early trade such as Tadoussac. In 1950, they were only beginning to be accepted by the Montagnais of the southeastern Labrador Peninsula, the Mingan, Natashquan, Romaine (Musquarro), and St. Augustine bands. Speck had used references to "our grounds" by a seventeenth-century Jesuit as evidence of Montagnais "ownership" of individual lands, despite clear evidence in the same account that people made decisions about where they were spending the winter according to practicalities and social contingencies (Leacock, 1954: 14-15).

In 1953-54, Edward Rogers studied hunting practices among the Mistassini Cree of the western Labrador Peninsula, and he also concluded that "a hunting territory system evolved with the introduction of a fur trade economy" (1963: 83). Prior to the fur trade era, a flexible "hunting area" system prevailed, whereby every winter a group would return from a summer gathering place to the same general area, but they would not observe precise boundaries or claim exclusive rights to resources.

The changes that took place in Montagnais-Naskapi society are not only in well-recognized features of material culture and religious life, but also in less obvious characteristics of social structure. The precise nature and timing of these changes varied in detail in different parts of the Labrador Peninsula, as one moves from the Mistassini-Cree groups in the west to the Montagnais groups of the St. Lawrence and the Naskapi groups of the north. Indeed, the fact that one can define these groupings in the first place follows not so much from Aboriginal distinctions among them as from the histories of their relations with different groups of Euro-Canadians – French and English, fur traders and fishing people, missionaries of different orders, and, more recently, lumbering companies, mining industries, and multinational enterprises. These last have been quick to seize on any differences they find within the Montagnais-Naskapi community in order to use them in divide-and-rule strategies in their moves to gain control of what have always been Indian lands.

Therefore, the fundamental unity of Montagnais-Naskapi history and culture is being obscured. Here, however, I shall deal with the Montagnais-Naskapi as one people and give in broad outline the nature of their society and culture as it was at the time of the Europeans' arrival (insofar as this can be reconstructed), as it developed during the fur-trading era, and as it is changing today. In my account I shall emphasize the way people relate to each other as they produce the goods upon which they live, i.e., the "mode of production" as the foundation upon which a group builds its particular cultural ways.

The Montagnais-Naskapi: Their Aboriginal Culture

Archaeological investigation documents the long history of hunting and fishing peoples in the Labrador Peninsula. Remains of campsites go back at least 5,000 years. Stone tool types changed slowly over time, and the overall record of continuity indicates that in all likelihood the early inhabitants were the direct ancestors of the present-day Montagnais-Naskapi.

The Montagnais-Naskapi population at the time of Columbus is estimated to have been over 4,000, and it was probably well over. This population was grouped in some twenty-five or thirty bands, each of which travelled up and down one of the large river valleys that mark the face of the Labrador Peninsula or hunted through the lands around one of the big interior lakes. People knew themselves and each other by regional names, such as the name of a river or lake, or of a food animal that abounded in a particular area. The name Montagnais was used by the seventeenth-century French for the many bands that summered at river mouths along the St. Lawrence, and the name Naskapi was used for those living to the north. Since dialect differences are but slight across the peninsula, and since cultural differences pertained mainly to the matter of which animals or fish were of greater importance in different regions, Frank Speck suggested the hyphenated term to designate as a whole the Montagnais, the Naskapi, and the bands near James Bay now known as Eastern Cree. Recently the term "Innu" has become widely used as well.

By far the best and most detailed description of early Montagnais-Naskapi culture is that written in the seventeenth century by Paul Le Jeune, director of the Jesuit mission at Quebec. Le Jeune's report is unusually valuable, since his commitment to Christianizing and "civilizing" the "savages" of New France led him to spend the winter of 1633-34 in a Montagnais lodge in order to learn to speak the language and to record the details of a life he sought to change. To be sure, by the time Le

Jeune worked with them, some of the Montagnais had been trading furs for metal tools and utensils, as well as some dried food, clothing, and blankets, for over a century, and his account tells of drunkenness and disruption around the French settlement. Nevertheless, Le Jeune's daily log of his experiences travelling with the Montagnais in the interior, and particularly his discussion of contrasts between Montagnais-Naskapi and French ways, shows that daily production was still mainly for direct use and sharing, and that involvement in the fur trade had not yet undercut the co-operative structure and values of Montagnais-Naskapi culture.

Economic Organization and Division of Labour

According to all early accounts by European explorers, traders, and missionaries, the means of production – the land itself and the animals, plants, and minerals on it – were collectively held by the Native peoples of the Labrador Peninsula. When food was short in one area, its inhabitants felt free to enter the territory habitually occupied by another group in order to hunt, with no more than the formality of asking and receiving permission. Each local group or band had an habitual cycle of movement through its homelands and a pattern of dispersal or cohesion according to the distribution and seasonal availability of game. Bands split into units of one or several multi-family lodges in lean seasons and came together with other bands when food was plentiful. In the summer, several bands usually gathered at lake or river shores to socialize, intermarry, and escape the mosquito-ridden woods. Two or more bands also joined forces for communal caribou hunts, or when seasonal foods, such as migratory waterfowl, were abundant. In a land of lakes, streams, and rivers, not to mention snow and ice, the availability of enough water for large gatherings was never a problem.

Everyone participated, according to age, gender, and ability, in procuring and processing food and in manufacturing tools, utensils, clothing, and shelter. All food and other necessities were freely shared. Therefore, with regard to freedom of access to the means of production and to the knowledge and skills to make use of them, as well as to the direct and "equal" participation in production and control over the distribution and consumption of basic goods, the Montagnais-Naskapi were communistic. I place "equal" in quotation marks to indicate that I do not mean literal equality or identity. The English language is attuned to assertions of "equal rights" as an ideal, by contrast with the reality of class distinctions that render such rights impossible, and it does not provide a term appropriate for a set of relations in which such rights are taken totally for granted. From all indications, acceptance of and respect for individual abilities and interests were great; in the past as in recent times, everyone must have contributed more of what he or she particularly liked to do.

Each sex had its specialties, but the division of labour was not rigid, and both women and men could do the basic work of the other when a situation called for it. Women were specialists in leather work; they tailored and decorated clothes, webbed snowshoes, made leather containers, and worked skins for lodge coverings if good bark was not available. Men specialized in wood work, making canoes, toboggans, snowshoe frames, snow shovels, and wooden utensils. Men chipped and ground stone into axes and other tools, but these were early replaced by traded metal, and the ethnographic record does not reveal whether or not women chipped their own knives and skin scrapers as they did among the neighbouring Inuit.

Men did most of the big-game hunting, although women also hunted as they needed or wanted to. Women set snares for hares, waterfowl, and other small game. When living in a Montagnais-Naskapi camp, I observed both women and men going out to check fish nets, as Rogers also noted for the Mistassini-Cree. Women gathered berries to bring into camp, though men who were short of food on a hunt must in the past, as recently, have taken advantage of any good berry patch they ran across.

Production was for direct use and consumption. True, there was always some trade. Good stone for tools must have been passed from hand to hand, because it is found archaeologically many miles from its original location. Ochre, widely used for decorating clothing, was also not found everywhere. In the southern part of the Labrador Peninsula, the Montagnais exchanged skins and meat for the corn and tobacco grown by their agricultural neighbours. However, such trade was not of great magnitude, nor did it undercut the structure whereby everybody had direct access to critical resources and directly controlled the distribution of what they produced.

Direct and equal production for consumption meant that there was full identity of interest between the individual and the group as a whole in Montagnais-Naskapi society. It was in everybody's interest to share. Stated in terms of our property orientation, to share one's catch one day meant the assurance of receiving part of someone else's catch another day. Stated in Aboriginal terms, it was simply inconceivable to hoard food when others were hungry. For all his Christian teachings, Le Jeune was chagrined when food was short in the winter and his hosts unstintingly shared an already depleted larder with others who came for help.

PLATE 7.1. Naskapi women in traditional dress, showing Inuit influence, 1902.
Courtesy of McCord Museum of Canadian History, Notman Photographic Archives.

When large amounts of meat were taken, strips were smoked or dried, part to be carried and part to be cached on storage platforms. People respected the stores of others, but it was taken for granted that those in sore need of food would help themselves and let the owners know.

The primary economic unit in Montagnais-Naskapi society was not a nuclear or extended family, but a multi-family group of some fifteen or so members. This might be called a "lodge group," since it consisted of several of what we call families who shared one large lodge. Within these working collectives there were no grounds for superordinate-subordinate relations between the sexes; instead, egalitarian relations prevailed. Such relations were made possible by the fact that, in contrast with hierarchically structured societies, women and children in no way depended on individual male family heads. The genders were dependent on each other as *groups* who exchanged and shared the goods and services each produced, but they were not bound by *individual* dependencies. There was always an available person of the opposite sex who could furnish a needed item, and there were no taboos on doing the work of the other sex. A man might be teased for collecting firewood, usually a woman's task, but not because the work was not valued; instead (in the incident recorded), it was because it showed he was not wanted by a woman. Having a spouse was pleasant and certainly more convenient than not, but sexual exclusiveness was not considered a part of marriage and divorce was easy. Moreover, in a very real sense children were considered a group responsibility, and orphans were eagerly adopted.

Social Organization and Decision-making

SOCIAL GROUPS

A close reading of the *Jesuit Relations* of the seventeenth century reveals four successively more inclusive levels of social organization. The basic unit on a day-to-day basis, as stated above, was the multi-family lodge group of some ten to twenty people. Several of these made up what might be called "winter bands" of some thirty-five to seventy-five people who stayed together when they could and who kept in close touch with each other if they had to split up and spread out to hunt over a wider area. Several of these, in turn, constituted the named group or band of some 150 to upwards of 300 people who came together during the summer at an interior lake or a river mouth. Finally, large summer congregations of up to 1,500 or more would gather, in the seventeenth century, around the forts and missions or to await incoming trading ships. These included other Algonquian-speaking people – Abenaki, Attikameg, Algonkin are mentioned – as well as Inuit. While they were drawn together by the fur trade, such gatherings probably had roots in old patterns of Indian trade and visiting.

Seasonally, then, people would come together in large groups and break up into smaller groups, balancing the enjoyment of social gatherings, on the one hand, with the availability of food on the other. Winter was often a difficult time. During the winter of 1633-34, which Le Jeune spent in the interior, the party of forty-five, in three lodges, moved camp twenty-three times between November 12 and April 22. The early winter was hard since the snow came late, and it was difficult to track down moose. One of the lodge groups separated from the other two to hunt over a wider area. People from other camps were even worse off, however, and came for help. Then snow fell heavily, and enough large game was killed so that some could be dried. In the spring the party split up again; some members hunted moose in the highlands, and others followed stream beds for beaver. All joined again at the coast to return to Quebec. Perhaps the last move was a response to the fur trade and the desire to take some beaver. The general account, however, when taken in conjunction with other accounts and with ethnographic, ecological, and archaeological data, indicates the pattern of seasonal movement to have been well established.

Membership in lodge groups, winter bands, and the larger band was flexible. It was important that the lodge groups be both congenial and balanced as to age and sex distribution, and there was always a good deal of moving about. Band membership was also flexible and the geography of the Labrador Peninsula allowed for easy shifting back and forth. A glance at the map will show that the rivers flowing to its different coasts all rise in the central lake plateau. These lakes were places not only for summer gatherings of people from different bands (particularly before the fur trade attracted more people to the St. Lawrence), but the lake plateau was also the site for winter meetings at times when game was plentiful. In fur trade times, people might decide to go downriver with another band and visit a different trading post, and there is no reason to think that such a pattern of easy movement between bands was not always the case.

MARRIAGE AND FAMILY

Exogamy, or marrying out of one's group into another, is a world-wide form of building friendly alliances. Band exogamy apparently characterized the Montagnais-Naskapi, although it is not clear whether the winter band or the band as a whole was the minimal exogamous unit. As previously discussed, marriages were preferably matrilocal, that is, the husband joined his wife's family, although this preference changed over the years. A Jesuit wrote that when a young man "saw that he was well received, he went to lodge in the cabin of his future spouse, according to the former custom of the Savages," and Le Jeune wrote that it was necessary to teach the girls as well as the boys if the "savages" were to be "civilized." Otherwise, "the boys that we shall have reared in the knowledge of God, when they marry Savage girls or women accustomed to wandering in the woods will, as their husbands, be compelled to follow them and thus fall back into barbarism or to leave them . . ." (*JR*, 5: 145).

There are many mentions in the *Jesuit Relations* of close relations between fathers-in-law and sons-in-law. (The Jesuits emphasized men in their reports and did not refer to the close mother-daughter relationships this implied). However, there are also references to married brothers living together, or fathers and sons, and when Strong worked with the Davis Inlet people in 1927, when they were as yet little involved in the fur trade, he found similar relationships. Was this just a matter of expediency? a response to personal preferences and/or to the needs for a balance in the size and composition of a group where there were more sons than daughters? Perhaps in part so, but collecting genealogies offers another explanation.

One's "cross-cousins" (in anthropological parlance) are one's mother's brother's children or one's father's sister's children. "Parallel cousins" are mother's sister's children or father's brother's children. This distinction is irrelevant in Euro-Canadian society, but it is most significant in societies based on exogamous clans. In such societies, where descent is counted on one side only, either that of the mother (matrilineal) or that of the father (patrilineal), one's cross-cousins can never be in one's own clan. Hence, they are marriageable. By contrast, one's parallel cousins on one's mother's side are always in one's own clan in a matrilineal society, and on one's father's side may be, and the reverse is true in a patrilineal society. The term for parallel cousin is often the same as that for brother or sister, while the term for cross-cousin often translates most closely into something like "sweetheart." This is so because not only *can* one marry one's cross-cousin in many societies, but also because cross-cousins are *preferred* marriage partners.

The reason a cross-cousin is a preferred spouse in a clan-based society is that economic, social, and political affairs are organized primarily through kinship ties. Cross-cousin marriages (where potential partners are congenial) serve two functions simultaneously. First, having an uncle or aunt as an in-law enables close personal relations to be maintained. Second, however, the principle of exogamy along with cross-cousin marriage means that this close relative also serves as a link with another clan, and a group is held together through a network of consanguine and affinal ties.

Although the Montagnais-Naskapi were not organized into formal clans, the combined principles of exogamy and cross-cousin marriage that are formalized in clan societies operated in theirs. When working with the Barren Ground and Davis Inlet bands, Strong found that parallel cousins were called by the same terms as brothers and sisters, and cross-cousins by a "sweetheart" term. Cross-cousin marriage was not uncommon, and my genealogies show that, although ruled out by Catholic law, cross-cousin marriage had occurred in the past at Natashquan. Furthermore, there was a "joking relationship" between cross-cousins, who would make bawdy overtures to each other publicly to the amusement of all present, since they were potential lovers.

My genealogies and life histories reveal further that cross-cousin marriage was closely related to the broader pattern of maintaining close sibling bonds. Both, when combined with the principle of exogamy, function to maintain close relations at the same time as cross-group ties are being built. In a superficially patrilocal move, a newly wed girl moved to Natashquan with her parents and four sisters. The sisters all married at Natashquan and formed a strong unit, sharing an outside cooking place at the summer camp and going upriver together with their spouses for the winter hunting and trapping season. A close group at Northwest River when I was there in 1951 illustrates cross-cousin marriage, albeit slightly indirect, along with "brother-sister exchange" marriage, a practice mentioned by Strong. A woman's son and daughter had married her brother's step-daughter and step-son, and all formed a close group.

These are twentieth-century family arrangements, but they are from bands that had retained much of their former lifestyle, so they throw light on some of the arrangements mentioned by the seventeenth-century Jesuits that contradict an ideal of matrilocality. The last example could be described as two men and their wives living with the men's parents by someone giving relationships – as the Jesuits did – only among men. Furthermore, matrilocality was probably never rigid. Personal preference and consideration of viable age-gender ratios must have always been important considerations in making choices about co-residential groups, and choices were necessarily always constrained by sheer circumstance and what living relatives a person had.

A man might take more than one wife if the women agreed. Le Jeune wrote, "Since I have been preaching among them that a man should not have more than one wife, I have not been well received by the women; for, since they are more numerous than the men, if a man can only marry one of them, the others will have to suffer. Therefore this doctrine is not according to their liking" (*JR*, 12: 165). It was acceptable for both women and men to have lovers, a matter of concern to the missionaries. Le Jeune wrote:

I told him that it was not honorable for a woman to love any one else except her husband, and that this evil being among them, he himself was not sure that his son, who was there present, was his son. He replied, "Thou hast no sense. You French people love only your own children; but we all love all the children of our tribe." (*JR*, 6: 255)

Thus legitimacy, so important to the French, was not an issue in Native society, and all children were cherished. Presumably always, as in recent times, they were inducted into adult occupations through observation, participation, and play. In any case, they were not punished. Le Jeune complained that this made their education by the Jesuits difficult:

The reason why I would not like to take the children of one locality in that locality itself, but rather in some other place, is because these Barbarians cannot bear to have their children punished, even scolded, not being able to refuse anything to a crying child. They carry this to such an extent that upon the slightest pretext they would take them away from us, before they were educated. (*JR*, 6: 153, 155)

An incident that occurred in 1633 showed that the cherishing attitude of the Montagnais-Naskapi toward all their children extended even to the French. A Montagnais man was looking closely at a drummer boy and his drum and was hit in the head with the drumstick, drawing blood. In Montagnais style, the onlookers asked for presents in recompense, but the French interpreter said, "Thou knowest our custom; when any of our number does wrong, we punish him. This child has wounded one of your people; he shall be whipped at once in thy presence." At this the Montagnais "began to pray for his pardon, alleging he was only a child, that he had no mind, that he did not know what he was doing." When the French persisted, "one of the Savages stripped himself entirely, threw his blanket over the child and cried out to him who was going to do the whipping: 'Strike me if thou wilt, but thou shalt not strike him.' And thus the little one escaped" (*JR*, 5: 219).

Families were kept small, as is usual for a hunting people. Two, three, and rarely more than four children contrasted with French families of eight, ten, or more. The record is silent, however, on methods used to control fertility rates.

GENDER RELATIONS

As previously stated, relations between the sexes were egalitarian. Husbands and wives each made their own decisions about carrying out daily activities, and, where group decisions were concerned, both participated. Le Jeune noted that "the women know what they are to do, and the men also, and one never meddles with the work of the other" (*JR*, 6: 233). However, in relation to personal affairs and social matters, the missionaries saw the women as holding "great power." Women's freedom actively to court men they liked, to divorce easily, and to have lovers though married is well documented because the Jesuits reported in detail on their successes and failures in attempting to change such a state of affairs.

The Jesuits complained about the fact that a man could not make decisions without consulting his wife. Le Jeune lectured one man, saying he "was the master and that in France women do not rule their husbands." Women had the major say, apparently, in the composition of winter bands. "The choice of plans, of undertakings, of journeys, of winterings, lies in nearly every instance in the hands of the housewife" (*JR*, 68: 93). However, in keeping with the principle of each gender making decisions about activities for which it was responsible, men made plans about short-run camp moves in relation to the exigencies of the hunt. Problems of serious moment to the group as a whole were discussed at length, and everyone's opinion was heard with attention. Women occasionally met separately to take up matters of particular interest to their gender.

True, women worked hard along with the men. Therefore, some European observers saw them in elitist terms, not as "ladies" who were respected but as drudges and slaves. It was those who came to know them and their society more fully who recognized the egalitarian nature of their status.

LEADERSHIP

There were no permanent chiefs in Montagnais-Naskapi society, and people who could be referred to as "leaders" were people whose influence rested on their wisdom and ability. They held no formal authority. Le Jeune describes a people who had "neither political organization, nor offices, nor dignities, nor any authority" (*JR*, 6: 231) and who "cannot endure in the least those who seem desirous of assuming superiority over the others" (*JR*, 16: 165).

They have reproached me a hundred times because we fear our Captains, while they laugh at and make sport of theirs. All the authority of their chief is in his tongue's end, for he is powerful in so far as he is eloquent; and, even if he kills himself talking and haranguing, he will not be obeyed unless he pleases the Savages. (*JR*, 6: 243)

Persons the Montagnais chose to speak of as go-betweens with the French were treated as chiefs or "captains" by the French, but they held no formal authority over their own people. When Champlain returned to the upper St. Lawrence in 1608, he accompanied an expedition of Montagnais, Algonkins, and Hurons who, with the benefit of French firearms, attacked the Iroquois at the edge of the lake Champlain chose to rename. Midway in the expedition, however, he encountered the well-known principle of autonomy among Native Americans with respect to the decision to go to war. The result of "some difference of opinion regarding the war," Champlain wrote, was that "only a part of them decided to come with me, whilst the rest went back to their own country with their wives and the goods they had bartered" (*JR*, 6: 231). People, both as groups and as individuals, had the full right to join or leave a war party if and when they chose.

Thus, decision-making was widely dispersed, and matters that were a problem to a group were discussed at length. The patience and respect with which all opinions were heard during serious discussions contrast with the rude teasing and joking that took place at other times. Between the two, effective working relations were managed.

RELIGION AND VALUES

Montagnais-Naskapi ideology underwrote egalitarian viewpoints and values. Humans were not seen as apart from and superior to nature; instead, in myth and story animals took human form, and humans and animals intermarried. An important story tells of the man who married the caribou god's daughter, and, as his son-in-law, helped cement relations between the people and the animals on which they depend heavily. Just as among the people no one held power over others, so also in the heavens there was no omnipotent figure. For example, in stories that taught the ethics of good behaviour, a leading figure who can be seen with his sister on the face of the moon, Djokabish, was the butt of laughter over the mishaps he brought upon himself through greed and lasciviousness. The most feared creatures were the Windigos, or cannibal monsters, who, one can surmise, objectified anxiety over the fear of cannibalism during hard winters when people faced starvation.

The high point of religious life was the specially built "shaking tent," in which everyone gathered to hear the shaman-priest converse with the gods and learn where good hunting might be found. Although Le Jeune claimed to have put an end to this ritual, I lay with my family in our tent at Northwest River in 1951 and listened to people leaving the shaking tent, chatting about what had just transpired. From the incidents told me the next day, I realized the extent to which the ritual served the social function of entertainment as much as the function of helping in the hunt.

Other ritual observances included respect for animals with special treatment of their bones; ceremonial drumming, usually by men but occasionally by women; and men's separate "eat all" feasts to ensure good luck in hunting. Le Jeune refers to women's separate feasts, but since he could not attend, their function is not recorded. The Montagnais-Naskapi shared the practice of "scapulamancy" with other Subarctic people. The cracks in a scorched shoulder blade of a caribou were read to determine where animals might be found. In 1951, upon observing some men examining the cracks in a bone that had been laid upon a stove, I realized that one function of the practice was to make the negotiation of different opinions easier in a society where consensus was continually sought and individual assertiveness shunned.

Interpersonal ethics stressed generosity, co-operativeness, and good humour. Individual interests and weaknesses were respected, but individual assertiveness was not. In discussing the last point, Le Jeune commented, "they place all virtue in a certain gentleness or apathy" (*JR*, 16: 165). However, this gentleness did not involve the constraint we might assume. Instead, lively good humour was important, and loud, sharp, and lewd teasing and ridicule were a source of enjoyment. Le Jeune noted that such "slander and raillery do not disturb their peace and friendly intercourse" (*JR*, 6: 247), and he marvelled that people's voices could become so sharp without their becoming angry. It was important to keep in good spirits, and laughter was a common reaction to misfortune. When Le Jeune became sick, he was told:

Do not be sad; if thou art sad, thou wilt become still worse; if thy sickness increases, thou wilt die. See what a beautiful country this is; love it; if thou lovest it, thou wilt take pleasure in it, and if thou takest pleasure in it thou wilt become cheerful, and if thou art cheerful thou wilt recover. (*JR*, 7: 191)

The Montagnais-Naskapi in the Fur Trade Era

In the sixteenth century, furs from Canada entered the European market and became important in the rivalries both among the different companies that were forming at the time and between France and England as nation-states. Lively trade transformed a product that had been useful to Native Canadians, but not especially important – the skins of small fur-bearers – into a product whose properties were virtually magical: a commodity that could be exchanged for tools of iron, for copper pots, for flour and dried fruits, for clothes and blankets, for liquor to assuage the trauma of a new and profound challenge to cultural autonomy and political independence, and, in time, for guns.

By the early seventeenth century, the trade had become of considerable importance to those bands summering on the upper St. Lawrence, and these bands in turn passed goods on to bands further north. The trade was also extremely disruptive. It brought with it the scourge of diseases such as smallpox, which killed thousands of people. It brought terrorization by the Iroquois, who had depleted the beaver in their own lands and ranged north for new sources. It brought the confrontation with powerful and proselytizing strangers that must have been deeply traumatic. And it brought alcohol that created anxieties even as it appeared to relieve them. Friction and conflict were particularly apparent around the French fort and settlement, in sharp contrast to the easy tenor of life reported by Le Jeune and others for the interior, even in cases where fairly large groups gathered together.

However, political stabilization followed the end of conflict between France and England over the control of Canada, and the focus of trade and exploration pushed westward. Although permanent trading posts were established along the upper St. Lawrence, at Lake St. John, at Lake Mistassini, and on James Bay by the end of the seventeenth century, posts were not established in the north and east of the Labrador Peninsula until the nineteenth century. Then, interior posts were established only long enough for the bands that summered on lake shores to become sufficiently dependent on trade to change their pattern of movement and come to coastal posts in the summer. Hence, the course of the centuries saw a relative stability for the Montagnais-Naskapi, based on a mixed subsistence and fur trade economy, until the pressure for industrial development that characterizes modern times invaded the Labrador Peninsula. This long period, varying in time depth from earlier to later as one moves from southwest to northeast, is generally known as the "fur trade era."

PLATE 7.2. Montagnais hunter, St. John, Quebec. Courtesy of the University Museum, University of Pennsylvania, NC35-13706.

Economic Organization and Division of Labour

The Montagnais-Naskapi took different stances toward the fur trade. Some individuals threw in their fortunes with the Europeans and attached themselves to the forts, mission stations, or trading posts. Most, however, apparently took enough furs to satisfy their basic need for iron tools and their modest desire for staple foods and some luxuries. They soon learned that the traders were as dependent on their labour as they were on the trade, and they turned this fact to their advantage when they could. In any case, they seldom trapped with the zeal and regularity that would have been necessary to satisfy the insatiable demands of the traders. In turn, the traders did what they could to make the Indians dependent on them. In the early nineteenth century, John McLean, who established a Hudson's Bay post at Fort Chimo, bemoaned the importance of the caribou to the Naskapi and their independence from the European traders. He wrote:

> As trading posts, however, are now established on their lands, I doubt not but artificial wants will in time, be created. They may become as indispensable to their comfort as their present real wants. All the arts of the trader are exercised to produce such a result, and these arts never fail of ultimate success. Even during the last two years of my management, the demand for certain articles of European manufacture has greatly increased. (1932: 262)

Thus, though it might seem that trapping furs for the market could be a simple adjunct to hunting for food, such was not the case. Instead, the hunting of small animals with little and often inedible meat for their furs was in conflict with the hunting of big animals for meat as well as with fishing and other basic activities. Though traders did take some moose and caribou hide, these were of little importance, and the leather was needed by the Indians themselves. Only the beaver was valuable for both food and fur, but even in areas where beaver abounded they could not alone support a population's needs without being seriously depleted.

Until well into this century, few Montagnais-Naskapi became full-time trappers. People continued to depend in great part on food from the land, and they worked out various compromises between the flexibility of movement that is required for the food quest and desired for social reasons and the permanence and isolation required for most efficient trapping. Nonetheless, that the Montagnais-Naskapi were to some degree becoming dependent on trade meant unavoidable changes in their economic and social life. Contrary to established practices of distribution for direct use and consumption, individuals did have to stockpile furs for trade. Exchange of these furs meant the sudden availability of a wealth of tools, food, and other essential goods. This meant that the direct and equal control by all adults over the total production process was challenged. Now, the economic interdependence of all members of family bands or multi-family lodge groups was undermined by the creation of important economic ties outside the group – by the emergence of a "public" economic sphere that had not previously existed. Concomitantly, the balanced reciprocity that had characterized the sexual division of labour was transformed – albeit slowly – into the dependence of women and children on male "heads" of economically independent family units. Although some women, especially widows, did their own trapping and trading, on the whole it was the men who participated in the new exchange sector of the economy. Furthermore, along with tools and food, trade brought in clothing, thereby reducing women's role in primary production. At the same time, mission teachings and trader and government practice both directly and indirectly encouraged the adoption of Western family structure.

These changes did not mean that strong collective ties became inoperative; such was far from the case. The power of beloved traditions was reinforced by the common ownership of lands and the continuing direct dependence on it for critical amounts of food. Although furs were individually owned, once they had been transformed into consumables these were shared generously. A distinctive economic and social mix of individual autonomy and collective responsibility continued to characterize relationships, both among individuals generally and between the sexes.

Social Organization and Decision-making

SOCIAL GROUPS AND THE "TRADING-POST BAND"

During the fur trade era, the "trading-post band" took shape as a loose network of increasingly independent nuclear families attached to a particular post. On the face of it, the emergence of the trading-post band as a major unit of Montagnais-Naskapi society simply meant that, in place of the former geographical focus for band membership – river-valley systems and large interior lakes – the focus became the trading post near which people gathered in the summer and to which they made short trips during the winter. Lying behind this change, however, the new and individualized dependence on an outside economic institution set in motion a fundamental transformation in the principles of group membership itself, from inclusive to exclusive and from co-operative to competitive.

Having said this, I must stress again that the changes outlined were slow, uneven, and far from complete. Pressures toward individualization and competition were opposed by the power of revered traditions and by difficulties the Montagnais-Naskapi faced that required the preservation of co-operative practices. First, the fur trade was tied to European market conditions and was not dependable; second, neither were the fur-bearers, which could be depleted by over-trapping. People had to be able to fall back on their own resources on both short-term and long-term bases and to move from more individualized to more collective practices. Third, under the best of circumstances, a hunting/trapping life in the north woods was difficult and required mutual support systems. Fourth, the Montagnais-Naskapi faced a long-term common fight to retain some control over their lands and their lives. And last, although they welcomed many of the technological benefits offered by the trade, as they observed Euro-Canadian culture many were sceptical about the social values and practices that contrasted sharply with their own. Facing opposing pressures, therefore, there were considerable variations as individuals and groups chose among available alternatives in efforts to strike some satisfactory balance.

Through the long fur trade era, from the sixteenth century in the southwest until the middle of this century in some parts of the Labrador Peninsula, great variations in land-use practices obtained. As late as 1950, family hunting territories were only beginning to be defined at Natashquan. At that time, people still formed small winter bands that stayed together in the interior, and the men laid only short temporary lines of twenty or so traps. At the same time, however, individuals had already experimented with laying permanent lines of several hundred traps, after the manner of the professional trapper. These had not worked out, apparently, perhaps partly because the best lands had been pre-empted by non-Native trappers.

With the fur trade, the economic importance of men's relations to trapping grounds and trading posts, in addition to policies of traders, missionaries, and government officials, such as introducing patrilineally inherited family names for keeping records, all encouraged the concept of men as "family heads." Concomitantly, the adoption of Western clothing and utensils went with laundering, cooking, and dishwashing as female responsibilities. Women and men had together put up lodges in the past, and these were periodically moved; stone boiling or pit roasting

MAP 7.1. Eastern Cree and Montagnais-Naskapi Bands of the Labrador Pennisula in the 1920s (Speck, 1931)

and cooking over an open fire had involved both sexes; each person had taken care of his or her own bark dish; and leather and fur clothing had needed no laundering. All this changed in accord with Western models for household servicing as woman's role. Nonetheless, the principle of individual autonomy in the making of decisions about one's own activities and in contributing to group decisions continued to prevail.

LEADERSHIP

In 1640, the Governor of Quebec called together some influential Montagnais men who were converts and, criticizing the failure of their people to live up to French marital norms, suggested they should elect some chiefs to govern them. The missionaries organized the election and encouraged the "captains" thus elected to use their authority to punish wrongdoers. Le Jeune reported to his superiors in Paris that a woman was made to return to the husband she had left by the threat of jail, and wrote:

> Such acts of justice cause no surprise in France, because it is usual there to proceed in that manner. But, among these peoples . . . where everyone considers himself from birth, as free as the wild animals that roam in their great forests . . . it is a marvel, or rather a miracle, to see a peremptory command obeyed, or any act of severity or justice performed. (*JR*, 22: 81, 83)

Shortly thereafter, a group of converted Montagnais, meeting in family council, decided to beat a young woman for speaking to a suitor against her parents' wishes, saying that the French had such a regard for the virtue of obedience that "if any one of them fail in it, he is punished. Parents chastise their own children, and masters their servants." The young woman's friends gathered around as she was being beaten, and they were lectured, "This is the first punishment by beating that we have inflicted upon anyone of our Nation. We are resolved to continue it, if any one among us should be disobedient" (*JR*, 22: 115).

Yet the institution of formal chiefly authority with the right to exact punishment went against the grain of Montagnais-Naskapi society. People of practical knowledge and social wisdom continued to be considered leaders, but they quickly lost their influence if they attempted to force their will on others. In later years when chiefs were elected as go-betweens with outsiders in accordance with Canadian government regulations, they held absolutely no authority within a band. In 1935, Julius Lips studied life in the Mistassini band and was told that a chief had responsibility for punishment. However, the band had chosen to get along without a chief for seven years when Lips was there, and he had difficulty trying to find actual examples of punishment. The people concerned worked out their own problems with the help of public opinion.

RELIGION AND VALUES

Most Montagnais-Naskapi became Catholics, although some Eastern Cree were converted by Anglican missionaries. They conducted their own Sunday services in the interior, and in the summer met with missionaries for baptism of newly born children and the formalization of marriages. They were selective in their beliefs, uninterested, for example, in the concept of original sin, and they continued to observe their own rituals. In particular, animals remained highly respected, especially the caribou, which to this day continues to be honoured. In addition to telling biblical tales, they kept alive their own traditional stories. At

Natashquan in 1950, I typed the story of Djokabish in the phonetic alphabet many of the band members had taught themselves to read.

The ethic that combines generosity and collective responsibility with anti-authoritarianism and respect for individuality also continues into the present.

The Modern Era

Like the fur trade era, the "modern era" cannot be defined in terms of exact dates; it varies from region to region across the Labrador Peninsula. Speaking broadly, the modern phase in Subarctic Canada started with the decline of the fur trade after the world depression of the thirties and the subsequent ascendance of lumbering, mining, and hydroelectric enterprises to economic dominance. In theory, "modernization" is supposed to raise the standard of living through employment, schooling, and improved health services and housing. In fact, it is threatening to transform independent and self-sufficient peoples into discriminated-against marginal populations in their own lands. In addition to lumbering and mining operations, since 1941 over twenty hydroelectric dams and plants have been built in the Labrador Peninsula. However, the resulting employment has at best been seasonal and underpaid; health facilities have been inadequate; and family allowances, old age pensions, and other governmental payments have not begun to make up for the losses resulting from the encroachment on Indian lands and the erosion of their subsistence base. The best-known example is James Bay.

In 1975, the Eastern Cree and Inuit signed over 400,000 square miles of their Aboriginal land rights for the building of a network of 170 dams and dikes by the James Bay Hydroelectric Project. In extensive negotiations, they agreed on $225 million to be allocated over twenty-one years in return, as well as government provision of housing with sewage and water systems in areas where people were to be relocated, and government support of trapping and subsistence hunting activities through an elaborately detailed plan for how such lands as remained available were to be used. Although the plan has worked to some extent, it has not enabled sufficient income and subsistence to be derived from the land, and the Cree have tried to augment their income through employment. Furthermore, the required monies were not allocated by the government for building relocation villages, and polluted water supplies caused an epidemic of childhood diarrhea that sometimes led to death. The Cree had to use a million of the dollars slated for economic development to provide clean water and another million to supply health services. Nor

MAP 7.2. Contemporary Eastern Cree and Montagnais-Naskapi Communities
(Charest, 1982; Rogers and Leacock, 1981)

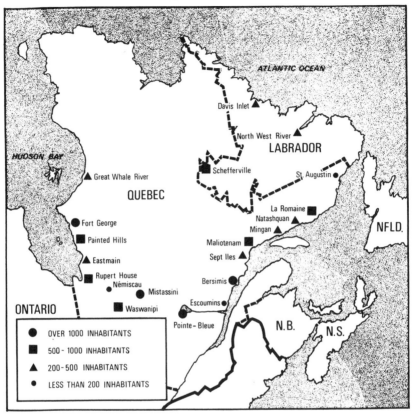

did the building of industrial enterprises on their lands lead to the availability of steady, well-paid jobs. The Cree are usually hired as guides,
woodcutters, and unskilled workmen prior to construction, and unskilled
labour during the construction of a particular project, but they are not
offered employment on subsequent projects.

At present, more than 12,000 Montagnais-Naskapi live in twenty settlements, either predominantly Indian villages or ethnically heterogeneous towns. Most continue to derive a part of their livelihood from fur
trapping and subsistence fishing and hunting. In the effort to provide for
their needs and to negotiate settlements on burgeoning developments,
they have formed several regionally based organizations. In the James
Bay area and in the northern Labrador Peninsula the Montagnais-
Naskapi are allied with the Inuit, and in western Quebec with the

Attikameg. On the one hand, mining and electrical interests try to hinder the development of broad alliances by playing on all possible differences of opinion as to how immediate and long-range problems can be solved. On the other hand, however, there are politically involved Montagnais-Naskapi who raise the necessity of alliance not only across Canada, but also with Indians of the United States and Latin America, before it is too late for indigenous peoples to retain some access to their lands and some right to determine the course of their own future.

Recommended Reading

Bailey, Alfred Goldsworthy

 1969 *The Conflict of European and Eastern Algonkian Cultures, 1504-1700: A Study in Canadian Civilization*, 2nd ed. Toronto: University of Toronto Press.

 A richly documented account of early relations between the French and the people of Acadia and the St. Lawrence Valley. Changes in Algonquian material culture, social and political life, religion, and art; problems of drunkenness and disease.

Charest, Paul

 1982 "Hydroelectric Dam Construction and the Foraging Activities of Eastern Quebec Montagnais," in Eleanor Leacock and Richard Lee, eds., *Politics and History in Band Societies*. New York: Cambridge University Press.

 Summary of hydroelectric developments in Montagnais territory. Discussions of ecological effects of dams and reservoirs and economic effects on hunting and trapping activities, and of sedentarization and proletarianization of the Montagnais.

Henriksen, Georg

 1973 *Hunters in the Barrens, The Naskapi on the Edge of the White Man's World*. Newfoundland Social and Economic Studies No. 12, Memorial University of Newfoundland. Toronto: University of Toronto Press.

 A full account of the Naskapi of Davis Inlet in the late 1960s. Contrasts between life in the interior as subsistence hunters during the winter and life on the coast as cod fishers in the summer.

Le Jeune, Paul

 1973 *Le Missionnaire, l'Apostat, le Sorcier: Relation de 1634 de Paul Le Jeune*. Edition critique par Guy Laflèche. Montréal: Les Presses de l'Université de Montréal.

 Selections from the accounts of the Jesuit Paul Le Jeune, Father Superior of the Residence of Quebec, who devoted himself to trying to understand Montagnais culture in order to change it into the French model; includes Le Jeune's record of the winter he spent in the interior in a Montagnais lodge.

Leacock, Eleanor

1954 "The Montagnais 'Hunting Territory' and the Fur Trade," *American Anthropologist*, 56, 5, Memoir No. 78.

A short, fully documented account of the major changes in band organization and land use that have taken place among the Montagnais-Naskapi from the seventeenth century to the mid-twentieth century. Details the effects of the fur trade on the development of the so-called family hunting territory.

1981 "Seventeenth-Century Montagnais Social Relations and Values," in *Handbook of North American Indians*, Vol. 6, *Subarctic*, ed. June Helm. Washington, D.C.: Smithsonian Institution.

Reconstruction of seventeenth-century Montagnais life according to the *Jesuit Relations*. Ecological adaptation, leadership and decision-making, social institutions and ethics, attitudes toward the supernatural.

Rogers, Edward S.

1963 *The Hunting Group-Hunting Territory Complex among the Mistassini Indians*. National Museum of Canada Bulletin No. 195, Anthropological Series No. 63. Department of Northern Affairs and National Resources, Ottawa.

Account of field research among the Mistassini Indians of south-central Quebec in 1953-54. Ecological and historical background, and mid-twentieth-century social and economic life. Status of "hunting territory" discussion.

Rogers, Edward S., and Eleanor Leacock

1981 "Montagnais-Naskapi," in June Helm, ed., *Handbook of North American Indians*, Vol. 6, *Subarctic*. Washington, D.C.: Smithsonian Institution.

Standard summary of Montagnais-Naskapi: regional variations, history, population, material culture, social organization, religion, bibliographic sources.

Savard, Rémi

1977 *Le Rire Précolumbien dans le Québec d'Aujourd'hui*. Québec: l'Hexagone.

Report of 1971 fieldwork among the Montagnais of Saint-Augustin, the easternmost settlement on the north shore of the St. Lawrence. Insight into Montagnais attitudes gained through the analysis of myths and stories. The essential social function of Montagnais humour.

Speck, Frank G.

1935 *Naskapi: The Savage Hunters of the Labrador Peninsula*. Norman: University of Oklahoma Press. Reprint, 1977.

An early account of Montagnais-Naskapi religious life and thought, based on fieldwork carried out in the teens and twenties. Interwoven with data on material culture and economic life.

Turner, Lucien M.

1979 *Ethnology of the Ungava District, Hudson Bay Territory, Indians and Eskimos in the Quebec-Labrador Peninsula.* Quebec: Presses Coméditex. Reprint of the 1894 account by a man who spent two years at Fort Chimo in the northern Labrador Peninsula, taking meterological, ecological, and ethnological notes on the area. Full data on material culture but no attempt to understand Naskapi social life on its own terms.

Additional References Cited

Cooper, John M.

1939 "Is the Algonquian Family Hunting Ground System Pre-Columbian?" *American Anthropologist*, 41: 66-90.

Innis, H.A.

1930 *The Fur Trade in Canada: An Introduction to Canadian History.* New Haven: Yale University Press.

Jenness, Diamond

1935 *The Ojibwa Indians of Parry Island: Their Social and Religious Life.* National Museum of Canada Bulletin 78, Anthropological Series No. 17.

1937 *The Sekani Indians of British Columbia.* National Museum of Canada Bulletin 84, Anthropological Series No. 20.

Jesuit Relations and Allied Documents

1906 71 Volumes. Edited by R.G. Thwaites. Cleveland: Burrows Brothers Co.

Leacock, Eleanor

1980 "Montagnais Women and the Jesuit Program for Colonization," in Mona Etienne and Eleanor Leacock, eds., *Women and Colonization: Anthropological Perspectives.* New York: Praeger.

1983 "Ethnohistorical Investigation of Egalitarian Politics in Eastern North America," in Elisabeth Tooker, ed., *The Development of Political Organization in Native North America.* 1979 Proceedings of the American Ethnological Society, Washington, D.C.

Lips, Julius

1937 "Public Opinion and Mutual Assistance among the Montagnais-Naskapi," *American Anthropologist*, 39: 222-28.

1947 "Naskapi Law," *Transactions of the American Philosophical Society*, 37, Pt. 4.

Lowie, Robert H.

1920 *Primitive Society.* New York: Boni and Liveright.

McLean, John

1932 *Notes of a Twenty-five Years' service in the Hudson's Bay Territory.* William S. Wallace, ed. Publications of the Champlain Society, 29, Toronto.

Speck, Frank G.

1926   "Land Ownership among Hunting Peoples in Primitive America and the World's Marginal Areas," *Twenty-second International Congress of Americanists*, 2: 323-32.

1933   "Ethical Attributes of the Labrador Indians," *American Anthropologist*, 35: 559-94.

Speck, Frank G., and Loren C. Eiseley

1942   "Montagnais-Naskapi Bands and Family Hunting Districts of the Central and Southern Labrador Peninsula," *Proceedings of the American Philosophical Society*, 85: 215-42.

Steward, Julian

1941   "Determinism in Primitive Society?" *Scientific Monthly*, 53: 491-501.

Strong, Wm. D.

1929   "Cross-cousin Marriage and the Culture of the Northeastern Algonkian," *American Anthropologist*, 31: 277-88.

CHAPTER 8

Hunting and the Quest for Power: The James Bay Cree and Whitemen in the Twentieth Century

Harvey A. Feit

Introduction

This chapter has been called "Hunting and the Quest for Power"[1] because it is about different quests for power and how they have interacted in the recent history of the James Bay region of northern Quebec. The key terms of this title are ambiguous; hunting means different things to the Cree than it does for other Canadians, and so, too, with power. The quest for power is a metaphor the Cree might use for the life of a hunter; it is also a metaphor Euro-Canadians might use for the goals of both northern developers and government bureaucracies.

The James Bay Cree region lies to the east and southeast of James Bay and southeast of Hudson Bay. It has been inhabited by the James Bay Cree since the glaciers left about 5,000 years ago. The Cree now number some 12,000 people and live in nine distinct settlements from which they hunt approximately 375,000 square kilometres of land. (The word "Cree" in this chapter refers specifically to the James Bay Cree.)

I visited the region first in 1968 when I began my doctoral research on hunters of the Cree community of Waswanipi. My interest in hunting arose from a concern for the relationships between Western societies and their environments. I had read often in the human ecology literature that Indians had a different relationship with nature, but I found the literature vague and somewhat romantic in its account. I thought an "on the ground" study of Cree/environment relationships could help revise the popular images of Indians as ecological saints or wanton over-exploiters and could develop a practical understanding of the real accomplishments and limitations of one Indian group's approach. I think I was able to partially accomplish this goal, but with Cree tutelage and encouragement I also learned things I had not foreseen. These are probably best described as lessons in the sacredness of the everyday and the practicality of wisdom.

When the Cree began their opposition to the James Bay hydroelectric scheme in 1972, they asked if I would present some of the results of my research to the courts and then use them in the negotiations. It was an unexpected happenstance that my study proved to be of some use to the Cree, and one for which I was thankful. I served as an adviser to the Cree organizations during the negotiation and implementation of the James Bay and Northern Quebec Agreement, regularly from 1973 through 1978, and on an occasional basis thereafter. This took me into a new set of interests in the relationship of the Cree to the government and toward a deeper interest in Cree history. The results of some of these experiences are described in the latter parts of this chapter.

The Contemporary Cree Hunting Culture

Cree Hunting Culture and Knowledge

An early ethnographer of the Eastern Subarctic, Frank G. Speck, called Indian hunting a "religious occupation." Several recent ethnographers have called it a culturally distinct science, an "ethnoscience." How can we understand Cree hunting, a way of life whose destruction would cause not only an economic and social crisis but a cultural and moral crisis as well? To answer such questions we must try to understand what meanings hunting has for the hunters themselves.

We can develop an understanding of how the James Bay Cree think about hunting and about themselves and their world by considering the different meanings conveyed by the Cree word for hunting. We will find that their concept of hunting is very different from the everyday understandings common in our own culture. However odd the Cree conception may appear to be at first, we will find that it not only has logic when understood in the context of Cree thought and action, but also that it has important affinities with the recent discoveries of ecological scientists working within our own culture. These analogies may help us to better understand Cree thought, although they will not make the Cree out to be scientists or transform scientists into effective hunters.

ANIMAL GIFTS

Nitao, the root of the Cree term that is roughly translated into English as "hunting, fishing, and trapping in the bush," is found in a series of words related to hunting activities. At least five basic meanings are associated with this root term for hunting: to see something or to look at something; to go to get or to fetch something; to need something; to want something; and to grow or continue to grow.

That hunting should be thought of as a process of looking or seeking is apparent to us as well as to the Cree. Hunting is typically a process of seeing signs of the presence of animals – tracks, spoor, feeding or living areas – and of then seeking to encounter the animals and to kill them. The proposition that hunting is "looking" emphasizes the uncertainty involved. The Cree view is that most animals are shy, retiring, and not easily visible, and hunting therefore involves an expectation as well as an activity. The hunter goes through a process of finding indications of possible encounters with animals; if the hunt is successful he fulfils his anticipation. We will see below how this anticipation plays a role in Cree thinking.

That a successful hunt should also be conceptualized as getting or fetching animals is also apparent, but part of what the Cree mean by this is different from what we would assume. To get an animal in the Cree view does not mean to encounter it by chance, but to receive the animal. The animal is given to the hunter. A successful hunt is not simply the result of the intention and work of the hunter; it is also the outcome of the intention and actions of the animals. In the process of hunting a hunter enters into a reciprocal relationship: animals are given to hunters to meet their needs and wants, and in return the hunters incur obligations to the animals. Thus the Cree conception of hunting involves a complex and moral relationship in which the outcome of the hunt is a result of the mutual efforts of the hunter and the environment. This is a subtle and accurate ecological perspective.

It may seem odd that animal kills should be conceptualized as gifts, and it is important therefore to note that Cree do not radically separate the concepts of "human" and "animals." In their everyday experience in the bush they continually observe examples of the intelligence and will power of animals. They express this by saying that animals are "like persons"; they act as if they are capable of independent action, and they are causally responsible for things they do.

For the Cree this is an everyday observation. Evidence of intelligence is cited from several sources. One type is that each animal has its own way of living or, as is sometimes said, its own way of thinking. Each responds to environmental circumstances in ways that human beings can recognize as logically appropriate. Each has its own preparations for winter: beavers build complex lodges; bears, dens; ducks and geese migrate. Each also relates to, and communicates with, members of its species. For example, beavers establish three-generational colonies built around a monogamous couple. Geese mate for life and have complex patterns of flock leadership. And inter-species communication is indicated by the intelligent response of animals to the efforts of the hunters themselves. Some beaver will place mud on top of a trap and then eat the poplar branches left as lure and a gift by the hunter. Hunters say their techniques have to depend on how fast an animal thinks. Further, each animal has special mental characteristics: beaver are stubborn and persistent, bear are intelligent, wolves are fearless, grouse are stupid. Further, animals have emotions and may be "scared" or "mad" when they avoid hunters.

That animals give themselves is indicated in part by their typical reactions to hunters. When a bear den is found in winter, a hunter will address the bear and tell it to come out. And bears do awake, come out of their dens sluggishly, and get killed. That such a powerful, intelligent, and potentially dangerous animal can be so docile is significant for the Cree. The behaviour of moose is also significant. Moose bed down facing into the wind, so that air does not penetrate under their hair. When a hunter approaches from down wind, he comes upon it from behind. A moose typically takes flight only after scenting or seeing a source of danger. It therefore rises up when it hears a hunter approach and turns in the direction of the noise to locate and scent the source. In this gesture, taking ten to fifteen seconds, the moose gives itself to the hunter by turning and looking at him.

The extensive knowledge Cree have of animals becomes, therefore, a basis for their understanding that animals are given. The concept of an animal gift indicates that killing an animal is not solely the result of the knowledge, will, and action of humans, however necessary these are, but that the most important reasons for the gift lie in the relationships of the givers and the receivers. Because animals are capable of intelligent thought and social action, it is not only possible for them to understand human beings, but for humans to understand animals. The actions of animals are events of communication that convey information about intentions. Saying that the animals are gifts therefore emphasizes that the hunter must adapt his hunt to what he learns from and knows about the animals. To see how this works we must examine the Cree world.

THE HUNTER'S WORLD

Because animals are gifts, it is appropriate to ask "Who gives the animal?" and the answer to this question leads us to important features of Cree logic and cosmology. Recurrent answers are that animals do not only give themselves, they are given by the "wind persons" and by God or Jesus.

Just as animals are like persons, so, too, are phenomena that we do not consider to be living. Active phenomena such as winds, water, as well as God and various spirit beings, are all considered to be like persons or to be associated with personal beings. And because all sources of action are like persons, the explanations of the causes of events and happenings are not in terms of impersonal forces, but in terms of the actions of one or more persons. Explanations refer to a "who" that is active, rather than to a "what" (Hallowell, 1955; Black, 1967). The world is therefore volitional, and the perceived regularities of the world are not those of natural law but rather like the habitual behaviour of persons. It is therefore possible to know what will happen before it does occur, because it is habitual. But there is also a fundamental unpredictability in the world as well: habits make action likely, not certain. This capriciousness is also a result of the diversity of persons, because many phenomena must act in concert for events to occur. The world of personal action is therefore a world neither of mechanistic determination nor of random chance: it is a world of intelligent order, but a very complex order, and one not always knowable by men. The Cree world of complex interrelationships is analogous to that of some ecological scientists, although the scientists use an organic rather than a personal metaphor.

For the Cree, the relationship of the wind persons to animal gifts is constantly confirmed by everyday experience. The wind persons bring cold or warmth and snow or rain, and with the coming and going of predominant winds the seasons change. They are responsible for the variable weather conditions to which animals and hunters each respond. The bear hibernates and is docile only in winter when the north wind is predominant. The geese and ducks arrive with the increasing frequency of the south wind and leave with its departure. In a myriad of other ways, the animals and hunters, and the success of the hunt, depend in part on the conditions brought by the winds.

Each of the four wind persons resides at one of the four points of the compass, and each has specific personal characteristics related to particular seasons, weather and animal patterns, hunting conditions, and success. When a hunter is asked by young men and women who have been away to school why he says that the animals are given by the winds, he often answers that they must come and live in the bush to see for themselves. It is demonstrated in the daily and yearly experience of the hunters, and it can be shared with anyone who will spend enough time in the bush.

Parallel discoveries of the relationships of animals, weather, and hunting can be found in hunting lore in our own society. But whereas this knowledge plays a role in our culture of hunting, scientists have devoted limited research effort to it. By contrast, such relationships are centrally important in Cree hunting practice, and they are encoded and highlighted by Cree concepts and in what we might call their science of hunting.

The concepts of the wind persons mediate and link several series of ideas that serve to order the Cree world in space and time. The wind persons are said to live at the four corners of the earth, thereby orienting space on a four-point compass. The wind persons also link God to the world. They are part of the world "up there," but they affect the earth down here. They thus link the spirits and God who are up there to the men and animals who live their lives on the earth.

"God" and Jesus are the ultimate explanation for all that happens on this earth, but He[2] also gives all the personal beings of the world intelligence and will in order to follow His Way, or abandon it. God alone gives and takes life, but beings are ultimately responsible for their actions. God therefore plays a key part in the gift of animals to hunters, but only a part. He is the leader of all things, and He is assisted by the wind persons and a hierarchy of leaders extending to most spirits, animals, and humans. The idea of leadership is persuasive in the Waswanipi world, and the hierarchy of leaders is spoken of as one of power. Hunting therefore depends not only on the hunter and the animals, but on an integrated chain of leaders and helpers acting together to give and to receive animals.

In this chain, human beings fit somewhere in the middle range, closely linked to those both above and below them. Human beings are mutually dependent on animals, who are generally less powerful than humans, and on spirit beings, who are generally more powerful. But the linkages are close and the positions flexible. As Cree myths indicate, some of the less powerful spirit beings were formerly human beings who have been transformed into spirits. Animals themselves used to be "like us," and in the "long ago" time of the legends they could talk with one another and with humans.

THE POWER OF HUNTING

The power of God and humans is manifest in the relationship between thought and happenings in the world. What God thinks or knows happens; His thought is one with happenings and thus He is all powerful. Spirit beings participate in this power to a lesser degree; they know only some of what will happen in the future or at a distance. Their thought and happenings frequently coincide. God and spirit beings may give their powerful knowledge to humans in dreams and in thoughts, and by signs in the world, but they never tell all that humans would like to know. People can often be said to "discover" their understandings rather than create them; and thought or insight may "come to us" as a gift from God and spirits, in waking thought or in dreams. Thinking and prayer may be one. The knowledge that spirits give anticipates the future with some real – but always unknown – degree of certainty.

Humans not only differ from animals by the degree of power they receive, but also from each other. Powerful and effective knowledge increases with age and with the care and attention individuals give to interpreting and cultivating their communications with God and spirit beings. These differences in power and wisdom are reflected in the patterns of leadership within human communities.

The meaning of power in the Cree perspective, therefore, differs in important ways from our own. We typically think of power as the ability to control others and/or the world. For the Cree it is more complex. Human knowledge is always incomplete, and there is often a gap between what humans think and what actually happens. In hunting, for example, a hunter will frequently dream of an animal he will be given before he begins to look for it. He may then go out hunting and find signs of that animal that confirm his expectation. When the things he thinks about actually come to be, when he is given the animal, that is an indicator of power. But humans never find that all they anticipate comes to be.

The power is a coincidence between an internal state of being (thought) and the configuration of the world (event), a congruence anticipated by the inner state and that this anticipation helps to actualize. Both the thought and the event are social processes. Power is not an individual possession, it is a gift, and a person cannot in this view bring his thought to actuality by individually manipulating the world to conform to his desires. And, at each phase of happenings in the world, humans, spirit beings, and other beings must sensitively interpret and respond to the communications and actions of the other beings around them. "Power" is a relationship in thought and action among many beings, whereby potentiality becomes actuality. Hunting is an occasion of power in this sense, and the expression of this is that animals are gifts, with many givers.

Power in this Cree sense may have analogies to our concept of truth, i.e., thought that comes to be. We might say that power is truth unfolding, rather than that power is control.

This complex understanding of hunting links intimately with basic Cree attitudes toward human life itself. The symbols conveying Cree concepts of hunting also order the Cree understanding of the life and death of animals and of the hunters themselves. The life and ultimate death of both the hunted and the hunters are as enigmatic for the Cree as they are for us. That humans should have to kill animals to feed themselves and their families in order to live and that humans themselves all die are fundamentally mysterious features of life. Both animals and humans participate in the mystery of death, and Cree symbols of hunting elaborate the mystery and bring the wonder of life and death into the world of everyday meanings.

The hunt is conceptualized as an ever-changing cycle at many levels. If a hunter is successful he will bring game back to his camp. Having received a gift, the hunter is under obligation to respect that gift by reciprocating with gifts of his own. These gifts go partly to other Cree, as most large kills are shared with kinsmen, neighbours, or with the community. By giving meat to others they are said to find more animal gifts themselves in return. The hunter also reciprocates to the spirits who have participated in the hunt, often by placing a small portion of the meat into the stove at the first meal of each day, so the smoke of the gift can go up the stove pipe as a sign of appreciation and respect to the spirits "up there." This return offering is part of an ongoing relationship of reciprocity: it not only expresses respect and repays an obligation, it continues the exchange as a statement of anticipation that the hunter will again receive what he wants when he is again in need. Many Cree rituals follow a similar structure.

Hunting is conceptualized as an ongoing process involving a delicate and ever-changing balance. When bad luck occurs, hunters turn their attention to other species, or they hunt in another area until the animals are ready to be caught again. If animals want to be caught and are not hunted, they have fewer young and more easily succumb to diseases or predation. Thus, proper hunting can lead to increases in the numbers and health of the animals. However, if a hunter kills animals that are not given, if he overhunts, then the spirits of that species will be "mad," and the hunter will have no luck. Thus, in hunting, the life and death of animals form a delicate reciprocal process.

The alteration in hunting luck brings us to the last of those meanings of the word "hunting." Hunters say that when they decrease their hunting they do so in order that the animals may cease being mad and may grow again. Hunting involves a reciprocal obligation for hunters to provide the conditions in which animals can grow and survive on the earth.

The fulfilment of this responsibility provides the main criterion by which hunters judge one another. In everyday conversation people speak extensively about the reputations and actions of other hunters. What is emphasized is hunting competence (Preston, 1975). A hunter who masters a difficult skill and through his ties with spirits receives hard-to-get gifts exhibits his competence and participates in power. Men and women who are respected for their exceptional competence are contrasted with those who take chances, who fool around with animals by not killing them cleanly, and who seek self-aggrandizement by large kills or wasting animals. The hunters who consistently have good luck but not excessive harvests also demonstrate competence because they maintain that delicate balance with the world in which animals die and are reborn in health and in continuing growth.

This image of the competent hunter serves also as a goal of the good life. The aims of both hunting and of life are, in part, to maintain a continuing sensitivity to and a balanced participation with the world, in which humans and animals reciprocally contribute to the survival of the other. The aim of life is the perpetuation of an ordered, meaningful, and bountiful world. This aim includes those now alive and those yet to be born. The social universe thus extends beyond the human world, beyond the temporal frame of an individual human life. Such a life leads from an awareness of the mystery of everyday life to the mystery of death, through competence to participate in power.

Hunting is not just a central activity of the Cree, nor is it simply a science or a formal ritual. Hunting is an ongoing experience of truth as power.

Hunting Practices: Subsistence Economy, Society,
and Ecological Management

Contemporary studies by anthropologists of hunting and gathering peoples can be dated to the mid-1960s when it was "discovered" that the hunting and gathering peoples of Africa and Australia were able to efficiently, abundantly, and reliably produce their own subsistence. This came as something of a revelation to both popular and professional images of hunting life. The hunting way of life was often thought to be precisely the opposite – inefficient, impoverished, and unpredictable. Following these findings, studies of the Cree tended to confirm the application of the new view to Subarctic hunters as well, although with some qualifications.

EFFICIENCY, ABUNDANCE, AND RELIABILITY OF
CREE SUBSISTENCE HUNTING PRACTICES

It was found that the hunters do not encounter game on a haphazard basis but that they carefully plan and organize their hunting activities. Hunting is organized into an annual cycle of activities so that each species of game is used at times likely to produce an efficient, abundant, and reliable supply of food.

Cree hunters know how to kill moose at almost any season of the year, but they tend to concentrate their hunting activities at several specific periods during an annual cycle. One period is during the fall mating period or rut, when moose call to attract partners and when they typically feed and drink in the mornings and evenings along the shorelines of streams and lakes. Cree hunters often look along the shores for signs indicating the places that moose have visited; they then wait or return at appropriate times to call the males to the location. After the rut, moose are not hunted extensively until snows have accumulated to significant depths. As the snow depth increases, the widely dispersed populations progressively concentrate and are often found on the hills where wind blows some snow accumulations thin. When the snow in the concentration areas exceeds one metre in depth, the moose tend to restrict their movements to a series of trails. Under these conditions moose move outside the trails reluctantly. If the moose do take flight, hunters on snowshoes can exhaust them by pursuit, until they stand their ground, face the hunter, and give themselves to him.

A third period of intensive moose hunting occurs in late winter when snow may melt and form a crust. The moose may be able to walk, breaking through the crust with each step, but if they run they tear the skin and tendons of their legs against the jagged edges of the crust. Again, they will often stand their ground and face a hunter.

Cree moose-hunting practices therefore depend on extensive knowledge of the actions of animals in relation to weather, habitat, and the actions of men. Hunting is concentrated on the occasions when moose most clearly give themselves to the hunters and when men can best fulfil their obligations to the moose by killing the animals efficiently and with a minimum of suffering.

As we would expect, the proficiency and knowledge of Cree hunters make their hunting quite reliable. They succeed on about 22 per cent of the days they search for moose, 88 per cent of days spent fishing, and about 50 per cent of days hunting beaver. The efficiency of the various activities was also substantial. The efficiency ratios for moose hunting run from 25:1 to 40:1 – each day of moose hunting provides food for twenty-five to forty active adults for one day, or for a family of four for one to two weeks. Beaver hunting returns average 7:1, and fishing, 4:1. Overall, Cree winter hunting activity efficiencies average 7:1.

Bush food provides hunters' families with 150 per cent of the calories they require, and it provides eight times the daily protein requirement. It also provides more than twice the required intakes of the nine other vitamins and minerals for which calculations could be run. These hunters also took purchased food with them into the bush camps, but the caloric value of bush foods produced was nearly four times greater than the calories available from store food.

Half the food produced is circulated in gift exchanges to kinsmen and friends back in the settlement, and some is kept for later village consumption. Those who give receive back other gifts of food, as well as gifts of other supplies and equipment. Bush food harvests have been estimated in the 1970s to provide from 25 to 55 per cent of the yearly energy needs of the various communities and at least 50 per cent of almost all required nutrients.

THE SOCIAL ORGANIZATION OF HUNTING AND THE
POWER TO MANAGE GAME RESOURCES

The Cree have a distinct system of rights and responsibilities concerning land, resources, community, and social relations – a system of land and resource tenure, and of self-governance. This system provides a means with which the hunters can fulfil their responsibilities to animals and spirits and contribute to the conditions necessary for their mutual survival.

Cree society is organized around principles of community, responsible autonomy, and reciprocity. The central resources of land and wildlife are not considered to be owned because people are born and die while the land continues. The land is passed on from previous generations and will be transmitted to future generations. The land and the animals are God's creations, and, to the extent that humans use or control them, they do so as part of a broad social community united by reciprocal obligations. These gifts and obligations are not solely individual; they involve the wider

MAP 8.1. Approximate Territory Areas of James Bay Cree Hunters

human community as well, so that all people have a right of access to land and resources to sustain themselves. This right extends to all Cree, and to others as well, but along with the rights go responsibilities to contribute to the continued productivity of the land and animals. The exercise and fulfilment of such responsibility require knowledge and a subtle responsiveness to the relationships with animals and spirits and imply a willingness to exercise self-control and participation in a community of responsibility.

The Cree are efficient enough at hunting that they could deplete the game. Regulation is both an individual and a community responsibility and is assisted through a system of stewardships. All the land on which they hunt is divided into territories that are under the stewardship of elders. The approximately 300 territories vary in size from about 300 to several thousand square kilometres, each supervised by a steward (see

Map 8.1). They are part of larger blocks, each associated with a particular Cree community. While rights to land and resources are distributed to the community as a whole, as a continuing society extending over generations, the stewards exercise authority over the territories in the name of the community and the common interest. The steward's authority is, in principle, spiritually sanctioned, thus obligating him to protect and share the resources.

In general, all members of a community have the right to hunt on any land on a short-term basis, while travelling through, while camping for brief periods, or while using small game or fish resources. However, extended and intensive use of the larger game resources is generally considered to be under the supervision and approval of the stewards.

Stewards generally grow up in a territory on which they hunt repeatedly over many years before they take over their role. During this time they build up extensive ties with the spirits of the land and acquire a vast knowledge of its resources. They are constantly aware of the changing conditions of the game populations. They note changes in the frequency of signs of moose, the numbers yarding together, the rates of twin births, and age and sex ratios. For beaver, they note changes in the number and size of colonies, size of litters, and the frequency of abandoned or new colonies. They can easily discuss these trends with an outsider, comparing present conditions with those of last year, the year before, or five years ago.

These trends are important to the stewards, and they discuss them with other stewards and elder hunters, comparing patterns in different territories and relating them to changes in weather, vegetation, and hunting activity. Some of the trends observed by the stewards are the same ones used by wildlife biologists to monitor game populations, although few biologists have such long-term and detailed knowledge. The trends are also important because they are communications from animals and spirits. Thus, if too many animals were killed in the past, the animals would be "mad" and have fewer young or make signs of their presence harder to find. This would indicate that the animals wish to give fewer of themselves, and, out of reciprocal respect, the hunters will take less than in the past.

The stewards use their knowledge to direct the intensive hunting of the animal populations on their territories. Each steward has the right to decide if the hunting territory will be used intensively in any season, how many and which people can use it, how much they can hunt of each key species, and where and when they can hunt. The stewards do not exercise these powers in an authoritarian manner. The responsibility of each

PLATE 8.1. Waswanipi Cree man hunting geese while travelling to get wood for his fall bush camp. Courtesy of H. Feit.

hunter is assumed, and each is given respect and considerable autonomy. Stewards usually act by suggestion and by non-personal public commentaries on the situation, and their knowledge, their spiritual ties to the land, and the sacred sanctions for their statements give them considerable influence.

The system is part of the network of social reciprocities. At the individual level, a system of giving privileges to hunters to join groups generally assures that each hunter has a place to hunt each year. For the community as a whole, the system permits the distribution of hunters and hunting to respond to the changes in the conditions of the game populations.

Typically, each steward inherits his position from a previous steward, and he has the duty to designate his successor. This places each steward within a chain of responsible authority that extends backwards and forwards. The land and animals are thus received also as gifts from previous generations, and the present hunters view their own actions as implying the same respect and responsibility to future generations.

In practice, the system of hunting-territory stewardships works to maintain an ongoing balance between harvests and game. This is generally possible for beaver and moose populations, and in some areas for marten. The system can apply to fishing, but communities may instead limit the numbers of fishing sites, the mesh sizes of the nets, and the length of fishing seasons (Berkes, 1977). For goose hunting along the James Bay coast, the Cree recognize adjacent groups of bays as goose-hunting territories under a "goose boss" who supervises a complex of hunting rules and restrictions designed not to scare the migratory geese away prematurely but to encourage their return on successive days and migrations (Scott, 1983).

Several studies supply quantitative evidence that the Cree system does work for the moose, beaver, fish, and geese populations, by keeping harvests below sustainable yields of the game populations. The best indicator of success is the relative stability of the game populations over the two decades during which estimates have been made. These data indicate that the long-term ecological balance sought by the Cree is, in general, maintained in practice. Furthermore, the Cree have been highly responsive to changing environmental and historical circumstances in pursuing a balanced hunt.

Moose began migrating into the James Bay region of Quebec only after vast forest fires swept the area in the last decade of the nineteenth century and the first decade of this century. The Cree had hunting territories prior to this time, and indeed probably had them periodically in the post-contact period and before the arrival of Europeans. The incorporation of moose into the system, however, depended on the development of a sound body of knowledge of moose behaviour and moose population dynamics and on creating effective types of restraints on hunting. Such systems were developed in the areas inhabited by dense moose populations between 1910, when the moose began arriving, and the 1950s, when intensive studies of Cree hunting began.

The Cree system has also responded to important demographic, technological, and economic changes. During this century the Cree have generally maintained viable game populations through a period in which numbers of Cree may have risen fivefold. To increase their food production they have intensified and diversified their use of some game populations but have also limited their bush food production to sustainable levels. They therefore now have to purchase a proportion of their food.

The more intensive harvesting has occurred with the aid of important additions to their technological repertoire, including improved rifles and shotguns, new traps, and some new means of transportation. But the use of this technology still depends on Cree knowledge, cultural values, and social practices. The technology, therefore, has not led to over-hunting, but rather to a more secure balance between men and animals.

The Cree have also maintained the balance despite periods of a shortage of cash. In such times they have done without some trade goods rather than exhaust animal resources. They have intentionally kept alive many traditional skills and crafts that could replace certain trade goods should these become unavailable. And they have continued to treat cash and trade goods as a socially modified form of property, using them for co-operative ends by integrating their distribution and consumption into the widespread reciprocal exchange practices.

The Cree have thus maintained their hunting and the animals of their region despite important changes in their environment and in historical circumstances. However, rare periods of breakdown in the balance of men and animals have also occurred.

The most serious of these happened in the 1930s, when beaver were severely depleted throughout much of northeastern Canada. This has been variously attributed to epidemic disease, to Native over-hunting, and to non-Native trappers. The reasons may never be known for all regions, and they probably varied from one area to another. In the southernmost portion of the Cree area, non-Native trappers, encouraged by high fur prices, entered the region from the railway 100 miles to the south, trapped out one place, and then moved on. Some of the Cree from this area say that they themselves trapped out the beaver because they did not see the possibility of maintaining animal populations if non-Native trappers continued to deplete their lands. It is significant that the only species over-hunted in this area were beaver and marten, the ones sought by non-Native trappers. Declining fur prices in the 1930s and the concern of the government for the ensuing plight of the Indians led to a closing of the area to non-Native trappers and a recovery of the beaver under Cree supervision between 1930 and 1950.

This example emphasizes the limits of the means at the disposal of the Cree for maintaining viable long-term balanced relations with animals. Culture and social organization of the Cree are effective aids for their self-governance, but they could not regulate or control the impact of what outsiders do on their lands. Further, where outsiders did not act responsibly and with respect, their activities threatened the animals and the Cree themselves.

The Cree recovered from the impacts of the intrusions of the twenties and thirties, but a crisis developed again in the 1970s when the government of Quebec started to build a massive hydroelectric project on their hunting lands. To understand the events of this second crisis, we have to turn from an examination of Cree culture and hunting to an account of Cree-white interactions.

The Cree Struggle to Maintain Autonomy in the Face of Government Intervention

Crises in the Fur Trade and Establishment
of a Government Presence

Many Cree today speak of the lives of their parents and grandparents at the turn of this century as being traditional. This century has seen greater change in their lives than earlier ones, primarily because other Canadians have intervened in their lives.

Fur traders have been present in the region since the mid-seventeenth century, and missionaries have visited most trading posts since the mid-nineteenth century, but the arrival of the government characterizes the twentieth century. Although these lands were purchased by Canada from the Hudson's Bay Company in 1870, the government presence was slow to be felt.

In the late 1920s the Quebec government's first intervention in the region occurred when it responded to requests to help solve the crisis created by white trappers. Quebec first made the killing of beaver by non-Indians illegal in the northern regions of the province, and then in the mid-1930s outlawed all killing of beaver. The Cree supported this closure, and some communities reached their own agreements to cease taking any beaver before the government took its decision.

When hunting resumed – after ten to twenty years depending on the region – the response had worked: beaver were numerous, they were no longer "mad," and they wanted to give themselves again. The Cree and the government thus agreed independently on the means and the timing for re-establishing beaver populations.

When beaver harvesting was again permitted, the federal and provincial governments jointly mapped the hunting territories and recognized the Cree stewards, whom they now called tallymen, because they were paid an honorarium to tally the number of active beaver lodges on the territory each year. The mapping and appointments were done in the communities at meetings of all the stewards, and the formal system of traplines thus established was clearly based on the already existing system of territories. However, there was a feeling among government agents that the territory system had broken down in part and that a more formal process had to be built into it. Thus, the stewards' annual tally of the number of beaver lodges was used by the government agent to calculate how many beaver could be caught on each territory. The steward would then be asked to allocate the harvest among the hunters he permitted to use his land. The government agents acted as if they were administering for the Cree a system of hunting and management.

For the Cree, the government was recognizing their own system and giving the stewards an additional source of authority that they could use to limit the hunting activities of people from outside their communities, including non-Natives, who often were less responsive to their spiritual and traditional authority. Frequently, what the agents suggested made good sense to the Cree hunters. Nevertheless, with their extensive knowledge of the resource populations, the Cree did not feel bound to follow the advice of government agents, which was based on simply following the trends in the number of lodges. Cree decisions were based on far more extensive knowledge.

In this respect, therefore, an important but not yet fully apparent conflict developed between the Cree and the government. The government thought that Cree hunting was regulated and supervised by government regulations and authority, and that they determined the Cree rights to hunt. The Cree thought the government had recognized their own system of tenure and self-governance.

The final element of the government response to the crisis of the 1930s was to establish a band government structure for each community and to start issuing rations and, later, social assistance. In the late 1930s and early 1940s the federal Department of Indian Affairs sent an Indian agent to each community to establish an official list of band membership – one band for each fur trade post – and to elect a chief and council. It appears that a chief and council system had been adopted in most communities before this time. In any case, a formal election system was now established under the Indian Act, which not only defined the size of the council but also its powers and those of the Minister of Indian Affairs. I have found no reports that the consequences of coming under the legislation were discussed with the Cree, and most of them describe the Indian agents' initial role as the giving out of surplus clothing and food, which was very much appreciated in the time of shortage. Cree accounts suggest that the band list was seen as a means of signing up for aid. The band council initially appears to have served as a source of information to the agent about who was in need of aid and of what kind, and as a representative group by which individual Cree could petition for assistance.

Nevertheless, these responses also represented a turning point in Cree society. They bound the Cree within the fabric of Canadian political society, law, and economy for the first time, and in circumstances that did not make the potential threats to their autonomy clear. The Cree were still exercising extensive control and autonomy in their hunting culture, but they were now doing so as part of the Canadian polity.

Government Assistance Turns To an Assertion of Dominance

Government presence in the region accelerated rapidly throughout the 1950s and 1960s as governments sought to "open the North." This involved making the region more accessible in order that its resources could be exploited by southern Canadians; it also involved extending the domains of government administration and authority. These changes were not intended to aid the Cree but to promote the interests of southern Canadians, and programs specifically affecting the Cree were not developed in consultation with them, aiming at their assimilation rather than at support for their culture and economy.

The expansion of the rail and road networks into the southern portions of Cree territory occurred in the 1950s and 1960s, and several mining towns were incorporated at that time. The towns, of 500 to 10,000 people each, occupied up to several square miles of land, and each disrupted one or more hunting territories. Their impacts on the Cree were neither foreseen nor considered in the process of planning.

The direct impacts on hunting spread more widely than the land immediately occupied. Hunters said animals became much less calm and less willing to be caught over large areas affected by noise generated by railways, road traffic, and airplanes now frequently traversing the region. Roadway shrubs were kept down by the use of powerful chemical sprays, despite the fact that moose and other game fed on these shrubs, and Cree fed on them. The Cree found several dead and sick animals, became cautious about consuming animals from the immediate vicinity, and successfully petitioned the governments to cease the spraying. Pollution from the mine waste waters and waste sediment ponds was also a problem. The Cree reported frequent finds of dead fish and aquatic animals and changes in the tastes of the animals over large areas.

The extensive Cree use of the environment and their knowledge of it made clear to them the extent of the impacts these developments were having, but no mechanism was established by governments or the companies to give them a voice in the projects. The meaning of the hunting territory system, upon which the government had built the beaver reserve system, was ignored. That the government did not consider the Cree system of land use and management as a system of land tenure and of rights, and that it did not consider that the government and developers as well as the Cree had mutual obligations, was becoming clear.

These development impacts reached near tragic proportions with the coming of the forestry industry. A pulp and paper mill went into operation in 1965, and its wastes were dumped into streams leading into a major river and lake network. In its initial operations this plant used a process that released a significant quantity of mercury into both the water and airborne effluents. The fact that inorganic mercury could be converted into deadly methylmercury through natural processes was not then known; it was discovered later at Minimata, Japan. In 1970, sampling of fish being sent to the commercial markets revealed that they had levels of methylmercury beyond those permissible for human safety.

Over the last fifteen years, several research projects have been conducted to determine the sources of mercury in the region, the possible evidence of its impacts on Cree health, and the implications for future use of fishery resources in the region. It was found that mercury levels are naturally high in several geological zones, but that the highest levels were downstream from the pulp mill. The plant has significantly reduced its releases of mercury, which now are slowly being buried by sedimentation. The impacts on people of methylmercury were hard to determine at the standards of scientific proof. However, the evidence is strong that the health of some Cree individuals was affected by the methylmercury.

In the 1970s the government advised the Cree to cease consuming the fish of the region. Because this recommendation itself would have severe consequences for the Cree diet and possibly their health, the Cree insisted on research to establish more precise norms. In 1978 specific recommendations for each affected community suggested a limited consumption of those species of fish with high methylmercury levels. The problem has not been stabilized, however, because of new fears that acid rain may be increasing the leaching of mercury from bedrock into the food chain. An irony for the Cree is that, while the governments improved medical services in the 1940s, within two decades these same governments promoted developments of the region that endangered their health and well-being.

The opening of the region to development projects not only affected the land, it affected the economic choices and pressures on the Cree. When fur prices declined in the 1950s, hunters began to meet the cash shortage by taking summer employment. They chose employment primarily in projects that were compatible with continued hunting, used their bush skills, allowed them to work in Cree groups, and were not organized by industrial time or authority structures.

The taking of these jobs provoked a new crisis. Agents of government saw this as the first step in an irreversible process of abandoning hunting for wage labour. This fit the common image of hunting as an unreliable, unproductive, and insecure means of living, and one that any rational person would willingly give up for a steady job and wages.

The Cree not only knew differently about hunting, but also about jobs. They had worked transporting goods for the Hudson's Bay Company, only to see the jobs disappear in the 1930s when airplanes came into use, just when they needed the incomes because of declining beaver populations. During their summer jobs in the 1960s they were aware of often being given the hardest work, of being paid lower wages than non-Natives, and of being the first fired. The non-Native sawmills, exploration companies, fisheries, and hunting outfitters for whom they worked were constantly failing or moving.

Government agents, however, operated on the belief, reinforced by our cultural assumptions, that the Cree had begun the transition from hunters to wage labourers. This view fit well with government policies of the period. Having discovered the poverty of many Native people across the country, the government placed emphasis on economic development, defined primarily as a need for jobs. It also fit well with plans to "develop the North" and with ignoring the impacts of those developments on the land and animals.

Government agents began withdrawing social aid and support services in order to speed the transition to wage labour. There was no consultation. These events made clear how the basic need for cash inputs to the hunting economy had made the Cree less autonomous, and how government agents could alter the possibilities of hunting by changing the conditions for receipt of government payments. Although the Cree continued to hunt, the number who did not pursue hunting as their main occupation rose significantly.

Other changes at the posts also influenced this process: the formation of reserves, the construction of permanent settlements, and the establishment of schools. Each of these factors contributed to the shift in economic opportunities, but none was decisive until the crisis in hunting.

Although some schooling had been provided earlier, during the 1960s a significant portion of Cree youths began to attend schools. The government tried to force Cree parents to send their children, sometimes threatening to cut social assistance if they did not. Most parents wanted their children to have some schooling, and an increase in the number of children also affected their willingness to send some to school. The trauma of schooling away from the reserves, in programs not significantly adapted to Cree culture, separated parents from their children in more than a physical sense. The longer children stayed in school the

PLATE 8.2. Waswanipi Cree woman preparing a beaver as her granddaughter watches. She will remove the pelt for commercial sale and cook the animal for sustenance. Courtesy of H. Feit.

harder it was for parents and children to understand each other. As people saw what was happening, up to one-third of a community's children were kept out of school each year to learn bush skills and the hunting way of life. Thus the Cree kept some control over the education of their children.

The result was not to limit the continuation of the hunting economy but to diversify the range of skills and interests of the young adults. The effect of schooling paralleled that of the crisis in hunting, creating a need for a more diversified economy, one in which both hunting and employment would be viable activities.

At the time, however, the economic conditions were making both choices difficult. By the early 1970s, real unemployment and underemployment had developed in Cree communities as opportunities for hunting and wage labour were too limited for the population.

This period was therefore one in which the government attempts to integrate the Cree into the labour market met very limited success; they had instead helped provoke an economic crisis. The Cree had moved toward an economy that would have to integrate employment and hunting within their own communities. The conflicts had created economic, educational, and social problems of profound concern to the Cree. However, the process had also created new resources for the Cree's continuing efforts to define their own future. An effect of schooling was to bring a young generation of Cree with high school, and some with higher education, back to the communities and into active roles in social and political life.

Quebec's Search for Power and Cree Opposition to the
James Bay Hydroelectric Scheme

When the government of Quebec announced its plans for hydroelectric development in the James Bay region in April, 1971, it followed its practice of neither involving the Cree in the decision nor examining the impacts of the development on them. When asked about the effects on the Cree and their rights, government spokesmen simply asserted that the project was to be built on provincial lands and would benefit the Native people.

Several young Cree leaders called a meeting of the leaders from each village to discuss the hydro project. The Cree at this time were comprised of eight separate communities and bands having no regional integration or political structure. At the meeting, all were opposed to the project because of the severe damage it would cause to the land and the animals, and to the Cree. In their view, the project was to serve whites, not Indians, who would not benefit substantially. They discussed ways to oppose the project and decided to organize within their own communities, soliciting support also from other Indian groups and from the public at large.

The Cree also attempted to get discussions going with the Quebec government and its crown corporations. They wanted to avoid complete opposition to the project and to see if modifications to plans might reduce its impact. However, the government refused to do anything but inform the Cree as the plans developed. The Cree were left with no choice but to oppose the project (Feit, 1985).

The Cree approached the federal minister to take action based on his trust responsibility for Indians, but he was reluctant. The Liberal federal government was politically allied with the Liberal Quebec government against a growing separatist sentiment in the province. Ottawa was therefore reluctant to take action that would appear as a federal intervention in provincial affairs. By the end of 1972, the federal cabinet had approved this position and labelled it "alert neutrality."

The Cree decided to use legal means to force Quebec into discussions. Joined by the Inuit of northern Quebec, some of whom lived on one of the rivers to be diverted by the project, in November, 1972, they initiated the longest temporary injunction hearing in Canadian history. Basically, the Native people had to prove that they had a *prima facie* claim to rights in the territory, that the project would damage their exercise of these rights, and that these damages would be irreversible and unremediable. They asked the court for a temporary injunction stopping construction until permanent injunction hearings could be completed.

The court hearings provided a detailed description of the project planned for the La Grande region. A 700-kilometre road was being built north across hunting lands belonging to six Cree communities. Airports and communication infrastructures would be needed as well as construction camps and a new town to house project headquarters. New mines and forestry operations were planned. The La Grande hydro complex involved diverting three major rivers into the La Grande River to increase its flow by 80 per cent. This required four main dams, 130 kilometres of dikes, and eight main reservoirs flooding 8,722 square kilometres (5 per cent of the land surface). The reservoirs would be filled in summer, and the water would be released in winter to produce electricity needed for heating requirements in southern cities; thus, water levels would vary all winter. The construction of power transmission lines would require the cutting of three or four corridors 960 kilometres long through the forest. And all this was envisaged as the first of three phases.

In the Cree view, many of the damages were like those they had previously identified from earlier developments, although now over a much larger area. In addition, the particular effects of flooding were of special concern because about 50 per cent of the wetlands of the region would be underwater, destroying important beaver and game habitat. The number of animals would therefore be significantly reduced, and the variability of water levels in the reservoirs would restrict the ability of many animals, particularly beaver, to re-inhabit the areas. Fish numbers would also decline, and a new balance of species could take up to fifty years to be re-established in the reservoirs. The vegetation destroyed by construction could take fifty to a hundred years to again become mature forest. In short, they argued that the hunters would suffer a serious and permanent loss of subsistence resources and a major threat to the continuity of their culture and society.

The Cree lawyers then argued that their clients had been exercising rights to the land since time immemorial, including the rights to hunt, fish, and trap, which constituted an Indian title over the land. The case was one of the most important on the concept of Aboriginal rights and Indian title until that time, and it was also one of the strongest such cases.

The government lawyers argued that the project would affect only a small percentage of the land directly, that it would improve its productivity in many respects, and that in any case the damages were temporary or remediable. They claimed that the Cree no longer lived primarily off the land, catching only 20-25 per cent of their food. The Cree lived in settlements, had houses, used manufactured clothes and equipment, and now ate purchased foods predominantly. They argued that Cree culture had been substantially transformed and replaced by Canadian culture. They said the Cree were dependent on government financial assistance and support for their settlements. They argued that the use of wildlife, especially beaver, was completely institutionalized by the government as a result of the establishment of beaver reserves. They claimed that a majority of the Cree now derived incomes from employment. Finally, they argued that the Cree had no Aboriginal title to the land, or at most had a right to some monetary compensation and small reserves such as were provided in other treaties made elsewhere in Canada. In November, 1973, Mr. Justice Malouf ruled that the Cree and Inuit people did appear to have an Indian title to the land; that they had been occupying and using the land to a full extent; that hunting was still of great importance, constituted a way of life, and provided a portion of their diet and incomes; that they had a unique concept of the land; that they wished to continue their way of life; that any interference with their use compromised their very existence as a people; and that the project was already causing much interference. He ruled that the province was trespassing. The ruling was a stronger affirmation of Cree rights than many people had thought would be possible at that time and forced the government to negotiate with the Cree.

To the Cree people in the villages the ruling was a great victory, but it was also a straightforward recognition of the truth – the truth about their way of life and values and about the dangers inherent in development conducted without their involvement and consent. It was also interpreted as a statement of good sense, reaffirming that relations between Cree and non-Natives could be guided by the principle of reciprocity that informs interrelations among all powerful beings in the Cree world (Scott, 1983, 1989). Reciprocity implied mutual respect for the needs and wants of others, ongoing obligations to others, and the possibility of sharing the land responsibly.

Cree Autonomy and the Aboriginal Rights Agreement

Negotiating Recognition of Aboriginal Rights

The Cree approached negotiations cautiously, despite all the effort they had put into trying to get meaningful negotiations started. They were in a difficult position as they were already experiencing the impacts of development, which had been permitted to continue while Mr. Justice Malouf's ruling was appealed.

Early in the negotiations the Cree formed their own political association, the Grand Council of the Cree (of Quebec) (GCCQ), with the chief and another leader from each community on its Board of Directors, and an executive group of four regional leaders. The Grand Council took over organization of the negotiations. However, the Cree people remained the final decision-makers as to whether to accept the results of the negotiation.

Components of the Agreement

With respect to project modifications, the negotiations concluded several changes to project plans.[3] The location of a main dam was changed. Funds were provided for remedial work to be undertaken as future impacts were experienced, and the negotiators described in some detail the project that could be built and agreed to authorize only a project conforming to this description. Because the project was still being planned, this assured that any future changes would require new approvals.[4]

These compromises reduced the direct consequences around the village of Fort George, now relocated to Chisasibi, and assured future participation for the Cree; but they also meant very substantial impacts on the land and wildlife of the region. Despite major efforts by the Cree, no other major project modifications could be agreed upon.

The government agreed to recognize the right of all Cree to hunt, fish, and trap all kinds of animals at all times, over all the lands traditionally

PLATE 8.3. Elderly Mistassini Cree hunter balloting during ratification vote on the James Bay and Northern Quebec Agreement. Courtesy of H. Feit.

harvested by them, on the understanding that their harvesting rights would be subject to conservation of wildlife. Conservation was an objective the Cree were pursuing on their own in any case, and they were careful to get an agreement on a definition that recognized their own needs.

In addition, it was agreed that Cree harvesting would take precedence over sport hunting and fishing by non-Natives. This priority was given effect through a series of measures, including exclusive hunting areas and species. Approximately 16 per cent of the land area of the region was set aside for exclusive Cree use, an area called Category II lands. From the government point of view the Cree recognition of the principle of conservation and of some non-Native access to wildlife made the provisions acceptable. From the Cree point of view the government recognition of their rights and of their priority of access to wildlife made the provisions acceptable.

Differences then arose over whether the governments or the Cree would have jurisdiction to implement these provisions. Whoever did would be bound by terms of the negotiations. But these provisions would have to be interpreted and applied to the changing conditions in the region each year, as game populations shifted and hunting activities varied. The Cree argued that the fact that game existed in the region today demonstrated the effectiveness of their management, and they claimed a right to manage the wildlife of the region. The representatives of Quebec and Canada argued that existing parliamentary legislation gave the responsibility to manage wildlife to the governments.

This conflict was resolved through two procedures. It was agreed that all parties would recognize the Cree system of hunting territories and that there would be a minimum of government regulation. Second, the provincial and federal governments would exercise legal authority and enforcement powers over most of the region, but only after receiving the advice of a co-ordinating committee composed equally of Native and government appointees. On the areas reserved exclusively for Native people, the Cree governments would act with the advice of the committee.

Both the Cree and the governments agreed that development had to be controlled. The Cree did not oppose all development, envisioning sharing the land with non-Natives, but they wanted the right to decide on whether specific projects should be permitted to go ahead, and if so under what terms and conditions. The governments argued that they had the right to final decisions authorizing future developments, and they wanted to avoid a situation in which the Cree could tie up a project in the court. The conflict over this issue was direct and not fully resolvable.

The insistence of the governments that the region be open for development limited the land base upon which the Cree could negotiate. The

MAP 8.2. Division of Cree Lands Under the James Bay and Northern Quebec Agreement

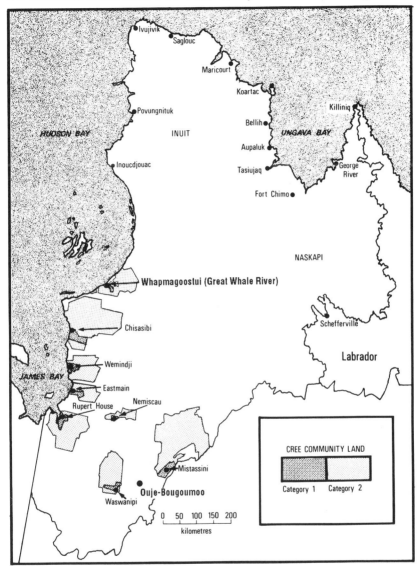

province took the position that land under Cree control should be limited to areas immediately around the settlements and to the adjacent hunting locations. The greatest amount of land the province would transfer to Cree control, Category I lands, was only 5,500 square kilometres, of the approximately 375,000 square kilometre region (Map 8.2).

The Cree sought in the negotiations to reduce their dependence on governmental authority and administration and to take more control of their own affairs through increased self-government. They therefore sought regional autonomy and self-determination through the formation of distinctive, ethnically defined governments and boards, which would assure Native control and administration of their affairs under the legal provisions established in the negotiations. This pattern was generally acceptable to the governments because it transferred the Cree from federal to provincial jurisdictions, and because Quebec was also prepared at that period to accept the decentralization of responsibility to regional boards and governments.

At the community level, the Cree got agreement that there would be special legislation for a Cree-Naskapi Act, extending the powers of their band councils as new community governments and replacing the provisions of the existing Indian Act.

The Agreement in Principle, reached after eight months of negotiation, was discussed periodically in each of the Cree communities, where the provisions were outlined in detail. People did not consider the draft agreement to be fair or just, but thought it would increase their chances of maintaining their culture, society, and economy, given the alternatives. The outcome was summarized by Chief Billy Diamond of the Grand Council of the Crees, in his speech to the press, announcing that all Cree communities had accepted the Agreement in Principle:

> The Cree People were very reluctant to sign an Agreement in Principle. However, after many meetings and many hours of meetings, the Grand Council of the Crees has received a mandate to sign an Agreement in Principle with the Quebec Government. . . . We feel, as Cree People, that by coming to an Agreement in Principle, that it is the best way to see that our rights and that our land are protected as much as possible from white man's intrusion and white man's use. We have always said that we wanted to maintain our way of life. We have always said that we want to pass the land on to our children. . . . We believe that even though we practised the traditional way of life, the aboriginal way of life, we believe this agreement supports and strengthens the hunting, fishing and trapping rights in/over all of the territory, and restricts non-native activity in that area. By the proposed agreement, we feel we have removed the worst effects of the Project to our way of life and the Cree People. . . . I hope you can all understand our feelings, that it has been a tough fight, and our people are still very much opposed to the

project, but they realize that they must share the resources. That is why we have come to a decision to sign an Agreement in Principle with the Quebec Government. (Diamond, 1977)

Implementing the Agreement and Enhancing Cree Autonomy

A definitive account of the results of the James Bay and Northern Quebec Agreement (JBNQA) cannot be made. The processes of implementing the agreement have been long and complex, and although the process has already extended over two decades, the outcome is not fully known. Nevertheless, I would emphasize four general aspects: (1) the agreement has considerably aided Cree hunting; (2) it has strengthened the Cree socially and politically; (3) government respect and support for the agreement have been mixed and uneven; (4) the Cree are more autonomous now than before the agreement, but real threats to Cree autonomy remain.

The protection and recognition of Cree hunting rights and the provision of income security payments for Cree hunters have enhanced the perceived viability of hunting as a way of life, and the participation of Cree in hunting has intensified. In 1975, about 700 families or single adults were hunting as a way of life. The number of intensive hunters increased following the agreement to approximately 900 and has since risen to about 1,200. Many of those initially taking up hunting were people who had been driven away by the difficulties of the 1960s and early 1970s. But those joining more recently are predominantly young adults, just starting careers as intensive hunters. The time spent in hunting camps has also increased, and the average number of days intensive hunters stayed in the bush hunting during a year increased by about 25 per cent after the income security program was begun. Most of these families now live seven months or more in bush camps.

The increased number of intensive hunters and the increased time they are spending in bush camps present complex challenges to the stewards of hunting territories, who want to assure these changes do not result in disrespectful over-hunting of game. In the initial year after the JBNQA, harvests of the most intensively used wildlife – geese, beaver, and moose – increased significantly. Stewards responded quickly to the dangers. They spoke widely of the problems in the villages, and re-organized their own hunting groups accordingly. By the second and third years geese and beaver harvests had returned to earlier levels. Moose and caribou harvests, which had initially increased the most (by 72 and 40 per cent, respectively), were no higher than earlier levels by the third year after the agreement. This adjustment of Cree hunting to a significant and rapid increase in the numbers of hunters and the length of time people spent in bush camps was a dramatic test and confirmation of Cree conservation practices.[5]

In terms of changes in social relations, several commentators anticipated that the increased cash available to both hunters and to the growing number of employed Cree might result in widespread increases in the independence of individual nuclear families and a reduction in extended social relations and reciprocity. They also thought there might be a change of hunting territories into forms of private property, as opposed to being a system of socially sanctioned stewardship of lands. These changes have not in fact occurred.

All sectors of Cree society maintain a high value and a strong preference for locally produced "bush foods." The desire for bush foods reflects the specialized knowledge, skill, and work that go into the harvesting of food animals and the recognized nutritional and health benefits of a fresh bush food diet. While hunters adjusted their harvesting effort after the agreement so as not to over-hunt intensively utilized game populations, they increased their harvests of some small game populations that would not be endangered by increased harvests. Increases in these harvests meant that the majority of families who hunt intensively not only have sufficient bush foods for their own needs, they continue to do the work necessary to make additional harvests of foods that they give to kin, friends, and those who do not hunt so intensively.

Access to hunting territories continues to be provided by invitations from hunting stewards, and the growing numbers of hunters are generally being accommodated through extended kin and friendship networks. Customary stewardship therefore continues to express social responsibility and mutual aid despite considerably more intensive use of lands (Feit, 1991).

In a society in which animals are sacred and labour is highly valued and a source of respect, social exchanges of bush foods and access to hunting lands are highly valued. The gifts of bush foods are a sign both of the continuing value of those foods and of the value of the social bonds that motivate the distribution and are confirmed by it. The fact that such exchange is less of a material necessity today highlights its social value.

The rapid increase in the Cree population has meant that while the number of intensive hunters has stabilized in recent years, the total population continues to grow, so that now less than half – between one-quarter and one-third – of the adult resident population are intensive hunters.

Almost all other Cree hunt, but on a variety of arrangements. Extensive linkages exist between families living most of the year in the settlements – and who hunt in evenings, on weekends, school breaks, and holidays, and between jobs – and those kin and friends who live most of the year in bush camps and for whom hunting is their primary activity. Those in the settlements often provide equipment and cash for those in the bush, while the latter provide access to the hunting camps and lands, advice and knowledge of hunting conditions, and regular gifts of food to those who live most of the time in the settlement. Hunting is critical to the identities and relations of nearly all Crees, and it binds together the diverse sectors of the communities.

Thus, even when much of the population works for wages and only hunts a part of the time, it is still the case that access to land and wildlife is provided through social reciprocity, not through market exchanges or individualized ownership. Hunting continues to be embedded in social and spiritual meanings and organization. Rather than cash and market conditions leading to an attenuation of social relations, hunting reciprocity continues to re-create wider social relationships, which are dominated by a desire to enhance a collective local autonomy in the face of the market forces that might otherwise transform Cree society.

Social linkages are also expressed in the growth of more formal community-based decision-making institutions. Under the agreement and the supplementary Cree-Naskapi Act, the Cree took over formal control of the many organizations that provided services in their communities, including school boards and health and social services boards. Initially, the organizations were taken over more or less in the form, and with the staff, that they already had when run by the governments. There was little time to make changes other than to transfer formal control, even though the agreement gave many boards enhanced powers.

With few Crees having the professional training to staff the service organizations in 1975, and with those Crees with experience in policy-making and governance of bureaucracies stretched to do all that was needed, it was not a surprise that changes to the policies, programs, and structures of the organizations were slow to develop. But Crees have got training on the job by doing the work alongside those with experience, and over time effective Cree control has grown and the policies and programs have become increasingly innovative (Salisbury, 1986).

At the same time, the Cree decision-making, which was initially centralized in the Cree regional government structures, has been devolving to local governments and administrations. In the villages, more and more school and health committees composed of local Cree users have started to play decisive decision-making roles. The result has empowered local people and provided them with enhanced skills and experience. Recently, various committees are beginning to ask how they should restructure the basic organizations themselves. These initiatives involve examining how distinctly Cree ways of working and relating can be structured into large organizations.

These processes have not been smooth or easy, and numerous mistakes have been made along the way. Nevertheless, the overall process has showed how an effective self-government can be established, even under difficult circumstances, where there was no time for advanced planning or proper preparation.

This process has also had important benefits for Cree community economies. The Cree takeover and expansion of the administrative services and programs have considerably increased employment opportunities in the communities. The thirty or so Cree who were fully employed as administrators before the agreement have been expanded to some 800 administrators and supporting employees. As more Cree develop the professional skills to replace additional non-Native teachers, nurses, and administrators, this number will grow.

It is clear, however, that the number of administrative positions will be insufficient to employ fully all those Cree in the rapidly growing population who do not hunt as a way of life. The Cree have therefore recently begun to emphasize the creation of Cree economic enterprises, especially in the communities. Such enterprises must be planned carefully, and they will develop slowly, partly because of systematic obstacles to their full participation in the regional resource-based economy from governments and large corporations. The structures the Cree are developing in this process frequently combine elements of modern business practices with structures adapted from Cree hunting society.

The economic development provisions of the agreement have not to date greatly benefited the Cree. Nor has the hydroelectric project contributed systematically to community-level economic development within the Cree villages. The economic benefits of the project have been directed to southern urban centres, and even the benefits for non-Cree inhabitants of northern Quebec have been less than expected. As a result there is a continuing high level of unemployment and underemployment in Cree villages.

Indeed, nearly all of the monetary provisions of the agreement have suffered negligence on the part of governments, and in some cases explicit subversion.[6] When the first major parliamentary review of the implementation of the agreement was conducted, five years after the signing in

1981, it was clear that the federal government had neither budgeted any special funds to meet its new obligations under the agreement, nor had it established any agency with responsibility for overseeing its role in the implementation processes. As a result of this review several initiatives were undertaken. In 1984, after three additional years of negotiation, the Cree-Naskapi Act was signed and passed into law, establishing local self-government for Cree (and adjacent Naskapi) communities, thereby fulfilling one of the obligations from the 1975 agreement.

As part of this supplementary negotiation a separate funding agreement was to be signed. It was a five-year accord that specified the basic annual financial obligations of Canada toward Cree governments, and it set out arrangements for annual adjustments over succeeding years – based on inflation and costing experience. The signing of the Cree-Naskapi Act provisions and the funding agreement (or Statement of Understanding, as it was called) were formally concluded at a Cree Annual General Assembly in the village at Eastmain in 1984. At the signing, questions about the federal government's commitments were raised by Chief Billy Diamond, who was wary of the failure of both the Canada and Quebec governments to meet earlier obligations. Before signing he said to the Minister of Indian Affairs and Northern Development, Douglas Frith:

> "I just wanted to make – to ask – one final point. . . . There was supposed to be five year block funding for the Cree-Naskapi Act. . . . and the Deputy Minister has refused to sign the Statement of Understanding in respect to the funding. Will the Minister now sign that Statement of Understanding and *commit the federal government* to those figures that were negotiated and arrived at; or will the Minister direct his Deputy Minister to sign on it? If they will not sign, will the Minister sign before September 1st, so that at least we are guaranteed continued funding for the next four years? . . ."
>
> The Minister responded, "I was prepared for this Chief Diamond, and show me the piece of paper and I will sign."[7]

Then the agreements were signed and the Minister handed over to the Crees the initial cheques for the cost of the first year of operations of the new Cree governments.

Despite this accord, strong disagreements arose over the funding for succeeding years. These differences centred on whether or not the agreement was binding on the government of Canada.[8] The Cree believe the agreement provisions are binding. The Department of Indian Affairs and Northern Development representatives stated at public hearings in

October, 1986, that the government of Canada "does not recognize [the Statement of Understanding] as a fully binding undertaking."

The disagreement was reviewed by the Cree-Naskapi Commission, the independent organization set up to report every two years to Parliament on the implementation of the Act. They reported:

> Having carefully considered the above facts and evidence, the Commission is of the opinion that the Statement of Understanding is both a moral and a legal obligation of Canada. Moreover, the Commission considers that Statement the principal fiscal arrangement which ties both Canada and the Cree and Naskapi nations to their financial obligations. The evidence is substantial and convincing. . . .
>
> It is difficult to believe that a federal department responsible for negotiating and implementing self-government arrangements with Indian nations, and charged with improving their conditions, could persistently misinterpret a negotiated arrangement of this nature. The Department's attempt to circumvent clear obligations . . . is unjust, and must not be allowed to continue. Such actions cannot be dismissed as merely an honest difference of opinion. (Cree-Naskapi Commission, 1986)

Similar attitudes and actions prevail in governments with respect to the exploitation of the natural resources of the territory. The governments of Quebec and Canada have repeatedly tried to avoid the obligations they have toward the Cree, and to the wider public, in the interests of facilitating large-scale projects that primarily meet the interests of private and public corporations.

Two major phases of hydroelectric exploitation are still planned in the James Bay region, the Great Whale River (GWR) project, and the Nottaway-Broadback-Rupert rivers (NBR) project (McCutcheon, 1991). The Cree continue actively to oppose both, with increased sophistication and with some surprisingly effective results.

The former project is at the stage during which environmental and social impact assessment is being conducted prior to the decision on whether authorization will be given to Hydro-Québec to proceed. The initial position of Quebec and Canada was that the government of Canada did not have to conduct an environmental and social assessment of the project before authorizing those aspects under federal jurisdiction, a view that explicitly abrogated provisions in the agreement as well as other federal legislation. The Cree took Canada and Quebec to court, and in 1991 the Federal Court of Canada ruled that the governments were attempting to circumvent and "free themselves from [their] duties and responsibilities." In another ruling by the Federal Court of Appeal the judge reminded governments that the JBNQA "was signed in good faith for the protection of the Cree . . ., not to deprive them of their rights" (quoted in Orkin and Hazell, 1991).

Unfortunately, these are not the only cases of governments unilaterally abrogating their obligations, and the Cree have been to courts on numerous occasions to try to force either Quebec or Canada to meet specific commitments or mutual understandings. The court processes are extremely time-consuming and costly, and therefore the outcomes are not fully successful.

But the pattern of government subversion of agreements, while not universal, is sufficiently widespread that it is a significant feature of the implementation process. One must assume that the governments have repeatedly chosen this type of action because they believe that the issues are so complex, and the processes are sufficiently drawn out, that public outrage will be muted and the public will forget.

Thus the struggles for public support are continuing to be fought in diverse arenas, ranging from Quebec City and Ottawa to New York and The Hague. At the same time, the proposed expansions of hydroelectric development have already begun to affect the Cree dramatically. For example, because the NBR project was initially expected to be built in the 1990s, and because there was a serious over-utilization of forests and wildlife further south in Quebec, an acceleration of the commercial cutting of forests and of the sport hunters' harvests of wildlife in the areas that would have been flooded was allowed and encouraged by Quebec, despite Cree opposition. Once the activities were established, the over-exploitation then spread throughout the James Bay region, even though the NBR project has been delayed by at least a couple of decades. These levels of resource use in northern Quebec are not sustainable, and they can only delay for Quebec as a whole the crisis caused by such exploitation. But the destructiveness of the ongoing exploitation of the region is being suffered now by the Cree.

Under the agreement forestry development was to be reviewed through Cree input to Quebec government forestry management plans. In practice, Cree input has not been sought at critical stages of the planning, and long discussions have not resulted in any significant modification to forestry practices or plans in the region. As a consequence of Quebec denials that forestry clear-cutting has a significant impact on the Cree, it has permitted forestry companies to cut without regard to the Cree hunting territory system. The scale of this exploitation now threatens some of the Cree traplines as effective hunting and conservation units. Several hunting territories have already been cut by over 40 per cent, and the cut on one trapline is already 80 per cent of the formerly commercially forested land (Beaulieu, 1993). This crisis continues to accelerate with the years. The rapid forestry development, as well as significant increases in non-Cree harvests of wildlife,[9] directly threatens the Cree use of lands and the fabric of Cree society and economy.

Therefore, even the gains made by the Cree with the JBNQA are constantly under threat. While many of the most important provisions of the agreement have been respected by governments, the erosion that has occurred is significant, and the threats to the Cree are unabated.

Conclusion: Continuing Resistance

The autonomy of the Cree communities has clearly been enhanced by the strengthening of the hunting economy and society, by the greater control of Cree government, services, and resources, and by their ability to initiate political, legal, and administrative action.

The need to continue the struggle for autonomy – and to enhance that autonomy in the face of government attempts to erode Cree power and rights – is also clear. The Cree now face several major threats. For one, the cash and natural resources available to the Cree under the agreement have proven inadequate. The Cree find they cannot invest funds for future generations and have sufficient incomes to meet the administrative, social, and economic development needs of the population. What looked like large sums are very modest in relation to the costs of social and economic development and self-government. The need for increased local economic development is urgent.

In addition, the large-scale resource exploitation projects are continuing on Cree lands. Future phases of hydroelectric development have been delayed but not abandoned, and forestry is having a massive impact. The limited regulation of resource development, known to be a problem when the agreement was signed, is becoming a major future threat to the revitalized hunting sector.

While the Cree have clearly come through the events of the last two decades a united people, more autonomous and better able to achieve their goals, it is also clear that their relationship to the governments and project developers is an ongoing problem. The process has strengthened the Cree ability to confront the problems that threaten them, but it has not fundamentally resolved those problems or provided a mutually acceptable new relationship between the Cree and the governments. The Cree hunters have hoped for a new relationship with Euro-Canadians, based on mutual respect for each other's needs, on a reciprocal and responsible sharing of the land and resources, and on a real process of communication and understanding. They are still waiting.

Notes

1. This paper draws on the work of many other scholars, both published and in personal communications. At the cost of leaving out many, I would like to note my general debt for ideas and information I freely incorporated into this chapter from: Philip Awashish, Fikret Berkes, Taylor Brelsford, Brian Craik, Rick Cuciurean, Billy Diamond, Peter Hutchins, Ignatius LaRusic, Toby Morantz, James O'Reilly, Alan Penn, Richard Preston, Boyce Richardson, Edward Rogers, Richard Salisbury, Colin Scott, and Adrian Tanner. Parts of the data cited in this paper were funded by grants from the Social Sciences and Humanities Research Council, the Canada Council Killam postdoctoral research program, and the Arts Research Board of McMaster University.

2. In the Cree language the word for God is not specific with respect to gender. But Cree, who are all Christians, generally use the masculine pronoun when speaking English. I follow their usage when paraphrasing their statements. In the text I generally also use the term "hunters," which is often taken as gendered. It is the case that most Cree hunters are males. But it should be remembered that many women also hunt, and that statements about hunters apply to women as well as men.

3. The James Bay and Northern Quebec Agreement was jointly negotiated by the Cree and the Inuit of Quebec. In this presentation only the aspects relevant to the Cree are discussed.

4. In fact, changes were agreed to later, including an agreement to relocate the site of the dam that had been moved back to its original location. A move to an alternative site other than that agreed to was requested by the corporation because construction at the agreed upon site proved to be technically impossible. Although a third site was available, the Cree agreed to let the original land be used, as long as construction camps were located further away. The decision appears to have been influenced by hunters' doubts about the survival of fish at the site given the changes in the flow of the river. The severity of the expected changes made construction there acceptable in the end. With the funds the corporation paid for the right to relocate the dam, the community relocated the village from Fort George Island to a new site at Chisasibi on the shore of the river.

5. The stewards of several communities were also trying to respond to the

impacts and disruptions caused by the construction of the first phase of the hydroelectric projects in these years. These impacts included those foreseen by Cree hunters, such as flooding and the opening up of lands to outsiders (see above), and others not foreseen by Cree or by governments, including a new source of increased methylmercury contamination of fish in the reservoirs and the downstream sections of rivers. See Orkin and Hazell (1991) for a summary of impacts.

6. One major exception has been the income security program, run by a specialized board of Cree and Quebec government appointees, which has demonstrated the possibility of strong commitment and co-operation by Cree and Quebec government representatives. Several other Cree organizations that receive their annual funding from governments also appear to be working under more stable arrangements in recent years.

7. The transcript of Chief Diamond and the Minister's public exchange is from the videotape recording of the signing ceremony, August 9, 1984. The text was published in the first biennial report to the Parliament of Canada by the independent Cree-Naskapi Commission (Cree-Naskapi Commission, 1986). Emphasis added.

8. The specific points of disagreement concerned the annual adjustments to the base subsidy for the following years and what conditions would apply for orderly transfer of funds to the Cree governments.

9. Sport hunters' harvests of big game have increased dramatically in the region, endangering the survival of these game populations. The Cree have been seeking effective responses from Quebec since the mid-1970s, and only today has the crisis been admitted by Quebec game managers. Whether it will be dealt with effectively is not yet clear.

Recommended Reading

Diamond, Billy
   1977 *Highlights of the Negotiations Leading to the James Bay and Northern Quebec Agreement.* Val d'Or: Grand Council of the Crees (of Quebec).
   1990 "Villages of the Damned: The James Bay Agreement Leaves a Trail of Broken Promises," *Arctic Circle*, November/December: 24-34.
             Invaluable accounts of the history of the JBNQA by the foremost Cree leader of the period. The former piece includes an outline summary of the agreement, the latter a critique of its implementation.
Feit, Harvey A.
   1991 "Gifts of the Land: Hunting Territories, Guaranteed Incomes and the Construction of Social Relations in James Bay Cree Society," *Senri Ethnological Studies*, 30: 223-68.

A review and assessment of the continuity of Cree social relations and hunting territories in the decade following the James Bay and Northern Quebec Agreement.

Francis, Daniel, and Toby Morantz

1983 *Partners in Furs. A History of the Fur Trade in Eastern James Bay, 1600-1870.* Montreal: McGill-Queen's University Press.

The first comprehensive history of the James Bay Cree in the period up to the twentieth century. An informative and readable account that challenges widely held assumptions.

Honigmann, John J.

1981 "Expressive Aspects of Subarctic Indian Culture," in *Handbook of North American Indians*, Vol. 6, *Subarctic*, ed. June Helm. Washington, D.C.: Smithsonian Institution.

A rich and balanced survey of values, ritual, and personal styles in Subarctic Indian cultures, including the James Bay Cree.

LaRusic, Ignatius, *et al.*

1979 *Negotiating a Way of Life: Initial Cree Experience with the Administrative Structure Arising from the James Bay Agreement.* Ottawa: Canada, Department of Indian and Northern Affairs, Policy Research and Evaluation Group.

A preliminary and critical evaluation of the formation of the initial Cree political and administrative organization. Identifies an extensive range of issues and problems for future research, but see Salisbury below.

McCutcheon, Sean

1991 *Electric Rivers, The Story of the James Bay Project.* Montreal: Black Rose Books.

An account of the James Bay hydroelectric project and its initial environmental and social impacts by an independent science writer.

Preston, Richard J.

1975 *Cree Narrative: Expressing the Personal Meanings of Events.* Ottawa: National Museum of Man Mercury Series, Canadian Ethnology Service Paper No. 30.

An extensive exploration of core Cree symbolic meanings and knowledge as revealed through the analysis of myths, songs, stories, and conjuring performances from Rupert House.

Richardson, Boyce

1979 *Strangers Devour the Land.* Vancouver: Douglas & McIntyre.

A richly personalized account of Cree hunting and the court case against the hydroelectric project, by a skilful journalist.

Salisbury, Richard F.

1986 *A Homeland for the Cree. Regional Development in James Bay, 1971-1981.*
      Montreal: McGill-Queen's University Press.

      A major review and synthesis of the organizational and economic changes
      in Cree society in the initial years following the signing of the James Bay and
      Northern Quebec Agreement.

Scott, Colin H.

1989 "Ideology of Reciprocity Between the James Bay Cree and the Whiteman
      State," in Peter Skalnik, ed., *Outwitting the State.* New Brunswick, N.J.:
      Transaction Publishers.

      A stimulating analysis of the Cree understanding of relations with white
      men, from the earliest contacts.

Tanner, Adrian

1979 *Bringing Home Animals: Religious Ideology and Mode of Production of
      Mistassini Cree Hunters.* St. John's: Memorial University of Newfoundland,
      Institute of Social and Economic Research, Social and Economic Studies No.
      23.

      A contemporary ethnography of Cree hunting emphasizing the
      ritualization of productive activities and the symbolic organization of the
      social life of hunters.

Vincent, Sylvie, and Garry Bowers, eds.

1988 *James Bay and Northern Quebec – Ten Years After.* Montreal: Recherches
      amérindiennes au Québec.

      Proceedings of a conference reflecting on a decade of implementation of
      the James Bay and Northern Quebec Agreement, with statements from many
      of the key indigenous leaders and government representatives.

Additional References Cited

Beaulieu, Robert

1993 Personal Communication on forestry statistics. Montreal: Cree Regional
      Authority.

Berkes, Fikret

1977 "Fishery Resource Use in a Subarctic Indian Community," *Human Ecology,*
      5: 289-307.

Black, Mary B.

1967 "An Ethnoscience Investigation of Ojibwa Ontology and World View," Ph.D.
      dissertation, Department of Anthropology, Stanford University.

Cree-Naskapi Commission

1986 *1986 Report of the Cree-Naskapi Commission.* Ottawa: Cree-Naskapi
      Commission.

Feit, Harvey A.

1978   "Waswanipi Realities and Adaptations: Resource Management and
       Cognitive Structure," Ph.D. dissertation, Department of Anthropology,
       McGill University.

1985   "Legitimation and Autonomy in James Bay Cree Responses to Hydroelectric
       Development," in Noel Dyck, ed., *Indigenous Peoples and the Nation State*.
       St. John's: Memorial University, Institute for Social and Economic Research.

Hallowell, A. Irving

1955   *Culture and Experience*. Philadelphia: University of Pennsylvania Press.

Orkin, Andrew, and Stephen Hazell

1991   *Second International Water Tribunal, Spring 1992, Case Document [on] The
       James Bay Hydroelectric Project, Quebec, Canada*. Ottawa: Canadian Arctic
       Resources Committee and Rawson Academy of Aquatic Sciences.

Scott, Colin H.

1983   "The Semiotics of Material Life Among Wemindji Cree Hunters," Ph.D.
       dissertation, Department of Anthropology, McGill University.

PART IV
The Western Subarctic

CHAPTER 9
The Northern Athapaskans: A Regional Overview

C. Roderick Wilson

Although the region strikes most southerners as definitely inhospitable, people have lived in the Western Subarctic longer than in any other part of Canada. As discussed in Chapter 2, bone tools discovered in the Old Crow region of the Yukon have been widely accepted as indicating human presence some 25,000 years ago. Some archaeologists think that other artifacts found in the region are much older. Whatever dates are ultimately demonstrated, Amerindian people have clearly lived in the region from "time immemorial."

The physical environment of the region can be characterized as the zone of discontinuous permafrost in western Canada. The southern half is boreal forest (spruce, fir, and pine, with some poplar and white birch) and the rest is primarily a transitional zone of boreal vegetation inter- mixed with patches of lichen-dominated tundra. (As a cultural region the Western Subarctic in places extends north of the tree line into the tundra because some Subarctic societies made extensive use of tundra resources.) In absolute terms the region receives little annual average

MAP 9.1. The Western Subarctic

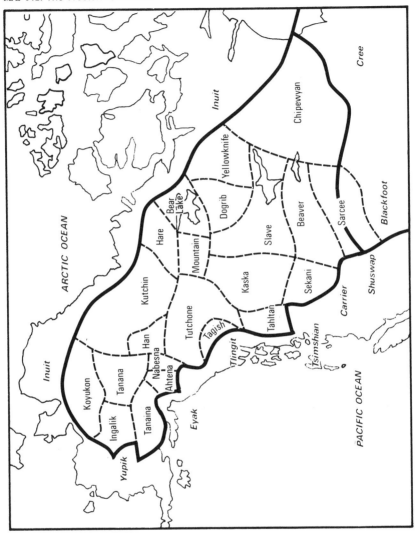

precipitation (about 40 cm), yet it has two of the largest river systems on the continent and innumerable lakes. The ground is snow-covered six months of the year, and few places have more than fifty frost-free days. Temperature extremes typically range from lows of –50° C to summer highs of over 20° C.

Large game animals, particularly caribou, constituted the primary resource base for Aboriginal peoples. Moose, goats, sheep, and even bison were locally important. Small animals (especially the snowshoe hare), fish, migratory waterfowl, and grouse were of secondary importance.

The entire Western Subarctic culture area is inhabited by Indians speaking a series of closely related Athapaskan languages. Linguists believe that these languages were undifferentiated as recently as 500 B.C. and that from their "ancestral" homeland they expanded further west in Alaska and eastward into the Northwest Territories and then southward. Some, notably the Apacheans, became physically separated from the others and ended up thousands of miles to the south, but for Northern Athapaskans, because of limited linguistic variation, communication is still possible across considerable distances. This implies frequent communication between people from different localities throughout the prehistoric past. Correlatively, the ethnographic evidence is that few Northern Athapaskan groups had significant relationships with non-Athapaskans. The exceptions are the Chipewyan (with Cree), the Hare and Kutchin (with Inuit), and the Kaska (with Northwest Coast groups).

In this context it seems significant that Northern Athapaskan kinship systems could be extended in such a way that usually one could find a "relative" even in bands quite far distant, and hence a legitimate basis for establishing a relationship. In general these people developed social strategies characterized by great flexibility and informal institutional arrangements. For example, leadership among the eastern Northern Athapaskans was largely situational: people were listened to or followed not because they had the power to make people obey but because they had demonstrated an ability to lead in that particular activity. An outstanding hunter might attract a considerable following; nevertheless, he had no permanent power. The overall picture thus was of individuals, family groups, and even larger groupings making short-term decisions about where and how they would live. These decisions were based on a large number of factors: the local supply of game, reports from elsewhere, degree of satisfaction with fellow band members, which relatives lived where, and so on. In the western part of the region, the existence of clans correlated with a more complex and formal social life; nevertheless, that life also was characterized by remarkable social flexibility.

Another key to Aboriginal Athapaskan society is its egalitarianism (autonomy and self-reliance are closely associated). This was true even among the most westerly Athapaskans who, like their maritime neighbours, had "chiefs." As McClellan and Denniston (1981: 384, 385) point out, these positions were conditional, and stratified rank was not possible for them until the fur trade period. The staples necessary for life were in general equally accessible, and the skills necessary to transform them into finished products were shared widely in the community. Although some people were more competent than others, and more respected, there was no basis from which an exclusive control over goods, and hence people, could develop. Even in the realm of spiritual power, the ultimate basis for any success and an aspect of life in which people varied conspicuously, the possibility of becoming a shaman was in principle open to all.

The initial contact of Canadian Athapaskans with Europeans was consistent with the general trend of the frontier moving from east to west. Direct trading contacts were made by the easternmost group, the Chipewyan, in 1714, while none of the westernmost tier of Canadian Athapaskans had direct contacts prior to 1850. There was not, however, a single frontier: Athapaskans in southern Alaska had trading contacts from 1741.

Helm (1975) makes the following points concerning the early contact process: European goods and diseases usually preceded direct contact with traders; the first-contacted tribes obtained guns and expanded their fur-collecting operations at the expense of their western neighbours; trading posts were welcomed by those living in the "new" territories; traders tended to act as peacemakers in this newly competitive context. The latter three points particularly contrast with Russian-Native relationships in Alaska.

The fur trade had numerous consequences, and it constituted a social revolution. The introduction of new goods, especially guns and traps, is salient. New social roles, such as trading chiefs, and changing social relationships are also striking. Perhaps most startling are features that are now identified as traditional, such as dog sleds, which were introduced during this period. Somewhat simplified, the guns, traps, and sleds enabled people to engage in old and new bush activities more efficiently, and the trading chiefs allowed traders to deal with the people more efficiently. However, the new elements made their own demands: a dog team in a year would eat thousands of pounds of fish, thereby increasing the "need" to obtain new goods such as fish nets and to harvest bush resources at a higher level. Further, an innovation frequently had a cumulative impact. The effect of the gun, an early trade item, in contributing to higher harvest levels becomes most evident after 1900. Nevertheless, these early changes were limited in scope, and the continuity with the past was evident. The ensuing way of life was remarkably stable for many groups for almost a century and a half. Even the general acceptance of Christianity resulting from the activities of Oblate and

PLATE 9.1. Chipewyan hunter with caribou he has shot, northern Manitoba. Courtesy Hudson's Bay Company.

Anglican missionaries was as notable for people's continued adherence to old beliefs as to new.

The impact of introduced diseases is not clear. Aboriginal population levels are not well known, nor are the consequences of the various outbreaks. Are they isolated events, as a narrow reading of the sources would indicate, or do they represent merely the documented cases of widespread epidemics? What is evident is that a number of new diseases (smallpox, scarlet fever, influenza, measles, venereal diseases, and tuberculosis – in rough chronological order) became common and that there were at times very high mortality rates, both because the new diseases were in themselves devastating and because in their wake small groups might well starve to death. Nevertheless, the recuperative powers of the population were such that the region as a whole appears not to have experienced significant demographic change until recently. With the advent of modern medicine some forty years ago, the Yukon and Northwest Territories have experienced the highest rates of population increase in Canada.

For most of the area, the fact that Native societies had become incorporated into Canada did not become a social reality until the early 1950s. There were two major exceptions. Much of the Beaver Indians' traditional territory, the Peace River country of northern British Columbia and Alberta, was arable. Farmers began displacing Natives *circa* 1890. Even more dramatic was the Klondike gold rush. Dawson alone had grown to 25,000 by 1898, while the Han "tribe," occupying adjacent portions of Alaska and the Yukon, numbered only about 1,000. The rush, and the government and commercial presence it created, resulted in an early marginalization of Native people in the Yukon to a degree that the people of the Northwest Territories generally have still not experienced.

A few generalizations about contemporary life are in order. First, for much of the region, most adults over about age forty have personal memory of what life was like before significant government-industrial presence. For some the "traditional life" is a still present reality. Second, as both Cruikshank and Ridington demonstrate, even for severely impacted groups, truly significant features of traditional life remain important.

Third, the treaties continue to be living documents. As Asch notes, there is active debate over how Treaties No. 8 and No. 11 should currently be interpreted, but both sides agree that they help define the constitutional debate on what it means to be Native in those regions. A unique element of this debate is Judge Morrow's 1973 investigation of the circumstances under which Treaty No. 11 had been signed in 1921, unique because at the time there were signatories to the treaty still alive and able to testify in court that the treaty had been everywhere presented as a gesture of friendship and goodwill and not, as a literal reading of the written text would indicate, a means of extinguishing Aboriginal title.

A fourth point is that Athapaskans have attempted both to maintain themselves as a distinctive people and to accommodate the powerful forces for change thrust upon them. The primary mechanism in the Northwest Territories for doing this, the Dene National Assembly, is profoundly rooted in traditional values. Membership, for instance, is open to all Natives, including Metis and Cree, as equally part of the community of people. Although they have had victories, they have not had the same success in establishing political legitimacy as have the Inuit in the eastern part of the Territories.

Our last point follows from this comment. The Inuit case is unique for Canadian Natives; they are numerically dominant in their region. The Dene, like most Natives in Canada, must find mechanisms other than a territorially based legislature for political accommodation. Presumably that means some form of limited, shared, or joint arrangement with Euro-Canadians. Their recent history demonstrates a willingness to seek workable solutions; will Euro-Canadians be as open to accommodation?

References Cited

Helm, June, *et al.*
  1975 "The contact history of the subarctic Athapaskans: an overview," in A. McFayden Clarke, ed., *Proceedings: Northern Athapaskan Conference*, Vol. 1. Canadian Ethnology Service Paper No. 27: Ottawa.

McClellan, C., and G. Denniston
  1981 "Environment and Culture in the Cordillera," in *Handbook of North American Indians*, Vol. 6, *Subarctic*, ed. June Helm. Washington, D.C.: Smithsonian Institution.

CHAPTER 10
Freedom and Authority: Teachings of the Hunters

Robin Ridington

A Classical Beginning

This chapter[1] is about the Dunne-za, but it is also about anthropology and about how my own practice of anthropology has developed through a combination of academic instruction and direct contact with Dunne-za teachers. Most anthropologists recognize that their discipline came from a parentage in the classics, but that recognition for me is more direct and literal. It is from my parents, Bill and Edie Ridington, that I learned the ways of thinking about other times and places that define me as an anthropologist. So, in a way, ontogeny recapitulates phylogeny. It is probably no accident that my own parentage replicates that of my chosen field.

Anthropology as a discipline arose in the nineteenth century when classicists in England, Germany, France, and, later, North America began to ask questions about what kind of people the ancients really were. How did they live, how did they govern themselves, how did kinship organize their societies? In England, Sir Henry Maine wrote a book on *Ancient Law*, the first anthropological study of another culture's system of governance. In France, Fustel de Coulanges wrote *The Ancient*

232

City, a portrait of social institutions in the cities of classical antiquity. These early anthropologists were classicists, in that the cultures they studied were known only from texts and from their physical remains. They were anthropologists, though, in the questions they asked of the texts. The English anthropologist E.B. Tylor put a name to what they were describing; it was the classical world's *culture*, "that complex whole that includes art, language, science, and any other habits or customs acquired by man as a member of society." Then in the 1870s, a classically trained American lawyer, Lewis Henry Morgan from upper New York state, was retained by the Seneca tribe to represent them in a land claim case. Morgan discovered that these Iroquois people were organized by ties of kinship (which he called consanguinity and affinity) generated through the female line. He remembered his classical studies. Before the rise of the city-state, Greek society, too, had been organized by a system of kinship. Morgan had a great insight. Here among the Native American tribes were societies organized in the same way that ancient societies had been organized. It was as if the ancient texts had suddenly come to life and spoken to him. It seemed to Morgan that he had found, in the Native Americans, his living ancestors. And so began a new form of what might be called neo-classical scholarship based not on ancient texts but on ethnography, the *production* of texts. Classics studies old texts, anthropology creates new texts, but they remain linked in the common purpose of interpreting between cultures. Classics works with the depth of time, bringing voices from the past to life. Ethnography works laterally, bringing us voices from our culturally distant contemporaries. A key difference has to do with the politics of the relationship. Classical voices don't talk back to us. Morgan's Iroquois most emphatically did talk back to him, as have all the other people ethnographers have studied. Classical authors were the sole and distant authors of the texts we study. The texts that anthropologists create from the ethnographic encounter are the product of a shared authority. They are a blend of voices. They are conversations. But then, the ethnographic encounter is not so different from those that produced many classical texts in their times. Plato spoke with Socrates and then wrote about the encounter. Heroditus, probably the first ethnographic writer, described customs different from his own throughout the world of classical antiquity.

For me, the relationship between classics and anthropology was immediate and personal. Growing up in the Ridington household, the classical world was always in view, both literally and figuratively. Reproductions of the Vaphio Cups from Mycene graced the mantelpiece. My father's photographs of the starry sky above the Parthenon are part of my earliest memories. Later, Agamemnon and Mycene and the Trojan War were as vivid to me as the American Civil War that I knew from visits to the nearby battlefield at Gettysburg, Pennsylvania.

But the most important lesson I learned from the classical world of my parents was how to ask questions. Beyond the immediate world of Westminster and Carroll County, Maryland, and of the United States of America are other worlds, other times, other places, and other cultures. How can we approach them? What can we learn about them? What can we learn about ourselves through them? These are the questions that continue to suffuse my own transformation of classical studies into anthropology. These are some of the questions I will explore during the course of this chapter.

Discovering Aboriginal America

I made my first contact with the world of people native to this continent in 1959. Like Columbus, I had not intended to discover a new world. It simply happened. I entered a country where the Indian presence remains strong. I entered with preconceptions and found them wanting. I began a trail of learning that is still ongoing. There is a bit of the Columbus in all of us whose traditions came from outside of North America. Columbus was not alone in mistaking the Native people of this continent for people he was expecting to find elsewhere. Columbus found Indians on an island in the Caribbean. I found Italian Boy Scout vandals in the forests of northeastern British Columbia. We were both wrong in interpreting what we saw in terms of what we were expecting. We were both taken by surprise.

I first came to Indian country through my friends, Eric and Jimmi Freedman, who had left Swarthmore College to test their skills and energy against the demands of life in a real wilderness. Less adventurous than they, I planned to join them for the summer and then return to college in September. They had written me with meagre instructions for finding them in the bush. "Drive to Mile 210 on the Alaska Highway, hide your car in the bush out of sight from the road, and follow a trail that leads about seven miles to where you will find us on a flat near where the Minnaker Creek joins the Prophet River."

Late in the evening, the friend with whom I was travelling and I found Mile 210 and manoeuvred my little blue Renault 4cv off the highway. We discovered a clearing in the bush and the remains of a campfire. Someone had left cans and bottles strewn about. Embedded in a nearby tree we discovered a rusty axe. From the same tree hung a pair of snowshoes, rusty traps, and coils of thin blue electrical wire. Some poles were lashed together enigmatically with twists of the same wire. Many of the spruce trees had been blazed with an axe. On some of them we discovered names, dates, and short messages written in pencil. A trail led away from the highway. It was similarly blazed and marked with pencilled messages. We managed to decipher some of the writing. One of the names was Johnny Chipesia.

In the woods of Sussex County, New Jersey, where our family has a summer home, I had also seen trees blazed with an axe. I was familiar with graffiti scribbled on blazes. This was usually the work of wayward Boy Scouts from one of the local camps. Kids from Newark, Passaic, and Montclair sometimes went crazy when they were turned loose in the woods. Some of them, I knew, were Italians. The name, Chipesia, sounded Italian to me. "Oh no," I lamented. "Even here in the wilds of northern British Columbia, the Italian Boy Scout vandals from Passaic have been here before me." I had always held vandals from the city in utter contempt. I respected the forest. I followed only the white blazes neatly painted by volunteers of the Appalachian Trail Club. I did not leave cans or bottles in the woods. I kept my axe bright and shiny. I did not litter the forest with junk. I respected nature. I was organized and civilized.

When I arrived at the place where the Minnaker joins the Prophet, my friends assured me that we were several thousand miles from the nearest Italian Boy Scout vandals from Passaic. They told me that Johnny Chipesia was a Beaver Indian, or as I would learn later, Dunne-za, one of the "real people" in his own language. He had already been down to check them out, and they had been to his home on the Prophet River Reserve at Mile 232 on the Alaska Highway. The flat where they were building the cabin was in his hunting and trapping territory.

Within a few weeks, a party of men and boys on horseback arrived at our little camp on the flat. Among them was the Italian Boy Scout himself, Johnny Chipesia. They asked what we had been eating. We showed them our sacks of whole grains, tubs of peanut butter, tins of Empress jam, and our hand-carved wooden bowls. As we talked, some of the boys rode their horses across the river and disappeared. Soon we heard the ping of a .22 calibre rifle shot. In less than an hour, the boys returned with a deer, neatly skinned and quartered. They built up the fire and impaled a rack of ribs on a green poplar pole pushed into the ground at an angle. After a largely vegetarian diet, we tore into the meat like hungry wolves. It was my first taste of deer meat. We were amazed. This was not New Jersey. These people were Indians, "real live Indians."

Until Johnny and the others rode into my life on that June day in 1959, I had not really thought of Native Americans as people living in a world that could connect to my own. Since that day, I have not been able to think about life in North America without reference to their existence. The contrast between their way of being in the northern forest and our own was immediately obvious. What had been difficult or impossible for us seemed effortless to them. Their visit was partly motivated by curiosity and the entertainment value we surely provided, but it was also a subtle assertion of their rights to the land on which we were squatting. They had come to show us what it means to be on Indian land. They were exercising their authority in a way we had yet to understand. They were showing us their freedom as well as their responsibility to the land.

Through this encounter, I first came into contact with the delicate discourse of a communication system that depends on establishing and maintaining mutual understandings. In this case, Johnny wanted us to know that this valley, although perhaps formally listed as crown land in a land registry office somewhere, was theirs because of the intimate knowledge they have of it. Their authority was vested in knowledge, not in a piece of paper. The ease he displayed in this place where we were as yet clumsy and ill at ease gave us the Indian message in a language more powerful than words. We began to understand that the land is theirs because of the way they know it. The rights they demonstrated by feeding us that day carried more authority than stacks of dusty documents in distant offices. Johnny's way of telling us we were on his land was to feed us from it.

Thus, in the cups of tea and freshly roasted meat we shared that afternoon, a mutual understanding began. I am sure the executives and engineers who decreed that seismic lines (oil exploration corridors) should be clear-cut through these crown lands never took tea with Johnny Chipesia. I doubt they entertained the possibility of any relationship to the land other than the documentary one of the land office registry and corporate balance sheet. Unlike a registered landowner who might very well have thrown us off his land at gunpoint, Johnny saw the needs that arose out of our ignorance and offered us the benefit of his knowledge. The deer meat we shared was sacramental, as was his implicit teaching about the freedom and authority that a deep knowledge of place conveys.

On the very first day, I had seen an Indian pack trail intertwined with seismic lines. I have followed the braided path of white and Indian trails ever since that time. I interpreted what I saw through the structure of my past experience. Italian Boy Scout vandals from Passaic were a category I knew from experience. Indians were as yet outside anything I knew. The

Indians I met that summer belonged to the northern forest country. Their thoughts, their songs, their ease of living in the bush took me back to a mythic time before the advent of history as I knew it. Their evident struggle to maintain themselves in a world of highways, seismic lines, towns, stampedes, alcohol, and government officials forced me to confront the forces of history I had taken for granted. As yet, I had little concrete knowledge of these forest people, but I could intuit from what I had experienced at least what kind of knowledge might be available to me upon further study.

Here in the forest north of the Peace River, I found a country still occupied by people whose right to the land was demonstrated, at least in their own thinking, by their knowledge of it. They had not paid cash for the land or possessed it by changing it, nor could they imagine selling it any more than they could imagine selling a part of their own bodies. Their right was the right of belonging. It was the right of knowing. Their relationship to the land was more complex, more deeply rooted, more spiritual, than simple material possession. The Indians knew that they and their ancestors had been on the land as long as the animals themselves. They were autochthonous, born of the land. I felt in them a sense of place I had never before experienced. Every person I had met before could say what place his or her ancestors had come from. The Dunne-za did not seem to be *from* anywhere. Although they could recall a complex pattern of movements within the Peace River country, it made no sense for them to think of being from any other place. As the summer drew to a close, I resolved to learn more of what it means to be truly native to a place. I resolved to study the source and nature of Dunne-za freedom and authority.

Because I grew up in Maryland, Pennsylvania, and New Jersey, I had never before made contact with "real live Indians." I had never experienced a natural land form or a climax community of plants and animals. Everywhere, the land and its life were transformed by farming and industry. History was written in the stones that settlers sweated and skidded from forest floors and heaped at the boundaries of their property lines. History was a resource to be mined from lodes of artifacts and documents. History was dead and gone from the breath of experience. It was about a past that would not return to life. Beyond history lay myth and legend, Athena and Dionysus and Agamemnon. Beyond the War between the States and the Magna Carta and the battle of Marathon lay this land of North America as it was before being shaped to the purposes of newcomers. Beyond European history lay the world of Indians, to me as yet a mythical dreamworld.

MAP 10.1. Dunne-za Nineteenth-Century Territories and Contemporary Communities

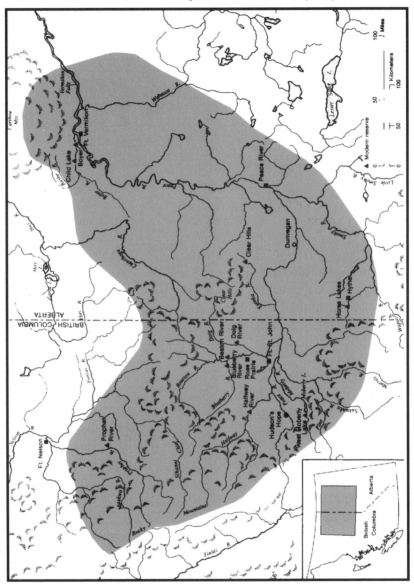

Reprinted from the *Handbook of North American Indians* (Washington, D.C.: Smithsonian Institution Press), vol. 6, page 351, reprinted by permission of the publisher.

Placing the Dunne-za in History

The Beaver Indians, as the Dunne-za are referred to in academic sources, speak an Athapaskan language closely related to those of Dene people in the Yukon and Northwest Territories, to the Sarcee language in southern Alberta, and more distantly to Navaho and Apache in the American Southwest. Older sources sometimes refer to them as Tsattine, the Athapaskan word for Beaver People. The Dunne-za translate the name they call themselves as "Real People." Today, about 800 people live on five reserves 70 to 250 km from the town of Fort St. John, B.C. The town itself has a fluctuating population depending on the boom-or-bust cycle in the oil industry. In 1981 it was 13,891 and served a surrounding area with an overall population of 26,000 (*The Canadian Encyclopedia*, 1985). Dunne-za territory once included lands adjacent to the Peace River extending from the Peace River Canyon, site of the present Bennett Dam, to Lake Athabasca. Their territory included a varied habitat and supported rich resources of game and fur-bearing animals.

Large areas adjacent to the river were either natural prairies or kept as parkland and prairie habitat by intentional burning. This practice allowed Aboriginal people to maintain large areas in subclimax vegetation without the labour-intensive activities normally associated with agriculture and animal husbandry. Ironically, such Aboriginal practices preadapted the Peace River area to agriculture. Animals available to the Dunne-za included bison, moose, elk, caribou, deer, grizzly bear, black bear, mountain sheep, mountain goat, beaver, and a variety of smaller fur-bearing animals, as well as Dolly Varden trout, whitefish, grayling, and jackfish. Bison were particularly important prior to contact and in the immediate post-contact period. North West Company traders used meat provided by Aboriginal hunters from the Peace River area to provision their activities in less productive areas.

European Influences

The North West Company established fur-trading posts along the Peace River between 1793 and 1821, until it was taken over by the Hudson's Bay Company. In the late eighteenth and early nineteenth centuries, Algonquian-speaking Cree people moved into much of the Peace River Athapaskan territory and came to occupy eastern sections of it exclusively by the beginning of the twentieth century. Anthropologist Pliny Earle Goddard obtained ethnographic and linguistic information from Dunne-za informants at Dunvegan, Alberta, in the first decade of the twentieth century. By World War Two the trading post at Dunvegan had been abandoned and most of the Dunne-za from the lower Peace had relocated to areas between Fort St. John and Fort Nelson, British Columbia.

Independent traders broke the Hudson's Bay Company monopoly during the last half of the nineteenth century and introduced new trade goods, including breech-loading rifles, such imported foodstuffs as flour, tea, and sugar, and manufactured clothing. Despite agricultural development in the area, which began in the twentieth century and developed rapidly following World War One, Aboriginal people were able to continue an independent bush life based on hunting and trapping well into the twentieth century in undeveloped areas, or those unsuitable for agriculture.

The Dunne-za obtained horses at the beginning of the twentieth century and quickly developed skills required to make them an important part of their adaptive strategy. A successful family could often accumulate a hundred or more horses. These were kept over the winter on rangelands that were part of the Dunne-za territory. Many of the habitat management techniques previously used for maintaining bison were easily transferred to horses. From late spring to early fall, horses gave hunting groups greater mobility and allowed hunters to bring meat back from some distance to a central location. Bands were able to move greater distances and carry more equipment with them through the use of pack horses. Oral traditions I collected in the 1960s document the impact of this new technology.

The Dunne-za experienced dramatic changes in their way of life when the U.S. Army Corps of Engineers built the Alaska Highway through their territory in 1942, making much of their territory accessible by vehicle for the first time. Heavy equipment made it possible for settlers to expand agricultural activity into areas previously unavailable for that purpose. Highway transportation encouraged the Dunne-za to make more frequent visits to the growing towns of Fort St. John and Fort Nelson. Exploration of Dunne-za territory for oil and gas began in the 1950s and had grown into an enormous industry by the 1960s.

During the time of first exploration and continuing to the present, the petrochemical industry has developed a vast infrastructure of seismic lines, winter roads, and all-weather transportation corridors, giving outsiders access to areas previously accessible only by trail. The roads have also made it possible for Dunne-za hunters and trappers to carry out their accustomed activities from fixed locations on reserves that are now some distance from suitable animal habitats. Like many other northern hunting people, they have been remarkably resilient and adaptable in their use of whatever tools are available and relevant to their situation at a given time. Just as horses were new a hundred years ago but quickly became part of Dunne-za culture, so motor vehicles are now very much a part of Dunne-za cultural competence.

From Hunt Chief to Prophet

As far as can be determined from ethnographic observation and oral tradition, the Dunne-za have always practised a form of leadership based on a person's skill and knowledge rather than on inherited or otherwise ascribed status. Leaders are people who "little bit know something," rather than "bosses" with the authority to give orders. Leaders are recognized in relation to particular tasks about which they have competence, not because of a belief in their overall superiority. This "task force leadership" is typical of Subarctic Athapaskan hunting peoples generally.

One of the leadership categories relevant to pre-contact adaptation was that of hunt chief or "Dreamer." According to oral tradition, the Dunne-za hunt chief was a person who could focus his dreams to visualize communal hunts that required the co-ordinated efforts of many people to drive and surround animals. Following the information he obtained through dreaming, the hunt chief directed people to particular roles in the hunt. He was a typical task force leader in that his authority pertained only to a situation about which he had knowledge. In this case, his knowledge came through the phenomenology of dreaming, something that has always been integral to Dunne-za adaptive strategy.

When the Dunne-za first came into contact with Europeans and the products of an industrial economy, they turned to hunt chiefs for leadership because of their ability to understand the pattern of unfolding events through their dreaming. Oral tradition describes how a Dreamer first predicted the coming of the white people and later identified images from Christian tradition as part of the knowledge that empowered these people and explained their technology. The Dunne-za continued to follow the teachings of Dreamers, whom they call prophets in English, until the 1970s. I was able to record the songs and oratory of Charlie Yahey, the last major figure in the prophet tradition. The Dunne-za credit prophets with bringing back songs from heaven. These Dreamers' songs continue to be the basis of Dunne-za ceremonial dances held to commemorate the journey to heaven of a community member who has died. The Dreamers' dances are also an important part of annual summer gatherings the Dunne-za continue to hold as "Treaty 8 Days."

Relations with Government

The government of Canada sent out treaty parties in 1899 to obtain the acceptance of Treaty No. 8 by Aboriginal leaders. While the government interpreted the treaty as a surrender of Aboriginal title, the Dunne-za viewed it as a treaty of friendship and a commitment by Canada to control unruly miners who had been disturbing their camps. Adhesions to the treaty continued to be taken between 1899 and 1910. Oral traditions from elders who were witness to these adhesions document a general suspicion about the motivations behind the treaty-making process. A point that treaty commissioners evidently used was that the treaty preserved the right of treaty Indians to hunt and trap on crown land, but it also reserved to the province the right to use and appropriate for its own purposes any lands other than those specifically reserved for Indians as a federal trust. Indians under Treaty No. 8 are different from those in the rest of British Columbia in that they maintain relatively unrestricted hunting and trapping rights on crown land. The Peace River is the only part of B.C. in which comprehensive treaties were signed.

Following the treaty, the Canadian government appointed Indian agents who worked closely with Hudson's Bay factors in negotiating trading relations with people whom they appointed to be chiefs. The Dunne-za called these agents *Dunne-za Mechi*, "Indian Boss." The name indicates that the Dunne-za knew full well that these people were agents of government policy rather than advocates for their well-being. The chiefs these bosses appointed became middlemen responsible for dealing with white authority as well as possible, considering their relative lack of power. The first agents set aside limited crown lands as reserves. One of these, IR-172, was located near the farming settlement of Montney just north of Fort St. John. The Dunne-za and Cree of the Fort St. John band called this land "the place where happiness dwells" because they used it annually as a summer gathering place.

After World War Two the Department of Indian Affairs established a nominal system of elected chiefs and councillors but in fact used the system as an instrument of rule by its own agents. The government system had little to do with the actual operation of Aboriginal government based on consensus among band members and the leadership of knowledgeable elders. Prior to World War Two, settlers in the Fort St. John area exerted considerable pressure on the federal government to remove IR-172 from Aboriginal reserve status. In 1945 the government evidently gave in to these and additional pressures for land by returning war veterans. They sent out agents to round up a quorum of male band members over

PLATE 10.1. Dunne-za leader and family, Peace River, Alberta (ca. 1911). Courtesy Glenbow Archives, NA-1440-8.

twenty-one years old, the people eligible to vote on band affairs (but not until 1960 in federal elections). On September 22, 1945, agent Joseph Gallibois took a document to the notary public at Rose Prairie, B.C. It indicated that a vote approving the surrender of IR-172 had been taken. Title to IR-172 was then transferred within the federal government from Indian Affairs to Veterans Affairs. The validity of that surrender became the subject of legal action against the government of Canada for breech of trust forty-two years after the surrender. The suit was denied at trial and is currently under appeal. I will discuss issues arising from it at the conclusion of this paper.

In the 1980s Aboriginal people of the Peace River area began to administer their own affairs and handle their relations with national and provincial governments directly rather than through the authority of an Indian agent. The Fort St. John Indian agency closed down and its functions were taken over by an Aboriginal organization, the Treaty Eight Tribal Association. This coalition of constituent bands made it easier for consensual decision-making and leadership to be integrated more effectively with overall Aboriginal strategies on issues such as hunting and trapping rights, Aboriginal title, the land question, and the administration of social and educational programs. While chiefs and councillors continue to be elected according to the provisions of Canada's Indian Act, these leaders are in fact supported by a deeply rooted Aboriginal view of leadership based on knowledge rather than by institutionally sanctioned authority. As political autonomy returned, people found the energy to strengthen cultural practices such as Dreamer's Dance songs, drumming, and dancing.

While strengthening their ancient sources of knowledge and power, the Dunne-za also learned about the resources of a wider world. Symbolically, at least, the range of their hunting activities expanded to include the entire spectrum of resources available to them in the larger North American cultural environment. While non-Natives generally failed to comprehend Dunne-za culture, Dunne-za leaders became practising ethnographers of theirs. The cultural practices the Dunne-za have adapted to their purposes range from evangelical Christianity to fashion design.

When I first began to do anthropological work with the Dunne-za in 1964, virtually no one there had a driver's licence or education beyond the elementary level. Now, a high school education is part of the normal adaptive competence. Like the prophets of old, who dreamed ahead to understand and interpret both European technology and the symbols of Roman Catholic Christianity, leaders today approach both educational skills and evangelical Christianity as resources about which an individual can obtain knowledge and power. Christianity, for those who practise it, has assisted its adherents in avoiding the life-threatening dangers that another European import, alcohol, brought into their communities. Dunne-za communities are now provided with generally adequate housing and social services. Materially, the quality of life is good. Game continues to be an important source of food, and hunting keeps people in contact with the bush and its skills.

Adaptive Strategies

Adaptive strategies are relative to the opportunities and limitations of an environment and to the cultural technology available at a particular time and place. Aboriginal people of the Peace River have been hunters of the boreal forest and prairie country for over ten millennia. The present-day Dunne-za inherit a cultural technology that has evolved as the environment itself changed from post-Pleistocene conditions to the present. Although the material tools for implementing Aboriginal technology have changed from fluted points and snowshoes to rifles and all-terrain vehicles, an underlying adaptive strategy, a way of thinking and acting in relation to one another and to the environment, has remained remarkably constant over the millennia. In an article on Peace River Athapaskan adaptive strategy, I wrote that:

> In thinking about hunting and gathering people who must move frequently from place to place . . . technology should be seen as a system of knowledge rather than an inventory of objects. . . . The essence of hunting and gathering adaptive strategy is to retain, and to be able to act upon, information about the possible relationships between people and the natural environment. When realized, these life-giving relationships are as much the artifacts of hunting and gathering technology as are the material objects that are instrumental in bringing them about. (Ridington, 1982: 471 [1990: 86])

To northern Native people, hunting is more than a simple matter of subsistence. It is a way of thinking about human beings in relation to the other beings of a living and sentient environment. Animals are more than food to sustain people's bodies; they are also sentient beings with whom humans must establish a sense of trust and understanding. Hunters touch the spirits of animals who give them life. They feel responsible to the animals they hunt in the same way that they feel responsible to one another. They respect the autonomy of their game as they respect the autonomy of other human beings. They do not take an animal against its will. Ideas about the relations of people to animals and natural forces are essential to the adaptive strategies of people who live by hunting.

Hunting people have evolved ways of thinking and institutions that balance individual autonomy with the interdependence of community living. They value knowledge as a source of personal power, but they also recognize that the stories a community holds in common are a fundamental source of all knowledge. They share information with one another in the same way that they share meat. Elsewhere (Ridington,

PLATE 10.2. Dunne-za family, Moberly Lake, B.C. (ca. 1919). Courtesy Glenbow Archives, NA-1463-19.

1988) I wrote about the distinctive blend of individualism and communalism that Peace River Athapaskans share with other boreal forest hunting people. The ways these people think and act are significantly different from those of people whose cultures are based on many years of experience with agricultural and industrial modes of production. I concluded that:

> Knowledge, power, and individual intelligence are keys to understanding the adaptive competence of northern hunting people. The individualism of these people is intelligible only in relation to *their* understanding that an individual's sentient intelligence must make contact with an intelligent organization of the environment at large. (Ridington, 1988: 110 [1990: 117])

These qualities of thought and action are best seen in Aboriginal modes of discourse, systems of government, and phenomenology. Based on my own observation of Peace River Athapaskan life over a thirty-year period, I believe that some essential quality of their ancient adaptive strategy continues to guide them as individuals and as communities in their relation to the contemporary physical and social environment. The following describes some of their experiences and adaptations during the post-contact period.

Discovering Anthropology

When I began fieldwork among the Dunne-za in 1964, I wanted to understand the cultural psychology of people who live by hunting. In August of that year I had been with the Dunne-za of the Prophet River reserve for about six weeks. I was camped with a small band of about two dozen people just off the Alaska Highway between Fort St. John and Fort Nelson, British Columbia. A large oil-drilling camp run by the Majestic Construction Company was less than two miles from our fires, but the distance between us could also have been measured in thousands of years. Our camp was an irregular cluster of tents, tepees, and brush-sided double lean-tos set on either side of a seismic oil exploration line cut through the brush by huge D-8 "Cats." The Indians called these tractors "kettles walking" in their language. The Indians were there to make drymeat. I was there to administer projective tests and collect data for a Ph.D. thesis.

In my research proposal I had said I would use the test results to examine the hypothesis that low-accumulation hunting economies are associated with high levels of a personality variable called Need for Achievement, or "N Ach," as it was referred to in psychologese. The idea was that people would be highly motivated to achieve in an economy where they had to hunt for uncertain resources. As it turned out, though, the Dunne-za were more secure in their hunting than I was in my research. They were doing very well at finding moose, while my testing was not going well at all. My "subjects" were reluctant to take the tests. When they did take pity on my desperate need to accumulate "data," their responses were minimal. Preliminary analysis indicated they were severely withdrawn, if not virtually autistic, but they did not act that way outside of the test situation. My questions, on the other hand, clearly revealed my own high level of performance anxiety. In order to elicit responses from them, I generally had to ask questions that were longer and more revealing than their answers. From time to time they suggested that they knew "Indian stories," which were much more interesting than the ones I wanted them to make up in response to the set of standardized pictures I had brought with me. For a long time I rejected their suggestions. These stories were not the scientific data I required. I should have remembered the lessons my parents taught me about the importance of mythology.

One day a tiny, frail old man was led into our camp by his grandson. He was Johnny Chipesia's father. I had met him before, first in the Fort Nelson hospital and later at the reserve, where people lived during the winter.

PLATE 10.3. Charlie Yahey, Dunne-za Dreamer, 1966, Halfway River Reserve. Courtesy R. Ridington.

He had been in and out of the hospital for several months, suffering from a series of heart attacks. Despite pressure from white doctors and the local school teacher to return to the hospital as the attacks became more frequent and more severe, he wished to be in the bush with his people. He needed moosemeat, wind, stars, his language, and his relatives, rather than the narrow white bed on which I had seen him perched cross-legged, like a tiny bird. His name was Japasa, "Chickadee," from which some well-meaning priest or Indian agent had derived the name Chipesia.

On the evening of his arrival, the old man suffered another attack. As he struggled and moaned, two of his grandchildren and two old men held him while they rubbed his arms and chest. A young daughter also came in to touch him. Outside the tent a circle of people watched in silence. Rain water, collected as it ran down the trunk of a living spruce tree, was sprinkled on the fire. Gradually he became quiet and passed into a normal sleep. A few people remained, to watch over him through the night and to keep a large fire burning.

The next evening, people gathered around the old man's fire after the day's work of hunting and preparing meat and hides. Johnny told a story about how he and the old man survived the terrible flu of 1918-19 that had killed many people. Then Japasa began speaking softly, apparently to himself, as if he were looking back into a dream to find the words. Johnny whispered a simultaneous translation into English for my benefit. It must have been important to him that I share this event. He wanted me to understand enough of what was going on at the time that I could discover its meaning later in my life. This is the essence of Japasa's revelation as related to me by his son. I have told it in my own words from notes I made later that evening.

My dad said that when he was a boy, about nine years old, he went into the bush alone. He was lost from his people. In the night it rained. He was cold and wet from the rain, but in the morning he found himself warm and dry. A pair of silver foxes had come and protected him. After that, the foxes kept him and looked after him. He stayed with them and they protected him. Those foxes had three pups. The male and female foxes brought food for the pups. They brought food for my dad, too. They looked after him as if they were all the same. Those foxes wore clothes like people. My dad said he could understand their language. He said they taught him a song.

At this point in the narrative, the old man sang the boy's song. He sang his medicine song. I did not know then that this song could be heard only when death was near to the singer or to the listener. I did not know he was giving up the power the foxes gave to him in a time out of time, alone in the bush in the 1890s.

My dad said he stayed out in the bush for twenty days. Ever since that time foxes have been his friends. Anytime he wanted to he could set a trap and get foxes. When he lived with the foxes that time he saw rabbits, too. The rabbits were wearing clothes like people. They were packing things on their backs.

The first night out in the bush he was cold and wet from the rain. In the morning when he woke up warm and dry the wind came to him, too. The wind came to him in the form of a person. That person said, "See, you're dry now. I'm your friend." The wind has been his friend ever since. He can call the wind. He can call the rain. He can also make them go away. One time when I was twelve, I was with my dad and some other people when we got trapped by a forest fire. One of our horses got burned and we put the others in a creek. My dad told all the people to look for clouds, even though it hadn't rained for a long time. They found a little black cloud and my dad called it to help us. In just about ten minutes there was thunder and lightning and heavy rain that put out the fire. We were really wet, but we were glad to be saved from the fire.

My dad sang for the rain to come a couple of days ago. He sang for it to come and make him well. That rain came right away. This morning he called the wind and rain. They came and then he told them to go away. He told them he was too old and he didn't need their help any more. He wanted to tell them he was too old and didn't need them. He said it was time to die. He told them they could leave him now.

After he had been in the bush twenty days he almost forgot about his people. Then he heard a song. It was coming from his people. He remembered them and he went toward the song. Every time he got to where the song had been it moved farther away. Finally, by following that song he was led back to his people.

After Japasa had told the story of his medicines the normal life of a hunting camp resumed. Men continued their hunting. They were very successful. Women were busy making drymeat and scraping hides. The old man stayed near his fire. From time to time we could hear the sound of his voice rising and falling in song like a distant wind. He had no more attacks. On the seventh day after giving away his medicines he remained well throughout the day. In the evening I returned to camp with some older men and boys after riding all day out to where a large moose had been killed. It took four pack horses to bring back the meat. The hunter's wife received it and then distributed meat to the other women of our camp.

Suddenly, it felt as if a wind were sweeping across the camp. It was a wind of alarm, of emotion, of change. I saw people flying toward Japasa's camp as if they were leaves in a wind. Their words were snatched away like cries in a storm. My fatigue and saddle sores from the day's ride vanished as I joined the flow of people. For the first time in my life I heard the rattle of death wrack a human body. People rubbed the old man as they had done before, but it was clear his breath would not return this time. A stillness came over us, then a gentle rain of tears. The tent was rolled back to make a kind of backdrop. The body was turned around to lie open to the sky. A friend and I dressed the old man's body in good clothes he had brought to be buried in. On his feet we placed a new pair of beaded moccasins, made for him by a young woman who had died the year before. The moccasins may have helped him follow her song on what I learned later was called "the trail to heaven." Wearing these new moccasins, the boy who knew foxes would be able to follow a trail of song to another camp.

After Japasa's death the tests seemed less important to me. I cared less about data relevant to the language of personality theory and more about data relevant to understanding the stories the old man had made known to me seven days before I heard his death rattle. In the years that have passed since I heard Japasa give away his songs, I have never again been close enough to death to hear a person sing the songs of his or her medicine. I have, however, listened to a wealth of Indian stories. I have studied them, dreamed them, told them, taught them, and made them my own.

The stories are windows into the thoughtworld of Indian people. Their time is different from ours. The old man and the boy circle around to touch one another, just as the hunter circles around to touch his game and the sun circles around to touch a different place on the horizon with every passing day. During the year it circles from northern to southern points of rising and setting. It circles like the grouse in their mating dance. It circles like the swans who fly south to a land of flowing water when winter takes the northern forest in its teeth of ice. The sun circles like the mind of a Dreamer whose body lies pressed to earth, head to the east, in anticipation of its return. The sun and the Dreamer's mind shine on one another.

On the evening when Japasa gave up his medicines, he gave me two stories as well. One was about how Indian people from far and wide used to gather in the prairie country near the Peace River to dry saskatoon berries. They came down the rivers in canoes full of drymeat, bear tallow, and berries. They sang and danced and played the hand game, in which teams of men bet against one another in guessing which hand conceals a small stone or bone. The other story was about frogs who play-gamble, just like people. He said he knew frogs because he once lived with them on the bottom of a lake.

The old man's stories recalled times that we would think of as being very different from one another. One we would call history – the other, myth. Written documents going back as far as the late eighteenth century describe Indians coming together to sing, dance, and gamble in the Peace River prairie country. We can use the traditions of historical scholarship to substantiate that what Japasa described really happened. There is no documentary or scientific evidence to indicate that frogs really sing and dance and gamble beneath the waters of a pond, but the old man said he experienced this, too. Because we lack documentary evidence, we are compelled to class his second story as myth. In our thoughtworld, myth and reality are opposites. Unless we can find some way to understand the reality of mythic thinking, we will remain prisoners of our own language, our own thoughtworld. In this world one story is real, the other, fantasy. In the Indian way of thinking both stories are true because they describe personal experience. Their truths are complementary.

Both of Japasa's stories were true to his experience. When he was a boy, Japasa knew frogs and foxes and wind. He knew their songs. He entered the myths that are told about them. He obtained power by joining his own life force to theirs. He knew them in the bush away from the society of other humans. He knew them in the searing transformation of his vision quest. He became their child, one of their kind. He saw them clothed in a culture like his own. He carried them through to the end of his life, and then he let them go.

Japasa also knew the social power created by his people when they came together in good times. At the time of his death both forms of power were strong all around him. Hunters were making contact with their game. Women passed the meat from camp to camp, making the people strong together. On the morning after he told us the stories of his medicines we saw a moose cross the seismic line within sight of camp. People said the animals were coming around the old man to say goodbye to him. They said they knew from the tracks that foxes came to his camp in the night. For seven days after Japasa let go of his powers the people were all around him. He became like the child he was before his vision quest. He was within the strength of his people when he left on the trail of a different song.

Historical events happen once and are gone forever. Mythic events return like the swans of spring. The events of history are unique and particular to their time and place. Mythic events are different. They are essential truths, not contingent ones. Japasa could be a frog or a fox and still be a person. He could know them as he knows himself. The foxes that came to Japasa before he died were the same as the foxes he knew as a boy. The wind came to him as a person, the foxes wore clothes and spoke in a language he could understand, the frogs gathered to drum and gamble. They gave this boy their songs as guides to the powers he would have as a man. Throughout his life he returned in his dreams to that visionary time-out-of-time. His powers were forces within him as well as forces of nature. The animal friends he encountered on his vision quest gave him the freedom to make intelligent decisions in the face of adversity. They gave his decisions an authority that others respected. As Johnny told me, Japasa could call the wind. His experience was always within nature, never in domination of it. Even in times of hardship he did not move against it. At the end of his life people and animals came together around him. When he died he returned to the mythic time, like the swans who fly south in the fall.

For northern hunting people, the possession of knowledge is more important than the possession of an artifact. Their technology depends on artifice rather than on artifact. They live by knowing how to integrate their own activities with those of the sentient beings around them. The most effective technology for nomadic people is one that can be carried around in their minds. Hunting people are able to create a way of life by applying knowledge to local resources. Their dreaming provides access to a wealth of information. It sets them free to make intelligent and responsible decisions. Their vision quests and their myths integrate the qualities of autonomy and community that are necessary for successful adaptation to the northern forest environment. The truths of the hunting way of life are essential, and unchanging from generation to generation. In spirit, they may very well reflect traditions of the distant ancestors we share with hunting peoples like the Dunne-za.

The mythic thinking of northern Native people combines the individual intelligence we all have as members of a common species with a cultural intelligence embedded in the wealth of knowledge they carry around in their minds. The exercise of individual intelligence defines the freedom of these people. The intelligence of their culture gives their choices meaning. Their stories tell them how to make sense of themselves in relation to a natural world of sentient beings. Their dreams and visions give direct access to this wealth of information. Individual intelligence and the intelligence of cultural tradition work together. Both are dedicated to making sense of human life in relation to the life of nature. These hunters act on the basis of knowledge and understanding, rather than on orders passed down through a social hierarchy.

European traditions strongly stress obedience to duly constituted authority. This authority is frequently intellectual, as well as social and political. We are more often taught answers than how to solve questions that come to mind. We are literal-minded in interpreting the meaning of experience in a hunting culture. We misunderstand myth by interpreting it as flawed history. For Aboriginal hunters, it is appropriate to place human life within nature. For people from a Judeo-Christian tradition, it is more common to place humans in a position of dominance over nature. For hunters, dreams and visions validate and explain the past in terms of present experience. For people from a literate tradition, written documents carry more authority than personal experience.

When anthropologists attempt to write the history of hunting people, we must find ways of recognizing the validity of personal experience without violating our own scholarly traditions of obtaining valid information about the past. We must be wary of dreaming up other cultures, but anthropologists can, perhaps, dream into the rich store of information that hunters have given us about themselves. The true history of these people will have to be written in a mythic language. Like the stories of Japasa, it will have to combine stories of people coming together with other people and those that tell of people coming together with animals.

When I heard old man Japasa speak in 1964 about his medicine animals, I knew with absolute certainty this man was neither lying nor deluding himself. It was I who indulged in self-delusion when I persisted in asking for data in a form that could not accommodate Beaver Indian reality. In his last days on earth, the old man gave me his vision of that reality. I hope that the trust he placed in me has been justified in some small measure by the work I have chosen to do in my life.

Discovering Freedom and Authority: The Teachings of the Hunters

The intelligence of northern hunting people continues to be based on information and action relevant to the possible relationships between people and environment, even when that environment now includes governments and multinational corporations, all-terrain vehicles and VCRs. The conversations of Subarctic hunting people continue to honour individual intelligence rather than that of the state. A person is still expected to "know something" through the authority of experience. He or she is also expected to exercise that knowledge in a socially responsible manner. Because hunting people exercise their individualism within a community of human and non-human relations, they do not suffer from the isolation and struggle of a "rugged" individualism like that described in its most extreme form by Ayn Rand.

In the 1970s one of the Dunne-za bands experienced a direct confrontation with an alien form of intelligence when an oil company drilled a sour gas well less than a mile from the village. Everyone experienced headaches, nausea, and irritability from its emissions of hydrogen sulfide gas. They tried to get "the authorities" to validate that experience with scientific tests, but experienced the nightmare of being shunted from one agency to another and being told that the white man's instruments could not document the harm they were experiencing beyond the reasonable doubt required in a court of law. Then in 1979, the well blew up and spewed a cloud of poison gas directly over the village. Fortunately, it happened early on a summer evening rather than in the dead of a winter night. They were able to evacuate safely. They then obtained an injunction that shut down the well, but the company applied to have it lifted.

Lawyers for the company argued that following the blowout the well was even less dangerous than it had been before. Lawyers for the Indians argued that their clients simply wanted time to move the entire village to a safer location, just as they would have done in response to a natural disaster in earlier times. The injunction hearing presented a classic confrontation between individual intelligence based on personal experience and the essentially non-human and amoral logic of a cultural intelligence removed from the human context.

Being witness to this confrontation between the intelligence of people from a northern hunting tradition and people whose lives are increasingly determined by the intelligence of essentially non-human cultural institutions has led me to think about our own freedom and authority in relation to theirs. For many thousands of years, human culture has been on a scale relevant to the values and perceptions of individual human beings. For the most part, the cultures of hunting and gathering people have informed them and furthered their understanding of the environmental conditions to which they have been closely adapted. Hunting and gathering cultures have particularly valued personal autonomy and the authority of individual experience. Traditional knowledge has generally furthered the human capacity for intelligent observation.

Human culture may be seen as a system of information or intelligence. This intelligence has informed the intelligence of individual human beings for millennia. With the rise of more complex social systems and particularly of those social systems dependent on an industrial adaptation to the resource potential of the planet, cultural intelligence has often come to work against the intelligence of individuals. Although the work of specialists is essential for developing the specialized knowledge on which such an adaptive system is dependent, it very often relates more to the requirements of the system itself than to the basic needs of individual human beings. Indeed, the high technology of our cultural intelligence has resulted in an obviously unintelligent capacity to destroy the entire species.

The simple desire of a band of former nomadic hunters to remove themselves from a source of poison gas they have experienced as hazardous brings into focus the more general hazard we all face, as we struggle to continue our lives as individuals and as a species in the face of an inhuman intelligence that has taken on a life of its own. The Dunne-za still think in terms of moving to a safer location, despite the limits imposed by industrial development of their former hunting and trapping lands, but those of us who were not raised in a hunting and gathering tradition realize that the group to which we belong is the entire species. The move we must make is not physical but evolutionary. Unless we are able to bring our culture's intelligence back to its traditional role of informing individual intelligence, all forms of intelligence may vanish from this world, as if they had never been. My contact with the world of the hunters has led me to consider fundamental questions about how we can use our intelligence to create a culture that is an adaptive tool rather than a threat to our survival. This is a critical task since what we do culturally could very well result in physical extinction. Northern hunting people view individual knowledge based on personal experience as empowering. Despite our vast cultural knowledge, we seem powerless to halt the degradation of our physical and social environment.

Northern hunting people learn to follow their own experience or that of knowledgeable leaders rather than written authorities or socially sanctioned bosses. They are profoundly egalitarian while being deeply committed to a communal responsibility that extends beyond relations between humans to that of the non-human persons who make up the natural environment. About a month ago, my wife Jillian and I were visiting our friends in "Beaverland," as we call it. At one point, Chief Gerry Attachie of the Doig River band gave me a piece of advice. He said, "Our old people tell us that whenever you take something from the earth, even a little root for medicine, put something back. That's because everything is alive." I nodded. "If you don't do that, you will grow old too quickly, even lose your mind." I thought about an entire generation, taking things from the earth and not giving anything in return. I thought about our way of life growing old too quickly. I thought about our culture losing its mind. "When I was a kid," Gerry said, "we used to make a joke about it. We'd say, 'We pay you back.'" He laughed, but I knew he was serious. This was a word of advice I should not ignore. What he said makes sense to me. What we take from the earth we must pay back. We must respect the planet's intelligence as we respect our own.

As an anthropologist, I owe an intellectual debt to my parents and to the Dunne-za. Both have profoundly shaped my understanding of anthropology. I hope that in the work I do I am paying them back for the education they both gave me so freely.

Note

1. In 1991 Western Maryland College asked me to deliver the first in a series of lectures that my parents, William and Edith Ridington, had endowed. I presented some of the material from this chapter in that lecture..

Recommended Readings

Faraud, Henri

    1866 *Dix-huit Ans Chez les Sauvages: Voyages et Missions de Mgr. Henry Faraud.* New York: Johnson Reprint.

        Father Faraud was one of the first people to write about Dunne-za culture. His objective was to convert them and persuade them to give up their Aboriginal religion. He wrote this account in part to obtain support for further mission work.

Goddard, Pliny Earle

    1917 "The Beaver Indians; Beaver Texts; Beaver Dialect," *Anthropological Papers of the American Museum of Natural History*, 10 (4-65): 201-546

        Goddard was a linguist specializing in Athapaskan languages. He collected considerable information on language during a short field trip to Dunvegan, Alberta. For many years his work was the only published source on the Dunne-za (Beaver Indians).

Ives, John W.

    1990 *A Theory of Northern Athapaskan Prehistory.* Calgary: University of Calgary Press.

        Using ethnographic information from Asch and Ridington, Ives compares kinship and social organization of Slavey and Dunne-za bands. The book provides a scholarly reader with models of how social organization is generated through kinship and marriage customs. While written for a largely anthropological audience, it might be of interest to the serious layperson as well.

Jenness, Diamond

    1937 *The Sekani Indians of British Columbia.* National Museum of Canada Bulletin 84. Anthropological Series No. 20. Ottawa.

        This is a classic study of the Rocky Mountain trench Sekani, close relatives of the Dunne-za, particularly those of the Halfway River band. Jenness provides information on social organization and religion as well as historic photographs and biographical sketches.

Moore, Patrick, and Angela Wheelock

    1990 *Wolverine Myths and Visions: Dene Traditions from Northern Alberta.* Edmonton: University of Alberta Press.

The Dene Tha are close relatives of the Dunne-za living in northwestern Alberta. This book presents wolverine and prophet stories in the original language, with excellent translations and an informative narrative describing the cultural context of the stories.

O'Neil, Marion

1928 "The Peace River Journal, 1799-1800," *Washington Historical Quarterly*, 19, 4: 250-70.

This journal is the first written account of Beaver Indians in the area of what is now Fort St. John. Although largely concerned with the fur trade, it does give information about a trading chief who may be the Dreamer, Makenunatane. See Ridington's use of this material in his 1988 and 1990 books.

Ridington, Robin

1978 *Swan People: A Study of the Dunne-za Prophet Dance*. National Museum of Man Mercury Series, Canadian Ethnology Service Paper Number 38. Ottawa: National Museums of Man.

This is a collection of stories relevant to the Dunne-za prophet tradition. It is probably available in most Canadian university libraries.

1981 "Beaver," in *Handbook of North American Indians*, Vol. 6, *Subarctic*, ed. June Helm. Washington, D.C.: Smithsonian Institution.

The *Handbook* is an authoritative reference source on the ethnology, ethnohistory, and archaeology of Subarctic First Nations.

1988 *Trail to Heaven: Knowledge and Narrative in a Northern Native Community*. Vancouver: Douglas & McIntyre.

This is a narrative ethnography describing the author's first and continuing experience with the Dunne-za.

1990 *Little Bit Know Something: Stories in a Language of Anthropology*. Vancouver: Douglas & McIntyre.

A companion to *Trail to Heaven*, this is a collection of articles about the Dunne-za Ridington published in anthropological journals.

Ridington, Robin, Howard Broomfield, and Myrna Cobb

1984 *In Doig People's Ears: Portrait of a Changing Native Community* (30 minute video documentary).

Additional References Cited

The Canadian Encyclopedia

1985 Edmonton: Hurtig.

Damas, David

1969 "Contributions to Anthropology: Band Societies," *Proceedings of the Conference on Band Organization*. Ottawa: Anthropological Series 84. National Museum of Canada Bulletin 228.

Fustel de Coulanges

1956   *The Ancient City*. Garden City, N.Y.: Doubleday (first published 1864).

Lewis, Henry T.

1982   *A Time for Burning*. Edmonton: Boreal Institute for Northern Studies Occasional Publication No. 17.

Maine, Sir Henry

1861   *Ancient Law*. London: J. Murray.

Morgan, Lewis Henry

1851   *The League of the Ho-de-no-sau-nee*. New York: Dodd Mead (reprinted 1904).

Ridington, Robin

1982   "Technology, World View and Adaptive Strategy in a Northern Hunting Society," *Canadian Review of Sociology and Anthropology*, 19, 4: 469-81. [Reprinted in Ridington, 1990.]

1987   "From Hunt Chief to Prophet: Beaver Indian Dreamers and Christianity," *Arctic Anthropology*, 24, 1: 8-18. [Reprinted in Ridington, 1990.]

1988   "Knowledge, Power and the Individual in Subarctic Hunting Societies," *American Anthropologist*, 90, 1: 98-110. [Reprinted in Ridington, 1990.]

1989   "Cultures in Conflict: The Problem of Discourse," *Canadian Literature*. [Reprinted in Ridington, 1990.]

Tylor, E.B.

1871   *Primitive Culture*. New York: Harper Torchbooks, 1958.

CHAPTER 11

The Slavey Indians: The Relevance of Ethnohistory to Development

Michael Asch

The Dene and the Pipeline:
Economic Development in the Canadian North

One important strain in anthropological thought is the notion that disciplinary expertise can be lent to the solution of problems in the "real world." As an undergraduate at the University of Chicago, I became acquainted with this perspective through a course I took with Dr. Sol Tax, widely known as a proponent of "action anthropology." This greatly influenced my decision to become an anthropologist. Yet, it was not until the mid-1970s that I was able to make a contribution to this aspect of the discipline.

The circumstances of my involvement were as follows. In the early 1970s, a consortium of multinational petroleum corporations decided to construct a pipeline to transport Alaskan and Canadian Arctic gas to markets in southern Canada and the United States. Named the Canadian Arctic Gas Pipeline Ltd. (CAGPL), the consortium proposed to construct an $8 billion line along the northern coast of North America and up the Mackenzie River Valley to northern Alberta. The region through which the pipeline was to pass included the homeland of two Aboriginal nations:

the Dene (Athapaskan-speaking Indians of the Mackenzie corridor) and the Inuvialuit (the most westerly Inuit of Canada). The government of Canada set up a commission of inquiry to ascertain the potential social and economic impact of this pipeline. Under Mr. Justice Thomas R. Berger this commission, called the Mackenzie Valley Pipeline Inquiry, spent more than two years listening to testimony from experts and community people. It concluded that the proposal should be shelved for ten years, and, in some respects at least, this recommendation was followed.

I became involved in the Berger Inquiry because I had done research among the Slavey regional grouping of the Dene in 1969-70. I had collected much information of the contemporary economy of the Slavey at Fort Wrigley ("pitzekin," or "Fort on the big rock" in Slavey) and Fort Simpson during my fieldwork and on their economic history. Yet the focus of my initial fieldwork had not been economic matters, but social organization and music.

My orientation to music and social structure was based on a complex set of factors, a part of which was my belief that understanding how other societies frame their world cognitively is crucial to the anthropological enterprise. I therefore chose in my doctoral research to focus on understanding how the Slavey conceptualized music sound and how they created structured musical compositions. This work resulted in the development of a model that described their music sound system and predicted, with some degree of accuracy, how compositions were structured (Asch, 1972, 1975). Yet I remained uncertain whether the model really mirrored Slavey perceptions or whether it was merely a creation that helped me to understand them. I felt I then had two choices: to try to solve this dilemma or to turn to a different sphere of Slavey life. I took the latter course. In focusing on economic activities I chose an aspect of Slavey life I believed I could understand in a manner similar to the Dene themselves. This was because the things of the economy as they see them are quite similar to the things I can see and, perhaps more importantly, because Dene talk much more about economic matters than they ever do about music.

For all that, I have not abandoned an interest in Dene cognition. In retrospect I see that my concerns ran deeper than just which focus to choose in analysis. The kind of cognitive mind-set I find myself interested in is not easily expressed by any group and requires a high degree of "native intuition." For this reason (I believe), I shifted my focus away from ferreting out the underlying cognitive framework (in the economic or any other sphere) of the Dene to working it out for our own society. Ultimately I have found that, for me, it is easier to use my intuition to grapple with the way in which we think than it is to figure out the "deep structure" of people from other cultures. It is not due to a belief that different ways of thinking do not exist or, as Rushforth (1986) attests, cannot be understood or discussed by non-Natives. Rather, it is that I do not seem to have a strong talent in that direction.

The Berger Inquiry dealt with the social and economic consequences of a major construction project on contemporary Native people. Crucial to this kind of evaluation is the status of the Aboriginal society: is it "dead" or "dying," or does it remain "viable"? At the heart of this matter lies our perception of hunting-gathering society. Dominant in academic thought today is an evolutionary view that sees such societies as of intellectual interest primarily because of the data they provide on the "past" of human history. Hunter-gatherers are in this view our "contemporary ancestors." Part of the intellectual baggage pertaining to this idea is the belief that such societies today are mere vestiges of their former statuses and, like vestigial organs, are about to self-destruct. Evidence for this conclusion appears to abound in transparently obvious symbols of precipitous assimilation. After all, the Dene now wear Western clothing, speak English, go to school, ride on snowmobiles and in cars, listen to country music, and complain about lack of disposable income. One could easily presume that fundamentally these are just poor people who happen to be Dene and not members of an autonomous culture.

The proponents of the pipeline firmly supported this view. On the basis of studies into the contemporary economy of the Dene and Inuit and by reference to some of the ethnographic literature, expert witnesses (including economists and sociologists) who appeared on behalf of the applicants argued that the traditional way of life was "dead" or "dying." As a consequence, they argued that in the near future the Dene would slip from high unemployment to endemic poverty. Seen in this context the pipeline was a good thing, for it would provide jobs enabling the Dene to make a "smooth" transition from a traditional existence to a middle-class way of life.

Because of my work at Fort Wrigley, I was asked by the Indian Brotherhood of the Northwest Territories (now renamed the Dene Nation) to provide evidence for the Berger Inquiry. However, it was not supposed to be about evaluating this way of thinking. Rather, it was to focus on ethnographic and historical evidence on land use and the fur trade. Indeed, my evidence was titled "Past and Present Land Use of the Slavey Indians." Yet, although the title never changed, the content did, for I found myself confronting an idea for which evidence was lacking.

Upon reading the data provided by the applicants' witnesses, I became convinced that something was fundamentally wrong with their work, for it did not jibe with my own recollections of the time I spent at Fort Wrigley. These people were being miscast as impoverished, marginalized Canadians, for, to paraphrase what Dr. Peter Usher stated about the Inuit, if these are poor people, they are the only ones who go to bed with stomachs filled with good meat provided from their own larders. It was a view that was further confirmed by the Dene themselves, for they argued almost unanimously in opposition to the immediate construction of the pipeline. Their reason? It would interfere with their traditional land-based activities. In short, the Dene were presenting the view that their traditional way of life (as currently practised) could remain viable in the modern world. The problem, as they saw it, was that the means to ensure this end were not in their hands. As a solution they proposed the creation of an autonomous polity (consistent with a statement of principles summarized in the Dene Declaration) and economic tools for protection and development of their economy (based in large part on the fulfilment of government promises respecting the finalizing of an outstanding land claim that arose from disagreements concerning the terms of a treaty signed in 1921-22).

If one agreed that their way of life was dead or dying, the point of view presented by the Dene could make no sense, and, indeed, the applicants characterized their assertions as "romantic" and "politically motivated." If, on the other hand, their assessment of their economy was taken to be valid, then their orientation could be understood as based on a realistic appraisal of the situation.

My testimony focused on determining which perspective was more appropriate and, although facts concerning these matters were used, did not present a story concerned with land use or economic history. In this respect, it represented my first attempt to grapple with how members of our society frame facts about Aboriginal peoples, for although one might argue that the assertions made by the applicants were merely "politically motivated," they appropriated a way of looking at Aboriginal peoples that dominates contemporary Western thought (including theorizing in anthropology). My work indicated that there was little factual basis for the assumptions made about the Dene as contemporary hunter-gatherers and sought to piece together an analysis that made better sense of the facts of cultural contact. It is a matter I have developed more fully elsewhere (Asch, 1979a, 1979b, 1982). However, it was also intended as a contribution to the process of the Berger Inquiry itself: independent factual evidence demonstrating that the contemporary way of life was not dying would help in understanding why the Dene did not want the pipeline built immediately and why they argued that, prior to its construction, a regime protective of their traditional way of life and controlled by them should be in place.

What follows is an edited and augmented version of my testimony at the Berger Inquiry, divided into three primary parts. The first focuses on economic history, establishing a theme about the course of development in the region. The second deals with the contemporary situation. This is followed by a final section evaluating solutions proposed by CAGPL studies in light of this evidence.

Although the analysis was confined to the region of the Slavey, broadly speaking the findings are relevant to the Dene as a whole.

Economic History – Aboriginal Period

At first glance it may seem inappropriate to consider that the Dene had an economy at all during Aboriginal times; there was, after all, no "marketplace." However, if we define the term "economy" in its most basic sense, as the production and circulation of goods, then it is clear that every society that survives in a material way from year to year must have an economy.

In the late pre-contact period the economy of the region was characterized by the dominance of small self-sufficient groups of approximately twenty to thirty related persons called by anthropologists "local groups." In order to maintain themselves, these groups relied on the harvesting of the many kinds of bush resources found in the region, including a wide variety of fish, small game animals, big game such as moose and woodland caribou, and a number of edible berries. As well, they relied on other products such as trees, which were important in constructing shelter, in transportation, and as fuel.

Given the nature of the terrain and the distribution of resources in the region, it is most likely that the local groups camped in winter near the shores of the larger lakes that dominate the region. Here, the small game and fish, the staples of the diet, could be found in most constant supply. Within these encampments, labour was organized along age and sex lines: men were primarily responsible for hunting big game and setting fish nets, and the women and children were responsible for the collection of small game. Women were also responsible for making clothing from local resources such as moose hide and rabbit skins.

PLATE 11.1. Slavey shaman (right), son (left), and Dogrib boy (centre), Fort Rae, N.W.T., 1913. Courtesy of the Canadian Museum of Civilization, 26079.

The primary techniques used in collecting animal resources were snaring with babiche or sinew, and entrapment. Moose and other big-game animals were hunted with bow and arrow, club, or spear when the prey were crossing water or open country. Fish were taken using fish nets made of woven willow bast or caribou babiche. Given this type of technology, large-game capture most often required co-operative labour in hunting parties. Co-operation was also important for women's production tasks.

Transportation in the winter at this time relied primarily on human labour and was accomplished almost exclusively on foot. Yet, paradoxical as this may seem, the use of this form of transportation resulted in more group travel than in the later period when dog power was used. The reason for this is simple: without dog teams it would be easier to bring people to the game than the other way around. Hence, in winter the people moved around more than in later periods and, in fact, may have travelled throughout the region in search of game, returning only occasionally to the fish-lake base camp. In summer the people travelled primarily by shallow-drafted canoes, sometimes made of moose hide. Travel included an annual trip to one of the major lakes where an encampment of perhaps 200 persons would be formed, probably around the times of the fish runs. Before winter the people would return to their small local groups.

Within local groups, bush resources were distributed on the basis of reciprocity or mutual sharing. Generally speaking, all participated equally in the good fortune of the hunters and all suffered equally when their luck turned bad. Although the distribution system was basically informal, there was some formality concerning the ways in which certain animals were shared in that specific parts were reserved for the hunter and persons closely related to his or her immediate family. In this way, individual ability could be recognized, but not at the expense of the collective good. Thus, it was the whole membership of the local group and not each family or each individual that defined the self-sufficient unit.

There is little evidence available from historical or archaeological sources concerning the circulation of goods between local groups during this period. However, an examination of the productive base of the land indicates that the region is not highly varied as to kinds of resources but is somewhat variable from year to year as to the actual distribution of these resources. Hence, the primary problem of circulation probably concerned the creation of a balance in any one year between local groups with resources surplus to their needs and those that did not have the minimum resources necessary for survival.

Theoretically, there are two ways in which this imbalance could be corrected: either surplus goods could be moved to people in need or people could move to areas in which a local surplus existed. Given the nature of the technology as well as the kinship system as reported by early travellers, it would appear that the latter solution was the case. Thus, the principle of mutual sharing of resources extended to include all groups in the region. This was done through a kinship and marriage system that linked all the people in a region into a single social unit and conveyed reciprocal rights and obligations concerning the use of resources in the region to all.

In terms of inter-regional or inter-tribal exchange, the little archaeological and historical evidence available indicates that trade between groups did occur: copper as well as implements of European manufacture are found in the region prior to the arrival of the European traders. However, nothing of the mechanisms of this trade is known.

Economic History – Fur Trade Period

Direct involvement with the fur trade began in the last decade of the eighteenth century. Although contact was established as the result of the competition between the Hudson's Bay Company and the North West Company for hegemony in Western trade, virtually none of the intense rivalry between the two trading companies was transferred to the region.

PLATE 11.2. Slavey Indian camp at Fort Simpson, N.W.T., 1934. Courtesy of the Canadian Museum of Civilization, 80042.

Here the North West Company maintained hegemony in the fur trade until 1821 when, with the amalgamation of the two companies, the new Hudson's Bay Company came into ascendancy. As a result, none of the disruptions in Native life that marked the period of competition in other parts of Canada appeared in the North, and, indeed, from the time of contact until roughly 1870 when the Bay lost its monopoly, the fur trade was marked by stability.

During the period of monopoly, the region was considered too remote to command much attention. Bay policy required that remote posts such as these remained self-sufficient in food provisions. Further, because of the depletion of furs by intense earlier competition, the Bay developed a conservation policy. At least from 1821 until 1850 it reduced trading in furs at all posts in North America, including those in this region. As well, supply lines at this time were maintained through the use of York boats and brigading from Winnipeg to the West, imposing severe restrictions on the amount of goods and furs that could be transported to and from the North.

Given such transportation and trading restrictions, goods available for trade at remote posts were limited in both kind and quantity. Of the goods available, the most important for the Indians probably were the new staples such as flour, tea, and sugar; metal utensils and implements; beads; blankets; tobacco and alcohol. In order to obtain these goods the Indians had to trade local resources. It would thus appear that production for the fur trade was not great and consisted mainly of supplying provisions rather than furs.

The economy of the Native people changed little during this period from its Aboriginal strategy. It was still "total" in that the people of the region, including Natives and Bay personnel, depended for their survival almost exclusively on local resources. This was achieved by Bay personnel through the exchange of trade goods for food and by the Natives through the continued use of a wide range of bush resources and the organization of the people into self-sufficient local groups. For the Native people, production, despite the new utensils and implements, was still primarily a collective activity: distribution of goods within and between local groups was still based on the principle of sharing. The only significant changes in Native economic life during this time were the adoption of certain trade-good items that made life a little easier and a shift in seasonal round to include both occasional trips to the trading posts for supplies at various times in the year and, especially later in the period, the occasional use of the trading posts rather than the major lakes as places for encampment during the summer.

With the sale of its territories in 1870, the Hudson's Bay Company lost its formal monopoly and with it an assured supply of furs at prices well below world market levels. In some areas of the Mackenzie region, such as Fort Wrigley and Fort Norman, monopoly conditions continued to obtain until as late as perhaps 1900. In other parts of the region, such as Fort Simpson and upstream, the effect of free traders further south was soon felt. Thus, William Hardisty, chief factor at Fort Simpson, as early as 1875 suggested that, while the Indians at Fort Norman "being in the centre of the District and far removed from the opposition . . . are still amenable to authority and generally work," the Natives in the Fort Simpson area ". . . would not deliver up their furs at the old prices. . . ." One reason was "the advent of free traders at Vermilion (in Alberta) and the exaggerated reports regarding them which have been carried all over the District."

To meet this new competition, the Bay needed to provide more trade goods and to provide them more cheaply. The major stumbling block was the continued use of a transportation system that was costly, inefficient, and taxed to capacity. To solve this problem (and perhaps spurred on by the development of an independent steam-transport system by the Roman Catholic missionaries), the Bay replaced the York boats with steam, first on the Athabasca in 1882 and then on the Mackenzie in 1885, and finally moved the major transshipment point to the North from Winnipeg to Edmonton after the completion of the rail link from Calgary to Edmonton in 1891. Between 1870 and 1890 transportation to the North was thus revolutionized.

Concomitantly, the Bay changed its strategy from one of monopoly in the collection of furs to the encouragement of competition. Their control now was seen to be in terms of virtual monopoly in transportation and retail sales, where it was felt that they could maintain a high level of profit.

Competition and the new transportation system, as well as the Yukon gold rush of 1898 and the rise in fur prices during World War One, resulted in the complete transformation of the fur trade. The kinds of goods available changed greatly. Among the new items introduced by the turn of the century were the repeating rifle, the steel trap, wide varieties of Western clothing, dogs and dog teams, and chocolates and other luxury items. As well, the quantities of traditional exchange items such as food staples, blankets, and metal utensils increased dramatically.

The new transportation system also meant that traders no longer depended on local resources for provisions. This new-found independence affected exchange relationships between traders and Indians. Natives still traded local resources, but whereas in the earlier period either provisions or furs could be used in exchange, now the Bay and the free traders alike manipulated exchange rates to encourage trade in furs. As early as 1871 the Bay limited the trade in percussion rifles to fur exchange, while allowing food and furs to be traded for common Indian guns. Late in the nineteenth century the Bay changed its standard of trade by doubling the exchange value of furs compared to provisions. The changing economic relationship was capped during the 1890s with the adoption of money as the medium of exchange and the concurrent demise of the old barter system.

As a result of these externally initiated developments in the fur trade, the Native economy in some areas had shifted by 1900 (and throughout the region by World War One) away from its virtual independence of trade goods to a situation where both trade goods and local subsistence resources were significant. Yet the internal organization of the economy did not change greatly. The primary economic unit remained the local group, which in most cases still wintered at fish lakes. Labour was still organized on the basis of age and sex; women and children were responsible for collecting small game, the men, for hunting, fishing, and now trapping.

Some changes in production resulted from the introduction of the rifle and the steel trap. Of these, perhaps the most significant was the new-found ability of individuals to maintain greater independence of others in their hunting and trapping pursuits. Yet, Aboriginal hunting techniques were still employed in collecting most game, including big-game animals, and co-operation therefore remained a significant component of production. As well, some changes occurred in the mobility of the people. The advent of the trapline, the year-round availability of provisions at trading posts, and the introduction of dog-team transport encouraged sedentism to the extent that during the early twentieth century many families built permanent dwellings at fish lakes and along traplines. To obtain supplies and trade furs, the men now made at least two trips to the trading posts during the winter, generally at Christmas and Easter. The women and children most often did not accompany the men to the posts but remained, as before, in the bush throughout the winter months. Summer travel was expanded by the introduction of motors on canoes and scows. The seasonal round now almost always included summer encampments at the trading posts.

Finally, the system of circulating goods among the people of the region remained virtually unchanged by the new fur trade conditions. Despite the increased individualization in production and the introduction of money into the economy, distribution both within and between local groups remained based on the principle of mutual sharing. Thus the main change in the distribution system of the region was the great increase in the amount of trade between the Native people and the traders.

Economic History – Recent Decades

The regional economy had been transformed by the new fur trade conditions from a "total economy" to one that relied both on local subsistence and on the use of externally produced goods that were exchanged for furs. However, this shift created no major changes in the internal dynamics of production and circulation within the Native economy. Nonetheless, as a result of this shift the standard of living was greatly raised. This must have made people feel quite wealthy. This rise in the standard of living, however, had an unexpected consequence: dependency. Now the stability and success of the economy were dependent in large measure both on external economic conditions, such as a high market price for furs in relation to trade good prices, and locally on the availability of a productive surplus in one resource, furs. The latter problem was chronic, and after the influx of whites into the North during the 1920s, it almost led to the collapse of the economy. On the other hand, the first aspect appeared at the time to be insignificant, for the relationship between fur prices and trade good prices remained stable through two world wars and the Great Depression. Yet, ultimately, it was this factor and not fur production itself that led to the collapse of the fur trade economy when, beginning after World War Two and lasting at least through the Korean War, there was a long depression in the value of furs and an astronomical rise in the prices of trade goods.

In the years immediately following World War Two, Native peoples hoped that fur prices would soon rise again. In the meantime, most people, supported in part by the general introduction of family allowance and old age pension payments during the late 1940s, maintained their fur trade economy focus. By the 1950s it became apparent that the fur economy would never return, at least not without direct government intervention. Thus, for example, the Territorial Council in January, 1956, unanimously passed a resolution that stated, in part:

> Whereas the real income derived from fur trapping in the Northwest Territories is less than one third of its pre-war level . . . and whereas it is not possible for a person to live and to provide the minimum needs of his family at the present prices of fur . . . (be it resolved that) the Commissioner be requested to ask the Minister of Northern Affairs and National Resources to request the Government of Canada most strongly to give immediate consideration to the provision of assistance to the people of the Northwest Territories through the establishment of an appropriate measure of support for the price of fur; or, alternatively, to take all possible measures at the earliest date to stimulate the economic development of the Northwest Territories so that alternative means of employment and income can be provided for these people. (Council of the Northwest Territories, 1956)

The federal government also took a general position in favour of economic development. To this end, Jean Lesage, Minister of Northern Affairs and Natural Resources, in 1955 proclaimed a new education program for the Northwest Territories, recommending the construction of school facilities in smaller centres and a program of hostel construction in larger ones to facilitate universal education. This solution was approved of by at least some of the band chiefs, for it seemed a way for the youth to overcome the problems of the contemporary economic situation.

By the early 1960s, grade schools had been constructed in virtually all communities in the region, and in most cases people moved into town where they would continue to receive benefits and could remain with their children. For the others, it was pointed out that:

> Forgetful children should not forget that school is compulsory and that missing school for five consecutive or separate times is liable to punishment. Parents who fail to send their children to school without serious reason and notification to the teacher are liable to be fined and jailed. Moreover family allowance payments may be cancelled upon report made by the proper authorities. Mark well, children, that missing part of the day accounts for a day's absence, in so far as the punishments are concerned. Therefore, do your share for your sake and that of your family. (*The Catholic Voice*, 1957: 5)

Given the economic conditions, the threat of the loss of family allowances must have been quite an inducement to those unwilling to volunteer to send their children to school. Voluntarily or not, most people had moved into town within one year of the opening of a winter-term school.

The new circumstances had a profound effect on the internal organization of the regional economy. The movement of people away from residence at fish-lake encampments and the introduction of direct family allowance payments, old age pensions, and other cash benefits directly to nuclear family heads and individuals completely undermined the economic rationale of the local group. Beginning no later than 1960, the nuclear-extended family, typically composed of an older married couple and their unmarried adult and younger children, became the primary self-sufficient economic unit.

While the overall economy still relied on both bush resources and trade goods, with the demise of fur itself as the means for obtaining trade goods, the internal organization of the economy was forced to shift into two virtually independent spheres of production and distribution: one for bush subsistence, the other for trade good subsistence.

Production and distribution for bush subsistence were little changed. Men were still responsible for hunting big game, fishing, and trapping; women, for the collection of small game and berries. However, the move into town meant that the men, who for the most part still retained their fish-lake hunting and trapping areas, had to travel long distances to obtain bush resources. On the other hand, permanent and enlarged local populations meant the eventual depletion of small game in the vicinity of communities and thus, ultimately, the virtual abandonment of winter collection activities by women.

Aside from the fact that the primary mutually sharing group was no longer the local group, the ideology of distribution in the bush resource sector changed little. Reciprocity still obtained in bush resource circulation both within the nuclear family and, where surpluses were available, between families that had co-resided within a single local group. Indeed, bush resources at times were shared within the community as a whole despite official counter-pressures against the ideology of reciprocity – for example, through government supervision of the distribution of game kept in community freezers.

The cash-trade goods subsistence sector also experienced pressures. In the past, furs alone had an exchange value sufficient for the trade good needs. With the collapse of the fur trade, people needed to obtain cash in addition to income received from trapping. In most cases, families relied on direct cash payments from the government to make up the difference: family allowances, old age pensions, and, in a few cases, welfare. In some families, some or all of the cash needed to live was generated by part- or full-time wage labour.

The cash-trade goods sector, regarding distribution, developed an ideology incorporating both Euro-Canadian and traditional Native features. On the one hand, the "production," the cash itself, was not shared except to purchase those trade goods necessary to fill the subsistence needs of the nuclear family; any income generated by family members in excess of these needs was considered the private property of the income earner, to be used individually on personal consumer items such as portable radios, record players, musical instruments, and amplifiers; for personal travel; or in some cases, to be buried as a useless thing. In rare instances, surplus money was lent (at no interest) to close relatives. It was never shared. On the other hand, traditional trade goods, especially food items, although now purchased with money rather than furs, were treated like bush resources and formed a significant part of the reciprocity system of distribution.

Movement into town also had a profound effect on mobility and travel. During the fur trade period women and children had remained fixed at fish-lake encampments throughout the winter, travelling extensively in summer. Now, aside from brief trips in summer, the women remained rooted throughout the year at the townsites. Here they resided, initially in houses that had been intended only for summer use, and later, in some cases, in government-built dwellings. Further, the winter round for men had reversed itself in that, rather than venturing from the bush into town a few times during the season to obtain trade goods, they now travelled from town to the bush a few times a year to obtain bush supplies. Finally, the younger children remained in the local communities for the whole year, and as they grew older they went on to the major centres to continue their education: many never experienced living throughout the winter in the bush environment.

In sum, the collapse of the fur trade and the concomitant rise of governmental intervention in the economic and social life of the people did not produce a qualitative shift in the focus of the Native economy away from its reliance on both local subsistence and the use of trade goods, although in recent years the latter has become increasingly important. The past forty years have been a period of marked change in the internal organization of the economy: production and circulation in the spheres of bush subsistence and cash-trade good subsistence became virtually independent of each other, creating what is known as a dual economy. Government policies introduced during the past forty years have themselves created fundamental changes in those aspects of economic organization pertaining to the size and composition of the self-sufficient economic units, mobility and travel, and perhaps most importantly, contact with the bush on the part of the younger generation.

The contemporary Native economy has not solved the problem of dependency on external agencies. Indeed, the problem has deepened: direct government payments have replaced productive labour as the main resource for obtaining trade goods – payments that are seen by most people, Native and non-Native, as handouts to the poverty stricken. In short, post-contact economic history is dominated by a single theme: the acceptance by Native peoples of immediate well-being in exchange for long-term economic dependence.

Economic History – Social Correlates

Changes in residence patterns or exchange relationships do not exist by themselves. The ideology about residence group formation exemplifies this. Slavey kinship structure is organized in a manner that unites residence with kin relatedness. That is, the local group traditionally was formed around persons with strong and mutually reinforcing kin ties.

Typically, these kinsmen were perceived to be related to each other in a manner that would discourage intermarriage among members. Solidarity, a sense of community, was established through a notion that persons who lived together were like what we would describe to be a "family." Regional bands were seen as groups of "families" that intermarried frequently.

The Fort Wrigley residents in the contemporary period are composed of members of three such former "families," each of which traditionally resided in a separate locale during winter. Intermarriage frequently took place between these families, and they together formed the primary group within which the Fort Wrigley regional band married.

The move into town created a single residence unit of what formerly was a regional band. What was its status? Were the three former bands amalgamated because they now lived together? Or were they to be considered three distinct entities that just happened to be permanently ensconced in the same locale? If the latter, intermarriage could continue, but at cost, since solidarity is based primarily on co-residence with kin. Without such mechanisms it might be difficult to maintain the peace when, as is inevitable in any social situation, friction arose between groups not perceived to be connected together. If, however, the first option were chosen, solidarity could be maintained through the creation of a new family structure, but the result would be the undermining of any possibility for intermarriage (for they would now all be considered members of a single family). In short, this could result in the inability of the group to reproduce itself.

While there was no conscious decision on this subject, the Fort Wrigley Slavey generally opted for the first course, transforming their kinship relations in a manner that would promote the idea of Fort Wrigley as a single family grouping. As well, they have tended to use such collective celebrations as drum dances (an event that brings together the whole community for group festivities at calendrical holidays such as Christmas) and feasts as a means to promote unity. They have used formal institutions such as the co-op to establish this idea.

Yet the move has had costs: the most important has been the effect on the reproduction of the social unit. The transformation of Fort Wrigley into one family lessened the possibility of finding an acceptable marriage partner. As a result, very few marriages have taken place, and these have generally been with members of other regional bands, as far away as Fort Good Hope (400 miles to the north). As well, bickering continues, despite the assertion of solidarity, for when disagreement occurs it is easy still to remember the former separate status of each of the family groups.

Social tension in Fort Wrigley is therefore higher than it was when people lived in smaller family units.

In short, the contemporary period has produced social and political dislocations derived in the main from the imposition of strong external influences on the Dene and from their need, in attempting to maintain their way of life, to accept short-term solutions that have long-term negative impacts.

Contemporary Social and Economic Problems

Industry-sponsored studies, best represented by Gemini North Limited (1974), suggest that nine major problems face northerners today: (1) alcohol abuse, (2) poor housing, (3) high welfare, (4) health-related problems, (5) poor educational opportunities, (6) increasing crime rates, (7) social stress and tension as related particularly to the rise of racism, (8) Native land claims settlement, and (9) poor recreational facilities.

I concur that these problems – except land claims settlement – exist and can be matched by many others. Yet, what is unmentioned is that these problems are surface manifestations of a pattern that has arisen out of the relationship between Native people and external agents – both governmental and business – during the past thirty years, a relationship best described as a massive intrusion of southern Canadian institutions, values, and powerful personnel into the ongoing social and economic processes of Native society. Many traditional Dene institutions and values have been put under tremendous strain, and this strain generates the surface problems.

Four examples of externally caused problems illustrate the strain on traditional institutions and values. The first two, education and welfare, are identified in the industry-sponsored studies. The latter two, wage employment and governmental insensitivity, are not mentioned as problems in these studies; indeed, wage employment is seen as a solution. The section concludes with some remarks concerning how Native people are working on both local and territorial levels to solve the problems we have presented them, an aspect of the contemporary situation conspicuously missing from the industry-sponsored reports.

One aspect of the education problem is the curriculum. The situation has improved somewhat from the period when the Alberta school curriculum was used, for today children are taught about their traditional culture as well as about contemporary southern Canadian society. Nonetheless, information about at least one aspect of their lives – their recent history – appears to be lacking both at the elementary school level and among recent high school graduates as well. Also, despite all the talk about respect for Native culture and courses concerning traditional crafts, it would appear that the elementary school curriculum stresses to teachers the position that Native culture is of the past and is today dead or dying, that children must learn that change is inevitable and that they should adapt to it:

> The North is experiencing increasingly rapid change. Clearly the learning program must do everything within its power to prepare people for change. In this sense the "future orientation" of the curriculum is of prime concern. Children can enquire into the past, as well as the present, but the overall objective must be in terms of using this information to try and predict what might be. (Department of Education, n.d.: 258, 259)

There are many other problems associated with the way in which education is organized, including the school year and compulsory attendance – issues of great importance today as children are still being forced from the bush and into the classroom.

The problem of welfare is not limited to the amount of pervasiveness of the payments themselves. Rather, it is importantly connected to whom they are given: to individual families. As noted, the traditional distribution system ensured that there was little wealth differentiation. This is still true of the distribution system related to the bush subsistence sector of the economy. On the other hand, the introduction of welfare payments in their present form has created the individualization of poverty and has helped to relieve the community of the traditional responsibility to help one another. The current form of the payments has undermined the values of the collective responsibility that is part of the reciprocal economy, and it has subtly led to the forced acceptance of the value, characteristic of our economy, of individual responsibility. In this sense, welfare represents a social intrusion that goes far beyond a mere question of dollars: like education, it creates a perfidious influence on the Native people to change their values.

The third problem area, wage labour, is closely related to the question of welfare. The introduction of permanent wage employment for only a small minority of people in the 1950s could have undermined the traditional value of economic equality by creating a class of rich and poor. However, during the 1950s and early 1960s, at least in Fort Wrigley, there was little temptation to spend large amounts of money; luxury consumer items were rather scarce. As well, since jobs went to responsible family heads, the excess money was often used for socially useful activities, such as supporting children attending schools in other communities, or was not used at all. Now there are many well-paying seasonal jobs, especially in oil and gas exploration. Virtually all go to young men and, at least in the case of Fort Wrigley, overwhelmingly to unmarried ones. Purchasing power has become concentrated in the hands of those with the fewest economic responsibilities. As a result, much of this income is spent on personal luxury items or on socially useless activities such as drinking parties. (Indeed, it would appear that the problem of alcohol abuse may in part be generated by the excesses generated through wage labour.) In addition, that payment goes to individuals has helped to create a distinction between the rich young men who work for wages and the seemingly poor young men who collect bush resources for the family. And yet, given the ways in which most wage-generated income is spent, the latter's activities are socially more useful both to the individual family and to the community.

In short, wage labour acts as a subtle influence to change values. It concentrates wealth in the hands of those who are least capable or willing to use it in socially productive ways. It can help to undermine respect for others who perform socially valuable labour. Under these circumstances, wage labour is often less of a solution than it is a problem.

The last in this litany of externally caused problems is government insensitivity. There are many examples of this in Fort Wrigley. Promises made prior to the move concerned, among other things, housing, water, and wood delivery; the government apparently now says they either were never made or could not have been kept even if a government representative made them on behalf of his employer. There is also the Mackenzie Highway, which the people of Fort Wrigley thought they had stopped, only to discover that it will now end there – the very circumstance they thought they had avoided by their agreement with the government (an agreement that derived from their own "impact study" of the effects of the road ending at the neighbouring community of Fort Simpson).

The common theme connecting these problems is that they are largely the result of the intrusion of southern institutions and values. Native people in the last thirty years have been under ever-increasing pressure to abandon their traditional way of life, to replace it with institutions and values like ours. Despite our conscious and unconscious efforts to effect this end, this process has not been completely successful, and many aspects of the traditional ways of life survive and even flourish. Although the pressure cannot be discounted, it is being resisted in the sense that Native people are not succumbing; they are working to solve these problems and regain control over their lives.

This response dates back at least as far as the first intrusion into Native political autonomy at the time of the so-called treaty signings in the 1920s. However, it has only been in recent years, with the rise of territorial political organizations – the Indian Brotherhood of the Northwest Territories and the Metis Association, for example – that the response has generated political power. This culminated in the land claim and in political statements such as the Dene Declaration through which Native people hope to regain control over their economic, political, and social institutions. Thus, the land claim is not a problem, as the industry-sponsored studies suggest; it is an attempt to find a solution to a whole range of problems.

It is ironic but significant to note that among the strongest supporters of the land claim are the young and well-educated, the very individuals the industry-sponsored studies suggest are most alienated from the traditional way of life and most willing to embrace the Western one. An overwhelming majority of young people do not want to abandon their traditional lifestyle, and they see the land claim settlement as a way to protect themselves in future from what has happened to their society in the past. The most important point is that they are not sitting around waiting for us to solve their problems; they have arrived at a proposed direction for a solution themselves. The question is whether we will allow them to take that path and make it work.

On a local level, the co-op in Fort Wrigley is an attempt to solve some problems. It is run by a Native board and operates so that many jobs are provided on a part-time basis, and preference is often given to heads of families. This provides equity in the distribution of income, ensures that money goes to responsible individuals, and enables people to spend time pursuing bush collection activities. Where local people have some control over the internal organization of economic institutions, those institutions can be run to maintain traditional values such as mutual sharing even in the cash sector of the economy.

Conclusion

The proposals regarding the pipeline were strikingly similar to the bargain proposed by the fur traders: immediate material well-being in return for long-term economic dependency. In one respect, this new bargain was quite different. The fur trade deal created maximum material benefit for Native people with minimal changes in their traditional economic activities and organization: the "new deal" required as a precondition the acquisition of the specialized skills necessary to obtain employment. In addition, the pipeline applicants anticipated the further erosion of the self-sufficient bush collection sector of the economy in favour of greater dependence on the cash-trade goods sector. According to the applicants, the desire of young Native men to have the relative "security" of wage employment would foster the dependence.

Whether wage employment is secure anywhere in Canada, given our economic system, is an open question. Of concern here, however, is that the petroleum industry will not be secure in the North over a long period. That is, just as the fur trade's viability depended on the availability of furs and a high world market price for them, so the viability of petroleum development will depend on the availability of oil and a high world market price for it. But what happens when the resource gives out, or we in the south find a cheaper source of fuel? What happens if the world market price of petroleum products declines to a point where it is uneconomic to exploit and transmit northern oil and gas to southern markets? The petroleum corporations, just like the fur traders before them, will pull out. They must leave if the proposition becomes uneconomic and, of course, that day inevitably will come.

What will happen to Native northerners? The history of the fur trade provides the answer: there will be a general collapse in the cash-trade goods sector of the economy. Yet the projections of the CAGPL-sponsored studies suggested that within the next decade:

> The economy of the Native people will have been transformed from its present situation in which there are two viable but independent sectors: one concerned with bush resource collection and the other with cash-trade goods subsistence; to one which is almost totally dependent upon the cash-trade goods sector. [and] . . . That a large segment of the Native community will consist of a highly trained labour force specializing in Petroleum exploration and related activities: a group unwilling or unable to use the bush as a means of obtaining subsistence.

The bargain the petroleum corporations were making is as follows: in return for reorganizing your labour force to suit our needs, we will provide you with employment for an indefinite period of time. As a result of our high wages, your people may well stop pursuing their traditional bush collection activities and therefore when we leave, as inevitably we must, there is a good possibility that you will be unable to sustain yourselves in your native land. It is against this type of proposition that Native people must protect themselves.

Yet, as the history of the fur trade shows, merely being participants in development will not accomplish this end. It is necessary that Native people have effective control over northern development, for only then can they decide which developments are in their own interests and provide safeguards to ensure that those aspects of their traditional economy they wish to maintain remain viable. A land settlement, should it follow the principles of the Dene Declaration, will provide this type of control.

Should a permit to begin construction of a pipeline be granted prior to a land settlement and the informed consent of the Native northerners, it will undermine their attempts to regain control over the direction of their society, for the single largest decision about their future will have been made without their approval. Thus the granting of a permit prior to a land settlement will exacerbate the present situation and undermine the initiatives that Native people have undertaken to solve their problems.

My research leads me fully to support the position of the Native people that there must be no pipeline before a land settlement. It is the only reasonable protection against the complexity of problems both already known and as yet anticipated that must inevitably accompany a development scheme of this magnitude.

Epilogue

In the spring of 1977, Mr. Justice Berger issued his recommendations (Berger, 1978). Singular among these was his position that the proposed pipeline should be shelved for ten years. Central in his decision was his acceptance of the view that the traditional economy of the Dene (and Inuit) could be maintained in contemporary times. The delay, in his view, was essential to provide time for the Native economy to be strengthened through controlled development. He recommended, among other things, the development of fur-processing facilities in the North and the infusion of the capital necessary to modernize the hunting-trapping sector of the Native economy.

Berger's vision was far reaching, but it failed to gain the political support essential to its full acceptance by government and industry. Government acted on only one aspect of his recommendations and then only partially – the idea of shelving the project. Rather than agree to a full moratorium, government and industry merely kept quiet on the subject for a time. In 1980, industry proposed a smaller line that would carry oil from Norman Wells rather than gas from the High Arctic. Approval was given (although it was agreed that the Native people would bear the highest cost and gain the fewest benefits) for, in a period of high oil prices and economic recession, it was seen to be in the national interest. Work on laying pipe along the route (which includes Fort Wrigley) began in the winter of 1984.

More recent resource extraction projects on Dene lands have proceeded without even cursory reference to Berger's recommendations. By using 1990s technology, staking diamond claims in the Dogrib region has been among the most rapid in history. As with the Cree of James Bay, the Dogrib decision to negotiate a comprehensive claim in their region was made in the face of rapid development on their lands without opportunity for their intervention.

The inability of the Dogribs to control this recent wave of development on their land also stems from the failure of the fourteen-year-long Dene-Metis comprehensive claim negotiation process. The 1990 Dene National Assembly refused to ratify the agreement-in-principle that would have followed the government-imposed requirement of extinguishing their Aboriginal title and treaty rights to achieve a claim settlement. With the failure of the claim, government removed the moratorium on development that had been in place during negotiation, and which had benefited (in the short term, at least) groups such as the Fort Good Hope Dene of the Sahtu region, who were able to seek petroleum exploration and development arrangements on their lands at more beneficial terms because their approval was necessary while the moratorium was in effect. Following from this experience, as well as observing the immediate effects of the 1984 Inuvialuit claim to the north, the two northern Dene regions elected to pursue regional claims as well. Essentially, two development options are available to Dene: settle a claim and co-operate in development activity, or, in the absence of a claims agreement, development will proceed without co-operation.

The other major avenue that Dene have investigated for controlling their lands and resources is the political sphere. They have participated in the process to reform the institutions of public government in the Northwest Territories, a process that has accelerated through the negotiation of the Inuit claim and its linkage with the establishment of the territory of Nunavut in the eastern Arctic. Dene are faced with the likelihood that they will not form a majority of the culturally diverse western Northwest Territories and have proposed measures designed to protect their political, economic, and cultural interests, such as residency requirements and double-majority votes on designated issues. However, most of these measures run contrary to the mainstream Canadian ideal of overt equality of treatment of all citizens within a region. The familiar Canadian alternative means of protecting ethnic minority rights is in geographical cultural enclaves, which can operate only in the specific instance of a region dominated by a single ethnic group, such as in Quebec and Nunavut. Thus Dene have undertaken the daunting task of promoting political arrangements unique in Canada, but not contrary to Canadian constitutional principles, against a backdrop of local and external interests that seek to establish structures familiar in the rest of Canada but which offer little protection for Dene interests.

However, two Dene regions argue that they have already negotiated a special relationship with the rest of Canada that guarantees protection of their interest: Treaties No. 8 and No. 11. Considerable research has been conducted and is ongoing to document the treaties as they were negotiated and to describe the nation-to-nation stature of the agreements. Through these treaties, Dene assert that their economic, land, political, and cultural rights were acknowledged in exchange for the promise of peaceful relations with non-Dene newcomers "as long as the sun shines and the river flows," a solemn promise that they have upheld. In general, they seek recognition of the rights they maintain through the treaties as they were negotiated and the fulfilment of the Canadian sovereign's treaty promises.

What Dene experience indicates above all else is the essential appropriateness of the Dene demand for control over decision-making on their lands. What they wanted was accepted by Mr. Justice Berger as reasonable. Yet within five years what they did not want started to take place while developments essential to their well-being remain shelved. Clearly, without local control, governments and other interests will have little incentive to pay attention to the legitimate, rationally founded arguments of the Dene themselves.

Recommended Readings

Berger, Mr. Justice Thomas R.
1977 *Northern Frontier, Northern Homeland: The Report of the Mackenzie Valley Pipeline Inquiry*, Volumes I and 11. Ottawa: Department of Supply and Services.

These volumes give a detailed account of the contemporary economy of the Dene and Inuit of the Mackenzie River Valley. Mr. Justice Berger also describes his views on the potential impact of the massive pipeline proposed by industry and makes specific recommendations, based on testimony from expert and community witnesses, on how to maintain a viable hunting-trapping way of life within a contemporary northern economy.

Brody, Hugh

    1981 *Maps and Dreams: Indians and the British Columbia Frontier*. Vancouver: Douglas & McIntyre.

        This volume presents a concise portrait of how the regional grouping of the Dene who live in northeastern British Columbia are working to maintain a traditional way of life based on hunting and trapping in the face of those who would transform their lands to extract resources. Written in a style that is accessible to the non-specialist, this work still maintains a high standard of scholarship and thus succeeds at explaining in a humanistic manner the central battle all northern Native groups now face.

Helm, June

    1961 *The Lynx Point People: The Dynamics of a Northern Athapaskan Band*. National Museum of Canada Bulletin 176. Ottawa: National Museums of Canada.

        The Lynx Point People are a group of Slavey Indians. Helm's monograph provides a useful summary of their way of life in the 1950s, as well as social and cultural changes. Of particular interest is her discussion of Slavey culture and values and their attempts to incorporate a commercial fishing operation into their way of life.

Helm, June, ed.

    1981 *Handbook of North American Indians*, Vol. 6, *Subarctic*. Washington, D.C.: Smithsonian Institution.

        The *Handbook* represents an authoritative reference source on the ethnology, ethnohistory, and archaeology of the Mackenzie Valley Dene. Among the essays on various regional groupings of Dene is one detailing the cultural history and way of life of the Slavey.

Honigmann, John

    1946 *Ethnology and Acculturation of the Fort Nelson Slavey*. Yale University Publications in Anthropology 33. New Haven: Yale University Press.

        This is a general account of traditional culture and society and of the effects of contact with Western societies as analysed from the perspective of the acculturation model. Honigmann emphasizes that in his view Slavey subsistence patterns result in a minimum of social and political complexity and in a high regard for individual autonomy.

Watkins, Melville, ed.

    1977 *Dene Nation: The Colony Within*. Toronto: University of Toronto Press.

        The book is composed primarily of edited versions of the testimony presented by witnesses called by the Indian Brotherhood of the Northwest Territories at the Mackenzie Valley Pipeline Inquiry. As such, it encapsulates the "case" presented by the Dene at those hearings. Among the specific contributions are pieces by Dene describing such matters as their education in

Western-style schools and by expert witnesses called by the Dene. Among
the latter, one can find the testimony of Scott Rushforth on evaluating country
food and, under the title "The Slavey Economy," a much reduced version of
the information presented in this chapter.

Additional References Cited

Asch, Michael I.
  1972 "A Social Behavioral Approach to Music Analysis," Ph.D. dissertation in
        Anthropology, Columbia University.
  1975 "Social Context and the Music Analysis of Slavey Drum Dance Songs,"
        Ethnomusicology, 19: 245-57.
  1979a "The Ecological Evolutionary Approach and the Concept of Mode of
        Production," in D. Turner and G.A. Smith, eds., *Challenging Anthropology*.
        Toronto: McGraw-Hill Ryerson.
  1979b "The Economics of Dene Self-Determination," in Turner and Smith, eds.,
        Challenging Anthropology.
  1982 "Dene Self-Determination and the Study of Hunter-Gatherers in the Modern
        World," in E.B. Leacock and R.B. Lee, eds., *Politics and History in Band
        Societies*. Cambridge: Cambridge University Press.
The Catholic Voice
  1957 A Monthly Publication of the Sacred Heart Mission. Fort Simpson,
        Northwest Territories.
Council of the Northwest Territories
  1956 Legislative Acts. Yellowknife, Northwest Territories.
Department of Education, Government of the N.W.T.
  n.d. *Elementary Education in the Northwest Territories: A Handbook for
        Curriculum Development*. Yellowknife, Northwest Territories.
Gemini North Limited
  1974 *Social and Economic Impact of Proposed Arctic Gas Pipeline in Northern
        Canada*. Study prepared for Canadian Arctic Gas Pipeline Limited.
Rushforth, E. Scott
  1986 "The Bear Lake Indians," in R. Bruce Morrison and C. Roderick Wilson,
        eds., *Native Peoples: The Canadian Experience*. Toronto: McClelland &
        Stewart.
Usher, Peter J.
  1972 *Fur Trade Posts of the Northwest Territories: 1870-1970*. N.S.R.G. – 14.
        Department of Indian Affairs and Northern Development. Ottawa.
Van Ginkle Associates Limited
  1975 *The Mackenzie: Effects of the Hydrocarbon Industry*. Study prepared for
        Canadian Arctic Gas Pipeline Limited.

CHAPTER 12

Understanding Yukon History: Contributions from Oral Tradition

Julie Cruikshank

Introduction

In northwestern Canada, an attentive listener will frequently hear contrasting explanations about features of landscape, life experiences, or events from the past. Some of these accounts appear in written documents; others are part of daily conversation. History books have conventionally taken their evidence about the past from written records. Until recently, oral testimonies have often been lumped together as "anecdotal," the very term suggesting that they lack a serious purpose.[1]

The area now known as the Yukon Territory has a history as ancient as the earth itself. There are many narratives about how the world began, some told by scientists, some by historians, and some by First Peoples whose oral traditions address similar questions. The stories told by elders and those told by scientists and historians have developed differently and depend on different sources, but both attempt to interpret how the world as we know it came to be. The discrepancies seem to provide striking evidence of how context affects interpretation.

My own interest in these questions began when I moved to the Yukon Territory in the early 1970s. As a recent graduate of an anthropology program where the ethical dilemmas inherent in anthropological research were much discussed, I was interested in working outside a university framework to see where my training might have practical applications. Like so many of my contemporaries, I was convinced of the relevance of anthropological questions but critical of positivist and objectivist approaches to the study of culture. I was excited by the energy with which these issues were discussed and debated in the Yukon Territory. Aboriginal organizations were preparing to begin negotiations for a settlement of outstanding land claims. Native band councils were proposing to take more control of educational programs and were asking for Native language curriculum. Indigenous people were testifying at federal inquiries into the social and economic impact of proposed pipeline projects. Discussions about land use, self-government, and cultural identity were part of everyday conversation in northern communities during those years.

In discussions with politically active Aboriginal women my own age, questions were regularly raised about whether an anthropology student could make useful contributions. At the time, we all tended to see anthropology's value as rather narrowly related to historical reconstruction in ways that might prove significant for land claims negotiations. The few ethnographic studies available in the early 1970s were carefully consulted by researchers preparing background documents for new programs, but because these books bore rather inclusive titles like *The Kaska Indians*, *The Han Indians*, and *The Upper Tanana Indians*, they tended to disappoint their new readership, especially women who found little of their experience reflected there.

Several women independently suggested that I might make a substantive contribution by working with their mothers or grandmothers recording life stories in a form that could be distributed to family members. Such an exchange seemed ideal to me because it gave me an opportunity to learn about how women's lives were changing at the same time as producing booklets authored by older women for their own families. Looking back, it is worth remembering that in the early 1970s political organization was engaging many young adult women, thereby making the task they were suggesting for me one that could appropriately be assigned to an outsider; a decade later, a significant number of Athapaskan women and men were doing their own cultural documentation.

During the following decade, then, with the support of Aboriginal organizations and under the direct supervision of elders, we produced a

number of booklets;[2] however, as I worked closely with teachers like
Mrs. Angela Sidney, Mrs. Kitty Smith, and Mrs. Annie Ned, my understanding of our objectives began to shift. Initially, I expected that by
recording life stories we would be documenting alternative perspectives
on events already chronicled in written documents – about the gold rush,
Alaska Highway construction, changing social and educational policies,
and changing land use. I thought of our work as a way of compiling
accounts that could be stored, like archival documents, for later analysis.
Although the older women responded patiently to my line of inquiry for a
while, they quite firmly shifted our emphasis to the "more important"
narratives they wanted me to record, essentially suggesting that my questions were not necessarily appropriate and that I needed to know more
before I could begin asking the right ones. Gradually, I came to see oral
tradition not as "evidence" about the past but as a window on the ways in
which the past is culturally constituted and discussed. When I returned to
graduate school a decade later, it was with an interest in learning how
these same issues were being discussed and negotiated in other parts of
the world where oral tradition remains a viable way not only of transmit-
ting knowledge about the past, but also of symbolically constructing the
present. Questions arising from many years of discussion with my Yukon
teachers, then, provide the basis for this paper.

Interest in what can be learned from orally narrated accounts has
grown enormously in recent years, particularly in North and South
America, in Africa, and in the South Pacific – all parts of the world
where oral and written sources are likely to report events in different
ways. The term "oral tradition," though, is often used to refer to two different things. Sometimes we use it to refer to a body of *material* – narratives and knowledge – retained from the past and known by elders.
Other times, we use the term to talk about a *process* by which that material has been handed down to the present. Both of these aspects are
important, but definitions like this may make oral tradition seem more
rigid than it actually is. Oral tradition is more than a body of stories to be
recorded and stored away, and it is not always passed on in the form of
complete narratives. Anyone who has spent time listening to Aboriginal
elders talk about their understanding of the past knows that oral
accounts are discussed and debated in small communities, that oral tradition itself is a lively, continuous, ongoing process, a way of understanding the present as well as the past.

Oral and written accounts not only speak from different perspectives,
they are passed along in different ways. Oral traditions survive by
repeated retellings, and each narrative contains more than a single

message. The listener is part of the storytelling event, too, and is expected to think about and interpret the messages in each story. Written accounts can be stored unchanged. Unless they are physically destroyed, they can be read and inspected by anyone who goes to a library to read them.

Like any system of knowledge, oral tradition has particular goals, methods, and questions, but they differ from those of European science or history. Beginning with different questions, oral tradition and written history provide us with different but equally valuable ways of understanding relationships among environment, animals, and humans. Because translation is such an imperfect process, it may be that cultural outsiders can best begin by trying to understand the *questions* raised by oral tradition rather than trying to extract quick answers or "facts" from it.

The writing of history has always involved collecting, analysing, and retelling stories about the past. The very act of collection, though, means that some stories are enshrined in books and others are marginalized. Rewriting history to include First Nations perspectives is a complicated process: it cannot be done by adding an introductory chapter to an existing history book. In Canada, for example, First Nations rightly point out that sandwiching a chapter on Aboriginal peoples between a chapter on geography and environment and a chapter on the fur trade gives a mixed message. It suggests that First Nations lived in the past and do not live on in the present. It traps them in history or even *prehistory*, a term that seems to suggest a time before history began. Dictionaries usually define prehistory as a time before written records, but for people who have always relied on the spoken word to pass on information, such a dictionary definition is not very meaningful. For Aboriginal peoples, these earlier periods *are* their history, and they reject the term "prehistory" as inappropriate.

Origins of Yukon Peoples: Two Kinds of Questions

One of the clearest examples of such dissonance can be found in interpretations of the earliest peopling of North America. Elders and archaeologists give different accounts of how humans came to be living in the area now called the Yukon. This happens largely because they begin with different questions, so the fact that the answers differ should not be surprising.

When Yukon elders talk about human origins, they are less concerned about *where* people came from than with *how* people came to be fully human – with how they learned to share power with other animals and other humans. In these accounts, the order in which events occurred is not always entirely clear or even very important, and the key figures differ in different parts of the Yukon. In the southern Yukon, for example, Crow created people, but he created them in a world where animals already existed. Animal Mother brought animals into the world quite independently of Crow, but at their birth she reminded them that they were "born from people" and should not trouble them. At the beginning of time, animals and humans could communicate directly with one another but were not entirely suited to living in the world together. Because animals and humans had to share the world, their first – and ongoing – task was to learn how to get along together and how to respect each other's powers.

Taken together, narratives about Crow, Animal Mother, and other prominent figures explore different aspects of a comprehensive world view. Even though chronology or sequence is not very significant in these narratives, *place* is important. One thing elders agree about is that creatures native to the Yukon were created here and that the Yukon has always been their home. Narratives told by Yukon elders convey a sense that time and space have some unity and are not easily separated. This picture contrasts with the one presented by Western science and history, where physical places are assumed to be distinct and separate, and where time is understood to follow a linear progression.

Archaeologists ask quite different questions about human origins, and consequently their conclusions differ. One major problem that interests archaeologists is when and how people first came to be living in North America. Consequently, they are more concerned than elders about ordering events in a sequence or establishing absolute dates. They are particularly interested in Yukon research because most of them believe that the ancestors of all Native American people once passed through the Yukon.

Archaeologists look for two kinds of evidence: physical remains (typically, human and animal bones), and what they refer to as material culture – objects deliberately or accidentally modified by humans. New stories are continually emerging from this material culture, stories about the 10,000-year period between the last ice age and the nineteenth century when the first Europeans arrived.

On a world scale, archaeological evidence suggests that humans originated in the warm, low latitude forests of Africa. As human populations spread out, they had to learn new strategies for survival, particularly as they moved north and encountered unfamiliar climates. Winters are extremely cold in the Subarctic, so before people could live in northern regions they had to master the use of fire. They also had to develop techniques for making tailored skin clothing and warm secure shelters.

There were fewer species of plants and animals than at lower latitudes and they were available only at certain times of the year, so people had to invent specialized hunting, fishing, and gathering techniques as well as methods for storing food. They probably developed specialized watercraft for travelling on large bodies of cold water. In the scientific study of human cultural development, archaeological evidence from the Arctic and Subarctic is very important because it documents a range of new skills people had to learn before they could pass *through* these environments to reach North America.

The most recent major glaciation, known as the Wisconsin, lasted from 30,000 to 10,000 years ago and covered most of Canada. Not all of northern North America was ice-covered, however. As Arctic waters became locked into ice, the shallow bed of the Bering Sea was exposed, joining northwestern Asia, Alaska, and northern Yukon in a large subcontinent called Beringia. Often described as a "land bridge" joining the Old and New Worlds, Beringia was actually a substantial land mass stretching 1,500 kilometres from north to south. With the melting of the glaciers, the seas rose again, eliminating entire plant communities and possibly driving out animals and humans who relied on them. Most archaeologists believe that people arrived south of the glacial barrier sometime between 15,000 and 12,000 years ago, though they disagree about the possible routes actually used to travel south.

The next several thousand years saw continuing changes in climatic conditions and corresponding cultural adaptations in northwestern North America. The early post-glacial period was characterized by a cold, dry climate with periodic flooding while lakes established their drainages. Archaeologists have named this cultural tradition "Little Arm" in the southwest Yukon, after the site where it was first excavated. Characteristic tools from this period were tiny razor-sharp microblades that could be mounted on a handle for very precise purposes.

A warming period began about 6,000 years ago and lasted for almost 3,000 years. This must have been a good time for human populations. Expanding grasslands and plentiful bison attracted a new population, probably from further northwest. This new tradition, again named after an early site where the characteristic tool assemblage was found, is known as "Taye Lake." Taye Lake traditions seem to have completely replaced those of Little Arm, except in the central Yukon where Little Arm culture seems to have persisted much longer. About 3,000 years ago, though, the climate suddenly became cooler and wetter and archaeologists can show how Taye Lake notched points were modified to deal with deteriorating conditions. Glaciers began to expand again,

impounding lakes that periodically emptied with disastrous results for downstream populations.

A final blow came with the eruption of the huge White River volcano 1,200 years ago. The thick ash layer, visible along river banks in the central Yukon, provides a clear marker between Taye Lake culture and the following cultural sequence, named "Aishihik" culture, which resembles Taye Lake but includes the addition of bows, arrows, and copper arrowheads. The climate continued to deteriorate until the end of the so-called Little Ice Age between 1600 and 1850, which produced the coldest temperatures in the previous 10,000-year period. These were the conditions first met by Europeans who provided our earliest written descriptions of North America – Martin Frobisher in the 1500s, Henry Hudson in 1610, Samuel Hearne in 1770, Alexander Mackenzie in 1798, and Robert Campbell in 1848.

A fourth, more recent cultural sequence, called "Bennett Lake," dominates the short period between 1800 and 1900 in the southern Yukon. It is marked by the appearance of trade goods, indicating involvement in the European fur trade. Because so much of the trade during the last several hundred years was in perishables, archaeologists investigating this period in the southern Yukon have come to rely increasingly on oral tradition in their work.

Comparing Oral and Written Records:
The Nineteenth Century

There are two kinds of remembered history from the late nineteenth-century Yukon, one oral and one written. These memories differ because the tellers had different goals and objectives, and consequently they interpreted events differently and emphasized different experiences. Written records from the Yukon do not go back so very many years – a few fur trade journals from the 1850s, travellers' reports from the 1880s and 1890s, a flood of letters and diaries from visitors who recorded their own stories during the Klondike gold rush. The histories constructed from these written records contain the visions of people who considered themselves explorers writing about their impressions of a land they thought they were discovering. In contrast, Aboriginal oral histories transmitted through narratives, songs, place names, and genealogies reflect an understanding of the land and events from people who have always considered the Yukon their home.

Even though both oral and written accounts refer to the past, they are usually told in order to make a statement about the present. In other

MAP 12.1. Yukon Native Linguistic Groups (after McClellan, 1975)

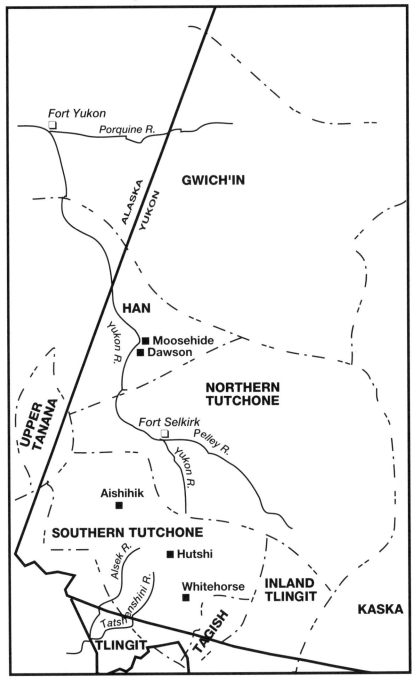

words, their purpose is to provide some background for explaining events that are happening now. They do this by emphasizing some events and leaving out others. Both written and oral accounts about the past are interpretations that may change as circumstances change. The topics discussed below refer to the past, but they also reflect issues that concern Aboriginal people now: *language, land use, material culture,* and *social life.* At another time in history, or in another setting, other topics might be considered more important.

Yukon Languages

Yukon languages belong to two distinct language families: Athapaskan and Tlingit. Tlingit is spoken both in southeastern Alaska and in the southern Yukon. Athapaskan languages include at least thirty distinct languages spoken in the Yukon, Alaska, Northwest Territories, northern British Columbia, and Alberta, as well as several spoken far to the south, including Navajo and Apache. Athapaskan languages spoken in the Yukon include Gwich'in, Han, Upper Tanana, Tutchone, Southern Tutchone, Tagish, and Kaska.[3]

Maps of the Yukon showing territorial boundaries usually have lines separating different languages. It is important to know several things about these maps. First, linguistic maps refer to language, not to separate territorial or political groups. While language boundaries may coincide with river drainages, these boundaries are only approximate and they are never as firm as they appear on maps. Nor can any map made in the present be completely accurate for earlier periods. People from Taye Lake, Aishihik, and Bennett cultures, mentioned above, probably spoke Athapaskan languages, but we do not know how similar their languages were to the languages now spoken in the southern Yukon. Nor do we know how many languages may have disappeared.

Second, it is important to remember that these are distinct languages, not dialects. Because there are eight different languages spoken in the Yukon and because English now has such prominence, the issue of language maintenance in contemporary contexts becomes complex. The Yukon Native Language Centre and the Yukon Aboriginal Languages Commission are both actively involved in these issues in the 1990s.

Third, even though names for Yukon languages are used more carefully now than in the past, they are still terms devised by outsiders. When the first European visitors arrived a century ago, they asked the people they met what they called themselves or what they called their neighbours and then transcribed what they heard somewhat uncritically.

Elderly speakers of Athapaskan languages now use quite different words to refer to themselves: they might call themselves *dän* or *den*, meaning "people," or they might refer to themselves by moiety names Crow (*Kajìt*) or Wolf (*Ägunda*). If they are from the southern Yukon, they might identify themselves further with reference to their clan – *Deisheetaan, Yanyeidí, Dakl'aweidí*, or one of the other prominent Tlingit-named clans. Because there are so many ways to refer to oneself, Yukon First Nations now use language names to distinguish regional differences. The expansion of the Yukon Native Language Centre programs in the 1980s and the Aboriginal Languages Commission in the 1990s indicates the significance language continues to have.

Land Use

Understanding past and present land use in the Yukon has been increasingly important for Yukon First Nations in recent years during ongoing negotiations of their land claims with the federal government. When elders talk about where they used to live, they usually describe their lives in terms of travel. Their understanding of land ownership is unlikely to include formal boundaries. Different headmen claimed ownership of particular areas on behalf of their extended family group, but they would not refuse access to visitors. In the late nineteenth and early twentieth centuries, families covered large distances each year, so members of one group might travel to several other parts of the country.

By the middle of the last century, people living in the Yukon were hunters and fishers who had made long-term and successful adaptations to a Subarctic environment. They depended on resources that varied from place to place and from season to season. These resources provided them with food, clothing, and shelter, but they had to be prepared to move and to adjust the size of their group as seasons and resources required. In spring, muskrats, beaver, and other fur-bearers were plentiful. In summer, salmon streams were teeming with fish. In fall, people might come together to intercept caribou herds or they might disperse into smaller groups to hunt moose. Meat from these animals was cached for winter when travel was more difficult. None of these movements was random. People travelled to familiar camping spots each year.

The number of people who might live together at one time varied depending on the season and the task. In winter, family groups spread out, but they made sure that each group was able to provide for itself. Each domestic unit required enough able-bodied adults to carry out necessary hunting and camp work and to look after dependent members. A group could not be too large: if there were some misfortune or a food shortage, having to feed large numbers could endanger the lives of every-one. Eight or ten people would be plenty to live together in winter under most circumstances.

At other times, resources could be harvested more efficiently in larger groups. For example, salmon migrating up the Tatshenshini and Yukon River systems arrived in large numbers during short periods of time. Families would converge from great distances during salmon runs to catch and preserve their annual supply of fish. Similarly, caribou hunting differs from tracking individual moose because caribou travel in herds and can be hunted most efficiently by families working co-operatively.

Mobility was critical. Every group needed to maintain a balance between people who were able to provide the necessities of life and those who were dependent. Each person began life as a dependent child, became a provider in adulthood, and became dependent again in old age. A grandmother, for example, might spend one winter with a group of her children and grandchildren and another winter with other family members. An able-bodied man or woman might join a group needing extra help. Families needed to be able to come together when food was plenti-ful and to spread out at other times. The key to successful hunting and fishing was this flexibility.

Material Culture: Technology and Arts

Museums tell stories, too. Because they collect physical objects, they preserve certain stories and ignore others. Because museums collect things, they encourage us to understand other cultures in terms of the physical objects people made and left behind. Yet, this emphasis on mate-rial things may say more about the societies that produce museums than about the societies producing the objects found in museums. Western societies certainly value material culture, and use the term "wealthy" to refer to people who have accumulated an abundance of material goods. This attitude differs from that of Subarctic peoples for whom extra pos-sessions were an encumbrance, slowing down travel.

Yukon material culture has sometimes been compared with that of the Pacific Northwest coast. Visitors to museums are familiar with the arts of Northwest Coast cultures through displays of magnificent totem poles, masks, and carved wooden boxes. By contrast, Yukon material culture may seem considerably less elaborate. It is not enough, though, to compare physical objects without considering reasons *why* coastal and interior material cultures may differ.

Coastal peoples were able to live in large, relatively permanent villages for one major reason: they had access to an incredibly rich and reliable renewable resource. Coastal salmon runs became established at the end of the last glaciation, and these fish have returned to the same rivers year after year, allowing people to count on their appearance every summer. Halibut, sea lions, other fish, and game also come within range of coastal villages each year, and shellfish are available all winter. Coastal subsistence strategies contrast sharply with those of interior Subarctic hunters because marine harvesting requires emphasis on population stability rather than mobility.

Subarctic peoples have always had a very different set of problems. To harvest their resources, they had to be prepared to move, so they developed a material culture based on principles that could be combined in a variety of ways. Portability was essential, so only absolute necessities were carried from place to place. Adaptability was also important: the principles underlying snare construction could be applied to snares for small animals like ground squirrels or large animals like moose and caribou. The critical issue was to learn the *idea* of how a snare is constructed and how it is used. Then, snares could be made as needed, not carried around. "Wealth" in such a culture is carried in one's head rather than on one's back. It is passed from one generation to another through oral tradition. It weighs nothing and can accompany a traveller anywhere, but it rarely appears in museums.

Part of the genius of Subarctic culture is the ability to take materials like bone, stone, wood, skins, bark, and copper and transform them into necessities like clothing and shelter, tools and transportation. Increasingly, young people are working with elders to learn more about the stories that objects can tell.[4]

Social Life: "Everyone Belongs"

At the foundation of nineteenth-century Yukon life are kinship and family. Throughout the world and during most periods of human history, people have relied on family ties to structure rules of behaviour and social obligations. We now take it for granted in Canada that governments are responsible for making available a number of basic services – health care, education, social and economic programs, and so on. Formerly, these services were provided by people who considered themselves to be part of one extended family.

Kinship can be traced in a number of ways, and people from all cultures have their own ideas about family that seem natural to them. In the

Yukon, elders say, Crow divided people into two groups at the beginning of time, Crow (*Kajìt*) and Wolf (*Ägunda*). Many societies in the world use a similar organizing principle, and anthropologists have devised the term "moiety" (meaning "half") to refer to this kind of organization. Membership in these groups is determined by birth. If you are an Aboriginal person in the southern Yukon, for instance, you belong to the same group as your mother; in other words, descent is matrilineal. This means that your father will always be a member of the opposite moiety from your own. By customary law, a person from one moiety can only marry someone from the opposite side. For two Crows or two Wolves to marry would be the same as for a brother and sister to marry, even if the individuals in question came from widely separated communities. Such unions were absolutely forbidden in the past and would still be frowned on by elders.

For Tlingit-speaking people in the southern Yukon, this becomes even more complicated because within each moiety there are further clan divisions, like *Deisheetaan* (a Crow clan), *Dakl'aweidí* (a Wolf clan), and several others. Members of any clan can usually name a common ancestor in the distant past, though they may not be able to trace all the genealogical links to that ancestor.

One of the great advantages of this system is that it gives people relatives everywhere. Even now, when young people go to visit another community, the first questions they are likely to be asked are "Who is your mother?" and "What is your Indian name?" Because names belong to specific clans and moieties, everyone will know from the answer whether the visitor is Wolf or Crow – in other words, where the visitor fits into the community.

Matrilineal descent was reinforced by a custom that encouraged a man to live with his wife's family after marriage, at least for a while. As long as a couple stayed with her family, a woman would continue to work with her mother, aunts, and sisters, and these women would raise their children together. Her husband would hunt in partnership with her brother, and being from opposite moieties, brothers-in-law might also become permanent trading partners. A man would also be responsible for providing for his wife's parents in their old age.

Living with the woman's family after marriage had other advantages. A man would come to know two hunting territories well – the one where he was raised as well as his wife's. A woman would retain detailed knowledge of berry grounds and the locations of vegetable roots and plants. Women's knowledge could be critical during particularly difficult winters when meat was scarce. Such knowledge must have been crucial during the bitterly cold winters of the Little Ice Age just prior to the coming of the first whites.

The Arrival of Strangers

Between 1840 and 1890, a number of visitors travelled to northwestern North America. Fur traders, missionaries, and scientists each had their own reasons for coming north. The accounts these visitors left behind suggest they came with expectations that they would acquire things they valued. Traders were interested in collecting furs. Missionaries were interested in collecting souls. Scientists wanted to collect and classify facts. Prospectors were intent on finding gold, and government-sponsored expeditions came with the intention of acquiring territories.

Whatever their motives for coming to the Yukon, most early visitors wrote down their observations and impressions. Their journals, letters, and reports have been valuable to historians writing about nineteenth-century Yukon. Frequently, though, the observer's comments tell us more about the journal writer than about the events or people the observer claimed to be describing. Yet the written observations of traders, missionaries, and scientists often became the basis on which policy decisions were made – by the Hudson's Bay Company, the church, and government. In this way, written documents based on cultural understandings from Europe or the United States often had real economic, political, and social consequences for the lives of Yukon peoples.

The Fur Trade

The fur trade is often discussed in history books as though it were a distinct *period* in Canadian history, as though it were an event or a series of events that occurred at some time in the past and then ended. Aboriginal Yukon trappers, on the other hand, regard trapping as an activity that began long before Europeans arrived and that continues to have social and economic importance in many communities. It is not a chapter of history that began and ended at some point in the past.

Indigenous people relied on fur-bearing animals for food, clothing, and shelter long before the European-based fur trade began. But as competing traders came to the coast of North America from Russia and from Britain, Natives' reasons for trapping began to shift from the domestic use of furs to their value as objects of exchange. Furs were the marketable resource that first drew outsiders to the North, the first industry to link Aboriginal communities with European economies. Because outsiders brought with them a range of goods to exchange for furs, trapping for trade gradually became a central activity for people living on the Yukon Plateau. Today, when elders talk about the traditional way of life, they are usually referring to a time when the fur trade was already well established.

A great deal has been written about the fur trade, but investigators begin their analyses with a range of different questions. Historians and economists, for example, usually write about the fur trade as a market-oriented business. They examine problems involved in the collection and transportation of furs from northern communities to urban centres. They look for linkages between fur production in Canada and fur markets in Russia, Britain, and the United States. Their emphasis is on the fur trade as an industry and their concern is to demonstrate how this fits into large-scale industrial economies.

Anthropologists, on the other hand, usually focus on how Aboriginal people have participated in the fur trade as producers. They look at the actual work done by men and women engaged in trapping and preparing furs, the kinds of exchanges made by trappers, the ways trappers organize their production of furs until those furs reach the trader. They look at the effects the fur trade has had on Native families, subsistence economies, and political organization.

Somewhere in between is a third approach that considers how the social relations between people involved in the actual exchange of furs have changed over time. Three quite distinct phases of trapping can be distinguished: the initial and long-standing Aboriginal trade networks; the arrival of international trading corporations by the 1840s; the proliferation of small independent traders during the early twentieth century. Some of the evidence about changes in trading relationships is available from written records; some comes from oral accounts.

A flourishing Aboriginal trade existed between coastal Tlingit and interior Athapaskan communities in northwestern North America long before the arrival of Europeans. The outlines of this trade are hazy because the earliest items of exchange – skins, seaweed, and oil – were perishable and rarely survive in the archaeological record. Recently, some archaeologists have turned to oral evidence to fill in some of the gaps in the material record.

Trade is especially likely to occur between groups of people who live in areas that are geographically and culturally distinct and where resources differ. Athapaskan people living on the central Yukon Plateau were separated by mountain chains from Coastal Tlingit in the southwest and from Arctic Inuit in the north. In each case, coastal peoples were able

PLATE 12.1. Mrs. Annie Ned, at her home in 1984. Courtesy J. Cruikshank.

to exchange products from the sea for skins and furs from the high country interior. Various Tlingit tribes – the Chilkat, Chilkoot, and Taku – made annual trips to the interior to trade, bringing such items as dried fish, oolachon oil, shell ornaments, and cedar bark baskets to exchange for tanned furs, moose and caribou hides, finished fur garments and sturdy moccasins, and Native copper. Further north, Gwich'in middlemen brought oil, bone, and tusks from the Arctic coast to exchange with inland people.

One of the most important aspects of this early trade was the opportunity it provided for social contacts. Such trade was organized through partnerships between traders from neighbouring groups. In a partnership between an Athapaskan man and a Tlingit man, for example, families sometimes arranged for one partner to marry the other's sister, thus cementing the economic relationship through family ties. Mrs. Annie Ned, born at Hutshi in the early 1890s, talks about her grandfather's long-term trading partner, Gasłeeni. She and her brother continued through the 1980s to maintain Gasłeeni's grave as a sign of respect for that alliance.

The commercial fur trade that came to dominate Aboriginal peoples on the Yukon River after the 1840s was driven by forces outside the Yukon and developed from two different directions – Russian traders from the west and British traders from the east. Both were originally drawn to the Pacific Northwest by the trade in sea otter furs. But the European fur markets had no limits: there were never enough furs to satisfy demands in Moscow, London, or Paris. By the mid-nineteenth century, sea otters were all but exterminated and trading companies turned their attention to the interior.

As long as commercial companies remained based on the Pacific coast, Aboriginal trade networks continued relatively uninterrupted. Russians dealt directly with Tlingit traders who, in turn, established their position as middlemen between Europeans and inland peoples. East of the Cordillera, the North West Company and Hudson's Bay Company had amalgamated by 1821 and were content to leave the Yukon as a buffer zone between themselves and the Russians on the Pacific coast. Like the Russians, they used middlemen to bring furs to their posts, and when the British leased southeastern Alaska from Russia in 1839, they adopted the same strategy of working through Tlingit traders.

From the east, though, the Hudson's Bay Company began a cautious two-pronged exploration into the Yukon after 1840, partly to find out what existed in this enormous area of land they considered unexplored and partly to try to head off competition from Russian traders working their way up the lower Yukon River. They established a post, Fort Yukon, at the junction of the Porcupine and Yukon rivers by 1847. When Robert Campbell built a second post, Fort Selkirk, at the junction of the Pelly and Yukon rivers the following year, he was astounded by the level of trading activity already taking place there between Tlingits and Athapaskans. The Chilkat tribe of Tlingits, in fact, interpreted his construction of that post as a direct attack on their Yukon River trading monopoly and destroyed it in 1852. The HBC wisely withdrew and resumed trading through the well-established Aboriginal networks, an arrangement that suited them well enough because it allowed them to maximize profits without disrupting social relationships in Native communities.

The nineteenth-century fur industry was based on ideas of fashion characteristic of a particular historic period in Europe. Beaver hats, stoles, muffs, and coats made of Yukon furs were a valuable commodity because of their scarcity, cost, and durability. But Europeans were not the only people interested in fashion. Yukon women experimented with designs made possible by new varieties of beads. Artistic traditions in these regions became more elaborate as women began working with different colours and textures, integrating new designs – floral patterns, especially – into established traditions. Ideas of beauty, fashion, and art, then, may have influenced the fur trade from several traditions, both Native and European. If furs fuelled a European fashion industry, the trade seems also to have fostered an indigenous artistic tradition in northern Canada.

After the expulsion of the Hudson's Bay Company, Aboriginal trade continued, much as in the past, with additional European trade goods reaching the Yukon River from distant posts. By the 1870s, other pressures – again from outside the Yukon – were signalling a new phase of trade. Rumours of mineral wealth on the Yukon River were attracting increasing numbers of white prospectors and trappers to the area, and Tlingits were finding it extremely difficult to retain their monopoly of the coastal passes by the 1880s.

The new independent traders saw little advantage in working within established trade networks. They began trading with individuals, extending credit to preferred trappers and binding individual trappers to exclusive trading relationships. By labelling some trappers as "better risks" than others for credit, this system emphasized new distinctions between people. Such arrangement also gave the trader more power than the trapper to decide which furs should be trapped. This imbalance increased as trappers gradually became dependent on consumer goods they could acquire only by trapping whichever furs were bringing good prices that year.

During the present century, new trade items like dogs, canvas tents, and wire snares all altered the kinds of work families had to do to continue their involvement in the fur trade. Competition with newcomers for land inevitably restricted the land base available for trapping. Government registration of traplines disrupted customary moiety, clan, and family trapping arrangements. More recently, the activities of animal rights groups have affected trapping economies across the North.

Missionaries: Victorian Values in the Subarctic

From 1840 to 1890, HBC traders and Church of England missionaries – most of them from England – were the main representatives from the outside world in contact with Yukon peoples. On the surface, traders and missionaries were in the North for very different reasons. In practice, they often worked closely together.

The earliest traders saw considerable benefit in working *with* indigenous cultural systems when those worked to their own advantage. Missionaries, on the other hand, came to the Yukon with a clear assignment to *change* Native peoples. In the 1850s, England had recently emerged from the Industrial Revolution with a strong conviction that it was the social, economic, and political centre of the world. If traders were bound to a European market, missionaries were swept up by a vision that they had a moral obligation to, as they saw it, "civilize" and Christianize peoples throughout the world by introducing everyone to the spiritual and cultural values of Victorian Britain.

Nineteenth-century Christian theology was concerned with fixed meanings – with the idea that there was only one truth. Consequently, missionaries were uninterested in spiritual traditions that guided people living in the Yukon, except when they identified traditions they wanted to alter. Yukon peoples, on the other hand, were quite open to new ideas and saw no necessary conflict between the idea of accepting the white man's God and retaining their own religious beliefs.

Ironically, the greatest conflict in the competition for souls came from within the missionary community. Two major agencies were in active competition west of the Great Lakes – the Church Missionary Society (CMS) associated with the Anglican Church and the Roman Catholic Oblates of Mary Immaculate (OMI). While both were active in the Yukon, Anglican missionaries were initially more successful there, largely because they developed an alliance with the Hudson's Bay Company during the critical expansion period in the nineteenth century.

Just as with the fur trade, we may ask different questions about missionary activity in hindsight. Recent scholarly activity has addressed the systematic expansion of missionary activity from Europe into North America and the uniformity of the program, despite internal conflicts and competition among the participants. Oral traditions from the Yukon focus on the variety of relationships that developed between Aboriginal people and particular missionaries. Individual missionaries brought distinctly different cultural and class backgrounds and different styles of

PLATE 12.2. Julia Kutug (Mrs. Robert McDonald) with her sons Neil and Hugh, and a friend named Mary. Courtesy Anglican Church of Canada, General Synod Archives, P7517-154.

operation to their task. Two who exemplify this are Robert McDonald and William Carpenter Bompas.

Born to an Ojibwa mother and a Scottish trader on the Red River, McDonald was one of several ministers to establish missions in northern Yukon by the 1860s. He was also one of the few CMS missionaries who did not come from England. McDonald shared the Church's enthusiasm for collecting converts but was less concerned than other missionaries with modifying the local Gwich'in culture he encountered. He had impressive abilities as a linguist, and with the help of his Gwich'in wife, Julia Kutug, he translated the Bible, the Anglican prayer book, and hymns into Gwich'in language, developing a writing system still preferred by some elderly Gwich'in speakers and readers. He trained lay readers and ministers and established a community-based church that continues to have great significance in the lives of Gwich'in people in the northern Yukon.

When McDonald became ill in 1865, he was succeeded by William Carpenter Bompas. Coming from an upper middle-class London family, Bompas was inevitably more influenced by conventional British values and more committed than McDonald to what he saw as civilizing and educating the local people. Where McDonald was happy to train lay priests, Bompas and his wife, Selina, began establishing schools in various parts of the territory where students could actually live under their supervision and tutelage for most of the year. The best known of these was the Chooutla school, which later became the Carcross residential school. Established shortly after the turn of the century, Chooutla continued as a residential school until the late 1960s.

Under Bompas, the mission program reflected an idea widespread in Britain at the time, that hunters were people whose progress to "civilization" (from the Latin *civitas* or city) would be hastened if they could be encouraged to give up hunting and to farm. This idea certainly served the interests of British colonial expansion by justifying repression of other ways of life in the service of expanding cities like London. Church policy took as one of its missions the transformation of hunters to farmers. Despite the dubious wisdom of pursuing agriculture in a Subarctic environment, extensive garden patches became part of the mission at Moosehide and at the residential school in Carcross.

Varieties of History

Other visitors besides traders and missionaries left written documents as well: scientists, mapmakers, and journalists, all determined to describe and classify the world they were encountering, left valuable documents behind. Written documents do give us an interesting snapshot of what nineteenth-century visitors saw, but what about the things they missed?

Older people in Yukon communities tell stories *they* heard about the earliest travellers. People on the upper Yukon, for example, had their own classifications for the visitors, calling them *K'och'èn*, or "cloud people," because of their pale skins. A number of ancient oral traditions tell of journeys made by men and women to another dimension of time and space where everything, including people and animals, is white. The white world is winter world where the characteristics of ordinary reality are reversed so that the traveller must undergo a re-education to understand what he or she is seeing. Some people reasoned that the *K'och'èn* were visitors from this world. They observed carefully and from a distance as the "cloud people" passed by in their boats. Many early reports from the upper Yukon River include sentences like, "Once again, we saw no Indians today." It is clear from oral histories, though, that indigenous people certainly saw the strangers.

Two major shortcomings confront us, then, when we try to learn about the history of Yukon First Nations during the 1800s exclusively from written documents.

First, we should remember that the Yukon was a dynamic and changing place by the time the first visitors arrived and began writing down their observations. In many cases, these visitors were documenting the consequences of European intrusion rather than features of Aboriginal lifestyle. By the 1800s the Tlingit and Athapaskan fur trade was tapering off. When large numbers of strangers began to arrive for the first time in the 1890s, many coastal Tlingit people were already working in canneries, and Athapaskan men and women were selling their labour to prospectors and travellers as well as taking advantage of the alternative trading relationships provided by recently established independent traders.

Second, most early reports from the southern Yukon provide observations from a narrow corridor along the Yukon River. A sharp contrast occurs when we listen to oral tradition. When elders talk about early centres of population in the southern Yukon, they always refer to Hutshi and Aishihik. When we turn to the written record, these places are rarely named because they are some distance from the Yukon River, far from the routes used by most white visitors.

Extending the Empire: The Gold Rush and Alaska Highway

By the 1870s and 1880s, prospectors were arriving on the upper Yukon River, many of them bringing expectations and experiences from the gold fields of California and British Columbia. Soon, the question of who actually "owned" the territory arose. It is very clear from written documents that this question was discussed only with reference to competing claims by Canada and the United States, with no reference to whether Aboriginal people might have legal claims to the land. Government officials were interested in adding new territories to those they already governed. The United States had purchased Alaska from Russia in 1867, and agreement was reached that the 141st meridian would be the boundary line with Canada. By the end of the century, though, increasing numbers of American prospectors were entering the Yukon River basin, many of them reluctant to be ruled by Canadian law.

Events surrounding successive gold rushes in California, British Columbia, the Yukon, and Alaska during the mid- and late nineteenth century continue to exert a peculiar fascination for Western audiences. This is particularly true of the Klondike rush, perhaps because its circumstances draw together so many elements essential to romanticized European and American views of the frontier. A singular glamour is associated with gold in any period of history, but its discovery in the Yukon, in 1896, coincided with a world depression and gave hope to thousands of unemployed men and women. It was called a "poor man's gold rush" because individual prospectors could go to the Yukon with relatively little capital, egged on by dreams of fortunes waiting to be found in the creek beds and gravel bars. All that seemed to be required was a willingness to take the risks involved in travelling to the extreme northwest corner of North America.

In hindsight, of course, we know that the Klondike gold rush was part of a much larger, less glamorous process – the expansion of the new Canadian state into what was seen as the margins of northwestern North America. Very few gold seekers even found claims to stake by the time they had completed the strenuous trip over the coastal mountains and down the Yukon River. The most permanent effect of the gold rush was the establishment of a framework for administration of the Yukon Territory from Ottawa, the new nation's capital. Institutions dating from this time continue to have far-reaching implications for everyone living in the Yukon.

This gold rush has produced an enormous literature, but in thousands of written pages we find very few references to indigenous peoples who watched the changes come and were affected by them. Between 1896 and 1900, tens of thousands of would-be prospectors and miners converged on one small area of the Klondike River. The vast majority came by the same route, climbing the Chilkoot Pass and then travelling down the Yukon River to Dawson City. We are left to imagine the impact of this torrent of visitors on Aboriginal peoples living along the route and at the site of Dawson City itself, because so few travellers even mentioned Native peoples in their journals.

Stories passed on by word of mouth, describing the gold rush from the perspective of indigenous peoples, are beginning to enter the written record. For example, a Tagish man named Keish (or Skookum Jim), his sister, and his nephews were involved in the original discovery of Klondike gold; their stories, handed down for many generations, are adding a different dimension to gold rush literature. Comparing such accounts shows how ideas about family and community organization – which differ from one culture to another – may influence the interpretation of events.

Some Aboriginal people became involved in packing, guiding, and providing food for prospectors. The Han people, located at the mouth of the Klondike River where prospectors converged, were most directly affected. For those indigenous people who remained observers rather than participants in the gold rush, the greatest effects included the breaking of the Tlingit fur trade monopoly; the impact of forest fires along the Yukon River; the arrival of independent fur traders; the expansion of missionary activity; the establishment of a state-administered justice system; the building of the White Pass and Yukon Route railway from Skagway, Alaska, on the coast to Whitehorse; and the running of a riverboat fleet between Whitehorse and Dawson City.

Most non-Natives left the country soon after the beginning of the century. In 1900, the total population of the Yukon Territory had climbed to over 27,000, of whom 3,000 were classified as Indian in the census. By 1912, the total population had declined to 6,000 and by 1921, to just over 4,000. The population remained relatively stable for the next twenty years: 4,230 in 1931 and 4,914 in 1941.

Fur prices remained high well into the 1930s. By then, a family's annual cycle included one or more trips to a trading post, and some families built log cabins near posts. There was some seasonal wage work on riverboats, at wood camps, with game guides, and on the railway. More children were attending residential schools. Nevertheless, basic social organization and coherence of long-standing lifestyles remained.

Before the Second World War there were no major roads and almost no mechanized vehicles in the Yukon. A few wagon trails remained from the flurry of mining activity in the early 1900s. A winter road paralleled the Yukon River from Whitehorse to Dawson City. Generally, most people travelled by foot, dog team, or boat, and they were separated from each other by several days' travel.

Then in April, 1942, three regiments of American soldiers arrived in Whitehorse with orders to build the Yukon section of the Alaska Highway. While a northern road system had been under discussion for some years, the threat of a military invasion from Japan accelerated the process dramatically. Between April, 1942, and December, 1943, more than 34,000 men were employed constructing the road through British Columbia, the Yukon, and Alaska. Once again, Native people were overwhelmed by large numbers of outsiders with radically different lifestyles.

This second "rush," as older people call it, marked the beginning of another new era. Its consequences were substantially more disruptive than those of the first rush, testing Native adaptability to the limits, often at great personal cost. Although the Alaska Highway was not the only factor involved in altering the old ways, its construction and use can be seen as a central thread in the changes after 1942.

Elders speaking out during both the Alaska Highway Pipeline Inquiry of 1977 and during the commemoration in 1992 of the fiftieth anniversary of Alaska Highway construction suggest that there were both short-term and long-term changes associated with the coming of the road. Short-term consequences included the inevitable impact of another brief population explosion as some 30,000 soldiers and construction workers arrived practically overnight. The range of responses has been documented elsewhere, including the excitement of new technology, new people, and new ideas, but also the devastation caused by epidemics and the dramatic increase in alcohol abuse.

The long-term changes occurred in two broad areas: first, in relationships between Aboriginal people and land, and second, in long-standing social institutions associated with kinship. The highway corridor permitted the possibility of systematic government administration for the first time. Because of extensive overhunting by soldiers, for instance, large areas of the southwest Yukon were set aside as a sanctuary, effectively barring Aboriginal people from their traditional hunting and trapping territories. State-imposed restrictions on hunting and trapping ultimately altered Aboriginal modes of production.

The highway also permitted new levels of social administration. A host of new agencies began to operate in communities, providing social assistance but often usurping roles formerly carried out by extended families – economic support, health care, education, and enforcement of rules. In the short term, many of these services were beneficial, but the cumulative effect of living in government-administered settlements with no economic base also contributed to social breakdown in many families.

Orally narrated accounts of Alaska Highway construction show that no single narrative captures the experience of Aboriginal people living through the changes of this century. Memories of wartime experience are contested and debated and discussion of these events has helped people to formulate their contemporary land claims position.

Continuing Importance of Oral Tradition in the 1990s

When Yukon Natives began doing research for land claims in the late 1960s, one of their initial objectives was to document their common, shared experiences as Yukon's First Nations. With the settlement of that claim, they are struggling to develop ways of working together while still recognizing traditional regional and cultural differences within the Yukon. They point out that they chose carefully when they selected the term "First Nations" to refer to themselves, because they *are* more than one nation and speak with more than one voice.

As the Yukon enters the 1990s, increasing attention is being paid to indigenous perspectives on the past, and the oral accounts of elders have at last begun to reach a wider audience. At the annual Yukon International Storytelling Festival, held in Whitehorse since 1987, elders speak to crowds of attentive listeners. Northern Native Broadcasting has produced videotaped documentaries on historical and contemporary issues and these are being transmitted across northern Canada on television. The Yukon Heritage and Museums Association has supported conferences on themes where both elders and academics participate and exchange ideas on topics of mutual interest. The Heritage Branch of the Yukon territorial government has funded First Nations in the Yukon to conduct their own oral history projects. The Yukon Native Language Centre continues to document languages, narratives, and history in indigenous languages and to ensure that these become part of the regular school program throughout the Territory. The Curriculum Development Program of the Council for Yukon Indians is developing a community-based curriculum for use in Yukon classrooms. Together, these initiatives are helping to ensure that the cultural heritage of First Nations is seen not simply as part of the past but as a continuing and growing force in the Yukon's present and future.

The endurance of oral tradition in the Yukon speaks directly to the strength and flexibility of Athapaskan and Tlingit ways of life. Recognition of the debts to old tradition is indispensable to the creation of new tradition. Through this process, First Nations are demonstrating the tremendous importance of storytelling in helping cultures undergoing rapid and complex changes.

Notes

1. Much of the material in this chapter is adapted from my *Reading Voices/Dan Dha Ts'edenintth'e* (Vancouver: Douglas & McIntyre, 1991). That book was funded by the Yukon Department of Education and was prepared with guidance from the Council for Yukon Indians, the Yukon Historical and Museum Association, the Yukon Teachers' Association, and the Department of Education.

2. Local publications included Sidney, Smith, and Dawson (1977), Sidney (1980, 1982, 1983), Smith (1982), Ned (1984).

3. For an excellent discussion of the history of Yukon languages, see McClellan *et al.*, *Part of the Land, Part of the Water*, Chapter 6. An overview of contemporary Yukon Native languages and issues associated with language maintenance, including personal statements about the ongoing importance of these languages, appears in *Speaking Out* by Southern Tutchone linguist Daniel Tlen.

4. During the summer of 1993, for example, Ingrid Johnson, a Tlingit woman with a degree in anthropology, worked with the MacBride museum in Whitehorse making an inventory of Tlingit beaded work in the collection and interviewing elders to learn their stories about women's artistic traditions.

Recommended Reading

Coates, Ken

1991 *Best Left as Indians: Native-White Relations in the Yukon Territory, 1840-1973*. Montreal: McGill-Queen's University Press.

      Using archival sources, an historian reconstructs Native-white relations during the nineteenth and twentieth centuries in the Yukon Territory.

Coates, Ken, ed.

1985 *The Alaska Highway: Papers of the 40th Anniversary Symposium.* Vancouver: University of British Columbia Press.

      An edited volume of papers analysing history and range of impacts of the Alaska Highway following the fortieth anniversary of its construction.

Cruikshank, Julie

1989 "Oral Tradition and Written Accounts: An Incident from the Klondike Gold Rush," *Culture*, 9, 2: 1-10.

1991 *Reading Voices/Dan Dha Ts'edenintth'e: Oral and Written Interpretations of the Yukon's Past.* Vancouver: Douglas & McIntyre.

1992 "Images of Society in Klondike Gold Rush Narratives: Skookum Jim and the Discovery of Gold," *Ethnohistory*, 39, 1: 20-41.

      These pieces discuss problems of historical reconstruction with reference to specific oral and written accounts.

Cruikshank, Julie, in collaboration with Angela Sidney, Kitty Smith, and Annie Ned

1990 *Life Lived Like a Story: Life Stories of Three Yukon Elders.* Lincoln: University of Nebraska Press; Vancouver: University of British Columbia Press.

      Three orally narrated life stories and analysis of how autobiography is socially and culturally constructed.

Duncan, Kate

1989 *Northern Athapaskan Art: A Beadwork Tradition.* Seattle: University of Washington Press.

A splendidly illustrated, well-researched book about Athapaskan women's artistic traditions in northwestern North America.

McClellan, Catharine

1970 "Indian Stories About the First Whites in Northwestern North America," in Margaret Lantis, ed., *Ethnohistory in Southwestern Alaska and the Southern Yukon: Method and Content*. Lexington: University Press of Kentucky.

An important article about the oral tradition, outlining methodological issues critical in the use of oral tradition as a source for historical reconstruction.

1975 *My Old People Say: An Ethnographic Survey of the Southern Yukon Territory*. Ottawa: National Museum of Canada Publications in Ethnology No. 6, 2 vols.

This is the classic ethnography for the southwest Yukon and provides the baseline from which all subsequent ethnographies begin.

1981a "Intercultural Relations and Cultural Change in the Cordillera," in *Handbook of North American Indians*, Vol. 6, *Subarctic*, ed. June Helm. Washington, D.C.: Smithsonian Institution.

1981b "Inland Tlingit," in *Handbook*, Vol. 6, *Subarctic*, ed. June Helm.

1981c "Tagish," in *Handbook*, Vol. 6, *Subarctic*, ed. June Helm.

1981d "Tutchone," in *Handbook*, Vol. 6, *Subarctic*, ed. June Helm.

These four essays in the *Handbook of North American Indians* provide authoritative accounts of ethnology and ethnohistory for the southern Yukon.

McClellan, Catharine, with Lucie Birckel, Robert Bringhurst, James A. Fall, Carol McCarthy, and Janice Sheppard

1987 *Part of the Land, Part of the Water: A History of Yukon Indians*. Vancouver: Douglas & McIntyre.

A highly accessible overview of Yukon ethnography prepared for a more general audience than McClellan's ethnography, cited above.

McDonnell, Roger

1975 "Kasini Society: Some Aspects of the Social Organization of an Athapaskan Culture between 1900-1950," Ph.D. dissertation, Department of Anthropology, University of British Columbia.

A reconstruction of the historical forces operating in the eastern Yukon and how they affected Kaska peoples in the early twentieth century.

O'Leary, Beth Laura

1992 *Salmon and Storage: Southern Tutchone Use of an 'Abundant' Resource*. Whitehorse: Government of Yukon, Heritage Branch.

This is a published Ph.D. thesis examining the relationship between salmon resources and subsistence strategies of people in the southwest Yukon. The work was carried out with members of the Champagne-Aishihik First Nation.

Slododin, Richard
  1962 *Band Organization of the Peel River Kutchin*. National Museum of Canada Bulletin 179. Ottawa.
  1963 " 'The Dawson Boys' – Peel River Indians and the Dawson Gold Rush," *Polar Record*, 5: 24-35.
        Detailed discussion of Peel River Gwich'in history during the late nineteenth and early twentieth centuries.

Tanner, Adrian
  1965 "The Structure of Fur Trade Relations," M.A. thesis, Department of Anthropology, University of British Columbia.
        A highly readable account of issues underlying the Yukon fur trade.

Tlen, Daniel
  1986 *Speaking Out: Consultations and Survey of Yukon Native Languages Planning, Visibility and Growth*. Whitehorse: Yukon Native Language Centre.
        Survey of the continuing importance of Aboriginal languages for Yukon people with recommendations for future programming.

Tom, Gertie
  1987 *Ekeyi: Gyo Cho Chu/My Country, Big Salmon River*. Whitehorse: Yukon Native Language Centre.
        Gertie Tom, a Tutchone language specialist, has written books in her language as part of her work with the Yukon Native Language Centre. This book focuses on place names and genealogy in the central Yukon where she grew up.

Additional References Cited

Emmons, G.T.
  1911 *The Tahltan Indians*. Philadelphia: University of Pennsylvania Publications in Anthropology, 4, 1.

Honigmann, John J.
  1954 *The Kaska Indians: An Ethnographic Reconstruction*. New Haven: Yale University Publications in Anthropology No. 51.

McKennan, Robert
  1959 *The Upper Tanana Indians*. New Haven: Yale University Publications in Anthropology No. 55.

Ned, Annie
  1984 *Old People in Those Days They Told Their Story All the Time*. Compiled by J. Cruikshank. Whitehorse: Yukon Native Languages Project.

Osgood, Cornelius

1971 *The Han Indians: A Compilation of Ethnographic and Historical Data on the Alaska-Yukon Boundary Area.* New Haven: Yale University Publications in Anthropology No. 74.

Sidney, Angela

1980 *Place Names of the Tagish Region, Southern Yukon.* Whitehorse: Yukon Native Languages Project.

1982 *Tagish Tlaagu: Tagish Stories.* Recorded by J. Cruikshank. Council for Yukon Indians and Government of Yukon.

1983 *Haa Shagoon/Our Family History.* Compiled by J. Cruikshank. Whitehorse: Yukon Native Languages Project.

Sidney, Angela, Kitty Smith, and Rachel Dawson

1977 *My Stories Are My Wealth.* Recorded by J. Cruikshank. Whitehorse: Council for Yukon Indians.

Smith, Kitty

1982 *Nindal Kwadindur: I'm Going to Tell a You a Story.* Recorded by J. Cruikshank. Whitehorse: Council for Yukon Indians and Government of Yukon.

PART V
The Eastern Woodlands

CHAPTER 13
Farmers and Hunters of the Eastern Woodlands: A Regional Overview

Mary Druke Becker

Environment

The portion of eastern Canada south of the boreal forest region forms a part of the Eastern Woodlands culture area. The land is richly forested with both deciduous and coniferous trees. Lakes and rivers are scattered throughout the region, and Indian territory has often been defined here by river drainage. The St. Lawrence River, linking the Atlantic Ocean to the Great Lakes, was an important feature in both the social and physical landscapes.

The environment richly provided numerous resources useful to its indigenous inhabitants. The forests were home to a number of animals desired primarily for their meat and hides, but also for other purposes. These included deer, bear, moose, rabbit, beaver, otter, muskrat, fox, wolf, raccoon, skunk, bobcat, and numerous fowl. These were hunted with bows and arrows or spears, or caught in traps, round-ups, or dead-falls. Edible fruits, nuts, roots, and, in places, wild rice were harvested. Europeans have always recognized that staples of the region in historic times, particularly corn, beans, and squash, were cultigens. What has

MAP 13.1. The Eastern Woodlands

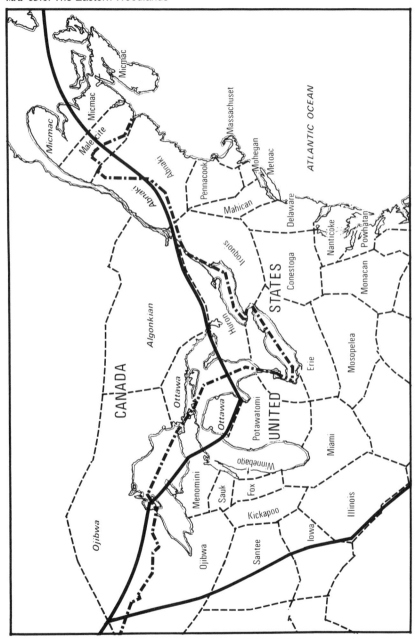

been recognized only more recently is that many other vegetable products were not simply gathered; the plants were in one way or another tended. Aquatic resources, including salt and freshwater fish, sea mammals, crustaceans, eels, and turtles, were also of major importance to most peoples in the region. Tools used for fishing were bone fish hooks, nets, harpoons, spears, and weirs. Animal skins and bones, wood and bark, clay and other such items provided the raw materials from which people created the things necessary for life: clothing; shelter; utensils for building, hunting, fishing, gardening, and the various domestic tasks; and objects that were decorative or recreational.

Social Organization

The people inhabiting the Canadian Woodlands during the historic period were primarily Algonquian and Iroquoian speakers. For the most part, Iroquoian-speaking people during the historic period were more intensive farmers than the Algonquian-speakers, who relied more heavily on fishing, hunting, and gathering. Friendly relations between Algonquian and Iroquoian peoples, when they occurred, often centred around trade, with corn and other agricultural produce going to Algonquians in return for meat, fish, and furs. The economies of both groups were broadly based, so that Iroquoians also engaged in fishing, hunting, and gathering, while many Algonquians practised horticulture. In noting the difference in emphasis, the reader should also note that in the warmer U.S. Woodlands, where horticulture was more reliable, the contrast between the two groups was less marked. Regardless of the particular emphasis, the subsistence activities of Woodlands people were intensive, providing enriched economies.

Inter-village contact was common, and a complex system of trails linked villages to one another and to hunting areas. Generally, Algonquians were more likely to use water transportation than were Iroquoians. Correspondingly, their birchbark canoes were light and efficient, while Iroquoians used bulkier elm-bark canoes.

Among Algonquian speakers, differences existed between inland dwellers and maritime peoples such as the Micmac. The latter had a band organization similar to that found in the Subarctic in that it was based on principles of friendship and cognatic relations, while inland peoples were more oriented toward totemic descent groups, usually patrilineal. Nevertheless, the maritime people may be considered to be more similar to Woodland cultural groups than to Subarctic ones, largely because of the intensive nature of their subsistence activities. Iroquoians were, and many still are, organized socially on the basis of matrilineal kinship, and membership in a lineage or clan depends on the affiliation of one's mother.

Most differences among Algonquian groups result from slight variations in ecological adaptation. This is obviously the case with many maritime/inland contrasts. Most differences among Iroquoians, also, can be related to ecological adaptations. Others are primarily related to historic and other factors: the hunting practices of the Mohawk of Oka/Kanesatake more closely resemble those of their Algonquian-speaking Algonkin and Nipissing neighbours than they do those of other Mohawk.

A division of labour existed. Men were primarily responsible for hunting, fishing, warfare, councils, building, manufacturing implements for hunting and fishing, and, among those involved in horticulture, clearing the fields. Women were responsible for gathering and for planting, cultivating, and harvesting. They also participated in fishing, cleaned fish and game, cooked, cared for children, and made clothing and household utensils.

Political organization among inland Algonquians took the form of local chieftainships. In some cases, as among the Passamaquoddy and Malecite, these chieftainships were patrilineally inherited. Among maritime people, leadership was band based, usually with one leader per band. Some Algonquian local groups united to form national or confederate councils, as in the case of the Abenaki Confederacy, composed of Malecite, Micmac, Passamaquoddy, and Penobscot. Iroquoians had local chieftainships, which in the case of the Six Nations (Mohawk, Oneida, Onondaga, Cayuga, Seneca, and Tuscarora) were based on both heredity and merit. Confederate structure is commonly associated with the Six Nations Iroquois, but it was typical of other Iroquoians also, such as the Huron.

History

When English and French explorers entered the region in the sixteenth century, Native people were thriving. Dire effects, however, followed contact with the strangers. Disease, smallpox, and other contagious illnesses for which people had no immunity cut back population drastically, as did the warfare centring on the fur trade. We do not know how many entire groups, let alone families and individuals, were completely lost during the very early historic period.

Other changes also were forthcoming. For many Iroquoians and Algonquians the fur trade resulted in a specialization in trapping and trading and less reliance on traditional subsistence practices. For some Algonquians horticulture became somewhat more feasible because they no longer had to break into small groups to search for food in times of

PLATE 13.1. (After Edward Chalfield) Nicholas Vincent Isawanhonhi, a Huron chief, holding a wampum belt, 1825. Courtesy of the National Archives of Canada, Ottawa, C38948.

scarcity and because, although horticulture was still less reliable than hunting in a relatively northern climate, there was now the security of an "outside" source of supplies in the event of crop failure.

Through time Christianity became common among many Woodlands people. Many Natives were induced by missionary efforts in the seventeenth and eighteenth centuries to move from their native territories to mission settlements. A number of communities and reserves in eastern Canada were formed in this way. Today, Christianity is found side by side with traditional religions in many Indian communities.

The map of Native people in eastern Canada has changed greatly during the historic period. Many groups were radically dispersed, some to points as distant as northern British Columbia or Mexico, as Euro-Canadian "pioneers" settled in their land, or as warfare with other Natives also attempting to cope with new conditions necessitated that they flee. Others were annihilated. Some groups originating in the U.S. moved to Canadian mission settlements or set up new communities when their own land was lost as a result of what were essentially European wars. Whatever their origins and however desperate their history, Woodlands Indians have survived and are an integral part of twentieth-century Canada. The following chapters provide more detail concerning the culture and history of these people.

CHAPTER 14
Iroquois and Iroquoian in Canada

Mary Druke Becker

Introduction

Iroquoian* speakers, including the St. Lawrence Iroquoian, Huron, Petun, and Neutral Indians, long inhabited what are now the provinces of Quebec and Ontario: according to their own oral histories, Iroquoians have been on "this island on a turtle's back" (the North American continent) since time immemorial. Their presence in Canada, however, was uneven during the historical period. By the twentieth century, except for some Huron and combined Huron and Petun (Wyandot), there were no descendants of the Iroquoians who had been known to French

---

* The terms "Iroquoian" and "Iroquois" can be confusing. "Iroquoian" generally refers first to a language grouping including northern Iroquoian speakers (discussed below) and southern Iroquoian speakers (Cherokee), and then to the culture of the people speaking Iroquoian languages. "Iroquois" refers to a specific group of Iroquoian speakers – members of the six nations comprising the political confederacy known as the League of the Iroquois.

missionaries and explorers in the sixteenth and seventeenth centuries. The present-day Iroquoian population of Canada consists mainly of people of the Six Nations (or, the Iroquois): Mohawk, Oneida, Onondaga, Cayuga, Seneca, and Tuscarora. These people moved to Canada from their homeland, in what is now New York state, from the late seventeenth through the early nineteenth centuries.

This chapter presents an introduction to the historic and, especially, the modern Iroquois of Canada. The approach is based on the interpretive perspective advocated by Clifford Geertz. Interpretive anthropology assumes that a particular action can have many meanings even within a single culture, and certainly across cultures. For example, a simple action like "blinking the right eyelid" (Geertz, 1973) could be an unintentional twitch, a wink, or a pretended wink; it could be done to mimic or ridicule someone, or for any number of other reasons. An interpretive anthropologist endeavours to determine which among the many possible meanings are attributed to particular actions by the people involved.

The interpretation of cultural phenomena usually requires looking beyond the obvious to make sense of the complicated symbolic meanings involved in interaction. In studies of cross-cultural interaction, this requires that one describe the ways that other people interpret what they do and experience. For example, Iroquois and Euro-Canadians often put different constructions on the same types of behaviour, a reality that has frequently caused mutual distrust, misunderstanding, and confusion.

Study of past Native cultures through historical sources is called ethnohistory, and interpretive anthropology can be especially helpful in ethnohistorical studies. It calls for an awareness of the cultural perspectives significant to the individuals involved in particular interactions. Through an analysis of sources, which may include manuscripts, printed documents, graphics, and oral traditions, the researcher must decide what was considered significant. Each such source, however, reflects the point of view of an individual. The object, then, is not merely to wade through all the separate points of view to find out what "really" happened, but to take into account features of the interaction itself, especially as, in most cases, the persons were themselves engaged in the interaction. Although ethnohistorical materials have limitations as sources of data, there are no limitations on the questions that may be addressed with their aid. A researcher is also free to compare data: the statements and observations made by an informant at different times may be weighed for consistency, and may be checked against information provided by others. Thus, the ethnohistorian does "fieldwork" among documents, observing and interpreting the interactions for which data are available.

The Historical Iroquoians of Canada

The first Iroquoian people of whom there is historical evidence are the St. Lawrence (or Laurentian) Iroquoians, first mentioned by Jacques Cartier in 1534 and last by Jean François de la Rocque de Roberval in 1543. Their identity and fate have long been an enigma to scholars. Algonquian characteristics in their culture have led to speculation that they were "Iroquoianized Algonquians." Most researchers, however, tend to categorize them as Iroquoians, probably descendants of those whose culture developed prehistorically in the region from Middle Woodlands culture. Those associated with the village of Stadacona (near present-day Quebec City) lived in seven to ten villages along the river between Ile aux Coudres and the Richelieu Rapids. The village of Hochelaga was on Montreal Island, as were two smaller settlements, apparently fishing camps. These villages were thriving when Cartier and Roberval travelled up the St. Lawrence. But by the time Samuel de Champlain arrived in 1603, the St. Lawrence Iroquoians had disappeared without trace. The Iroquoian-speakers that Champlain mentions are Huron. The Huron were to become the dominant Iroquoian group with whom the French had extensive contact until 1650, when they, too, disappeared.

The Huron were divided into five confederated tribal groupings – Attignawantan, Attigneenongnahac, Ahrendarouon, Tahontaenrat, and Ataranchronon – and, meeting at least once a year to renew their alliance, they occupied a rich area of coniferous and deciduous forest west of Lake Simcoe and east of Georgian Bay. Other Iroquoian-speaking peoples with whom the French were familiar in Canada during the early seventeenth century were the Neutral, Wenro, and Petun.

The Neutral, so named by the French because of their tendency to remain neutral in the wars between the Huron and Iroquois, comprised five groups – Attiragenrega, Niagagarega, Antouaronon, Kakouagoga, and Ahondihronon – occupying from twenty-eight to forty villages lying south and east of Huronia. The relation of the groups is not known in detail, although evidence indicates that they formed a confederacy or shifting alliance of tribes. The Neutral disappeared when, in 1647, the Seneca attacked one of their villages because its people had allowed a Seneca to be captured by the Petun in Neutral territory.

The Wenro are commonly associated with the Neutral and, at one time, were allied with them. Apparently, the Wenro were located close to Seneca country, in two villages near present-day Lewiston, New York. They moved to Huronia in 1638 because they felt threatened by the

Iroquois; having split with the Neutral, they were then without military support to defend themselves.

At the beginning of the seventeenth century, the Petun lived southwest of Huronia, in what are now Ontario's Nottawasaga and Collingwood townships. The Petun were composed of two nations: the Wolves and the Deer. They were very similar to the Huron, especially the Attignawantan, except that they grew large amounts of tobacco, so much, in fact, that they have been called the Tobacco Nation. A number of Huron settled among the Petun in 1649. The combined Huron and Petun were eventually displaced in warfare against the Iroquois.

The Iroquoian-speaking peoples lived primarily in sedentary villages that were moved every ten to twelve years when conditions (e.g., soil exhaustion) warranted. In some cases, multiple village settlements developed: two or three villages formed a cluster usually designated by a single name. Within a village, people lived in communal longhouses, averaging eight by thirty metres in size and built of post frames covered by strips of elm or cedar bark. The arched roofs had coverable holes to allow release of smoke from the fires lining the centre of each house. Usually, two families shared a fire. Compartments formed of boards with supports suspended a distance from the ground lined both sides of the longhouse. Each family slept and stored clothing and goods in a compartment. Storage for dried foods and firewood was located at each end of the longhouse and under sleeping platforms. As Iroquois kinship was matrilineal and residence was matrilocal, each longhouse was inhabited by a group of related adult women, their spouses, and children.

Within villages, the main organizing units were matrilineally grouped women, who directed communal activities such as planting and gathering, and councils of peace and war chiefs, the former arbitrating internal disputes and making alliances, the latter deliberating on military actions. Decisions in council were generally made by consensus. No one was bound by a decision, however, although social pressure acted to induce acceptance of decisions made.

Sex and age were important determinants of economic activity. At least during the later historic period, the division of labour resulted in a mental association of men with forests and women with clearings, an association fundamental to the way Iroquoian people structured their world.

Women, aided by children, did most of the agricultural work and the gathering of fruits, other vegetable foods, and firewood. Women also made wooden utensils, pottery vessels, and clothing. The clothing consisted of moccasins of soft leather for both sexes; breechcloths, complemented by leggings and mantles in winter, for males; and skirts, with leggings and mantles in winter, for females. All clothing was made of tanned animal (usually bear or deer) skin. When European goods were introduced, cloth was sometimes substituted for leather.

Iroquoian men were hunters, fishermen, councillors, and warriors. In spring, summer, and winter (primarily late winter and early spring), men went on hunting expeditions, using bows and arrows to take deer, moose, bear, mountain lion, and similar large game. More casual hunting, in late spring and early summer, focused on small game, e.g., otter and beaver. Fishing, by net, lance, and weir, was undertaken primarily in spring. Meat, fish, and some vegetable foods were commonly dried for storage. Men made hunting, fishing, and war tools, built homes and canoes, cleared new fields, and traded, negotiated, and warred with other nations. They had much greater contact with the world outside their villages than did women. However, Algonquian-speaking people sometimes wintered near Iroquois villages, giving women some opportunities for contact with people outside their own village and nation.

There were, of course, variations on this cultural pattern. For example, although Hochelagans were characterized by the same subsistence and settlement patterns as other Iroquoians, Stadaconans were not. Corn was much less, and fish much more, important to Stadaconans than to other Iroquoians and, hence, these people were less sedentary. Large numbers of Stadaconan men, women, and children travelled in summer to Gaspé Peninsula to fish for mackerel. Others travelled east and north, toward Saguenay, to hunt white whale, seal, porpoise, and, possibly, walrus.

The Neutral and the Petun differed from the Huron in growing tobacco, which they traded extensively with their Algonquian neighbours. The Neutral followed different hunting practices than did the Huron: they entrapped deer, several at a time, in enclosures established in an open space where they could be killed easily, while the Huron generally hunted one deer at a time. Furthermore, the Neutral apparently did not wear clothing as consistently as did the Huron. Two French missionaries, Daillon and Lalement, wrote that Neutral men sometimes did not wear breechcloths, although one mentioned that the women usually were clothed, at least from the waist to the knees.

Lalement noted three ways in which the Neutral differed significantly from the Huron, with whom he was more familiar. He categorized the Neutral as "taller, stronger, and better proportioned" than the Huron. He remarked on a difference in burial customs, involving a longer mourning

period among the Neutral, noting that the Huron brought bodies for burial immediately after death, while the Neutral waited until the "very
latest moment possible when decomposition has rendered them insup-
portable." Lalement's third comment is blatantly ethnocentric:

> In going through the country, one finds nothing else but people who
> play the part of lunatics with all possible extravagances, and any
> liberties they choose, and who are suffered to do all that is pleasing
> to them, for fear of offending their demon. They take the embers
> from the fire and scatter them around; they speak and shatter what
> they encounter, as if they were raving, – although in reality, for the
> most part, they are as self-collected as those who do not play this
> character. But they conduct themselves in this way, in order to give,
> they say, this satisfaction to their special demon, who demands and
> exacts this of them, – that is to say, to him who speaks to them in
> dreams. . . . (Thwaites, 1896-1901, 21: 187-231)

This behaviour, further discussed below, was not significantly different
from that considered appropriate to dreaming among the Huron and Iroquois, although Lalement was struck by its prevalence among the Neutral.

Jesuit and Recollet missionaries left fairly rich records on Huron
beliefs. The Huron believed that the universe was inhabited by other-
than-human beings as well as by humans. It was important to appease
these beings, including those associated with animals, so that one's life
would run smoothly. They believed that the dead went to a haven in the
West, travelling there via the Milky Way. Every ten years or so, the dead
of a village were disinterred and brought by clan segments (groups of
matrilineages) to a large feast at which the bones were reinterred in an
ossuary pit. Often this "Feast of the Dead" coincided with the movement
of a village to a new location. It served an integrative function, uniting
village members both living and dead, and it allowed for the formal
expression of personal grief. The Neutral had a similar ceremony.

The Huron had very sophisticated attitudes toward dreams, believing
that they reflect a person's subconscious desires. Dreams were commonly analysed by shamans, and every effort was made to fulfil them,
symbolically if not literally. Each winter there was a three-day festival
called *ononharioa* ("the upsetting of the brain"), in which villagers
"feigning madness" recited their dreams and demanded fulfilment of
them. French missionaries were amazed by this ceremony, often interpreting it as demonstrating the "primitive" nature of the Huron. Psy-
choanalysts might view it as an effective cathartic practice, allowing

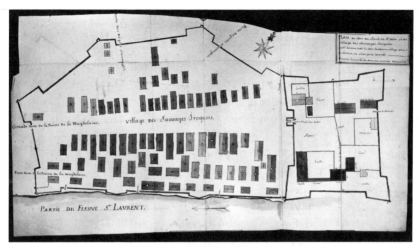

PLATE 14.1. Plan du Fort de Sault de St. Louis Villages des Iroquois (Kahnawake), mid-eighteenth century (Ayer M.S. Map 211 in Ayer M.S. 299). Courtesy of the Edward E. Ayer Collection, The Newberry Library, Chicago.

for the expression of suppressed wishes. It also resulted in a redistribution of wealth: many objects deemed necessary for fulfilling a dream were not returned.

Herbal medicines were used to cure some types of diseases; others, however, were believed to be caused either by other-than-human beings who had been upset or by sorcerers intent on causing harm. When such illnesses were diagnosed, ceremonies of supplication might be conducted to appease the angry beings, or incantations and extractions of foreign elements from the sick person's body might be undertaken if it was believed that a sorcerer was responsible.

Sorcery was considered a very real phenomenon, and the belief provided a valuable tool for social control: leaders, for example, were discouraged from grasping too much power lest they be categorized as sorcerers. Sorcery also affected the Huron evaluation of Jesuit missionaries, who claimed to be power holders. Because spiritual power was respected, missionaries were both valued and feared – feared especially because the power of the Jesuits to bring disease did not escape Huron attention.

Disease ravaged the Huron and other Iroquoian peoples after contact. The Huron population decreased from about 20,000 to about 9,000 after smallpox epidemics in the 1630s. Although other factors were more directly responsible for their final disappearance, the effects of disease should not be underestimated. It seems probable that the St. Lawrence Iroquoians were destroyed primarily by disease and warfare and that

survivors took refuge among other groups, eventually losing their identity. Their demise may have been precipitated by their attempts to play a
dominant role as middlemen in the fur trade. The Stadaconans tried, for
example, to keep Cartier's party from going to Hochelaga in 1535, telling the French that they might meet death if they did. In one view, the
Stadaconans were destroyed by either the Hochelagans or the Algonquians in about 1580, and the Hochelagans were later attacked by the
Mohawks.

By the early seventeenth century, the French trade had become important to other Iroquoians, affecting their relations with other Native
peoples and, often, playing a role in their disappearance. For example,
the Huron were an important link between the French and people to the
north and west. As trade concerns became increasingly important,
nations of the Iroquois confederacy, particularly the Mohawk (who were
already involved in the Dutch fur trade), became interested in the French
trade. With the aid of guns and ammunition provided by Dutch traders,
they waged war against the Huron, other Iroquoians, and the Algonquians in a push to widen their trade networks. In 1649, after a series of
devastating defeats, the Huron abandoned their villages; the Wenro, who
had taken refuge among the Huron in 1638, shared their fate. Many were
killed or captured by Iroquois raiding parties; others took refuge with
neighbouring tribes; some even went to live among the Iroquois, who
accepted the refugees in an effort to increase their own numbers. A number of Huron, however, banded together for the severe winter of 1650 at
Gahendoe (Christian) Island. Of these, about 300 settled under French
protection at Ile d'Orleans near Quebec City. They moved to the mainland six years later and their descendants, often referred to as the Huron
of Lorette, remain there. Others took refuge among the Petun, who later
were also displaced by the Iroquois. The combined Huron and Petun
became known as Wyandots (the Huron name for themselves being
"Wendat") and settled at various sites in the Great Lakes region. Today
some live on the Wyandotte Reservation in Oklahoma; others live near
Sandwich, Ontario.

In 1647, warfare between the Iroquois and Neutral intensified, and by
1652 most Neutral had fled their villages. The last remnants identified
historically were a group shown living south of Lake Erie on a map dated
1656. The Iroquois did not move into the territory vacated by the displaced Iroquoians; they used the area for hunting, trading, and travel during war. The first permanent Iroquois settlement in what is now Canada
began in 1667 and was not directly related to the wars.

The People of the Extended Households

In the seventeenth century, the Iroquois inhabiting what is now New York state were a confederacy of five nations – Mohawk, Oneida, Onondaga, Cayuga, and Seneca. Their image of themselves was spatial – a long-house with the Mohawk as the eastern door and the Seneca as the western. Their name for themselves was "Kanonsionni" ("the League of the United [or Extended] Households"). Another Iroquoian-speaking nation, the Tuscarora, joined the confederacy after being driven from their homes in North Carolina, in about 1713.

The nations of the Iroquois League were culturally similar to the other Iroquoians. They were primarily sedentary people, practising agriculture for their staples of corn, beans, and squash. During the seventeenth and eighteenth centuries, the villages were composed of matrilineal longhouses. Matrilineages were grouped together to form clans, usually designated by the name of an animal. For example, the Bear, Wolf, and Turtle clans were present in all of the nations. Longhouses gave way, in the late eighteenth and early nineteenth centuries, to wooden frame houses occupied by extended families. Longhouses continue to be used for political and ceremonial functions.

The typical sex-based division of labour was in effect among the Iroquois; in later times, however, as game became scarcer, men became more involved in agriculture. The village was the primary focus of activity for women, older men, and children. Younger men often spent summers away from the village, joining war parties or attending councils. In late fall, early winter, and early spring, they were often away hunting. Women and children might accompany them on short expeditions. Fishing was done on rivers and streams in or near the village.

Like the Huron, the Iroquois saw their universe as composed of both human and other-than-human beings – from the smallest insects to beings such as Panther, the Thunderers, Grandmother Moon, and the Creator, whose power could be used for good or harmful purposes. Hence, many rituals and ceremonies, including medicine rituals, were designed to appease these beings, to get them to use their power in helpful ways, or both. As an extension of this attitude, reciprocal alliances were a vital part of Iroquois interrelations: the League itself was an alliance of nations, and the Iroquois were proud of, and diligent in maintaining, the covenant chain alliance with the British. An Iroquoian symbol of the alliance was the linking of arms. Although Iroquois political practices were very similar to those of Canadian Iroquoians, their confederacy, designed to regulate matters between nations of the League and external affairs involving other nations, was much stronger than any alliance among any other Iroquoian nations.

Chieftainships among the Iroquois during the seventeenth, eighteenth, and nineteenth centuries were hereditary (matrilineally); they remain so among some Iroquois groups. Primogeniture was not a feature of succession, merit being an important consideration in determining who among the descendants of a leader would take his or her place. The Iroquois League was, and is, led by a council of chiefs commonly called sachems. According to the Iroquois, the confederate council, since its foundations, has been composed of forty-nine (some say fifty) chiefs. Each chief is given the name of the person he succeeds when he takes office; hence, the names of the current chiefs are those of the original founders of the confederacy. A roll call of sachems is recited at each condolence council, where a deceased chief is mourned and a successor installed in his place. This roll call emphasizes the merging of the past with the present, as the recitation recapitulates the kinship basis of the confederacy. The matron of the lineage holding a vacant chieftainship selects a successor and presents him to the council for acceptance. Theoretically, the council may veto the matron's choice, but this rarely, if ever, happens.

Village chiefs, who may or may not also be confederate chiefs, also inherit their positions matrilineally. Most Iroquois communities now have elective councils, as well as hereditary ones. The two types often vie with one another for recognition of legitimacy.

The League of the Iroquois allowed for local autonomy while providing a League-wide forum for airing problems and plans. This balanced structure provided for considerable diversity. Because a goal of unanimity in decision-making was actively sought, council negotiations were prolonged. The process of deliberation revealed highly valued positions. If neither side could persuade its opponents, discussions would be discontinued. Groups would often act on their own. Occasionally, rifts between parties became strong, in some cases leading to the splintering of communities. Some modern Canadian Iroquois communities were formed under such an impetus. Links were, however, usually maintained with the village of origin.

Decision-making usually took place first within the appropriate council at the village level. For example, if the issue involved peace, it would be discussed by the council of peace chiefs; if war, by the council of war chiefs; if planting, by the council of women. If the members of the council were of one mind, and if the matter was of concern to the village as a whole, a general village council, attended by all adult males, would be

MAP 14.1. Iroquois Settlements circa 1784

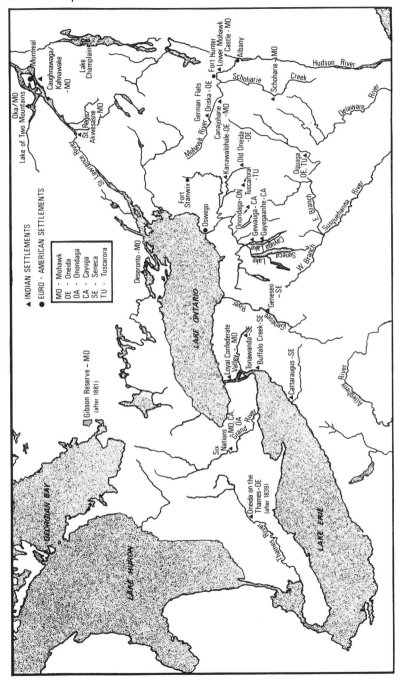

held. Women's opinions were expressed by a male speaker. If unanimity was achieved at the village council and the issue affected other villages within the nation, a general council of these villages would be held, usually in the village where the matter was raised. Again, if all were in agreement, and if the matter involved the confederacy, a confederate council would be held. Steps in the process might be skipped, if appropriate. Although the same council and confederate structures are not in operation among all Iroquois people today, the process of decision-making, the emphasis on unanimity, and the resultant structuring of alternatives are features of both elected and hereditary councils.

At the time of European contact, the Iroquois had considerable inter-tribal contact. Those whose villages lay along the Mohawk River travelled extensively by water, even to Lake Erie and the St. Lawrence River. The elm-bark canoe, the principal vehicle, was portaged overland from one body of water to another. Trails were used for warfare, hunting, and overland trade (in skins, wampum, corn, copper, and so on).

Iroquois Settlements in Canada

There are seven Iroquois settlements in Canada: Kahnawake/Caughnawaga, Oka/Kanesatake/Lake of Two Mountains, Gibson, St. Regis/Akwesasne, Six Nations/Grand River, Tyendinega, and Oneida on the Thames. A reserve of Mohawk descendants (Michel's Band) existed in Alberta until the members enfranchised in 1958, losing their Indian status.

Kahnawake, the oldest of the Iroquois reserves in what is now Canada, started in 1667 as a Jesuit mission settlement, primarily of Mohawk and Oneida. Located across the St. Lawrence River from Montreal, the original settlement was called Kentaké by the Indians, La Prairie by the French. The inhabitants moved the settlement further west on the south side of the St. Lawrence three times between 1676 and 1716. Finally, they formed the settlement called, by the French, Mission Sault St. Louis, and, by the Iroquois, Kahnawake ("at the rapids,") after a Mohawk settlement in the Mohawk Valley (present-day Fonda, New York) from which some of the settlers had come.

From the beginning, contacts were maintained with Iroquois in New York. During winter, most of the people settled at Kahnawake dispersed, many to hunt near their former villages, which they visited and where they encouraged dissatisfied kinsmen and friends to join them in the northern settlement. Mohawk who hunted and traded along the

St. Lawrence were also encouraged by Indians and missionaries to settle at the Jesuit mission; hence, the settlement grew rapidly, causing much concern to people remaining in the Mohawk Valley.

During the nineteenth century, the traditional division of labour continued to some extent at Kahnawake, even after hunting and warfare ceased to be viable activities for males. In the late nineteenth century, men began working in the high steel industry in major cities. Many returned to Kahnawake from such places as Brooklyn on weekends or during longer breaks. High steel work has been interpreted as a cultural substitute for the high-risk activity of warfare. Today, Kahnawake men are primarily high steel workers, factory workers, employees of the reservation government, and small-scale farmers.

Oka/Kanesatake, too, began as a mission settlement. When Indians at La Prairie moved in 1676, some went to a Sulpician mission that finally settled on the north side of the St. Lawrence River, near Montreal. The settlement, known in Algonquian as Oka and in Mohawk as Kanesatake, is occupied by Iroquoian and Algonquian speakers. It consisted of three tribal villages – Algonkin, Nipissing, and Iroquois – which were often seen as one village served by a single mission. Iroquois agricultural practices greatly influenced the Algonquian at Oka. In turn, the Algonquians influenced the hunting practices of the Iroquois. Beginning in the mid-nineteenth century, however, cutting and selling timber from the settlement began to replace hunting as an economic activity, particularly among the Iroquois. In using the land for this purpose, the Natives of Oka/Kanesatake met with resistance, which they considered unjustified, from the Sulpician order, which also claimed the land. As a result, after 1881 some Iroquois moved to Gibson Reserve, a land grant about fifty kilometres east of Georgian Bay, in an attempt to secure a more secure land base.

St. Regis was originally a mission settlement called Akwesasne (Mohawk: "where the partridge drums"), formed in the mid-eighteenth century. Accounts of its origin differ. Some maintain that conflict at Kahnawake led to the establishment of this spin-off settlement; others hold that the critical factor was crowding. Akwesasne is now a reserve in Quebec, Ontario, and the state of New York. As a result of the Jay Treaty of 1794, which exempts Natives from some boundary considerations, many Mohawks consider the international border of interest only as it affects the source of treaty annuities. Agriculture and hunting were early means of subsistence at Akwesasne, but agriculture became the mainstay by the late nineteenth century. Today, small farms are less viable; hence, subsistence agriculture has been replaced by high steel work, factory employment, small business enterprises, and employment by tribal governments on the reserve.

In the late eighteenth through mid-nineteenth centuries, some Mohawk of Akwesasne, Kahnawake, and Oka/Kanesatake participated in the fur trade in western Canada, acting as guides for the North West and Hudson's Bay companies. Some of them formed Michel's Band, and settled not far from Edmonton, Alberta; others formed small communities along the foothills of the Rocky Mountains. Both groups intermarried with non-Iroquois, principally Cree. Today, although some realize that they are also descended from Mohawk, most identify themselves as Cree.

Some Iroquois settlements were formed in Canada as a result of the American Revolution. Many Iroquois, viewing American settlers as a threat to their land and security, supported the British during the war. Moreover, many Iroquois held that it was the British, rather than the Americans, who were their true partners in the covenant chain. Despite promises from British officials, Indian interests were not protected during the peace negotiations. The 1783 treaty between the United States and Great Britain made no provisions for Indians: it divided land, including Native land, between the two nations. The Iroquois, who had been assured that they would be compensated, were determined to see that this promise was kept.

British officials in Canada were aghast at the outcome of the treaty, and it was their responsibility to appease the Indians and keep them as allies. In 1783, Frederick Haldimand, Governor General in Canada, arranged for a land grant north of Lake Ontario at the Bay of Quinte. Many Iroquois, however, sought land nearer Iroquois country – such land was found west of Lake Ontario on the Grand River and was purchased by the British crown from the Mississauga Indians for the Mohawk and others of the Six Nations who had supported the British during the war, or who otherwise desired to settle there. A grant for this land was given by Haldimand in October, 1784. The British identified the villages at Bay of Quinte and Grand River primarily as Mohawk, although the Six Nations settlement included a number of Onondaga, Cayuga, and Seneca, and some Tuscarora and Oneida. At that time the Indians at Six Nations identified themselves largely as Mohawk, from the village of Canajoharie in the Mohawk River Valley, and Mohawk and Oneida, from the village of Oquaga in the Susquehanna River Valley.

At both settlements, agriculture was the primary economic activity, supplemented by hunting until the early nineteenth century, when game became particularly scarce. At that point, work in neighbouring towns began to take the place of hunting in the economy.

Oneida on the Thames was formed in about 1839 as a result of the policy, adopted in the United States in the 1820s, of removing Indians west of the Mississippi River. Indians in New York state were among those pressured into moving and, while most resisted, some Iroquois wished to go. Most of the Oneida who left at that time settled near Green Bay in what is now Wisconsin. Some, however, came to Canada, where they continued farming and hunting.

Sorting the Winks and Twitches

In doing ethnohistorical research and ethnological work among the Iroquois of Canada, I have been impressed by common threads in the tapestry of intercultural relations between Indians and Euro-Canadians, particularly on a governmental level. Two themes are striking: first, that Euro-Canadian participation in Indian affairs has often been interpreted as assistance by the Euro-Canadians and as interference by the Indians; second, that the relationship existing between the two groups has also been variously interpreted – as alliance of sovereign peoples by the Indians, as dependence by Euro-Canadians.

The Natives of Kahnawake confronted a threat to their land base in the 1760s, when the Jesuits claimed Sault St. Louis as their own. One issue that brought the matter to a head was the question of revenues from settlement property leased to non-Indians. The Natives held that their ancestors had moved to the settlement with the understanding that the land, although held in trust by the Jesuits, was their own, in place of land left behind. The Jesuits, however, held that the settlement land was their property. The Natives sought help in resolving the matter. The Governor General's ruling, based on a grant from Louis XIV dated May 31, 1680, maintained that the lands had been granted to the Natives for as long as they inhabited them, and that it was to revert to the crown if the Natives should leave the settlement. The Kahnawake Iroquois frequently refer to this ruling when defending their position of sovereignty over their land. They had tried to use the assistance of the British government in securing their land base, and they were satisfied with the outcome.

A similar case at Oka/Kanesatake, however, worked out differently. In the nineteenth century, members of a Roman Catholic order, the Sulpicians, insisted that the Natives did not have the right to cut timber on what the order claimed was Sulpician land. This claim was shocking to the Natives, who considered the land theirs. They requested that the government of Canada assist them. Although ruling after ruling has favoured the Sulpicians, on the basis of a 1717 grant, each judgement states that the Natives have rights to use and occupy the land. No formal provisions for implementing these rights have been made, the assumption being that the Sulpicians would provide for them. Subsequent Sulpician actions were far from satisfactory, however. Moreover, much land at Oka/Kanesatake was sold to Euro-Canadians by the Sulpicians, alienating the land from the Natives. Two efforts were made by the Canadian government to offer alternatives. One was that in 1881 land near Georgian Bay was purchased for the Iroquois as a reserve in place of Oka/Kanesatake. The land was far from the quality of land at Oka/Kanesatake, however. About one-third of the Natives moved to Gibson Reserve, although some later returned to Oka/Kanesatake. The Iroquois remaining at Oka/Kanesatake pressed securance of their rights there. A second effort was that the Department of Indian Affairs took what officials believed to be a final step in the matter in 1945, when they purchased the original settlement from the Sulpicians for the use of the Natives. The motives of the officials were honourable: they wished to settle what had become a persistent problem for the Natives. However, they overlooked one significant factor: the Indians were not party to the agreement. Given the dissatisfaction over the issue in the first place, this only served to cause further problems. In addition, the agreement did not make Oka/Kanesatake a reserve and, therefore, did not provide for securing the land to the Natives in the proper sense. In this case, in which Natives sought control over land, the approach of the federal government emphasized the lack of control held by the people. We will see below what further implications this has had at Oka/Kanesatake. By excluding Indian participation in the decision-making, by acting for, rather than with, the Natives, the government of Canada before and after Confederation has opened many such decisions to uniform protests by Iroquois.

In a different example, a company was formed in 1832 to open the Grand River to navigation by dredging a canal. Investors were difficult to find, however, so Six Nations Reserve money ($160,000) held in trust by the federal government was invested with the permission of the Lieutenant-Governor of Upper Canada. This money was lost as the Grand River Navigation Company went bankrupt when rail transport became available. The Indians had opposed opening the river to navigation; moreover, their money was invested without their approval. Such interference has been highly resented. They have appealed repeatedly to the government of Canada for compensation and have brought the case before the courts. Rulings, such as an 1894 order-in-council, recognize that the Indians are entitled to compensation. The question of who should provide it, the government of Britain or that of Canada, remains open; it is being pressed by the people of Six Nations Reserve. Both this case and that at Oka seem to the Iroquois to represent the Canadian government as interference rather than assistance.

Indian interpretation of the role of external government in Indian affairs is not always so uniform, however. In 1924, at the Six Nations Reserve, an elected council was approved and the hereditary council was locked out of the council house by members of the Royal Canadian Mounted Police. The action was undertaken with the approval of people on the reserve who opposed extremes advocated by the hereditary council; it was categorized as gross interference by that council. The elective council has remained in power. Both exist on the reserve, however, and provide counterbalances to one another. Although the Canadian government recognizes and negotiates with the elective council, "the hereditary council is still important as a kind of standing committee for airing grievances and organizing resistance against Canadian regulation" (Shimony, 1961: 95).

The participation of external governmental bodies in internal Iroquois politics has not been uncommon in Canada. Elected and hereditary councils are also present at Oneida on the Thames. Generally, the two are rivals. They are, however, superseded by a general council attended by all people of the reserve. The reserve at St. Regis is served by three governmental bodies: elective councils on both the Canadian and United States sides of the reserve, and a hereditary council representing the Mohawk as the eastern branch of the Iroquois Confederacy. These three bodies are independent, mutually exclusive, and parallel systems, which co-operate in certain matters and compete in others for recognition by external parties. The elective councils are recognized as legitimate by both the Canadian and American governments; however, while neither government accepts the hereditary council as a valid governing body, neither can ignore it. Both systems maintain their independence from the governments of Canada and the United States – rights they perceive that they have, as independent people. They have had to fight for these rights, though.

In their dealings with the government of Canada, the extent of Iroquois control over their resources has often been questioned. Issues involving land at Six Nations provide examples. The grant that the Native people at Grand River received from Haldimand in 1784 was not registered. This oversight led to fifty years of discord about the nature of the grant. No mention was made in the grant document of the land being held in trust; therefore, the Natives assumed that, as they had expected, the land had been given to them unconditionally, as they were valued British allies. When officials who had not been involved with the Iroquois during the American Revolution came to power, however, they interpreted the relationship as one of dependence rather than alliance. The Iroquois at Six Nations, however, continued to view the land as reimbursement for land and other property lost in the war. Moreover, they did not consider it full reimbursement, continuing to press for further compensation.

The Six Nations people became aware of the British interpretation after the Mohawk leader, Joseph Brant, with power of attorney from the chiefs, began leasing and selling land in the settlement to Euro-Canadians. When Brant requested that the sales be confirmed by the government for the protection of the purchasers, his request was refused because officials, notably John Graves Simcoe, Lieutenant-Governor of Upper Canada, believed that the land was held in trust for the Indians, not granted in fee simple. Brant resisted this interpretation, as did many other Indians of Six Nations. Brant argued that the land belonged to the Indians to do with as they chose, and that the sales were necessary to ensure a source of livelihood since hunting was no longer profitable and agriculture in the settlement needed improvement. Simcoe opposed Brant's arguments, citing the Royal Proclamation of 1763, which stated that no land could be purchased from the Indians except through the crown. However, Simcoe's superior, Lord Dorchester, favoured Brant's arguments, and eventually sales that Brant had made were "registered and sealed" although new sales were forbidden. Brant continued to press the issue of unconditional control, and sales continued to be made until January, 1841, when land at Six Nations was surrendered to the British crown to be administered for the "sole benefit" of the Indians. The land sales had not been supported by those Six Nations people who felt that steps should be taken to prevent sale of land in order to secure it for posterity. In maintaining this position, they approached the government for aid in preventing the land from being alienated. In response, the government increased its control over Six Nations affairs, a result that went far beyond what had been desired.

Such disputes over control of land are not wholly a thing of the past. In a more recent case, the control of the Mohawks of Kahnawake was challenged when Canada and the United States undertook to build the St. Lawrence Seaway. The Iroquois, angered that land given to their ancestors and confirmed as theirs in the dispute with the Jesuits would be taken from them and flooded, waged a legal battle. They were especially incensed because this seizure threatened their perception of sovereignty. Non-Natives, pressing for and securing a ruling of eminent domain, considered the expropriation of the land to be necessary for the greater good of the people of Canada and the United States. For the Iroquois, the question was not simply one of what was good for the whole. Not only were they unconvinced that the development was a good thing, they were convinced that they were not being considered as part of the whole, that their interests were not being taken into account. This suspicion has been a nagging one for Natives in their intercultural relations with Euro-Canadians. So often it has appeared to them that their welfare as a people has been considered little, if at all, by Euro-Canadians wanting to accomplish something for themselves and making decisions with little or no input from Natives. The Seaway battle was lost by the Iroquois.

Conclusion

Interactions between Iroquois and Euro-Canadians have often been frustrating for both parties. The examples given demonstrate that the actions of governments in Indian affairs were seen differently by each party: generally, as interference by the Iroquois and as assistance by Euro-Canadians. The context of interaction between Iroquois and external governments has consistently been defined by the Iroquois as the need of independent allies to be mutually supportive and by the external government as the need to express good will to a semi-helpless people.

One sees the effect of layer upon layer of cultural and interpersonal misunderstanding and misinterpretation, complicated by changes among the actors and among the circumstances of action. Natives strive for control over their lives and land, although how this is done is at issue in disputes among themselves. Moreover, they feel that the Euro-Canadian governments have a responsibility to act *with* them to protect their interest, this responsibility arising from the relations of the Iroquois as Euro-Canadian allies. Euro-Canadian governments, on the other hand, have interpreted the relationship between Natives and themselves as one of dependence of the Iroquois upon them, with the governments' working for Natives for their benefit and protection. Underlying this is the assumption that, because of lack of education, lack of sophistication, and their general "mode of life," Natives are open to being swindled and otherwise taken advantage of, and it is for their protection that certain policies are undertaken, even at times contrary to their wishes. The persistent misunderstandings have had yet another unfortunate result: they have created a mythology, on either side, that views the other as, at best,

PLATE 14.2. Sculpture of a Mohawk Warrior entitled "Par for the Course," by Peter B. Jones. Courtesy of the Woodland Cultural Centre.

misguided and, at worst, mendacious. The resolution of existing conflicts and prevention of future ones must depend on participants in interactions accepting that the same types of behaviour can be variously interpreted: actions derive differing meanings from differing cultural perspectives.

The implications of the layering of different interpretations of cultural interaction resulted in violent confrontation at Oka/Kanesatake in 1990. Throughout the twentieth century, Native people of Oka/Kanesatake have pressed for recognition of their rights over land there, without satisfaction. Frustration finally resulted in conflict at Oka/Kanesatake in the summer of 1990 as the town of Oka sought to expand a municipal golf course onto land claimed by the Natives. John Mohawk, a Seneca negotiator for the Iroquois Confederacy, has interpreted the militancy that resulted as indicative of a "loss of hope" that matters could be settled through negotiations. Barricades were constructed by Natives to keep workers from cutting trees for the expansion. Allying themselves with Mohawks of Oka/Kanesatake, Mohawks of Kahnawake barricaded the Mercier Bridge, blocking easy access to Montreal. A confrontation ensued between provincial police (Sûreté du Québec) and Natives. As members of the Sûreté du Québec pushed their way past the barricades at Kanesatake with weapons drawn on July 11, 1990, onto land occupied by armed Mohawks, shots were fired and a police officer, Marcel Lemay, lay dead. It is unknown who fired the shots that killed Lemay. The Sûreté du Québec withdrew and a heated, armed, often racially tense stand-off lasted throughout the summer months while efforts toward negotiations were made.

Although numerous divisions were manifested among the Native people of Oka/Kanesatake, particularly over the involvement of the militant nativist Mohawks of what is known as the Warrior Society, there was a remarkable degree of consensus spanning political differences over the issues of autonomy, claim to the land, and assertion of control over their own affairs and resources. As in cases in the past the support of allies was sought by the Natives. A large number of other Native people were quick to show their support. The federal government of Canada was approached, as were the British crown and the European Parliament. As with negotiations in the past, however, attempts to solve the problem were taken by the Canadian government *for* the Native people involved with limited consultation with them. The land under contention, for example, was purchased by the federal government so that expansion of the golf course is no longer in the hands of local politicians in Oka as it had been. This has done little to address the issue of Native claims over this land, however.

Non-Native Canadian interests were also divided. The issue of Quebec separatism following the defeat of the Meech Lake Accord for constitutional reform in Canada was just below the surface of negotiations. Claims of Native sovereignty took on new meaning for Canadians as relations of Québécois to the federal government began to be called into question. Ironically, French-speaking citizens of Quebec failed for the most part to appreciate any similarity between their assertions for autonomy from the federal government and Native claims of sovereignty.

The confrontation continued for three and a half months and ended on September 26 when Natives behind the barricades, realizing that face-to-face combat was futile, walked out from behind the barricades "to go to their homes." Arrests and legal battles ensued. The persistence of the people behind the barricade, however, put Oka/Kanesatake on the map, so to speak. It brought the complex issue of Native claims to sovereignty not only to the attention of Canadians but to many in international arenas.

This may have been advantageous to all parties. There are acknowledgements in the speeches of Native leaders and Canadian officials after the crisis that they have been talking past one another and must take a careful look at the issue of sovereignty, which has been at the basis of many of the relations between Native and non-Native people in Canada for hundreds of years. It remains to be seen whether this is merely rhetoric or represents a genuine recognition of the complexity of relations of Iroquoian people with the government of Canada and the fact that they have been viewed through different coloured glasses by people involved in negotiations. It is hoped that it is more than rhetoric and that reflection on these matters will bring parties "in touch with the lives of strangers" who live next door.

Recommended Readings

Bechard, Henri

    1976 *The Original Caughnawaga Indians.* Montreal: International Publishers.

        A history that focuses rather narrowly on the earliest settlers at Kahnawake, representing, however, a careful combing of the *Jesuit Relations.*

Blanchard, David S.

    1980 *Kahnawake: A Historical Sketch.* Kahnawake: Kanien'kehaka Raotitiohkwa Press.

        A brief, somewhat idealized history of Kahnawake, with good illustrations. Valuable as an introduction that provides some non-conventional perspectives.

Cruikshank, E.A.

    1930 *The Coming of the Loyalist Mohawks to the Bay of Quinte.* Papers and Records of the Ontario Historical Society. 26.

Careful exploration of the initial settlement at Bay of Quinte (Tyendinega) referring especially to documents in the Ontario Historical Society.

Desrosiers, Leo Paul

1947 *Iroquoisie.* Montréal: Les Études de l'Institut d'Histoire de l'Amérique Française.

Very good study of the Iroquoians of Canada prior to 1646.

Johnston, Charles M., ed.

1964 *The Valley of the Six Nations: A Collection of Documents on the Indian Lands of the Grand River.* Toronto: University of Toronto Press.

A valuable sourcebook of transcriptions of documents pertaining to Six Nations/Grand River.

Morgan, Lewis Henry

1972 *League of the Ho-de-no-sau-nee or Iroquois.* Secaucus, New Jersey: The Citadel Press. (First published 1851.)

Provides scholarly analysis and description of the League of the Iroquois by the "father of American anthropology." Also contains much ethnographic information about material culture. Although modern work has added much new information, and often from a different perspective, Morgan's volume remains a basic reference tool.

Quinn, David B.

1981 *Sources for the Ethnography of Northeastern North America to 1611.* Canadian Ethnology Service Paper No. 76. Ottawa: National Museum of Man Mercury Series.

Discussion of sources of early material pertaining to the Indians and Eskimos of what is now Canada, including detailed summaries of the sources.

Shimony, Annemarie

1961 *Conservatism Among the Iroquois at the Six Nations Reserve.* Yale University Publications in Anthropology 65. New Haven, Connecticut.

Excellent, focused ethnography of Six Nations Reserve.

Speck, Frank G.

1923 "Algonkian Influence Upon Iroquois Social Organization," *American Anthropologist*, 25, 2: 219-27.

Very good study of results of interactions of Algonquian- and Iroquoian-speaking people at Oka.

Thwaites, Reuben Gold, ed.

1896-1901 *Jesuit Relations and Allied Documents.* 73 vols. Cleveland: The Burrows Brothers Company.

A major source for information on the Iroquoians of Canada. The relations were written by Jesuits to their superiors in Paris and then published in pamphlet form, in French, in attempts to raise money for Jesuit missions in Canada. Much information can be combed from them, if one realizes that the writers were Jesuits proselytizing among what many considered to be "heathens." (In French, with English translations.)

Tooker, Elisabeth
 1964 *An Ethnography of the Huron Indians, 1615-1649.* Bureau of American Ethnology Bulletin 190. Washington, D.C.
  A very good, basic source of ethnographic information about the Hurons, making frequent comparisons between Huron and Iroquois cultural practices.

Trigger, Bruce G.
 1969 *The Huron: Farmers of the North.* New York, Chicago: Holt, Rhinehart and Winston.
  An introductory volume about the history and culture of the Huron. Serves well as a quick and easy reference.
 1976 *The Children of Aataentsic: A History of the Huron People to 1660.* 2 Vols. Montreal: McGill-Queen's University Press
  Provides the most current and detailed information on the Huron.

Trigger, Bruce G., ed.
 1978 *Northeast.* Vol. 15 of *Handbook of North American Indians.* Washington, D.C.: Smithsonian Institution.
  An excellent, basic source of information about the history and culture of Indians of northeastern North America, including the Iroquois and Iroquoians of Canada. Contains articles written by major scholars.

York, Geoffry, and Loreen Pindera
 1991 *People of the Pines.* Toronto: Little, Brown & Company (Canada).

Additional Reference Cited

Geertz, Clifford
 1973 *The Interpretation of Cultures.* New York: Basic Books.

CHAPTER 15
The Micmac: A Maritime Woodland Group

Virginia P. Miller

My graduate training in anthropology was influenced by the writings of Sherburne F. Cook, Robert Heizer, and Martin Baumhoff, Western anthropologists who took ecological and historical approaches to the study of culture. When I moved to the eastern Maritime provinces in the mid-1970s and wanted to familiarize myself with the Micmac people and their culture, I began reading available source material in the Public Archives of Nova Scotia. There I learned how little was known about this large and complex group.

Why was this the case? Until recently, few anthropologists, with the notable exceptions of Frank Speck and Wilson and Ruth Wallis, had bothered to study the Micmac and other eastern Maritime groups. Apparently, this neglect was due to the common opinion that, because of the 500 years of contact between these Natives and Europeans, the Micmac were essentially acculturated and no cultural information remained to be recorded. The renaissance of interest in Native cultures by Natives themselves as well as by anthropologists has refocused interest on eastern

Maritime peoples. Not only can cultural and historical information still be recovered from Micmac elders today, but the ethnohistoric method enables reconstruction and reinterpretation of Micmac culture.

The path to reconstructing "traditional" Micmac culture has not been entirely smooth, however. Several problems exist in the data available for ethnohistorians to use. One of these is that the Micmac were first contacted by fifteenth- and sixteenth-century European fishermen, who were illiterate and recorded no observations of the Natives. Luckily, the contact they had with the Micmac was largely offshore, consisting of an exchange of material culture items, and the non-material culture changed little. Further, once written records did begin about 1600, they were written by male priests, adventurers, and traders; hence, information on female aspects of culture is incomplete. But the seventeenth-century reports are otherwise fairly complete, and they were written by reasonably objective men whose independent accounts verify each other's work. What this chapter defines as "traditional" culture is really early seventeenth-century Micmac culture.

This account is written from a functional ecological perspective, using the methodology of ethnohistory. Sources include archival material, published primary sources, archaeological and linguistic material, and my own fieldwork and interview notes. A picture emerges of quite a different culture from a typical hunting and gathering culture, hence the terms "Maritime" and "Woodland" in the chapter title.

Traditional Culture

Micmac is one of a number of languages belonging to the Algonquian language family. The language seems to have been particularly closely related to that of the Malecite, neighbours to the west, and to the Passamaquoddy of Maine. Long ago, the Micmac people left the Great Lakes area – probably the source of the Algonquian language family – and migrated into what is now the eastern Maritime area of Canada. Here they developed their historic culture from the Woodland tradition, already reflecting the coastal-inland pattern that was to characterize their movements in historic times.

A glance at a map will reveal that the Micmac people were a solidly maritime group: Nova Scotia is a peninsula connected to the mainland by a narrow isthmus; Prince Edward Island is an island in itself; and the parts of New Brunswick and Quebec occupied by the Micmac extend along the coasts of these provinces. Some Micmac also occupied the southern and western areas of Newfoundland. Many rivers and streams ran through

Micmac territory, providing easy access to the sea. In recent years, scholars have paid increasing attention to maritime hunting and gathering groups, as it has become apparent that these groups are significantly different from their inland counterparts. Maritime groups not only have more species to draw on as food sources since they are able to use both land and sea resources, but the greater variety of resources available to them means increased flexibility in the event of the failure of any particular species. Abundant and relatively stable food supplies permit greater population densities to develop, possibly resulting in the development of more complex cultures than among inland hunting and gathering groups at corresponding latitudes. With the Micmac spending more than half the year living on the coast, it has been estimated that as much as 90 per cent of their diet came from the sea. Seventeenth-century European accounts testify to the almost incredible abundance of food available during the annual runs of fish and eels and during the seasonal migrations of birds. Equally important to the food quantities is that the Micmac had the intimate knowledge of their environment required to allow them to develop appropriate technology to exploit the food sources for their needs. Their use of both the lush sea and land resources may best be illustrated by an examination of their seasonal round.

In the spring, the Micmac settled in villages along the coast. Here they remained until fall, living in nuclear family units in conical birchbark wigwams erected and painted with colourful designs by the women; extended families might live together in large, rectangular, cabin-shaped birchbark structures. Summer village sites were chosen for their proximity to fresh water and to marine food sources such as shellfish beds. Often a village was situated at the mouth of a river to permit easy travel by birchbark canoe to other coastal locations or to inland locations to hunt or dig ground nuts. Good campsites were returned to year after year.

The Micmac diet during this time consisted principally of products from the sea, with less reliance on land animals and plants. Food was never a problem from spring through fall. Oysters and clams were collected easily. With fish traps built across river and stream mouths, the Micmac took ample quantities of smelt, alewives, sturgeon, and salmon, as these fish returned to fresh water to spawn. Large fish and lobsters were attracted at night with torches and were taken using bone-tipped harpoons. Coastal ocean fish such as cod, plaice, skate, and striped bass could be caught with bone hooks and lines or taken by weirs constructed in bays, although ocean fish apparently did not play a significant part in the diet. Fish were prepared for eating by the women, who cooked for the entire family. Fish were roasted whole on the coals or between the prongs

MAP 15.1. Micmac Political Units and Colonial Sites

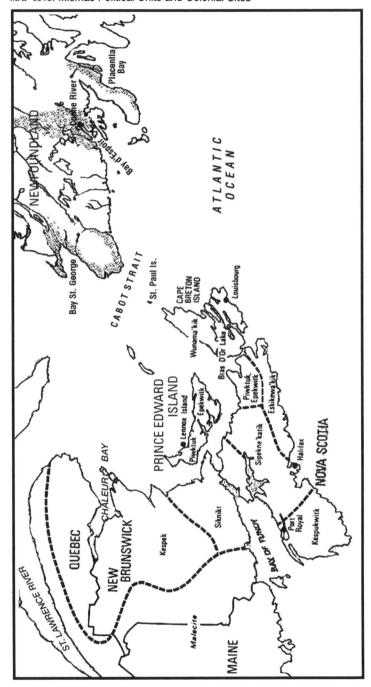

PLATE 15.1. Traditional caribou skin canoe, constructed at Conne River, Newfoundland, as a part of a provincial museum project. On the left is Michael Joe, Sr., and on the right is Martin Jeddore. Courtesy David Quinton, 1981.

of a split stick over the fire. They might also be boiled in birchbark containers by dropping hot stones into the water. Women also preserved some fish for the winter by smoking them.

Birds, particularly ducks and geese, migrated in such numbers that they were easily snared, clubbed, or shot with bows and arrows. At night, torches were used to awaken and confuse sleeping birds, which fluttered around the torch while the Micmac knocked them down with sticks before wringing their necks. Eggs gathered from birds' nests along the coast or from offshore islands were an important food in the spring. In summer, men also ventured out in canoes to hunt small ocean mammals such as porpoises; from time to time, they hunted small whales, and early sources tell us that people also ate beached whales. Seals found along the coast were clubbed.

Land animals, too, such as moose, beaver, bear, and caribou, were hunted sporadically with bow and arrow, harpoon, or traps during the winter months when fish were not so readily available. In mid-summer, strawberries began to ripen, followed by blueberries and cranberries.

PLATE 15.2. Mrs. Alexander
Mitchell in Micmac ceremonial
dress, Burnt Church Reserve,
New Brunswick, twentieth
century. Courtesy of the
New Brunswick Museum.

Women collected these as well as digging the ground nuts that became suitable for use through late summer and fall. Dried berries and ground nuts were stored for the winter.

In late summer, camps were moved inland, away from the impending harsh coastal winter storms. The men went ahead by canoe to choose and clear a winter campsite adjacent to a river or stream, while the women had the responsibility for transporting the household goods using backpacks and tumplines before once again setting up camp, this time covering their wigwams with birchbark, mats, and skins to fortify them against the approaching winter cold. When the fall eel runs began, great numbers were taken either in traps or with leisters. Eels, still today a favourite food among the Micmac, were roasted or boiled and eaten fresh; quantities were also smoked for the winter. The fall bird migrations once again provided an important food source for the Micmac.

As winter settled in, the hunters turned their attention to land animals. Despite the heavy reliance in the diet on fish and sea products, hunting was regarded as the most prestigious way of obtaining food, and all men aspired to be good hunters. The Micmac had their own breed of hunting dog, which they used to locate, track, and harass game; a good hunting dog was a valuable possession and its sacrifice for a feast bestowed a great honour upon guests.

Moose were hunted with bow and arrow or taken with snares set across game paths. During the fall mating season, male moose could be lured within shooting range by the clever use of a birchbark moose call mimicking the call of a female, while the hunter carefully poured water from a birchbark container into a pond in imitation of the sound of a female urinating. Winters with heavy snowfalls were the easiest times to take moose, however, since the deep snow slowed the heavy animals' flight while the hunters pursued swiftly and easily on snowshoes. Following a kill, the hunter marked the spot by breaking nearby tree branches, then returned to camp and dispatched the women to fetch the kill. Women prepared moose meat, like other meat and fish, for eating, either by roasting chunks on sticks placed near the fire or by stone-boiling in a birchbark container or wooden kettle. These large wooden kettles were fashioned by alternately burning, then gouging out the burnt centre of a fallen tree. Because of their size and weight, the wooden kettles were not portable; they remained in the spot where they were fashioned, thus often determining campsites. Soups prepared by stone-boiling were the mainstay of the diet; according to early Europeans, the soups were very fatty but apparently quite nutritious and substantial, for they caused the Natives to "live long and multiply much." A delicacy was the roast head of a young moose. Meat not consumed fresh was sliced thin by the women and smoked for future use. Finally, Micmac women pounded, then boiled, moose bones to yield "moose butter," a fine white grease regarded as a great delicacy that also served as a basic provision when travelling or hunting. Animal bones were not given to the dogs or thrown into the fire for fear that the animal's spirit would take offence and warn others of its species against allowing themselves to be taken by hunters.

Traditionally, beaver were hunted year-round. During summer and fall, beaver were taken in deadfall traps or shot with bows and arrows as they fled a beaver house destroyed by a hunter. Winter hunting of beaver was more difficult, although it increased in response to the fur trade; traders preferred the heavier winter pelts. Early accounts relate that in winter hunters used their dogs to sniff out the beavers' escape routes under the ice, then chopped holes through the ice to reach their arms into a beaver house, where they grabbed the beavers one at a time by their tails, flipping them onto the ice and clubbing them. Beavers might also be harpooned, shot with an arrow, or seized and clubbed as they tried to escape. In this way, all the beavers in a lodge might be killed.

Other land animals were taken as they were available throughout the year, but particularly in winter. Fat bears preparing to hibernate in the fall were a favourite food; in winter, they were smoked out of hibernation and killed. Caribou were present in Micmac territory, but only in Newfoundland were they an important food, as in other locations they remained in remote or barren areas. Smaller animals such as muskrat and otter were taken, usually with deadfall traps.

The seal was important in the Micmac diet, and several species were taken. Seals were hunted opportunistically year-round as they were encountered, but during the winter whelping season great numbers could be found and clubbed on the rocks and islands off the coast or on ice floes. Men probably left the inland winter groups in pairs or in small groups to return by snowshoe to the coast for the seal hunt. Both seal meat and the oil that women rendered from the fat were relished. The oil was stored in moose bladders, then drunk straight or served as a relish at feasts; it was also used as a body ointment and for hair grease. Following the seal whelping season, the people relied for sustenance on their stored and cached foods in addition to hunting land animals, until early spring signalled the move back to the coast to begin the annual cycle once again.

The Micmacs' seasonal round described above represents a generalized situation; there was undoubtedly variation with the locale and the season. For example, although we may propose a general coastal-inland pattern of seasonal movement for the Micmac, in no part of their territory were they ever very far from the sea; it was possible for hunters to leave the inland camps in winter to venture to the coast for a few days or a week of seal hunting, or for everyone to leave temporarily to collect maple sap. Doubtless, families went off singly or in small groups temporarily to hunt or exploit a particular resource in another locale, or even took off on junkets to visit relatives or friends in other settlements.

Social and Political Organization

A Grand Chief, or "sagamore," presided over all the Micmac people. Normally the residence of the Grand Chief was on Cape Breton Island, Nova Scotia, but in 1605, when the French settled Port Royal on the Bay of Fundy in Nova Scotia, the Grand Chief resided in that area. Contemporary French accounts of this individual, named Membertou, describe a truly exceptional person. A tall, majestic, bearded man, Membertou combined the capabilities of political leader, fearless warrior, and powerful shaman to make him a very powerful individual who merited the respect of all the Micmac. Among the chiefly duties of Membertou was the calling of Grand Council meetings of all lower chiefs and respected men when a decision had to be made on matters affecting the entire nation.

Micmac territory traditionally was divided into seven political districts, each governed by a district chief. The names of these districts, insofar as they are known, reflect natural features.

Sipekne'katik (Shubenacadie) means "ground nut place."
Wunama'kik (Cape Breton Island; Micmac of Newfoundland also affiliated with this district) means "foggy land."
Piwktuk (Pictou) means "where explosions are made."
Epekwitk (Prince Edward Island) means "lying in the water."
Eskikewa'kik (east coast of mainland Nova Scotia) means "skin dressers' territory."
Kespek (Gaspé) means "the last land."

Duties of the seven district chiefs included calling district council meetings as required, touring the district to meet and confer with lower chiefs, feasting visiting chiefs, and attending and participating in Grand Council meetings. An important function of the district chiefs was the annual re-apportionment of hunting territories to family heads within the district; these hunting territories were re-assigned as family sizes changed. Generosity and concern for others were qualities admired in the district chiefs, some of whom made it a point to dress poorly themselves while giving away their best possessions and furs to their followers as a way to cultivate love and respect.

Beneath the district chiefs were the local chiefs, whose territories were defined geographically, bounded by rivers or other natural features. Each of the local chiefs headed a group composed of his bilocally extended family and probably some unrelated individuals as well who chose to ally themselves with him. Group size was probably about thirty or forty at a minimum, although contemporary reports exist of much larger groups; these larger groups may have been temporary aggregations made possible by a seasonal increase in food resources. Local chiefs were assisted in their leadership duties by local councils of male elders.

Micmac society was ranked socially. Beneath the three levels of chiefs was a group that can best be termed "commoners." This group included the family members and other followers of the local chiefs, people who followed the directives of their chiefs and who organized their daily lives along the lines of a sexual division of labour. Common men spent their time hunting, fishing, participating in war raids, and manufacturing and repairing equipment for these activities; they constructed fish traps and weirs and made their own bows, arrows, spears, clubs, and all other wooden items, including cradleboards and long-stemmed pipes. They were also responsible for manufacturing birchbark canoes and snow-shoe frames, although the women corded the snowshoes. If a man were a good hunter and warrior, with age he might accrue respect and prestige and receive the satisfaction of having some influence in the village council of elders. Some duties of Micmac women have already been mentioned; they transported household goods when moving camp, then set up and maintained camp. They brought home the kill and had responsibility for cooking the food and for preserving food for winter by smoking or drying it. In addition, they dressed the skins before manufacturing clothing and moccasins, which they might decorate with porcupine quills. Women collected plants and dug ground nuts for food and medicine. They manufactured household items such as birchbark containers and reed baskets, and they wove mats. And, of course, they bore and cared for the children. Like common men, common women might gain respect as they grew older, either as the wives of good hunters or warriors, or in recognition of their skills as herbal curers, or for other outstanding and valuable qualities.

Slaves were at the bottom of the Micmac social order. Slaves were not commonly found in hunting and gathering societies; their presence is testimony to the lush food resources in the maritime environment, for slaves were individuals who did not contribute actively to the food supply, yet they had to be fed nonetheless. Slaves were taken in war, though not all captives became slaves. Adult male captives were frequently killed on the field of battle, but some were allowed to live and were taken home. A few of these may have been given to the women to torture, but others became assistants to the women around the camp and were forced to do menial chores such as fetching firewood or water. Female and young captives, however, were often adopted into the tribe and treated humanely despite their status as slaves. Slaves who tried to escape and were apprehended were put to death.

As in most hunting and gathering societies, kinship was traced bilaterally with perhaps a patrilocal emphasis in post-marital residence and a patrilineal emphasis in inheritance of chiefly positions. The large, bilocally extended families comprising the local groups of Micmac ensured that each nuclear family could call on a sizable group of closely knit kin in the event of misfortune. Similarly, the bilateral kin groups provided a large network of relatives to facilitate adoption of orphaned children.

That age differences were important to the Micmac was reflected in their kinship terminology: terms of address differentiated between older and younger brothers and between older and younger sisters. A single term was used to address both mother's brother and father's brother.

Both parallel and cross-cousins were addressed with the same terms used for siblings, suggesting that the incest taboo extended to these relatives.

Life Cycle of Individuals

Large families were a source of joy and pride to the Micmac, who welcomed all children although they are said to have rejoiced more at the birth of a son than a daughter. If a woman became pregnant while she was nursing a child she might induce an abortion, claiming that she could not nurse two children at the same time. However, the Micmac were not known to practise infanticide, perhaps another reflection of the ample food supply. Children of both sexes were indulged by all adults.

At an early age, both boys and girls began to learn the tasks later expected of them as adults. Girls learned the female tasks in life by helping their mothers around camp, caring for younger children, gathering firewood and water, and bringing in and processing game. With their mothers, they also tanned skins and made clothing; men's clothing included a loin cloth, leggings, cloaks, removable sleeves, and moccasins. Women's clothing was similar, though for more formal occasions it was elaborately decorated and coloured garments were worn. When women desired ornamentation, they pierced their ears and wore bracelets of shells and porcupine quills; men relied on face paint for special occasions such as feasts or war raids. When girls reached puberty, it is likely that some sort of puberty rite was held to observe the occasion, since the Micmac did practise menstrual seclusion for adult women, and, until the twentieth century, pubescent girls were sent to a designated older woman for instruction on how to conduct themselves as adults. Boys learned men's tasks from their fathers, making weapons and items necessary for hunting and fishing, and accompanying their fathers on the hunt. When a boy killed his first sizable game, usually a moose, his family held a feast to celebrate the boy's skills as a hunter.

When a boy reached young adulthood, he began to look for a wife, most frequently in another village. After a young man found a girl who pleased him, he approached her father to ask for the girl's hand. If the father agreed and the girl was willing, the young man then spent a year in bride service, showing himself to be a good hunter and provider and generally a responsible adult. During this time, the prospective groom lived in the wigwam of his future in-laws, although sexual contact with his betrothed was prohibited. After a year, if the father approved of the young man's behaviour and abilities and the girl still agreed, a wedding feast featuring game brought in by the young man was held. Wedding speeches praised the groom and recited his family genealogy. Following the wedding feast, the couple were free to move to the groom's village, to remain with the wife's parents, or to establish a new household. Family circumstances and personal inclination presumably influenced where the couple would live.

The arrival of children served to formalize the marriage; if a wife bore no children within the first few years of marriage, her husband was justified in divorcing her or in taking a second wife. Apparently adultery was rare. The Micmac practised levirate marriage: a childless widow was sometimes taken as a wife or a second wife by the deceased husband's brother or other close relative. (This practice is common in non-Western societies where marriage is regarded as a contract between groups rather than as an alliance between two individuals.)

Polygyny was not uncommon among the Micmac, although normally only men who were good hunters or chiefs would have more than one wife. Chiefs needed more than one wife simply because the hospitality duties of chiefs required more than one woman to do the work of preparing for feasts and generally maintaining a relatively elaborate household. More than one wife also meant more offspring, and hence more supporters for the chief.

Micmac men were most respected who had shown themselves to be good hunters and good family men. A brave warrior also commanded much respect and admiration among the Micmac, whose warring tendencies have not been greatly recognized in ethnographic accounts. The Micmac were enemies particularly of the New England Algonquian groups and the Mohawk, although they also fought the Malecites and the Inuit from time to time. They travelled overland or canoed long distances to raid these groups and in turn were raided by them. Palisaded villages close to the western edge of Micmac territory in what is now New Brunswick testify further to the warlike nature of traditional Micmac society. The Micmac recognized some individuals as *ginaps*, war leaders.

Activities

The Micmac held feasts with dancing on numerous occasions, ranging from a son cutting his first tooth to a daughter's marriage and to funerals of family members. Outside the family circle, "eat-all" feasts were held before a hunting party set out; at such feasts, all available food was consumed, certainly indicating the optimism felt by hunters and non-hunters alike regarding the likelihood of bringing home game. War parties feasted before setting out on a raid. Men ate first at feasts, while women, children, and those not able to war ate afterward.

Waltes, a gambling game involving flipping marked bone discs on a wooden platter, was a favourite adult diversion. Storytelling served as a means of preserving tribal history and legends, for the amusement and education of both children and adults. Young men doubtless pitted against each other their skills with bow and arrow and competed in feats of physical endurance. When the weather permitted, young men of Cape Breton might undertake canoe trips to Newfoundland, stopping overnight on St. Paul's Island.

Death and Burial

In pre-European times, Micmac men in particular lived very long lives; individuals over 100 years old were not uncommon. But when a man knew his death was imminent, he would summon his family and friends and proceed to give his own funeral feast and oration. Guests would bring gifts of skins, weapons, and dogs, and exchange gifts with the dying man as he disposed of his material property. Dogs were important at funerals because they were killed and served at the funeral feast.

More commonly, when an individual died without holding his own funeral feast, relatives and friends would begin a general weeping and wailing; this might last several days, depending on the prominence of the deceased. If burial had to be postponed, the body was embalmed before being wrapped in skins or in birchbark painted red and black, then placed on a scaffold for a period of up to a year. At an appropriate time when numerous friends were gathered, the body was buried in the ground accompanied by gifts and personal possessions. Grave goods for men might include items such as weapons, knives, skins, and sacrificed dogs. Ornaments and domestic items such as mats, bark containers, and spoons might be interred with women. A funeral feast with speeches in praise of the deceased was followed by dancing, completing the funeral rites. In some instances, property of the deceased, including his wigwam, dogs, and other items, might be burned. Mourning lasted about a year, during which time the bereaved painted their faces black and trimmed their hair short.

Beliefs and Religion

The Micmac worshipped the sun because they believed that the sun had created the earth and everything on it. Traditionally, it is said that the

Micmac would face the sun at dawn and at sunset, with arms extended, and pray for the sun's blessing. The sun and the moon, both heavenly bodies, seem to have been regarded as manifestations of the Great Spirit, a concept shared with other Algonquian tribes. Souls of the dead ascended to the land of the dead by climbing the Milky Way. In the Micmac pantheon, there were a number of lesser deities beneath the Great Spirit; these were thought to be human in form, but to be immortal and to have supernatural powers they employed to assist mortals. Glooscap was the most prominent of these and seems to have served as an assistant to the Great Spirit. Glooscap spent time on earth, during which he created natural features of the land inhabited by the Micmacs. Some accounts say that Glooscap created animals. Glooscap also instructed the Micmac in making tools and weapons before he departed the earth, after foretelling the coming of Europeans and promising to return to help the Micmac in the event of war. On the lowest level of the Micmac pantheon were supernatural monsters and beasts, who harmed or destroyed people and consequently were feared and dreaded. "Little people" were friendly beings helpful to mortals. They were thought to live in the woods.

Religion and spiritual beliefs thus permeated all aspects of life. This is further demonstrated by the fact that the duties of religious leaders included predicting future events, directing hunters in the quest for game, and curing the sick. Shamans were typically men. Women who had passed menopause might become shamans, although this seems to have been rare. Shamans were powerful and influential people who ranked close behind chiefs in Micmac society; an individual combining shamanic abilities with chiefly qualities, as Membertou did, was regarded as particularly powerful.

Sweating was regarded as a way of cleansing and purifying adult males, who periodically gathered in a wigwam around a shallow pit containing fire-heated stones. At intervals they poured water on the stones to make steam, before finally running out to jump into a nearby lake or roll in the snow. When they dressed after sweating, they were refreshed both physically and spiritually.

Some illnesses could be cured by the use of plant and herbal medicines, but for a persistent illness, or for one with no apparent physical cause, the shaman was summoned. The shaman arrived in the sick person's wigwam bringing his medicine bag, his badge of office; it contained items such as curious stones or miniature weapons thought to be imbued with magical powers and therefore sacred to the shaman. The shaman proceeded to exorcise a malevolent being or supernaturally intruded object from the patient by singing and chanting to his spirits while dancing around the patient, pausing periodically to blow or suck on the affected body part to drive out the evil spirit causing the illness. After the ceremony, the shaman might announce that the patient was cured; if such was the case, the family rewarded him with furs and other gifts. A successful shaman might receive so many gifts for his services that he did not have to hunt for his own food, thus becoming a full-time religious specialist. Doubtless, many part-time specialists existed as well. If, however, after the curing ceremony, a shaman realized the patient's case was hopeless, he would announce that death was imminent. Food, water, and general care were then withdrawn from the patient, and, if several days passed and the patient did not die, it is said that cold water was poured on his abdomen to induce the predicted death. It was in this way that the early French priests saw their chance to discredit the shamans and win converts to Catholicism. When the Grand Chief Membertou lay near death in 1610 after a shaman's vain attempts to cure him of dysentery, the priests succeeded in curing him. The grateful Membertou then allowed himself and his followers to be baptised in the Catholic faith.

Acculturation

Adaptation that the Micmac people had evolved over hundreds of years allowed them to flourish and prosper in the climatically harsh but food-rich environment of eastern Maritime Canada. The complementary division of labour among male and female adults facilitated everyday life; the alliances and kinship networks brought about by marriages between bands and bilateral kin reckoning helped to bind the people together locally, while the Grand Chief, the Grand Council, and the system of political districts facilitated unified action of the Micmac people on political matters. The seasonal round permitted optimal use of resources. With frequent feasts and dances for a variety of occasions, regional and Grand Council meetings providing an opportunity for visiting friends and relatives, and other social activities and pastimes, even war raids, life must have been full and eventful. From the early accounts of the culture, one gets the impression that the Micmac had made an eminently satisfactory adjustment to life. Into this setting came the first Europeans.

It is very likely that the earliest Europeans were fishermen who, in their continuous quest for fish stocks, preceded Columbus across the Atlantic. Probably these fishermen first visited Newfoundland, then, at a slightly later date, pressed further west to discover what are today the Maritime provinces. Undoubtedly they sometimes landed on these strange shores in search of fresh water or game, but also out of curiosity.

That they came into contact with the Micmac people and established trading practices at a very early date is borne out by an encounter of the French explorer Jacques Cartier around the Bay of Chaleur in New Brunswick in 1534, when Cartier's ship was hailed by a party of Micmac waving beaver skins on sticks in an effort to attract the Frenchmen's attention and have the opportunity to trade their skins for European items. Cartier reported that the Micmac were so eager to trade that they exchanged even the skins off their backs for French goods.

Doubtless much contact and trade occurred during the sixteenth century throughout Micmac territory, but because the fishermen were illiterate for the most part, we have very few references and descriptions of the Micmac during this time. However, the fur trade in the eastern Maritime area of Canada was considered sufficiently lucrative that Samuel de Champlain established a post at Port Royal in Nova Scotia in 1605 for the purpose of fur trading, and sources on Micmac culture increase after this time. During the seventeenth century, trade intensified: hundreds of thousands of beaver, moose, and other skins were taken out of the Maritime area before the fur trade came to an end in the late eighteenth century.

To the dismay of the Natives, more than trade items came with the fur trade. Initially they welcomed the Europeans and the goods the Europeans offered in exchange for furs. Copper kettles and metal knives and axes were superior to the fragile pottery and stone cutting tools the Micmac had manufactured. As years of trade and contact with Europeans wore on, however, the Micmac found that both they and their culture were changing, and not in beneficial ways.

Probably the earliest disruptions in Native culture and lifestyle began well before 1600; as the Micmac became caught up in the fur trade, they found that the trade demanded changes in their entire lifestyle and seasonal round. Trading ships were present in the waters off the maritime coasts only during the summer months. If the Micmac wanted to participate in the fur trade, they had to give up their summer hunting and gathering pattern and instead spend the time loitering along the coast waiting for trading ships. This lifestyle change in turn drastically affected their winter diet; they were unable to accumulate their normal summer food stores and were thus forced to rely for the winter on whatever dried foods they received in trade and managed to save. Trade food items, an important commodity to the Micmac, emphasized dried vegetables such as corn, peas, beans, ships' hardtack biscuit, and even prunes. Most of these were consumed as they were received, leaving only stores of hardtack biscuit for the winter. Often the Micmac found themselves in a desperate situation before spring.

In addition to dried foods, another trade item the Micmac learned to demand at an early date was alcohol, which affected their culture and population detrimentally. With the wine and brandy they received in trade, the men held drinking bouts during which fights broke out, sometimes leading even to murder. Women, too, held drinking parties in the woods, separate from the men because the women feared the physical violence of the men's drinking parties. However, groups of women drinking in the woods served as a lure for sailors from the fishing ships who found the inebriated women easy sexual prey. Thus the value placed on female chastity and sexual fidelity was disappearing by the mid-seventeenth century, while the Micmac population was incorporating a number of offspring of mixed parentage.

The introduction of alcohol and the changes in diet, combined with exposure to unfamiliar European diseases, had to have had an effect on the Micmac people physically. Despite the presence of European epidemic diseases in the general region prior to 1600, there is no clear evidence of their sweeping through the Micmac population. Instead, from their statements to Europeans in the early 1600s, most likely local outbreaks of European maladies occurred among various groups of the Micmac, causing increased mortality rates. In addition, the Micmac themselves, as well as contemporary European observers, noted the effects of the dietary change on their general health: lung, chest, and intestinal disorders were increasingly common, especially in winter. Also related to the dietary change was an overall reduction in life expectancy. By the end of the seventeenth century, long-lived individuals were quite rare, and those were individuals who deliberately eschewed the European foods and lifestyle in favour of a traditional diet.

A final consequence of changing lifestyle and changing diet was the diminishing family size observed among the Micmac as early as the seventeenth century. Large families and polygyny became less common after 1600. One reason for this was that, as Micmac men spent less time hunting and more time drinking and dissipating, they could not support more than one wife. Impotence resulting from the great amounts of alcohol consumed may also have been a contributing factor in reduced family size. Meanwhile, the miscellaneous accidents and injuries that had occurred in pre-contact times continued into post-contact times, but with greater effect for they acted on a population with a diminishing birth rate. Because of the general decline in health and the overall diminishing numbers of the mature population, polygyny gave way to monogamy as the standard marriage form. Any children born were more likely to die before reaching maturity, thus perpetuating the downward spiralling trend in the population.

Nobody, much less the Micmac themselves, could foresee the great toll that these factors of changed diet, the introduction of alcohol, and European diseases would have on the Micmac population. But even before written records began for the eastern Maritime area, shortly after 1600, it is apparent that the Micmac population had been heavily depleted. As a Jesuit priest in Nova Scotia summarized the situation in 1611: "these countries . . . are very sparsely populated, especially those . . . which are near the sea; although Membertou assures us that in his youth he has seen *chimonutz*, that is to say, Savages, as thickly planted there as the hairs upon his head" (Thwaites, 1896, 1: 177). The Micmac population continued its decline for over 200 additional years, until it reached its nadir somewhere around 1850, leaving a population of about 3,000. For the period between 1600 and 1850, the declining trend is particularly well documented in a rich assortment of published primary sources and unpublished archival material. Using materials from these sources, we will focus on Nova Scotia with some attention to the other provinces.

The French were the first to send permanent settlers to the Maritimes area. French Acadians began to arrive shortly after the establishment of Port Royal, and they settled first in that vicinity, later extending their settlements along the Bay of Fundy and the isthmus of Chignecto, which connects Nova Scotia to New Brunswick.

After the signing of the Treaty of Utrecht in 1713, the French tried to strengthen their hold on Acadia by building a fortress at Louisbourg on Cape Breton Island in eastern Nova Scotia. From Louisbourg, the French further cultivated friendship with the Micmac people, giving them gifts while inciting them to commit hostile acts against the English, who were at the same time attempting to establish their own foothold in Acadia. The French incitement was successful, and the seeds were sown for permanent mutual dislike and distrust between the Micmac and the English. Hostilities between the two were quite intense during the first half of the eighteenth century, escalating into a so-called "Indian-English War" between 1722 and 1726, during which the Micmac took great delight in harassing and seizing English ships and fishing boats. The Micmac even carried out an attack on Port Royal, held by the English, at this time and the English countered by initiating a campaign of genocide against all Micmac people, which was to last more than fifty years.

English attempts at genocide took various forms: they served poisoned food to the Natives at a feast in 1712; they traded contaminated cloth to some Micmac in 1745, setting off an epidemic that caused the deaths of several hundred; they sent groups of English soldiers to roam Nova Scotia and destroy Micmac camps, murdering the Natives without regard to sex or age. The English even imported companies of Mohawks and New England Algonquians, traditional enemies of the Micmac, to track down and kill them. All these tactics cost the lives of an uncalculated number of Micmac.

Despite the open hostilities between the English and the Micmac people, it was the French, the Micmacs' friends and allies, who unwittingly brought more harm to the Micmac than all the English efforts. The French had settled Nova Scotia, and their close contact with the Micmac meant that any diseases contracted by them also spread to the Natives. Thus, in the early 1730s, Micmac around Louisbourg suffered a severe smallpox epidemic. In the years that followed, outbreaks of other European diseases also occurred among the Micmac in the vicinity of Louisbourg. But the most disastrous epidemic came with the arrival of a French fleet in Halifax harbour in 1746. At this time, all of mainland Nova Scotia had fallen into English hands, and this French fleet had been dispatched in an attempt to recapture the lost territory. Unfortunately, the huge fleet, consisting of a total of sixty-five ships transporting more than 3,000 soldiers, had encountered poor sailing conditions while crossing the Atlantic. Most of the ships had been sunk or otherwise dispersed, and the crossing had been greatly delayed. When the remnants of the fleet, roughly a dozen ships, reached Halifax harbour, the men on board were suffering from a highly contagious fever, probably typhus, which had broken out at sea. While the fever caused the deaths of over 2,000 French soldiers, it wreaked even greater havoc among the Micmac people, a large number of whom had gathered at the harbour to trade with the arriving Frenchmen. Contracting the fever, the Micmac in the area were decimated. Moreover, the fever spread rapidly through the western part of Nova Scotia, an area especially densely populated in aboriginal and early post-contact times. One reliable account of this epidemic estimated that it brought death to approximately 4,000 Natives, or about one-third of the Micmac people of Nova Scotia.

This typhus epidemic of 1746 decimated the Micmac population in western Nova Scotia, but it really marked only the beginning of the deaths of increasingly large numbers of Natives. The English genocide campaign, begun in the early 1700s, intensified after 1749, when they established the city of Halifax in an attempt to maintain their control over mainland Nova Scotia. It is a testimony to the great numbers of the tribe that when the English settlers arrived in Halifax three years after the great epidemic they still found numerous Micmac people. Probably these had moved here from the east after the epidemic, since the Halifax area was reportedly a favourite hunting ground. Despite the ongoing campaign of genocide in other parts of Nova Scotia, the newly arrived settlers found the Micmac around Halifax hospitable. One of them wrote home to England that "when we first came here, the Indians, in a friendly manner, brought us lobsters and other fish in plenty, being satisfied for them by a bit of bread and some meat."

Cordial relations were short-lived, however, possibly because the head of the new settlement, Colonel Edward Cornwallis, seems to have been prejudiced against the Natives from the beginning. While admitting that he found the Micmac initially "peaceable," he ordered his troops to clear a space thirty feet wide around the settlement and erect a fence; he then built a fort nearby. Perhaps because such actions were not lost on the Micmac and perhaps because of French incitement, several incidents occurred that seemed to Cornwallis to justify punitive action.

During the summer and early fall of 1749, some Micmac harassed an English settlement in eastern Nova Scotia and captured several ships. For the British, the last straw came at the end of September, when a party of men sent to cut wood for a government sawmill across the harbour from Halifax was attacked and five of them murdered by Micmac. Cornwallis wasted no time: the very next day, October 1, 1749, he met with his Executive Council to discuss this hostile situation. Openly declaring war on the Micmac, Cornwallis felt, "would be in some sort to own them a free people, whereas they ought to be looked on as Rebels to His Majesty's Government." So the Executive Council decided to give orders to all Englishmen in the province "to annoy, distress, and destroy the Indians everywhere." At the same time, Cornwallis established two companies of volunteers to scour the entire province in search of Micmac. He placed a bounty of ten guineas on every Micmac killed or taken prisoner; the following summer, the bounty was increased to £50. Despite the size of the bounty, only a very few payments were made, perhaps, as one newspaper put it, because of "the care of the Indians in carrying off their dead." The campaign had its effects on the Micmac people in numbers killed, but also in causing the population to shift its campsites and movements away from English settlements, for, again, as a settler put it, "our soldiers take great pains to drive [the Micmac] away and clear the country of them."

The campaign became so uncomfortable for the Micmac that several chiefs, including the Grand Chief, came to Halifax in 1752 with overtures of peace and concluded a peace treaty that year with the English. However, it was an uneasy peace as long as the French remained in Nova Scotia to incite the Natives against the English and as long as the Micmac themselves remained numerous and powerful enough to threaten the English presence. Four additional treaties were negotiated over the next quarter-century between the Micmac and the English, as both sides violated treaties.

Despite these treaties, the English campaign against the Micmac was pursued relentlessly. In 1756, the English renewed their bounty offer, and volunteer companies as well as individual Englishmen continued to hunt and kill Micmac people wherever they were found. The following is one account of the massacre of a Micmac encampment in Nova Scotia in 1759:

Intelligence had reached Annapolis . . . that a hostile Micmac village existed on Green Point. . . . Major Rogers with his celebrated Rangers at once advanced in pursuit . . . they espied, through a spy glass, the object of their search. Here they encamped for the night, sleeping on the ground as was their custom. Leaving the men there, Rogers went in the morning, before daylight, to reconnoitre the village by moonlight. Arriving near the property of the late Sheriff Taylor, he surveyed the Indian settlement of wigwams with its rude inhabitants now engaged in festive entertainment, wholly unaware of the presence, almost in their midst, of a British soldier preparing for battle. After all was quiet, Rogers, joined by his men, attacked the sleeping encampment, killing the chief on the spot. Thus surprised and having no effective weapons of defense the Indians fled in disorder before the disciplined pursuers, who followed them along the shore. (Clayton 1966: 7)

And this, of course, was only one such exploit perpetrated by one volunteer company. These companies did not keep records of how many Micmac they killed in such a manner, but historical records reveal that the English employed such volunteer companies from at least 1744 to at least 1761, giving us some indication of a considerable number.

After 1780, pressure on Micmac lands intensified as increasing numbers of settlers poured into the eastern Maritime area, clearing and fencing land. Many of these were United Empire Loyalists, who chose to resettle in Canada rather than remain in the rebellious American colonies, and invariably they chose to settle in the most desirable locations. Often these lands were traditional Micmac hunting or fishing spots. Moreover, the settlers put increasing pressure on available game as they hunted moose as a replacement for beef cattle, which were not plentiful in Nova Scotia or New Brunswick at the time. As hunting and gathering opportunities declined and disappeared for the Natives and as the fur trade dropped off after 1780, the Micmac people found themselves without food or goods to trade for food. The result, of course, was starvation, and great numbers of Micmac, particularly those in Nova Scotia, succumbed to starvation well into the nineteenth century.

Reports of Micmac suffering from hunger date from as early as 1775 in Nova Scotia, when some settlers in the western half of the province appealed to the government on behalf of "several poor Indians, who from bad Success in hunting were in Great Distress." A few years later, a bill to "prevent the Destruction of Moose, Beaver, and Muskrat in the Indian hunting Ground" was introduced into the legislature, but it was defeated. Meanwhile, non-Native poachers in Cape Breton reportedly killed nearly 9,000 moose and caribou in the winter of 1789 alone. After 1790, when a series of unusually mild winters served to reduce further the number and quality of fur-bearing animals, accounts of outright starvation among the Indians became common. Even small game such as birds and rabbits was scarce, and numbers of Micmac began to congregate around white settlements for food. Settlers in one area of Nova Scotia complained in the fall of 1793 of large numbers of Micmac who not only begged food, but who had also become "extremely troublesome" to the point of stealing and slaughtering settlers' stock for food.

The situation became so desperate that, as one settler put it in his petition of January, 1794, "a great many Mickmacks have died for want of victuals . . . notwithstanding the little they get from the superintendent . . . if they have not some more general relief they and their wives and children must in a few years all perish with cold and hunger in their own country."

Finally, at the Indian superintendent's urging, the Nova Scotia government established a committee in 1800 to study the Micmacs' situation and make recommendations for dealing with it. The only outcome of this committee was the establishment of a small sum set aside annually for relief of the Natives. At first set at £150 and then gradually increased until it reached £300 in the years just preceding Confederation, the sum was never sufficient to cover the food, clothing, and medical attention the Micmac people needed. The very first year that goods were distributed, the government agent in Antigonish reported that, while the Micmac in his jurisdiction were certainly in a miserable condition, some of them "entirely naked," the goods allotted were insufficient for the needs of the overwhelming number of Micmac who turned up for the distribution. And the suffering and deprivation went on at least until 1867, when the federal government assumed responsibility for the Natives.

Of course, Micmac people were dying from causes other than simple starvation and exposure during this time. The malnutrition and cold they suffered and the excessive consumption of alcohol by some contributed to lower resistance to diseases. During 1800 and 1801, there was a wide-spread epidemic of smallpox, possibly contracted from some recently arrived Scottish immigrants who landed at Pictou. Reports of the epidemic came in from all around the province. Micmac families fled to the woods from their usual haunts, hoping to avoid the smallpox, but this movement had two bad consequences: it spread the disease to other Micmac and it prevented them from collecting relief supplies issued in the settlements. Both these factors contributed to additional suffering. Smallpox was only the first well-documented European disease to affect the Micmac during the nineteenth century, and it recurred several times. As it recurred, all Micmac came to fear this disease greatly, in at least one instance refusing blankets that they thought had been in contact with smallpox patients. Since the early years of the century, the government provided inoculations against smallpox and encouraged the Natives to take them, but the Micmac disliked and avoided the vaccinations, which doubtless contributed to the smallpox mortality.

Whooping cough, measles, typhus, typhoid fever, and numerous outbreaks of unspecified ailments labelled simply as "sickness" are all recorded as causes of death among the Micmac during the first half of the nineteenth century. It appears that outbreaks of diseases occurred locally, and when settlers in the vicinity were made aware of such an outbreak they notified the Indian superintendent, who in turn called a doctor to attend the ailing Natives. An example of this procedure is provided by an epidemic of infectious hepatitis that swept through Micmac camps around southern New Brunswick and mainland Nova Scotia in 1846 and 1847. Transmitted by frightened Micmac fleeing infected camps, the disease brought considerable suffering and painful deaths to "a number" of them before medical doctors were summoned. Because of the "threatened annihilation" of Micmac people living around Dartmouth, Nova Scotia, the government built a temporary hospital to isolate victims and bring the epidemic under control. But the conditions in which infectious hepatitis flourishes – poor hygiene, inadequate diet, substandard living conditions – testify once again to the mid-nineteenth-century living conditions of many Micmac people and, thus, to their vulnerability to all manner of disease.

Infectious diseases such as these run their course, for better or worse, in a relatively short period of time; lingering, wasting diseases among the Micmac began to be reported about the middle of the nineteenth century. Tuberculosis, the most prominent of these, may have been present since prehistoric times, but received first notice in 1841 when a settler reported in a letter to the Lieutenant-Governor of Nova Scotia that "many [Micmac] have died off with consumption." The frequency and intensity of this dread disease spread as tuberculosis brought death to Micmac of all ages and even entire families. The incidence of tuberculosis peaked shortly after 1900, but its continued presence was largely responsible for keeping the Micmac population at a constant low figure until the 1940s.

The pattern described for Nova Scotia generally was similar to events in New Brunswick. The Micmac of Prince Edward Island were entirely landless until 1870, when money was raised to purchase Lenox Island for them. Following Confederation in 1867, the federal government established reserves for the Natives, while the Newfoundland government in the early 1870s surveyed a reserve for Micmac families residing at Conne River. All the Micmac had a low profile through the later years of the nineteenth century and into the twentieth century. Government funds did not provide for them well and they survived as best they could in a variety of economic activities. Some families sold hand-crafted baskets or porcupine quillwork to tourists; they also made butter tubs, coal pick handles, axe handles, and hockey sticks to sell to local residents. Some men worked cutting wood for sawmills, as labourers on the railroads and in the dockyards, or in fish and lobster canneries. Some acted as hunting guides. Others farmed while their wives were domestic workers. And doubtless some families camped on settlers' property, moving from place to place and picking up a living in a semi-traditional manner. The First and Second World Wars offered escape from unemployment or underemployment through enlistment, as did the Korean and Vietnam wars.

In 1969, the status Micmac of Nova Scotia joined to form the Union of Nova Scotia Indians, while the New Brunswick Micmac formed the Union of New Brunswick Indians. Both began administering their own programs on the reserves. They also began documenting land claims, a process that paid off in part when the federal government agreed that part of Big Cove Reserve in New Brunswick had been taken over illegally in 1879, while the Wagmatcook Reserve in Nova Scotia was awarded $1.2 million for reserve lands also illegally alienated. Another significant

PLATE 15.3. Rita Joe, P.C., C.M., is a Nova Scotian Micmac elder and celebrated poet. She has been appointed a member of the Privy Council and has received the Order of Canada, among other honours and awards. Courtesy David Mahoney.

PLATE 15.4. Micmac RCMP Constable Steve Michael of Indianbrook, Nova Scotia, receiving an RCMP reward for suicide prevention in Maritime communities, 1993. Courtesy of Micmac-Malisseet Nations News Association.

settlement came in 1993 when the Micmac people of Pictou Landing Reserve in Nova Scotia were awarded $35 million in compensation from the federal government for failure to prevent pulp waste pollution of their reserve shoreline. The Federation of Newfoundland Indians was formed in 1973 and worked for recognition of the Natives living in Newfoundland, who had been virtually ignored by government when Newfoundland came into Confederation in 1949. Success came in 1984, when the federal government registered the Micmac people living at Conne River, Newfoundland, under the Indian Act. Since then, conditions have improved for these people and a land claim has been filed seeking compensation for the loss of their traditional territory in southern Newfoundland. Micmac people have also had success in reclaiming their traditional hunting and fishing rights in recent years, as is demonstrated by the 1990 case of the Micmac moose hunters in Nova Scotia. Since 1985, Bill C-31 has provided opportunity for some non-registered Natives, including Micmacs, to apply for registration under the Indian Act.

In 1994, social problems still exist for the Micmac. Donald Marshall, Jr., a young Micmac man in Nova Scotia, encountered discrimination in the judicial system in 1971, when he was wrongfully convicted of murder. After serving eleven years in prison, he was released and acquitted after a new trial. Marshall subsequently received financial compensation from the province. Other social problems include substance abuse and a high suicide rate on many reserves. In New Brunswick, Big Cove Reserve has attempted to reduce a particularly high suicide rate by a combination of government-sponsored community programs and the revitalization of traditional cultural values.

Educational and employment opportunities on reserves still need improvement. The Micmac people are working to improve their situation through self-government and Native control of finances and decision-making. Along with this have come growing Native awareness and pride as shown by the increasing number of powwows and Native dancing, drumming, and chanting groups on reserves.

In 1993, a total of 20,500 registered Micmac people lived both on and off reserves in the five provinces. Despite the massive lifestyle changes and attempts to acculturate them, the Micmac after 500 years remain separate from the larger society. Their culture today is an amalgam of traditional Native values and contemporary white values.

Recommended Readings

Denys, Nicholas

1672   *The Description and Natural History of the Coasts of North America* (reprint, 1908, Toronto: Champlain Society).
Contains the classic seventeenth-century account of the Micmacs and their culture. Also interesting as it contains an early description of acculturation in the Micmac culture between 1634, the year of Denys's arrival in Acadia, and 1672, the year the book was published.

Hoffman, Bernard G.

1955   "Historical Ethnography of the Micmac of the Sixteenth and Seventeenth Centuries," Ph.D. dissertation in Anthropology, University of California, Berkeley.
The best ethnography available. Done using the ethnohistoric method and based on a thorough combing of all archival materials, the work is sometimes repetitive; if anything, it errs by being over-complete.

Jackson, Douglas, and Gerald Penney, eds.

1993   *"On the Country": The Micmacs of Newfoundland.* St. John's: Harry Cuff Publications Limited.
Provides a good historic overview of the Micmac people of Newfoundland.

LeClerq, Chretien

1691   *New Relations of Gaspesia, with the Customs and Religion of the Gaspesian Indians* (reprint, 1910, Toronto: Champlain Society).
Another of the classic seventeenth-century accounts. More complete than Denys, although parts of LeClerq's book may be based on Denys.

Lescarbot, Marc

1609   *The History of New France* (reprint, 1911-14, Toronto: Champlain Society).
One of the most valuable of all the seventeenth-century accounts of the Micmac as it is the earliest. Also more complete than Denys.

Thwaites, Reuben Gold, ed.

1896   *The Jesuit Relations and Allied Documents.* 73 vols. Cleveland: Burrows Brothers.
Especially volumes I, II, and III, for the years 1610-16, as they contain Father Biard's early observations and speculations on the Micmac.

Wallis, Wilson, and Ruth Sawtell Wallis

1955   *The Micmac Indians of Eastern Canada.* Minneapolis: University of Minnesota Press.
The standard modern ethnography of the Micmac, but uneven as it combines information from the seventeenth-century accounts with data from Wilson Wallis's fieldwork in 1911. Cited here because Hoffman is not generally available.

Additional Reference Cited

Clayton, Hazel Maud Snow
    1966 *Down Nova Scotia Way.* Digby, Nova Scotia: privately printed.

PART VI
The Plains

CHAPTER 16
Myths and Realities:
An Overview of the Plains

C. Roderick Wilson

No Aboriginal people on earth have so captured the popular imagination as have the "historic" Plains Indians. Frozen in mid-nineteenth century by strips of Hollywood celluloid, or for our grandparents by dime novels and Wild West shows, the Plains Indian has for millions become "The Indian." So much is this the case that Indians from culture areas thousands of miles distant at times feel compelled to don Plains-style feather headdresses and assorted other finery – so that others will recognize them as Indians.

Non-Indian devotees of Plains culture are found around the world. Black celebrants at Mardi Gras in New Orleans and throughout the Caribbean annually celebrate by means of elaborate costume, song, and dance an essentially mythic kinship with Plains Indians. European Boy Scouts devour both highly romanticized popular works and technical treatises on Plains Indians, with some scrupulously following every possible detail in creating their own medicine bundles and actually becoming, in their own minds, members of their chosen tribe. Some North

MAP 16.1. The Plains Culture Area

American hobbyists spend thousands of dollars and hours in perfecting historically accurate costumes and dances, and in performing. A number of Canada's national myths have to do with events by which Plains Indians were incorporated into the Canadian state: the North-West Mounted Police protecting Canadian Indians from unscrupulous American whiskey traders; the Canadian Pacific Railway, the ribbon of steel that tied Canada together, being made possible by the pacification of the warriors of the Plains; the stark contrast in levels of violence on the

Canadian and U.S. frontiers. In myriad ways, both conscious and unconscious, the dominant Indian image, in Canada and the world, is that of the Plains Indian of about 1850.

What relationship, if any, exists between the popular image and the reality?

There are several ways to answer the question. One is to emphasize that the stereotype has virtually no relationship to the reality of the time that Indians have occupied the region. In the 12,000 or more years of its existence, the economic basis of Plains society changed substantially. The earliest known Plains dwellers appear to have relied mainly on spears to dispatch the large animals they hunted. Three major technological innovations transformed Plains hunting prior to the advent of the European: the spear thrower, the bow and arrow, and the buffalo pound. Each brought new efficiencies to the hunt and in turn affected the life of the people. The real Plains Indians thus are part of a millennia-old pattern of dynamic change and development, of adjusting to major shifts in climate and environment, to altering frequencies of game population (including the extinction of major species such as the mammoth, mastodon, and ancient species of buffalo), and to new hunting tools that demanded new skills and new forms of social co-operation. The stereotype, in contrast, has no roots and does not speak to change. In fact, it denies change.

To further emphasize this point, it can be noted that the list of "tribes" on the Canadian Plains during the "classic" period is substantially different from what it was earlier. (1) Assiniboine (Stoney) people broke off from the Yankton Sioux and thereafter associated largely with the Cree. Three hundred years ago they lived in Minnesota at the edge of the parklands and Plains, hunting both deer and buffalo, and engaging in some horticulture. (2) Blackfoot, like the Cree and Saulteaux, speak an Algonquian language. They probably have lived on the Plains for a substantial period of time. (3) Although recent evidence indicates that Cree have lived in the parkland regions of the West for some time, the Plains Cree came into existence and moved onto the Plains through involvement in the fur trade. (4) Saulteaux, who refer to themselves as Bungi, could as well be called the Plains Ojibwa. They also may have moved on to the Plains in early historic times. (5) Sarsi are Athapaskan speakers from the north who became buffalo hunters associated with the Blackfoot in recent times. Thus, of five tribes inhabiting the Canadian Plains in 1850, only one was probably not a newcomer. If one considered the Metis a tribe, the case is even stronger. Conversely, three tribes that in late prehistoric times lived in the region, the Kutenai, Shoshone, and Atsina (Gros

PLATE 16.1 Assiniboine warrior. Courtesy Saskatchewan Archives Board, R-A4945-1.

Ventre), had been displaced by 1850. Again, the stereotype gives no sense of dynamic changes in the region.

Another indicator of the discrepancy between the stereotype and the tradition of Plains culture is the extent to which life changed as a result of the horse and gun. Each in turn increased the efficiency of the hunt. People not only could get more food and hides quickly, they could also carry bigger tipis and more goods, men could keep more women productively working and so were more likely to be polygynous, infant mortality dropped and women at least were likely to live longer, and so on. Perhaps most significantly, high status now depended on having horses, creating a new impetus for raiding – and with the gun the level of violence increased dramatically. In addition, as Foster points out, life on the Plains was no longer autochthonous; the Europeans were also there. Although Plains life in 1850 was still grounded in the past, in many regards it was conspicuously different from anything that had gone before.

The stereotype, however, was not wholly invented. There were buffalo-hunting nomads who sought visions, counted coup, and ate pemmican. Dempsey writes graphically of Blackfoot in this period, and much of what he describes could also be said of other Plains tribes. Although Dempsey's portrait corresponds quite substantially with elements of the stereotype, major differences include: (1) as a generalization dealing with typical patterns, it allows for the fact that people's real behaviour is quite variable; (2) it recognizes that real Blackfoot had a past and that their present is markedly different from their life a century ago; and (3) in recognizing that today's changed Blackfoot are rooted in the life and values of the past, it implies that they have a future as a culture. Its implicit denial of an authentically Indian future is perhaps the most damning feature of the stereotype.

This discussion originated in a consideration of the popular stereotype of the Plains Indian. Part of our argument about the pervasiveness of this image is that it has affected also the perceptions of government officials and academics. Carter's chapter contains a thorough and depressing analysis of the extent to which the stereotype was one of the factors that effectively prevented Plains Cree from becoming productive farmers in the late 1800s. Unfortunately, what she documents for this group could easily be extended in both time and place.

Carter also mentions, almost in passing, that the Plains stereotype has affected the view of historians. She could have mentioned anthropologists as well, and any other academics who have discussed these people. The personal example she provides is straightforward: her research of the facts dispelled the presuppositions with which she started. Some connections are not so easily traced, however. One of our unfinished tasks is to rethink not only our national and regional history, but also the disciplines themselves.

We conclude with the observation that the Plains stereotype has been, and continues to be, a factor in the Indian-government relationship in Canada. Although there are earlier treaties, the formal treaty-making process that created the modern reserve system is fundamentally a phenomenon of the Plains. That is where the numbered treaties started, and most treaty Indians still live in the Prairie provinces. The necessity of settling the Canadian Plains, of protecting them from a neighbour whose vision of manifest destiny conflicted with our own, and of tying the nascent nation together prompted the treaties. The treaties and reserves were also a product of the U.S. Plains, a deliberate attempt to avoid the bloodshed and expense associated with the U.S. frontier; such events as that of the Little Bighorn, where the Seventh Cavalry was routed by concentrated Indian forces, loomed large. It is no accident that Canadian reserves, generally, are both smaller and more scattered than are reservations in the U.S.

The treaties called for reserves. The government not only established reserves for the treaty Indians but for thousands of non-treaty Indians who did not live on the Plains and with whom the government saw no necessity of signing treaties. But the reserve system, as legislated by the Indian Act, embodies an assumption that Indians are not competent to govern their own affairs, that land and money must be held by the government in trust for them. The Plains stereotype, it must be remembered, is in part a fusion of two conflicting stereotypes, both held by Europeans for centuries – the Indian as the uncivilized and barbaric savage and the Indian as the noble savage, the untutored child of nature. Noble he may be, but in the eyes of the law, a child. Most Canadians would be shocked to realize the domination that Indian agents legally exercised on reserves until recently, as well as the reluctance that is still frequently encountered among professional "carers-for-Indians" to allow their "noble charges" the simple dignity of running their own lives. The fact of the non-adult legal status of the Indian is central to most of the public controversies concerning Indians in recent years. The Plains stereotype does not alone explain the history and current conditions of Canadian Indians, but it certainly served, and continues to serve, to reinforce unfortunate tendencies toward paternalism.

CHAPTER 17
The Blackfoot Indians

Hugh A. Dempsey

The Ethnographic Blackfoot

Environment and Economy

The Blackfoot territory during the historic period after 1750 was vast: it ranged from the North Saskatchewan River to the Missouri River, and from the Rocky Mountains to the present Alberta-Saskatchewan boundary. Near the latter part of the nomadic era, the northern range shrank to the Battle River, as the Blackfoot withdrew in the face of Cree pressures and as the decreasing buffalo herds congregated farther south.

Blackfoot territory was primarily short-grass plains interspersed by deep coulees and streams bisecting it in an east-west direction. A number of these watercourses dried up completely during the summer months. Lakes often were so alkaline that the water was virtually undrinkable. Most of the river areas and lakeshores were devoid of timber. When groves of trees were found, they became favourite wintering areas.

The large mammals in Blackfoot country were the buffalo, grizzly bear, black bear, antelope, deer, elk, mountain sheep, and mountain goat. Of these, the Blackfoot were interested primarily in the buffalo, calling its flesh *nitapiksisako*, or "real meat," implying that all other meat was inferior. Besides being used for food, the buffalo was the source of many articles of utilitarian and religious use, such as lodge covers, tools, clothing, drinking vessels, storage containers, expungers, and shields.

Lesser mammals were used as food only when buffalo was unavailable. These included porcupine, rabbit, and squirrel. The Blackfoot rejected all fish as food; they considered these creatures to be part of an evil Underwater World. Ducks, geese, partridge, and swans were sometimes eaten, and fowls' eggs were collected for food.

Similarly, a wide variety of berries and edible roots were gathered by the women: most prominent were the saskatoon or sarvice berry, chokeberry, bull berry, high and low bush cranberry, gooseberry, pin cherry, raspberry, strawberry, wild turnip, wild onion, bitter root, and camas root. Other plants had a practical or medicinal use: bearberry and the inner bark of the red willow were smoked, as was a form of wild tobacco. Because of its bitter taste, the latter was mixed with herbs and, in later years, with commercial tobacco.

The weather in Blackfoot country was marked by hot dry summers and long cold winters, with warm chinook winds providing some respite during winter. Spring was often cool and wet, interrupted by late blizzards, while autumns were warm, dry, and pleasant; the term "Indian summer" was most appropriate for the region. Spring and summer saw violent thunderstorms, to which were attributed religious significance. The first thunderstorm of spring heralded a ritual of the medicine-pipe owners, while the thunder itself was considered to be a powerful deity. Death by lightning was not uncommon.

Under ideal conditions an abundance of food could be found by the Blackfoot; they could also starve during periods of drought or blizzards. If the Blackfoot went into their winter quarters and the buffalo remained far out on the Plains, if prairie fires drove the herds out of the area, or if blizzards prevented the hunters from leaving their camps, hunger and privation would result. As nomads they could not store large quantities of food and thus were dependent on a regular supply of fresh meat. In autumn some meat was cut into long thin strips and sun-dried, but this provided emergency rations for relatively short periods of time. Other dried meat was pulverized and mixed with crushed, dried sarvice (saskatoon) berries and hot fat, producing pemmican. This, too, provided a limited but important source of food in winter.

PLATE 17.1 Blackfoot warriors. Courtesy of the Canadian Museum of Civilization, 73462.

Buffalo were killed in a variety of ways. The prehistoric Blackfoot used the steep cliffs near the foothill streams as buffalo jumps. Those not killed by the fall were quickly dispatched by hunters. This system of hunting was practised for thousands of years. With the introduction of the horse and the gun, it gradually fell into disuse and was abandoned during the mid-nineteenth century.

Another method of killing buffalo was the "surround." When hunters located a small herd they crept forward, sometimes disguising themselves as wolves or buffalo calves, and when they were close enough they picked off animals on the outer fringe of the herd. If they were lucky the herd merely milled in a circle instead of running away, and the hunters might kill several animals before the buffalo finally took flight.

But perhaps the most thrilling way to kill buffalo was on horseback. When the Blackfoot acquired the horse in the early 1700s they quickly learned how to ride among a herd at a full gallop, picking a fat cow and killing it with an arrow or lead ball. Specially trained horses were guided by the knee pressures of the hunter and often would press so close to the quarry that the hunter's leg would be touching the buffalo. So valued were these buffalo runners that they had no other duties to perform.

Smaller animals and birds were hunted on foot, young boys killing rabbits and partridges as part of their education in learning how to stalk and shoot. Young water birds were sometimes caught by teenage girls who waded among the reeds. Picking berries and digging roots were entirely the women's responsibility, although a teenage boy usually accompanied them to protect them in case of attack by bears or other animals. The berries were either stewed or sun-dried and saved for winter use.

Because of the movement of the buffalo and the availability of products at certain seasons of the year, the Blackfoot followed an annual cycle in their travels. In winter they gathered in small bands along wooded river bottoms, often near the foothills where they were within easy reach of the buffalo. There they stayed in one place for weeks at a time, particularly when hunting was good. In such winter camps, tepees (or tipis) were strung out for miles among the protective cottonwoods of a river valley. Each band might have a separate camp but remained within a mile or two of another camp for mutual protection against enemies.

In the spring, the people moved out into the prairies, sometimes in small family groups or bands, depending on the movements of the buffalo. Some would go deep into the foothills to cut new tepee poles or travois poles, while others went to trading posts or killed enough buffalo to make new lodge covers. By early summer they congregated in larger camps, comprising whole tribes, so that the Sun Dance and other rituals could be held. When gathered in such large numbers they seldom remained in one spot for more than a week, as their horses soon grazed off all the nearby grass. After the ceremonies they wandered off in small groups again, picking berries, drying meat, and making pemmican to sell to the trading posts. In the early autumn they completed their fall trade and chose their winter campsites. Often these were in close proximity to buffalo jumps, which provided them with a source of food as long as buffalo stayed in the area.

During all this period, of course, there always were small family groups that wandered off to visit other tribes and young warriors who went to raid enemy horse herds, but the general practice was to follow the movement of the buffalo.

Social Organization

The Blackfoot nation is made up of three tribes: the Blackfoot, or *Sik-sik-a'*, meaning "black foot" or "black feet"; the Blood, or *Kai-nai*, meaning "many chiefs"; and the Peigan, or *Pi-kuni*, meaning "scabby robes." The latter was further subdivided into the North and South Peigan tribes. Allied to the nation, thus forming the Blackfoot Confederacy, were the Sarcees and the Gros Ventres, the latter separating and becoming an enemy in a dispute over stolen horses in 1861.

A number of myths explain how the Blackfoot tribal names came into existence. The most popular is that at one time they were an unnamed group that took possession of the foothills and Plains but found themselves beset by enemies on all sides. To control the area they agreed to divide into three groups – one to guard the northeastern frontier, another to protect the southeast, and a third, the southwest.

After some time had passed an Indian from the northern tribe decided to visit the other two, to see how they were living. On his way he passed over a large area burned by a prairie fire and when he reached the southeast camp, his moccasins were black with ashes. Entering the village, he asked a man who was the chief. "I am," said the Indian. Another Indian stopped and said, "I am the chief," and soon the northerner was surrounded by several Indians, all claiming to be chiefs.

"I shall call your tribe 'A-kainah,' or Many Chiefs," he said, "for everyone here seems to be a chief." The Crees gave this tribe the name of Red People, for the ochre they spread on their clothes, and this was later translated as Blood People, or Bloods.

These Blood Indians looked at the visitor's moccasins and said, "Very well, you have given our tribe a name, so we will reciprocate; your people shall be called 'Siksika,' or Blackfoot Indians."

The man then went to the southwest Indians where their territory was rich in buffalo. The people had become lazy and the women had tanned their hides so badly that men were walking about with pieces of dried flesh and hair on their robes. "I shall call you 'Apikuni,' or 'badly-dressed robes'," he told them; over the years the word became corrupted to Peigan. Collectively these three tribes were called "Sakoyitapix," the "prairie people," or sometimes the "Nitsitapix," the "real people."

Because the nation is divided between the United States and Canada, a number of contradictions have arisen regarding spelling of tribal names. For example, Canadians generally and Indians on the Peigan Reserve in southern Alberta use the term "Peigan," while in the United States it is spelled "Piegan." But most controversial has been the correctness of

MAP 17.1. Blackfoot Reserves

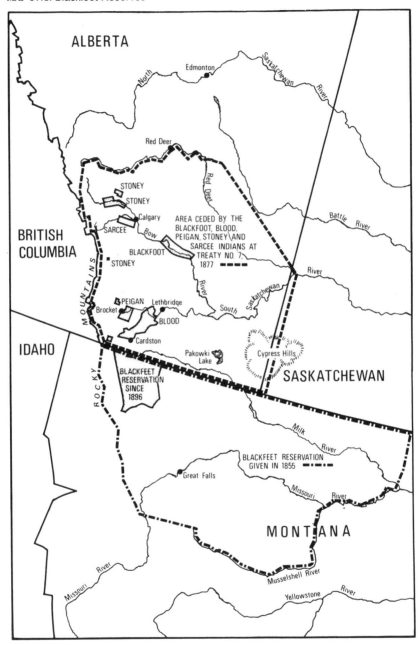

"Blackfoot" or "Blackfeet." Some academics and historians have insisted that one term is correct and the other is wrong but no evidence exists to support either thesis. The word *sik-sik-a* is taken from two root words: *Sik-si* from *siksinum* or "black," and *ka* either from *okat* (foot) or *okats* (feet). When the Indians signed a treaty with the Americans in 1855, the document identified the "Blackfoot Nation" but was signed by four "Blackfeet"; similarly, in the Canadian treaty the term "Blackfoot Tribe" was used, but an adhesion to the document was signed by "Blackfeet." Today, most Canadians, anthropologists, and Indians in Canada use the term "Blackfoot," while many Americans and Indians in the United States use "Blackfeet." Therefore, both terms appear to be acceptable as long as the user is consistent.

The smallest political unit among the Blackfoot was the band, usually having an extended family as its nucleus. Those bands that had particularly good leaders or seemed to be constantly lucky in the hunt attracted people from other bands until they became so large that they might have to split in two when they became uneconomic. Others that experienced misfortunes sometimes disappeared completely as their members gradually drifted away to other groups. For example, a band of Bloods called the Followers of the Buffalo kept growing in size because of its wise leadership and every few years a group would break away, forming such new bands as the Many Fat Horses, the All Tall People, and the Knife Owners. On the other hand, the Bear People lost their leading men in a battle in 1872 and the survivors went away to join other bands.

Blackfoot bands received their names because of some distinctive feature or attribute of their members, or because of some incident. For example, when blizzards caused starvation among a band isolated in the foothills, its members were forced to subsist on fish to survive. As a result they became known as the Fish Eaters. Another band received the name of Gopher Eaters through a similar experience. Other names, like All Black Faces or All Short People, were purely descriptive. The names could change, too, if an old one became outdated or if a new incident occurred. After settling on their reserve, the Followers of the Buffalo were renamed Camps in a Bunch while the Shooting Up band was renamed the Interfering band. The latter was based on a humorous incident caused when a river changed its course, leaving the band without water; joking friends said its members had interfered with the stream by taking all the water for tea.

A band was a self-contained unit small enough to find food yet large enough to protect itself from enemy attacks. It had a leader recognized as the political chief; another man was the war chief. During normal times the political chief controlled the movements of the band, but should there be danger from enemy attack or other causes, the war chief immediately assumed control.

The political chief took the role of chief magistrate, presiding at council meetings, giving instructions to the camp police, and settling disputes within the band. His police were members of one of the warrior societies.

When a boy reached his early teens he joined one of these societies made up of comrades his own age. Then, about once every five years, his society took over the membership of the group that was older than themselves and transferred their membership to a new group of younger persons. In this way every man in the camp could belong to a society of people his own age. Those who were between twenty and twenty-five, or between twenty-five and thirty, were most often chosen to act as camp police. They patrolled at night, acted as guardians during buffalo hunts, and protected the band while on the trail. They also carried out the edicts of punishment decided by the chief. For example, a thief might be banished from the camp, or a man who went out alone to hunt buffalo and frightened the herds away might have had his horse seized and his riding gear destroyed.

Whenever several bands joined together to hunt or to camp in winter, one of the leaders was recognized as the head chief; he presided at all council meetings. There was no single head chief of a tribe, but if an entire tribe was together, one man was chosen during that time as the presiding authority over the camp. Yet if the tribe should suddenly be faced with danger the head chief would be replaced by a war chief for the period of danger, just as was done in smaller bands. For example, Red Crow was considered to be a great chief of the Bloods in the mid-nineteenth century, but if the camp were threatened by an enemy, White Calf became the war chief and had complete control over the warrior societies.

Council meetings were usually attended by the head chief, the war chief, and the heads of leading families. Decisions were made by consensus, rather than by majority vote, and the head chief seldom tried to give direct orders to the other councillors. He knew they were too proud and independent to be intimidated and that they could always withdraw from the camp if they disagreed with him. Instead, the head chief tried to win adherents through oratory; when he felt that he had enough support, he would announce his own intentions. If there was a dispute as to whether the camp should move north or south, the chief might present his arguments, gain support, and then say that he was going south. He did not order the others to follow, but he knew that they probably would go with him.

Religion

Religion pervaded almost every aspect of daily life. A woman beginning her quillworking would say a prayer; an old man awaking in the morning would sing a prayer of thanks; a person before eating placed a small morsel of food in the ground for the spirits.

The Blackfoot believed that their entire universe was inhabited by spirits, some good and some evil. One of the greatest of these was the Sun, who was the head of a holy family consisting of his wife, the Moon, and their boy, the Morning Star. The thunder spirit also was a powerful deity, while even a lowly mouse had its supernatural role. A strangely twisted tree or an unusual rock formation was considered to be the manifestation of spiritual power and, as a result, passersby left offerings for good luck.

Often the most important spirits were those directly related to an individual's experiences. A young teenage boy, for example, might go on a vision-seeking quest, looking for a spiritual helper for his future years. He would go to a secluded place and, if he was particularly daring, to an area of great danger, such as a high precipice or a burial ground. Constructing a crude rock shelter, he lay down with a pipe beside him and fasted and prayed for four days. During that time he hoped that he would slip into a trance and that a spiritual helper would come to him. Sometimes it would be an animal in the form of a man, while at other times a creature itself might speak to him.

A famous leader, Red Crow, was hunting gophers with his bow and arrow while still a small boy. As he lay near a gopher hole he fell asleep and in his dream the gopher spirit came to him and promised to help him if he would only go away and leave him in peace. "When you go against an enemy," advised the spirit, "take a blade of grass and stick it in your hair. Then you'll never get hit" (Dempsey, 1980: 10). Red Crow followed this advice and although he was in thirty-three battles, he was never struck by an enemy or wounded in a fight.

As a result of their visions, young men wore amulets or ornaments in their hair or around their necks. Crowfoot kept an owl's head in his hair, while others could be seen wearing the skins of animals or other objects that represented their spirit helpers. Usually, each had specific songs and rituals performed by the owners. The objects themselves were unique to the individual; when he died they were buried with him.

Some men had visions of benefit to the whole tribe, rather than just to themselves. Usually, such people already were recognized as holy men and, as a result of their dreams, they created sacred pieces called "medicine bundles." This is a generic term for any objects wrapped together and used for ritualistic purposes. Some medicine bundles contained war shirts decorated with scalps or weasel skins; others had animal skins, fossilized ammonites (known as "buffalo stones"), or other parts of costumes. But perhaps the most common was the medicine pipe, which was a long pipestem decorated with eagle feathers. The pipe had no bowl, as it was not for smoking but for performing a dance to bring good luck to the tribe or to help someone who was sick. Medicine-pipe men – the owners of the pipes – led a lifestyle distinctive from others in the tribes; they wore their hair in a certain way, painted their faces, carried the pipe on its own travois, and had many taboos. These men were considered to possess the spiritual power to keep evil spirits away from the tribe and to help those in need. Although they did not constitute a society, they would gather together periodically to open their pipe bundles, perform the dances and rituals, and renew their vows. Every spring after the first thunderstorm, each medicine-pipe bundle was opened in response to the call the owner believed he had received from the thunder spirit.

Besides these revered medicine pipes, lesser pipes were individually owned. Most common was the black-covered medicine pipe, which was small enough to take to war and often was presented to a fledgling warrior by an older relative.

Medicine pipes and other medicine bundles originated in visions but, unlike personal amulets, could be transferred or sold. If a man wished to become a bundle owner, he went to someone who had such a bundle, offered to smoke with him, and announced that he wanted it. The owner could not refuse, so a price was arranged and a formal transfer ceremony took place.

The most ancient of Blackfoot medicine bundles was the beaver bundle that, according to legends, was given to a hunter who was camped by St. Mary's Lake in what is now northern Montana. The man was killing too many birds and animals, so one day when his wife went for water a Beaver Man came out of the lake and captured her. Later she led a procession from the lake to her husband's lodge, this group consisting of the Beaver Man, the Sun, and the Moon. The hunter was told that if he would stop killing game unnecessarily, his wife would be returned to him and he would be given a medicine bundle. Then, one by one, animal and bird skins were taken from the walls of his lodge and he was taught the songs and ceremonies for each. These were wrapped together with sweetgrass and face paint to make the beaver bundle.

Most medicine bundles contained a few standard items, such as braided sweetgrass used for incense and ochre to paint the user's face.

The rest of the objects were worn or held during the ceremonies, usually with each accompanied by its special song. The whole bundle was contained within a large rawhide case that hung on a tripod behind the owner's lodge in the day and was carried inside above his sleeping place at night. Prayers and songs, as well as the burning of incense, were performed each morning and night.

Medicine bundles also were used by the various secret societies of the Blackfoot. Most common of these were the warrior societies, discussed earlier. Each member of a warrior society had his own bundle, which was simply a packet of paints and the costume he needed for his society's dances and ceremonies. A society had one or two leaders, each of whom had a distinctive headdress and face paint. For example, a head man in the Raven Carriers society wore a coyote skin and had an eagle feather in his hair; while he danced, he carried a long red stick trimmed with cloth and feathers.

Although females did not normally take an active role in most societies, the Blackfoot were unique in that they had one society exclusively for women. It was called the "Motoki," popularly translated as Old Women's Society, but, more accurately, it should be called the Sorority. Like the Longtime Medicine Pipe, the society came to the Blackfoot from the Mandans in 1832, but it has been given a mythical origin relating to the actions of a white crow among a buffalo herd.

The primary function of the Motoki was to acknowledge the importance of the buffalo to the Blackfoot people. In their rituals the women took the roles of buffalo killed by hunters and paid homage to the power of the buffalo spirit. The primary intention was to appease the spirits so that the tribe would have good luck in its future hunts. Among the costumes worn by the women were headdresses made of scalps from old buffalo bulls and worn by leaders of the society.

The Sun Dance

As can be seen, religion among the Blackfoot ranged from personal visions and a constant concern with the supernatural to more structured societies involving the combined actions of several people in performing rituals and ceremonies. The most complex of all ceremonies, the Sun Dance, or "Okan," involved an entire tribe. This festival lasted for several days and had social and political overtones besides its purely religious function.

The term Sun Dance is a misnomer, for this implies a simple dance to the Sun spirit rather than a series of religious ceremonies. The Blackfoot term for the Sun Dance, "Okan," refers to the centre pole of the Sun Dance lodge – the most sacred object of the ritual.

The basic purpose of the Sun Dance was to allow everyone to reaffirm faith in the Sun spirit. Its nucleus consisted of constructing a lodge, presided over by a holy woman, where various dances and rituals were performed. The assembling of the entire tribe also became the occasion for the secret societies to perform their dances or to exchange their memberships, for medicine-pipe bundles to be opened, for war exploits to be recounted, and for the self-torture ritual to be performed. None of these latter ceremonies was a part of the Sun Dance but, because they were performed at the same time, they were inextricably linked to the ritual itself.

The decision to hold a Sun Dance was made by a pure woman – i.e., a virgin or faithful wife – who had a male relative in danger of losing his life. A husband might be ill or a son may not have returned from a raid. The woman made a public vow that if the person's life was spared, she would sponsor a Sun Dance. Then, if her prayer was answered, she began preparations for the summer festival.

The sponsoring of a Sun Dance was expensive, so relatives and the extended family began to assemble blankets, horses, and other gifts to be given away. Others sought out a woman who had previously sponsored the ritual and made arrangements for her to transfer her medicine bundle, called the Natoas bundle, to the new sponsor.

The Sun Dance was held in July, as soon as the sarvice (or saskatoon) berries were ripe, for they were needed for sacramental purposes. A site was chosen by a warrior society in consultation with the chiefs – the location offering good protection against enemies, providing good grazing, and being close to the buffalo.

During the first several days while bands assembled, the people enjoyed themselves gambling, horse racing, and visiting. The Motoki then held its ceremonies in the centre of the camp circle, building a lodge of travois and tepee covers that served as their home during the four-day ritual. On the last day, the women had a public dance and gave away gifts to visitors and friends.

By this time the grass near the camp had been grazed over by the hundreds of horses, so a new campsite was chosen four or five miles away. At that location, warrior societies, such as the All Brave Dogs, Pigeons, Horns, or Prairie Chickens, held their dances. At last the holy woman moved her lodge inside the camp circle, decorating its base with green boughs to signify that she was beginning her fast.

The main sacrament of the Sun Dance was the buffalo tongue. While fasting the holy woman was instructed by the former bundle owner how to cut the tongues into thin strips and smoke-dry them over the fire. During the four days that the holy woman remained in her lodge, she could not touch water, even to wash, for this was believed to cause rain. Instead, she wiped her face with a muskrat skin and prepared for the building of the main lodge. On the first day of her fast a huge sweatlodge was built just outside the northern edge of the camp. This lodge was made of fifty willow sticks and was painted half black, for night, and half red, for day. Then fifty stones were heated in readiness for the sweat. This lodge symbolized the actions of Scar Face, a legendary Blackfoot who had visited the Sun spirit and had his scar removed in such a sweatlodge.

When the stones were in readiness, the holy woman and her teacher went to the lodge and sat beside it while their husbands went inside. While water was being placed upon the stones and the men sweated in the steam, the holy woman painted a buffalo skull with the symbols of the Sun, Moon, Morning Star, and Sun Dogs; later it was placed at the base of the Sun Dance pole. Women never entered a sweatlodge, so when the men came out the party returned to the holy woman's lodge to finish the fast.

These ceremonies were repeated for the next three days and each morning the participants moved to a new campsite. Finally, at the end of the fourth day, they arrived at the site of the Sun Dance ceremonies.

The following morning a warrior society left the camp in search of a forked tree that would serve as the holy centre pole. When they found one they returned to camp as though they were scouts who had discovered an enemy camp. Then the others in the warrior society crept up to the tree; when it was cut down, they attacked it as though it was a fallen enemy. The tree was taken back in triumph to camp, there to be laid on the ground in readiness for the building of the lodge. Others in the camp built the frame of the lodge, which was similar in shape to a circus tent. At last the holy woman ended her fast and went to the unfinished lodge where she prayed over the centre pole before it was raised in position.

Among some tribes that practised a Sun Dance, the building of the lodge was done with little ceremony; with the Blackfoot, however, the raising of the pole was the highlight of the entire ritual. Guns were fired in the air, men gave war whoops, and everyone yelled joyously as the forked pole was fitted in place and the rails from the outer walls fastened to it. The happy mood continued as scores of people, young and old, collected green branches to place around the lodge as an outer wall. This part of the ceremony symbolized the beginning of new life, just as their faith in the Sun spirit was being renewed. Normal taboos were relaxed as young men lifted unmarried girls and sweethearts onto their horses as

PLATE 17.2. Sun Dance camp near Gleichen, Alberta. By the 1920s Blackfoot persisted in holding such ceremonies as the Sun Dance. Traditional travois were replaced by wagons and democrats. Courtesy Glenbow Archives, NA-336-7.

they went to collect the greenery. By sunset the lodge had been completed and was ready to be sanctified. With the building of the lodge, the work of the holy woman was finished and her fast was over. She provided a huge feast for the camp, at which time her family gave gifts to everyone who had helped. One particular symbol of opulence was the pathway between the holy woman's lodge and the Sun Dance lodge; when the woman travelled that route, it was carpeted with blankets and robes provided by her family. The farther the carpet of goods extended, the greater the prestige; after the ceremony, the objects were given away.

That night, four warriors would build a small bower within the Sun Dance lodge and remain there all night, singing their holy songs. In the morning, men known as weather dancers lined up in two rows facing each other and, with faces elevated toward the sun, performed their ceremonial dance. Various warrior societies also performed public dances. The Sun Dance lodge was considered to be a holy place, so activities taking place there were believed to bring good luck.

A warrior might proclaim one of his war deeds and re-enact the entire episode in pantomime; if he lied or exaggerated, people believed that he would not live to see another summer. Young men who had made vows had skewers thrust through slits cut in their breasts and backs. The skewers in front were fastened to lines attached to the centre pole, while those at the back were used to suspend a shield or buffalo skull. As he danced the young warrior had to thrust himself backward in order to tear the skewers free from his chest and then to wrest the obstruction from his back. This ritual sometimes is referred to as "making a brave," implying that one did it to become a warrior. This is not true; the ordeal was suffered by a young man who had made a vow to the Sun for the good health or protection of someone in his family. It was an act of gratitude to the Sun spirit for answered prayer.

The Sun Dance was in sharp contrast to other more individualistic aspects of Blackfoot religion. The use of personal amulets and medicine bundles was a much older practice. Only with the acquisition of the horse and the availability of leisure time could the Blackfoot develop such a complex series of rituals as those of the Sun Dance.

Myths and Legends

In an attempt to explain the phenomena around him, the Blackfoot created many myths and legends, some of them based on spiritual or supernatural experiences. Myths explained the origins of medicine bundles and painted tepee designs; they recounted the exploits of great warriors; and they told of the origin of man himself.

The most common type of legend was one related to a trickster-creator, whom the Blackfoot called Napi, or the Old Man. Napi was responsible for the creation of the world, for making the first man and woman, creating life and death, and making all the flora and fauna in Blackfoot country. Yet Napi was not a god who was revered by the Blackfoot; rather, he was a supernatural personification of man, with all his wisdom and foolishness, his bravery and cowardice, his honesty and greed. Some of the tales cause the listeners to double over in laughter as Napi is outwitted by an opponent or does something foolish.

There are many tales about Napi, such as those explaining why the bobcat has a flat face, the skunk has a striped back, and how man became superior to buffalo. These stories were told partly for entertainment, but also to explain to young people the world around them, to allay their fears of strange phenomena, and to teach them the customs and mores of the tribe. Through these stories children learned about good and evil, about the folly of greed, and about the importance of making wise decisions.

The Blackfoot were known for their extensive legends about the stars. Most stars were said to have had their origins on earth as Indians who had used their supernatural powers to join the Sky People. Even the Blackfoot tepees pay homage to the stars; on the upper ears or flaps of most lodges are white circles depicting Ursa Major and the Pleiades. In fact, a Blackfoot painted tepee is rich in mythology; its main design is often the result of a vision. Another element of the design may relate to the Morning Star or to the butterfly, the spirit of sleep.

Stories about great warriors almost inevitably are rooted in supernatural feats. The Blackfoot believed that if a man performed some brave or important deed, he succeeded only because of the spiritual help he received. Crowfoot, the head chief of the Blackfoot, was said to have received his power from the owl's head he wore in his hair; Red Old Man, a great Blackfoot warrior, had a mouse as his spiritual helper. When faced with a crisis these men often had visions or were led from danger by an animal or bird. One of the most famous stories among the Blackfoot deals with the warrior named Low Horn, who was killed by Crees in the 1840s. According to tales, bullets could not kill him, and he died only when an enemy drove an elk's antler into his ear. After his death the Crees burned Low Horn's body, but an ember exploded from the fire and turned into a grizzly bear that attacked the Crees. As they fled, a thundercloud overhead sent down lightning bolts to kill even more Cree. Later, the Blackfoot believed that Low Horn was reincarnated in a young boy who ultimately became a medicine man among the Bloods and died there in 1899.

Warfare

The Blackfoot were in an almost constant state of warfare during the historic period. On one hand, they coveted the rich horse herds of the Crow, Shoshoni, and Nez Perce tribes to the south and southwest. To the north and east the Cree and Assiniboine preyed on the Blackfoot herds and also envied the heavy concentration of buffalo in Blackfoot hunting grounds. Therefore, if war parties were not out raiding the tribes to the south, the Blackfoot were being attacked from the north. To the southeast they sometimes came into contact with the Sioux.

Generally the Blackfoot went to war for booty or revenge. If the former was the reason, a small war party might set out on foot, in expectation of capturing enemy horses and returning in triumph. Killing an enemy was not their primary objective and, in fact, scalping was not considered to be among the most heroic of deeds. Rather, a warrior was praised for his audacity and fearlessness in battle. A man named Sleeps on Top was remembered because he rode into a conflict armed only with a club and when he saw two mounted enemies he deliberately knocked one off the left side and the other off the right, just to show his bravery. Young warriors entering an enemy camp at night took the horses tethered to their owners' lodges, not just because they were the best animals, but to display their skill as raiders.

Most Blackfoot went on raiding parties between the ages of thirteen and twenty; after that time most were content to hunt and to breed horses, but others continued to go to war until they were old men. For them wealth in horses was less important than the glory and excitement of war.

Revenge parties were entirely different from raiding parties. Usually a revenge party was formed after an enemy war party fell upon a helpless camp of Blackfoot and killed several people. When this occurred grieving relatives called on fellow tribe members to form a huge war party, sometimes consisting of 200-300 men. If the killing had been done by a Cree, the Blackfoot made no attempt to seek out the actual murderers; they were satisfied to kill other Cree in revenge. Often, non-Natives did not understand that this practice also applied to them. If, for example, a whiskey trader killed a Blackfoot, then the deceased man's relatives might kill the first non-Native they could find.

Other types of raids, which were less frequent, were those made upon tribes trespassing on Blackfoot hunting grounds. The Kutenais, Pend d'Oreilles, and Flatheads, who lived across the mountains, travelled to the prairies once or twice a year to hunt buffalo but usually sent scouts ahead to avoid conflict. If the Blackfoot learned of their presence, either a temporary peace treaty was made or the mountain tribe was forced to retreat. Similarly, frequent hunting parties of Cree and Halfbreeds were deeply resented because of their incursions. The Halfbreeds were particularly disliked because their huge, organized hunts resulted in the wholesale destruction of buffalo herds. As very little Blackfoot intermarriage with non-Natives occurred during the nomadic period, the Halfbreeds (as the Blackfoot call them) always were associated with the enemy Cree.

Family Life

When a child was born, the baby was given a personal name by its mother; if a girl, it was sometimes based on the first thing the woman saw when the child was delivered: Sky Woman, Spider, or Kit Fox Woman. This might become the girl's official name, but more often a male member of the family, an uncle or grandfather, would select a name based on his own war experiences. The Blackfoot believed that the warrior must have had supernatural help to win a battle, so good luck was attached to the name. This is why so many Blackfoot women had such warlike names as Killed at Night, Double Gun Woman, Attacked Towards Camp, or Stabbed Twice. Others had names associated with the namer's spiritual helper: Elk Woman, Big Rabbit, Fisher Woman, or Yellow Squirrel.

Boys were given their first official name when only a few days old. Most often an older member of the family would announce his right to choose the name, and, when he was ready, he would perform a ceremony and go into a sweatlodge to sanctify his choice. The name he chose was based on the man's war or religious experiences but was recognized as a child's name, such as Shot Close, Little Child, or Berries. This name was used until the boy was old enough to earn an adult name on the warpath or in hunting.

Boys and girls played together until they were about five years old, at which time their formal education began. Girls learned to carry out simple chores, like collecting firewood and water or looking after younger children. The boys were taken in hand by an uncle or older brother and taught to use a bow and arrow, guard and round up horses, follow game trails, and become good riders. The first time a boy killed food for the lodge, such as a rabbit or partridge, the father announced the achievement throughout the camp and sponsored a feast for his comrades.

There were no special puberty rites among the Blackfoot. When the girl began her menstrual periods, she was taken away to a separate shelter where she remained; the Blackfoot believed that a woman at this time would bring bad luck if she stayed in the lodge with the hunters. They felt that her scent would be carried by the hunters and frighten the game away.

When boys became twelve or thirteen, their comrades or older brothers often gave them derisive nicknames, like Lately Gone or Little Shine, to encourage them to go to war to earn an adult name. On their first expeditions boys went as servants, making fires, cooking, repairing moccasins, and looking after the camp. They did not take part in the actual raid and received no share of the plunder, but if they acquitted themselves well they might receive an adult name and be invited to go on further war parties. At this age, the name chosen would be one that belonged to the family. Names were considered to be material possessions; when a person died, his name was the exclusive property of the extended family until it was taken by someone else. If a man had gained a particularly outstanding war record or had died under heroic circumstances, the name might be reserved until someone in the family performed a notable deed of valour.

For example, a warrior named Crowfoot was killed while on a peace expedition to the Shoshoni in 1828; because of the circumstances, his name was revered within the family. Not until the 1840s did a younger relative perform a deed of sufficient daring for him to take this name.

When a young man reached marriageable age he began a courtship, often meeting a girl on her way to get water or gather wood, or near her tepee at night. Clandestine meetings were discouraged by the girl's parents, as virginity was held in high esteem and had religious significance. A young man, particularly if he was handsome, might spend hours combing his hair or painting his face in a place where he was sure to be seen by the girl of his choice.

Marriage was arranged in a number of ways, depending on the wealth and social status of the participants. Most frequently, negotiations were held between the father of the girl and his prospective son-in-law, or between the two male parents. Once an agreement was reached there was an exchange of gifts, with the groom and his family making a payment of about double the amount received. In some instances where the families were poor, the boy might agree to work for his father-in-law for a year, herding his horses, hunting, and performing other duties. Usually, however, the bride moved to her husband's camp, her family providing her with a new tepee and the furnishings. These were considered to be her property and, in the event of a separation, she kept the lodge and all household utensils. Polygamy was common, and the number of wives was limited only by a man's wealth. Men commonly had two or three wives, while one chief at the treaty of 1877 was said to have had ten wives. Normally the first wife was the senior member of the female household and was referred to as the "sits beside him" wife. She directed the duties of the lodge and accompanied her husband to feasts and ceremonies. It was not unusual for a man to marry two or more sisters, with the belief that they could live together in harmony, while an older brother might marry the widows of a younger brother should that man die or be killed. Polyandry – the practice of a wife having more than one husband – did occur from time to time, but an overabundance of women due to male death in hunting and war made this an infrequent event.

If a woman proved to be lazy or unfaithful a man could divorce her simply by sending her back to her parents and demanding the repayment of the gifts. A woman also could leave her husband, but only on the grounds of extreme cruelty or neglect. Most often if a bride returned home she was promptly sent back to her husband so that the family would not suffer the humiliation of being accused of having raised an incompetent daughter.

In daily life there was a clear division of labour between men and women. The wives were responsible for pitching and striking the tepee, packing, cooking, manufacturing and decorating most clothing, caring for infants, training girls, and for the general maintenance of the lodge. The men provided food, protected the camp, manufactured some objects related to religion and war, looked after the horses, and carried out raids on enemy camps. The men painted the exterior designs on the lodges, although women were responsible for decorating liners, backrests, and parfleche bags. Women did virtually all of the beadworking and quill-working; men painted religious symbols on shields, robes, and rattles, and carved or produced instruments of war.

When a man was dying he was dressed in his best clothes and his personal possessions were placed around him. After he died the camp was abandoned, as the Blackfoot believed that his spirit would haunt the area before leaving for the sand hills. His lodge was sometimes sewn up and used as a death lodge; otherwise the body was placed in a tree or on a hill for burial. It was not buried underground, for the spirit had to be free to come and go. A man's horse might be killed to provide transportation when he finally left for the spirit world.

When a man died, women mourners cut off their hair, gashed their legs, sometimes cut off a joint of a finger, and wailed ritualistically in sorrow. Male mourners cut their hair and left the camp, either on a raid or to visit another band. During this period of mourning, men wore old clothing and lived simply, and women carried out their mournful wailing at frequent intervals for up to a year.

The clothing worn by the Blackfoot was similar to that of other northern tribes. In fact, persons were known to walk into an enemy camp and not realize where they were until they heard a strange language being spoken. In 1810, fur trader Alexander Henry the Younger, when describing Blackfoot men, said:

> Their dress consists of a leather shirt, trimmed with human hair and quill-work, and leggings of the same; shoes are of buffalo skin dressed in the hair; and caps, a strip of buffalo or wolf skin about nine inches broad, tied around the head. Their necklace is a string of grizzly bear claws. A buffalo robe is thrown over all occasionally. Their ornaments are few – feathers, quill-work, and human hair, with red, white, and blue earth, constitute the whole apparatus. (Coues, 1897, 2: 525)

In 1833, when Prince Maximilian saw the Blackfoot on the Upper Missouri, he described women's clothing as consisting of a dress:

... coming down to their feet, bound round the waist with a girdle, and is often ornamented with many rows of elks' teeth, bright buttons, and glass beads. The dress wraps over the breast, and has short, wide sleeves, ornamented with a good deal of fringe. . . . The lower arm is bare. The hem of the dress is likewise trimmed with fringes and scalloped. The women ornament their best dresses, both on the hem and sleeves, with dyed porcupine quills and thin leather strips, with broad diversified stripes of sky-blue and white glass beads. (Maximilian, 1906: 249)

Of course, for everyday wear, both men and women had plain, unadorned clothing. The women, in particular, required such costumes when butchering or skinning buffalo. Children's clothing was virtually a miniaturization of adult costumes, though very young boys and girls went entirely naked in summer. However, the Blackfoot were extremely modest and even in the warmest weather a man would retain a breechcloth while a woman would simply unfasten the sides of her dress below the arms to create a cooling effect.

The average Blackfoot tepee was made of twelve to fourteen buffalo skins and required as many as twenty-three poles of lodgepole pine. The tepees were erected upon a basic foundation of four poles tied together at the top, the others being laid against them. The tepee always faced east, both as a protection against the prevailing winds and for religious reasons, in order to face the rising sun. The ears of the lodge, which regulated the draught, were controlled by two poles fitted through eyelets cut into the upper corners of the ears.

Some wealthy men had lodges made of thirty buffalo skins. These dwellings were unique structures, used only by warriors who had performed great feats of a dual nature, i.e., killing two enemy with a single shot. The lodges were so big that they were made in two sections, each forming a single-horse travois load. Such a lodge had two entrances and two fireplaces, one of the latter being reserved for religious purposes. Such a tepee was an obvious sign of opulence.

Prior to the acquisition of the horse, lodges were much smaller, as they had to be dragged about on dog travois. The travois was made by tying two pieces of lodgepole pine together at the top; this was placed at the pack animal's neck, with the poles dragging on either side behind. A net or rack between the poles behind the animal provided the means for carrying several hundred pounds of goods. The only other method of transporting goods was in packs carried by dogs, horses, women, and sometimes men. The Blackfoot did not use canoes.

Although life was difficult for the nomadic Blackfoot, they still enjoyed themselves whenever the opportunity arose. Winter nights were spent telling stories – Napi tales to the children and war experiences and culture tales to adults. Some people would be invited for an All Smoke Ritual, which lasted from sunset to sunrise, each participant singing his or her own religious and personal songs in turn, taking breaks from time to time to smoke or to eat. Some gathered to gamble, playing the hand game for hour after hour as they sang the accompanying gambling songs. Young men rode around the camp after sunset, singing songs beside the lodges of the wealthy in the hope that they would be fed.

There were plenty of games for children – hide and seek, archery contests, races, throwing mud balls, or sliding down hills on sleds made of ribs. A popular game for young boys was to pretend that they were a war party. Two scouts would be sent ahead to see if they could find some meat drying on a rack in their own camp and then, on a signal, the boys raced forward and helped themselves. Often, the scouts were seen by their mothers and instead of getting dried meat, the boys received a severe clubbing from the owner of the lodge.

Besides sledding in the winter, boys played a spin top game, whipping rocks on ice to make them spin and to knock their opponents out of a circle. They pretended that their rock was a warrior and their opponent was an enemy; if they knocked the rock away, it became their prize. Another winter game was held as a contest to see who could throw a long stick, called a snow snake, the farthest. Properly hurled, the snake could slide for hundreds of metres along the crust of the snow.

Horse racing was popular with young and old. Some men trained horses that were used only for racing. Large amounts of goods and possessions might be bet on the outcome of races. In some instances, the Blackfoot made a temporary peace with other tribes just to hold horse races.

A pastime of the women, besides shinny and gambling, was to have working bees, which gave them the opportunity to visit and tell stories. Sometimes they got together to make a new tepee for one of their friends or a prospective bride, while in other instances several quillworkers could bring their own work to a lodge where they could visit and drink tea while they were working. In times of peace when the buffalo were plentiful, life became pleasant. During these brief periods people took time out from their labours to play, gamble, sing, and visit.

Blackfoot History

Pre-Contact Period

Some controversy has existed about the earliest hunting grounds of the Blackfoot. Considerable credence has been given to an account given by a Cree Indian to explorer David Thompson in the winter of 1787-88. The Cree man, who had been adopted by the Peigans, claimed that the Blackfoot had lived in the woodlands near the Eagle Hills, in present-day Saskatchewan, and had wandered from there onto the Plains. Other information suggests that in the 1600s the Shoshoni and perhaps the Crow were in possession of southern Alberta and that the foothills area was occupied by a band of Kutenais. A smallpox epidemic in the early 1700s is said to have severely depleted the Kutenais and left the region vacant for the Blackfoot to occupy.

There can be no doubt that the Blackfoot were absent from southern Alberta and northern Montana in the 1600s, but this does not necessarily mean that they were a woodland people. At that time frequent fires kept the prairies free from tree growth right to the bank of the North Saskatchewan River. It is therefore probable that the Blackfoot occupied the region from the Bow River to the North Saskatchewan for countless generations before they moved south. As a people without horses they could move only short distances at a time and did not require a vast hunting area. Furthermore, their culture is almost completely devoid of woodland traits, even though these characteristics have persisted among the Plains Cree, who are known to have had a woodlands origin.

The Eagle Hills may well have been included in the Blackfoot hunting grounds, for this area was simply an extension of the Plains region. The depletion of the southern tribes by smallpox coincided with the Blackfoot acquisition of the horse and the gun, and a southern movement became practical; even at that date the foothills were one of the finest hunting regions in the district and offered the added advantages of mild winters and chinook winds.

The Blackfoot did not see a white man until the mid-1700s, but by then they already knew about him and his inventions. When the first traders arrived on the shores of Hudson Bay in the late 1600s, they bartered metal objects, beads, and other goods to the local Indians. These passed from tribe to tribe until they reached the Plains. Such utensils as knives, axes, and pots were bought by the Blackfoot from middlemen, usually Crees. One of the most important objects they obtained was the gun, for it was unknown to their enemies to the south. With it they were able to make the Shoshoni and other tribes flee in terror.

During this same period, between 1700 and 1725, the Blackfoot also obtained their first horses. These were descendants of those brought by the Spanish when they invaded Mexico in the 1500s. Over the years the animals had been acquired by the southern tribes and were passed north-ward. David Thompson was told how the Shoshoni first attacked the Blackfoot using horses that "they rode, swift as the Deer, on which they dashed at the Peeagans, and with their stone Pukamoggan (clubs) knocked them on the head" (Glover, 1962: 241-42). But the Blackfoot soon acquired the horse as well, and by the time the first white man, Anthony Henday, visited them in 1754 they were skilled riders.

Fur Trade Period

By the late 1700s, the first trading posts of the British had been built within reach of the Blackfoot; by the 1790s, posts such as Fort Edmonton and Rocky Mountain House were located at the edge of their hunting grounds. Because their territory lacked good water routes and had few beaver or fur-bearing animals, the traders had no reason to build forts south of the North Saskatchewan River. As a result, the tribes were able to acquire European trade goods but were free of non-Native influences and were not obliged to alter their hunting and subsistence patterns as did some of their northern neighbours.

During this time the Sarcees, who were an offshoot of the woodland Beaver tribe, became allies of the Blackfoot, as did the warlike Gros Ventres from the south. The Blackfoot had good relations with the British, although the Gros Ventres proved to be intractable and ultimately destroyed a trading post before withdrawing to the southern part of their hunting grounds, in what is now eastern Montana.

In 1806 the Blackfoot had their first experience with white men travel-ling the Missouri River. In that year the Lewis and Clark expedition was returning from the Pacific when they became involved in an altercation with the Peigans and killed a man. For the next quarter-century anyone coming up the river was considered to be an enemy. Not only were the Blackfoot incensed about the killing, but they soon discovered that American fur-gathering methods were quite unacceptable. Whereas the British companies established forts and encouraged the Indians to hunt and trap, the Americans operated independently, with the trappers and mountain men invading Indian hunting grounds and doing the trapping themselves. The Blackfoot believed that these men were thieves and treated them accordingly.

In 1831 the reign of terror ceased when the American Fur Company finally made peace with the Blackfoot tribes and built Fort Piegan on the upper waters of the Missouri. From that time on the Blackfoot became keen traders who pitted American against British to get the best prices for their robes, furs, and dried meat.

The population of the Blackfoot tribes varied considerably over the years during the nineteenth century, being affected primarily by smallpox epidemics in 1837 and 1869, and measles and scarlet fever epidemics in 1819 and 1864. In 1823 the populations were estimated to be 4,200 Blackfoot, 2,800 Blood, and 4,200 Peigan, but in 1841, just after the smallpox epidemic, it was reduced to 2,100 Blackfoot, 1,750 Blood, and 2,500 Peigan. The tribes made a rapid recovery, and in 1869, just before the next epidemic, there were 2,712 Blackfoot, 2,544 Blood, and 3,960 Peigan. After a further loss of numbers in 1869-70, the tribes maintained a relatively stable population until they settled on their reserves.

Treaties and Reserves

The first treaty with the Blackfoot was made by the American government in 1855. At that time consideration was being given to building a railroad across the Plains and clear title was required to Indian lands. In the treaty the Blackfoot surrendered the major part of the Montana plains in exchange for exclusive hunting grounds, annuity payments, and other benefits. Two additional treaties, although never ratified, were made in 1865 and 1869, and the vast reservation was cut down in size by executive orders of 1873 and 1874 and by agreements in 1888 and 1896. These pacts were made almost exclusively with the South Peigan tribe, as the Bloods, North Peigans, and Blackfoot considered themselves to be "British" Indians.

Within a few years of the signing of the 1855 treaty, non-Natives began trickling into Montana Territory. First there were free traders, missionaries, and government officials. Then the discovery of gold along the mountains brought in a flood of prospectors, merchants, and ranchers. The opening of steamboat navigation on the Missouri provided easy access as far upriver as Fort Benton.

This influx resulted in a number of clashes between Indians and settlers, reaching such proportions by 1866 that Montanans were referring to the troubles as a "Blackfoot war." The events culminated with an attack in January, 1870, by the United States cavalry, under command of

Major Eugene Baker, upon a peaceful camp of Peigans. The soldiers, looking for Mountain Chief's camp where they expected to find a number of men wanted for murder, mistakenly attacked Heavy Runner's camp, killing 173 persons; the majority were women and children. This event became known as the Baker massacre.

The attack drove a number of camps to the Canadian side, but there the Indians were exposed to the unlimited sale of whiskey by American traders at such posts as Fort Whoop-Up, Standoff, and Slideout. Catholic missionary Constantine Scollen observed, "The fiery water flowed as freely . . . as the streams running from the Rocky Mountains, and hundreds of the poor Indians fell victims to the white man's craving for money, some poisoned, some frozen to death whilst in a state of intoxication, and many shot down by American bullets" (Morris, 1880: 248). The traders operated with impunity on the Canadian side because the territory had been recently transferred from British to Canadian jurisdiction and no means of maintaining law and order existed. Finally, in 1874, the North-West Mounted Police were sent west to put a stop to the illegal traffic. The police established friendly relations with the Blackfoot, and in 1877 the Canadian government successfully negotiated Treaty No. 7, the Blackfoot Treaty, with the tribes that had chosen to live in Canadian territory. In the treaty the Indians gave up all rights to their hunting grounds in exchange for reserves (in the United States they are called reservations), annuity payments, and other benefits. Besides the Blood, Blackfoot, Peigan, and Sarcee Indians, their mortal enemies, the Stoneys, also signed the treaty.

By 1880 the buffalo herds had been virtually exterminated in Blackfoot territory as the result of extensive slaughter by white hide hunters and the increasing incursions of Crees and Halfbreeds from the north. The buffalo had been the staff of life for the Blackfoot. With its destruction they had no recourse but to go to the reserves.

In Montana, the South Peigans went to the Blackfeet Indian Reservation, while in southern Alberta the Bloods settled on their reserve – the largest in Canada – south of Fort Macleod, the Peigans near Pincher Creek, and the Blackfoot east of Calgary.

Although each tribe developed along separate lines after that date – particularly where two countries and two separate administrations were involved – there were many similarities in their history. All were obliged to turn to farming and ranching as a means of livelihood; log houses replaced tepees; Catholic, Methodist, or Anglican missionaries built boarding schools and took children away from their homes; and the

PLATE 17.3. Anglican Mission, Blackfoot Reserve, 1900. Although teachers were dedicated, students faced massive cultural conflicts as well as the threat of tuberculosis because of the confined facilities. Courtesy of the Glenbow Museum, NC 5-61.

ration house became the centre of reserve life. Both governments expected the Indians to become self-supporting through farming within a few years, and when this did not happen the authorities turned to a welfare system to keep them fed and quiet. Few, if any, long-range programs were introduced, and for many Indians it was as though time were standing still. Many believed that the governments were simply feeding them until they all died off from such common diseases as tuberculosis, venereal disease, and scrofula.

The introduction of ranching in the 1890s improved the lot of many Indians, for they found parallels between buffalo hunting and cattle raising. However, when the agricultural industry became mechanized, capital was required, which the Indians did not have, and the problems of severe winters left many destitute and unable to cope with the demands of the dominant society. To them the reserves became a haven from the avariciousness, discrimination, and hostility they experienced in neighbouring towns. In Canada, efforts were made between 1907 and 1921 to force the Indians to surrender large parts of their reserves. The Peigans gave up almost a third of their reserve in 1909 and the Blackfoot ended up losing

about half of their reserve. Only the Bloods resisted all attempts to give up parts of their reserve. In Montana the Blackfeet were allotted individual lands in 1907, and the unclaimed areas were sold. In 1918 the Indians were given permission to sell their allotments, and as a result, the reservation became a checkerboard of Indian- and white-owned lands.

Recent Trends

Little progress was made on the reserves until after the Second World War. Prior to that time, children were sent to residential schools and came out either to farm or to go on welfare. The Sun Dance continued to be the main ceremony, and the warrior societies still met to hold dances and rituals. During the first half of the twentieth century the reserves became a mixture of the old and new. The elders still wore braids and spoke only in Blackfoot, while young men dressed in modern clothes, participated in rodeos, and tried to find work on or near the reserve. Government policies discouraged anyone from getting an education beyond the age of sixteen. Some exceptional ones did become nurses and teachers, but most merely subsisted within the protection of their reserves. The mortality rate was high, particularly among infants, and the average life span was less than half of the national norm. Although conditions were depressed and depressing, people still enjoyed family life, visiting, dancing, and participating in Indian events.

After the war the governments of both countries began to provide more funds for better schools, improved health services, economic development, and the encouragement of self-reliance. In the 1960s the first graduates of integrated schools began to assume more significant roles in the community. Most employees on the reserve were Indians, including band managers, welfare officers, public works staff, police, and teachers. With a better education some chose to leave their reserves to work in nearby cities, although they usually returned after a few years.

Attempts were made during this period to introduce new industries to the reserves, with only moderate success. Such businesses as a pencil factory, mobile-home plant, post-peeling plant, commercial potato industry, retail stores, moccasin factory, and other firms have been opened. Some existed for only a few months but others carried on their work successfully, employing dozens of people from the reserves.

Although opportunities for education and employment improved, many serious problems remained. The extension of liquor privileges to the Blackfoot during the 1960s caused a traumatic social upheaval,

which, while levelling off at a later date, remains a serious problem. Welfare and a lack of employment on the reserves also continue as major difficulties. Yet most Blackfoot would prefer to put up with a welfare system and lack of employment, rather than leave their extended families and go to the alien world of the cities.

On the other hand, as the Blackfoot assumed more responsibility for their own affairs, they have taken over many jobs formerly performed by outsiders. One will find Indian accountants, managers, police, teachers, social workers, road crews, and office staff carrying out their tasks diligently and efficiently. Members of tribal councils serve on many boards and committees, both on the reserve and off, for the benefit of their people. Still others have gained favourable reputations as artists, musicians, rodeo performers, and in other related fields.

By the 1970s the introduction of television began to make rapid inroads into the daily lives and culture of the Blackfoot. English soon replaced Blackfoot as the primary language in many households and the communication of oral traditions was abandoned. The Sun Dance virtually died out on most reserves, to be replaced by secular Indian Days. Pan-Indianism began to replace tribalism as the dances, songs, and even some of the ceremonies were borrowed freely from other regions. However, a consciousness of their unique history and culture soon resulted in the formation of museums, cultural centres, dancing clubs, and other activities, which were designed to help preserve elements of the past. Even the Sun Dance reappeared and conscious efforts were made to interest young people in Native culture.

Current Challenges

The 1980s and 1990s have seen rapid changes in the lifestyle of many members of the Blackfoot nation. On one hand, the effects of higher education and professionalization are being felt on all reserves. There are Indian lawyers, educators, administrators, and other professionals who are directing their attention to their tribes. At the same time, the loss of language and culture has become so widespread that attempts have been made to stem the tide. Language courses are being offered on all reserves and attempts are being made to interest young people in cultural programs. These have not been very successful as the pervasive influence of television has virtually eliminated the Blackfoot language from many homes.

As part of a political and cultural awareness, the Blackfoot tribe has officially changed its name to the Siksika Nation, while the Peigans are being called both the Peigan Nation and the Pikuni Nation. The terminology for the Blood tribe and the Blackfeet Indians of Montana has remained unchanged. The allied Sarcee tribe is now called the Tsuu T'ina Nation.

Although the economies of all reserves are still basically rural, some attempts have been made to provide basic retail services to tribal members rather than relying on nearby towns. On the Siksika Reserve, the tribal administration offices are located in a large structure that also includes a shopping mall. Among the Indian-run businesses there are a supermarket, cafeteria, furniture store, video store, video arcade, and laundromat. Nearby is a service station while behind the mall is a pottery manufacturing plant. Scheduled to open on the reserve are a chartered bank and a post office.

Similarly, the Blood Reserve has an administration building and a small mall with a supermarket, cafeteria, and bank. By the early 1990s, the reserve also had three service stations. The Peigan Reserve has a store, service station, and craft shop, while the Indians in Montana are still served by white merchants in Browning – a town located on the reservation.

The establishment of Indian-owned businesses has resulted in a significant loss of trade on the part of nearby merchants and has caused some tension. However, the trend appears to be toward more such services as tribes attempt to find additional sources of income on their own reserves.

Similarly, efforts are being made to provide more educational facilities on reserves. The majority of students are still being educated in nearby integrated schools but all reserves now have their own facilities for teaching elementary and high school courses. The Blood Reserve, in particular, has placed considerable emphasis on Indian-run schools where language and culture courses can be included in the curriculum. In addition, the Bloods operate Red Crow College, which is affiliated with Lethbridge Junior College, while the Siksika have courses offered on the reserve by Mount Royal College of Calgary.

Many Indians from the region are attending colleges, their numbers limited by a cutback in federal government spending. Also, the University of Lethbridge has a Native Studies program especially directed toward Blood and Peigan Indians.

In the economic and social spheres, the situation on most reserves has not greatly improved in recent years. Alcohol and drug offences continue to be a major social problem while unemployment remains in the 75 to 80 per cent range. Yet, some progress has been made through rehabilitation programs, and gradually intoxication is becoming less and less socially acceptable. Many social dances and meetings are now completely alcohol-free at the insistence of those sponsoring the gatherings.

All reserves are now virtually self-governing. No Indian Department or other federal officials reside on reserves and the bulk of employees – administrators, accountants, outside workers, etc. – are Native. Decisions of tribal councils still must be approved by the government, but usually this is merely a formality. The reserves, in varying degrees, are also assuming responsibility for education, social welfare, and the administration of justice.

A Personal Note

My own approach to Blackfoot research has undoubtedly been governed by the situation that brought me into contact with the tribes in the first place. In 1948, as a newspaper reporter, I began to cover the activities of Indian political movements, during which time I met a Blood Indian girl whom I later married. As a result. I was constantly exposed to Blackfoot history and contemporary Indian-white relations as part of my daily life. The extension of my interests to that of writing Indian biographies arose when I began to question why such men as Crowfoot and Red Crow were such respected leaders. I soon discovered that biographies were excellent vehicles for relating Native history; the political and social events of the period became the background for the study, while the more personal aspects of a man's life provide a level of human interest that could not be covered in a formal history. Tragedy and triumph become more significant when they are related to a man's career.

In order to write Indian biographies, one is basically an historian, but one must be familiar with related fields of anthropology, political science, and even geography. The information from these other disciplines are then interpreted from an historian's perspective.

Recommended Readings

Dempsey, H.A.

1972 *Crowfoot, Chief of the Blackfeet.* Norman: University of Oklahoma Press.

1978 *Charcoal's World.* Saskatoon: Western Producer Prairie Books.

1980 *Red Crow, Warrior Chief.* Saskatoon: Western Producer Prairie Books.

> Dempsey is best known for his biographic works. Although they deal with individuals, they are placed in an historic and cultural context and so relate to wider, even contemporary issues. Red Crow, for instance, is portrayed as a

political realist who adjusts to the reserve system but at no point loses his
Indianness.

Ewers, J.C.

1958 *The Blackfeet: Raiders on the Northwestern Plains.* Norman: University of
Oklahoma Press.

This is by far the most important book on the Blackfoot in the pre-reserve
period. Also of interest to students of cultural change is one of his other
publications, *The Horse in Blackfoot Indian Culture*, published in 1955 by
the Smithsonian Institution, Washington, D.C.

Grinnell, G.B.

1962 *Blackfoot Lodge Tales.* Lincoln: University of Nebraska Press.

Originally published in 1892, this is a classic on traditional Blackfoot
culture.

Hungry Wolf, Beverly

1980 *Ways of My Grandmothers.* New York: W. Morrow.

This contemporary Blackfoot writer is not to be confused with Adolf
Hungry Wolf, a prolific German-born Californian often assumed to be
Indian.

Long Lance, Buffalo Child

1928 *Long Lance: The Autobiography of a Blackfoot Indian Chief.* New York:
Cosmopolitan Book Corporation.

In spite of the title, the book is a fictionalized account of Blackfoot life by
a mixed black-Indian-white journalist from North Carolina who worked
among the Blackfoot.

Mountain Horse, Mike

1979 *My People the Bloods.* Calgary: Glenbow Museum.

Written during the 1930s, this book provides a fascinating Native
viewpoint of history and culture as seen through the eyes of one of the first
graduates of the local mission school system.

Wissler, Clark

1910 "Material Culture of the Blackfoot Indians," *Anthropological Papers of the
American Museum of Natural History*, 5, 1: 1-175.

1912 "Social Life of the Blackfoot Indians," *Anthropological Papers of the
American Museum of Natural History*, 7, 1: 1-64.

1913 "Societies and Dance Associations of the Blackfoot Indians,"
Anthropological Papers of the American Museum of Natural History, 11, 4:
359-460

1918 "The Sun Dance of the Blackfoot Indians," *Anthropological Papers of the
American Museum of Natural History*, 16, 3: 223-70.

Intended for the specialist, these are the most comprehensive works on the
Blackfoot and make extensive use of field data.

Additional Sources Cited

Coues, Elliott, ed.

1897 *New Light on the Early History of the Greater Northwest: The Manuscript Journals of Alexander Henry and of David Thompson, 1799-1814*. New York: Francis Harper, 2 Vols.

Dempsey, H.A.

1981 "The snake man," *Alberta History*, 29, 4: 1-5.

Glover, Richard, ed.

1962 *David Thompson's Narrative, 1784-1812*. Toronto: Champlain Society.

Maximilian, A.P.

1906 *Travels in the Interior of North America*, in R.G. Thwaites, ed., *Early Western Travels*, Vols. 22-24.

Morris, Alexander

1880 *The Treaties of Canada with the Indians of Manitoba, the North-West Territories, and Kee-Wa-Tin*. Toronto: Willing and Williamson.

CHAPTER 18
The Plains Metis

John E. Foster

Introduction

During the 1870s, Louis Riel, the noted Metis leader, estimated the Metis population of western Canada at more than 25 per cent of the total Native population (40,000 Indians; 15,000 Metis). Such relative numbers, in addition to events in the Red River Settlement at the time of the first Riel Rising ("The Transfer") in 1869-70 and during the Saskatchewan Rebellion fifteen years later, denote historical prominence for the Metis. This historical prominence and their distinctiveness from the Indians elicit questions about the nature of their way of life and the historical factors responsible for their origins. Prior to the establishment of the fur trade the metis did not exist. * Yet as the golden era of the fur trade waned on the western Plains, the Metis comprised over one-quarter of the Native

---

* The term "metis" designates those communities the historical actors saw as distinct from both Indian and Euro-Canadian communities in the fur trade era. The term "Metis" was and is the labelling term used by some metis communities to identify themselves.

414

population. They were a startlingly successful socio-cultural adaptation to a particular socio-economic environment.

Until recently, studies into the origins and nature of metis communities have tended to emphasize their "mixed-blood" heritage and to view the metis as a "widespread" phenomenon in the fur trade, arising "naturally" out of the social interaction between Indians and Europeans (Giraud, 1945). More recent works point to the view that, rather than being a widespread and natural phenomenon, the metis as communities were an infrequent, if not unique, socio-cultural product of particular events and circumstances (Peterson, 1978). Yet as occasional as the appearance of new metis communities may be in the historical record, in at least two instances, in the Great Lakes region and on the Canadian Plains, they flourished. Their appearance would appear to be related to alterations in the circumstances of the fur trade, which, for some participants, constituted new opportunities. Of the few metis communities that arose during the nearly four-century history of the fur trade in Canada, perhaps the largest and most familiar is the Metis of the prairie-parkland in what is today the Canadian West.

The Disciplinary Context

The disciplinary basis of study in this chapter is historical rather than anthropological. The objective of historical study is an understanding of how the historical actors, in this instance the Plains Metis and their neighbours, perceived, understood, and acted upon their experiences. To obtain this understanding, the historian identifies relevant sequences of events in the context of particular circumstances. The patterns of behaviour that emerge are analysed in terms of the logical associations that constitute explanation. Frequently, because of gaps in the historical record, the historical explanations that result are the "best" case rather than the "only" case possible.

The historian's sources of data are surviving documents. Historical analysis emphasizes the consistencies and inconsistencies found within a document and among related documents and evaluated in terms of the historian's other experiences. The historian's analysis is not necessarily tied to a methodology that could be identified as belonging to a social science discipline. In historical analysis, empathy for the protagonists as much as rigorous logic should be reflected in sensitive and mature judgements that constitute historical explanations. In historical works of note, it is no accident that links of social class and/or ethnicity frequently tie the historian to his or her subject matter. Some historians would argue that a unicultural chain linking historical actors to recorder to historian provides a richness of experience that results in analysis and explanation capable of revealing the fullest range of complexities and the subtlest of distinctions involved in particular human experiences.

A quick perusal of scholarship bearing on the Metis in recent years demonstrates that, with notable exceptions, scholars in disciplines other than history have made the significant contributions to the field. Historians, essentially "middle-class" and/or English-speaking, appear to have had difficulty in perceiving experiences of substance in the lives of the Metis. In part, the problem lies in the fact that the Plains Metis, with the exception of Louis Riel, have authored few of the documents that record their history. Most existing records were written by "outsiders." Yet the skilled historian should be capable of a document analysis that would guard against the biases inherent in such sources. The critical factor explaining the poverty of significant historical results is the historian's inability in this instance to draw upon the same wealth of personal experience in analysing his subject matter. The socio-cultural distinctions between a twentieth-century historian in Canada and a British-born Hudson's Bay Company officer, during the period of modernization after 1820, are minimal in comparison with the distinctions between the same historian and a Metis buffalo hunter of that earlier era. This sense of the inadequacy of the historian's socio-cultural perspectives for analysing the documents bearing on the Metis has led some historians to search out new perspectives.

Some recent historical works have emphasized the benefits to historians to be derived from a quantification approach. Analysis of census documents, parish records, and "Halfbreed Scrip" records have shown much in terms of Metis demography. The historical writings of Douglas Sprague and Gerhard Ens are useful examples. Others have turned to the findings and approaches of other disciplines to provide suggestions. In doing so they do not seek to abandon the strengths of their own disciplinary approach: rather, they seek new perspectives from which the contents of familiar documents can be analysed to give forth understandings not apparent previously in historical analysis. It remains to be seen whether these perspectives will prove useful.

As with all study there is a personal dimension to the selection of subject matter. Experiences in my youth, expressed in the words of the dean of western Canadian historians, W.L. Morton, played a role: "Teaching inspired by the historical experience of metropolitan Canada cannot but deceive, and deceive cruelly, children of the outlying sections. Their experience after school will contradict the instruction of the history class . . ." (Morton, 1980). These explanations offered in the official histories did not seem to match the social reality I perceived in the surrounding community. The schoolyards of post-World War Two western Canada reflected ethnocultural groups not evident in Canadian history texts. More frequently, where I expected historical explanation the official texts simply chose to ignore the subject. Where were the eastern Europeans, the Asians, and the Native peoples? Inevitably, my quest for explanations of the nature of my community led to an interest in "beginnings." This interest breached the barrier of the transfer and settlement to the pre-1870 world of peoples who were ancestral to a significant number of westerners today. And the historical explanations that have emerged since are not those that reading in the official histories would have predicted.

Origins

The origins of the Plains Metis are to be seen in the appearance of *les gens libres* (freemen) about the posts of the St. Lawrence-Great Lakes trading system extended to the valleys of the Red, Assiniboine, and North Saskatchewan rivers in the closing quarter of the eighteenth century. Some *engagés Canadien* (contracted servants) ended their employment in the interior rather than at Montreal. Coming together in two or three household bands, they supplied provisions and furs to the forts. Their survival and, in time, flourishing way of life required the active co-operation of the traders in the trading posts and, at the very least, the toleration of the Indian bands with whom they shared the prairie-parkland region. The explanation for the historical events and circumstances encouraging the appearance of these *gens libres* is to be found in part in fur trade experiences farther east in an earlier era.

When Western Europeans first contacted Western Hemisphere Indians with a view to trade rather than to settle, similar commercial systems marked their behaviour. From the coast of Brazil in the 1500s to the shores of Hudson Bay in the latter part of the seventeenth century similar trading systems announced the presence of Europeans. Coastal factories warehoused goods and furs for transshipment after Indian traders arrived from the interior to participate with their European counterparts in the ritual of exchange known as the fur trade. The French with Samuel de Champlain extended this coastal factory system up the St. Lawrence to Quebec in 1608 and later, after the formation of alliances with members of the Huron Confederacy, to Montreal after 1641. The Huron were masterful traders, gathering furs from throughout the Great Lakes region and the Canadian Shield beyond and transporting them to Montreal. French "factory representatives," known as *coureurs de bois* ("woods runners"), journeyed sometimes illegally between Montreal and the Indian villages, facilitating trading contracts between particular Huron traders and particular Montreal merchants. In their role as brokers, they behaved in a manner that would win the approbation of their Indian hosts. They joined them in war; they shared their material good fortune; and they married women of the leading trading families, strengthening social ties to the band. The children of such unions, raised in Huron villages, grew to maturity as Huron. The very few raised in the colony of New France would grow to maturity as *Canadien*. There was little or no room for a metis community to arise quickly in the coastal factory system of trade.

The identity of individuals performing the role of the Indian trader in the St. Lawrence-Great Lakes trading system was irrevocably altered when Iroquois attacks in the winter of 1648-49 initiated the destruction of Huronia. In the aftermath, the French and the successors to the Huron, the Ottawa, attempted to re-establish the coastal factory system. Social and political circumstances in the Great Lakes region would not permit it. The Iroquois, allied first to the Dutch and then to the English at New York, harassed the hunters on the Shield and the Indian traders journeying to and from Montreal. During the half-century following the destruction of Huronia, Indians ceased to perform the tasks of the Indian trader. The coastal factory system of trade gave way to the *en dérouine* fur trade (itinerant peddling).

The essential diVerence between the coastal factory system and the *en dérouine* fur trade saw Euro-Canadians* replace Indian traders in the task of trading furs from the hunting bands and transporting them to Montreal (Nute, 1966; Peterson, 1978). From a principal post in the Great Lakes area, such as Michilimackinac, under the command of a military oY cer appointed by the royal government in France, individual bourgeois (merchants) dispatched small parties of men *en dérouine*, to trade with the hunting bands on their home grounds. These trading parties were led by a *commis* (clerk) whose success as a broker was essential to the success of the *en dérouine* trade. Similar to the *coureur de bois* of a previous era, the *commis* found it useful to join his Indian suppliers on some of their war junkets, to share his material good fortune with them, and to take a country wife from among their womenfolk.

---

* Although these people were mostly *Canadien*, they did not remain exclusively so. In later years their numbers included non-French Europeans and even a few non-local Indians.

For those *commis* who succeeded in establishing enduring house-holds, the country wife could be of critical importance. In addition to sup-plying the vital social linkages to some of the bands, her economic skills could be essential in maintaining the *commis* in his broker role. In time, successful *commis* could emerge as bourgeois. The circumstances of the bourgeois appear to have been characterized by large households that occupied pivotal positions in the networks of extended families found throughout the Great Lakes region. In such extended families many sons functioned much as did Indian hunters and trappers: those sons most tal-ented as commercial brokers, however, succeeded their fathers as *commis*. Daughters were sometimes given in marriage to bourgeois and *commis* in order to establish an alliance. The communities of Great Lakes Metis that arose out of this process survived Britain's conquest of New France by extending their kin ties to include British merchants who sup-planted French and *Canadien* bourgeoisie after 1763. The appearance of American settlers – not traders – a half-century later would mark the demise of the Great Lakes Metis.

The En Dérouine Trade in the West

A variety of factors, including distance and time, necessitated alterations in the *en dérouine* fur trade to make it functional in the *pays de la mer de l'ouest*, the interior Plains over the height of land beyond the Lakehead. By 1680, the French had penetrated to the Lakehead; yet a hiatus of a half-century would follow before they would move farther west in strength. Historians have seen in La Verendrye's achievements the activ-ities of a fur trader masquerading as an explorer and a colonizer (Morton, 1929). Perhaps an equally effective understanding would emphasize La Verendrye's solutions to the logistics problems. The supplies of side pork and corn that sustained the fur brigades from Montreal could not supply the brigades beyond Kaministiquia and still contribute to the sustenance of brigades returning to Montreal. Wild rice (actually a grass), harvested by the Indians in the shallow areas of the lakes of the region west to Lake Winnipeg and traded at a series of provisioning posts marking the route westward, became the basis on which the St. Lawrence-Great Lakes trad-ing system expanded to the Great Plains.

The Seven Years' War caused a momentary retreat from the western lands before the British merchants, known as "pedlars," returned with renewed vigour. In the violent and bloody competition that ensued among rival syndics of pedlars, the *en dérouine* system was an effective tool. In time, the logic of monopoly inherent in the European end of the fur trade asserted its wisdom with the emergence, by the 1780s, of the North West Company to dominate the Montreal trade. Over the next four decades it would use the *en dérouine* system as an effective competitive tool against the Hudson's Bay Company. In these circumstances, the *en dérouine* system was also important as a means of solving the perennially critical problem of provisioning personnel.

The high profits of the North West Company rested on the annual labour-intensive canoe brigade carrying furs from the "Eldorado" of the fur trade, the Athabaska country, to Grand Portage and later Fort William at the Lakehead, to be exchanged for trade goods canoed from Montreal. This brigade could not complete the round trip in the seasons of open water if it had to hunt or fish its way across a sizable portion of the continent. Caches of provisions in posts at strategic locations along its route of travel were essential to its success. In addition, many of the *engagés* who paddled the canoes of this and the Saskatchewan and Red River brigades had to be fed during at least part of the winter months. It was for this reason that North West Company posts of the parkland region gave priority to provisions as well as to furs in their trading activities.

The problems and costs involved in provisioning personnel encouraged North West Company wintering partners (bourgeois) to supply small parties of men with goods to go *en dérouine* with bands of Indians "pounding" buffalo in the parkland during the winter months. (The "pound" was an enclosure of wood and brush into which buffalo were driven and/or enticed to be killed. Where terrain permitted the "jump," a cliff over which buffalo were driven was used. With the advent of the horse the "surround" was used with increasing frequency.) This practice, in addition to reducing demands on the posts' provisions, allowed the men to encourage the Indians to trade furs and surplus provisions at the fort of their employer.

The Emergence of the Plains Metis

By the 1780s some older *engagés*, who had taken country wives from bands with whom they had wintered, chose to become free on the Plains and live out their lives primarily as buffalo hunters. As these men were frequently past their physical prime, and as they tended to have large families who were provisioned at the expense of the post, the bourgeois would view positively such a cost-saving step. The usual practice of the fur companies was to give their *engagés* their freedom at Montreal, far from where some of them might be tempted to initiate a competing trade.

On the Upper Saskatchewan, however, the vast distances from the north-west to Montreal precluded all but the best financed and organized from adopting such a course of action.

The trading Indians, Cree and Assiniboine who had carried furs to the Hudson's Bay Company posts on Hudson Bay, found themselves with-out a middleman role when the venerable old Company followed its new rival, the North West Company, into the interior after 1773. Previously, these bands had hunted buffalo in the parkland regions during the half-year they were not engaged in the annual journey to the coastal factories. With the end of their annual trading journeys they began to hunt buffalo year-round. During the late spring, summer, and early autumn they fol-lowed the herds from the parklands out onto the prairie. Their adaptation to year-around buffalo hunting was facilitated through the use of the horse, a superior means of hunting buffalo that had appeared a half-cen-tury earlier among the Blackfoot to the south and west. The horse would prove to be a technological innovation of significant consequence.

The Cree and Assiniboine bands who became year-round buffalo hunters became less dependent on European goods. Their appearance at the provisioning posts along the North Saskatchewan River became less frequent and more irregular. The fur trade could not be adequately pro-visioned by such suppliers. Freemen with their greater interest in Euro-pean goods remained in relatively close contact with the provisioning post. Their importance to the North West Company was reflected in the higher prices they received and in the services extended to them that were not given in the Indian trade. In time the Hudson's Bay Company looked to the bands of *gens libres* to provision themselves as well. Mutual dependence tied the trader and the freeman hunter. Thus the households of the freemen proved admirably suited to fill the provision-ing niche in the western fur trade. From their first appearance their behaviour distinguished them from the Indians. They pursued buffalo and beaver with an assiduity that the Indians believed to be unnecessary. The Cree of the region were tolerant of these newcomers with whom they had ties of kinship. They came to identify the freemen as "O-tee-paym-soo-wuk," "their-own-boss." In time the newcomers would become the Plains Metis.

More by implication than by explication, an earlier generation of his-torians tended to see the Metis as products in large part of "Indianized" or "failed" Euro-Canadians. Influenced by the sense of rascality and out-lawry associated with the *coureur de bois* of an earlier era, historians saw French-Canadian males who established Metis households as choosing the licentious freedom of Indian ways rather than succeeding to the family and citizenship responsibilities of their own heritage (Saunders, 1939; Giraud, 1945).

Recent research, in contrast, would suggest that the choice of these men in "going free" with their families in the interior was not a function of "Indianization" or of a "failed" Euro-Canadian; rather, it was the expression of a deep-rooted Euro-Canadian ethos of that era in the context of the western fur trade at the end of the eighteenth century (Moogk, 1976). To these men, work in the service of others was a temporary circumstance, tolerable only until one found the means of establishing himself as his own master, as a man of consequence. One behaviourial expression of this ethos, in the context of the St. Lawrence-Great Lakes trading system on the western Plains at the end of the eighteenth century, was the freeman. Those *gens libres* who established enduring households that were succeeded by a later generation of buffalo hunters became the Metis. Thus, a significant dimension in the heritage of the Metis is an ethos that heavily influenced the lives of adult males whose cultural founts were pre-industrial France and Britain.

Another source contributing in some instances to the appearance of the Plains Metis were those active servants who did not leave their employment but established households in neighbouring Indian bands. Such "house" Indian bands were a feature of the fur trade throughout its history. The households of servants in these bands were marked by frequent changes in personnel. Over half a century later an Anglican missionary described the household circumstances of these "unskilled" servants in the fur trade:

The Hon. Company's servants seldom continue more than 3 years at the same post, and often only one. In the summer the whole of their time is occupied in voyaging upon the rivers, carrying out the furs which they had traded in the winter from the Indians; and returning with a new outfit for the trade of the ensuing year. . . . When a young voyager comes to his winter quarters, he finds he wants many things to fit him for this new existence which he has entered upon. He wants his leather coat, trowsers, mittens, duffle socks and shoes, all then must be made and kept in repair. He has not time to do this himself; he applies to an Indian who has got some daughters, or two or three wives. . . . thus the unfortunate voyager forms his connexion with the natives and raises an offspring. He may continue here two or three years, and enjoy the benefit of his helpmate. He goes off in the summer, returns in the autumn, and perhaps finds the same young woman given to another. This does not distract his mind, he forms another connexion as speedily as possible; by this time he believes he cannot get on without a woman. The next time he leaves his winter quarters, he perhaps is sent to a post 600 or 1000 miles from his former wives. . . . The same course is run until old age and grey hairs are upon him. . . . (Cockran, 1975)

For these men the centre of their social world was the society of their workmates. Here they evaluated themselves in terms of how they felt they measured up to particular masculine virtues. It was in this society over half a century later that the demi-legendary Paulet ["Little" or "Tiny"] Paul emerged:

[He was] a giant in stature and strength, . . . with a voice like thunder and a manner as blustery and boisterous as March, eyes like an eagle and a pair of fists as heavy and once, at least, as deadly as cannon balls. . . . When the different brigades met at York Factory, and the question which could produce the best man, came to be mooted over a regal [*régale*] of Hudson's Bay rum, he was ever the first to strip to the waist and stand forth to claim that honour for the Blaireau ["Badgers," name of the Saskatchewan York boat brigade]. . . . Such encounters, off-hand at first no doubt, and having their inspiration in the rum keg, came to be a recognized institution of the trip. . . . [Michael Lambert] was the darling of the Taureaux ["Bulls," name of the Red River York boat brigade]. . . . They liked Poulet [*sic*] because he was a hard man to beat, but they adored Michael because he could beat Poulet [*sic*]. . . . There was Jimmy Short, otherwise known as Checkam, who could put up an ugly fight. . . . He too had stood up for the honour of the Taureaux against Poulet [*sic*], but only to be knocked out. Still he had lived to tell the tale and that alone was an honour not to be despised. (Gunn, 1930)

The evidence is not conclusive about the extent to which these men and their households contributed to the Plains Metis tradition. In several instances, their descendants took treaty as Indians during the 1870s.

The Red River Metis

The confluence of the Assiniboine and Red rivers (downtown Winnipeg today) was the heart of the Red River Settlement, and the settlement itself played a major role in the history of the Plains Metis as possibly a

MAP 18.1. Metis Settlements and Migrations

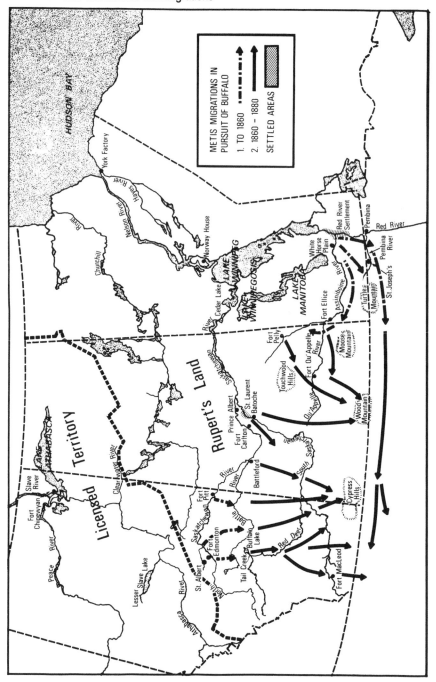

majority of the Metis were found within its boundaries and hinterland. The heterogeneous nature of the settlement's population coloured Metis experience. The settlement divided at the junction of the two rivers with the Metis (numbering approximately 55 per cent of the population in 1835) and a few *Canadien* households occupying narrow river lots to the south and west of the fork. To the north, down the Red River toward Lake Winnipeg, lay the river-lot farms of the other metis people in Red River, the "Hudson Bay English" (30 per cent of the population, 1835), at Kildonan, the original Selkirk settlers (numbering 8 per cent, 1835), and at St. Peters, the Indian village (Saulteaux and Swampy Cree numbering 7 per cent, 1835). Religion and language marked the basic division between "French and Catholic" and "British and Protestant" in Red River, although the two metis communities could make themselves understood in Cree or Saulteaux. Churches, schools, and the instruments of local government such as courts and the appointed Council of Assiniboia underlined distinctions between Red River and the circumstances of Metis living on the Saskatchewan.

The Metis hunting about the junction of the Red and Assiniboine rivers had welcomed the appearance of the Highland Scots crofters, the original Selkirk settlers, in the spring of 1812. Although these settlers were assisted by the agents of Lord Selkirk and the Hudson's Bay Company, the settlers were appreciated as a ready market for surplus buffalo meat and pemmican as well as for fish and water fowl. Yet the settlers' involvement in the competition between the North West Company and the Hudson's Bay Company polarized positions. The North West Company convinced the Metis that the settlers and the Hudson's Bay Company were usurping Metis lands. Almost inevitably, violence escalated to the Battle of Seven Oaks, June 19, 1816, when a party of Metis, commanded by the British-educated metis son of a Nor'wester, Cuthbert Grant, killed more than twenty of a mixed party of settlers and Company servants, including the colony governor, Robert Semple. The legacy of this battle coloured relations between "French and Catholic" and "British and Protestant" for the next century.

The end of competition in the fur trade in 1820 witnessed the victory of the revitalized Hudson's Bay Company over the North West Company. Yet a majority of the officers in the new concern were former "Nor'westers." These Highland Scots merchant-adventurers based in Montreal had been more than able successors to the *Canadien* and French merchants, extending the St. Lawrence-Great Lakes trading system to the Arctic and Pacific coasts. Their élan and esprit de corps had all but defeated the Hudson's Bay Company when their own shortcomings, a deficiency of system and regulation, made them vulnerable to the "modern" managers who took control of the Hudson's Bay Company in 1810 (Rich, 1960). For these new men, effective management emphasized the efficiency of the process involved rather than the social interests of the participants. In the face of such management objectives the deficiencies of the pre-industrial ways and means of the Nor'westers were glaringly evident. They were defeated by the commercial superiority of modern management in the conduct of the fur trade.

The victory of the Hudson's Bay Company marked the dramatic beginning of a new era for the inhabitants of the old Northwest. The governor and committee of the Hudson's Bay Company, besides emphasizing modern business practices to control costs and maximize long-term profits, envisaged a settlement at the junction of the Red and Assiniboine rivers in harmony with the interests of the fur trade. Stimulated in part by the philanthropic efforts of Thomas Douglas, Earl of Selkirk, the settlement received support from the Company even before it passed into the hands of the Company in 1835. In a letter in 1822 to their principal officer in Rupert's Land, the governor and committee explained their reasons for encouraging a migration of metis peoples to the Red River Settlement:

> It is both dangerous and expensive to support a numerous population of this description [metis] in an uneducated and savage condition, and it would be impolitic and inexpedient to encourage and allow them to collect together in different parts of the country where they could not be under any proper superintendence. (Governor and Committee, 1938)

Throughout the 1820s, Metis families drifted into the settlement to squat for the most part with Company approval on river lots to the south and west of the forks. There they commenced the annual pattern of activities that would mark their way of life in Red River.

The Buffalo Hunt

Late in spring, most Metis left their river lots, some with small plots planted with root vegetables and barley, harnessed oxen or horses to their two-wheeled Red River carts, and set out south to the rendezvous point near Pembina, on the border with United States territory. Only the elderly, the sick, and the crippled remained at home. Many households, having a very skilled buffalo hunter or more than one hunter, hired

PLATE 18.1. Gabriel Dumont, buffalo hunter and military leader (ca. 1880). Courtesy Glenbow Archives, NA-1063-1.

engagés, no doubt from among kinsmen, to drive additional carts and to participate in the processing.

At Pembina, a general assembly of the hunters met to select officers and promulgate basic rules. Images of the militia in New France and Lower Canada are suggested both in the selection of officers and in the promulgation of hunt rules. The first order of business was to choose ten *capitaines* who in turn would each choose ten *soldats*. The foremost of the *capitaines* was the hunt leader, variously styled as the "War Chief" and "le Président." In addition, ten guides were selected from among the hunters past their physical prime. No doubt the selection of the ten captains and the ten guides reflected the socio-political concerns of the Metis in terms of the major extended families in the community; but no documentary evidence has been found, as yet, to confirm such a pattern.

Social and political authority among the Metis was a function of an individual's achievements – his reputation – and it was characterized by limited powers, in terms of both duration and extent, authorized by the community. On the buffalo hunt each guide and each captain commanded for a day. In a cycle of ten days all of the guides and captains would have command of the hunt. At dawn, the raising of the hunt flag above a guide's cart signalled his command for that day. With camp struck, carts packed, and livestock harnessed or herded, the hunt, in two or more lines of carts abreast, set out on a course determined by the guide-of-the-day. The captain-of-the-day positioned his soldiers ahead, abreast, and to the rear of the line of march. The soldiers sought buffalo, but they were also on guard against the Dakota (sometimes known as the Sioux), who claimed the resources of the lands on which the Metis frequently hunted. Two soldiers always rode together: by riding away from each other at a gallop or toward each other they could signal the hunt as to whether buffalo or Dakota had been sighted. Whatever the quarry the hunt flag was lowered, passing authority from the guide and captain-of-the-day to the hunt leader. At any hint of danger the carts were circled with shafts inward to corral the stock. If buffalo were sighted the hunters assembled in line abreast under the command of the hunt leader.

Slowly the line of hunters advanced. Severe sanctions in the rules of the hunt awaited any brash hunter who broke the line to rush the herd. At the quarter-mile mark the command *allez* launched the hunters forward into a crescendo of gunfire, stampeding buffalo, galloping horses, and exulting or cursing hunters. Clouds of dust, permeated with the smell of sweat and blood, would part momentarily to reveal possibly a downed rider lying lifeless or perhaps seeking assistance from those nearby. Others, surprisingly unaware of the chaos and confusion about them, closed with their prey. At the command *allez*, the individual hunter, astride his prized mount, had galloped forward. His horse then chose a target and closed with it. When nearly abreast of the buffalo the hunter in a single fluid motion lowered the barrel of his gun, fired his ball, and dropped a personal article, usually an article of clothing, to mark his kill. Instinctively his horse sidestepped the tumbling carcass and sought out another target while the hunter on his mount's back reloaded. Pouring a "guesstimated" amount of gun powder from his powder horn into the barrel of his gun, the hunter then spat a lead ball, from those he carried in his mouth, into the barrel. The charge was rammed home with an abrupt smack of the butt on the saddle pommel or the hunter's thigh. Holding the gun upright until his mount closed with another quarry the hunter, again in a single fluid motion, lowered the barrel of his gun and fired.

In a matter of minutes the hunt for the day was over. The dust and noise receded to reveal hunters busy butchering their kill. From two to five buffalo would be killed by each hunter, depending on ability and particular circumstances. Later, when repeating rifles were introduced in the closing years of the 1860s, kills of over twenty-five buffalo for one hunter would be recorded. Beginning with his last kill the hunter began butchering the carcasses in preparation for the women to dry the meat and manufacture pemmican. Cut into strips the meat was hung on racks to dry in the sun and over fires. When dried meat was pounded to flake into a coarse powder and an equal amount of melted fat was added, together with berries and other edibles in season, the resulting product was pemmican. Cooled and sewn into ninety-pound buffalo-hide bags, pemmican could be transported and stored with ease. The Company's provisioning posts on the North Saskatchewan and the Red and Assiniboine rivers purchased pemmican and dried meat for their own needs, with the surplus being delivered to Norway House to provision the York boat brigades and for transshipment to northern posts to supplement the diet of fish.

In terms of preference Metis hunters and Plains Indians chose the meat of the heifer or young cow. With the horse this target could be selected with much regularity. In terms of buffalo numbers this behaviour contributed substantially to the demise of the buffalo.

The hunt remained a dangerous undertaking. In addition to the accidents associated with it there was the hostility of the Dakota. In most instances, violent confrontations were relatively short-lived and involved small numbers. In July, 1851, however, the hunt from White Horse Plain, a Metis settlement a few miles to the west of Red River, came under sustained attack. They withstood the onslaught with only one dead and a few wounded while inflicting casualties that forced the Dakota to break off the action. On this occasion the Metis had corralled their stock behind the encircled carts while the women and children took positions behind them. The men charged forward the distance of a gun shot to scrape gun pits in the prairie sod. From these vantage points they kept the attacking Yankton Dakota from destroying their stock and thus, at the very least, leaving them stranded on the prairie. The *Canadien* priest who accompanied the hunt stood astride a cart, crucifix in one hand, tomahawk in the other, exhorting his flock to persevere. The Metis victory at Grand Coteau confirmed in their own minds their paramountcy on the prairie west of Red River.

The return of the summer hunt to Red River saw "recognized hunters" rather than individual hunters negotiate the sale of their pemmican and dried meat, at prices that remained low and varied little over the years. The recognized hunters appear to have been in many instances the heads of extended families with whom the Company sought influence. A smaller autumn hunt left the settlement late in October or early November to provision the Metis for the winter months. It was sufficient to sustain the leisurely round of visits among kinsmen, punctuated by celebrations associated with numerous weddings. During these months not a few Metis found themselves, over the years, increasingly attracted to the illicit trade in furs.

The summer hunt returned to Red River Settlement usually in time to harvest what insects, drought, or floods had allowed to grow on their small plots of cultivated land. To sustain their stock over winter each settler looked to the mile of land behind his river lot for hay. For some families this hay was insufficient. Each year they joined others waiting for the local Council of Assiniboia to declare the opening date for haying on the prairie lands beyond the hay privilege. Having spotted a likely area prior to the beginning of haying, the hunter and his family rushed to the area on the appointed date, claiming all the hay that he could encircle in a single day's cutting. The introduction of mechanical reapers in the late 1850s gave some farmers in Red River a notable advantage over Metis hunters.

The "Free Trade" Controversy

Before 1820, in the shadow of the competing fur trade giants, a few enterprising traders, apparently linked to Great Lakes Metis families, had managed to establish small trading operations in the valley of the Red River. With the end of competition, the victorious Hudson's Bay Company, using a variety of successful carrot-and-stick techniques, stifled the illicit trade. Geographical isolation was the essential circumstance maintaining the Company's monopoly for the next two decades. Routes to outside markets, other than those of the Company, were either too difficult or too dangerous to sustain commercial links. Besides, the Company tied the Metis to their interests with a sinecure for their leader, Cuthbert Grant, entitled "Warden of the Plains" and paying £300 per year. As a result, the Company took little interest in the exchange of furs between

Indians and their Metis kinsmen, for most if not all the furs eventually found their way to the Company's warehouses. But with the end of geographical isolation, the Company viewed such exchanges in a far more negative light.

In 1844, Norman Kittson, a Canadian, opened a post for the American Fur Company at Pembina on the Red River, a few yards south of the international boundary. A knowledgeable trader, with kin ties to the Marion family that linked him to the Metis, Kittson would not fall victim to the Company's competition as his predecessors had. His post would become a beacon to enterprising young Metis who would see in its existence opportunities their fathers had known but which in recent years had seemed to recede before their grasp. In time, the Red River Metis leader, Cuthbert Grant, would lose his following, giving way to younger men who would challenge the Company's hegemony.

Within a decade of the end of the fur trade competition in 1820 the Hudson's Bay Company had slashed expenses, in part, by reducing its purchase of "country provisions" and regularizing continuing purchases to the point where there was little variation in amount or price from year to year. Thus, by the 1830s the Metis found their market for pemmican and dried meat satiated. Between 1820 and 1840 the population of Metis doubled. At Red River in the same period the number of carts involved in the hunt grew from 540 to 1,210. As the Company dealt only with recognized hunters in purchasing the produce of the hunt, it was increasingly difficult for young men to find the means of succeeding to this status and the social prestige and the financial rewards it entailed. By the 1840s "opportunity" for many young Metis males, as it was defined in terms of their own cultural traditions, was shrinking. No doubt many Metis regarded the construction of Kittson's post as a godsend.

From the time of their first appearance on the western Plains in the latter quarter of the eighteenth century the *gens libres* had traded furs with Indian kinsmen. While such exchanges acknowledged socio-economic ties between kinsmen, there could be, as well, a commercial dimension to the transactions. Both Indians and freemen in the period before 1820 were aware that the trading companies paid higher prices to freemen than to Indians to encourage further the freemen's demonstrated diligence in pursuing both provisions and furs. In some circumstances this price difference could be exploited by Indians through their freemen kinsmen. In these occasional trading activities the freeman kept alive the image of the *commis* conducting an *en dérouine* trade. This image was a cultural legacy to which the Metis of the Red River region could turn when the promised rewards of the buffalo hunt became increasingly difficult to realize and when Kittson's post seemed to provide a means to return to the entrepreneurial ways of the past.

The Hudson's Bay Company's opposition to the free traders culminated in the Sayer trial of 1849. Guillaume Sayer and three other Metis were accused of trading furs in violation of the Company's charter. A "committee of ten" Metis, probably headed by Louis Riel *père*, assembled an armed mob of 300 Metis to surround the courthouse and give expression to their views. The trial proceeded with Sayer being found guilty, largely on the basis of his son's testimony. The Company's chief factor at Red River, John Ballenden, satisfied with a legal victory in the courts of Rupert's Land in support of the Company's charter, addressed the court, requesting additional charges against Sayer be dropped and punishment suspended. When the court agreed, a French-speaking member of the jury, misconstruing developments, rushed to the courthouse door to cry *"le commerce est libre."* His words were greeted with a *feu de joie*, much self-congratulatory back-slapping, and general merriment. Before their eyes the Company's officers saw legal victory dissolve into commercial defeat. Henceforth, the Company would have to meet the challenge of the free traders through appropriate business techniques and not with the legal canons of its charter. The Metis in turn felt they had successfully asserted their hinterland interests in the face of the agents of the London metropolis who, in defining new opportunities for themselves, seemed to deny it to those residing in the region.

The Metis victory at the Sayer trial was expressed in the 1850s with the appearance of successful free traders such as Pascal Breland and Louis Goulet. Besides strengthening the settlement's commercial ties with St. Paul in Minnesota Territory, they extended business links southwest toward the Missouri, west toward the Qu'Appelle Valley, and north toward the North Saskatchewan River.

The Buffalo Robe Trade

Years earlier, in the decade after 1800, American fur traders on the lower reaches of the Missouri River identified buffalo robes, cow pelts taken between the middle of November and the middle of March, as a marketable product in the growing cities of northeastern North America. While there was no market in Europe, North Americans valued buffalo robes as sleigh throws and bedcovers and sometimes as a raw material for the manufacture of winter boots and coats. From a few hundred robes a year before 1820 the market expanded to more than 100,000 robes a year a half-century later. After 1850 the heads of several extended families among the Metis emerged as traders (*bourgeois*) whose networks of hunters and their families, *hivernants* (winterers), chose to winter on the prairie at wooded oases such as Moose Mountain, Wood Mountain, and, in time, the Cypress Hills, rather than return to river lots at Red River or St-Albert in the Saskatchewan country. By the 1870s encampments such as Tail Creek and Buffalo Lake south of Fort Edmonton numbered several hundred *hivernants*.

As the nineteenth century advanced eastern institutions other than buffalo robe buyers became aware of "opportunities" in a land previously thought fit only for nomadic hunters and fur traders. Their agents soon put in an appearance. Roman Catholic and Protestant missionaries who earlier had been in Red River now jostled each other on the upper reaches of North Saskatchewan River and beyond. Canadian settlers appeared, as yet in small numbers, in Red River and, as Overlanders, traversed the Plains to cross the Rocky Mountains into British Columbia. Members of the British gentry as tourists sought adventure in the wilds of the fur trade West. Government-sponsored expeditions led by John Palliser and H.Y. Hind gathered data on hinterland resources that the outside world avidly sought. Interests other than the fur trade were preparing their assault on the resources of the Northwest. In Red River the closing years of the 1860s were marked by the failure of farm and hunt, necessitating the importation of relief supplies from Canada and the United States. Such events raised questions about future opportunities for the Metis.

The Transfer and the Aftermath

The "Transfer" in 1870 of the Hudson's Bay Company's territories to the control of a recently created country, the Dominion of Canada, marked the loss of the Northwest's last vestige of independence from the modern world. This "conquest," which had been evolving over the previous half-century, would be consolidated in the next decade and a half. In Red River, Louis Riel's defiance of the Canadian Lieutenant-Governor-designate, William McDougall, in 1869 and his establishment of a provisional government marked the assertive action of a community determined to secure its interests in the new order. Not a few Metis traders opposed Riel out of fear that his actions would disrupt the robe trade. Yet others saw Riel's provisional government as assurance of and opportunity for the future. Riel and the Metis behind him did not limit their political frame of reference to themselves. They saw the other communities of the old Northwest, together with the Metis, having legitimate corporate interests that the Canadians would have to recognize if the

PLATE 18.2. Scrip Commission meeting at Hudson's Bay Company post, Lesser Slave Lake, 1899. Courtesy of the RCMP Museum, Regina, NA-949-18.

old inhabitants, as communities, were to survive and to prosper in the new order. In 1870, negotiations with representatives of Riel's provisional government culminated with the Canadian government's passing of the Manitoba Act (styled the Manitoba "Treaty" by Riel and the Metis). In this legislation, Riel and his government believed they had determined the political and constitutional structure necessary for the corporate survival of the old communities. The Canadians, for their part, felt they had granted in a more formal fashion what they believed they had always been prepared to grant: the rights, privileges, and responsibilities of individual citizenship (Morton, 1956a). In the Canadian pantheon of truisms, "opportunity" was primarily a function of individual merit and not corporate privilege. The Canadians believed that, in terms of equity, circumstances demanded a period of wardship for the Indians through the treaty system before full citizenship could be extended. For the Halfbreeds, including the Metis, the problem of equity was supposedly acknowledged in the provision in the Manitoba Act for 1.4 million acres to be reserved for the children of "Halfbreed heads of families."

The year 1874 witnessed the departure of the last hunt from the Red River Settlement. In the same year the trickle of Metis migrating westward became a flood. The Manitoba Treaty had not achieved what Riel and his followers felt they had successfully negotiated with the Canadians. A number of the migrants journeyed southwestward to Dakota Territory, creating the temporary large settlement of St. Joseph before continuing westward to Montana Territory. More journeyed westward to the Qu'Appelle Valley and the environs of Fort Ellice and Fort Pelly. Many continued northward to the valley of the South Saskatchewan, a couple of days' journey south of Prince Albert, to establish the parish of St. Laurent with the tiny village of Batoche in its midst. A few traders, such as Louis Goulet, journeyed westward to the Metis indigenous to the Saskatchewan country. For many Metis in Red River the exodus westward was the pursuit of opportunity in the robe trade. But for others the migration was fundamentally a flight from what the future appeared to hold in Manitoba and a search for an opportunity to establish a base from which the objectives of the Manitoba Treaty could be retrieved from failure.

Much has been written on the Saskatchewan Rebellion of 1885. In the more recent historical literature there has been a tendency to find fault with the actions of the Canadian government, seeing them as provoking the violent responses of some Indians and Metis who had legitimate grievances (Stanley, 1963, 1964). A recent revisionist work has presented evidence to question both the culpability of the government and the "blamelessness" of Metis actions (Flanagan, 1983). Were the Metis not to a major extent authors of their own misfortune in placing themselves under the leadership of the erratic Louis Riel? Recent writings on Indian motives in the Rebellion suggest that, while they acted independently of the Metis, they aspired to ends similar to those expressed by the Metis at the time of the Transfer and that the Metis believed they had enshrined in the Manitoba Act (Tobias, 1983). The fundamental aspiration of both Metis and Indians in 1885 was to be recognized as corporate entities and to be guaranteed a relevant role in the West's future as such. For the Canadians, with their emphasis on individual rights and responsibilities, such corporate aspirations constituted unfair privilege. The defeat of the Metis on the battlefield at Batoche on May 12, 1885, ended for a half-century their collective purposeful pursuit of this objective.

Dispersal, frequently to the fringes of the dominant society, marked the fate of many if not most Metis in the half-century following the Rebellion. Some in the area of Winnipeg chose to emphasize things "French" and "Catholic" in their heritage as a means of retaining a distinct identity and defining a corporate role for themselves in the settlers' West. Others sought strengthened ties with kinsmen on the Indian reserves. The research to determine with some precision who among the Metis did what after 1885 has been initiated only recently. It would appear that little of permanent benefit accrued to the Metis from the government's program of Halfbreed scrip. The expression "the road allowance people," referring to Native families living in rough cabins on crown lands, reflects the fate of many.

The New Order

The dominant ethnic element among the settlers who surged onto the prairie lands in the fifteen-year period from 1896 to 1911 was Ontarian. They saw property ownership as a fundamental value, and they believed it should be widely dispersed throughout society. Universal adult male suffrage was the political means by which governments were disciplined to act as agents of this community. Others, such as Americans and those of the British Isles, held very similar views and found opportunities to act upon them in the Canadian West. In time these traditions would blend to create distinct western Canadian views. A series of Halfbreed scrip land grants were made between 1870 and 1900 to facilitate Metis adjustment to this new order.

The conditions and terms under which land was made available to the Metis varied during the period scrip was granted. In many instances, the 240-acre land grants were sold to speculators who were able thus to establish large blocks of homestead lands for their own speculative purposes. In many other instances, when terms permitted, the Metis took money scrip entitling them to $240. A suggestion of ignorance or irresponsibility on the part of the Metis is often associated with the decision to take money scrip.

It was not, however, until Marquis wheat became widely available to western farmers after 1900 that grain farming offered a reasonable chance of success. Without the certainty of grain harvests from year to year, the agricultural future of the West was limited to livestock. In the years prior to 1900 the agricultural response of the Metis, with its emphasis on livestock and mobility, could be viewed as effective as that of any ethnic group. When it is remembered that the Metis were eligible as well for homestead entry, then the decision to take money scrip becomes an effective adaptive response rather than evidence of ignorance or irresponsibility.

At the moment our impression of Metis agricultural practices after 1885 highlights a home base near a prairie lake or slough with small plots of land planted to grains and root vegetables. The produce of the gardens was supplemented by gathering the eggs of waterfowl or hunting and snaring birds and animals found in the vicinity. Livestock – a few cattle and horses – were moved as pasturage and other factors dictated. In such circumstances, particularly when the home base was protected by a homestead entry and open range was still available, it made sense to take money scrip rather than acquire more land. With capital to purchase the requirements of semi-nomadic agriculture, such as wagons, harness, portable stoves, and tents, survival was enhanced. When it is noted that the value of fur shipped from Edmonton remained greater than agricultural produce until after 1900, then the survival value of Metis agriculture is readily apparent. They could continue to harvest furs as they had done during the era of the buffalo hunt. Only later, when crown lands filled with homesteaders and grain farming could be conducted with some certainty of success, did the decision to take money scrip rather than land scrip appear to be a mistake.

An essential problem for the Metis early in the twentieth century was their lack of access to capital to enable them to complete the transition to sedentary agriculture with an emphasis on grain. They lacked social connections that might have unlocked some financial doors; they lacked expertise in Canadian political ways that might have opened others. Finally, they emerged from the period of the Halfbreed scrip grants without ownership of significant amounts of land. Many Metis communities were doomed to exist as islands of enduring poverty that did not accompany their settler neighbours into the "good life" following the pioneering era. With the end of open land, with the establishment of the viability of settled farming, and with the loss of an institutional basis for expressing their corporate identity, large numbers of Plains Metis were dispersed northward and westward into the region of the boreal forest to join kindred peoples to eke out difficult lives on the fringes of settlement.

With the onset of the Great Depression in 1929, efforts were rekindled to resurrect *la nation métisse.* A notable example in Alberta saw an enfranchised Indian, Joseph Dion, the son of an Indian agent, Jim Brady, and the son of an early Edmonton businessman, Malcolm Norris, acknowledge their Native heritages by identifying their personal interests with those of the Metis people. The result was the creation of the Metis Association of Alberta. In 1938 the Saskatchewan Metis Society came into existence.

Food, clothing, shelter, and medical treatment were dominant concerns in the agitation of Dion, Brady, and Norris. Questions of cultural survival were viewed as irrelevant when questions of physical survival were uppermost. The Metis Association of Alberta succeeded in having the provincial government, in December, 1934, establish a Royal Commission "To Investigate the Conditions of the Half-Breeds of Alberta" under Justice A.F. Ewing. The result of the Ewing Commission's hearings was the Metis Betterment Act, 1938.

The question can be asked whether this Act was an improvement over the Manitoba Act of 1870. The Metis Betterment Act established eight Metis colonies at different locations in northern Alberta. In imitation of

PLATE 18.3. Frank Moberly, guide, near Jasper Alberta (ca. 1920). The Moberlys and other Metis residents of the Jasper region were evicted when it became a national park. In the 1970s their descendants gained a land settlement north of Jasper. Courtesy Glenbow Archives, NA-3187-7.

the federal government and its views of Indian reserves, the colonies were to constitute a protected environment in which the Metis could be instructed in "the intricacies of modern society." It was hoped that within a few years the success of the legislation was to be reflected in the disappearance of the colonies and the assimilation of the Metis into western Canadian society. The Metis would become fully participating individuals in the life of the dominant society. A similar view was expressed by many if not all the leaders of the Metis community.

The 1960s witnessed an upsurge in activity among the Metis in western Canada. In 1961 court action was launched against the province of Alberta for its refusal to pay royalties on resources, particularly oil and gas, removed from Metis settlements. In 1965 the Metis of northwestern Ontario formed an organization that would become known as the Ontario Metis Aboriginal Association. In 1967 the Saskatchewan Metis Society amalgamated with the Metis Association of Saskatchewan, while in the same year the Manitoba Metis Federation united the Metis of that province who could trace their organizational roots to 1887 and the formation of l'Union National Métisse Saint Joseph du Manitoba.

In the 1970s organizational growth continued in northeastern British Columbia and in the Northwest Territories. At the national level the Metis associations of the three prairie provinces would form the Native Council of Canada. In 1981 they would leave the NCC to form the Metis National Council (MNC).

At the national level the MNC continued to press for federal responsibility that would lead to constitutional recognition, self-government, and a land base. At a series of first ministers' conferences during the 1980s the MNC believed it had accomplished its initial objectives, with the Metis Nation Accord to be included in the Charlottetown Accord, but the Canadian electorate's resounding defeat of the constitutional referendum in 1992 and its savaging of two of the three mainline parties in the federal election of 1993 appear to have ended constitutional reform for a period of time. Other strategies, if not altered objectives, may suggest themselves in the wake of an apparently angry, awakening electorate targeting what they define as "special interests" and a professional middle class that appears to have profited handsomely by brokering the interests of these special interests. For the angry electorate, national and provincial institutional leadership has betrayed the traditions of fairness and opportunity for the individual tax-paying citizen. Special interests have become "citizens plus" at the expense of others. This altered perception of special interests could well prove to be the greatest challenge for Metis leadership at both the national and provincial levels.

At the provincial level a significant effort emphasized Metis participation in government action directed at the educational and social problems experienced by many Metis. In Alberta a series of "framework agreements" between the provincial government and the Metis Nation of Alberta (MNA – formerly the Metis Association) aspires to promote joint planning and joint action on the part of the parties involved. To this end a joint committee, involving senior provincial government and MNA officials and co-chaired by individuals of each interest, is responsible for strategic planning and monitors the progress of the various sub-committees. While the provincial government may be simply seeking more effective delivery for its programs at a time when increased hostility toward government performance is being expressed by many in the electorate, the MNA sees in these agreements the experiences that will eventually lead to constitutional recognition, self-government, and a land base.

The task for Metis organizations in the 1990s is to convince an increasingly negative electorate, nursing its own sense of betrayal and victimization, that such aspirations for the Metis constitute fairness rather than privilege.

Recommended Readings

Brown, J.S.H.
   1980   *Strangers in Blood: Fur Trade Families in Indian Country.* Vancouver: University of British Columbia Press.
   An excellent study of nineteenth-century fur trade officers' families, suggesting the concept of patrilocality to explain why children of these families did not become Metis.
Ens, Gerhard
   1988   "Dispossession or Adaptation: Migration and Persistence of the Red River Metis, 1835-1890," *Historical Papers.* Ottawa: Canadian Historical Association.
   A challenge to those who would see the Metis essentially as victims.
Flanagan, Thomas
   1983   *Riel and the Rebellion: 1885 Reconsidered.* Saskatoon: Western Producer.
   A controversial revisionist work on the causes of the 1885 Rebellion.
   1992   *Louis Riel.* Ottawa: Canadian Historical Association, Booklet 50.
   A brief survey by the current leading authority on Riel.
Foster, John E.
   1994   "Wintering, the Outsider Adult Male and the Ethnogenesis of the Western Plains Metis," *Prairie Forum*, 19, 1.
   The question of origins is examined.

Giraud, Marcel

    1945 *Le Metis Canadien*. Paris: l'Institut d'Ethonologie. Translated by George
        Woodcock as *The Metis in the Canadian West*. Edmonton: University of
        Alberta Press, 2 vols., 1986
        The fundamental study on the Plains Metis.

Hargraves, J.J.

    1871 *Red River*. Montreal: Printed for the author by John Lovell.
        The son of a Hudson's Bay Company chief factor, the author had a
        familiarity with Red River and the fur trade West unrivalled by any other
        non-resident. His description of the buffalo hunt complements that of
        Alexander Ross (below).

Innis, H.A.

    1975 *The Fur Trade in Canada*. Toronto: University of Toronto Press.
        The classic statement of the staple trade thesis in terms of the fur trade.

MacLeod, M.A., and W.L. Morton

    1963 *Cuthbert Grant of Grantown: Warden of the Plains of Red River*. Toronto:
        McClelland and Stewart.
        This study of the first prominent leader among the Plains Metis is a useful
        depiction of the Red River Metis at mid-century.

Metis National Council

    1993 The *Métis Nation*, 2, 2. Ottawa: Metis National Council.
        A sophisticated expression of a Metis perspective on their history and
        current issues and circumstances.

Morton, W.L.

    1956a "Introduction," in W.L. Morton, ed., *Alexander Begg's Red River Journal and
        other Documents Relating to the Red River Resistance of 1869-70*. Toronto:
        Champlain Society.
        This is the best scholarly history of the Transfer, 1869-70.

    1956b "Introduction," in E.E. Rich, ed., *London Correspondence Inward from Eden
        Colvile, 1849-1854*. London: Hudson's Bay Record Society.
        The best scholarly history of the Red River Settlement from 1840 to 1855.

Peterson, Jacqueline

    1978 "Prelude to Red River: A Social Portrait of the Great Lakes Metis,"
        Ethnohistory, 25, 1: 41-67.
        A seminal article in the study of the Metis, it is fundamental to any
        scholarship on the subject.

Ray, A.J.

    1974 *Indians in the Fur Trade: Their Role as Hunters, Trappers, and Middlemen in
        the Lands Southwest of Hudson Bay, 1660-1870*. Toronto: University of
        Toronto Press.

The first, and still essential, study to delineate an Indian history in the fur trade West.

Ross, Alexander
  1972 *The Red River Settlement: Its Rise, Progress, and Present State.* Edmonton: Hurtig.
        A former fur trader who retired to the Red River Settlement with his Okanagan wife and their children. This folk history account, originally published in 1856, contains the most useful description of a buffalo hunt in the primary sources.

Sawchuk, Joe, Patricia Sawchuk, and Theresa Ferguson
  1981 *Metis Land Rights in Alberta: A Political History.* Edmonton: Metis Association of Alberta.
        The most useful survey of Metis history in the twentieth century with a focus on Alberta.

Sprague, Douglas
  1988 *Canada and the Metis, 1869-1885.* Waterloo, Ont.: Wilfrid Laurier Press.
        For many readers a "victims" and "oppressors" history.

Sprenger, Herman
  1972 "The Metis Nation: Buffalo Hunting vs. Agriculture in the Red River Settlement (circa 1810-1870)," *Western Canadian Journal of Anthropology,* 3, 1: 158-70.
        An excellent challenge to the view that the hunting ways of the Metis were inappropriate in the context of agricultural opportunities at Red River.

Stanley, G.F.G., *et al.,* eds.
  1985 *The Collected Writings of Louis Riel/Les Ecrits complets de Louis Riel.* Edmonton: University of Alberta Press, 5 vols.
        Self-explanatory in terms of importance for the period of the Transfer and the Rebellion.

Van Kirk, Sylvia
  1980 *"Many Tender Ties": Women in Fur Trade Society in Western Canada, 1670-1870.* Winnipeg: Watson and Dwyer.
        The most thorough and definitive historical study of women in the fur trade.

Additional References Cited

Campbell, Marjorie
  1973 *The North West Company.* Toronto: Macmillan.

Cockran, William
  1975 "To the Secretary of the Church Mission Society from Rev. W. Cockran, Red River Settlement, July 25, 1833," in L.G. Thomas, ed., *The Prairie West to 1905.* Toronto: Oxford University Press.

Foster, J.E.
  1983 "The Metis: The People and the Term," in A.S. Lussier, ed., *Louis Riel and the Metis*. Winnipeg: Pemmican.
Governor and Committee of the Hudson's Bay Company
  1938 "To George Simpson from the Governor and Committee, London, February 27, 1822," in E.E. Rich, ed., *Journal of Occurrences in the Athabaska Department by George Simpson 1820 and 1821, and Report*. Toronto: Champlain Society.
Gunn, J.J.
  1930 "The Tripmen of Assiniboia," in *Echoes of the Red*. Toronto: Macmillan.
Moogk, P.N.
  1976 "In the Darkness of a Basement: Craftsmen's Associations in Early French Canada," *Canadian Historical Review*, 57, 4: 399-439.
Morton, A.S.
  1928 "La Verendrye: Commandant, Fur Trader and Explorer," *Canadian Historical Review*, 9, 4: 284-98.
Morton, W.L.
  1980 "Clio in Canada: The Interpretation of Canadian History," in A.B. McKillop, ed., *Contexts of Canada's Past: Selected Essays of W.L. Morton*. Toronto: Macmillan.
Nicks, Trudy
  1980 "The Iroquois and the Fur Trade in Western Canada," in C.M. Judd and A.J. Ray, eds., *Old Trails and New Directions: Papers of the Third North American Fur Trade Conference*. Toronto: University of Toronto Press.
Nute, G.L.
  1966 *The Voyageur*. St. Paul: Minnesota Historical Society.
Rich, E.E.
  1960 *The History of the Hudson's Bay Company*. London: Hudson's Bay Record Society.
Saunders, R.M.
  1939 "The Emergence of the Coureur de Bois as a Social Type," *Canadian Historical Association Annual Papers*.
Stanley, G.F.G.
  1963 *The Birth of Western Canada: A History of the Riel Rebellions*. Toronto: University of Toronto Press.
  1964 *Louis Riel*. Toronto: Ryerson.
Tobias, J.L.
  1983 "Canada's Subjugation of the Plains Cree, 1879-1885," *Canadian Historical Review*, 64, 3: 519-48.

CHAPTER 19

"We Must Farm To Enable Us To Live": The Plains Cree and Agriculture to 1900

Sarah Carter

Early in September, 1879, at Fort Carlton, North-West Territories, Plains Cree chiefs Atakakoop, Mistawasis, and Ketawayo, with five councillors, met with Edgar Dewdney, the recently appointed Commissioner of Indian Affairs. The chiefs were frustrated that promises of agricultural assistance, made to them three years earlier in Treaty No. 6, were "not carried out in their spirit" (Anon., 1879: 26). They stated that they intended to live by the cultivation of the soil, as "the buffalo were our only dependence before the transfer of the country, and this and other wild animals are disappearing, and we must farm to enable us to live." They insisted that government had not fulfilled its part of the treaty in assisting them to make a living by agriculture and that what had been given them made a mockery of the promises made in 1876. This was by no means the first effort of these chiefs to place their concerns before government officials, and there were similar expressions of dissatisfaction and disappointment throughout Manitoba and the North-West Territories.[1]

444

Such evidence of the strong commitment of the Plains Cree to agriculture seemed startling to me when I set out to explore why agriculture
failed to provide a living for residents of arable Indian reserves in western Canada. The standard explanation, one firmly embedded in the non-
Aboriginal prairie mentality, seemed compelling: that Aboriginal people
of the Plains never had any inclination to settle down and farm despite
concerted government efforts and assistance. I originally approached the
topic with the argument in mind that agriculture was the wrong policy, for
the wrong people, at the wrong time. Before I was too far along in my
research, however, I found that there was little evidence of agriculture
floundering because of the apathy and indifference of Aboriginal people,
although it was certainly the case that this view was consistently maintained and promoted by the Department of Indian Affairs and later by
many historians. Yet from the time of the treaties of the 1870s and well
before, Aboriginal people were anxious to explore agriculture as an alternate economy when they began to realize the buffalo were failing them. It
was not government negotiators but the Aboriginal spokesmen who
insisted that terms be included in the treaties that would permit agricultural development. Aboriginal people of the western Plains were among
the earliest and largest groups to attempt agriculture west of the Red
River Settlement. Like most other "sodbusters," Aboriginal farmers
were inclined to become commercial farmers specializing in grain. The
fact that they did not had to do with government policy and intent, not
with Aboriginal choice and inability.

My topic and approach is the product of a number of influences,
including the work of "new" social historians who, beginning in the
1960s, argued that history should be not only the study of elites but of
ordinary people as well, and of the day-to-day as well as the dramatic
events. The new social history stressed that non-elites – ethnic minorities, women, the working class, and non-literate peoples – sought in various ways to transcend the limitations placed on them and were not
hopeless victims of forces beyond their control but rather coped creatively with changing conditions. While Arthur J. Ray, Sylvia Van Kirk,
and John Milloy cast Native people in a central role as active participants in the history of the pre-1870 West, the same could not be said of
the more modern era. In the dominant narrative histories of the West in
the post-1870 era, Aboriginal people all but disappeared after they made
treaties and settled on reserves. The story of the establishment of the
rural core of the prairie West was inevitably told from the point of
view of the new arrivals, with little mention of the host society, and generally a record of positive achievement was stressed and the casualties

of development were downplayed. Studies of late nineteenth-century imperialisms, which increasingly drew regions into a transcontinental network, provided context for understanding that what happened in western Canada was not unique, but was part of a global pattern of Western expansion.

Aboriginal Adaptations to the Northern Plains

The Plains culture that evolved over centuries in western Canada seemed far removed from the sedentary lifestyle of farms, fields, and fences that began to alter forever the prairie landscape in the late nineteenth century. The Plains Cree, the northernmost people of the Great Plains of North America and one of the last Aboriginal groups to adopt Plains culture, developed a lifestyle that was well suited to the predominantly flat, treeless landscape and to the northern Plains climate of extremes and uncertainties. Particular habits of movement and dispersal suited the limited and specialized nature of the resources of the northern Plains (Bennett, 1990: 41-79). The Natives exploited the seasonal diversity of their environment by practising mobility. Plains people moved their settlements from habitat to habitat, depending on where they expected to find the greatest natural food supply. All aspects of life hinged on this mobility; their tepees, for example, were easily taken apart and moved, and their other property was kept to a strict minimum so that they would be unencumbered. As homesteaders were later to learn, basic necessities such as good soil, water, game, and fuel rarely came together in many Plains areas, and this combined with the great variability and uncertainty of the climate to make mobility central to the survival of the indigenous peoples of the Plains. Many of the earliest homesteaders on the Plains found that they could not stay put either, certainly not at first; they sought off-farm jobs, especially during the "start-up" years, or they were obliged to try several localities in their search for basic necessities. External inputs in the way of seed-grain relief, subsidies, or rations were often necessary as the resources of a fixed locality could not always sustain the inhabitants.

The buffalo was the foundation of the Plains economy, providing people not only with a crucial source of protein and vitamins but with many other necessities, including shelter, clothing, containers, and tools. Aboriginal life on the Plains followed a pattern of concentration and dispersal that to a great extent paralleled that of the buffalo. But Plains people were not solely hunters of buffalo. To rely on one staple resource alone was risky in the Plains environment, as there were periodic shortages of buffalo, and it was mainly the gathering and preserving work of

PLATE 19.1. Cree camp near Saskatoon (ca.1900). Courtesy Saskatchewan Archives Board, R-B1016.

women, based on their intimate understanding of the Plains environment, that varied the subsistence base and contributed to "risk reduction," a role the immigrant women to the Plains would also acquire. Mid-summer camp movements were determined not only by the buffalo but by considerations such as the ripeness and location of saskatoon berries, the prairie turnip, and other fruits and tubers. Many of the foodstuffs women gathered were dried, pounded, or otherwise preserved and stored for the scarce times of winter. Women fished, snared small game, caught prairie chickens and migratory birds, and gathered their eggs. A high degree of mobility was essential for people effectively to draw on the varied resources of the Plains.

Nineteenth-century European observers tended to see the Great Plains as a timeless land, as a place without history, its people unaffected by any outside forces and leaving no mark of their presence upon the land. Captain William Butler, who described the Plains in 1870 as a great ocean of grass, wrote that "This ocean has no past – time has been nought to it; and men have come and gone, leaving behind them no track, no vestige of their presence" (Butler, 1968: 317-18). European observers saw Plains people as living at the mercy of natural forces and failed to appreciate the sophisticated adaptations to the environment and the many ways in which resources were altered, managed, and controlled. Methods such as the buffalo pound, like the Huron enclosures and Beothuk drivelines for capturing deer, have been described as a form of animal management. There is evidence that people of the northern Plains were concerned with keeping up buffalo herd numbers as they periodically burned the grasslands in the autumn to keep forage levels high (Duke, 1991: 60). This burning increased yields, encouraged spring grass growth earlier, and induced buffalo into favoured areas of fresh, young grass. Fire was used to influence buffalo movement – to direct a herd to a kill site and to keep buffalo away from fur trade posts so that Europeans could not provision themselves. Fire was also used to protect valuable stands of timber.

Well before the treaties of the 1870s some Plains people, particularly the Cree and Plains Saulteaux, had begun to raise small crops and to keep cattle to smooth out the seasonal scarcities that were increasing as the buffalo receded westward. As the homesteaders were later to learn, however, especially those who attempted farming before the development of dry-land farming techniques and early-maturing varieties of grain, yields from cultivated plants were highly unpredictable, and a more flexible economy that combined agriculture with hunting and gathering was the most feasible until the disappearance of the buffalo in the late 1870s. Agriculture was a far more ancient and indigenous tradition on the Plains than the horse culture, which was a much more fleeting episode. The Cree were acquainted with cultivated plant food and techniques of agriculture through several of their contacts, most notably the Mandan, Arikara, and Hidatsa who maintained a flourishing agricultural economy on the upper Missouri. There is evidence of an agricultural village on the banks of the Red River near the present-day town of Lockport, Manitoba, that dates from between A.D. 1300 and A.D. 1500 (Putt, 1991: 64). The Blackfoot were found by the earliest of European fur traders to be growing tobacco.

Aboriginal people of the Plains were not as "passive" as the landscape; their world was not static and timeless. The archaeological and historical records suggest that on the Plains learning new ways took place regularly, that there was much adaptation and borrowing among people, and that changes occurred constantly. The Plains Cree, for example, had a history of making dramatic adjustments to new economic and ecological circumstances, modifying the ways in which they obtained their livelihood. With the establishment of fur trade posts on Hudson Bay after 1670 the Cree, along with their allies the Assiniboine, quickly seized the opportunity to function as middlemen to the trade (Ray, 1974). With the expansion of European fur trade posts inland in the late eighteenth century, the Cree took advantage of a new economic opportunity and worked as provisioners of buffalo meat to the trading

PLATE 19.2. Cree from the File Hills Reserve, Saskatchewan (ca. 1914). Courtesy Saskatchewan Archives Board, R-B 1854.

companies. The Cree showed themselves to be remarkably flexible in rapidly adjusting to the rewards and demands of different environments – the forest, parklands, and Plains. The branch that became the Plains Cree readily adopted many of the characteristics, techniques, and traits of Plains buffalo and horse culture (Milloy, 1988). Aboriginal people such as the Cree were accustomed to making dramatic adjustments to new ecological and economic circumstances, and there is no inherent reason to believe that they could not have made adjustments to the new order of the post-1870 era by becoming full participants in the agricultural economy. The fact that they did not was due not to their own choice; rather, there was a refusal to let them do so as they were denied access to the opportunities and resources that would have allowed them a more independent existence.

While the Aboriginal people of the Plains required assistance and instruction to establish a farming economy, they had certain advantages that the new arrivals did not enjoy. They had an intimate knowledge of the resources and climate of the West. They were much better informed on rainfall and frost patterns, on the availability of water and timber, and on soil varieties. They had experience with locusts, fires, and droughts. Aboriginal farmers might have had a better chance than many of the settlers from the humid East. Many of these never could accept the discomforts and conditions, and they departed, and even for those who remained acclimatization could take several years. Settlers from elsewhere might well have benefited from the knowledge Aboriginal people of the Plains had to offer. One settler in Saskatchewan, who had previously worked as a trader, consulted an Aboriginal friend by the name of South Wind when he wanted to locate his homestead in the 1880s, and he learned, for example, how to use fire to protect stands of timber and how to replenish the hay swamps. He later found local legislation regarding fire to be a "positive evil" and wrote that "our legislators should have had old South Wind at their Councils."[2] Accounts of such consultation are, however, very rare.

As early as the 1850s European travellers to the Plains reported that the Cree were concerned about the scarcity of buffalo, that many were anxious to try agriculture and wanted assistance in the way of instruction and technology (Spry, 1968: 125n, 136, 432). They were well aware that the buffalo hunt was no longer going to sustain them. With the demise of the fur trade, agriculture appeared to be the only option. During the treaty negotiations of the 1870s Plains people sought government aid to make the transition to an agricultural economy. In return for their offer of an opportunity for peaceful expansion, Aboriginal people asked that they be given the instruction and technology that would allow them to farm. Aboriginal spokesmen did not see any inherent conflict between their distinctive identity and active participation in an agricultural economy. Circumstances obliged them to cease to live as their ancestors had done, but they did not therefore cease to be Aboriginals. Like the Natives of the older provinces of Canada, they were in favour of agriculture, resource development, and education, which would assist them to survive, but they did not, for example, intend to abandon their religious ceremonies and beliefs. Euro-Canadian observers consistently insisted on seeing Plains people as hunters, gatherers, and warriors incapable of adopting agriculture.

A Crop of Broken Promises: The 1870s

The people who are the main focus of this study are those of the Treaty No. 4 district of southeastern Saskatchewan, who settled on reserves in the Touchwood Hills, File Hills, and along the Qu'Appelle River. Most were Plains Cree, collectively known as the *mamihkiyiniwak*, the Downstream People, although Assiniboine, mixed Cree-Assiniboine (Young Dogs), and Plains Saulteaux also settled here. Although these people form the main focus, evidence was also drawn from the Treaty No. 6

MAP 19.1. Saskatchewan and Assiniboia Districts, circa 1900

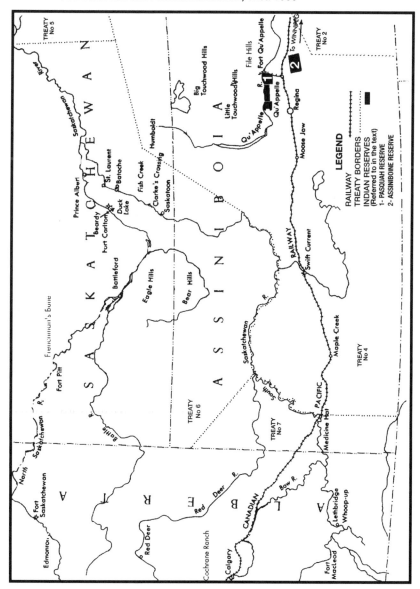

district, settled primarily by Plains Cree known as the Upstream People. In the later 1870s, the earliest years of Indian reserve settlement in present-day Saskatchewan, farming proved nearly impossible despite concerted efforts. For some bands, farming was never to be successful because of the nature of the reserve site itself. Other bands received high-quality agricultural land that was later to excite the envy of other settlers. The earliest instructions to surveyors was that care should be taken to ensure reserve lands "should not interfere with the possible requirements of future settlement, or of land for railway purposes." At that time what was seen as the "fertile belt," and the proposed route for the Canadian Pacific Railway, ran northwest along the Assiniboine and North Saskatchewan rivers. Land further south was considered arid and unlikely ever to be wanted by settlers, so many reserves, such as those along the Qu'Appelle River, were surveyed there. But when the CPR route was changed in 1881 and rerouted through the south, many of these reserves were located near or on the railway route, in the midst of what it was hoped would become the settlement belt and the heart of a prosperous agricultural economy.

Farming in the 1870s proved to be nearly impossible because the implements and livestock promised in the treaties were inadequate. Ten families, for example, were to share one plough. Bands varied in size, numbering between seventeen and fifty families, but regardless of size, each was offered only one yoke of oxen, one bull, and four cows. To earn a living from the soil, a yoke of oxen was required by every farming family. As one Plains Cree chief pointed out in 1879, it was perfectly ridiculous to expect them to get on with so few oxen, that every farmer in the Northwest, however poor, had his own yoke of oxen, that "We are new at this kind of work, but even white men cannot get on with so few oxen" (Anon., 1879: 28). In addition to the overall inadequacy of the agricultural assistance promised in the treaties, government officials were reluctant and tentative about distributing what was promised. The people prepared to farm expected their supply of implements, cattle, and seed immediately, but officials were determined to adhere strictly to the exact wording of the treaty, which stated that implements, cattle, and seed would be given to "any band . . . now actually cultivating the soil, or who shall hereafter settle on these reserves and commence to break up the land." Aboriginal people could not settle until the surveys were complete, and in some cases this took many years. They could not cultivate until they had implements to break the land, yet these were not to be distributed until they were settled and cultivating. Government officials shared the belief that the distribution even of those items promised in the treaties could "encourage idleness," and there was concern that the implements and cattle would not be used for the purposes for which they were intended.

There were also problems with the quality and distribution of seed grain. In the earliest years the seed arrived in a damaged state and was received in mid-summer when the season was far too advanced for planting. Acres sometimes lay idle because there was no seed available, and more land might have been broken had there been seed to sow. It was also learned after a number of years that people cultivating the reserves had to be supplied with some provisions in the spring during ploughing and sowing. The people of Treaty No. 6 had successfully bargained for this during their negotiations, but no such promise had been made to the people of Treaty No. 4. Although David Laird, Lieutenant-Governor and Indian superintendent for the North-West Superintendency, recommended in 1877 that some provisions be distributed in the spring to Treaty No. 4 bands, this request was struck from the estimates in Ottawa. It proved impossible for more than a few to remain on their reserves and cultivate as the others were obliged to hunt and gather provisions for the group to survive. Once seeding was finished, and sometimes even before, many residents of the reserves were out on the Plains, leaving behind only a few to tend the crops.

Aboriginal farmers were hampered in their earliest efforts by the kind of ploughs they were issued. By the late 1870s, Manitoba farmers had learned that American ploughs, especially the John Deere, with its chilled-steel mouldboard, were far superior for western conditions than the Ontario models. The Indian Department, however, continued until 1882 to purchase only Canadian-manufactured ploughs, which proved to be unsatisfactory. There were problems keeping in good repair the implements and wagons that were distributed, as they frequently broke down, crippling operations. Wooden parts were sometimes replaced by the farmer, but the breakage of metal parts was much more serious, as reserve farmers did not have access to blacksmiths, who were also required to point, or sharpen, ploughshares. Other equipment and livestock supplied by contractors under the terms of the treaties were clearly inferior, and Aboriginal people simply refused to accept some of it. An 1878 commission of investigation found Winnipeg Indian commissioner J.A.N. Provencher guilty of fraud in the awarding of contracts and it was discovered, among other things, that it was standard practice to furnish the Indian Department with "the most inferior articles" (Titley, 1986). In 1879 one observer described the carts and wagons supplied to but refused by Treaty No. 6 people near Fort Carlton as "the poorest description of Red River carts, which have been used by freighters up to this point, and are really unfit for further use; while the waggons are literally falling to pieces." The axes, "miserably small," were also refused (Anon., 1879: 29).

Perhaps the most scandalous example of corruption was in the cattle sent to a great many reserves in the late 1870s. They received wild Montana cattle, which were unaccustomed to work and could not be hitched to the plough. The milk cows given out were of the same description. The Fort Carlton bands were astounded when these cattle were brought to them from Montana, when tame cattle could have been purchased at Prince Albert or Red River. Most of them died over the first winter of 1878-79. Some choked themselves when tied in stables; others could not be fed because they did not take to the food. As one Plains Cree chief stated, "We know why these Montana cattle were given us; because they were cheaper, and the Government, thinking us a simple people, thought we would take them" (Anon., 1879: 28). He was correct in this as it became clear during the 1878 investigation that individuals in Winnipeg had profited by purchasing these creatures from Montana at about half the rate that they actually charged the Indian Department.

Aboriginal farmers laboured under other disadvantages as well. In these earliest years there were no grist mills located near reserves, and the wheat they raised was of no use to them without milling facilities. With the disappearance of the buffalo, their main source for all their apparel also vanished. They lacked clothing and footwear, which one official described as the greatest drawback to their work. To cover their feet they cut up old leather lodges, but these too rapidly diminished. Often hungry, weak, and ill, people could not work no matter how willing.

There was little progress in agriculture in the years immediately following the treaties of the 1870s. Early on, government officials insisted that this had to do with the indifference and apathy of Aboriginal people, who wilfully rejected an agricultural way of life and inflexibly and stubbornly insisted on pursuing hunting and gathering. Through idleness they were creating their own problems. An explanation that belittled and deprecated the abilities of the Aboriginal farmers absolved the government of any responsibility in the matter, and it was to be the favoured explanation of department officials well into the twentieth century. During these initial years of government parsimony, indifference, and outright corruption an opportunity was lost. Many of those who wished to farm found it impossible and became disheartened and discouraged. Had the government shown a genuine interest, some steps toward the creation of an agricultural economy might have been taken during the years before 1878-79, when the food crisis, brought on by the total disappearance of the buffalo, became severe. There was much distress, suffering, and death throughout the Northwest by 1878, although reports of starvation were systematically denied by government officials and the western press, as such news could damage the reputation of the region as a prospective home for thousands of immigrants. Once again, Aboriginal people were portrayed as chronic complainers with imaginary grievances, and they were blamed for having "not made the usual effort to help themselves."[3]

The other legacy of the years immediately following the treaties was the sense of betrayal felt by Aboriginal people who had expected government assistance in the difficult transition to an agricultural economy. As Chief Atakakoop stated in 1879, "On the transfer of the country we were told that the Queen would do us all the good in the world, and that the Indians would see her bounty. With this message came presents of tobacco, and I took it at once; and I pray now that the bounty then promised may be extended to us." Three years after the treaty the chief was convinced that the "policy of the Government has been directed to its own advantage, and the Indians have not been considered so much." These chiefs had made several representations to government authorities, "but they were as if they were thrown into water" (Anon., 1879: 28).

Chief Pasquah, from the Pasquah Reserve in southeastern Saskatchewan, had presented Joseph Cauchon, Lieutenant-Governor of Manitoba, with similar grievances and concerns a year earlier.[4] His people, though willing to farm and diversify their subsistence base, had no cattle to break and work the land, no seed to sow, and no provisions to sustain them while at work. Aboriginal people had reason to feel that they had been deceived and led along a path that ended in betrayal, that their treatment constituted a breach of faith. They were getting the clear impression that the treaties were made simply as a means of getting peaceable possession of the country without any regard to their welfare. As Aboriginal spokesmen grasped every opportunity to implore the government to assist them to make a living by agriculture, department officials increasingly reacted by blaming the Natives for their misfortunes and portraying them as troublemakers and chronic complainers, incapable of telling the truth.

The Home Farm Experiment

In the wake of alarming reports from the Northwest of destitution and starvation, an ambitious plan to both feed and instruct Aboriginal people in farming was hastily contrived in Ottawa in the fall and winter of 1878-79. A squad of farm instructors, mainly from Ontario, was sent west in the summer of 1879. They were to establish "home farms" at fifteen sites in the Northwest: six in the Treaty No. 4 district and nine in the Treaty No. 6 district. At these farms, located on or near the reserves, the instructors were to raise large quantities of provisions to support not only themselves, their families, and employees but also the neighbouring Aboriginal population. Their farms were to serve as "model farms" for Aboriginal observers, and in addition the instructors were to visit the reserve farmers from time to time to assist them in breaking, seeding, and harvesting and in building their houses, barns, and root houses. At two "supply farms" in the Treaty No. 7 district large quantities of produce were to be raised, but the farmers at these sites were not given the additional responsibility of instructing Aboriginal farmers.

The home farm plan was hastily and poorly conceived in Ottawa by people without any knowledge of Aboriginal people or of the region's soil and climate. The men chosen as instructors were unfamiliar with conditions of life in the West and knew nothing about Aboriginal people. They had to be provided with both guides and interpreters. As one Aboriginal spokesman stated, it only made sense that a farm instructor be a man "from the country, who understands the language, and with whom I could speak face to face, without an interpreter" (Anon., 1879: 28). The official rationale for not choosing local people was that "strangers" were likely to carry out their duties more efficiently, would not have their favourites, and would treat all fairly and alike. It is also clear, however, that the position of farm instructor was a patronage appointment, and all were chosen by Sir John A. Macdonald, the Canadian Prime Minister, from a list furnished by Laurence Vankoughnet, deputy superintendent-general of Indian affairs. In addition, the tasks assigned the instructors were beyond the resources and capabilities of any individual, however well acquainted he might be with conditions in the Northwest. It soon proved that the instructors had great difficulty establishing even the most modest farms. The government found itself responsible for the support of instructors, their families, and employees, who ran farms with such dismal returns that they contributed almost nothing to the expense of running them. It was also soon discovered that the farmers simply could not attend both to their own farms and to assisting on reserve farms. The instructors seldom visited the reserves and lacked even basic knowledge about the people they were to instruct. The program turned out to be an administrative nightmare. Difficulties with personnel arose early, and the program was characterized by resignations and dismissals. The instructors were angered by government decisions to charge them for the board of themselves and family, and also to charge them for food they consumed that they had raised themselves.

Beset with all of these difficulties, the home farm program floundered. In the House of Commons, government critics hammered away at the plan. They claimed that the instructors were incompetent carpetbaggers, but the central criticism was that there should be no such expenditure on the Aboriginal people of the Northwest, as this was encouraging idleness when they should be made to rely solely on their own resources. One member of Parliament argued that the program was an enormous waste of money because efforts to "civilize Indians" were inevitably doomed to failure.[5] Government defenders of the program argued that the essential problem lay with Aboriginal people, who were "idlers by nature, and uncivilized." In the opinion of Prime Minister Macdonald they were not suited to agriculture, as they "have not the ox-like quality of the Anglo-Saxon; they will not put their neck to the yoke."[6]

There were many vocal critics of the home farm program in the Northwest as well. Non-Aboriginal residents viewed the program as unfair, because too much was being done to equip Aboriginal people to farm, more than was available to the true "homesteaders," upon whom it was felt the prosperity of the region depended. The home farm program ingrained the idea that Aboriginal farmers were being lavishly provided with farm equipment and other assistance that was "conducive to the destruction of self-reliance, and calculated to give them a false impression of what the Government owed them." In the wake of the food crisis in the Northwest the government had begun to provide modest rations to reserve residents. Indeed, some of the farm instructors found much of their time taken up issuing relief in the form of "musty and rusty" salt pork in exchange for assigned work. Many non-Native residents were critical of the distribution of rations, which they saw as a reward for idleness and as unfair because it gave Aboriginal farmers an advantage over other struggling farmers.

The home farm program had a very brief life in its original form. By 1884 the department had officially retired the policy, which had already undergone much modification. Farm instructors remained and their numbers increased, but their own farms were to consist of no more than a few acres and they were to concentrate on instruction. New recruits were no longer brought from Ontario at great expense, but were men from the Northwest.

The Pioneer Experience: Agriculture in the 1880s

All who attempted farming on the Plains in the 1880s experienced frustration and failure. Crops during this decade were damaged year after

PLATE 19.3. Native farmers (ca. 1906-10). Courtesy Provincial Archives of Manitoba-Edmund Morris, G11-510.

year by drought and early frosts. Prairie fires became a serious hazard, consuming haystacks as well as houses, stables, and fences, and hampering the abilities of farmers not only to winter cattle but to carry out the whole cycle of farming operations. There was a high rate of homestead cancellation, and many of the community experiments of ethnic, religious, working-class, and aristocratic groups did not survive the decade.

A major difference between the Aboriginal farmer and his neighbours was that while the newcomers had the option to leave and try their luck elsewhere, the reserve residents had little choice but to persevere, as under the Indian Act they were excluded from taking homesteads. Aboriginal farmers could not obtain loans because they were not regarded as the actual owners of any property, however extensive and valuable their improvements might be, and they had difficulty obtaining credit from merchants. Because of many of the technicalities and prohibitions of the Indian Act, Natives were prevented from doing business or transacting even the most ordinary daily affair. They were deprived of the right to do what they chose with nearly everything they acquired by their own personal industry. People who came under the Indian Act were prevented by a permit system from selling, exchanging, bartering, or giving away any produce grown on their reserves without the permission of department officials. A pass system, imposed initially during the 1885 Rebellion but continued well into the twentieth century, controlled and confined the movements of people off their reserves. Those who wished to leave the reserve were obliged to acquire a pass from the farm instructor or Indian agent declaring the length of and reason for absence. The most recent arrivals to the country had far more rights, privileges, and freedom than the original inhabitants.

Despite these restrictions and the drought, frost, and prairie fires of the 1880s, reserve farmers in some localities made significant advances in the 1880s. Several of the problems that had hampered reserve farming in the past had to some extent been ameliorated. Through a "cattle on loan" policy, for example, many bands had considerably increased their numbers of work oxen, cows, steers, heifers, and bulls. Under this system the department "loaned" a cow to an individual who was to raise a heifer, either of which had to be returned to the Indian agent. The animal became the property of the individual, although the agent's permission was required to sell or slaughter. Reserve farmers also had increased access to grist mills in the 1880s as the department initiated a program of granting bonuses to individuals who would establish mills in the Northwest. Recipients of the bonus were obliged to charge Aboriginal customers a little less than ordinary customers for a ten-year period. The department also displayed greater concern to supply the services of blacksmiths, which bolstered agricultural operations.

Reserve farmers began to acquire some of the up-to-date machinery necessary to facilitate their operations. Mowers and rakes were the most common purchases. Some reserves were fortunate in their abundant hay supplies, and a number of bands sold hay on contract to other reserves, to settlers, and to the North-West Mounted Police. Selling hay was one of the very few opportunities for outside employment available to reserve residents. These machines were purchased with their own earnings or through pooled annuities. They were not purchased for them by the department. Agents and farm instructors in the 1880s felt that access to mowers and rakes was essential for all bands, not only those that sold hay. As stock increased on the reserves, mowers and rakes were necessary to provide enough hay. Reapers and self-binders were also acquired during this period. The self-binder lessened the danger of being caught by frost during a protracted harvest, and it also reduced the waste experienced in binding with short straw. Such machinery permitted farmers to cultivate a larger area. By the late 1880s on some reserves in the districts of Treaty No. 4 and Treaty No. 6, farmers were beginning to see some significant results of their labour, and they had produce that they wished to sell: predominantly cattle, grain, and hay.

Like other prairie women of this period, Aboriginal women helped in the fields during peak seasons such as haying and harvest, but otherwise the business of grain-farming was predominantly a male activity. Women continued to harvest wild resources such as berries, wild rhubarb, prairie turnip, and birch sap, and they hunted rabbits, gophers, and ducks (Dion, 1979: 114-16). Because of increased settlement, the pass system, and calls for the restriction of Aboriginal hunting rights, these opportunities became increasingly constricted. Aboriginal women were eager to learn new skills and to adopt new technology. By the late 1880s the wives of many of the farm instructors acquired the title of "instructress" and they, as well as the wives of missionaries, taught skills such as milking, butter-making, bread-making, and knitting. Women adapted readily to these activities, but a chronic shortage of raw materials made it difficult to apply what they had learned. While the women knew how to make loaf bread, for example, they did not have the proper ovens, yeast, or baking tins, so they continued to make bannock, despite government attempts to abolish it from the diet as it required more flour than loaf bread. They seldom had yarn with which to knit. There were no buttons for the dresses the women made. They were often short of milk pans, although they made their own using birchbark. One instructress reported in 1891 that the greatest drawback was "their extreme poverty, their lack of almost every article of domestic comfort in their houses, and no material to work upon."[7] They lacked basic necessities such as soap, towels, wash basins, and wash pails, and had no means with which to acquire these.

The log dwellings on reserves in this era and well into the twentieth century were invariably described as "huts" or "shacks" that were one-storey and one-room. The roofs were constructed with logs or poles over which rows of straw or grass were laid. They were chinked inside and out with a mixture of mud and hay and had clay stoves but no flooring, and tanned hide was used for window covering. It was impossible to apply lessons of "housewifery" in such shacks. In publications of the Department of Indian Affairs, however, Aboriginal women were often depicted as poor housekeepers who wilfully ignored instruction in modern methods. They were blamed for the poor living and health conditions on the reserves. Explanations that stressed the incapacity of Aboriginal women to change, like those that disparaged the farming abilities of the men, absolved the government of any responsibility for the poverty of the reserves.

The Pressure of Competition

As Aboriginal farmers acquired the technology required by western conditions and as they began to increase their acreages and their herds, they also began to pose a threat as competitors in the marketplace. By the late 1880s, farmers in parts of the Northwest were complaining loudly about "unfair" competition from Aboriginal people. It was widely believed that government assistance gave Aboriginal farmers an unfair advantage. Non-Aboriginal settlers had the misconception that reserve farmers were lavishly provided with livestock, equipment, government labour, and rations, and did not have to worry about the price at which their products were sold. There was absolutely no appreciation of the disadvantages they laboured under as farmers, or of how government regulation and Canadian laws acted to stymie their efforts. Editorials in the *Fort Macleod Gazette* regularly lamented "Indian competition," which was injuring the "true" settlers of the country. If the Siksika (Blackfoot), Kainai (Blood), Pikuni (Peigan), and Tsuu T'ina (Sarcee) were "cut loose" from the treaty, support could be given to their industries, according to the *Gazette*, but it was "pretty hard to ask the people of the country to contribute toward the support of a lot of idle paupers, and then allow them to use this very support for the purpose of taking the bread out of the settler's month [*sic*]."[8]

It was argued in the *Gazette* throughout the 1880s and 1890s that Aboriginal people should not be permitted to compete with the settlers in the sale of hay, potatoes, or grain. Any evidence that they were successful in securing contracts was used as proof that they had underbid non-Natives. There was no consideration that their product might be superior, as was certainly the case with the hay purchased by the North-West Mounted Police, who often noted in their reports that the best hay was bought from reserve farmers.[9] In a letter to the editor in July, 1895, one local resident claimed that "it is altogether unfair to allow these Indians to enter into competition with white men who, even with hard work, find it difficult to make both ends meet and provide for their families." Evidence of unfair competition was used by the editors of the *Gazette* to bolster their larger campaign of the later 1880s to have Aboriginal people moved to one big reserve, an "Indian territory" out of the way of the Euro-Canadian settlements. It was argued that Indian policy had been a failure as Aboriginal people "had not made a single step toward becoming self-supporting."[10] There was apparently no recognition of the fact that it was impossible to become self-supporting to any degree unless they were allowed to sell their products.

Concerns about unfair "Indian competition" were echoed in other parts of the Northwest as well. The residents of Battleford and district were particularly strident in their objections to the competition of the Plains Cree in the grain, hay, and wood markets. Here, as well as in the district of southern Alberta, there was concern that reserve residents not become successful stock-raisers as the supply of cattle to the Indian department for rations was a vital source of revenue for many settlers. In 1888 the editor of the *Saskatchewan Herald* (October 13) of Battleford denounced any plan to "set the Indians up as cattle breeders, encouraging them to supply the beef that is now put in by white contractors."

Here, as in other districts, Aboriginal farmers were in competition with new settlers for hay land. Because of the predominantly dry years of the 1880s hay was very scarce some seasons. Off-reserve areas where reserve farmers had customarily cut hay became the subject of heated disputes. Non-Aboriginal residents of the Battleford district successfully petitioned the Minister of the Interior in 1889 to limit the hay land available to Aboriginal farmers off the reserves, despite the fact that the Battleford agent had warned that there would be no alternative but to decrease stock on the reserves. Many influential people in the West had a direct interest in the continuation of rations and in seeing that Aboriginal people were not self-supporting. Large operations like the W.F. Cochrane Ranch in southern Alberta found a sizable market for their beef on the neighbouring reserves. In his correspondence to department officials he naturally objected to any reduction in rations, arguing that this meant that their lives, and well as their property and cattle operation, would be in danger.[11]

The Peasant Farming Policy: 1889-1897

In 1889, Hayter Reed, Commissioner of Indian Affairs in Regina, announced that a new "approved system of farming" was to be applied to Indian reserves in western Canada. Reserve farmers were to reduce their area under cultivation to a single acre of wheat and a garden of roots and vegetables. Along with a cow or two, this would sufficiently provide for a farmer and his family. They were to use rudimentary implements alone: to broadcast seed by hand, harvest with scythes, bind by hand with straw, thresh with flails, and grind their grain with hand mills. They were to manufacture at home any items they required, such as harrows, hayforks, carts, and yokes. This policy complemented government intentions to subdivide the reserves into small holdings of forty acres each. Publicly, the subdivision of the reserves and the peasant farming policy were justified as an approach intended to render reserve residents self-supporting. Individual tenure, it was claimed, would implant a spirit of self-reliance and individualism, thus eroding "tribalism." Hayter Reed argued that the use of labour-saving machinery might be necessary and suitable for settlers, but Indians first had to experience farming with crude and simple implements. To do otherwise defied immutable laws of evolution and would be an "unnatural leap." In Reed's view, Aboriginal people had not reached the stage at which they were in a position to compete with white settlers. [12] Another argument forwarded against the use of labour-saving machinery was that rudimentary implements afforded useful employment for all.

Clearly, however, there were other reasons for the peasant farming formula and for allotment in severalty, reasons that were understood and appreciated by non-Aboriginal settlers. The *Saskatchewan Herald* (August 20, 1887) applauded the policy for the Aboriginal farmer:

> Thrown thus on himself and left to work his farm without the aid of expensive machinery he will content himself with raising just what he needs himself, and thus, while meeting the Government's intention of becoming self-sustaining, they at the same time would come into competition with the white settler only to the extent of their own labour, and thus remove all grounds for the complaint being made in some quarters against Government aided Indians entering into competition with white settlers.

This was a policy of deliberate arrested development. The allotment of land in severalty was viewed by officials, as well as by Prime Minister Macdonald himself, as a means of defining surplus land that might be sold (Tyler, 1979: 114). Severalty would confine people within circumscribed boundaries, and their "surplus" land could be defined and sold. Arrested development was a certain means of ensuring that much reserve land would appear to be vacant and unused.

Despite the protests of Aboriginal farmers, Indian agents, farm instructors, and inspectors of the agencies, the peasant farming policy was implemented on Plains reserves beginning in 1889. Officials were not to authorize the purchase, hire, or use of any machinery. Even if people had purchased machinery before the policy was adopted they were still to use hand implements. Farmers with larger holdings were to use the labour of others rather than revert to the use of machinery, or they were to restrict their acreages to what they could handle with hand implements alone. Officials in the field were dismayed by the policy that robbed the farmers of any potential source of revenue. They argued that the seasons in the Northwest were simply too short for the use of hand implements, which meant a loss in yield at harvest time and resulted in a much reduced supply of hay. Agent W.S. Grant of the Assiniboine Reserve protested that "the seasons in this country are too short to harvest any quantity of grain, without much waste, with only old fashioned, and hand implements to do the work with." In his view the amount of grain lost in his agency through harvesting with hand implements would be of sufficient quantity to pay for a binder in two years.[13]

Aboriginal farmers were profoundly discouraged by the new rules. It was widely reported that many refused to work with the hand implements and gave up farming altogether. One farmer from Moose Mountain declared he would let his grain stand and never plough another acre, while another gave up his oxen, his wheat, and the reserve.[14] Other aspects of the program, such as the home manufactures idea, were unrealistic and unworkable. Homemade wooden forks, for example, were simply not strong enough for loading hay, grain, or manure. They were to make their own lanterns, but agents protested that people could not look after their cattle at night without proper lanterns. At headquarters in Ottawa it proved impossible even to acquire some of the old-fashioned implements, such as hand mills, destined for the Aboriginal farmers. But Reed was not sympathetic to or moved by the objections and complaints, and he refused to give in to the "whims of Farmers and Indians." He advised that losing some of the crop or growing less grain was preferable to the use of machinery. If grain was being lost, the solution was for farmers to confine their acreage to what they could handle. Department employees were not to convene or be present at meetings with Aboriginal farmers, as this would give "an exaggerated importance" to their requests for machinery. They risked dismissal if they refused to comply with peasant farming policy.

Effects of the Restrictive Policy

The policy of deliberate discouragement of reserve agriculture worked well. By the mid-1890s, per capita acreage under cultivation had fallen to about half of the 1889 level and many serious farmers had given up farming altogether (Carter, 1990: 260-63). In 1899 a resident of Prince Albert, William Miller, Sr., wrote to the Minister of the Interior that in passing through the Duck Lake and Carlton reserves, he noted "no less than five fields [which can] be seen from the trail now without a bushel of grain sown in them . . . that previously used to be an example to the settlers around."[15] Peasant farming, severalty, and measures such as the permit system combined to undermine and atrophy agricultural development on reserves. The Canadian government acted not to promote the agriculture of the indigenous population but to provide an optimum environment for the immigrant settler. Whatever Canada did for its "wards" was subordinate to the interests of the non-Aboriginal population. Government policy was determined by the need to maintain the viability of the immigrant community.

Aboriginal people protested policies that affected them adversely, as they had from the 1870s. They raised objections to government officials, petitioned the House of Commons, sent letters to newspapers, and visited Ottawa. But the outlets for protest were increasingly restricted. Grievances related to instructors and agents rarely went further. Agency inspectors were, as mentioned, not allowed to hold audiences with reserve residents. The published reports of agents and inspectors were to divulge only that "which it was desired the public should believe."[16] Visiting officials such as the Governor General, who were usually accompanied by journalists, were taken only to select agencies that would leave the best impression. Department officials, particularly those in the central office, shared the view that Aboriginal people were chronic complainers not to be believed and a people who would go to extraordinary lengths to avoid diligent work.

Hayter Reed and the peasant farming formula were disposed of the year after Wilfrid Laurier and the Liberals came to power in 1896, but the damaging legacy of the policy was to be felt for years to come. Laurier was fortunate in coming to power just at a time when a constellation of factors, including rising world wheat prices, increased rainfall on the prairies, innovations in dry-land farming techniques, and massive immigration allowed a wheat economy to prosper in western Canada. Aboriginal farmers, however, had little place in this new age of prosperity. By the turn of the century agriculture did not form the basis of a stable reserve economy, and after that date the likelihood faded even further as the new administrators of Indian Affairs promoted land surrenders that further limited the agricultural capacity of reserves. The fact that there was "vacant" and "idle" land on many reserves, to a great extent the result of the peasant farming years, conveniently played into the hands of those who argued that Aboriginal people had land far in excess of their needs and capabilities. Government policy was that it was in the best interests of all concerned to encourage reserve residents to divest themselves of land they held "beyond their possible requirements," and the policy received widespread support in the western press and from farmers and townspeople. Residents of towns near Indian reserves regularly submitted petitions claiming that these tracts retarded the development and progress of their districts. Such pressure resulted in the alienation of many thousands of acres of reserve land, often the best land, in the years shortly after the turn of the century. The economic viability of reserve communities was deliberately eroded by the dominant society, mainly through government policies.

Aboriginal farmers, who lost the opportunity to participate in commercial agriculture in the 1890s, did not regain any ground in the early twentieth century. Cree historians Edward Ahenakew and Joe Dion both describe a pattern in their communities of an initial interest in agriculture and stock-raising that was atrophied because of the weight of regulation and supervision. They fell further behind in technology as well as training, as they did not have access to either the formal or informal agricultural education programs of the wider farming community. The reserves remained pockets of rural poverty. Twentieth-century visitors to reserves often found Aboriginal people living in the midst of farmland that was not cultivated at all, was leased to non-Natives, or was worked with obsolete methods and technology. It was generally concluded that they were a people who had been unable to adapt to farming, who stubbornly clung to the past, and who were impervious to "progressive" influences despite years of government assistance and encouragement. The initial enthusiasm of many for agriculture and the policies of deliberate discouragement have been obscured and forgotten.

A 1966 survey of the social, educational, and economic conditions of the Aboriginal people of Canada, headed by anthropologist Harry B. Hawthorn, found that some of the most depressed reserve communities in the country were in agricultural districts of the prairies where there appeared to be land for livestock or crops. Investigators described what few farms there were as marginal or sub-marginal, or the land was leased to neighbouring non-Aboriginal farmers, or farming had been abandoned altogether. Although in recent decades there has been some expansion of agricultural and livestock industries, many of the old obstacles remain, such as the limitations of the Indian Act. The process of settling outstanding treaty land entitlements in Saskatchewan will eventually expand reserve holdings for economic development, but here, too, old obstacles remain. Members of the non-Aboriginal public continually question the Office of the Treaty Commissioner about the wisdom of such measures, insisting that "Prairie Indians were never farmers, only hunters and warriors. Why should they get land for farming now? They . . . will only waste good farmland."[17] Such attitudes remain deeply embedded, and collective amnesia continues, as it remains important to deny that Aboriginal people could ever make proper use of such a valuable commodity as land.

Notes

1. "North-West Territories" was the form used until 1912, when it became the present "Northwest Territories."
2. National Archives of Canada (NAC), Saskatchewan Homesteading Experiences, MG 30 C 16, vol. 3, 790.
3. *Saskatchewan Herald* (Battleford), April 26, 1879.
4. NAC, RG 10, vol. 3665, file 10094, interpreter to Joseph Cauchon, June 1, 1878.
5. *House of Commons Debates*, 1884, 2: 1105 (Philipe Casgrain).
6. *Ibid.*, 1107 (John A. Macdonald).
7. NAC, RG 10, vol. 3845, file 73406-7, T.P. Wadsworth to Hayter Reed, February 17, 1891.
8. *Macleod Gazette*, August 16, 1887.
9. Annual Report of Commissioner L.W. Herchmer for 1889, in *The New West: Being the Official Reports to Parliament of the Activities of the Royal [sic] North-West Mounted Police Force from 1888-89* (Toronto: Coles Publishing Company, 1973), p. 6.
10. *Macleod Gazette*, December 7, 1886.
11. NAC, Hayter Reed Papers, W.F. Cochrane to L. Vankoughnet, September 6, 1893, file W.F. Cochrane.
12. NAC, RG 10, vol. 3964, file 148285, Hayter Reed to A. Forget, August 24, 1896.
13. *Ibid.*, W.S. Grant to Reed, October 1, 1896.
14. *Ibid.*, J.J. Campbell to Reed, October 8, 1896, and Grant to Reed, October 1, 1896.
15. NAC, RG 10, vol. 3993, file 187812, William Miller, Sr., to the Minister of the Interior, July 21, 1899.
16. NAC, RG 10, Deputy-superintendent letterbooks, vol. 1115, Reed to J. Wilson, August 3, 1894.
17. Peggy Brezinski, Review of *Lost Harvests*, *Anthropologica*, 34 (1992), p. 267.

Recommended Readings

Ahenakew, Edward

1973 *Voices of the Plains Cree*. Ruth M. Buck, ed. Toronto: McClelland and
      Stewart.
          Through his fictional character Old Keyam, Ahenakew (1885-1961)
      presents a vivid portrait of life on prairie reserves, especially of the crippling
      effects of the weight of government policies and regulations.

Carter, Sarah

1990 *Lost Harvests: Prairie Indian Reserve Farmers and Government Policy*.
      Montreal: McGill-Queen's University Press.
          An analysis of agriculture on prairie reserves from the treaties to World
      War One.

Dion, Joseph

1979 *My Tribe the Crees*. Hugh Dempsey, ed. Calgary: Glenbow-Alberta Institute.
          An account of the early years of settlement at Onion Lake and Kehiwin.

Dyck, Noel

1991 *What is the Indian 'Problem': Tutelage and Resistance in Canadian Indian
      Administration*. St. John's: Institute of Social and Economic Research, Social
      and Economic Studies No. 46.
          A critical examination of past and present relations between Aboriginal
      people and governments in Canada, with emphasis on prairie Canada.

Elias, Peter Douglas

1988 *The Dakota of the Canadian Northwest: Lessons for Survival*. Winnipeg:
      University of Manitoba Press.
          A detailed analysis of the different economic strategies adopted by the
      Dakota, including the farming bands at Oak River, Birdtail, Oak Lake,
      Standing Buffalo, and White Cap.

Milloy, John S.

1988 *The Plains Cree: Trade, Diplomacy and War, 1790-1870*. Winnipeg:
      University of Manitoba Press.
          An analysis of the complex trade and military patterns of the branch of the
      Cree that became a Plains people. Milloy argues that the Plains Cree culture
      flourished in the era to 1870 and was not undermined by their contact with
      European fur traders.

Ray, Arthur J.

1974 *Indians in the Fur Trade: Their Role as Hunters, Trappers, and Middlemen in
      the Lands Southwest of Hudson Bay, 1660-1870*. Toronto: University of
      Toronto Press.

The first and most significant revision of fur trade history, placing the emphasis on the role of Aboriginal people. Ray explored how the Cree and Assiniboine were involved, the extent to which they shaped the trade, and the effects of the fur trade on these societies.

Sluman, Norma, and Jean Goodwill

1982 *John Tootoosis: Biography of a Cree Leader.* Ottawa: Golden Dog Press.

Tootoosis, from Poundmaker Reserve in Saskatchewan, gives an account of the obstacles facing reserve farmers, of government efforts to effect land surrenders as well as the strategies adopted to circumvent these.

Tobias, John L.

1983 "Canada's Subjugation of the Plains Cree, 1879-1885," *Canadian Historical Review,* 64, 4.

An important revisionist analysis of traditional interpretations of Plains Cree actions and strategies in the immediate post-treaty years.

Additional References Cited

Anonymous

1879 *Chronicles By the Way: A Series of Letters Addressed to the Montreal Gazette Descriptive of a Trip Through Manitoba and the North-West.* Montreal: Montreal Gazette Printing Co.

Bennett, John W.

1990 "Human Adaptations to the North American Great Plains and Similar Environments," in Paul A. Olson, ed., *The Struggle for the Land: Indigenous Insight and Industrial Empire in the Semiarid World.* Lincoln: University of Nebraska Press.

Butler, William F.

1968 *The Great Lone Land.* Edmonton: Hurtig Publishers. (First published, 1872.)

Duke, Philip

1991 *Points in Time: Structure and Event in Late Northern Plains Hunting Society.* Niwot: University of Colorado Press.

Hawthorn, H.B., ed.

1966 *A Survey of Contemporary Indians of Canada: Economic, Political, Educational Needs and Policies.* Ottawa: Indian Affairs Branch.

Putt, Neal

1991 *Place Where the Spirit Lives: Stories From the Archaeology and History of Manitoba.* Winnipeg: Pemmican.

Spry, Irene, ed.

1968 *The Papers of the Palliser Expedition, 1857-60.* Toronto: Champlain Society.

Titley, E. Brian
1986 "J.A.N. Provencher: A French-Canadian Carpetbagger in Manitoba," paper presented to the Canadian Historical Association, University of Manitoba.
Tyler, Kenneth J.
1979 "A Tax-Eating Proposition: The History of the Passpasschase Indian Reserve," M.A. thesis, Department of History, University of Alberta.
Van Kirk, Sylvia
1980 *"Many Tender Ties": Women in Fur Trade Society in Western Canada, 1670-1870.* Winnipeg: Watson and Dwyer.

PART VII
The Plateau

CHAPTER 20
The Plateau: A Regional Overview

Douglas Hudson and Elizabeth Furniss

The Region and Its People

The Canadian portion of the Plateau culture area is essentially the same region as that defined locally in British Columbia as "the interior." This area is bounded on the west by the Coast Range and on the east by the Rockies, and comprises a series of interconnected plateaus and north-south valleys that extend south into the United States. With a history of extreme glaciation, the interior is now environmentally diverse and includes seven biogeoclimatic zones ranging from sagebrush deserts to sub-boreal spruce forests.

The Plateau is also linguistically diverse, with four different language groups located here. The Athapaskan-speaking nations (with the exception of the Nicola) are found in the northern Plateau and are linked both linguistically and culturally to their northern neighbours of the Western Subarctic. They probably represent a southern expansion into the Plateau. The Salish-speaking peoples of the central and southern interior, like their Sahaptin neighbours in the extreme southern Plateau, may represent a northward migration from the Great Basin region of the United

MAP 20.1. The Plateau Culture Area

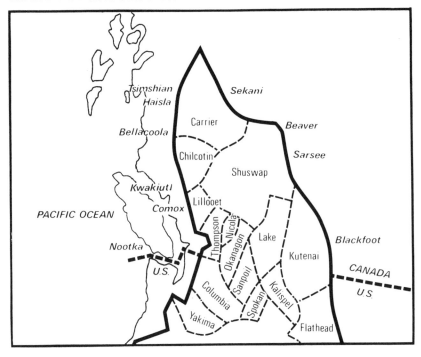

States in post-glacial times. The Kutenai of southeastern B.C. and northern Idaho and Montana are a linguistic isolate.

Over time, due to disease, displacement, migration, and population growth, populations shifted and territorial boundaries were modified. A number of historic population shifts are directly related to European-introduced epidemics. Smallpox destroyed up to half the Sanpoil in 1782-83, swept through the southern Plateau in both 1800 and 1832, and caused the extinction of a Carrier band in the Ootsa Lake region in 1837. The most devastating smallpox epidemic occurred in the winter of 1862. The overall Indian population of B.C. was reduced by a third, and among the Shuswap alone seven bands along the Fraser River were virtually wiped out. Chilcotin bands moved eastward to occupy land formerly held by the Shuswap; in turn, the southern Carrier moved southward into formerly Chilcotin territory. By the 1800s the Nicola were absorbed by the Nlaka'pamux (Thompson), while in more recent times most of the Lakes Indians removed to the United States. The groups in the Canadian Plateau are indicated in Table 20.1.

Table 20.1
Plateau Language Groups

Language Family	Language	Sub-grouping
Salish	Lillooet	Upper Lillooet
		Lower Lillooet
	Thompson	Upper Thompson
		Lower Thompson
	Shuswap	Fraser River
		Canyon (Chilcotin R.)
		Lake (Shuswap Lake)
		North Thompson
		Bonaparte
		Kamloops
	Okanagan	North Okanagan
		Similkameen
		South Okanagan
	Lakes	
Athapaskan	Carrier	Central Carrier
		Southern Carrier
	Babine	
	(Northern Carrier)	
	Chilcotin	
	Nicola	
(none – an isolate)	Kutenai	Upper Kutenai
		Lower Kutenai

In 1977 the Plateau had 17,161 status Indians, of which 5,314 (31 per cent) resided off reserve. The area contains 32 per cent of the B.C. Indian population.

Plateau Cultural Patterns

The Native societies of the Plateau region show a high degree of cultural diversity, making it somewhat challenging to identify typical Plateau cultural patterns. One of the key features characterizing the Plateau region is the availability of abundant runs of salmon. This feature can be used as a basis on which to identify a common cultural pattern that distinguished

PLATE 20.1. Plateau Indian fishing for salmon on the Fraser River, Lillooet, B.C. Courtesy of the Provincial Archives of British Columbia, HP68625.

Plateau groups from their neighbours. Other dominant cultural features of the Plateau in the 1800s were: the establishment of semi-permanent winter or summer villages, and the existence of kinship groups within each band that exercised ownership over resources and strictly regulated access to them.

Plateau groups gained access to salmon through three major river systems: the Fraser, Skeena, and Columbia. Salmon, however, were not evenly distributed throughout the region. While most Native groups on the lower Fraser had access to all five species of salmon, those communities situated on the upriver watersheds were almost totally dependent on single runs. The size of these individual runs could vary tremendously from year to year. For example, a recent four-year cycle of sockeye runs in the Stuart Lake watershed was estimated at 589,600, 35,500, 26,800 and 24,500. Groups such as the Stuart Lake Carrier coped with these regular fluctuations in salmon availability by travelling to different watersheds to obtain salmon through fishing or trade with neighbouring Carrier bands. Other Plateau groups, such as the southern Carrier and the upper north Thompson Shuswap, had fewer salmon resources or the salmon were less accessible. Consequently, most of these groups followed a more mobile lifestyle in which game and freshwater fish were of primary importance and in which permanent villages were lacking. These groups are the exceptions to the typical pattern of Plateau cultures.

Plateau groups followed a similar annual round of subsistence activities. In the summer, families congregated along major rivers to trap and process salmon for the winter months. Many different species of berries were collected and dried into small cakes. In the southern Plateau roots, especially bitterroot and camas, were important to the diet and were steamed in underground pits. In the fall, families dispersed to the mountain regions to hunt large game and to prepare dry meat for the winter. Deer were the most important large game animals hunted in the southern Plateau, while before 1850 caribou were the most important large game animals in the northern Plateau. The caribou range has since shrunk due to a warming trend, and moose have now become plentiful and an important source of meat in northern regions. In the winter, those groups having access to abundant salmon resources congregated in semi-permanent villages, where stores of dried salmon sustained them through the cold months. Other groups, such as the southern Carrier and north Thompson Shuswap, dispersed into small groups of perhaps two to three families and turned to ice-fishing and rabbit-snaring for subsistence. In the lean months of early spring, when resources were at their lowest, families might sustain themselves on black lichen or the sugar-rich inner rind of the jackpine before travelling to distant lakes to trap the spawning trout and suckers.

Trade was also important to the economy of Plateau groups. The Wet'suwet'en (Bulkley River Carrier) and Ulkatcho Carrier had close social and economic ties with the neighbouring Northwest Coast societies. The Ulkatcho Carrier obtained salmon from the Nuxalk (Bella Coola) and often wintered with relatives among this nation. Some Wet'suwet'en Carrier spent the winter months with the Gitksan at the village of Hazelton, and in the springtime Wet'suwet'en occasionally travelled to the Nass River to participate in the oolichan fishery alongside the Nisga'a.

Plateau groups in the 1800s recognized several different levels of social organization. The most important social group, in terms of day-to-day domestic activities, was the extended family, which hunted, fished, and gathered materials necessary for survival. Groups of related families that used a common territory constituted a band, which was named after the territory it occupied. Each band had from one to several villages that were occupied in the winter months. The village group was an intermediary level of social organization made up of closely related families. Most Plateau groups had these three levels of organization, although the social and economic significance of each varied between groups. Most of the Carrier, in addition, had a fourth level of social organization in the form of matrilineal clans. Some Plateau groups, such as the Chilcotin and Shuswap, had a sense of common tribal identity, while others, such as the Carrier, recognized neither tribal nor linguistic unity.

Kinship among the Plateau groups, with the exception of some of the Carrier, was reckoned along bilateral lines – that is, it was traced through both the father's and mother's lines. Rules of local group exogamy meant that people were compelled to marry outside of their village group, and often outside of their band. Bilateral kinship, the rule of exogamy, and the ethic of sharing and providing assistance to kin resulted in the creation of a network of relatives throughout the region who could be called upon to provide food, assistance, and access to hunting and fishing grounds when resources in one's own territory were scarce.

Being able to trace kinship ties was not necessarily enough to enable a person to gain access to resources in different territories. Equally important were how closely one was related and how one was related. This brings up the third defining feature of Plateau groups: the existence within each band of kinship groups that exercised exclusive rights to access and use valuable resources, with those groups most dependent on the rich salmon resources having the most formally developed and restrictive systems. Plateau societies have not remained static over time, however, and over the centuries there may well have been fluctuations in the degree to which specific ownership rights were exercised by kinship groups. The discussion here relates to Plateau cultures during the 1800s.

Among most Plateau groups the most productive salmon-fishing sites were controlled by specific individuals or families. Access to these sites was restricted to close kin only. Groups such as the Lillooet (Stl'atl'imx), in addition to individual or family fishing stations, also had fishing sites open only to village members, while the less productive fishing stations were open to anyone. The Shuswap along the Fraser River also recognized the exclusive rights of families to salmon-fishing stations. Berry grounds, while open to all the Shuswap nation, were nevertheless strictly controlled by the hereditary band chief in whose territory the grounds were situated. The chief would allow harvesting to proceed only when the berries were sufficiently ripe. Eagle cliffs and deer fences were owned by individuals and were inherited by the closest kin. In contrast, the northern and central Carrier bands were divided into matrilineal clans

PLATE 20.2. Kutenai Indian family, ca. 1914. Note the influences of neighbouring Plains groups in dress and tepee styles. Courtesy of the Provincial Archives of British Columbia, HP73839.

whose hereditary chiefs exercised exclusive control over specific tracts of land, including not only salmon-fishing stations but also hunting and trapping grounds and berry patches. Only clan members were permitted to use the resources in these territories. Although the Plateau groups differed in the type of kinship groups that developed to restrict access to the resources – and, as in the case of the Shuswap, the different levels of social organization were associated with control over different resources – most included some dimension of restrictive, exclusive control. On this basis Plateau groups can be distinguished from Subarctic Native cultures.

Plateau cultures varied also as a result of their interaction with neighbouring nations. During the early 1800s, as a result of the intensification of social and trade relations between the interior and coastal nations, the traditions of clan organization, social classes recognizing a nobility, and potlatch ceremonialism began to spread from the Northwest Coast societies to the southern Carrier, Chilcotin, and Shuswap. These groups simultaneously incorporated and modified these traditions. Clans, for example, became bilateral in order to fit the system of social organization operating in the new settings. Although the ethnographic information is limited, it appears that each dominant family within a band became associated with a clan, and by the mid-1800s Shuswap families were exercising ownership rights to fishing stations in the name of their clan. The clan system never became fully entrenched among them, though, and it began to disappear after the rapid population decline brought about by the 1862 smallpox epidemic. Clans, however, have a longer history of existence among the northern Carrier, and persist today among both the northern and central Carrier. Debates continue today as to whether these matrilineal clans are an archaic feature of Carrier culture or were introduced to the northern Carrier during the late eighteenth century through contact with the Gitksan. In the southern Plateau, the Kutenai were greatly influenced by their associations with the Plains nations. The Kutenai regularly travelled across the Rocky Mountains to hunt for buffalo, and much of their technology, such as tepee and dress styles, as well as their Sun Dance ceremonialism, bears the Plains cultural influence.

Origins

To a nation composed mainly of immigrants, questions of origins and "first arrivals" seem important. Many non-Natives, for example, enjoy studying their personal family history and tracing their roots back generations to different countries of origin. Archaeologists share these concerns with "first arrivals" and seek to answer questions regarding the origins of Native peoples in North America. To indigenous peoples, however, these questions are irrelevant; indigenous peoples have always been here. Plateau Indians explain origins in terms of how the earth was transformed by ancestral beings and how people separated from the rest of nature, receiving mortality as the price for guaranteed salmon runs, sunlight, and other things. Archaeological and indigenous approaches to the issue of origins are rooted in different cultural perspectives on the past; both address the reality that Indian people have occupied the Plateau for a long, long time.

Like other Interior Salish, the Okanagan trace their origin to the actions of the Creator, or Old One. Specific features of the landscape, though, are attributed to the actions of Coyote, whose wanderings resulted, among other events, in the introduction of salmon to the Columbia River system. Coyote is also responsible for the absence of salmon in the Similkameen River. Once Coyote was denied a woman he sought from the Similkameen people. In retaliation he dammed the mouth of the Similkameen River, forever blocking the passage of salmon. The presence today of kokanee, a land-locked salmon, in the Similkameen suggests that salmon once did ascend its waterways to spawn, but a rock slide at some unknown time forever eliminated the runs. The contrast between indigenous and non-Native interpretations of the significance of landscape symbolizes the different cultural approaches that the two groups use to conceptualize history.

Colonial Political Economy

The colonial presence in the Plateau is relatively recent. It was not until the first decade of the 1800s that trade posts were established in the northern Plateau, although European trade goods had become part of the material culture by the late 1700s. From the northern interior posts the traders explored further south, Simon Fraser reaching the mouth of the Fraser River in 1808 and David Thompson the mouth of the Columbia in 1811. Through these explorations the fur trade gradually expanded into the Plateau, and by 1821 a string of trading posts had been set up. The fur trade relied heavily on Indian participation. The forts depended on Natives not only as suppliers of furs, but also as providers of salmon, on which the forts based their subsistence. Natives also served important roles as messengers and labourers. While the fur trade did initiate some changes in technology and land tenure, its overall effect on Plateau cultures was minor, and Native/trader relations were relatively balanced.

This tenuous equilibrium was shattered with a series of gold rushes in the British Columbia interior during the 1850s and 1860s. The Cariboo gold rush alone drew thousands of miners northward into Shuswap and Carrier territories. At the same time the smallpox epidemic of 1862 struck the Plateau region, wiping out entire bands and causing dramatic depopulation among the Native groups, who had no natural immunity to the disease. Natives were outnumbered by miners and were displaced from their hunting grounds, and hydraulic mining practices damaged or destroyed a number of valuable salmon spawning beds on which these groups depended. The major interior gold rushes ended by the 1870s, and in their wake came colonial administrators and settlers.

The central and southern Plateau contained rich agricultural lands. By the 1880s much of the cultivatable land had been pre-empted. As farms and ranches were established and fences erected, Plateau groups lost access to some of their hunting territories and fishing stations. The 1860 Land Ordinance had prohibited the pre-emption of Indian villages and fields, but even this minimum protection of Native rights had been ineffectual. Due to the lax administration of the times, on a number of occasions settlers were able to pre-empt Native homesteads and cultivated

PLATE 20.3. A group of Chilcotin Indians in Lillooet, B.C., may have been employed as ranch hands in the surrounding area. Courtesy of the Provincial Archives of British Columbia, HP90320.

fields. After 1866 the land rights that were extended to settlers were denied to Indians. While non-Natives could apply for free grants of land, Indians were prohibited from using the pre-emption system at all. The failure of governments to recognize Aboriginal rights to hunting or fishing grounds, and to sign treaties to formally acquire Indian lands, further exacerbated Indian/settler land conflicts. Small reserves were established in the late 1800s, but the issue of Aboriginal title continued to be ignored by governments.

By the 1880s Indian agents had arrived and were attempting to implement the terms of the Indian Act. Government control over Indian fishing, hunting, and trapping was extended in the following decades. Fishing by means of nets, fences, and basket traps was outlawed by federal fisheries regulations, hunting was restricted, and trapping was brought under government control. B.C. Native leaders continued to lobby for government recognition of Aboriginal title, and their campaign gained momentum in the 1910s and 1920s. In response, in 1927 the federal government passed legislation to make it illegal for Indians to collect or donate money for the purpose of pursuing land claims.

Plateau groups responded in a variety of ways to these forces of change. Many Natives took advantage of the economic opportunities created by the colonial economies and played an important role in the gold rushes, working as miners, guides, and freighters. As the agriculture industry developed, Natives took jobs as cowboys, farm labourers, and migrant harvesters. As well, many families incorporated small-scale cattle- and horse-raising into their round of economic activity, sold their stock on the local market, and successfully competed with non-Native ranchers. Natives also played significant roles in the transportation industry, hauling supplies by team and wagon into the northern interior and the Chilcotin plateau. Native labourers cut ties and timbers and freighted supplies during the construction of the Canadian Pacific Railway in the 1880s, and later for the Grand Trunk and Pacific Great Eastern railways in the early 1900s. Ironically, these railways also signalled the end of Native employment in small-scale freighting; further, the railways undermined Native rights by enabling non-Native settlement and the expansion of resource industries into previously isolated regions.

The colonial economy had varying impacts in different regions of the Plateau. Shuswap and Okanagan territories were settled early, and these groups responded by developing a mixed economy in which wage labour and stock-raising existed alongside trapping, hunting, and fishing. Other groups, such as the Chilcotin and Carrier, occupied lands more marginal to non-Native interests and were able to maintain a measure of control over their lands, continuing to follow a subsistence lifestyle based primarily on hunting, fishing, and trapping. With the rapid growth of the logging industry in the post-World War Two period the lifestyle and cultures of these more remote groups have begun to be significantly disrupted.

Contemporary Issues: Resource Conflicts

A number of resource conflicts in the Plateau emerged as significant issues in the 1980s and 1990s. North of the town of Lytton, at the confluence of the Fraser and Thompson rivers, the Stein Valley became a focal point for conflicts between the Nlaka'pamux (Thompson) and forestry companies. The Stein Valley is an area of much cultural significance, with pictographs, camps, trails, and other sites of historical and cultural importance to the Nlaka'pamux. Proposals to carry out logging activities in the valley are still under negotiations. Other Plateau regions have similar histories.

Fraser River fisheries and water flows have also emerged as significant issues in the 1990s. Carrier bands along the Nechako River, a major tributary of the Fraser River, have been outspoken in their opposition to plans by the Aluminium Company of Canada (ALCAN) to complete a hydroelectric project, known as Kemano II. A series of hearings on impacts on this part of the watershed commenced in 1993. Members of one Carrier band, the Cheslatta Carrier, with its traditional territories at the headwaters of the Nechako River, were relocated from three villages at Cheslatta Lake in the early 1950s to allow the lake to be used as a water spillway. Today the Cheslatta argue that the completion of the hydroelectric project would re-create the devastating economic and social problems that arose during the 1950s consequent to their relocation, a legacy the Cheslatta argue has lasted to the present.

The Fraser River system, at the heart of the Canadian Plateau, is heavily industrialized, and a number of bands have raised more general concerns about deteriorating fisheries because of water pollution. A related issue is the twinning of existing rail lines along the Fraser and Thompson rivers and the possible damage this may cause to salmon habitat. Construction requires either digging into the hillsides or expanding into the river by filling in sections. Further, many of the areas slated for expansion run through Indian reserves, many of which contain villages, cemeteries, and fishing stations. In response to this crisis, Indian bands from the lower Fraser Valley to the headwaters of the Thompson River formed an organization, the Alliance of Tribal Councils, to oppose what has become known as the CN Twin Tracking project. The Alliance crosses a number of different languages and traditional political jurisdictions. The main concerns of the Alliance centre on potential loss of reserve lands, cemeteries, and heritage sites, increased rail traffic, reduced access to traditional fishing sites, and potential loss of spawning habitats in upriver regions.

Part of the concern is that events of 1913 might be repeated. Railway construction along a stretch of the Fraser River known as Hell's Gate resulted in tonnes of rock being blasted into the river, obstructing the passage of migrating salmon. Salmon runs in the Fraser River system were almost eliminated. To many interior Indian groups, it was a time of great deprivation.

In the late 1980s the Alliance of Tribal Councils (now known as the Alliance of Tribal Nations) initiated court action to prevent construction of the second rail line, and the matter is now before the courts.

Contemporary Social Issues

One of the most important issues discussed among Canadian Aboriginal peoples in recent years has been the impact of the Indian residential school system. Indian residential schools were a joint venture of the federal government and various religious denominations. They existed for over a century, the last ones closing only in the 1970s. Native children were removed from their homes and were raised in church-run boarding schools, where they were taught Christian beliefs and morality as well as agricultural, trade, and domestic skills. The explicit goal of the schools was to remove children from the "harmful" cultural environment of their families so as to prevent the transmission of cultural knowledge, values, and beliefs.

Native people in the Plateau region are now examining the long-term psychological and social consequences to their communities of the residential schools' assimilation program. In 1991 the Cariboo Tribal Council hosted a four-day national conference that served to galvanize public and media attention to the issue. Many people spoke about their own experiences at the schools and the suffering they underwent as a result of being separated from their families, subjected to harsh physical punishment, denied the right to speak their Native language, and indoctrinated with messages of personal and cultural inferiority. Many Native leaders today link the residential school experience to social problems faced by many reserve communities, problems that range from alcoholism, suicide, sexual abuse, and family violence to low self-esteem, loss of initiative, and enforced dependency.

A number of Plateau communities have taken steps to address these issues by developing their own social programs and systems of justice rather than turning to outside governmental agencies for assistance. In 1980 the Spallumcheen First Nation became the first Indian band in British Columbia to sign a child welfare agreement with the province. In an effort to stem the apprehension of children from the community by provincial human resources workers, the Spallumcheen band council persuaded the provincial government to recognize its authority and responsibility for providing for the care of its own children and for the support and treatment of families in crisis.

The need for a separate justice system, controlled and operated by First Nations, was emphasized in the 1993 report of the provincial Cariboo-Chilcotin Justice Inquiry. The report documented a number of cases in which RCMP officers abused their authority and applied excessive force and intimidation in their interactions with Native people. In several Lillooet communities these problems are being partially addressed through the creation of a community-based tribal police force, which has assumed authority for maintaining law and order within the reserves. These interim initiatives are being pursued as part of a more general project by Plateau groups to affirm their right to self-government through the negotiated settlement of outstanding Aboriginal title claims.

CHAPTER 21

The Okanagan Indians

Douglas Hudson

Background

The Okanagan Valley of south-central British Columbia and northern Washington is home to the Okanagan Indians. Originally the term referred not to people, but to a place. Literally meaning "head of the river," in reference to the farthest point that salmon could ascend in the Okanagan system, it indicated a spot near the traditionally important fishing site of Okanagan Falls. The people simply called themselves *ski-luxw*, people, although nowadays they also call themselves Okanagan.

The Okanagan watershed includes the Similkameen and Methow rivers; these areas are inhabited by Okanagan people who have distinct dialects. Very closely related are the languages of three other "tribes," actually better thought of as dialects: Sanpoil-Nespelem on the Columbia River, Colville in the Colville Valley, and Lakes (or Sinixt) in the area of the upper Columbia River, Arrow Lakes, and Slocan Lake in B.C. All these dialects are thought of as comprising the Okanagan-Colville language group.

Table 21.1
Okanagan-Similkameen Bands

Band Name	Band Membership (1986)
Okanagan (also known as Head of the Lake)	960
Westbank	262
Penticton	445
Osoyoos (or Inkameep)	199
Lower Similkameen	237
Upper Similkameen	34

Okanagan Society as Network

Okanagan people interacted with each other and with neighbouring groups on the basis of social rules and tradition in a variety of activities. Three main settings, or frameworks, for interaction can be identified: (1) economic activities, (2) social and political activities, and (3) religious and ceremonial activities. These are analytic categories; in life they were not mutually exclusive. Thus, salmon fishing was an economic activity in that fish were caught and processed; it was a social activity because the people assembled were also engaged in any number of informal activities; and it had religious aspects in that a ritual specialist conducted ceremonies to celebrate the return of the salmon.

Okanagan people moved extensively throughout the region to participate in various economic, social, and ceremonial activities, utilizing a network of relatives and friends. This system ensured that people and food were redistributed, an important feature in a land characterized by seasonal and local variation in resources. It also ensured that the key fishing sites were available to numbers of people. Ultimately any speaker of the Okanagan-Colville language could be considered a potential friend. This network was a major feature of Okanagan society. To understand how it worked – and continues to operate – we need to examine its economic, social, and ceremonial basis.

MAP 21.1. **Okanagan Locations**

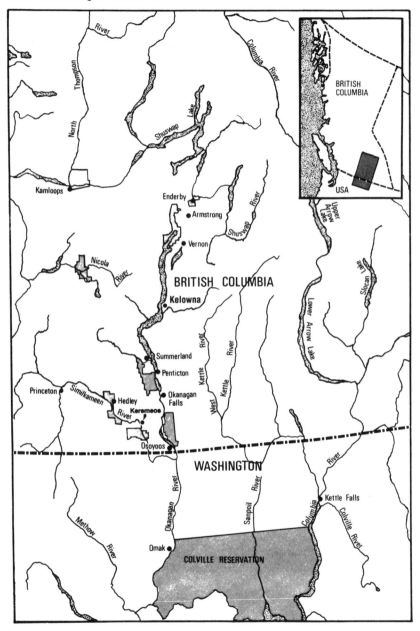

Okanagan Society: Economic Activities

The economic basis of Okanagan society centred on a few key locations where resources could be harvested by relatively large numbers of people at specific times of the year. The most important of these were fishing sites, especially for salmon. The annual subsistence cycle involved extensive movement in the summer and fall and a more sedentary existence during winter, a season of important ceremonies.

Fishing

Most Plateau groups had direct access to productive fishing sites. Streams and lakes provided trout, kokanee, sturgeon, suckers, and a variety of other fish. In the late summer and fall salmon ascended the major rivers to spawn in small tributaries. The canyons through which they passed became important fishing places. The restricted number of canyons in the region meant that people from a large region gathered at them. The most important sites were Shuswap Falls, Okanagan Falls, and Kettle Falls. An 1865 account by Charles Wilson, a member of the Northwest Boundary Commission, outlines their importance:

At the *Okinagan River* a weir, constructed of slight willow wands, was found, which extended right across the stream and at one end had an enclosure into which several openings were left; the remainder of the weir, being nearly, if not quite, impassable, all salmon passing up the river found their way into a sort of "cul-de-sac," where the Indians were busily engaged in spearing them. At the *Kettle Falls* of the Columbia and *Great Falls* of the Spokane, salmon are caught in a large wicker basket, suspended from the rocks at one end of the falls, and projecting slightly into the water. At the foot of the rock there is an eddy, and the water coming down with less force at this point, the salmon here make their chief effort to leap the falls, the greater number, however, fail to clear the rock, many leap right into the basket, whilst others strike their noses against the rock and fall back helplessly into the trap below. (1865: 297)

Salmon fishing was controlled by a salmon chief, who directed the construction of the traps and weirs and performed a ceremony to mark the capture of the first salmon. The first Salmon Ceremony symbolized the community's dependence on salmon and the need to maintain a proper relationship with it. Under the guidance of the salmon chief, the

PLATE 21.1. Salmon-fishing camp, Shuswap, B.C. Note the salmon drying on the racks in the foreground. Courtesy of the Provincial Archives of British Columbia, HP22936.

first salmon caught was cooked and distributed to members of the assembled community. Its bones were returned to the river to maintain the cycle.

The salmon chief also had general supervisory powers, as the following observation from 1865 indicates:

> One blow from their practised hands settles the account of each fish, which is then thrown out on the rocks and carried to the general heap, from which they are portioned out to the different families every evening by a man known as the "salmon chief". . . .

Prohibitions underscored the practical and symbolic importance of salmon. Swimming was banned upriver from the weir, and menstruating women and recent widows and widowers could not come near the weir or eat salmon.

Men built the weir, often to the accompaniment of special songs to ensure success, but the processing of fish fell to the women. While a weir could collect thousands of fish, the availability of female labour to cut and dry the salmon provided an upper limit on the actual number of fish that would be taken. Each family tried to obtain enough salmon to last the winter; some obtained a surplus that could be traded to neighbouring villages for other commodities. As people from miles around gathered at the major sites, these aggregations became festive scenes. They played games (like *lehal*, or "stick game"), raced horses or on foot, traded, talked, and looked around for potential mates. Depending on circumstances, these gatherings could last from June into October.

While salmon were the most important fish in the Plateau, others also had their place. Kokanee were taken at numerous creeks throughout the Okanagan. The Similkameen supported abundant trout, Dolly Varden, and greyling. In spring, suckers were caught in traps as they migrated from lakes to streams. White sturgeon were caught in the major lakes and streams. Ling cod, or "devil fish," were taken in winter with hand lines.

Gathering

Roots, berries, and other plant parts were collected in season from spring to fall and were used for food, drinks, and medicine. Bitterroot (*spitlem*) was most important and was gathered by women in April and May in upland areas. A First Roots Ceremony was held in the southern Okanagan to celebrate the gift of new food and highlight the passage from winter to spring. Turner (1978: 27) provides a description of the ceremony:

> The traditional bitter-root digging grounds of the Penticton people are located up Shingle Creek, west of Penticton, in two high flatlands locally known as Pierre and Roddy Flats. Each year in May when the bitter-root flowerheads appeared, four of the purest maidens of the village were selected to go out hunting and fishing. At the same time, four other women were chosen to pick the first Saskatoon berries, and four young men selected to go out hunting and fishing. When these first harvesters had collected enough roots, berries, and game, a large feast was held to thank the foods for returning once more for the benefit of the people. After this feast, anyone in the village could go out to get bitter-root or Saskatoons.

Like fishing, the harvesting of bitterroot in the spring provided opportunity for people to socialize, tell stories, and exchange goods after the winter months. April itself is called *spitlemtem*, "bitterroot month."

The types of plant foods available to particular groups varied, but most villages had access to bitterroot and abundant berries. In the south, particularly in Washington, camas was an important resource and productive areas attracted people from considerable distances.

Hunting

Okanagan country contained large and small game animals that were either hunted or trapped. Animals hunted included deer, elk, bighorn sheep, and bear. Smaller game used for food included rabbits, marmot, and beaver. There were four great annual hunts: in spring, for deer and sheep; in late fall, for deer, sheep, elk, and bear; in mid-winter, for deer; and late in winter, for sheep. Noted hunters directed collective activities. Success in hunting was seen as the outcome of knowledge and adherence to proper ritual. For example, hunts might be preceded by purification in a sweat lodge.

Networks

Men and women worked together in economic endeavours in a complementary way. In general, men built weirs and hunted while women processed resources and gathered plant foods. Stored food belonged to women, giving them effective control over the household economy and the exchange of food. Both sexes were essential in functioning households.

The very nature of Okanagan social organization linked local production groups in various kinds of exchange. For example, the Ashnola area of the Similkameen was an important mountain sheep habitat. The Ashnola people invited not only neighbouring Similkameen bands but other Okanagan people as well as Thompson and Nicola tribespeople to join the hunt. Osoyoos people went as far as Kettle Falls to dig camas bulbs, and they traded bitterroot, hemp, and blankets to the Thompson and Shuswap Indians for salmon.

Okanagan Society: Social and Political Activities

The basic residential unit of Okanagan society was the village, a cluster of houses containing related people who used the area's resources in common. Villages were occupied primarily during winter; the rest of the year was spent at seasonal hunting, fishing, and gathering camps. The winter village sites were located in protected valleys. People referred to themselves as occupants of a particular winter village. The actual placement of houses in the village depended on the availability of firewood, and through the years a village might move up or down a valley as wood supplies were depleted.

Houses were most commonly built over an excavation of two or three feet and covered with tule mats. Some resembled tepees, while others, housing several families, were oblong in shape. Another structure, less common but still in evidence, was the pit-house, a circular, semi-subterranean lodge covered with turf.

A village contained several special-use structures in addition to its dwellings. A short distance from the houses, small huts were constructed for menstruating women or girls entering puberty. Here they stayed, away from direct interaction with the main camp. Several sweat lodges might also be in evidence, with separate lodges for men and women. Food was stored in raised caches or pits dug into sandy ridges.

Village Organization

Local village autonomy was a feature of Plateau culture. While villages were linked through linguistic and social ties, each retained its independence. For the Okanagan, several house groups, perhaps scattered in contiguous settlements, were seen as a community under the direction of a chief. The chief, usually male, derived his power from his status as a "worthy" man from his family's high status, his knowledge of village affairs, and his ability to merit the respect of others. A chief was followed because of his attributes and did not have power to force people to do his will. Because extensive kinship ties linked most members of the community, a chief was also a person who had a large number of relatives upon whom he could call for assistance and support. The chief's status and knowledge were important in maintaining community relations and ensuring that economic and ceremonial tasks were carried out for the benefit of the whole community. Chieftainship could be inherited; the Okanagan placed great emphasis on the order of birth, and the first-born son of a chief was a prime candidate to be named successor. A council of elders drawn from the community advised the chief and helped choose the successor.

If the community consisted of more than one settlement, each local residential cluster also had a headman, who took on some of the tasks of chief. A headman had responsibility to direct the group in successful hunting by his dream power. Further, each house group in a settlement had a "house leader" – usually the eldest male – who represented the house group in dealings with the rest of the community. In parts of the southern Okanagan the chief did not give directions himself but through a spokesman. However, the informality of daily living and the required seasonal movements mitigated against the formalizing of power.

The chief functioned in a variety of capacities. A salmon chief directed the construction and operation of a fish weir, and a shaman directed activities during winter dances and healing ceremonies. Thus it may be appropriate to view chieftainship not as general, but to see chiefs and headmen as managers of a series of specific activities – economic, social, political, and ceremonial – for which they had the required knowledge, ability, and respect.

The essence of the Okanagan political system is evident in the observations made by a fur trader in the early 1800s:

> The government, or ruling power among the Oakinackens (Sinkaietk) is simple yet effective, and is little more than an ideal system of control. The chieftainship descends from father to son: it is, however, merely a nominal superiority in most cases. Their general maxim is, that Indians were born to be free, and that no man has natural right to the obedience of another, except he be rich in horses and has many wives; yet it is wonderful how well the government works for the general good, and without any coercive power to back the will of the chief, he is seldom disobeyed: the people submit without a murmur. (Walters, 1938: 94)

That chieftainship was to some extent inherited raises the question of whether, or to what extent, social classes existed. The Okanagan did not have a rigorous division into a high and low class. Rather, there were families whose members were considered to be of high status and morality, while other families had "lost their history." In other words, gaining authority was partly based on prestige, which in turn reflected proper conduct, and was partly based on institutional factors, such as being an eldest son. Those who had no history had lost, through accident or poor choice, the respect of the community and thus lacked relatives who would attest to their character and rights to particular positions. In a sense they had lost their place in the kinship system.

Ownership

Okanagan communities were kinship-based, and all rights of ownership and access to resources must be seen in this light. Property could be corporeal or incorporeal. Corporeal property refers to tangibles like land and material objects. The group – family, village, or band – owned resource areas in the sense that its members reproduced rights of access and control over them. Others could participate, but only with permission. Chiefs managed, and in that sense owned, resource areas, but the extensive ties that united Okanagan people created a social universe of friends, relatives, and neighbours. Thus, in a sense, the region and its resources were owned by all Okanagan collectively, with local resources controlled by various kinship and residential groups.

Incorporeal property, such as guardian spirits, songs, and dances, was owned by individuals, in that they alone had the right to perform a particular dance or song. However, there was also a social, or group, aspect to this ownership. Names were seen as the property of families, and particular names were inherited or transmitted within kin groups. Possessors of particular names, though, could confer them on others if compensated – although again the names stayed within particular families. Special songs and dances might also be transferred from a parent to a child.

Social Units

Although the nuclear family – the husband-wife pair and their unmarried children – existed in traditional Okanagan society, it was economically and socially submerged in the extended family that was the basic social unit and the primary unit of production and consumption. A household was usually an extended family and might consist of two brothers and their wives and children, or of an older couple with their married children, or of "cousins" living with their families. A rich man might establish a polygynous family (multiple wives).

The kindred (all one's relatives traced through the families of both parents) were important to the Okanagan. Kin provided security and protection; in neighbouring villages there would usually be at least one member of one's kindred, or *chichops*, "relatives." Another category of kin was the *kalh*, the descendants of a particular grandparent or great-grandparent. For example, two people who are descendants of the Okanagan person known as Quinisco would consider themselves *kalhquinisco*, with special obligations of mutual respect and support. Membership in a *kalh* is traced through male and female lines.

Kinship Terms

Okanagan kinship terms were organized on different principles than those of English. (1) Different terms were used by male and female speakers. Therefore, the sex of the speaker was important. Males and females defined social relations in different ways, as reflected in the use of kinship terms. Not all terms differed, however – just those for very close kin. (2) Different terms were used for older and younger siblings, indicating that age was important (recall that the eldest son was most likely to inherit his father's position). (3) Sibling terms were extended to cover children of parents' siblings (people whom an English speaker would call "cousin" were called "brother" and "sister"). This reflects the social basis of kinship terms in all societies; parents' siblings' children are in the same kindred as ego and therefore called by a term reflecting common membership in a social group and best translated as "person of my generation in my social group."

The determination of potential mates was another aspect of Okanagan kinship. Genealogies were the topics of extended conversations. As one person commented, "First and second cousins are *skuit*, just like your own brother and sister. You can't marry them. Perhaps you can marry a third cousin." That marriages were arranged helped to ensure that they took place between families of similar social standing. The parents initiated the proceedings with a series of small exchanges, some of which predated the actual marriage, while others continued for years after. These economic exchanges gave the marriage stability by emphasizing that marriage was the concern of the group.

Life Cycle

The Okanagan life cycle emphasized several key events and periods in one's life, starting with birth.

Birth

The birth of a child received special recognition. One of the earliest descriptions of an Okanagan birth ceremony came from an account in 1865:

> After childbirth, the women have to live apart for about thirty days, frequently washing themselves, and, before joining the others, they have to wash all their clothes and undergo general purification. A small lodge is erected about ten or twelve paces from the large or family one, and in this the woman lives during the period of her seclusion, which is kept with great strictness, notwithstanding the close proximity of her friends and relations. When the time of childbirth is felt to be approaching, the woman goes out and plucks a sprig of the wild rose, which she places upright in the ground of the lodge and fixes her eyes upon it during the pangs of labour, which, it is believed, are alleviated by this ceremony. The rattles of the rattlesnake are also frequently used as a medicine to procure ease in the same cases. (Wilson, 1865: 294)

Following their seclusion, mother and child were welcomed back into the community by the elders. In some cases a few relatives and close friends gave an informal feast. For the next few years the baby was carried in a cradle. The infant received a temporary name during the first year, then an ancestral name was conferred, usually by a grandparent. The name had to be purchased if a person using it was still alive. The name could come from either the mother's or the father's side. Boys often received names of animals and girls of plants.

Childhood

In childhood boys and girls gradually learned the distinctions between male and female roles. Education was largely informal, through observation, oral history, and comments from elders. Tales were used to teach children, and to remind adults, about the importance of proper conduct. Parts of the physical landscape were used as reference points for information, where events were associated with natural rock formations or other features.

Boys learned to hunt and fight. Their first animal kill went to the elders for redistribution, thus reinforcing the power of the group over the individual. Similarly, girls learned skills needed to perform successfully as adults – the techniques of gathering and root-digging, for example. Children's play emulated tasks and roles to be performed later as adults. For example, they might play with miniature fish weirs.

Adults forced children to take early morning swims in icy water and sweats in lodges to build their character and prepare them for the change from childhood to adulthood, which was signalled by the guardian spirit quest.

Guardian Spirit Quest

The transition from childhood to adulthood was an important event for males and females at puberty. Just prior to the onset of puberty, boys went into the countryside to obtain a guardian spirit, which came in a vision. This quest sought the transfer of power from the natural to the social world and, if successful, a boy had a spirit helper for the rest of his life. Boys prepared for the quest by fasting, sweating, and physical exercise.

After preparation, a boy went to an isolated area and sought for four days the vision of a guardian spirit. One man, as a boy, dove to the bottom of a lake every day for three days without achieving a vision. On the fourth day, a human figure appeared, announcing that it was a particular animal, and from that day on the boy would be able to draw on its power in times of need. This power, *sumix*, had to be sought and obtained prior to or at puberty. After puberty the search would prove fruitless. Not all who sought a guardian spirit found one, and those who obtained one did not become fully aware of its power until later in life. Thus the quest of a guardian spirit, whose assistance was essential to adult success, came just at the point when boys faced manhood.

Girls also received instruction at puberty, going to special places of retreat. These places often were the tops of large, flat rock formations that even today are marked by the circle of rocks placed around each girl in her vigil.

Marriage

Parents arranged the marriages of their children, initiating a series of exchanges. An early exchange might feature the parents of the boy giving fish and meat (symbolic of male activities) to the parents of the girl, who in turn gave roots and berries. After marriage, a couple usually lived in the village of the husband, although the social network provided for other residential options.

It was during adulthood that the power of a personal supernatural began to be revealed, requiring a man to "dance out the power" at a winter ceremony. It seems that social maturation was paralleled by spiritual maturation. Thus marriage and participation in winter ceremonies marked the complete transition to adult male status in Okanagan society.

Death

The deceased were buried in talus slopes. Special belongings, perhaps copper pendants or dentalia, were interred also. Death brought an obvious end to a person's direct participation in society, but names borne by the deceased remained in the extended family or kindred and were transferred to descendants. The birth of children who were given ancestral names maintained the family over generations; the use of previous names reinforced a world view in which the past merged with the present in a common social sphere.

Male-Female Relations

Children were born into well-defined male and female roles; by the onset of puberty, they had a good notion of their place in society. While the kinship system emphasized the importance of tracing relatives through both the father's and the mother's sides, a tendency to stress male relations existed. This "patrilateral bias" was reflected in residence patterns, the political system, and elsewhere. Women, however, did control stored food, giving them some power. The relationship between males and females in Okanagan society was expressed as being similar to two fir trees growing up beside each other: one, a male tree, was tall, with few limbs; the other, a female, was low with heavy limbs.

Okanagan Society: The Ceremonial Framework of Action

The tension between individual rights and collective responsibilities ran as a constant theme through Okanagan society. This is perhaps best expressed in concepts and ceremonies where power (*sumix*) is in focus. Through the spirit quest an individual acquired power, but the community, probably through a shaman, guided the individual to use that power to benefit the community.

Although spiritual power was a dominant aspect of many Okanagan ceremonies, secular ceremonies also occurred. The following types of ceremonies can be identified. (1) Renewal ceremonies (such as the first-root and first-salmon ceremonies) emphasized the continuation of important food resources. (2) Redistributive ceremonies were secular and included naming ceremonies and a more elaborate distribution called the potlatch. (Perhaps "potlatch" is a term best reserved for the formal exchange ceremonies among Northwest Coast groups; while the Okanagan redistributed goods and food at a number of social occasions, none are actually called potlatches. It also appears that those Okanagan who recalled potlatching saw it as something peripheral to traditional Okanagan culture but part of the culture of the Thompson and Shuswap Indians.) (3) Power ceremonies, including the Winter Dance and the Medicine Dance, focused on spiritual matters.

Winter Dance

The most important Okanagan ceremony, one in which spiritual power was a key element, was the Winter Dance, held when people gathered in their winter villages.

According to the Okanagan view of the world, the power, which one acquired through the guardian spirit quest, required dancing or else the possessor would die. Power itself was not equally distributed. Only males obtained it, and it had two levels: power that could be used to protect oneself, and power that could be used to help – or hurt – others. Not everyone had this second curing power, and some used it to harm people; sickness, for example, might be attributed to natural causes or to the direct actions of a malevolent shaman. The distinctions between the two main types of spiritual power are reflected in the Okanagan terms *chuchuin* and *sumix*. *Chuchuin* ("voice" or "whisper") meant that a voice came to a person during the guardian spirit quest, giving him a supernatural helper. But that person had no real *sumix*, or power, merely a spirit helper. *Sumix* came when a person was older – usually when one's hair turned white.

Different animals conferred different kinds of power. Most power came from grizzly bear, cougar, blue jay, rattlesnake, and eagle – all of which gave the possessor the power to cure. Blue jay also gave power to find drowned or lost people.

To perform at a winter dance required several steps. A neophyte had a power dream in which the guardian spirit required a dance. He then sought the service of a ritual expert (shaman, or medicine man) as master of ceremonies. A central post was erected in the dance lodge, and, in some cases, the lodge was ceremonially swept to purify it. The neophyte then danced before the assembled group and distributed gifts. Other people then expressed their power in dance.

Summary

The continued operation of Okanagan society and culture required a successful and efficient technology and a flexible and workable social system that enabled people to gather in great numbers at appropriate times, yet facilitated the movement of people between different areas and villages. Traditional Okanagan society was held together in a variety of ways. Through a multitude of social ties, primarily based in kinship, most Okanagan were linked and could enlist aid from people in numerous places. Collaborative activities such as deer hunting and salmon fishing facilitated inter-group exchanges. Participation in ceremonies involving large groups of people reinforced mutual systems of meaning and identity.

Post-Contact Change in Okanagan Life

The earliest changes in Okanagan life associated with European contact were in their fashion profound, but they were incorporated into ongoing patterns with relatively little disruption. The fur trade did not threaten Indian ways of organizing social relations, of using the land, or of developing power. The most disruptive events of the early and mid-1800s were the diseases that left devastation and demoralization in their wake.

Until the 1860s the Okanagan Valley represented a means of getting somewhere else – a route for shipping furs and trade goods to distant markets or a passageway to beckoning gold fields. The 1860s brought prospectors and ranchers, both representing a new kind of claim on lands traditionally used by Indians. A customs post was established at Osoyoos in 1862; a trading post and store were opened in 1866 at Penticton; and more land became pre-empted by ranchers and settlers. The pressure grew on the government to restrict the movements and land holdings of the Indians in the region. What had been Indian territory became plots of land owned by Euro-Canadians. Other parcels of land were surveyed as Indian reserves, a process that took years to complete because of conflicts between the B.C. government and Ottawa.

Economic Changes

As the Okanagan region became incorporated into an expanding Canadian society and economy, Indian labour became more important for economic activities dominated by non-Indians. These included ranching, farming, logging and sawmilling, and other activities.

It is significant that Indians were quick to engage in economic activity on an ownership basis. Freighting and ranching were two such enterprises in which Okanagan Indians were conspicuously active. However, Indian cattlemen raised stock on common range lands open to all ranchers (called a commonage) south of Vernon only until access was curtailed, largely due to pressures from non-Indian ranchers. Similarly, Indian cattlemen drove stock from Keremeos to Princeton for seasonal grazing until their use of "free range" was also curtailed. Some Okanagan reserves were large enough that some cattle could still be raised, but they could never become competitive with non-Indian ranchers.

While some traditional economic activities remain important for many Okanagans, fundamental changes have taken place. Many of the ancient fishing places are no longer viable. Okanagan Falls has been dammed; Kettle Falls was flooded by the construction of Grand Coulee dam in the 1930s; and the number of salmon reaching the Okanagan River system has diminished following the construction of dams along the Columbia River. Weirs and fish traps were banned by the Canadian government around the turn of the century, and they were destroyed by fisheries wardens throughout the Okanagan. Urbanization and the rerouting of streams have further diminished fish production.

Religious Changes

The continuation of winter dances, guardian spirit quests, and other activities associated with spirit power was anathema to the missionaries who moved into the Okanagan Valley. Adherents of spirit power were at one time forbidden to attend churches and winter ceremonies were condemned. Given the Okanagan belief that power had to be danced out, the result of banning spirit dances was predictable. Without the traditional form of releasing power, people were felt to have died because of pent-up pressures. Few guardian spirit quests have been carried out for decades, although the belief that power still exists as a force beyond human control persists. The guardian spirit quest was a culturally recognized means of transferring power from the natural and supernatural worlds to the human world, where it became, in a way, social. A balance between power possessed by humans (as spirit power) and untapped power in the natural and supernatural worlds existed. But that balance has been broken by the suppression of spirit dances, and an overabundance of power is felt to exist outside of human control.

In recent years, there has been a resurgence of winter dances and of practices generally that foster a uniquely Indian identity.

Social and Political Changes

There were some elements of conflict between Okanagan and Europeans from the beginning. An extreme example occurred in 1858 when passing American prospectors massacred twelve Okanagan Indians. More typically, however, frontier society in the Okanagan was characterized by mutual good will and co-operation.

During the late 1800s the economic, political, and social activities of the Okanagan Indians and the Euro-Canadian immigrants became intertwined, with a myriad of reciprocal exchanges. Early writers point to close relations between Indians and non-Indians in the Okanagan, although ignoring the issue of fundamental differences of political power. A description of Penticton as late as the 1920s reads: "At that time we, of the town, lived much closer to our Indian neighbours than we do now. We knew each other by name, stopped to chat on the street and we played together. We depended on hay cut on the reserve or winter pasture for our horses. We bought wood and buckskin gloves from them" (Sismey, 1976: 19).

The Euro-Canadian settlers and their descendants have since created their own version of Okanagan history, one that talks about the material exchanges but sets aside the early social and marriage relations between Indians and non-Indians. The result has been a certain fabrication of social distance between two groups, one readily accepted by more recent immigrants to the Okanagan who know little or nothing of early settler history aside from the official versions.

While informal relations between Okanagan and immigrant neighbours were generally mutually beneficial, formal relations were characterized by changes over which Indians had little control and to which they frequently objected.

The traditional system of leadership was altered by the imposition of external political frameworks. First, Catholic missionaries introduced the Durieu system in B.C. Indian villages about 1875. This system called for Indian church leaders in each village under the supervision of the local priest. Each village had a church chief with captains under his command. Although the ideal was to appoint already established chiefs, the church chiefs were appointed by the priest and were directed to enforce his commands concerning morality and conduct. The influence of the Church declined after the B.C. courts intervened in 1892 following a Lillooet case in which forty lashes were imposed for adultery (Knight, 1978: 247).

A second major change occurred when the Department of Indian Affairs established a system of elected chiefs and councillors to run band affairs. Most of the chiefs elected in this fashion were male, but in 1953 the first woman was elected to the Penticton Indian band council. All Okanagan bands now elect chiefs and councillors.

After Euro-Canadian penetration of the Okanagan, much of the responsibility for services shifted to non-Okanagan institutions, and it became difficult to retain many cultural practices. The residential schools played an important part in undermining the teaching of traditional culture. Children began to spend most of the year in a residential school some distance from their home village. Forbidden to speak their languages, the children became isolated from the teachings of their parents and elders. Older Okanagan people retain the experiences of residential school life: cooking, washing clothes, splitting firewood, growing crops, and instruction in a foreign language (English). Perhaps with the best intentions, the residential schools operated on the premise that the Indian child should be separated from his or her own Indian traditions and family for most of the year.

In the 1870s, frustrated with government inaction on Indian land claims and faced with increasing alienation of Indian lands by settlers and ranchers, some Okanagan and Shuswap people argued for a co-operative venture. Through armed force and a possible association with Chief Joseph and the Nez Perce, then fighting the U.S. government, a resolution to outstanding grievances would be forced. A meeting at the head of Okanagan Lake in 1877 resulted in the formation of a Shuswap-Okanagan Confederacy. No armed resistance came, however, and the nascent confederation was effectively broken up by the Indian Reserve Commission and priests, who made agreements with individual bands and split the movement.

The governments of B.C. and Canada argued for decades about the sizes of B.C. Indian reserves and struck a committee in 1912 to settle the issue. It held meetings with Indians, chambers of commerce, and other interested parties, and presented a four-volume report in 1916, confirming the boundaries of some reserves, adding to others, and, most importantly, reducing some. In the Okanagan, of 146,427.66 acres of reserve land, the commission cut off 18,536.8 and added 2,600.

To the federal and provincial governments, the issue of reserves was settled. To the Indians, the process by which reserves were diminished was seen as questionable, and bands began research to substantiate claims that some cut-offs were done without the band's permission and that compensation was due. In the 1980s the federal and provincial governments came to an agreement to settle the issue of cut-off lands, and several bands have received compensation. In 1981, for example, the Penticton band received 4,880 hectares of land and $13 million to resolve their cut-off losses. The issue of compensation to Okanagan bands for loss of access to commonages in the early 1900s may also be an issue for the 1990s.

In 1916, several B.C. bands formed an organization called the Allied Tribes of B.C. This organization included the Okanagan. At that time, however, no resolution of land claims issues was possible.

Okanagan involvement in political movements continued throughout the twentieth century. In the late 1960s, Okanagan people were involved in the formation of the Union of B.C. Indian Chiefs. In the 1970s, a majority of the bands in the Okanagan Valley formed the Okanagan Indian Tribal Council, with an office in Penticton. This in turn became part of the Central Interior Indian Tribal Councils, representing interior B.C. Indian bands and tribal organizations. The political picture is more complex today; in the 1980s and 1990s a number of umbrella organizations have emerged. Another important movement rooted in the 1960s and 1970s involving Okanagan people was the Indian women's movement.

Contemporary Resource Use Conflicts

Like other indigenous groups in British Columbia, Okanagan bands have been involved in land and resource use issues. While water levels are an issue throughout the Okanagan Valley, they are of special concern to the Osoyoos band at its southern, downstream, end. Disputes over recreational uses of the Okanagan watershed have resulted in road blockades, especially in areas where road access is through Indian reserves (e.g., Penticton). Potential impacts on archaeological sites are of increasing importance to Okanagan and Similkameen bands, and current research is directed at the identification and protection of indigenous heritage sites in the Okanagan-Similkameen region. This includes village locations, pictographs, ceremonial sites, and parts of the landscape with special cultural meaning. For example, some natural rock formations are discussed as places where Coyote travelled, fished, and carried out various activities. These culturally defined places on the landscape serve as aids in understanding Okanagan-Similkameen cultural history, topography, and ecology. Since 1993, some of my own research has involved working with members of the Upper Similkameen band and an archaeologist in describing and understanding the dimensions of this cultural landscape and discovering how oral traditions, archaeology, and indigenous cultural definitions of the land intersect.

Education

In the past decade, a number of bands and tribal councils have moved toward administering their own educational programs, with the inclusion of indigenous language and culture components. In the late 1970s and early 1980s especially, the issue of representations of Okanagan culture and history emerged as an important issue. To deal with this, a writing and education centre, the En'owkin Centre, was established by the six bands of the Okanagan Tribal Council in 1981 in Penticton.

An important element of the En'owkin Centre is its international school of writing, established to assist First Nations writers and associated with the University of Victoria. The issues of "voice," of cultural representation, and of developing literary styles that extend and connect with traditional modes of representation are important themes at the Centre.

Fieldwork: A Personal Perspective

My fieldwork in anthropology has involved working with a number of groups in the Pacific Northwest and adjacent interior: first with a Carrier band in the north-central interior of B.C. as part of my Ph.D. program (although I later returned to carry out research for the tribal council in the area); and then with Okanagan and Similkameen communities in the southern interior for a year with an educational project (the Okanagan Indian Curriculum Project). My research after that involved land ownership and occupancy studies with the Nisga'a and Taku River Tlingits in the northwestern part of the province, and work with Dunne-za and Saulteaux in the northeast on the cultural importance of a specific part of the Peace River area. More recently, in 1993, I returned to the Similkameen to carry out research associated with the interests of one of the bands and to continue with some of my earlier research questions.

Involvement with these different communities and their histories has caused me to rethink some of the issues in anthropology and to appreciate the different ways in which various communities sought to maintain traditions and control of land – and the ways in which anthropology itself is in a dialectical relationship with these different histories. For example, my work in the Okanagan was as a researcher and curriculum developer for the Okanagan Indian Curriculum Project, involving bands of the Okanagan Tribal Council and school districts, and in that capacity I collected ethnographic and historical data for use in developing educational material more culturally relevant than that in the public schools. As the first full-time employee of the tribal council, I had to develop a new orientation. Abstract anthropological concepts were of little interest to them and my anthropological framework had to be reworked to meet local needs.

The earlier work with the Carrier had been at a time when industrial changes were threatening their traditional economy, as logging competed with hunting and trapping for common habitats. The research with them documented what they had been saying for years – that an important hunting, trapping, and fishing economy rooted in Carrier social institutions and values continued to be economically viable. This was of potential use to the band for educational or legal purposes. It also allowed me to mount an argument (Hudson, 1983) to the effect that Steward (1955) had overstated the extent to which Carrier people had become like the local Euro-Canadian population through acculturation.

The Okanagan people also were attempting to deal with some local problems; one was that Indian history had been reduced to meaninglessness in a region that eulogized the first white settlers. Encouraged by tourist industry that advertised the presence of primitive Indians, the settler society had denied an Indian history in presenting its own.

As a final note on fieldwork, the question of reciprocity must be stressed. In my view anthropological research will increasingly involve debate between what are seen as the intellectual requirements of the discipline and the practical needs of Aboriginals who draw on anthropologists to collect data. The aims of anthropology as a discipline are perhaps not enough to justify research, and one of the tasks of anthropologists will be to integrate academic and practical anthropology, merging theoretical problems from the classroom with practical problems defined by Indian people.

Recommended Readings

Carstens, Peter
    1991 *The Queen's People: A Study of Hegemony, Coercion, and Accommodation among the Okanagan of Canada.* Toronto: University of Toronto Press.
        A critical study of the social and political history of a contemporary northern Okanagan community.
Cline, Walter, *et al.*
    1938 *The Sinkaietk or Southern Okanagan of Washington.* L. Spier, ed. General Series in Anthropology, Vol. 6.
        A collection of articles on the Okanagan Indians of Washington state, based on research in the 1930s.
Lutz, H.
    1991 *Contemporary Challenges: Conversations with Canadian Native Authors.* Saskatoon: Fifth House
        A collection of interviews with Native authors, including one with an Okanagan author.
Ray, Verne
    1939 *Cultural Relations in the Plateau of Northwestern America.* Publications of the Frederick Webb Hodge Anniversary Publication Fund, Vol. III. Los Angeles: The Southwest Museum.
        A classic overview of the basic elements of Plateau culture.
Robinson, Harry
    1989 *Write it on Your Heart: The Epic World of an Okanagan Storyteller.* Compiled by Wendy Wickwire. Vancouver: Talonbooks/Theytus.

1992 *Nature Power: In the Spirit of an Okanagan Storyteller.* Vancouver: Douglas
       & McIntyre.
       Two collections of stories of Okanagan culture and history based on
       interviews with an Okanagan storyteller.
Spencer, Robert, Jesse Jennings, *et al.*
1977 *The Native Americans.* New York: Harper and Row.
       This volume contains an overview of the Sanpoil and Nespelem of the
       southern U.S. plateau; useful for comparative purposes.
Teit, James, and Franz Boas
1930 "The Okanagan." In *The Salishan Tribes of the Western Plateaus.* Bureau of
       American Ethnology, 45th Annual Report.
       A classic account of Plateau culture, although sometimes with an
       overemphasis on Thompson materials.
Turner, Nancy, Randy Bouchard, and Dorothy Kennedy
1980 *Ethnobotany of the Okanagan-Colville Indians of British Columbia and
       Washington.* Victoria: Occasional Papers of the B.C. Provincial Museum, No.
       21.
       An account of Okanagan plant use, with extensive ethnographic
       information.

Additional References Cited

Allison, Susan
1976 *A Pioneer Gentlewoman in British Columbia: The Recollections of Susan
       Allison.* Margaret Ormsby, ed. Vancouver: University of British Columbia
       Press.
Hill-Tout, Charles
1978 *The Salish People,* Vol. 1, *The Thompson and the Okanagan.* R. Maud, ed.
       Vancouver: Talonbooks.
Hudson, Douglas
1983 "Traplines and Timber: Social and Economic Change among the Carrier
       Indians of Northern British Columbia," Ph.D. dissertation, Department of
       Anthropology, University of Alberta.
1990 "The Okanagan Indians of British Columbia," in J. Webber, ed., *Okanagan
       Sources.* Penticton: Theytus.
Kennedy, Dorothy, and Randy Bouchard
1985 "Salish, Interior," *The Canadian Encyclopedia,* Vol. III. Edmonton: Hurtig.
Knight, Rolf
1978 *Indians at Work.* Vancouver: New Star Books.
Sismey, Eric
1976 "Okanagan Days," Okanagan Historical Society, *40th Report.*

Stewart, Julian

 1941 *Recording Culture Changes Among the Carrier Indians of British Columbia.*
      Explorations and Field-work of the Smithsonian Institution in 1940.
      Washington, D.C.: Smithsonian Institution.

 1955 *Theory of Culture Change.* Urbana: University of Illinois Press.

Turner, Nancy

 1978 *Plant Foods of British Columbia Indians, Part 2, Interior Peoples.* Victoria:
      British Columbia Provincial Museum.

Walters, L.

 1938 "Social Structure," in W. Cline *et al., The Sinkaietk or Southern Okanagan of
      Washington.* L. Spier, ed. General Series in Anthropology, Vol. 6.

Wilson, Charles

 1865 *Report on the Tribes Inhabiting the Country in the Vicinity of the 49th
      Parallel.* Transactions of the Ethnological Society, London, New Series,
      Vol. 4.

 1970 *Mapping the Frontier: Charles Wilson's Diary of the Survey of the 49th
      Parallel.* George Stanley, ed. Toronto: Macmillan.

CHAPTER 22

The Carrier Indians and the Politics of History

Elizabeth Furniss

Introduction

The Carrier Indians are a northern Athapaskan-speaking people whose Aboriginal territory stretches across the central interior of British Columbia from the Rocky Mountains in the east to the Coast Mountains in the west. This region, part of the vast interior Plateau, is characterized by generally flat or rolling terrain. Thick forests of spruce, pine, and fir cover the ground, interspersed with numerous large and small lakes, streams, marshes, and meadows. This is the homeland of eighteen Carrier First Nations,[1] each having from one to several reserve villages. Carrier people today are employed in a variety of occupations: they are hunters, fishers, trappers, traditional healers, hereditary chiefs, grandmothers, teachers, politicians, students, lawyers, loggers, and secretaries. Many Carrier people continue to speak their Aboriginal language, and cultural values and beliefs, spiritual concepts, and patterns of family and community organization continue to distinguish the Carrier from other Native nations and from non-Native society in Canada.

I first was introduced to Carrier people in 1985, when I was hired by the Nazko First Nation to conduct ethnographic research on the history of an ancient Aboriginal trade route. The trail, known to the Carrier as the Grease Trail and to non-Natives as the Alexander Mackenzie Heritage Trail, recently had become the focus of government-sponsored tourism development. Alexander Mackenzie's journey down the trail in 1793 was being celebrated as a landmark in Canadian history. In contrast, the Native heritage of the trail had been minimally represented, if not ignored, in the promotional materials. I was hired to produce a documentary video that would provide some balance to the interpretation of the trail's historical significance.

It soon became apparent, though, that the problem of interpretation of the trail's history was not simply one of the omission of Native content. My anthropological interpretation of the trail's Native heritage conflicted sharply with that produced by the trail developers. Somewhat to my surprise, my video sparked heated debates about which was the "true" history of the trail. Through the events of that summer I became interested in the politics of history, especially as they relate to Indian–non-Indian relations in Canada.

History is defined here as a body of knowledge about the past. There is no one "true" version of history; instead, each history is a subjective interpretation of the past. Consequently, many different histories exist, each shaped by the present cultural values, beliefs, and interests of the person creating the account. This does not mean that there are no facts of history. Events do occur. Where historical accounts vary is in which events of the past are highlighted and which are ignored, and in how the significance of these highlighted events is interpreted. The construction of historical accounts involves this process of selecting and interpreting the significance of past events, and this process is fundamentally mediated by the cultural context.

For example, public school history textbooks typically represent Canadian history in terms of the "discovery" of North America by individual explorers, whose courage, perseverance, and faith enabled them to surmount overwhelming obstacles, often represented in terms of a harsh environment and "hostile savages," to bring about ultimately the foundation of the nation of Canada. These histories celebrate some of the key values of contemporary Euro-Canadian culture: individualism, self-reliance, and advancement through hard work, struggle, and self-sacrifice. The early explorers, however, did not achieve these feats alone. They relied heavily on the assistance provided not only by fellow countrymen and women, but also by Native people who served as guides, interpreters, and labourers. Nevertheless, this collective achievement is portrayed in individual, male terms; the figure of the explorer-hero embodies all of the cultural values that guide the contemporary lives of Euro-Canadians. It is significant to look at the events that are not discussed in these textbook histories. These include the Canadian government's less than honourable treatment of Aboriginal peoples and, in regions such as British Columbia, the systematic failure of governments to address the issues of Aboriginal title and rights. The phrase "history is written by the victorious" is sometimes heard, and it is relevant here. This refers to one of the most important political functions of official, government-sanctioned histories, which is to validate events of the past and to legitimate existing institutions and relations of authority within a state. Contentious issues in history often are erased from the historical record. Alternately, the image of the "hostile savage" serves to rationalize Indian-European violence as a natural and inevitable result of the progress of civilization; the image of the friendly Indian assisting the European explorers serves both to suggest Indian approval of the colonial project and to mask the fact that conflicts have permeated events in Canada through the past four centuries.

Histories, however, can function to challenge governmental authority and to draw attention to unresolved historical problems and injustices that occurred in the past. In the summer of 1993 the southern Carrier First Nations used the opportunity of the Mackenzie bicentennial celebrations being held in British Columbia to critique popular conceptions of history. Carrier First Nations leaders were widely quoted by news media when they stated that to celebrate Mackenzie was to celebrate the start of 200 years of colonization and genocide of Aboriginal peoples.

All historical accounts, then, are shaped by the cultural context in which they are produced. The fact that all histories are relative does not mean that anthropology cannot contribute to the understanding of past events. On the contrary, it places anthropology in a unique position among the social sciences. It allows us to explore how different cultural contexts have shaped people's constructions of history, how these versions of history function to make sense of current social relations, and why, therefore, conflicting views of history often become the subject of intense debate.

The accounts of Native cultural history produced by anthropologists also are relative accounts. Anthropological accounts are shaped not only by the anthropologist's cultural situation, in most cases as a member of the dominant society, but also by his or her adherence to a particular theoretical tradition, which defines what questions are important to ask about cultural history. Consequently, it is important for anthropologists, when writing histories, to include some kind of commentary on the conditions, personal and professional, that have shaped the production of their own knowledge. For example, adherence to a particular school of thought, such as materialism, will result in an anthropologist posing different questions and interpreting data differently from an anthropologist using an idealist orientation.

My interests in anthropology, Indian–Euro-Canadian relations, and the politics of history emerged from several different sources. I entered graduate studies in anthropology after receiving an undergraduate degree in the sciences. My primary reasons for turning to anthropology were motivated more by intellectual questions than by ethnographic interests: I wanted to explore the basic question of why people in different cultures hold different beliefs, and why, under certain circumstances such as revitalization movements, people undergo rapid "changes of mind." I had originally planned to return to the more pragmatic field of biological science – and get a secure job with the government – but I enjoyed anthropology so much that I decided to continue on. After a summer living at Nazko and conducting research on the Grease Trail's history, and after completing my Master's degree, which was based on ethnographic research on a contemporary revitalization movement in the Shuswap community of Alkali Lake, I then moved to a city in the central interior of British Columbia. There I took the position of land claims researcher with the Cariboo Tribal Council, which at that time represented both Shuswap and Carrier First Nations, and where I remained for four years. During this time, through developing friendships with Native people and through witnessing the realities of life in a frontier town, my eyes were opened to the dynamics of Indian–non-Indian relations, which, coming from a middle-class upbringing in a virtually homogeneous Euro-Canadian town on Vancouver Island, until then I had not experienced. As a result, I turned to the study of Indian–Euro-Canadian relations and the politics of history, not only as a means of pursuing some academic questions about the nature of culture and society, and about the manner in which knowledge is shaped by relations of unequal power, but also as a way of contributing to a broader practical understanding of some of the problems in their relations with the majority Canadian society that have had tragic consequences for many Native people.

This chapter is centred on the theme of history, and it is relevant to an understanding of the Carrier people today for two different reasons. First of all, history is important as an analytical device. It is both difficult and problematic to reconstruct a "traditional" culture of the Carrier. Instead, their earlier culture is best understood in an historical framework. Through the eighteenth and nineteenth centuries the Carrier were introducing important changes in their culture and socio-political organization, and differences in these areas continue to distinguish different subgroups today. In reality, Carrier culture was and is dynamic and heterogeneous, and cannot easily be described in terms of a list of traits that has remained static through time. Furthermore, in this respect Carrier culture is typical. Culture, as a system of beliefs, values, and practices that characterizes a group and enables its survival in a particular setting, must be continually adaptive to changes in the social and ecological environment. Over the millennia Native societies in Canada have been continually adjusting their cultures to such changes.

Anthropologists have been especially interested in studying the Carrier because of the opportunity they provide to explore the process of cultural change. The classic ethnographies of Morice (1893a, 1893b), Jenness (1943), and Goldman (1940, 1941, 1953) discuss Carrier culture and the manner in which different subgroups, over the last 200-300 years, have adopted the ideas of status hierarchies, clan organization, and potlatching through contact with Northwest Coast societies. In the first section of this paper I provide a brief sketch of nineteenth-century Carrier culture, its regional differences, and the innovations that people were introducing to their culture during this century.

History is important to this discussion for a second reason. History has become a key political resource in the Carrier's struggle to gain government recognition of their Aboriginal rights to land, resources, and self-government. Through these claims First Nations leaders are challenging the official histories that have been promoted by governments, that have been learned in school textbooks and in popular writings, and that exist as common-sense knowledge among the general Canadian public. These accounts typically portray Native societies of the past as "primitive" groups of people who originally had no form of land ownership or concept of property rights, and who now have lost their culture under the impact of European colonization. In contrast, Carrier leaders are seeking to show the legitimacy of pre-European contact forms of government and land ownership, and also the existence of distinct Native cultures in the present. These different representations of Native culture and history are now being vigorously contested in the courts, on the blockades, and in the media. In the second part of this paper I focus on two examples of the contemporary politics of history: the Gitksan and Wet'suwet'en land claims case, and the Nazko and Kluskus First Nations' protest over the development of the Mackenzie Grease Trail.

Carrier Culture and History in the Nineteenth Century

Sources of Information

This chapter relies on written accounts, rather than on primary research of Carrier oral traditions, to reconstruct the culture of the nineteenth-century Carrier. Oral traditions, such as the *kungax* of the Wet'suwet'en, contain a wealth of ethnohistoric information. Some of these traditions have served as primary sources of information for anthropologists such as Jenness (1943) in his reconstruction of Carrier history. In this sense, oral traditions and written anthropological accounts to a degree are interwoven. However, many oral traditions, representing Carrier perspectives on their culture and history, have yet to be fully explored in anthropological studies and would be an important addition to the literature.

The earliest written accounts of the Carrier can be found in the letters, diaries, and journals of the European explorers and fur traders. Alexander Mackenzie, in 1793, was the first European to enter Carrier territory. Both he and Simon Fraser, who explored the Fraser River in 1808, left journals of their explorations, and these journals contain valuable descriptions of Carrier life and customs. By 1807 the North West Company had established trade posts in the region, and the journals of fort employees contain notes on the local Carrier people. Records from Roman Catholic missions serve as additional sources of information.

The most comprehensive written accounts presently available on the nineteenth-century Carrier are found in the writings of the Oblate missionary Adrien Gabriel Morice. Morice arrived at Stuart Lake in 1885 and over the next fifty years published a wealth of ethnographic and linguistic studies. Comprehensive ethnographies are found in Jenness's study of the Wet'suwet'en, or Bulkley River Carrier, based on fieldwork conducted in the 1920s, and in Goldman's publications on the Ulkatcho Carrier, based on fieldwork during the winter of 1935-36. In these and other studies (Duff, 1951; Hackler, 1958; Hudson, 1972, 1983; Kobrinski, 1977), anthropologists have focused much of their attention on three main questions. How can we account for regional differences in Carrier culture? Why have some bands adopted ideas of status hierarchies, clans, and potlatching, while others have not? By tracing the adoption of these ideas by the different Carrier groups, what can we learn in general about how and why cultures change?

There have been two basic approaches to these questions. The first, the materialist approach, emphasizes the role of material and economic factors in shaping culture and cultural change. The ecological environment is believed to impose limitations on the forms of culture that may develop within it. Groups occupying similar environments – arctic tundra, boreal forests, prairie grasslands, tropical rain forests – develop similar technologies and strategies for subsistence, which in turn influence the patterns of social organization and the values and beliefs that develop. Because the technological and subsistence components of culture develop as adaptations to a particular ecological setting, they become the core features of that culture. These features tend to be stable over time, as long as ecological factors remain constant. Consequently, both cultural differences and cultural changes are explained in terms of the variation in economic or ecological factors. For example, diversity among the Carrier subgroups is explained in terms of the differential access that groups had to large, predictable salmon runs, which allowed a higher degree of sedentism and the development of forms of socio-political hierarchy. A critically important assumption of the materialist approach is that humans have a universal drive to maximize their material wealth and that, given the opportunity, they will strive to exert control over and restrict others' access to valuable resources. This image of "economic man" is a belief rooted in the cultural context of Western capitalism. To what extent these motives for human behaviour hold true in non-Western cultures is an important question that requires further study.

In contrast, the idealist approach emphasizes the role of ideas and values in shaping culture and cultural change. Culture is seen as the product of the creative activity of individuals, and culture changes when individuals consciously experiment with new ideas, social institutions, and traditions. However, in this approach individuals are less motivated by individual economic incentives than they are by social or cultural considerations. Second, the core features of a culture consist in the cluster of ideas, values, and beliefs, which then constrain how culture will change. If new traditions and practices are incompatible with existing values and beliefs, they will either be rejected or reformulated to fit into the cultural context.

One example of the different orientations of the materialist and idealist approaches lies in the question of the causes for the mobility of Native hunting societies in Canada. The materialist approach interprets mobility as a consequence of ecological factors, specifically the absence of sufficient resources in any one location to permit groups of people to stay in one place for extended periods. The assumption is if people could develop a sedentary lifestyle, they would. However, the contemporary southern Carrier, although many are not engaged full-time in hunting, fishing, and trapping activities, continue to have a highly mobile lifestyle. People often are on the move, travelling between the bush, their homes on the reserves, and to the homes of family and friends on other reserves and in distant cities. The high value that people continue to place on mobility indicates that social and perhaps symbolic factors are important in motivating people to travel. Idealist approaches would explore this by looking at the meaning and significance of travelling to the Carrier people themselves, and by linking this to core ideas and values within the culture.

These two approaches, however, are not mutually exclusive, and materialist and idealist approaches are often used in conjunction. Both materialist and idealist theoretical orientations appear in the following discussion of the early Carrier, and each provides a useful although partial account of Carrier culture and society in the period of early European contact.

Who Are the Carrier?

At the time of first European contact the Carrier did not recognize a level of socio-political unity at the tribal level (by "tribal" I mean a group generally defined on linguistic and cultural grounds). Nor did these bands have a name to designate the collective of Carrier-speakers. Instead, the most general and enduring level of social inclusion was the regional subgroup or band. Each band was a territorial group consisting of closely related families that used the resources in a specific region. Each band was known to itself, and to others, by a name taken from the group's territory, with the added suffix *whoten*, sometimes abbreviated to *t'en*, meaning "people of."[2] For example, the Nazkot'en are the people of the Nazko River, or the river flowing from the south (*naz* = south, *koh* = river). In the mid-1800s there were approximately fourteen bands; in 1994 there are eighteen. These bands have been remarkably stable over time. Of the named bands that existed over a century ago, the majority are still in existence today (Table 22.1).

The fact that the Carrier, at the time of European contact, had no common name and no sense of socio-political unity at the tribal level does not mean that bands were isolated groups. Rather, the different Carrier bands were closely interconnected through extensive bonds of kinship, through social and economic relations, and through ties of shared history, culture, and language. Nineteenth-century Carrier society was not a precisely bounded unit; rather, it was a society defined by a diffuse network of social relations that stretched across a wide territory. These networks were created and reinforced by frequent intermarriage between close and

Table 22.1
Carrier First Nations, 1993

Southern Carrier:	Ulkatcho, Kluskus, Nazko, Red Bluff
Central Carrier:	Lheit Lit'en, Stoney Creek, Nak'azdli, Tl'azt'en Nations, Takla Lake, Nadleh Whuten, Stellaquo, Cheslatta Carrier, Broman Lake
Northern Carrier:	Hagwilget, Moricetown, Nee-tahi-buhn, Babine Lake, Burns Lake

SOURCE: Department of Indian and Northern Affairs.

distant bands, by ties of reciprocal obligations among kin, and by frequent travel by individuals to visit relatives in other regions. In extreme
circumstances, individuals from different bands might mobilize together
for common political action, such as to launch a war raid. In these cases,
individuals were not motivated by a sense of obligation to an abstract
"tribal" identity, but to kinfolk who had been wronged and who now
needed assistance. These cross-cutting networks of kin, and the constant
movement and interchange among people, created a situation in which
ideas and knowledge were continually circulating through the region.
Viewing Carrier society as a diffuse network, rather than a homogeneous
bounded unit, is critical to the later discussion of the way in which historical factors have contributed to regional cultural diversity.

   The idea of the Carrier as a united linguistic and cultural collective
was the creation of early fur traders, missionaries, and linguists. The
name Carrier has been used since first European contact by Mackenzie in
1793. The term originated with the Sekani, who referred to the neighbouring bands as *aghelhne*, or "the ones who pack." This name was
derived from a funeral ritual in which a widow gathered and carried with
her the cremated remains of her spouse, which after a one- to two-year
period were then ritually disposed. It is unclear how all-encompassing
the Sekani term was meant to be; it is likely that the Sekani included in
this category only those bands with whom they had immediate social
relations. In the early nineteenth century, European observers listed only
the central and southern bands in this category. By the end of the nineteenth century, through anthropological and linguistic studies, the idea of
the Carrier was extended to include all of the bands presently categorized. Thus it is by virtue of historical circumstance that the name Carrier
came about. If early European traders had arrived not from the northeast

via Sekani country but from the south via Shuswap territory, the Carrier might be known today Carrier as Yu'nahena, the name by which the Shuswap knew the bands to the north. If the newcomers had arrived from the west, via Gitksan country, the Carrier might be known today in general as Akwilget, a name the Gitksan used specifically for the Wet'suwet'en and their village Hagwilget.

The creation of new social categories is an important way of ordering social relations when previously isolated groups come into contact with one another. It was critical for early European fur traders, as a prerequisite for communication and business, to be able to identify the languages spoken by Native trappers. Thus the creation of the category "Carrier," defined on linguistic and later cultural grounds, was a logical consequence of the nature of the European trader/Native trapper relationship.

With the influx of Europeans into their territories, the Carrier, like the traders and missionaries, were forced to create new social categories as a means of representing themselves to others. In the course of developing relations with Europeans the Carrier responded not by creating a new tribal identity but by developing a new level of social identity expressed in the term *dakelh* (often recorded in fur trade and missionary records as "Takully"). *Dakelh* is a contraction of *'uda ukelh*, and literally means "people who travel by water in the morning." *Dakelh*, in the 1800s as today, translates semantically as "Indian." As neighbouring Native groups such as the Shuswap, Chilcotin, and Nuxalk are included in this category, *dakelh* constitutes a more global, pan-Indian identity that distinguishes the Carrier and other Native peoples from non-Indians. The creation of this category underscores the autonomous orientation of the different bands and absence of any all-encompassing political identity in this period.

The term "Carrier" today has evolved to become a significant and meaningful category of identity for many people, who identify themselves as members of the Carrier nation not only on the basis of extensive kinship connections, but also due to strong cultural similarities. The name "Carrier" also has become commonplace among non-Natives, anthropologists, and linguists, and it remains an important category for describing basic linguistic and cultural similarities that existed, and continue to exist, among these bands. Nevertheless, some regional differences in culture and language persist. In fact, linguists and anthropologists have long perceived a significant degree of internal diversity among the Carrier. In 1893 Morice, using linguistic and geographical criteria, divided the Carrier into three subgroups: lower, upper, and Babine. Morice went so far as to speculate whether the Babine dialect should be

MAP 22.1. Carrier Territory and Contemporary First Nations

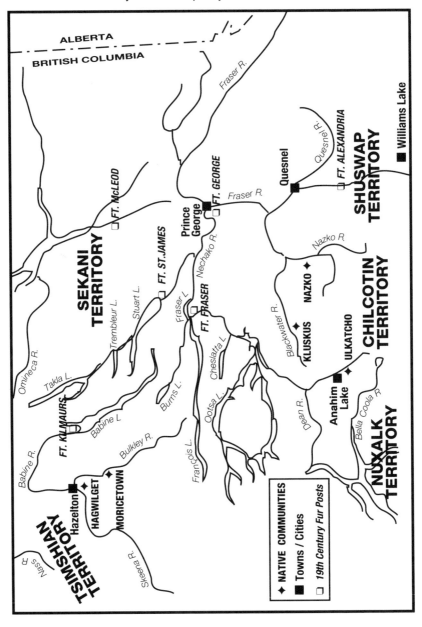

considered a separate language. Contemporary linguists agree, and have reclassified Babine as a distinct northern Athapaskan language.

. Cultural differences, specifically forms of socio-political organization, also distinguish the different Carrier bands, both in the nineteenth century and today. While Morice's lower Carrier are organized into autonomous, flexible extended family groups of bilaterally related kin, the more northerly (Morice's upper and Babine) bands are organized into matrilineal clans whose hereditary chiefs exercise ownership over specific territories. In this essay I use a combination of linguistic, geographical, and ethnographic criteria to distinguish the Carrier into northern, central, and southern subgroups (Table 22.1). Today the different Carrier bands continue to display a high degree of political autonomy, as is evident in the fact that the eighteen First Nations are divided among three distinct political organizations or tribal councils.[3]

Geography, Climate, and Resources

Much of Carrier territory lies within the boundaries of the interior Plateau, a region of flat or gently rolling terrain. The northern and western region of Carrier territory is mountainous, particularly along the Bulkley River, which is flanked by the Hazelton Mountains to the west and the Skeena Mountains to the east and north. The climate is typically continental. Summers are moderately warm and dry, with an average daytime temperature of 22° C, while winters are cold, with daytime temperatures occasionally dropping to −40° C. Early autumn frosts begin in late August, and by early November snow is on the ground. By April much of the snow has disappeared, although spring freezes continue until early June.

Carrier territory is dominated by the sub-boreal spruce forest, a broad biogeoclimatic zone that serves as a transitional area between the northern boreal forests, the Douglas fir forests to the south, and the subalpine forests in the mountainous regions. White/Engelmann spruce, interior Douglas fir, and lodgepole pine are common throughout the region, and willow and black cottonwood often are found along river banks. The mountainous regions that border Carrier territory, with their colder climate and heavier snowfall, are covered by spruce and subalpine fir interspersed with open meadows and grasslands.

The most important animals that the nineteenth-century Carrier used for subsistence were caribou, moose, grizzly and black bears, beaver, and rabbits. Grizzly bears, hoary marmots, and mountain goats were hunted in the mountainous regions to the north and west. Animals

PLATE 22.1. Salmon weir and traps, Fort St. James (ca. 1900). The men are facing downstream. Basket traps are placed on the upstream side at openings in the weir. Courtesy British Columbia Archives and Records Service, 96785 (G-3743).

trapped chiefly for their fur included beaver, muskrats, wolves, black bears, martens, fishers, otters, wolverines, fox, lynx, coyotes, and mink. A variety of birds, including swans, geese, ducks, grouse, and loons, were also used for food. Numerous large and small lakes, rivers, streams, and marshes are scattered over the landscape, and freshwater fish such as trout, whitefish, carp, and suckers were important components of the diet.

Salmon was a particularly important resource. There are two primary drainage systems in Carrier territory: the Fraser River and the Pacific. Much of the region is drained by the Fraser River and its tributaries, while to the north and west the Bulkley, Babine, and Dean Rivers drain into the Pacific Ocean. Salmon ascend both of these drainage systems to spawn, dividing up into separate runs in different tributaries and again into separate stocks or races within particular watersheds. The sizes of the runs vary between watersheds, and each run varies also in regular cycles of between four to six years, salmon being abundant in the peak year and less abundant or scarce in intervening years.

Subsistence Strategies and the Annual Round

All three Carrier subdivisions followed a similar pattern of seasonal activity. Throughout the year the most important economic unit was the family, a group of related individuals who worked together to provide the essentials for survival. Families moved through the region in regular patterns, harvesting resources that were seasonally available and hunting and fishing whenever necessary. With the exception of the summer months, when families gathered together for the salmon fishery, families tended to be widely dispersed. As a result of this mobile lifestyle, a complex network of trails existed through the region connecting villages, seasonal campsites, and hunting and fishing grounds. Trails also extended into the territories of neighbouring bands and tribal groups, with whom the Carrier carried on an active trade.

Some activities were predictable and gave structure to the seasonal round. In the summer, many families congregated at fishing stations to harvest and dry the salmon for winter. Salmon were harvested with weirs and traps, or with spear or net. A weir of woven sticks was erected partially or completely across a river to block the passage of fish. Large conical baskets, perhaps five to six metres in length and one and a half metres in diameter, were placed at the various openings of the weir. Traps often were set at night, and by morning could contain hundreds of fish. Salmon were gutted, split, and suspended on poles to dry over smouldering fires. The dried salmon either were stored in underground cache pits or were packed flat into bales and placed in elevated caches. The salmon-fishing season typically began in July and could extend into September or October, depending on the abundance of salmon and the amount needed. Many different species of berries were collected during the summer months and were dried into cakes and stored for later use.

In the fall, families dispersed to distant regions to hunt for caribou, beaver, bears, mountain goats, and marmots. Hunting technology consisted of bow and arrow, spears, deadfalls, and snares. A variety of snare designs were used, each specific for the animal being sought. Snares for small animals were made of sinew; those for larger animals were made of strips of caribou hide.

A number of families might gather together for the caribou hunt. Fences several kilometres in length were constructed by attaching long poles horizontally to trees. These fences gradually converged to a small corral. Families worked together to drive the caribou along the fences and into the corral, where the caribou then were killed by waiting hunters. In the summer, hunters used smouldering fires to attract caribou, which were drawn to the smoke in their attempt to escape the torment of mosquitoes.

Meat from the fall hunt was dried for winter use, and skins were processed and sewn into robes and winter clothing. Through most of the year people travelled mainly on foot, packing their goods and supplies on their

PLATE 22.2. Azel of Ulkatcho spinning sinew (ca. 1922). Sinew is made from long tendons that run along the backbone of large animals. The material is split into fine strands, then several strands are twisted together by rolling between the palms. Courtesy of the Canadian Museum of Civilization, 55690.

backs using a tumpline. Once the snow fell people shifted to travelling by snowshoes and toboggans. Canoes made of spruce bark or cottonwood also were used.

As the winter progressed and large animals became more scarce, attention shifted to ice fishing and rabbit snaring. People also made occasional trips back to the summer villages to retrieve stores of dried salmon. Winter camps were set up adjacent to good rabbit-snaring grounds and where the supply of firewood was plentiful. During the winter families continued to camp on their own, occasionally joining with two or three other families if the resources were plentiful. Some Ulkatcho families stayed during the winter with relatives among the Nuxalk (Bella Coola), while some Wet'suwet'en wintered at the Gitksan village of Hazelton.

The period between late winter and early spring was the most difficult. Winter stores of food were almost gone, warmer temperatures and melting snow made travel difficult, and game was scarce. Families sustained themselves by ice fishing using net, spear, and set line. The inner bark of the hemlock was scraped, roasted, and its fibres pounded into a pulp to form small dried cakes. These could later be softened with water and consumed. Black lichen, growing abundantly on the dead lower branches of pine trees throughout the region, often was used as an emergency food. The lichen was mixed with water and shaped into cakes, then roasted by the fire.

As the spring progressed, families congregated along lakes and rivers, where nets, fences, and basket traps were used to harvest spawning trout and suckers. As the days became longer and warmer, plants sprouted new growth and the sap began running in the trees. Plants such as wild parsnip were roasted, peeled, and eaten, and the bark of pine trees was cut and the sugar-rich sap scraped off and consumed. The roots of tiger lilies, which grow abundantly along rivers and streams, were roasted in underground pits. Waterfowl returned from the south and were snared, as were beaver, muskrats, and squirrels. Families dispersed and continued to hunt before gathering again at summer villages in July.

Regional Differences

Within Carrier territory, regional differences in the availability of salmon enabled the central and northern bands to establish permanent villages and have a more sedentary lifestyle during the summer months. Each band had two or more permanent villages situated at the sites of salmon-fishing stations. Both the northern and central bands relied on salmon as a principal source of food.

PLATE 22.3. Gaffing salmon at Moricetown on the Bulkley River (ca. 1952). The harpoon has a detachable foreshaft attached with a leather thong. This prevents the fish from coming free or breaking the shaft when caught. Courtesy of Royal British Columbia Museum, Victoria, B.C., PN3272.

The rivers in the northwest, including the Bulkley River and Babine River, as well as Babine Lake, support the largest and most predictable salmon runs in Carrier territory. The watersheds of the Fraser, including Stuart, Trembleur, Francois, and Ootsa lakes, also support large salmon runs, although the sizes vary substantially from year to year. When salmon were abundant the Carrier groups in this central region gathered in permanent summer villages to harvest the fish for the winter; when the salmon were scarce people travelled to watersheds of adjacent bands, or across to Babine Lake, to acquire salmon from relatives or through trade.

Salmon resources in southern Carrier territory were much more unevenly distributed. Although major runs passed up the Fraser River, only moderate runs entered the Blackwater River, along which most of the southern Carrier bands were centred. Significant runs entered the Quesnel River, but these runs were subject to extreme fluctuations from year to year. As a result, the southern Carrier did not rely on salmon as a principal food source and followed a more mobile lifestyle than the other Carrier groups.

Each Carrier band had one or several central gathering places. Although these may be called villages, in reality people gathered here for only a small portion of the year. Further, villages had different significance among the northern and central bands as compared with the southern bands. Among the former, villages were places for gathering in the summer months, for harvesting salmon, and for organizing clan activities and hosting potlatches. Among the southern bands, villages were more temporary. The Nazko, Quesnel, and Alexandria Carrier each had a village on the Fraser River, and these villages were occupied briefly during the salmon-fishing season. In the early nineteenth century the Ulkatcho Carrier, who had recently incorporated the traditions of clan organization and potlatching, had several villages: on the Dean River, at Qualcho Lake, and at Gatcho Lake. As potlatching became more important, so did the significance of the villages. By the late nineteenth century, due to dramatic population decline, only one of the villages, at Gatcho Lake, remained. In the 1930s the village continued to be occupied only intermittently through the year.

In short, the functional significance of villages differed from band to band. Periods of co-residence varied according not only to ecological factors, namely the availability of sufficient salmon to sustain large groups of people for long periods, but also due to cultural reasons. Unlike the Ulkatcho band, the other southern Carrier bands had not incorporated the potlatch complex and had less cultural incentive to remain together in the villages for extended periods.

Social and Political Organization

Bands were the most widespread and common groups among the Carrier. Nevertheless, bands had no permanent political leaders, nor were they closely united in terms of political action. In terms of day-to-day domestic activities, the individual families within a band were the most important units. Among the southern Carrier, the family also was the most important political unit. The central and northern bands, however, had matrilineal clans, which served as the most important political units. The following characterizations of the social and political organization of the nineteenth-century Carrier to a large extent remain true today.

Southern Carrier families were highly autonomous, flexible, extended groups of bilaterally related kin. The Carrier term for the extended family was *sadeku*, or all those individuals related through the grandfather. Because of the tendency for patrilocality – the wife joined the household of her husband – the core of the extended family group usually consisted of a group of brothers, their spouses and children, and married sons' wives and children. At any one time, though, the household unit engaged in hunting or fishing might be as small as a nuclear family or as large as to contain three generations. The composition of households changed due to ecological factors, expanding in times of food abundance and splitting apart in times of shortage. Households changed composition for social reasons as well. Some individuals might leave to defuse an interpersonal conflict, while others might leave to visit other relatives or other sections of the country.

The extended family was led by the *detsah*, or headman, usually the oldest person in a line of siblings. He was considered the spokesman of the group, and he co-ordinated the tasks of hunting and fishing. In keeping with southern Carrier values of autonomy and egalitarianism, the headman's authority was informal. His continued leadership depended on his ability to make sound decisions and on the continued support of his relatives. The headmen, along with *duyunne* or shamans, were the most influential political figures in southern Carrier society.

Each extended family was associated with a particular hunting territory, although their rights to these territories were not exclusive and any band member could hunt wherever he wished. Rights to specific salmon- and trout-fishing stations, however, were considered family property. Individuals were expected to marry outside of the *sadekuka*, or descendants related through the line of great-grandfather, and marriages between the different bands, as well as with the neighbouring Chilcotin and Nuxalk, were common. As a result, each individual could trace a network of relatives through a wide territory. This created, in effect, a safety network of kin who could be called upon to share food and access to hunting and fishing territories in times when fish or game was scarce in one's own territory.

In contrast, the most important political units among the northern and central Carrier bands were the matrilineal clans. The northern Carrier were divided into several clans, which were further divided into a number of houses.[4] Membership in both the clans and the houses was determined through matrilineal descent. Each house was led by a hereditary chief who, on behalf of his house, exercised ownership and stewardship over specific hunting and fishing territories and controlled access to these resources. Only those families that could trace membership to the house were permitted to use these territories. The house chief was responsible also for settling disputes among families, for providing help to destitute house members, and for representing the interests of house members to other houses and clans.

The notions of social hierarchy and rank were expressed not only through the position of house chief but also through the ownership of titles and crests, which bestowed status to their holders. Each house owned a number of titles and crests. House crests were publicly displayed on totem poles, houses, and ceremonial regalia, and were tattooed on house members' chests and wrists. The crests represented animals, natural features, mythical beings, or manufactured objects, and were infused with spiritual power. The chief and most of the nobility of the house also owned at least one personal crest, which could be bought and sold.

The potlatch (or the Feast, as it is known by the northern Carrier) was a central institution in the social and political life of the northern Carrier. It provided the political vehicle for the public validation of chieftainship, for transferring and confirming property rights, and for conferring high status to individuals via titles and crests. Through amassing and giving away goods, and thus the creation of a system of ongoing credit and debt, the potlatch served the economic function of the continuous redistribution of resources through the community. It served the social function of reaffirming the solidarity of kinship groups and for maintaining social networks based on reciprocity and alliance. Potlatching and house activities occurred primarily in the summer months, when families were gathered together in the villages for the salmon fishery.

In the nineteenth and early twentieth centuries the clan and potlatch-rank systems varied slightly among the central Carrier bands. Here clans were not subdivided into houses. While the Wet'suwet'en and Babine Lake Carrier both had five clans, the central bands had various numbers of clans. The central bands, as well as the northern band at Babine Lake, no longer required clans to be exogamous; this became a matter of choice. As among the northern Carrier, the clans of the central bands were divided into nobility and commoners. The nobility owned titles associated with specific hunting and fishing territories, over which they controlled access. Titles were inherited along matrilineal lines and were publicly validated through potlatching.

In summary, Carrier groups in the northern and central regions displayed characteristics that anthropologists consider typical of Plateau cultural groups: high reliance on salmon as a principal food and the establishment of permanent villages. In contrast, the southern Carrier are best described as having a typical Subarctic culture, with their high degree of mobility, flexibility in social arrangements, informal political institutions, situational leadership, egalitarianism, and emphasis on values of individualism and autonomy.

These regional differences among the Carrier are, in part, a product of local ecological adaptation. The availability of a rich, stable resource base, salmon, plus the fact that the best sites for salmon harvesting were restricted to a few key locations, enabled not only a more sedentary lifestyle, but also the development of a local elite, the clan and house leaders, who successfully exercised control of the means of production. The surplus in resources allowed for the creation of a system of ceremonial feasting, a central component of which was the giving away of large quantities of goods. However, while the environment enabled the development of socio-political hierarchy and potlatching, we can refine our understanding of Carrier cultural change by viewing these developments as a result also of historical factors. These developments are the product of the flow of ideas and practices from neighbouring nations and their creative adaptation into Carrier culture.

Carrier Cultural Change

How can we account for the existence of socio-political hierarchies and potlatching among some Carrier groups but not others? First of all, the northern bands are believed to have incorporated the ideas of social rank and status, and potlatch ceremonialism, through their contact with the neighbouring Gitksan, with whom they had close social and economic relations. In the early nineteenth century the Gitksan, a Tsimshian-speaking group of the upper Skeena River, held the lucrative position of middlemen in the Wet'suwet'en trade with the coastal Tsimshian. The Wet'suwet'en and Gitksan frequently intermarried and participated in each other's ceremonies. The five Wet'suwet'en clans were linked with the four Gitksan clans for the purposes of regulating marriage and potlatching. From the Wet'suwet'en and Babine Lake Carrier the ideas of socio-political hierarchy and potlatching were picked up by the Carrier bands to the east and south.

How long have the Carrier been organized into matrilineal clans? The existence of matrilineal clans does not necessarily lead to the development of social hierarchies, and as a result the adoption of matrilineality may have been a separate phenomenon. The question of the antiquity of matrilineal clans among the Carrier and other Athapaskan groups is still debated within anthropology. Dyen and Aberle (1974), based on their lexical reconstruction of proto-Athapaskan kinship terminology, believe that matrilineality is the ancient and original form of social organization among Northern Athapaskans. In contrast, Goldman (1941) and Steward (1960) believe that matrilineal clans were adopted by the Carrier at the same time as the ideas of socio-political hierarchy and potlatching, and that bilateral organization was the original system among the Carrier. These latter ideas, which are based on material and ecological explanations, are explored in this section.

The question of exactly when ideas of social rank, status, and pot-latching were adopted by the Carrier is difficult to answer, particularly when relying only on the scattered documentary sources left by early European observers rather than Carrier oral traditions. Steward, using a materialist approach, believes that the introduction of these ideas and practices among the Carrier occurred two to three decades before direct European contact. By the last two decades of the eighteenth century, Carrier bands were trading indirectly with European trading ships on the coast through Gitksan middlemen. The new source of wealth in furs was the trigger for the adoption of these new forms of social and political organization. When coupled with the abundance of salmon in northern Carrier territory, people now had sufficient resources to be able to host potlatches, which required a surplus of both foods and material goods to give away during the ceremonies. Along similar lines, Goldman believes that with the advent of the maritime fur trade, intermarriage intensified between the Carrier and the Gitksan as a way of solidifying trading relations. As the Carrier married into high-ranking families among the coastal nations, the ideas of social rank and clan organization were incorporated into Carrier society. Now high-ranking families could claim exclusive control over trade with the high-ranking Gitksan families, and the emerging Carrier elite used this system to exert control over these valuable trade networks.

The ideas of socio-political hierarchy, clan organization, and potlatching were adopted by the more southerly Ulkatchot'en. For reasons that remain unknown, the other bands to the east, the Kluskus, Nazko, and Quesnel (Red Bluff) Carrier, did not incorporate these traditions. As the Ulkatchot'en incorporated the idea of clans, however, the principles of clan membership were modified to fit in with the Ulkatcho emphasis on bilateral social organization.

This emphasis on bilaterality was reinforced by the close economic and social relations that the Ulkatcho Carrier had with the coastal Nuxalk. As among the Wet'suwet'en and Gitksan, these relations intensified in the late eighteenth century with the inception of the maritime fur trade, when the Nuxalk assumed the role of middlemen in the southern Carrier trade with the European trading ships. While the Nuxalk lacked clans, their society, too, was organized around the principles of bilateral descent. In addition, the Nuxalk held to principles of social rank and status, which were demonstrated through the individual ownership of crests. These crests were inherited along bilateral lines among the nobility of Nuxalk society, and the crests were validated through potlatch ceremonies.

The Ulkatchot'en, then, through their social relations with both the northern Carrier and the Nuxalk, were exposed to a wide variety of ideas about social organization, wealth, status, and principles of land owner-ship, ideas that were in a state of flux with the changes being introduced by the maritime fur trade. From this mélange of possibilities, the Ulkatchot'en adopted the ideas of clan organization, social rank, and pot-latching, but remodelled these practices to suit their own needs and to fit into existing principles of social organization.

When clans were first introduced into Ulkatcho society in the early nineteenth century, they became associated with specific extended fami-lies. Clan affiliation was determined along bilateral rather than matri-lineal lines: a child could choose to belong to his father's or mother's clan, or both. The extended family, now under the rubric of the clan, lived in the same village, where its members jointly hosted potlatches and shared common fishing and hunting territories, even though the bounda-ries of these territories were never sharply drawn. However, after a few generations the clans evolved to be primarily ceremonial organizations rather than land-owning units, in contrast to the clans of the central and northern bands.

To strengthen their trade alliances with the Nuxalk, the Ulkatcho Car-rier also incorporated the ideas of status and rank through ownership of personal titles and crests, which were validated through potlatches. However, like the clans, among the Ulkatcho Carrier the inheritance of these titles and crests occurred along bilateral lines, as among the Nux-alk, rather than along matrilineal lines, as among the northern Carrier.

In short, in incorporating clans, potlatches, and status distinctions through ownership of crests and titles, the Ulkatcho Carrier were not sim-ply passive recipients of foreign cultural traditions. Instead, they actively modified these ideas while making changes to their own cultural prac-tices. Clan organization and potlatches greatly declined in importance after the drastic reduction in population caused by the 1862-63 smallpox epidemic and after the sharp drop in fur prices in the 1930s, which left few individuals with sufficient wealth to host regular potlatches. Further, not all individuals were equally involved in the potlatch system. The idea of social hierarchy failed to take root in Ulkatcho society partly due to its conflict with the fundamental Ulkatcho values of individualism and egal-itarianism. However, in the last few years the Ulkatcho Carrier have begun to revive the clan system in their community, where they are remo-delling the clans once again to fit the contemporary context.

Values and Beliefs

Despite differences in socio-political organization, a core set of values and beliefs that characterized nineteenth-century Carrier culture can be identified. The Carrier's survival as hunters, fishers, and gatherers depended on each individual having extensive knowledge of the land and its resources. Material technology was less important than the knowledge of how to construct and apply this technology efficiently. This knowledge consisted of a detailed understanding of animal habits, population cycles, climate, and topography. Knowledge was built up during an individual's lifetime in a number of ways. First, it was acquired through practical experience. As a child grew to adulthood he learned, through observation and through trial and error, the techniques of hunting, fishing, and trapping and the unique features of the animal populations, vegetation, and geography in his particular territory. Second, an individual's knowledge of the land and its resources was expanded through sharing information with other household members, with other families temporarily camped together, and with groups of travellers encountered on the trails. As a result, Carrier culture placed strong emphasis on individual responsibility and autonomy, at the same time valuing the importance of communication and social co-operation.

While survival depended on practical knowledge, it was also important for people to live according to certain standards of conduct. The Carrier believed that all animate and inanimate objects in the world had a spirit. The people's survival depended on their ability to maintain balanced relations with all of the spirits in the land; if they did not, animals would not give themselves to the hunter. Balanced relations were kept by living according to certain ethical standards and by performing appropriate rituals. These ethical concepts were encoded in oral traditions, which served as primary educational devices for children's moral training.

A person was expected to show respect for the foods and materials he or she used, to not waste any of these resources, and to perform certain rituals after a successful hunt. An individual was expected to be generous, and to always share meat from the hunt with other households and provide assistance to others when needed. The person was expected to be modest and not to boast of his achievements or predict success in the future, whether it be an upcoming hunt or the birth of a new child. Emphasis on individualism and autonomy was especially strong among the southern Carrier. No individual was believed to have the authority to tell another what to do; rather, each person was responsible for choosing his own course of action. Gossip and social exclusion served as effective mechanisms for social control. In extreme cases conflicts were resolved by household groups or camps splitting apart and moving to different regions. If one lived by these values and codes of behaviour, the person would be fortunate in hunting and would enjoy good health. Misfortune or ill health was seen as the person's failure to live by these codes of behaviour, or his breaking of a taboo.

Boys and girls might explicitly seek out direct contact with an animal spirit through the adolescent guardian spirit quest. These quests were an important component of the rites of passage to adulthood among the central Carrier. Among the Wet'suwet'en and southern bands, however, the guardian spirit quest was optional. In any case, spirits came to the individual through dreams, providing the person with knowledge of where to look for game or of events that were to happen in the future. People with especially strong connections to animal spirits might become shamans, who had extraordinary healing powers.

The Impact of Colonialism

The Fur Trade

The Carrier were quick to become involved in the expanding land-based fur trade with Europeans. The first fur trade post to be established in British Columbia was Fort McLeod, built in 1805 by the North West Company. The fur trade soon expanded into central Carrier territory with the building of three forts: Fort St. James and Fort Fraser in 1806, and Fort George in 1807. In 1821 the North West Company merged with the Hudson's Bay Company. The same year saw the establishment of Fort Alexandria on the Fraser River in southern Carrier territory. Fort Alexandria was built as the terminus of the newly established overland supply route from the Columbia River. The fort collected furs from the Carrier, Chilcotin, and Shuswap. Fort Kilmaurs, on Babine Lake, was built the following year, drawing trade from both Carrier and Sekani trappers.

The forts were established in strategic locations, being adjacent to Carrier villages and salmon-fishing stations. The transportation of goods and supplies from both the eastern and Columbia River posts was a slow and difficult process, and the forts were forced to rely on local foods – almost exclusively salmon – for survival. The fort personnel obtained salmon either by directly harvesting the fish from the river or through trade from the local Carrier. The forts' reliance on local resources, access to which on occasion was strictly controlled by the Carrier, plus the availability of the Aboriginal trading networks with coastal nations gave the

Carrier a significant degree of control in their relationship with the European traders and precluded the Carrier from becoming dependent on the forts for food or supplies. Two other forts, Fort Chilcotin (1829) and Fort Kluskus (1844), were constructed in southern Carrier territory in an effort to intercept the coastal trade; both forts failed in these efforts and were eventually closed.

The European fur trade instigated several changes in the economic and social organization of the Carrier. By the early twentieth century, southern Carrier families had extended their concept of family ownership of fishing sites to include rights to specific trapping areas. Individuals remained free to hunt anywhere in the band area. A similar process occurred among the central Carrier, where families began to exert control over trapping territories, thus weakening the system of clan-based land ownership.

With the introduction of new technologies and goods, such as guns and ammunition, steel traps, axes, kettles, blankets, and cloth, the Carrier became inextricably linked to the economic system of the colonial society. The Carrier continued as active trappers through the late nineteenth century and well into the twentieth century. Through the trapline registration system, introduced in British Columbia in the 1920s, individuals became the "registered" owners of traplines, bringing Carrier practices more fully under the restrictive control of the provincial government. Nevertheless, trapping has played an important role in the Carrier economy through to the present.

The Expansion of the Colonial Frontier

The gold rushes of the 1860s represented the second wave of expansion of resource industries into Carrier country. The Cariboo gold rush of 1858-64, followed by the Omineca rush five years later, brought thousands of miners into Carrier territory via the Skeena and Fraser rivers and resulted in the establishment of permanent transportation corridors in the region. The free traders who arrived with the miners brought an end to the Hudson's Bay Company's monopoly over the interior fur trade. Behind the prospectors and free traders came colonial administrators, who sought to impose government authority by regulating mining claims and land pre-emptions and by keeping law and order on the new frontier. In the 1880s Indian agencies began to be established in the British Columbia interior, and Indian agents set out to regulate and restrict the lives of Native people according to the regulations of the Indian Act.

The 1860s also saw the decimation of the Carrier population by small-pox. The southern Carrier bands were especially hard hit by the epidemic. A Carrier band in the Bowron Lakes area east of the Fraser River was wiped out by the epidemic, while other bands were reduced to fractions of their former level. As the gold rushes ended, a number of miners stayed in the region, pre-empted tracts of lands, and established ranches and farms. Settlement in Carrier territory, however, remained sporadic until the construction of the Grand Trunk Pacific Railway between Edmonton and Prince Rupert in 1914. This triggered a land boom in central and northern Carrier regions, and settlers and land speculators pre-empted land and established small towns along the railway belt between Prince George and the Bulkley Valley. Economic development in northern British Columbia remained minimal until after World War Two, most of the settlers supporting themselves through small-scale logging, saw-milling, farming, and trapping.

Carrier Economic Changes

Although the Carrier had been employed in wage labour since the establishment of the fur trade posts, wage labour became a much more important component of the economy after the 1860s. Carrier people found periodic work as ranch labourers and cowboys, as guides and packers along the gold field trails, as workers in the coastal salmon canneries and the interior sawmills, and as construction crews on the roads and railways being built in the region. Some families took up cattle raising on a small scale and kept herds of horses that they used for packing supplies through the country.

By the early twentieth century the Carrier had developed a mixed economy based on hunting, fishing, trapping, seasonal wage work, and small-scale stock raising. The Carrier responded to disruptions in any one of these economic pursuits by shifting emphasis to other activities. For example, after the virtual collapse of the salmon fishery in 1913 and 1914, families turned more attention to trapping and hunting. Wage work became more scarce during the 1930s, and again after World War Two due to the mechanization of ranching and logging operations, causing families to shift once again to hunting and fishing. Government assistance programs, including old age pensions, family allowances, and social assistance, were made fully available to Indians in the 1940s and 1950s, and served as sources of income that augmented rather than replaced hunting and trapping activities.

Changes in Beliefs and Values

Religious colonization of the Carrier began with the establishment of two Roman Catholic missions, one in 1867 near Williams Lake and a second in 1873 at Stuart Lake. The goals of the missionaries were ultimately to bring about submission of the Carrier to the religious authority of the Church and to convert the Carrier to Catholicism and to a settled, agricultural existence. The establishment of two Indian residential schools, St. Joseph's Mission near Williams Lake and Lejacq residential school at Fraser Lake, facilitated these plans. Children as young as five were sent to the schools, where they remained for ten months of the year, and often until the age of sixteen. The intent of the residential school system was to remove the children from their homes so as to block the transmission of cultural values and practices. At the schools the children were taught basic literary skills as well as cooking, sewing, farm labour, and a variety of trades. While the residential schools interfered with the transmission of culture to the younger generations, the schools nevertheless failed in their original goal, which was the assimilation of Native people into Canadian society.

The Carrier, in their typically pragmatic orientation to outside influences, nominally converted to Catholicism and welcomed the periodic visits by travelling missionaries while retaining many aspects of their own spiritual beliefs. By the early twentieth century the guardian spirit quest was no longer practised among the southern bands, although periods of ritual training still persisted for adolescent boys and girls. Many people today continue to believe in the power of dreams, and shamans occasionally are called upon to help individuals who are suffering from extraordinary illnesses. The relative isolation until recent times of the Carrier communities from the impacts of logging, mining, and settlement has facilitated the retention of their language, culture, and subsistence lifestyle.

Colonial Authority: Restriction of Aboriginal Rights

With the exception of small areas on Vancouver Island and in northeastern B.C., governments did not sign treaties formally transferring the land from Native nations in the province. While settlers were encouraged to take up free tracts of land, after 1866 Native people were prohibited by law from pre-empting land, and the Carrier in the Bulkley Valley and Quesnel areas were powerless to prevent some of their homesteads, campsites, and graveyards from being pre-empted by non-Native settlers. After 1871 the provincial government in British Columbia refused to address the issue of Aboriginal title. Instead, it sought to quell Native protests by establishing reserves throughout the province. Reserves for the various Carrier bands were allotted between 1871 and 1902. Final adjustments to the sizes of reserves in the province were made through the 1916 federal/provincial Royal Commission on Indian Affairs.

By the turn of the century Aboriginal hunting and fishing rights increasingly became subject to government regulation by game wardens and fisheries officers. The federal Fisheries Act outlawed the use of weirs, basket traps, and nets for salmon fishing on inland rivers. These regulations began to be enforced with vigour as the commercial salmon fisheries developed in the late nineteenth century, and particularly after the 1913 Hell's Gate slide, in which debris from the construction of the Canadian National Railway filled the Fraser River, almost completely blocking the salmon from returning to their upriver spawning grounds. Federal fisheries officers destroyed salmon weirs on Babine Lake in 1905 and 1906 but eventually reached a compromise with the seven Carrier bands on the Babine Lake, Stuart Lake, and Nechako River watersheds, in which the bands agreed instead to fish by net. On the Fraser River, under the scrutiny of local fisheries officers, some Carrier families switched to fishing for salmon by dipnetting, a much more time-consuming and laborious method.

Expansion of the Forest Industry

Up until the 1940s, settlement throughout most of Carrier territory was sparse. The Carrier remained in control of most of their territory despite the fact that the governments had failed to negotiate Aboriginal title settlements. This situation changed after World War Two with the expansion of the forest industry. By the 1960s small logging and sawmilling operations had become obsolete, and larger companies were supplying wood to the major pulp and sawmills in the interior towns. As the economy boomed and opportunities for work increased, the population of non-Natives in the region expanded. Increased competition for work, plus the requirement for more highly skilled labour, led to the gradual exclusion of Natives from employment in the industry. As the industry expanded, clear-cutting pushed further into regions previously isolated from settlement. In the past the Carrier had been able to respond to downturns in the industrial economy, whether trapping or wage labour, by placing more emphasis on their hunting and fishing activities. Now this very backbone of their economy was threatened with the loss of the forests to the logging industry. The historic failure of governments to recognize and address Aboriginal title now became a critical issue. In the 1970s the Carrier began a new era of political struggle with the Canadian state as they launched direct protests over the unresolved matter of Aboriginal title and rights. The question of history is at the centre of these debates.

The Politics of History: Two Contemporary Examples

Carrier bands today have adopted a variety of strategies to press for government recognition of Aboriginal rights and title. One is the use of the Canadian court system, with the rationale that the legal recognition of Aboriginal title would force the Canadian and provincial governments to negotiate land settlements. A second strategy is the use of direct political action, including the staging of blockades and the use of the media. The goal of these acts is to generate sufficient attention and public sympathy to pressure governments into direct negotiations of Aboriginal rights and title.

The essence of Aboriginal claims is this: Native leaders argue that before European arrival each nation had its own system of land ownership and government, through which resource use and social conduct were effectively regulated. Native leaders assert that their rights to land and self-government have not been relinquished, but only suppressed, in the course of European colonization, and that these rights persist today. Native leaders draw attention to the continuity of cultural traditions from past to present to demonstrate their continuing status as distinct societies within Canada.

These representations of culture and history, though, are subject to challenge and debate. The common-sense belief of non-Native Canadians is that Native societies of the past were "primitive" groups who had no form of land ownership or concept of property rights. Most non-Native Canadians believe that today Native people either have lost their culture under the impact of Western society, or that their culture survives in the form of arts and crafts, ceremonies and dances, and eco-spiritualism, all aspects of culture that non-Native Canadians can appreciate comfortably without having to consider the unresolved question of who owns the land. One recent example of these conflicting views of history can be found in the Gitksan and Wet'suwet'en land claims case.

The Gitksan and Wet'suwet'en Land Claims Case

In 1984, fifty-one hereditary chiefs representing the houses of the Wet'suwet'en and Gitksan peoples initiated legal action in the British Columbia Supreme Court. Through this action the chiefs asked the court to recognize their past and ongoing ownership and jurisdiction over their traditional territories covering 54,000 square kilometres in northwestern B.C. The court case began in May, 1987, and ended in June, 1990, and was the longest Aboriginal title case heard in Canadian history. The case was also unique with respect to the extensive historical evidence provided by the hereditary chiefs themselves. The core of this evidence consisted of the Gitksan *adaawk* and the Wet'suwet'en *kungax*, oral histories that document their ownership of land and resources in specific territories. Through this evidence, and that provided by anthropologists and historians, the court was told of the Gitksan and Wet'suwet'en clan and house systems, of the authority of the clan and house leaders, and of the critical role played by the potlatch in regulating and affirming Gitksan and Wet'suwet'en political, social, and economic life. The Gitksan and Wet'suwet'en argued that, despite the colonization of British Columbia, they have not relinquished their Aboriginal title, and that their traditional systems of law remain in effect in their territories and continue to order life in their contemporary communities.

Nevertheless, in his controversial and much discussed decision (McEachern 1991), the judge, Mr. Justice McEachern, put forth a fundamentally different view of history. The judge stated that the nineteenth-century Gitksan and Wet'suwet'en were a "primitive people without any form of writing, horses, or wheeled wagons." According to the judge, the Gitksan and Wet'suwet'en had only a rudimentary form of social organization, barely any degree of culture, and lived a marginal existence in which starvation was common and life was "nasty, brutish and short." McEachern concluded that the Gitksan and Wet'suwet'en no longer have a distinct Native culture because not all the people continue to hunt and trap and because many participate in wage labour, own automobiles, and consume store-bought food. Ultimately, the Aboriginal title claim of the Gitksan and Wet'suwet'en peoples was rejected.

This view of history is rooted in a colonial ideology framed on the nineteenth-century theory of cultural evolution, which holds that all societies can be ranked on a scale of progressive evolution from "primitive" to "civilized." Native societies are "primitive" and occupy the lowest rungs of this scale of evolution, while European societies are "civilized" and occupy the highest position. "Primitive" societies, according to this theory, are not only weak, poorly organized, and precarious, but are inherently less morally worthy than "civilized" societies. The implicit suggestion is that because "civilization" is both inevitable and advantageous, the colonization of North America, the bringing of "civilization" to the continent, and the domination of Native societies has been in Native peoples' best interests.

These views conflict sharply with those of contemporary anthropology. Native societies are no less highly evolved than European societies; rather, they have evolved differently, and have developed complex ways of adapting to their specific environments. For example, the changing nature of Carrier social organization in the late eighteenth and nineteenth centuries is not a sign of the indeterminate, unorganized state of "primitive" societies, nor is it an indication that, through these changes, the Carrier "lost" their "traditional culture." Instead, these modifications in social organization were adaptive strategies that enabled the Carrier to solidify trade relations and pursue their economic interests. The judge in this case viewed Native culture to be static, defined by a series of traits that existed in some mythical past but that have now all but disappeared. In contrast, anthropology today emphasizes the dynamic nature of culture and the manner in which people are continually adapting their culture to their changed circumstances. For example, trappers now use trucks instead of snowshoes to get to their traplines. To the judge, this was a sign of their loss of their culture. However, while the form of transportation may have changed, its function remains the same. Modern vehicles serve a critically important function of enabling the Carrier to maintain their older cultural pursuits.

In short, not only does this view of history emerge from a cultural context of nineteenth-century European colonialism, but it serves the political function of justifying and maintaining the status quo of Native-government relations in Canada. In his conclusion, Mr. Justice McEachern, in adhering to a belief in objective history, rejected the Gitksan and Wet'suwet'en perspectives on their history as "not literally true." He failed to consider the possibility that there are many different perspectives on history, and he failed to consider how his own view of the Gitksan and Wet'suwet'en was shaped by a colonial ideology and by archaic beliefs about culture that have been rejected by contemporary anthropologists.

The Nazko and Kluskus Carrier and the Mackenzie Grease Trail

A second example of the importance of politics of history in contemporary Carrier life is in the Nazko and Kluskus Carrier's protest over the
development of the Mackenzie Grease Trail. The Mackenzie Grease
Trail is an Aboriginal trade route, possibly thousands of years old, that
runs over 300 kilometres between southern Carrier territory and the Nuxalk villages on the Pacific coast. Southern Carrier people refer to the trail
as the Grease Trail. This name comes from the large quantities of oolichan oil that the southern Carrier obtained through trade with the coastal
Nuxalk. Alexander Mackenzie travelled along the Grease Trail in 1793
to reach the Pacific Ocean. Mackenzie since has become celebrated as
the first European to traverse the North American continent north of
Mexico and to thus establish symbolic claims to the territory that would
later become Canada. Many non-Natives today refer to the trail as the
Mackenzie Trail, the Mackenzie Grease Trail, or the Alexander Mackenzie Heritage Trail.

The different names for this trail are symbolic of the debates that have
since arisen over the trail's historic significance. In the early 1970s a
national non-profit organization devoted to the preservation of natural
areas for public use began efforts to have the route officially designated as
a heritage trail. In 1982 the federal and provincial governments signed a
formal agreement to develop and preserve the Alexander Mackenzie
Heritage Trail. The trail has been promoted as an important symbol of the
birth of the Canadian nation-state. Its main historical significance is
deemed to lie in Mackenzie's successful completion of his transcontinental voyage.

In contrast, the thousands of years of Native history of the trail and
the trail's continued importance as a transportation route linking the
homesteads, fishing camps, and hunting and trapping territories of the
contemporary Carrier people have played a secondary role in the trail's
promotional campaign. Given the depth of Native history in the region,
the Carrier see Mackenzie's contribution to the historical significance of
the trail as minor. While the Mackenzie Grease Trail has been promoted
as a symbol of Canadian national identity, to the southern Carrier it has
become a symbol of their struggle to maintain the integrity of their communities and to exert control over developments in their midst.

The concept of developing the trail as a heritage route arose in 1974.
Spurred on by the dedicated efforts of two volunteer organizers, in the
following years the trail development plan slowly took shape. Both the
provincial and federal governments undertook feasibility studies on the

trail's development. The location of the original trail travelled by Mackenzie was far from obvious, due to the many horse and wagon trails that
crisscrossed the area. With close reference to Mackenzie's published
journal, between 1978 and 1979 the "official" trail was identified and
cleared, and an informal plan was drafted for the development and interpretation of the historic sites along the route. A comprehensive hiker's
trail guide entitled *In the Steps of Alexander Mackenzie* was published in
1981 by the non-profit organization.

The Nazko and Kluskus First Nations, however, knew little of these
plans, and neither band council had been formally approached for input
or approval for the development concept. This was so even though the
official trail crossed through eight Nazko and Kluskus Indian reserves
and through the entire Nazko and Kluskus traditional territory over
which the two First Nations recently had prepared a comprehensive
claim. "Native heritage sites," including historic villages and graveyards
both on and off reserve land, were prominent features of the interpretive
scheme. Yet no information had been provided to, or sought from, the
local First Nations about how these heritage sites were to be identified,
interpreted, and protected. In short, despite the need for the political support of the Carrier First Nations, there existed a complete lack of communication between the trail's developers and the local bands about the
development.

These events followed on the heels of the recent incursion of logging
into southern Carrier territories. Up until the 1970s the Nazko and
Kluskus people had remained largely sheltered from the industrial developments in the central interior, and they continued to live a hunting, fishing, and trapping lifestyle in family homesteads dispersed along the
Blackwater River. In 1974, however, logging began in the Nazko Valley,
and roads began to be built in the Nazko and Kluskus hunting and trapping territories. The Nazko and Kluskus people erected a road blockade
and created sufficient media attention and political pressure to secure a
short-term moratorium on logging. Eventually, however, logging proceeded, and the clear-cutting of the forests severely disrupted the economy and integrity of the communities. With this recent loss of control
over their traditional lands fresh in their minds, the Nazko and Kluskus
chiefs interpreted the development of the Grease Trail as the theft of their
last remaining resource: their culture.

In 1979 the Nazko and Kluskus chiefs began a series of formal meetings with the provincial and federal government agencies in which the
chiefs attempted to negotiate the terms of their participation in the trail's
development. By virtue of their Aboriginal title and their authority over

reserve lands, the two First Nations demanded that they be included in the decision-making structure on an equal level to that of the provincial and federal governments. Second, they requested control over the manner in which Native heritage resources were defined, interpreted, and developed. After a prolonged series of negotiations, however, these terms were not met. Rather, the First Nations were told they would have the same opportunity for input as other "public interest groups." When the chiefs informed the government agencies that no trespassing on the reserves would be allowed unless an agreement was reached, the trail developers, in a classic example of the rewriting of history, began steps to reroute the official trail to bypass the reserves. Although discussions between the government agencies and the Carrier First Nations periodically occur, this situation of conflict remains essentially unresolved, and the development of the trail continues to proceed with the lack of support of the Nazko and Kluskus First Nations.

Nevertheless, the trail developers continue to use symbols of Native culture and history in their promotional materials. In these representations, as well as in newspaper stories and magazine articles describing the trail, Native people alternately are erased from the landscape or are assigned secondary roles that only enhance the main plot line: that of the celebration of European "discovery" and settlement of Canada. Mackenzie is portrayed as a courageous explorer of an uncharted land. When Natives do appear in these accounts, they are seen either as helpers or as hostile savages who thus enhance the spectre of Mackenzie's heroism. The contemporary Native communities along the trail are either ignored or they themselves are promoted as tourist attractions – the once hostile Indians are now friendly hosts who are willing to share their culture with visitors.

The history reproduced through the Mackenzie Grease Trail development is but one example of a pervasive genre of history, the frontier history, that is found in public school textbooks and on the shelves of bookstores and libraries across Canada. Frontier histories serve the political functions of celebrating Canadian national identity while legitimating the colonization and domination of Native peoples. The image of early Canada as an empty wilderness heroically conquered by the first pioneering settlers serves to erase Native people – and the unresolved issue of Aboriginal title and rights – from historical consciousness. In the case of the Mackenzie Grease Trail, the presentation of contemporary Native people as friendly hosts allows tourists to appreciate the richness of Carrier culture without having to learn of the ongoing protests of the Nazko and Kluskus people and of the controversy that has surrounded the trail development since its inception.

Summary

Conflicts over historical representations have become almost common-place in Native peoples' struggles with the Canadian state. These conflicts have given rise to renewed discussions among anthropologists about their moral obligations to the First Nations with whom they undertake research and to the consequences of advocacy work to the discipline. While the ability of anthropologists to resolve these on-the-ground conflicts is questionable, one of the main contributions that anthropology may make is to develop a better understanding of the cultural contexts in which different versions of history are created and contested. In order to understand the issues that concern the Carrier and other First Nations today, we need to pay increasing attention to the subtle ways in which the ideas of history and images of Indians that permeate popular beliefs among the non-Native Canadian public reinforce the oppressive system of relationships that First Nations leaders are now seeking to challenge.

Notes

1. I use the term "First Nation" rather than the older term, "Indian band," to refer to the political groups defined by the Indian Act and the Department of Indian and Northern Affairs. In addition, I use the terms "Aboriginal" and "Native" to refer to the Aboriginal people in Canada generally; I use "Indian" specifically when I wish to evoke the beliefs and attitudes that non-Natives hold regarding Aboriginal peoples in Canada.

2. In the following pages the words presented in italics are Carrier terms that have been written in the orthography developed by the Summer Institute of Linguistics (Antoine *et al.*, 1974).

3. The Ulkatcho, Kluskus, Nazko, and Red Bluff First Nations belong to the Carrier-Chilcotin Tribal Council; Hagwilget, Moricetown, and Nee-tahi-buhn belong to the Wet'suwet'en; while Takla Lake, Nadleh Whuten, Stellaquo, Nak'azdli, Stoney Creek, Tl'azt'en Nations, Burns Lake, Cheslatta Carrier, and Broman Lake belong to the Carrier-Sekani Tribal Council. In 1994 Lheit Lit'en and Babine Lake were independent.

4. The term "house" is used here to refer to a socio-political group that may or may not reside in the same dwelling.

Recommended Readings

Gisday Wa and Delgamuukw

1989   *The Spirit in the Land: The Opening Statement of the Gitksan and Wet'suwet'en Hereditary Chiefs in the Supreme Court of British Columbia, May 11, 1987*. Gabriola, B.C.: Reflections.

An introduction to the history of the land claim and a summary of contemporary Gitksan and Wet'suwet'en societies, their major institutions, and systems of authority and land ownership.

Goldman, Irving

1940   "The Alkatcho Carrier of British Columbia," in R. Linton, ed., *Acculturation in Seven American Indian Tribes*. New York: D. Appleton-Century.

A summary of Goldman's ethnographic study of the Ulkatcho Carrier, focusing on social, political, and economic life.

1941   "The Alkatcho Carrier: Historical background of crest prerogatives," *American Anthropologist*, 43, 3: 396-418.

An analysis of the adoption of the clan and potlatch-rank systems among the Ulkatcho Carrier through their contact with the Nuxalk (Bella Coola) and northern Carrier.

1953   "The Alkatcho Carrier of British Columbia." Manuscript. Victoria, B.C.: Royal British Columbia Museum.

A comprehensive ethnography of the Ulkatcho Carrier, based on fieldwork conducted in the winter of 1935-36. Focuses on social and economic life, religious beliefs, shamanism, and oral traditions. Available from the Royal British Columbia Museum, Victoria, B.C.

Jenness, Diamond

1943   *The Carrier Indians of the Bulkley River: Their Social and Religious Life*. Washington, D.C.: Bureau of American Ethnology, Smithsonian Institution.

This is a detailed discussion of the Wet'suwet'en social and political organization, religious beliefs, and shamanism, based on three months of fieldwork among the Wet'suwet'en Carrier in 1924-25.

Kew, J.E. Michael

1974   "Nazko and Kluskus: Social Conditions and Prospects for the Future." Manuscript. Quesnel: Nazko Band Office.

A concise ethnographic summary of the contemporary Nazko and Kluskus Carrier, based on a year-long period of ethnographic field research. Focuses on the social and economic impact of the proposed expansion of logging in Nazko and Kluskus territories in 1974. Available from the Special Collections Division of the University of B.C. main library, as part of the *Report on the Nazko and Kluskus Bands from the Nazko-Kluskus Study Team*.

Morice, Adrien G.

1893a "Notes Archaeological, Industrial and Sociological on the Western Denes,"
Transactions of the Canadian Institute (1892-93).

A detailed account of Carrier material culture, with emphasis on the
central Carrier. Includes a list of Carrier bands and villages in the mid-1800s.

1978 *The History of the Northern Interior of British Columbia.* Smithers, B.C.:
Interior Stationery.

A very readable overview of the history of the region, with many
references to Carrier history, culture, and the Carrier's evolving relationship
with European traders and missionaries. Based on Morice's experience as a
missionary at Fort St. James on Stuart Lake.

Tobey, Margaret L.

1981 "The Carrier," in *Handbook of North American Indians*, Vol. 6, *The
Subarctic*, June Helm, ed. Washington, D.C.: Smithsonian Institution.

A summary of Carrier culture at the time of European contact, plus
detailed bibliographic list.

Additional References Cited

Antoine, Franscesca, Catherine Bird, Agnes Isaac, Nelly Prince, Sally Sam, Richard
Walker, and David B. Wilkinson

1974 *Central Carrier Bilingual Dictionary.* Fort St. James: Carrier Linguistics
Committee.

Duff, Wilson

1951 "Notes on Carrier Social Organization," *Anthropology in British Columbia*,
2: 28-34.

Dyen, Isidore, and David F. Aberle

1974 *Lexical Reconstruction: The Case of the Proto-Athapaskan Kinship System.*
New York: Cambridge University Press.

Hackler, James

1958 "The Carrier Indians of Babine Lake: The Effects of the Fur Trade and the
Catholic Church on their Social Organization," M.A. thesis, Department of
Anthropology, San Jose State College.

Hudson, Douglas

1972 "The Historical Determinants of Carrier Social Organization: A Study of
Northwest Athapaskan Matriliny," M.A. thesis, Department of
Anthropology, McMaster University.

1983 "Traplines and Timber: Social and Economic Change Among the Carrier
Indians of Northern British Columbia," Ph.D. dissertation, Department of
Anthropology, University of Alberta.

Kobrinsky, Vernon
   1977   "The Tsimshianization of the Carrier Indians," in J.W. Helmer, S. Van Dyke,
          and F. Kense, eds., *Problems in the Prehistory of the North American
          Subarctic: The Athapaskan Question.* Calgary: University of Calgary
          Archaeological Association.
McEachern, Allan
   1991   *Reasons for Judgment: Delgamuukw v. B.C.* Smithers, B.C.: British
          Columbia Supreme Court.
Morice, Adrien Gabriel
   1893b "Are the Carrier Sociology and Mythology Indigenous or Exotic?"
          *Proceedings and Transactions of the Royal Society of Canada for the Year
          1892*, series 1, section 2, Vol. 10.
Steward, Julian
   1960   "Carrier Acculturation: The Direct Historical Approach," in S. Diamond, ed.,
          Culture in History: Essays in Honor of Paul Radin. New York: Columbia
          University Press.

PART VIII
The Northwest Coast

CHAPTER 23
People of Salmon and Cedar: An Overview of the Northwest Coast

Margaret Seguin Anderson

The Native cultures of the Pacific coast of Canada developed in a rich natural environment. Villages and camps in sheltered harbours close to salmon spawning routes also allowed access to shores and shoals with halibut, cod, herring, oolichan, shellfish, and marine mammals. Unique localized resources were exploited by each tribe, and even by each village, but frequent contacts between neighbouring groups along the coast stimulated sharing of ideas, techniques, and institutions throughout the area, creating the patterns that outsiders have designated as Northwest Coast culture.

The evolution of knowledge, tools, and techniques permitted an effective adaptation to the maritime zone; the Aboriginal patterns of such items as halibut hooks have never been bettered. The permanent villages of large red cedar plank houses located in protected sites throughout the area were built by skilled carpenters and embellished with carvings that have received recognition as masterworks of great artistic traditions. Well-built canoes sixty feet and more in length carried the people to their

MAP 23.1. The Northwest Coast

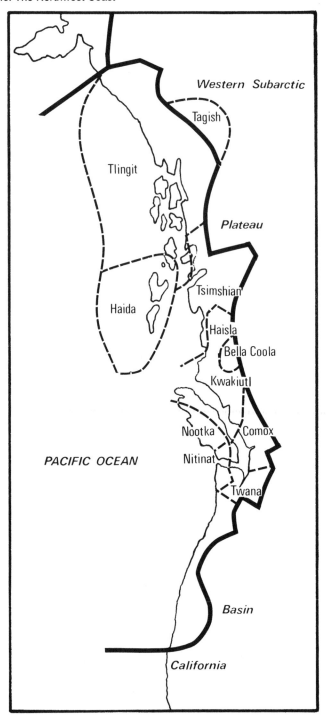

fishing sites, to collecting territories for shellfish, berries, bark, and roots, to hunting areas for land and sea animals, and to other villages for purposes such as weddings, feasts, and, occasionally, raiding. A few trails, such as the famous grease trails in the north, penetrated the thick rain forests that barred movement past the beach rocks up the steep mountain slopes that plunged into the fjords.

Ownership of the territories was vested in local corporate groups of kin; control of territories and access to resources were gained by inheritance of a ranked name/title among all the groups, and in some could also be obtained through marriage, as a gift, or as a prize of war. Inherited differences of rank associated with economic and supernatural privileges were substantial among all the groups. Chiefs had the power to allocate resources, command labour, make alliances, and even to take the life of a slave.

Shamans used both an extensive natural pharmacopoeia and supernatural abilities to cure illness. The natural remedies were potent, and the social cohesiveness created for a patient by the dramatic shamanic performances healed illnesses of the spirit as well as of the body.

The religious beliefs of all the groups emphasized contact with supernatural beings who controlled wealth and life itself. Humans endeavoured to establish relationships with supernatural powers through ceremonial activities, notably ritual purifications, feasts, potlatches, and winter dance ceremonies. Ritual occasions drew on the power of artistic traditions to create lavish events in which setting, costume, oral literature, drama, song, and dance expressed the profound spirituality that pervaded the cultures. Gift-giving feasts called potlatches manifested the wealth and power of the great chiefs, who had the ability to mediate with supernatural powers. Winter ceremonial dances, often lasting months at a time, represented the supernatural forces that created order, brought wealth, and ensured the continuity of the group.

The intrusion of Europeans into the Northwest Coast brought few changes for the first 100 years from initial contact in the late eighteenth century. The early explorers traded iron tools and other European goods for furs and Native artifacts, but they did not seek to alter the pattern of Native cultures. The first European goods obtained were integrated into the traditional cultures as prestige items and useful tools in Native technologies. But the explorers set the stage for more radical changes by demonstrating the potential profit to be made from the furs traded by the coastal Natives, especially the fur of the sea otter, which could be sold for huge profits in China. A busy maritime fur trade was quickly established, reaching its greatest magnitude in the decades around the turn

of the nineteenth century. The early nineteenth century saw the establishment of permanent trading posts along the coast; the sea otter population was depleted by the 1830s. The trade shifted to the furs of land
animals, many of which were obtained from interior groups, and the
coast traders reaped large profits as shrewd middlemen. Though the
profits of the trade were high, the cost was also great. A number of Old
World diseases were introduced, taking a huge toll among the Native
population. Smallpox, tuberculosis, influenza, and venereal diseases
swept through whole tribes, sometimes reducing the population to a
small fraction of its former level. Unscrupulous traders anxious to
obtain scarce furs traded alcohol and firearms, which made hostilities
between traditional enemy groups much more lethal.

At the present, many British Columbia First Nations are entering a

Even greater changes occurred as missionaries, adventurers, gold
miners, and settlers entered the area in large numbers in the mid-
nineteenth century. Many of the intruders had an exaggerated sense of the
glories of "civilization," and little understanding or tolerance for the
complex cultures of Native people. Rights in land were not acknowledged, and resources were appropriated without apology or compensation. British Columbia entered Confederation in 1871, which placed the
Native population under the existing Indian Act, and small reserves were
provided for each local group. In most cases the allocation was unilateral,
involving little consultation and no agreement by the Native group.
Though Native title had not been extinguished by any treaties or agreements (except for a few groups in the southern and northeastern parts of
the province), the province refused to enter negotiations to do so. A few
groups pressed their claims repeatedly, notably the Nisga'a in the north.
In 1973, a decision in the Nisga'a case (referred to as the *Calder* case)
was finally issued by the Supreme Court of Canada. Although the decision was split, the federal government was forced by the narrowness of
this decision and the implications of the case presented around the same
time by the James Bay Cree to recognize a continuing Native title.

At the present, many British Columbia First Nations are entering a
process of negotiating Aboriginal claims to their traditional lands
through a recently established procedure. After over a century of refusal
to acknowledge any Aboriginal rights, the province agreed in the 1990s
to participate in the negotiations; however, the process is expected to
prove extremely lengthy. As of this writing in mid-1994, no settlements
have yet been reached; an announcement that a settlement of the Nisga'a
negotiations is due this year may signal a breakthrough, but this is not yet
established. The Gitksan and Wet'suwet'en groups in the watersheds of

PLATE 23.1. Of all the Northwest Coast populations the Haida were the most devastated by diseases introduced by Europeans. Ninstint on Anthony Island was already abandoned by 1901 as a result of population depletion from epidemics, the forest beginning to reclaim the site. Courtesy of Royal British Columbia Museum, Victoria, B.C., PN 837.

the Skeena and Bulkley rivers have declared their intention to pursue the judgement in their case to the Supreme Court, which has agreed to hear the case; the *Delgamuukw* case (named after the first of the list of hereditary chiefs who are the plaintiffs) is a suit for ownership and jurisdiction over the hereditary territories of the chiefs. The decision at the first level was a rejection of these claims, issued in language that echoed nine-teenth-century social evolutionism to a degree that has appalled many observers; at the appeal level the court partially reversed the complete rejection of the rights of the Gitksan and Wet'suwet'en, but the judgement offered them little of substance. When the case is decided by the Supreme Court it is likely to be the most significant decision in the area of Aboriginal rights since *Calder*. The current situation in B.C. is very com-plex. On the one hand both the federal and provincial governments are defendants in *Delgamuukw* and are pursuing their defence strongly, denying all rights claimed by the plaintiffs. At the same time, however, the federal government is undertaking new initiatives such as the Aboriginal Fisheries Strategy, an attempt to work with First Nations communities in developing fishing plans that recognize their rights in accordance with court decisions such as the *Sparrow* decision;[1] and the provincially established B.C. Treaty Commission is organizing hearings to settle the outstanding claims.

The extravagance of potlatches during the nineteenth century was often viewed with astonishment and dismay by outsiders, particularly those bent on fitting Native people into the mould of Victorian civiliza-tion; the disruption of traditional, established rank relationships among chiefs and the huge surplus of wealth that entered Native economies dur-ing the fur trade are now thought to have created stresses and imbalances in the traditional system, leading to lavish competitive potlatching as a way of re-establishing social order. Toward the end of the last century, the potlatch was outlawed by the Canadian government, causing it to go underground and curtailing the scale of the events. The masks and para-phernalia associated with the potlatches and winter ceremonials were confiscated, destroyed, or sold to collectors, and fines and prison confine-ment were sometimes levied in an attempt to enforce the law. Despite almost universal conversion to various Christian denominations, the tra-ditional functions of the feasts were continued by many groups through this period, and, with the dropping of the prohibition during the 1950s, the feasts and dances are once again public celebrations in many Native communities, and have increasingly become a major feature at public occasions in urban communities across the province. For example, the 1994 Commonwealth Games held in Victoria featured a Queen's baton carved by three Northwest Coast artists, a huge commemorative totem pole was raised for the games, and several Native dance groups were fea-tured in the opening ceremonies.

Native languages were vigorously suppressed by the agents of Cana-dian authority as well. Until the 1940s, and even later in some areas, standard policy in many schools was to administer corporal punishment to pupils who spoke in their Native tongues. Inevitably, the policy succeeded, to the extent that there are now very few Native speakers of any of the languages of the Northwest Coast under the age of forty. Official policies and public attitudes have reversed, but unless the language programs now offered in the schools are given much higher priority, the languages will not long survive. The Royal Commission on Aboriginal Peoples has heard numerous submissions on the topic of language revitalization, and strong recommendations are anticipated. Universities and colleges in British Columbia are becoming aware that the languages and cultures of First Nations are significant subjects for research and teaching, and there are increasing opportunities for students in these areas. The new University of Northern British Columbia has made First Nations Studies a featured program, and will begin offering undergraduate and graduate degrees in the field when it officially opens in 1994, including a complete degree program offered in partnership with the Wilp Wilxo'oskwhl Nisga'a in the Nass Valley; the Nisga'a have declared their readiness to welcome outsiders to their territories and to teach them their language, culture, and history.

As the fur trade declined in significance and the economy of British Columbia began to focus on the lumber industry and the commercial fishery, Native people on the coast continued to fish, hunt, trap, and engage in other traditional activities, but they also entered the new industries in substantial numbers. Native men fished commercially during the salmon run while Native women worked long hours in the canneries scattered along the coast, to which families moved for several months of the year. The economic cycle of the developing resource industries was frequently boom/bust; labour shortages during the boom periods made entry into wage labour both easy and attractive for Natives, who comprised a large proportion of the population of the province. The centralization and intensive capitalization of many industries and the rapid expansion of the immigrant settler population have decreased the significance of Native participation in all industries, and economically marginalized Native individuals and communities.

The absolute number of Native Indians in British Columbia fell during most of the nineteenth century, reaching a low point of under 25,000 in 1929. Though the Indian population is now greater that it was before initial contact, it comprises less than 3 per cent of the population of the province. There are close to 200 bands in British Columbia, many with a membership of under 500 persons; since Bill C-31 was proclaimed in 1985 a large number of individuals have regained status, and this new membership has increased pressure on reserves, as well as increasing the proportion of off-reserve members. The greatest proportion of the population is along the coast, as it was in Aboriginal times. About 50 per cent of the registered Indians reside on reserves, which are the smallest in area per capita of any province in Canada. Each band is governed autonomously, with funding for some programs provided through the federal Department of Indian Affairs. In the last two decades, tribal associations have been formed in a number of areas on the coast, bringing together a number of bands to lobby and to provide a link in the administrative chain. Economic development, improved facilities and educational opportunities, access to resource rights, and the settlement of the land claims are the primary foci. As noted above, there have been few settlements at this time, and almost the entire province of British Columbia is under claim.

There has been an increasing tendency for First Nations groups to be sought as allies by environmentalist groups opposed to development of areas of the province. The west coast of Vancouver Island around Clayoquot Sound was the scene of a major confrontation between those supporting logging of the forests of the area and those opposed to any cutting of one of the last standing old growth forests in North America. The province has established CORE (Committee on Resources and the Environment) processes to negotiate land-use plans in this and other contentious areas, and for the Clayoquot the result was a proposal to preserve a percentage of the Clayoquot Sound area as parkland and to tighten regulations on logging practices in other areas; the initial plan was prepared without thorough consultation with the Nuu-Chah-nulth peoples of the region, but as these groups have been involved more of the general public seems to have accepted this "Clayoquot Compromise." ALCAN's proposal for "Kemano Completion" is another issue in which environmentalists and First Nations communities have been allied; this is the proposal by ALCAN to re-direct a high proportion of the remaining flow of the Nechako River through its dam system and to install further turbines to generate additional hydroelectric power at its Kemano generating station. The proposal is opposed by environmentalists as a further threat to the watershed and the ecology of the Fraser River system into which the Nechako drains, by commercial fishing interests on the coast because of the perceived threat to major stocks of salmon, and by the Cheslatta Carrier people, whose territories were flooded by the original dam in the 1950s. The federal and provincial governments are holding hearings on the case now, but the mandate of the hearings is only to recommend ways to ameliorate the environmental impact since both governments have already given approval for the further water diversion despite recommendations by federal fisheries scientists against the project. There are numerous other areas of the province, such as the fight over the Stein Valley, the "Save the Tat" campaign (the Tatsenshini is one of the last remaining wild rivers; a mining proposal threatened its pristine beauty), and the Lyell Island blockades, in which similar alliances have been forged between First Nations and their neighbours, and it may be anticipated that this will continue as the symbolic capital of aboriginality is sought by environmentalists. At the same time, however, the First Nations of the region are making plans for sustainable economic development on their territories after their claims are settled, and this generally includes careful harvesting of resources.

Note

1. In 1990 the Supreme Court of Canada unanimously reversed the conviction of Ronald E. Sparrow of the Musqueam band on twenty-five charges under the Fisheries Act. The court ruled that the crown had not proved that Aboriginal rights to fish for food had been extinguished by the Fisheries Act and affirmed the priorities set by the 1980 case *Jack v. the Queen*; that is, conservation of species is the first priority, followed by Indian fishing, with non-Indian commercial fishing next and sports fishing in the lowest priority.

CHAPTER 24

Understanding Tsimshian Potlatch

Margaret Seguin Anderson

This chapter will focus on the Tsimshian feasts, which, with the feasts of other Northwest Coast groups, are referred to as "potlatch."[1] Gift-giving feasts were widespread on the Northwest Coast at the time of contact and were sometimes very elaborate and lengthy during the nineteenth century. They continue to be an important focus and in the past decade have increased in frequency and prominence. Although there have been numerous descriptions and analyses of such feasts, none seemed to provide an integrated account that "made sense" of either the traditional or current Tsimshian feasts that I read about and saw. In particular, the literature gives little insight into the symbolic value of the actual events to the Tsimshian.

Accounts of traditional Tsimshian feasts (*yaokw*) have emphasized their importance in structuring social and economic relations, but have given little insight into the significance of details of the feasts, displays, and orations involved, into the logic or pattern of the symbols as selected and ordered in time and space, or into connections with the symbolic value of elements in other aspects of Tsimshian culture. I refer to these aspects of the feasts when I speak of the symbolic value of the actual events to the Tsimshian. I will attempt here to interpret Tsimshian feasts by tracing connections between elements found in the feasts and other aspects of the culture. I focus on the relationships among the Tsimshian belief in reincarnation, traditional attitudes toward other realms of power – including spirits, animals, and supernatural beings – and, most significantly, the relationship between an individual and his father's clan. The appreciation of these relationships makes the potlatch of the traditional Tsimshian understandable not only as a means of perpetuating a social structure, and as a viable economic system, but as a vision of the Tsimshian fulfilling their obligations of reciprocity to the powers of all the worlds in their own cosmological system. Furthermore, the shape of the modern feast system and the significance of its continuity for over 200 years are clarified when seen in this context.

The reader of an ethnographic essay may not always be aware that it is an intensely personal account, not an impersonal presentation of objective "facts." It is sometimes equally difficult for an author to convey effectively the extent to which her background, interests, and the history of her particular research effort have shaped the final presentation. The following personal information seems relevant here: I am not Tsimshian; I am a linguist by training; I taught in a Department of Anthropology for nineteen years; I began work on Tsimshian culture in the village of Hartley Bay, British Columbia, at the invitation of members of the community, to work with a local language program, and six years later married a man from that community; and I am a woman.

As a linguist, I am concerned always with language, and most particularly with *meaning* in language; as a linguist who taught for many years in an Anthropology Department, I am concerned with the meaningfulness of *cultural* phenomena. My approach to understanding the feast system starts from an assumption that the Tsimshian are not just "doing something" in the feasts, but that they are also "saying something." Trying to understand how the Tsimshian interpret the messages of feasts implies building a Tsimshian "cultural philology." One way to do this is to "de-construct" meanings from context and exegesis, and then to "re-construct" an enriched interpretation. Successive layers of such interpretation act to focus understandings of the parts and the whole. The end product is also an exegesis, or contextualization, which becomes a part of the new context of interpretation. Each fragment of information provides part of the interpretation for the others. This sort of approach is sometimes referred to as *hermeneutic*; it is an instance of a trend in the social sciences that Geertz describes: ". . . many social scientists have turned away from a laws and instances ideal of explanation toward a cases and interpretations one, looking less for the sort of thing that connects planets and pendulums and more for the sort that connects chrysanthemums and swords" (1983: 19).

Constantly probing for meaning in the activities of anyone is occasionally disconcerting. The difficulties have been ameliorated in my work in Hartley Bay because the feast system is viewed as important and interesting there, and because I first met people in the village while I was working on their language program. Though I am not Tsimshian, being in a Tsimshian village feels comfortable, intellectually and practically; perhaps, as a woman, I felt more at home in a place where women are relatively potent than I did in "my own" milieu at the university, where the power structure was generally overwhelmingly male.

The research for this work has included five years of intermittent residence in Hartley Bay over a fifteen-year period. During that time I have sought an understanding of the nature of current feasts in that community and have discussed oral traditions with many elders, a number of whom have died during this time. I have also assembled recollections of activities in the community over the past seventy years. Textual material collected in Hartley Bay by William Beynon has provided some independent documentation from the 1940s and 1950s. Texts and descriptions of feasting traditions from other areas, especially Garfield's ethnographic work at Port Simpson, have been consulted and discussed with community members, but most of the materials that originated in other locales are considered foreign; similarities are seen as interesting, but do not compel integration.

The interpretation that follows is intensely local, in that the material from Hartley Bay vastly outweighs that from other communities and sources. Paradoxically, much of the locally derived interpretation should prove to hold in its general contours for other Tsimshian groups, as well as the linguistically related Gitksan and Nisga'a. The material reveals patterns grounded in conventions of discourse and linguistic structure that were shared by all speakers of the Tsimshianic languages. These patterns comprised the process by which Tsimshian people defined "otherness" and "us-ness." They were productive of unique practices and histories as they interacted with the existing context in each locale, but I hope that the patterns themselves express some of the shared understandings that constitute the unique genius of Tsimshian culture.

The Context of the Study: The Tsimshian

Traditional Tsimshian chiefs conducted themselves with the formality and concern for protocol now associated with international diplomacy. Each territory was held to be a world apart, distinct in history, custom, and law; to enter the territory of another village (or even of another lineage segment) was to enter a foreign land. The inhabitants of each domain figured as reciprocal, symbolic "others," providing an important component of a view of the universe as a place of many worlds. The people of each village emphasized the foreignness of outsiders by epithets (both polite and pejorative), and by descriptions of the exotic practices of each. Actual and classificatory kinship relationships penetrated the insularity of each village. Knowledge of other groups was often intimate and detailed. Ideas, customs, and objects moved easily between groups, but adoption of foreign customs was framed by the premise that, once adopted, the customs were no longer foreign; they were placed within the local meaning system. If a chief received a privilege such as a dance from a neighbouring chief, the privilege and the story of its acquisition became a part of the interpretive context for his own group – part of their story. If the other group understood it differently, that was the natural result of their foreignness. As long as each chief had a legitimate claim to the use of the privilege, interpretations were correct for respective worlds, and this would be affirmed at performances. The external form was shared, as was the understanding that allowed the local interpretations to co-exist. Foreigners might be seen as capricious, and potentially dangerous, but not as wrong in being foreign.

Generalizations became broader as distance increased, and all the groups beyond the Northern Kwakiutl were merged as *didoo* ("down there"). Details of shared kinship and history were known, but had to be constantly revitalized in order to continue to hold force in structuring interactions.

People who arrived late on the coast, and who seemed to live in ships rather than houses, became known as *'amsiwah*, or "driftwood people"; their peculiarities became known far and wide, most notably the absence of women among them. The Tsimshian have come to know a great deal about the *'amsiwah*, of course, and we have become a very significant "other" group for them; yet only occasionally have we *'amsiwah* understood the Tsimshian in the context of the local meaning systems in which they continue to live.

MAP 24.1. Tsimshian Communities (data from Duff, 1959)

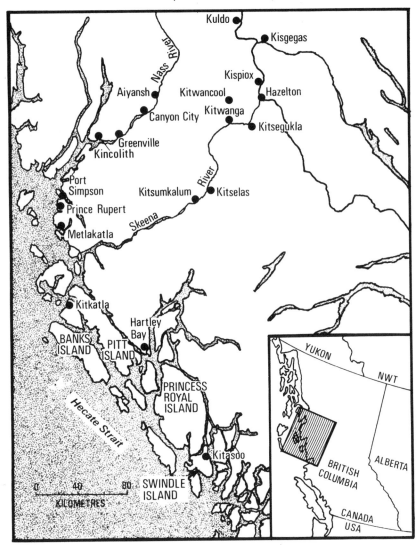

The Tsimshianic Groups

The Tsimshianic-speaking peoples occupied territories along the Nass and Skeena rivers and their tributaries and estuaries, extending to the islands and coast to the south. There were four major linguistic divisions:

the Nisga'a on the Nass; the Gitksan on the upper Skeena, above the canyon at Kitselas; the Coast Tsimshian on the lower reaches of the Skeena and the adjacent coast; and the Southern Tsimshian, who extended Tsimshian culture as far south as modern-day Klemtu.

The four Tsimshianic divisions were united by closely related languages. Boundaries between the divisions were marked by the linguistic patterns themselves, by distinctive ecological contexts in each division's territories and the annual cycles attuned to those contexts, by different emphases in ritual activities, and by the political context and relationships to foreign groups maintained by each. The boundaries were bridged by long-established travel and trade relations, intermarriage, feasting exchanges between certain chiefs, and occasional conflict.

There were up to four exogamous clans in each village, designated by the principal totemic crests of each: blackfish and grizzly bear, raven and frog, eagle and beaver, and wolf and bear. A clan might include several distinct lines that traced origin to separate ancestors whose exploits were recounted in the lineage history; these lines maintained mutual exogamy but did not consider themselves directly related, and they sometimes hosted each other at feasts and in various ways interacted as mutual "others." The local segments of these lineages were the groups that held territories and feasted as units. Depending on the size of the local segment there might be one or more houses headed by chiefs who had inherited names carrying economic and ritual privileges. The chiefs had established relative ranks, which determined their rights to precedence in political interactions.

The territories belonging to a local segment of a clan were administered by the chiefs, each of whom inherited control over a specific territory with the name of his maternal uncle. Women also held names of high rank, inherited from their own mothers and maternal aunts, but it was unusual for a woman to hold a territory-controlling name, though she might hold the privilege of managing certain resources such as berry-picking grounds. Generally, each clan represented in a village had control over sites for each type of available resources in an area, but one local lineage segment often held the highest-ranked names and controlled the bulk of the territory.

Large red cedar plank dwellings housed each of the local lineage segments; if the group were large and several chiefs were of high rank there might be several such houses for a segment. The residents of each house were usually a group of men closely related through their mothers, with their wives, children, dependents, and slaves; such a group was the unit of production and consumption. The man bearing the highest-ranked name was deemed to be the owner of the house, but he took counsel with the holders of the other ranked names in his house in making decisions about matters that bore implications for the power and prestige of the house. Matters of mutual interest, such as defence, were discussed with the chiefs of the other houses in the village as well. Succession to the highest-ranked names was a matter of concern to chiefs in other villages, and was validated by guests assembled from a wide area. Individuals who did not hold high-ranked names associated with territories could join one of the houses to which they were related.

All changes in social relationships were declared and legitimated by property distributions and feasts. The major focus of feasting among the Tsimshian groups was the cycle that began with the death of a chief and culminated with the installation of his heir, who was generally the eldest son of his eldest sister. The cycle generally included a memorial feast, the feasts associated with the erection of a memorial pole and the building of a new house, and the final feast of name assumption. When the deceased was the head of a local lineage, guests were generally invited from all groups with which political relationships were maintained. The prestige of the local lineage and the maintenance of its economic and political power were dependent on the success of events, including distribution of sufficient wealth to demonstrate control over their territories.

Chiefs were responsible for relationships with other villages and with foreign tribes such as the Haida, Tlingit, and Haisla. They also bore responsibility for keeping their group in balance with the supernatural beings who controlled the continuation of food and wealth. Each lineage had inherited relationships to supernatural beings encountered by the original holders of their names. Animal species such as bear, salmon, seal, and mountain goat were governed by their own chiefs who demanded proper respect. Named locations were also occupied by powerful supernatural beings who controlled the wealth of the area and the safety and success of those who visited. Accounts of ancestral interactions with supernatural beings were an integral part of the assumption of a ranked name. Such events were depicted by the crests that were carved and painted on the houses, poles, and specified household goods of each chief; some powers might also be dramatized in performances, which involved masks, costumes, songs, and dances exclusively owned by the lineage. Some of these crest privileges were common to all members of a lineage; others were restricted to those holding a particular, highly ranked name.

Winter ceremonial performances and dances brought supernatural powers into the Tsimshian worlds. The old Tsimshian form of winter ceremonial was the *halait*, which was firmly integrated into the rank structure. Chiefs controlled supernatural power for their people, manifesting their abilities in dramatizations of a special set of names. A series of four winter ceremonial dances had apparently been entering the Tsimshian system via the Northern Kwakiutl connections at Kitimat and Bella Bella in the late pre-contact period. Two of these were open to all ranks, but two were restricted to particular chiefs.

Another form of relationship with supernatural power was the province of the ritual specialists known as shamans, some of whom were also chiefs. Shamans practised several sorts of healing based on Tsimshian understandings of the nature of illness. Part of their responsibility was to combat the effects of witchcraft, which was surreptitiously practised by disaffected individuals.

The material culture of the Tsimshian was a magnificent manifestation of this intricate, coherent, symbolic vision. The privilege of owning and displaying many treasures was restricted to those with sufficient rank to respect them properly by distributing property; other items were limited to those with supernatural powers, such as shamans and members of the secret societies. The large houses were carved and painted with designs representing the crests of the house owner, fronted with complex poles erected in honour of past chiefs. Everyday objects such as clothing, baskets, canoes, fish hooks, and storage boxes were finely made, frequently displaying complex symbolic decoration. The sculptural style of Tsimshian carvers has been acclaimed, and their creations were sought by other groups during traditional times as avidly as by modern collectors.

The relationships of the Tsimshian to the land, to their neighbours, to the supernatural beings, and even to themselves were ultimately radically transformed by the intrusion of Europeans and Euro-Canadians. Initial contacts with explorers and maritime traders did not undermine the traditional patterns; the goods received in trade were incorporated into the cultures as useful items in traditional technologies or as prestige items in the system of crest privileges. But sea otter furs proved tremendously valuable and led to rapid development of a maritime trade. The sea otter was brought to the edge of extinction within five decades. The trade shifted to land furs, which the Tsimshian acquired by direct trapping and by controlling the trade of interior groups, reaping large profits as middlemen.

A land-based trading post was established by the Hudson's Bay Company in Tsimshian territory at the mouth of the Nass River in 1831 and moved in 1834 to Fort Simpson. The chiefs who controlled the trade became even more wealthy, and the nineteenth century was probably the period of greatest opulence for the Tsimshian. Huge amounts of wealth entered the Native economy and a ready supply of iron tools allowed the carvers to reach even higher standards and greater productivity. At the same time, established relationships of rank were destabilized by new aggregations around the trading post, which brought together chiefs who had not previously had stable political relationships through the feast system. There were extraordinary mortality rates because of diseases such as smallpox, measles, influenza, and venereal infections. Frequent deaths encouraged the promotion of multiple claims as names became vacant, leading to some competitive potlatching.

Other influences entered the area. In 1857 a lay preacher for the Church Missionary Society named William Duncan came to Fort Simpson. He began by learning the language of the Coast Tsimshian; he was ultimately to convert most of the Coast Tsimshian and Southern Tsimshian people and to build a new community with them at Metlakatla, a traditional Coast Tsimshian site. Metlakatla was a great success, and nearby groups actively sought missionization.

Duncan fought the *halait*, but awarded various badges and the insignia of new power that replaced it. Church activities, hymn singing, participation in brass bands, sports days, village offices, and clubs were all enthusiastically embraced by the Tsimshian who joined Duncan. Shamanic healing was denounced, but Duncan made available substitute services, and the use of traditional medicines not accompanied by ritual performance was not prohibited. Duncan did not forbid the telling of stories, and he was of the opinion that several demonstrated knowledge of the Flood and other biblical events. Property distributions for display were denounced, but Duncan himself obliged the same rank system by granting positions of authority to chiefs in the new community structure and by collecting property and redistributing some of it through the chiefs. Duncan did assign English-type last names, which were transmitted patrilineally, but did not forbid the remembrance and transmission of the Tsimshian names, nor apparently of feasts at which they were bestowed, as long as the format included Christian prayers and distribution of presents only as payments. The chiefs also had leading roles as public speakers and as Duncan's counsellors. Duncan's intransigence was difficult for many of the church workers who came to work with him, but it was quite consonant with the behaviour the Tsimshian expected of a chief. A Christian Tsimshian social pattern was forged from the desire of the Tsimshian to retain their territories and power and from Duncan's visionary Christianity.

PLATE 24.1. Metlakatla, B.C., showing the eastern portion of Metlakatla with cannery buildings on the left. Courtesy of the Provincial Archives of British Columbia, HP55799, C-8105.

Duncan stayed at Metlakatla for twenty-five years, drawing increasing numbers to the village and the Christian Tsimshian life. Duncan became hugely influential because of his great success, but he never lost his intransigence in the face of what he saw as error. This led him into difficulties with authorities in the church; in 1887 he left to start a New Metlakatla in Alaska, with over 800 Tsimshian people. The land to which they moved was far from traditional territories they had continued to use for hunting and fishing, and many firm converts chose to remain in B.C. Old Metlakatla reverted to a small village, and the populations of other villages were restored.

During the late nineteenth century the Tsimshian saw an influx of gold seekers, adventurers, and a few settlers. By then the Aboriginal nations were no longer treated as sovereign. When B.C. entered Confederation, small reserves were allocated to each village, and the Tsimshian groups came under the provisions of the Indian Act without ever having signed treaties; none of the groups have abandoned claims to their traditional territories. The Nisga'a have pressed their Aboriginal claim with tenacity, leading the government at one point to pass a law against the raising of funds to finance such activities. The Nisga'a claim was finally heard by the Supreme Court of Canada. Despite an ambiguous decision issued in 1973, the case was one of the major factors that set the stage for serious negotiations between the federal and provincial governments and the

First Nations of British Columbia. The current British Columbia treaty process has its roots in these events.

The Tsimshianic languages were used during initial missionization but were suppressed by later missionaries, educators, and administrators. Southern Tsimshian is now spoken by only a couple of individuals. There are few speakers of the other Tsimshianic languages under the age of thirty. Official suppression of the languages has been abandoned, but they are unlikely to continue as living systems unless they are given substantial artificial support; while positive steps have been initiated, the revitalization of these languages and other Canadian languages is not yet a policy priority.

The Tsimshian participated actively in the development of the modern economy of their homeland. Their success in the modern commercial fishery is particularly notable, but Tsimshian people also made contributions in areas such as logging, transportation, and commerce.

The Symbolic Structure of the Traditional Tsimshian Yaokw

The preceding section has established a context. In this section I weave threads of association between some traditional Tsimshian religious premises and symbolic associations and the traditional *yaokw* as the central Tsimshian social institution. The model of symbolic analysis has its roots in philology, as discussed above. Because of constraints on length, three sections of the argument are presented only in précis; the fourth section is presented in greater detail to illustrate the sort of evidence available.

i. The Tsimshian local matriclan, which was the functioning feast group, was a *waab* (house). A house is symbolically a box, a container. Persons were not *in* a *waab*, they *were* the *waab*.

The matrilineage is imagined as a house, which is a container motif, like the box containing preserved food and/or wealth. The participants in a feast are assigned places within the house. The feast "empties" the house. Houses are much like persons: built by father's clan, named at a potlatch after the building, and carved and painted with the crests of the lineage (Garfield, 1939: 276). In fact, the significant "members" of the lineage are not particular individuals but the "social persons" of the ranked names. Individuals are required to carry the names, but the structure of the lineage is the structure of the names. From this perspective individuals are indeed contained, *in* a name. This interpretation of the significance of containers is quite different from that in recent work developed from a psychoanalytic perspective (Dundes, 1979; Fleisher, 1981), which suggested that the potlatch on the Northwest Coast was a manifestation of "anal erotic character traits."

The Tsimshian see themselves as forming the container, rather than as inside it; their concern is not with excretion *per se*, but with the restoration of real beings to their proper worlds and with the preparation of an "empty container" to receive new wealth.

ii. A *waab* included individuals who were more and less "real." A "real" person (*Sm'oigyet*, "chief") held a high name, passed to him/her matrilineally; each name was associated with an origin story, crests, songs, dances, and economic powers. Becoming "real" depended on lifelong participation in the property distributions at *yaokw*. Relations between groups, whether human villages or different species, were mediated by their respective real people.

That *Sm'oigyet* literally translated as "real person" has often been noted. "Reality" is not an absolute, but should be seen as a cline: slaves are outside the cline; commoners are less real than chiefs; chiefs can be ranked from less to more real. Real animals can appear in human form in the human world. Occasions are also more and less real; real occasions are those in which real beings interact, altering the world. Real people were those who had been "shown to the people" and "pushed up" since childhood; who had "fed the people" by giving feasts and distributing property; who had "put on a name" entitling them to social and economic prerogatives; who "could talk to the people"; and whose conduct, particularly on "real" occasions, affected the entire lineage.

Communication and negotiation within and among human groups was channelled through these real people. Decisions within a *waab* were made by the ranking name-holder with the support and advice of his councillors, who also partook of the quality. If there were several houses in a local clan, the ranking members of each, led by the highest-ranking name-holder, managed the affairs of the local clan. Relations between local clans were arranged by the highest-ranked persons in the village, in consultation with advisers and with the consent of the ranking name-holders from the other local clans. Consent was given by participating in public feasts and ceremonies at which decisions, particularly concerning successions to names, were announced. Relations with other Tsimshian groups, including trade, marriage, and settlement of disagreements, were similarly channelled through the real people, usually the highest-ranked name-holder(s). Relations with non-Tsimshian, including notably the Nisga'a and the Gitksan (speakers of Tsimshianic languages, but not

PLATE 24.2. High-ranking Gitksan women dressed in ceremonial regalia that includes frontlets, Chilkat blankets, and dance aprons, 1910. Courtesy of Royal British Columbia Museum, Victoria, B.C., PN 3929.

called Tsimshian), Haida, Tlingit, and Northern Kwakiutl groups, were essentially "royal" affairs. These interactions were particularly delicate, even potentially violent if mishandled. Apparently the early missionaries and traders were also thought to be "real." Collison (1915: 9) mentions that "in the spring (April) of 1860, Mr. Duncan first visited the Nass River. He was well received at the lower villages, where several of the chiefs feasted him and gave him presents of furs."

Since the real people were responsible for dealing with other groups for the entire constituency (house, lineage, village), their conduct was important to the group. Failure of any sort was an indication that standards were not being maintained. Failure in fishing or hunting demonstrated that the real people among the animals were not prepared to acknowledge the claims of the human group. A wound or an accident signalled a loss of prestige and potency – if relations with other powers were correct then the accident would not have occurred. Generally, when an accident happened to a real person, distributions of property served to inform other real beings that any defect had been remedied and were a part of the cure, along with increased self-discipline. The person was said to "wash" by making these distributions. Failure to be treated appropriately at a feast (being called later than appropriate, or given less than proper in relation to others) had also to be answered – otherwise it was evident that the individual or group belonged at the level accorded them, and the prestige of the person slighted was actually diminished. Since such a loss of power would affect the individual's influence with *all* other real beings and reflect on all members of the lineage, demands for rightful recognition were not mere self-aggrandizement.

Individuals with more reality were more potent. Relations with beings in all worlds were required, and these were mediated by the real beings. Interaction of a real being entailed simultaneous effects on the less real beings under his sway – for example, if the chief of the spring salmon willingly entered a river where fishermen were waiting, so would his tribe.

iii. In addition to the Tsimshian tribes and other human groups they were acquainted with, Tsimshian recognized other societies. Each animal species had its own village, with "real people," commoners, and slaves, similar to Tsimshian villages. Food animals came to the Tsimshian by the animals' own consent, directed by their chiefs. There were also villages for human ghosts, with similar social structure. However, spirits of both animals and humans were subject to reincarnation. Actions taken on animal bodies in human villages influenced the animals in their own villages. Complete, respectful consumption of animal bodies was required to ensure the health of the animals. Proper reincarnation among humans was dependent on human feasting. The consequences of actions in one domain could be observed in the others. Real animals in their villages were aware of actions taken by humans; human shamans were especially adept at perceiving other worlds.

Whether we interpret them as literal or metaphoric statements, their myths indicate that traditional Tsimshian did not view the universe anthropocentrically: they were aware of parallel worlds, some inhabited by animal people and some by supernatural powers, as exemplified in the story of "The Prince Who Was Taken Away by the Salmon People" (Boas, 1916: 192 *et seq.*), which also shows the way in which actions in one world had consequences in the others. The story tells us that a young prince who had taken a bit of dried salmon from his mother's box to feed a slave during a famine was taken by the salmon to their village. The salmon village had houses carved with figures of spring salmon, the largest inhabited by the old chief of the spring salmon, who had been ill with palsy for two years:

> The sick chief ordered his attendants to spread mats at one side of the large fire. They did so. Then the Prince went and seated himself on the mats which had been spread for him by the chief's attendants. As soon as he was seated on a mat, behold! an old woman came to his side, who touched him, and said, 'My dear Prince!' Then she questioned him. 'Do you know who brought you here?' The prince replied, 'No' – 'The Spring Salmon have brought you here, for their chief has been sick with palsy for over two years, because your mother has kept him in her little box for over two years. When you unfolded the salmon the other day, the chief got a little better because you did so.'

Though the other worlds were very like the world of the Tsimshian, there were also clear refractions of structure. In their domain, animals perceived themselves as human and perceived humans as powers or foreigners (never, apparently, as food animals). The salmon come to the world of the Tsimshian to fish for their own salmon, which are to us the leaves of the cottonwood tree, and while there, their salmon bodies are food in turn for the Tsimshian. As long as the proper respect was shown to the salmon caught, and as long as the fish was completely consumed (and any bones, etc. burned afterwards, or returned to the water), the salmon would return.

Each world (each village) was as "real" as the others. Relations between each village/world were the particular responsibility of the real people and the real beings, and also of shamans, who were especially adept at discerning the state of affairs of other worlds and at negotiating with them, frequently being given tokens of supernatural power from other worlds. A real person who put on a high name was connected to other worlds through the tokens of contacts made by his predecessors in the name with real beings – tokens such as songs, dances, crests, and power. These treasures and potent connections were maintained in perpetuity by the feast system.

Among these other worlds were villages of ghosts. Although the details of the traditional understanding of reincarnation are no longer clear, the concept is still firmly held in Hartley Bay, and evidence from the Gitksan suggests that in Aboriginal times the parallel to the worlds of the animal people was close. That is, a *baa'lx* (person reincarnated) also preferred to come back to a person who is generous at feasts.

> iv. Tsimshian saw symbolic associations between fathers, foreigners, animals, and supernatural. A father contributed food to his wife and children, members of a *waab* different from his own, as animals fed their bodies to humans, who lived in a world other than their own. Just as the real animal remained in its own village, the reality of a father remained a part of his own *waab*. Members of father's clan had special ritual duties to a child and were paid by the child's matriclan for these duties at feasts.

Though the most significant category of kinship relations for Tsimshian was the matrilineal clan to which an individual belonged, the *kswaatk* ("where you come from," your father's side) was extremely significant in an individual's life as well. The name given to a child was supposed to have been selected from a set of names belonging to the matrilineage, but it should also have reference to the side of the father. Throughout life, services were performed by "father's side," or "father's sisters," including the naming of the child, piercing of ears, birthing, mourning, and all medical treatment. Services such as housebuilding and pole- and canoe-carving were also to be purchased from the father's clan. In turn, an individual returned respect to the father's side – "paying" when a crest of the father's side was displayed, giving food to a member of the father's clan who returned blankets or other goods to the giver, being supported by a member of father's side in some dances, and paying for the many services provided. By a careful comparative analysis of kin terminologies from Tsimshian, Haida, and Tlingit, Dunn (1984: 5) established several symbolic associations:

From the Tsimshian perspective a set of binary opposition serves to set the Haida and the Tlingit apart. . . . The Haida are symbolic male, while the Tlingit are symbolic female. The Haida are elder, the Tlingit younger. The Haida are animal, supernatural, and unfamiliar, while the Tlingit are human and 'known,' i.e. related. For the Tsimshian the Haida are 'father' while the Tlingit are 'little sister.'

The association of fathers with supernaturals, animals, and foreigners (Haida especially) allowed the Tsimshian to maintain reciprocal relations with supernaturals and animals in their own world through the feasts and payments made to the father's side. Powers, good relations with animal real people, and success were gifts from the supernatural – first received from a supernatural father, then passed on matrilineally. The father/benefactor is inevitably located by the end of the story in a different world/village than the child/receiver, who has a token of the gift embodied in a name, story episode, song, dance, crest object, etc. (There are few Tsimshian tales of human males marrying supernatural women, and none that I know of resulted in children. In a matrilineal system, children of such a union would not, of course, be Tsimshian anyway). The continued potency of the gift from the supernatural father was contingent on a continued relationship with the benefactor in the other world.

The set of payments and services also allowed for clear delineation of rights in persons, despite mixed residence patterns. Since any service performed by a member of a person's father's lineage was promptly and publicly paid for by members of the mother's lineage, there was a clear statement of group affiliation. Each residence unit necessarily included members of other clans, but even a long-term resident belonging to another clan was an outsider, while a visitor from an allied house/clan from a distant village was immediately accorded a place fitting his/her status.

The traditional feast system was central as the context for keeping and building relations of power. The names were an incarnation of powers that were socially manipulable. One interesting possibility is that the guests at a *yaokw* might have been receiving food and gifts in an inversion of the bestowal of gifts by non-human real beings, in fact, instead of those beings. Gifts from the non-human real beings included food, wealth, and crests. Since gifts must be publicly acknowledged, and eventually the giver should become a receiver, by their participation in feasts the hosts (real human beings) keep relations of power and dependence

PLATE 24.3. Tsimshian men building a traditional canoe on the beach at Metlakatla. Courtesy of the Provincial Archives of British Columbia, HP55797, C-8103.

valid with the other real beings (represented by real human beings who were guests, instead of real beings from other worlds).

As animal food had to be consumed for animals in their villages to be reincarnated and healthy, humans had to "eat" the wealth held in a lineage for more wealth to return. This was particularly important at death, which was the centre of Tsimshian feast activity. By feasting, in which one's father's clan received wealth, the integrity of power in other worlds was ensured and future wealth for the clan was possible. Wealth was returned to enable future wealth, as animal food was consumed to enable future reincarnated animals. One effect of the feast, then, was to return substance accumulated in a *waab* to the fathers, reuniting the fathers' substance with their own reality, which is part of their own matrilineal *waab*.

Payments for services and gifts were given throughout life to members of one's father's clan. The great potlatches were generally given at the time of assumption of a name at the death of one's predecessor (usually mother's brother). Contributions to this endeavour were collected from all the members of one's group. The guests were persons of sufficient reality from other clans in the same village, other Tsimshian villages, and foreign groups. Property was distributed according to the rank of the guests as payment for specific services performed (burial, putting on a name, carving a pole, etc.) and for validating the *yaokw* by attending. The clan was in fact emptying its wealth to its fathers, since the services were performed by members of father's clan, and since classificatory kinship terminology made brothers and sisters of clan members, so that each of the guests was *kswaatk* to the host or his siblings, all of whom contributed to the feast. By giving to fathers the clan is simultaneously giving to the supernatural animals with whom fathers are symbolically associated, thus restoring their (supernatural animals') worlds by reuniting substance with reality.

If the *yaokw* centred on emptying a clan after the death of a name-holder, it simultaneously was involved with the filling of the name by the incarnation of a new name-holder, who had the responsibility to "bury" his predecessor in the name and was thus generally the host of the event. It is by understanding this that we can understand why the clan had to be emptied. Just as a hunter had to be clean – to fast and to purge himself – before hoping to encounter animals, a new name-holder had to empty himself in order to attract the supernatural from whom the powers of his new name came. Otherwise, the name-holder came to the supernatural full of things acquired by his predecessor through his connection to the same supernatural, holding part of the substance of the supernatural that had never been restored.

If the term "incarnation" for the elevation of the new name-holder is taken seriously, it may be useful to see the assumption of the name as the final stage in the reincarnation that was begun at birth. The services of naming performed by the father's clan make it likely that this is appropriate, as does the comparison with the closely related Gitksan, who make it explicit that a person should take the name of his/her *baa'lx*. If this was indeed the final step in reincarnation, it is interesting to recall the story of "The Princess Who Rejected her Cousin" (Boas, 1916: 185 *et seq.*). The relevant material is too long for quotation, but a general summary with a few quotations is necessary to show its significance for the argument to be developed (my summary notes are in square brackets):

A very long time ago there was a great village with many people. They had only one chief. There was also his sister. They were the only two chiefs in the large town. The chief also had a beautiful daughter, and the chief's sister had a fine son . . . they expected that these two would soon marry . . . the girl rejected the proposal . . . but the young prince loved her very much, and still she refused him. . . . the princess wanted to make a fool of her cousin . . . [she led him on, and asked him to show his love, first by cutting his cheeks, and by cutting off his hair – which was dishonourable as a mark of a slave.

He did as she wished, but then she rejected him and mocked him]. . . . 'Tell him that I do not want to marry a bad-looking person like him, ugly as he is;' and she gave him the nickname Mountain with Two Rock Slides, as he had a scar down each cheek . . . the prince was so ashamed and left his village with a companion . . . he came to a narrow trail and went along it, finally meeting an old woman in a hut who knew him and his story. She told him he would soon come to the house of Chief Pestilence, and told him how to behave so that Chief Pestilence would make him beautiful. The prince did as she told him and became as beautiful as a supernatural being . . . when he came back his companion was just bones, but he took him to Chief Pestilence and he was also made beautiful . . . they returned to their own village . . . the princess wanted to marry him . . . he then mocked her . . . she went with a companion . . . they met a man who asked them which way they intended to go, and the princess told him they were going to see Chief Pestilence. . . . She passed by him, and did not look at him, for she was ashamed to let any one look at her . . . [they got to Chief Pestilence's house, but with no counsel such as the young man had received, she went to all the maimed people in the house who called her, and was maimed and bruised . . . they eventually returned to their own village, where the princess lay in bed, and finally died.]

This story may be interpreted as a story of two types of death and rein-carnation, one proper and the other socially censured. If the relationship between the prince and the princess is remembered, it will be apparent that the young man who "went away" (died) had behaved properly in life, and we may assume that the old woman whom he encountered on his path represented his father's clan, aiding him in the other world. The young woman, on the other hand, had humiliated the prince, *the son of her father's sister* (who was the person who would ordinarily help at the bur-ial, mourn, and participate in a mortuary feast as guest). She met with no helpful guide on her travels; she did encounter a man, who may have been a representative of her father's side, but he offered her no counsel because she was too ashamed to talk to him. If this interpretation is accu-rate, it establishes the central symbolic nexus or rationale for the feasting of the Coast Tsimshian, which primarily centred on the mortuary feast and the elevation of an heir: *to make it possible for the lineage members to be reincarnated properly.*

Several expressions and customs in current use are clarified in the con-text of this interpretation. First, people who are more real are *kswaatk* to a wider group of people. "Big" people thus provide services to and receive gifts and payments from more people. This was apparently also true in the past; Boas indicated rules for the "support" of dancers (1916: 512) that show that a much wider group of people treated a person with a big name as *kswaatk*. In certain dances it was (and is) necessary for onlookers to hold up dancers. Each dancer is supported by a noble who is of the same clan as the father of the dancer – so that during an encounter with a supernatural in this world one is supported by one's *kswaatk*, who also supported one in such an encounter in other worlds, helping one to be properly restored to this world. The more real a person, the more potent was the connection with supernatural.

Another example of a current usage that is both clarified in this context and contributes to an understanding of the traditional symbolism is that if a person makes a gift of food to another and then eats from the gift, it is said that "You'll get sores." The process of "incarnation" may have been continuous, requiring constant good relations with supernaturals. This would explain the traditional emphasis put on "washing" if a real person had an accident or made a mistake, and the expectation that real people should be physically without defect. One washed away shame by distributing property, usually to *kswaatk*. The vilest insult that could be hurled by a traditional Tsimshian was that a person was *wah'a'yin*, or "his scabs don't heal" (the literal translation is "without healing"). In English texts this is glossed as "without origin" or "having no relatives." These two glosses may imply that such a person had no *kswaatk* to provide treatment for injuries in return for payment, and, perhaps in the light of the argument above, that there was also no supernatural connection to give potency to the person's name – that, in fact, the person was not real.

The Tsimshian knew that they were real and that their villages were real. No place was at the centre of the Tsimshian universe, but all places are equally centres. The Tsimshian also knew that they had a duty to partake of the gifts received from other worlds and to return gifts to those worlds through their fathers, who connected them to those other worlds.

Modern Feasts

Although one of the most significant functions of the inter-tribal feasts was the protection of territories, the real threat to Tsimshian territorial sovereignty after the middle of the nineteenth century did not come from other Tsimshian or Native groups but from the encroachment of white resource appropriation and settlement and the failure of the province to acknowledge the validity of the original ownership. The set of "others" to be considered in the world had shifted so that the most significant rival was Canadian society at large. The patterns of asserting claims vis-à-vis the new power remained within the Tsimshian tradition. Councils of chiefs now drew from all the tribes, forming organizations to press land claims and other crucial issues. One of the most significant organizations was the Native Brotherhood of British Columbia, which held its first meeting in Port Simpson on December 15, 1931. Delegations from Masset, Hartley Bay, Kitkatla, Port Essington, and Metlakatla, B.C., attended. By 1936 the efforts of such active organizers as Chief Heber Clifton of Hartley Bay and Chief Edward Gamble of Kitkatla had brought in branches from Vanarsdale, Klemtu, Bella Bella, Kitimat, Kispiox, Kitwanga, Skeena Crossing, and Hazelton.

The Local Context: The Gitga'ata

The modern Tsimshian village of Hartley Bay is located at the entrance of the Douglas Channel in the southern portion of Tsimshian territory. The village was established in 1887 by a small group of people who had their traditional territories in the same general region, centring on their winter village, about twelve miles north of the present village.

From the 1860s to the 1880s the Gitga'ata joined the mission village of Metlakatla, probably residing there in the winter and travelling to their own territories for the balance of the annual cycle. When Duncan left Metlakatla to begin his community again in Alaska, the founders of Hartley Bay established a new permanent village in their own territories, but a village that was as strict as Duncan might have wished. From the beginning the community defined itself as a progressive, Christian, Tsimshian village, with equal emphasis on each aspect of their definition. A council of chiefs wielded a firm hand over all aspects of daily life in Hartley Bay during its early decades, and all of Duncan's rules were enforced until the middle of the twentieth century, when curfews and Sunday work prohibitions were relaxed somewhat.

The first reserves for the village were allocated in 1889, with additional allocations by the Royal Commission on Indian Affairs in 1916. The chiefs at Hartley Bay steadfastly refused to participate in the process, insisting instead on a settlement of their title to their entire traditional territory, which the Commission would not discuss. At the present time the village of Hartley Bay is engaged in the land claims process with the other Coast and Southern Tsimshian villages.

Feasting was apparently continued without interruption. Recollections of elders from Hartley Bay indicate a firmly ensconced modern

MAP 24.2. Sites in the Territory of Gitga'ata

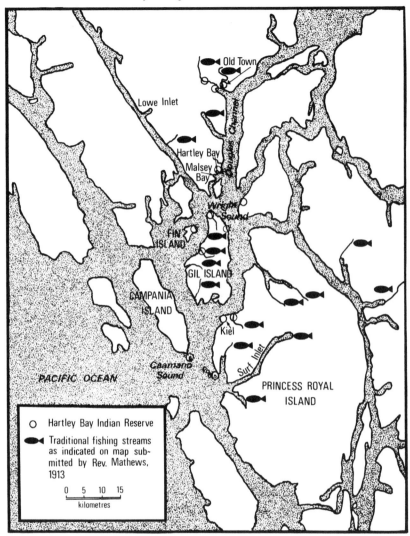

feast tradition early in this century. The feasts were of the sort considered respectable by Duncan; they still begin with prayers. The feasts given were solemn when the occasion was a memorial and light-hearted when the occasion was not so serious. The person who was to inherit a name generally "buried" his uncle, including sponsoring the memorial feast and paying the members of the father's side who had prepared the body and supplied the coffin. Marriages were arranged by the families, in some cases as late as the 1960s, and generally still maintain clan exogamy or include a clan-adoption process to maintain the formal structure of exogamy.

Traditionally, the names within a clan were ranked; the relative rank was displayed most prominently at feasts, when guests were seated in positions according to rank. The convention of recognizing the highest-ranked chief in the strongest clan in a tribe as the chief of the village was widespread. This practice is followed at Hartley Bay at the present time; the hereditary chief of the Gitga'ata is Wah'modm, the highest name of the Blackfish. The same individual also holds another high Blackfish name, Nta'Wi'Waab. This individual, John Clifton, is the hereditary chief of the Gitga'ata. The chief of the Eagle clan at Hartley Bay until his death in 1982 was Louis Clifton, John Clifton's eldest brother. (Traditionally, of course, brothers would not have been in different clans; John Clifton was taken by the Blackfish clan during the life of his father, but also retains his Eagle name.) Louis Clifton has been succeeded in his Eagle name by his sister's son, Charles Robinson. The holder of the highest-ranked Raven name in that Gitga'ata lineage is Heber Clifton, who currently resides in Prince Rupert. His younger brother, Chief William Clifton, is the highest-ranked resident Raven chief. Both of these men are sons of the late Louis Clifton. There is not an active Wolf clan at Hartley Bay; the group became very small, and apparently all members have been adopted as Blackfish. Within each clan there is a recognition that lesser names were also traditionally ranked among themselves, but little regular use is now made of these relative rankings.

The interpretation of traditional feasts offered above was that they were a mode of discourse, a way of creating messages and expressing the social order to members of the group and to other groups. The organization of the feast discourse conforms to conventions of discourse structure observed in some conversations at the present time in Hartley Bay. Very briefly, the convention of conversation is that the event (conversation or feast) cannot end until consensus is reached and expressed. In the conversations to which it applies, this means that a listener can subtly compel modifications in a statement by declining to provide a supportive closure to the conversation; in feasts, it means that the appropriate guests must be present and participate for the feast to fulfil its function.

The discourse convention includes the understanding that it is inappropriate to hold discussions with persons who do not have a proper authority to speak on a matter. It was manifested in the dealings of the Gitga'ata with the Royal Commission on Indian Affairs, which visited

Hartley Bay in 1913. "The Indians were asked to give testimony as to the character of the reserve, population, etc., etc., but they flatly refused to do so" (Campbell, 1984: 27). Eventually, a request for lands was submitted by a missionary in the village.

The current feasts at Hartley Bay continue to function as discourses, following the traditional patterns. However, the discourse currently gains interpretation in the historical and structural context in which the Tsimshian are now placed.

A Unique Feast

The Raven Feast of Chief Billy Clifton, on January 2, 1980, was in many ways typical of current feasts at Hartley Bay, but in a few respects it was a unique event. The feast was hosted by Billy Clifton, who is ranked as the highest resident chief of the Raven clan in Hartley Bay. The most unusual feature of this event was the adoption by Mr. Clifton of his uncle, Chief John Clifton, as a member of the Raven clan.

Ordinary feasts are based on a well-understood pattern in which the guests ratify the acts of hosts. Their presence is an acknowledgement of the right of the host clan to present their claims. Implicit in the Raven feast of Chief Billy Clifton was a violation of these expectations. It was not an ordinary right of the Ravens to take a member of the Eagle or Blackfish clans as a member (and Chief John Clifton was already a member of both these clans). This adoption was extraordinary and required explicit affirmation to be successful.

The process of adopting Chief John Clifton and putting a Raven name on him was marked by several modifications of ordinary feast procedures. The primary orator for the Raven clan, Ernest Hill, delivered a prologue speech, which "made sense" of the adoption. He addressed the concerns of the Ravens, indicating that the new Raven would help their clan, and he made an explicit claim that the adoption would make all the clans work together and was good for the entire village, including the Blackfish and Eagles.

The adoption allows Ravens to put claims on John Clifton, thus potentially infringing on the exclusive claims of the Eagles and Blackfish. In ordinary feasts, the clan of the father is asked to put the name on the individual. The names are then paid off, which gives the father's clan restitution for that service, as well as for raising the child. The adoption of Chief John Clifton as a Raven, and the putting on of his Raven name, was performed by members of both the Eagle and the Blackfish clans. They thus showed that they were willing to share rights in him with the Ravens. The involvement of both clans in this adoption makes it clear that the namers are *kswaatk*, not only in the sense of father's clan but in the more general sense of "where you come from." Chief John Clifton was being taken from both the Eagle and Blackfish clans, and members of both ratified the adoption by participating.

This feast, then, presented a new kind of claim couched in a traditional form; a "new tradition" has been forged. This new tradition celebrates the unity among members of the village and it is incarnate in the person of the chief who participates in all three clans. Symbolically, three have become one, and low has become high. I have couched the process in those terms deliberately because I would argue that the symbolism is distinctly Christian, not as a replacement of traditional symbols but as an interpretation of them. Christian symbols are the sensible interpreters of traditional Tsimshian symbols in this village, which has never wavered from the Christian Tsimshian course set when the people came back from Metlakatla.

The new structure has appeal at this time, particularly for members of the Hartley Bay community who were not tightly integrated into the traditional rank hierarchy. The privilege of names has been extended to most members of the village, but the stock of ranked names is running out. Chief John Clifton is perhaps the only member of the community who could have creatively re-formed symbolic structures in this way. The political context of the village now is a united one, confronting the next round in the struggle to retain their territories not from rival chiefs but from a non-Tsimshian government. This feast may be a manifestation of the context within one village, in which the chief and the united people are "One Step Higher," which is the English translation of the Raven name given to Chief John Clifton.

Current Issues and Future Challenges

During the 1990s the community of Hartley Bay faces many of the issues confronting other First Nations: effective governance, access to economic opportunities and management of resources in their territories, local control over education, and the urgent concerns of ensuring cultural and linguistic vitality for future generations. In the area of governance, Hartley Bay is exploring forms of internal and external political organization that will meet the aspirations of the community. At present the community still relies on a chief and council system for internal governance, elected under the "band-custom" provisions of the Indian Act. The community is working on mechanisms to involve members of the band who are not resident on-reserve in community governance. Some of this is a response to a recent court decision in which it was deemed illegal to exclude non-reserve band members from participation in elections, as well as to the growing proportion of members resident off-reserve due to the addition of members under Bill C-31. However, a number of local factors are also involved, including a shrinking absolute number of on-reserve residents due to increasingly constricted economic opportunities; whereas the Hartley Bay School had seventy-eight children enrolled in grades K-10 in the late 1970s, in 1994 there are fewer than fifty children in the school. At the level of the Tsimshian Tribal Council there has been a move to involve the hereditary chiefs in decision-making and to represent through them the unity of the Tsimshian Nation in negotiations with governments. This has not been effected consistently at this point; one of the difficulties has been that the long-term suppression of the feast system has made identification of the currently entitled name-holders difficult in some communities, and the traditions of generosity, respect, and authority that underpinned the system have been considerably eroded.

Shifting management priorities and the downward spiral of employment and income in both forestry and fisheries have been difficult to combat. For example, Area Six, the fisheries management area closest to Hartley Bay, has been almost entirely closed to commercial fishing in recent years, which local people attribute to favouritism toward sports fishing interests from Kitimat on the part of policy-makers. This has made it uneconomic for fishing vessel owners to reside in the community. At the same time there is pressure to decrease the number of days for commercial fishing in nearby areas such as the mouth of the Skeena River; one reason is that while there are large available stocks of some species such as sockeye (millions of these fish return to the Skeena River each year), other stocks that migrate at the same time are small (some runs number under 2,000), and the current technology available to the commercial industry does not allow for selective harvest. It is ironic that a century ago the federal government systematically destroyed fish weirs and fish traps that had been used by Aboriginal communities for millennia on the grounds that they were a threat to the conservation of the species; these same technologies are now being touted as remedies to the obvious problems confronting the mixed-stock fisheries. However, those individuals and groups with extensive investments in the current fishing industry are deeply concerned about the impact of such schemes on their futures. The Aboriginal fishing strategy and community rather than individual licences are being used to re-orient harvesting away from the current industrial model. Hartley Bay received a community licence for harvesting herring roe-on-kelp several years ago, and this is one of the economic projects that offers some potential; the Tsimshian Tribal Council employs fisheries guardians and is training community members in fisheries management. The future of this key economic sector is likely to be very turbulent.

Logging reserve lands and developing a tourism business at a former village site are other current projects that Hartley Bay is pursuing to establish a solid and more diversified economic base. As a member community of the Tsimshian Tribal Council, Hartley Bay is working with other Tsimshian villages on issues such as land rights, management of fisheries and forestry in their territories, repatriation of Tsimshian cultural objects from museums, and the development of educational programs, including Tsimshian language and culture programs. The greatest certainty as the community moves into the twenty-first century is that many of the issues they confront will remain unsettled for a long time.

Note

1. This chapter summarizes my 1984 monograph on feasts. My field research was supported by grants from the Contract Ethnology Programme of the National Museum of Man and the Social Sciences and Humanities Research Council of Canada. While aspects of the interpretation presented here have been discussed with members of the community of Hartley Bay, and a copy has been submitted to the band council of that village, the interpretation, and any errors, are entirely my responsibility. Spellings of Tsimshian terms follow the system outlined in Dunn's *Practical Dictionary of the Coast Tsimshian Language*. Original spellings have been retained in quotations from other authors.

Recommended Reading

Adams, John W.
1973 *The Gitksan Potlatch: Population Flux, Resource Ownership and Reciprocity.* Montreal: Holt, Rinehart and Winston.

A discussion of the Gitksan system within the cultural ecological framework based on fieldwork in the mid-1960s. Adams argues that the Gitksan redistributed people to territories and resources by the assignment of individuals to groups through the feast system. The description of current feasts is detailed.

Barbeau, Marius

1929 *Totem Poles of the Gitksan, Upper Skeena River, British Columbia*. National Museum of Canada, Anthropological Series No. 12, Bulletin 61, Ottawa.

Along with *Totem Poles* (1951), this is one of Barbeau's longer and more enduring contributions to the study of the cultures of the Northwest Coast.

Berger, The Honourable Thomas R.

1981 "The Nisga'a Land Case," in Berger, *Fragile Freedoms: Human Rights and Dissent in Canada*. Toronto: Clarke, Irwin.

A thorough and clear presentation of the struggle for recognition of the Nisga'a claim to hereditary lands. Berger represented the Nisga'a before the Supreme Court of Canada; though the panel split 3-3 (with one abstention on technical grounds) the case was one of two that set the stage for serious land claims negotiations throughout Canada.

Boas, Franz

1916 *Tsimshian Mythology*. Thirty-first Annual Report of the Bureau of American Ethnology, Washington, D.C.

A rich collection of Tsimshian material as collected by the Tsimshian James Tate. Boas provides extensive annotation and a description of traditional culture based on information in the myths.

Duff, Wilson

1959 *Histories, Territories and Laws of the Kitwancool*. Anthropology in B.C., Memoir No. 4. British Columbia Provincial Museum, Victoria.

A record of the information considered significant by the people of a Gitksan village; significant because of the collaboration involved in producing it as well as for the information presented.

Garfield, Viola

1939 *Tsimshian Clan and Society*. Seattle: University of Washington Press.

An extremely valuable discussion of traditional and developing social organization by an important contributor to the scholarship of the area.

Robinson, Will, and Walter Wright

1962 *Men of Medeek*. Kitimat, B.C.: Northern Sentinel Press.

Stories from a Tsimshian elder; considerable material of interest in understanding world view and social organization.

Seguin, Margaret, ed.

1984 *The Tsimshian: Images of the Past, Views for the Present*. Vancouver: University of British Columbia Press.

A collection of recent scholarship from diverse perspectives focused on a single group; includes important material on feasts, shamanism, history, and culture change.

Usher, Jean

1974 *William Duncan of Metlakatla: A Victorian Missionary in British Columbia.*
Publications in History 5. National Museum of Canada.
A scholarly analysis of the activities of this intriguing missionary.

Additional References Cited

Campbell, Ken

1984 "Hartley Bay: A History," in M. Seguin, ed., *The Tsimshian: Images of the
Past, Views for the Present.* Vancouver: University of British Columbia
Press.

Dundes, Alan

1979 "Heads or Tails: A Psychoanalytic Study of Potlatch," *Journal of
Psychological Anthropology*, 2, 4: 395-424.

Dunn, John Asher

1984 "International Matrimoieties: The North Maritime Province of the North
Pacific Coast," in M. Seguin, ed., *The Tsimshian: Images of the Past, Views of
the Present.* Vancouver: University of British Columbia Press.

Emmons, George T.

1907 *The Chilkat Blanket.* Memoirs of the American Museum of Natural History,
Vol. III, Anthropology, Vol. II. December.

Fleisher, Mark

1981 "The Potlatch: A Symbolic and Psychoanalytic View," *Current
Anthropology*, 22, 1: 69-71.

Geertz, Clifford

1980 "Blurred Genres," *American Scholar*, 49, 2: 165-79.

CHAPTER 25
From Kwakiutl to
Kwakwa ka'wakw

Peter Macnair

Introduction

Of the linguistic groups occupying the Northwest Coast, the Kwakiutl are probably the most widely known. The term describing them has been rendered in many ways: Kwakiutl, Kwawkewlth, Kwagyol, Kwagiulth, and Kwagutl, to cite a few, and all are attempts at transcribing the Native term *Kwagu'ł*. The exact meaning of this word remains obscure despite attempts by Native speakers, anthropologists, and linguists to provide a translation. It is, however, a proper name used to describe one of about twenty linguistically related village groups, the "Fort Rupert tribe."

Herein lies a problem, for the other village groups have always objected to being called "Kwakiutl." Even today a man from the village of Kalokwis on Turnour Island will feel insulted if you call him "Kwakiutl," for he knows himself to be "Lawit'sis," one of the "Angry Ones." A solution to this terminological problem has recently been suggested by Indians themselves. The main dialect spoken by the twenty village groups is Kwak'wala, and a suitable and accurate descriptive term has emerged, that being Kwakwa̲ ka'wakw, which roughly translates "those who speak Kwak'wala."

The term Kwakwa̲ ka'wakw has been promoted by the U'mista Cultural Society at Alert Bay, the most populous of the Kwak'wala-speaking villages, and it has entered the literature in their language publications and more recently in a fine analysis of one of the great carvers from the area, *Smoky Top: The Art and Times of Willie Seaweed*, by Bill Holm. It is therefore appropriate to promote and use the term Kwakwa̲ ka'wakw even though initially this might appear more cumbersome than the more familiar "Kwakiutl."

The Kwakwa̲ ka'wakw today comprise about twenty village groups, or "tribes" as these were called by the pioneer anthropologist Franz Boas. Each functioned relatively independently of the others, although there were many social and ceremonial occasions that brought them together. Despite the ties of language and culture, in pre-contact and early historic times internecine war was known among the Kwakwa̲ ka'wakw, in revenge for the murder of a chief or to avenge an insult.

The territorial boundaries claimed by the Kwakwa̲ ka'wakw today include the east coast of Vancouver Island from Campbell River to Cape Scott, and from there, the exposed western side of the island south to Cape Cook. As well, they occupy the mainland north from Campbell River to Smith's Inlet. This area is one of myriad islands and waterways and of deep fjords penetrating the Coast Mountains.

Dense coniferous forests, where red cedar, hemlock, Douglas fir, and spruce dominate, fill the landscape, except for river bottoms where such deciduous trees as red alder and cottonwood flourish. The evergreens sweep to the very water's edge, denying a safe landing to canoe-borne travellers over much of the littoral. At the same time, there are expansive sheltered beaches covered with broken white clamshells glinting brilliantly in the summer sun, clearly marking areas of long habitation and use. The largest of these are the permanent winter village sites identified by shell middens in some cases up to six metres in depth. Archaeologists are only beginning to analyse Kwakwa̲ ka'wakw sites in any systematic way, but radiocarbon dates indicate human occupancy for at least 8,000 years. Such antiquity does not suggest that the Kwakwa̲ ka'wakw themselves have been present continuously for that long period, but it clearly indicates that people have exploited the area for millennia.

In times past, travel was achieved mainly by water, although trails did cut across certain peninsulas and penetrated the Coastal Range. Canoes, ranging in length from two metres through twenty, were the means of

PLATE 25.1. Early in the twentieth century most Kwakwa̱ ka̱'wakw lived in cedar plank houses and followed a traditional lifestyle. The village of Blunden Harbour welcome figures were erected on the beach front. These served to welcome guests invited to witness ceremonial occasions and attend potlatches. Courtesy of Royal British Columbia Museum, Victoria, B.C.,PN 258.

access, and every Kwakwa̱ ka̱'wakw was a skilled paddler, familiar with the rhythm of tide and vagaries of weather. Families moved throughout a considerable territory during the yearly round as they exploited resource areas reserved exclusively for their own use. All the accoutrements for daily living were crowded into canoes as people moved from berry-gathering stations to clam beds to halibut-fishing stations and to the broad rivers and seemingly insignificant streams where the five species of Pacific salmon spawned.

Material Culture

Most readers have some sense of the material culture of Northwest Coast Indian groups. Large plank houses, totem poles, spectacular masks, ocean-going canoes carved from giant logs are familiar images, and the Kwakwa̱ ka'wakw versions of these are unique, reflecting a deep under-standing of the environment and its potential to feed, house, and clothe.

Of all the trees found on the North Pacific coast, the red cedar is the most significant to Native inhabitants. Light, relatively strong, straight grained, pungent with decay-resisting oils, red cedar wood is tractable at the hands of a skilled carpenter or carver. Planks as wide as two metres and ranging to more than ten metres in length can be split from a cedar log with careful use of a battery of yew wood wedges tapped gently with a stone hammer. Admittedly, planks of a two-metre width were rare, but they did exist, and they were viewed as great treasures, carefully maintained by their owners. Cedar planks clad the house frames found in the permanent winter villages and could be removed to erect temporary shelters in the summer fishing camps.

Planks were also used to construct almost every description of container. Kerfs were cut nearly through from opposite sides of a board and these were then steam-heated to soften the wood enough so it could be bent to a ninety-degree angle. Three kerfs accurately laid out on a smooth plank created a four-sided box, the final side of which was pegged or sewn together. A bottom was similarly applied and, if required, a lid was fashioned. In their roughest form, such boxes could be used for temporary storage of food or gear, but most were carefully crafted and painstakingly decorated with engraved geometric designs or painted with representations of crest figures.

Most were so skilfully constructed that they were watertight and thus functioned as water buckets, cooking boxes, or containers for other liquids. Others were used to store dried or smoked fish, shellfish, berries, fruits, and roots. Still others were "boxes of treasures" in which ceremonial regalia were respectfully stored. Infants were bound into slat cradles, versions of the boxes, and the dead were placed in rectangular chests that functioned as coffins.

While every Kwakwạ kạ'wakw had basic carpentry skills, specialists tackled monumental carving tasks. Canoe makers served long, demanding apprenticeships before they could successfully create the balanced, flowing lines of a cedar log canoe. Again, steaming was a technique employed by the canoe maker; more than seventy centimetres could be added to the width of a large canoe by spreading steam-heated wood. But greater skills were in evidence before the spreading took place, for the canoe maker had to know in advance how the dimensions of his craft would shift during the widening process and anticipate and accommodate these in the carved form arrived at before steaming.

Other artisans achieved renown as carvers and painters, producing an incredible array of ceremonial objects from red cedar, yellow cedar, alder, and yew, to name the preferred species. Accepted fiction is that each village had a single carver to supply its needs, but clearly there were several in each, often sharing projects such as the carving of totem poles or large masks. Apprentices to the established carvers were inevitably sons or nephews, which allowed for the development of village substyles within the general Kwakwa̱ ka'wakw art form.

This general form, reflected in both the sculptural and two-dimensional painting traditions, is in most cases clearly distinguishable from that of other Northwest Coast linguistic groups. It is based on a simpler archaic style practised at the time of European contact known as "Old Wakashan," but it assumed a distinctively flamboyant quality, incorporating more complex carved planes and more elaborate painted detail in the last quarter of the nineteenth century.

Iron was known to the people of the Northwest Coast at the time of European contact, although its use was not exclusive, for Captain Cook noted both iron and stone blades in coincidental use during his voyage of discovery in 1778. However, as metals became more available through the burgeoning trade, shell, stone, and bone blades were invariably replaced with those of steel or copper. Significantly, though, the ancient tool forms were retained; today, elbow adzes, D-adzes, chisels, and straight and curved bladed knives are still in use.

Not only the wood of the cedar was vital to the Kwakwa̱ ka'wakw. Bark and roots were equally important. In the spring, six- to eight-metre lengths of bark were stripped from young cedar trees, and then the smooth inner layer was split away using small flexible bone spatulas. The desired bark was then bundled for easy transport and storage. Both red and yellow cedar bark were gathered, the latter preferred for the manufacture of the capes, skirts, and blankets constituting the clothing worn by the Kwak'wala speakers in pre-contact times.

Industrious preparation of the bark was required before a comfortable garment could be produced. Using a whalebone beater, women would pound the flat strips of bark until the fibres began to separate, imparting a supple softness. Strips so prepared were then woven on a single bar loom into final form.

Other cedar bark was not pounded as for clothing. Instead, thin strips of even width were manufactured and, using a checker weave technique, fashioned into mats. Some were designated as coverings on which food was served, some functioned as sleeping mats, some provided extra insulation on walls or served as bedchamber partitions, while still others covered canoes, protecting these delicate craft from a hot summer sun that threatened to split the thin sides of the dugout.

The roots and branches of the cedar, and of other conifers such as spruce, were also important and provided material for withes (used for sewing planks together) and for burden baskets. Every object had a well-defined function. Openwork baskets made from tough cedar root not only allowed shellfish to drain while they were gathered; once the basket was filled, it was vigorously plunged in and out of the sea a few times to clean the sand and grit from the outer surface of the shells.

Food and the Annual Cycle

The sea dominated the daily routine and yearly round of the Kwakwa̱ ka'wakw. While certain land mammals such as deer and elk and a variety of fowl, including ducks, geese, and grouse, were important food sources, the ocean provided the bulk of the protein-rich diet of Northwest Coast people. Such shellfish as clams, cockles, abalone, and mussels were significant, and other bivalves, univalves, and crustaceans were taken when needed. Of sea mammals, only seals were significant; whales were not hunted.

Just as the cedar tree dominates the material culture of the Kwak'wala speakers, salmon typifies their diet. Five species of Pacific salmon spawn in the streams and rivers of Vancouver Island and the adjacent mainland, and their runs range from spring through December. Various techniques were employed to secure the fish, predominantly traps, weirs, nets, and harpoons. Most such fisheries were near the mouths of rivers or somewhat upstream.

Oil content differed considerably among the species, and Spring, Sockeye, and Cohoe salmon were favoured for fresh consumption, while the Pink and, most importantly, the Dog salmon were preserved. The latter species has a lesser fat content that the others, lending itself well for preservation. In early times, extended families would cure literally thousands of Dog salmon in smokehouses; thus preserved, the fish would keep in a cool, dry environment for several months. Other fish, such as halibut, were nearly as important as salmon, and still others like lingcod, flounder, herring, and rockfish offered welcome variety. A small ocean-run smelt, the oolachon, which returned in early spring to spawn in two major rivers in Kwakwa̱ ka'wakw territory, was netted by the tonne, and from its body an oil was rendered. This prized oil was used as a condiment, greatly enhancing the flavour of barbecued salmon. It was traded widely with other groups and given to noble guests at special feasts.

The Kwakwa̱ ka'wakw diet was supplemented with a reasonable choice of vegetal products. While agriculture was not practised, family groups owned resource areas where clover, cinquefoil, and other roots were systematically gathered, and berry patches where salmon berries, thimbleberries, and, most importantly, salal berries were gathered. Such berries were enjoyed fresh, but their year-round availability was assured through a process of mashing the berries and sun-drying the mixture into flat square sheets. Spring brought a variety of shoots, providing a welcome change from winter's fare. The cambium layer of the hemlock tree, scraped and processed into cakes, offered a form of starch.

Everything considered, the Kwakwa ka'wakw lived in an area relatively abundant in food. But successful exploitation of the environment depended on an intimate knowledge of its potential and its seasonal vagaries, as well as on a sophisticated technology with which to recover and preserve available foods. Popular accounts suggest that the people of the Northwest Coast occupied a paradise where food-getting was a simple and assured matter. A careful examination of Native accounts indicates that this is not the case; every day of the year saw a good portion of the population involved in some aspect of the food quest. Long winter storms could prevent travel by canoe for days on end, and rationing was a concern of every household. Although clams and other shellfish were usually available at door-front, some winter villages contained populations exceeding 500 persons, and an immediate resource could be quickly threatened. The villages of the Da'naxda'xw and Dzawada'enux tribes were located on mainland rivers where harsh, ice-bound winters were not unusual. Stories of privation and even starvation are part of the histories of the Kwakwa ka'wakw and other Northwest Coast peoples, and an easy life was far from assured.

Contact

Early explorers and traders very much relied on Indians to provide them with fresh fish. The first direct contact many Kwakwa ka'wakw people had with whites must have occurred in 1792 when Captain George Vancouver circumnavigated the island that now bears his name. His landing at the 'Namgis village he called Cheslakees was indeed eventful, and a reasonable description of its inhabitants and their lifeways survived in his journal and that of his staff botanist, Archibald Menzies. The English chartmakers were surprised to discover goods of European manufacture in the hands of these people, whose village was located on a high terrace above the mouth of the Nimpkish River. Muskets of Spanish manufacture were handled with confident ease by the 'Namgis and there was no lack of iron among them. The botanist Menzies observed a pewter basin, on the bottom of which was engraved the name of a French ship, which only three months earlier had put into Friendly Cove on the central west coast of Vancouver Island. The villagers were clearly familiar with Maquinna, the Nootkan chief of Yuquot, or Friendly Cove, who figured so prominently in the British and Spanish voyages of discovery.

At the time of European contact the Kwakwa ka'wakw possibly numbered as many as 8,000. Large villages such as the one Vancouver described certainly seemed to contain about 500 individuals. This can be considered a large population for the area occupied, given that these people were not agriculturalists. The Indians generally responded favourably to the presence of whites in the early contact period. Trade goods were welcomed, and although some aspects of the alien's technology were superior, the Natives remained in ascendancy and very much in control.

Things began to change as the sea otter population dwindled. It was the dense, soft pelage of this marine mammal that attracted a host of British, European, and eastern American vessels to the coast following the Spanish and British discoveries of 1774 and 1778. By 1825, the maritime fur trade had just about ended, but it was replaced by a land-based trade, spearheaded by the Hudson's Bay Company. By 1849, Fort Rupert was established on northern Vancouver Island, almost at the epicentre of the Kwakwa ka'wakw world. Profound changes rapidly followed – some positive but others horrifyingly tragic.

The wide, shallow, sandy, protected harbour was chosen by the Hudson's Bay Company because of its proximity to a coal seam able to service the needs of steam-powered vessels, which were by then increasingly important in Company operations. Although an ancient village site, at the time it was used only seasonally by two Kwakwa ka'wakw village groups. About two years after the fort was established, four closely related tribes moved their winter residence to the site. The leading and highest ranking of these four was the Kwagu'ł. (Presently, this name has succeeded to describe all four. As indicated earlier the term "Kwakiutl" was rendered from this specific tribal name.)

Because of their proximity to the fort, the Kwagu'ł quickly became middlemen in the land-based fur trade. As their riches grew, so did their prestige, and in effect Fort Rupert became the ceremonial centre of the Kwakwa ka'wakw. Theatrical performances became more elaborate as privileges were acquired from the Heiltsuk, Owikeno, Haida, Tlingit, and Tsimshian neighbours to the north through intermarriage. The "Old Wakashan" art style became more elaborate and flamboyant as both the two-dimensional, and to an extent sculptural, art styles of the northern groups gained exposure among the Kwakwa ka'wakw.

By 1860, Indians were still very much masters of the area that was to become British Columbia, although the effects of tuberculosis, venereal disease, alcohol, and gun powder were evident in declining population figures. Tragedy and terror marked 1862, irreversibly hammering Native populations of the North Pacific coast. In that year, smallpox was introduced at Fort Victoria, and within two years it had killed more than one-third of the Indian population of what is now B.C.

Still, the Kwakwa̱ ka̱'wakw held on, so that by 1886, when the young anthropologist Franz Boas first visited B.C., traditional lifeways were still essentially intact, and if not, certainly remembered by the Kwak'wala speakers. Boas's introduction to Fort Rupert was fortuitous for he there met village resident George Hunt, who was fluent in both Kwak'wala and English. Hunt was unique, born of an English father employed by the Hudson's Bay Company and of a high-ranking Tongass Tlingit woman who, coming from a matrilineal society, introduced a number of northern privileges to the Kwakwa̱ ka̱'wakw. Yet Hunt was in many regards culturally a Kwagu'ł, his status increasing when he married a Kwakwa̱ ka̱'wakw woman.

Hunt was available to interpret and explain as the pioneering anthropologist attempted to define Kwakwa̱ ka̱'wakw society. Boas struggled to describe the essential functioning social unit in anthropological terms, eventually discarding gens, clan, or sib, and applying the Kwak'wala term *numaym* (hereafter spelled *namima*). A linguistically satisfactory translation of this word is not possible, though Boas offered the suggestion "brothers" as a reasonable alternative. *Namima* implies an extended lineage group, all of whom descend from a single mythic ancestor. Several *namima* constitute a village group, or "tribe" as Boas termed such units. The *namima* functioned more or less independently, each having specifically defined resource areas that only they could exploit. Further, their ceremonial prerogatives were jealously guarded, though they could be transferred through either the male or female line in marriage.

An example of origin stories is here appropriate. One *namima* of the 'Na̱mg̱is tribe, which now resides at Alert Bay, was descended from a mythical halibut and a Thunderbird who occupied the mouth of the Nimpkish River at a time when the world was young and animals could change at will into human form and back again. The monster halibut swam ashore, transformed into a man, and commenced the construction of a house. Alone he was able to insert four houseposts into the ground, but he could not place the two massive roof beams he had prepared atop the posts. Lamenting the fact, he sat at river's edge when suddenly he felt a presence. He turned to discover a Thunderbird, landed on a boulder in the river. The bird readily agreed to assist and, grasping a beam in his talons, flew into the sky and put it into place. The man-transformed-from-halibut thanked the bird and indicated he wished the bird were a man as well. "O but I am," the Thunderbird replied, throwing back his beaked headdress to reveal a human face. Then the mythic bird removed his headdress and his feathered, winged cape and threw them into the sky where they returned to the middle heavens where Thunderbirds dwell. Together the two became the founders of a 'Namgis *namima* and ever since their descendants have had the right to display such images on house frontal paintings, on carved houseposts or house frontal posts, on ceremonial settees, or on dancing blankets. Masks may also be employed in an elaborate theatrical tableau to re-enact the adventures of these mythical forebears.

Such imagery filled the daily and ceremonial lives of the Kwakwạ ka'wakw at the time of European contact. Each person was aware of his or her origins and secure in the knowledge that his patrimony was assured.

Social Organization and Ceremony

In routine daily activities, the individual identified primarily with his or her extended family, which occupied a separate house; several of these closely related households constituted the *namima*. Inheritance of positions within the *namima* was based on primogeniture, and a system of ranking was evident. But the system extended beyond the *namima*, for the *namima* themselves were ranked within the tribe. Finally, the tribes were ranked so that there emerged a first-ranking chief of the first-ranking *namima* of the first-ranking tribe, under whom the remaining nobility of the Kwakwạ ka'wakw were ranged. This hierarchical system operated *only* in the ceremonial context; no political or economic power was vested in the hierarchy.

The ranking system was complex, for not all members of one tribe were positioned above all of those in the next ranking tribe. If the system were schematized, the first-ranking chief of the first-ranking *namima* of the *third*-ranking tribe would occupy a higher position than that of the fifth-ranking chief of the fourth-ranking *namima* of the *second*-ranking tribe. In actual fact the system did not function strictly according to the theoretical model, because the individual fortunes of participants were always a factor. The system was also very much threatened in the late nineteenth century when positions became vacant simply because no rightful heir existed. Because of a declining population, upstarts began to claim positions not normally accessible, and they were able to force their suits through individual financial backing. Until the 1880s, significant economic control was the exclusive domain of the *namima* chief. During this decade, however, individuals of lower status were able to enter the whites' economic system, earning money in the growing fishing and lumbering industries and gaining the wherewithal to attempt access to vacant positions.

The complex economic system governing the ranking system and relating to ownership of ceremonial privileges was the potlatch, an institution that characterized all Northwest Coast Indian societies. The potlatch *was* society; it was all-inclusive, encompassing things economic, political, social, religious, ritualistic, and ceremonial. Simply stated, a potlatch involved a payment of goods and food to assembled guests gathered to witness a host's claim to ancestral rights or hereditary position. The transfer of rights from one generation to the next, the acquisition of privileges through arranged marriage, or the assumption of a new position could only be concluded through such public events. Thus, the guests, or witnesses, were the ultimate arbitrators; by accepting gifts, they validated the claims of their host and confirmed his status.

Certain jealously guarded privileges confirmed by potlatching were evident at all times; others were revealed only in ceremonial context. An example of the former would be a house belonging to a *namima* member. It would have a name, possibly a design painted on the façade, houseposts generally carved to represent mythic ancestral figures, and other architectural details designated as inherited prerogatives. These details would always be available to the casual observer; they were part of the daily village scene.

On the other hand, there were privileges shown only at special times of the year. Primarily these were dance dramas, incorporating a highly developed stagecraft. The Kwakwa̱ka̱'wakw identify two distinct dance cycles, the Ṫseka, or Red Cedar Bark Dance, and the Tła'sala, or Chief's Dance. Of these the Ṫseka is the more important, and it incorporates the *hamatsa*, or cannibal dance, which has come to characterize the Kwakwa̱ka̱'wakw winter ceremonial.

In the *hamatsa* sequence, the main performer is inspired by the spirit of a man-eating monster and first appears in a frenzy, hungering for human flesh. As the dance progresses, the *hamatsa* is gradually tamed and brought back to a state of normalcy. Rigorous training is required prior to the first public appearance of the dancer. The individual selected for initiation spends up to three months in relative seclusion, attended only by members of the *hamatsa* society. During this period he learns songs and dance movements especially created for him. Ritual bathing and fasting at one time were part of the initiation that enhanced contact with the cannibal spirit.

Once the initiate was trained, guests were invited to witness his first performance. His entry into the dance house was preceded by the shrill of whistles that represented cries of various spirits. Attendants guarded him yet were often unable to restrain his frenzy as he suddenly darted into the audience to attack an onlooker. He might actually bite that individual, drawing blood. The movements of his hands, face, and feet acted out words of his song, most of which described his hunger for and eating of human flesh. In time his passion was assuaged, through the calming gestures of certain designated participants. Eventually he left the dance floor, to be replaced by performers wearing bird-like masks representing the mythical attendants of the cannibal spirit.

Many variations are seen in *hamatsa* performances and these represent individual privileges. Certain dancers might enter the house holding a corpse in outstretched arms. In the most dramatic enactments, a number of veteran *hamatsas* might rush onto the dance floor and appear to devour the corpse.

It is safe to say that nearly all such acts were simply marvellous theatre; those bitten by the *hamatsa* had agreed to be so mutilated beforehand and were later paid handsomely for their willing participation. While it is possible that in the distant past morsels from desiccated human corpses were swallowed, a more usual practice was to substitute animal flesh. Similar stagecraft was evident in the many dances that followed the *hamatsa* performance. In one, a singing woman climbed into a box that was then placed in the fire. As the box was consumed, her voice gradually faded away and in time her charred bones were raked from the coals. Four days later she reappeared, obviously unaffected by her ordeal.

Again, the ingenuity of the dance masters must be admired. Unknown to the audience, the box had no bottom and once inside the woman lifted a trap door concealed in the earthen floor of the dance house. She crouched in an excavated chamber and sang through a tube that carried her voice to the edge of the fire, giving the appearance that she was still in the box. After the guests had left the house, she was retrieved from her hiding place and later presented at a suitably dramatic moment.

Other props impressed the viewers: masks suddenly opened to reveal an entirely different creature; giant mechanical frogs hopped around the floor; flights of birds flew around the dance house; puppets emerged from unexpected places. Knowledgeable observers expected such dramatic surprises and obviously delighted in them. At the same time, uninformed onlookers were often unaware of the stagecraft involved and especially

PLATE 25.2. Potlatch at Alert Bay. Guests are assembled to hear the words of the speaker, who is recording the privileges and claims of his chief. When the speeches are concluded sacks of flour will be distributed to the assembled guests. Courtesy of Royal British Columbia Museum, Victoria, B.C., PN10067.

objected to aspects of the *hamatsa* performance that involved the apparent consumption of human flesh.

In fact, this last was one of three major objections to traditional Kwakwa ka'wakw lifeways expressed by early authorities and that heralded a radical and unhappy change in the lives of these people. The federal government was petitioned to legislate against the "heathen" practice of "cannibalism," and support for this position was garnered through lurid reports in the popular press.

The second concern expressed by authorities related to the traditional form of Kwakwa ka'wakw marriage. Often such unions were arranged when the intended bride and groom were still infants, or when the bride was considerably younger than her husband-to-be. Advantageous unions were sought by both parties, though it was the bride who brought, as her dowry, privileges in the form of dances, songs, and names. These were held by the groom's family, in most cases, for eventual distribution to the children in time born to the couple. The groom's family was required to make payment for these prerogatives, and in the historic period the principal unit of payment was a woollen blanket, commonly known as the "Hudson's Bay Blanket." In earlier times, cedar-bark blankets, boxes, and canoes were the standard media of exchange.

The authorities saw such transactions from their own narrow Victorian perspective as the buying and selling of women. The fact that such arranged marriages were central to the social fabric of the Kwakwa̱ ka̱'wakw was entirely lost on those who sought to control the destinies of their charges, and pressure was applied to the Canadian government to curb the heathen practice.

The final concern of early missionaries and Indian agents was the great, ostentatious display of wealth that accompanies any formal Kwakwa̱ ka̱'wakw transaction. In certain potlatches, as many as 10,000 blankets were given away, an incredible wealth for any individual to amass in the nineteenth century, especially if he were an Indian. The potlatch host appeared to be impoverished at the end of his great display of gift-giving. In a material sense he was, and elderly people today can recount how, as children, they returned to their houses to find them devoid of all but the most essential possessions. Virtually everything – furniture, clothing, utensils – had been given away. Such actions were clearly contrary to a way of life the authorities were trying to force on the Indian of British Columbia. They conceived the Indians as a new peasantry who would lead quiet, industrious lives in nuclear family units, contributing to the Canadian economy as docile labourers.

From the Kwakwa̱ ka̱'wakw point of view, giving away one's possessions was not an impoverishment – it was the only way of gaining prestige. To give away wealth was to be wealthy. Not only did the individual rise in stature through such actions, so did the entire *namima*, for it was the extended family that worked, often years in advance, to amass the goods and food required for distribution at a large potlatch.

But the administrators were unable to appreciate the reality and validity of the Kwakwa̱ ka̱'wakw way and so, through a series of legal actions, began to undermine the basic structures of Northwest Coast society. In 1884, federal legislation banned the potlatch and its attendant dances, and in time prosecutions were entered against individuals who continued to engage in traditional ceremonies. The bitter culmination of more than three decades of pressure by a series of local Indian agents occurred in 1921 when more than twenty high-ranking Kwakwa̱ ka̱'wakw nobles were found guilty of contravening the Potlatch Law and were sentenced to terms of up to six months in Oakalla Prison.

Confused and betrayed, the Kwakwa̱ ka̱'wakw nonetheless held on to old traditions in secret. An ingenious chief went from one household to another in Alert Bay distributing goods while whispering the traditional business he was conducting to senior members of each family. When accosted by the Indian agent, he simply reminded the agent of the date and noted that he was giving away Christmas presents. People slipped away to remote villages around which sentries were placed to warn of police patrolling by boat and there conducted what today are referred to as "bootleg potlatches." So, while admittedly in reduced form, the potlatch tradition was maintained.

In 1951 the Indian Act was rewritten and the section banning the potlatch was quietly omitted, not formally repealed as B.C. Indians would have preferred. The anti-potlatch legislation almost achieved what it was intended to do; it certainly tore away most of the traditional social fabric of the Kwakwa ka'wakw people. Nonetheless, determined men and women continued to speak their language despite being forbidden to do so while attending residential schools in their youth. The training of young men as *hamatsas* continued in remote villages, though the initiation was not as prolonged or as rigorous as it was in the past. Marriages, while not "arranged" in the traditional sense, were still marked with the transfer of privileges brought as dowry by the bride. Centuries of skills relating to knowledge of wind, tide, and season and the relation of these to the salmon fishery were finally recognized in the 1940s, when fishing companies allowed Indians to captain and operate fishing vessels rather than allowing them no more status than deck crewmen.

Few individuals outside the Indian communities offered much support of the old ways, and indeed the Kwakwa ka'wakw themselves were divided on whether the old ways should be retained. By 1950, three generations of anthropologists had made their reputations studying the Kwakwa ka'wakw, and major museums in North America and Europe were filled with treasures once the objects of fierce pride.

Following the end of World War Two, some rebirth of traditional lifeways was encouraged by outside agencies. Notably, this came as support from the Museum of Anthropology at the University of British Columbia, and later the British Columbia Provincial Museum, which employed the Kwakwa ka'wakw carver Chief Mungo Martin. The last dozen years of his life were spent refurbishing old totem poles and carving new ones for these institutions. In addition, he built a ceremonial house on the grounds of the Provincial Museum, carved new masks for use, and dedicated the house with a formal presentation of certain of his dances that culminated in a potlatch distribution. Finally, potlatching was again public and acceptable.

PLATE 25.3. At a recent Kwakwa̱ ka̱'wakw potlatch, the cannibal bird mask representing the "Crooked Beak of Heaven" is worn by a participant. Courtesy of Royal British Columbia Museum, Victoria, B.C., PN 15381-27.

Personal Experience among the Kwakwa̱ ka̱'wakw

An outsider visiting any Kwakwa̱ ka̱'wakw village in the fifteen years following 1951 would be apt to receive very mixed impressions of the state of traditional culture. As a young and new employee of the Provincial Museum, my own introduction to the 'Na̱mgis village at Alert Bay in 1966 was made easy, as I was in the company of the late Helen Hunt, adopted daughter of Chief Mungo Martin. The people of her generation and those older than she were celebrating the completion and dedication of a traditional ceremonial house in that village. Men and women who had known "Dr. Boas," and some of the children of his associate George Hunt, participated in the event. We saw old men dance *hamatsa* who had been trained as rigorously in their art as were those described in the works published by Boas and Hunt some seventy years previously. Siblings of the woman "burned" in the fire, described earlier, were present, and remembered. At the same time, children from the nearby residential school were herded into the dance house to witness events that were almost as unfamiliar to them as they were to their non-Indian teachers.

At that first visit to Alert Bay, Helen Hunt not only introduced me to the potlatch, she quite literally escorted me to the community, found a place for me to stay, and introduced me to people. This was, however, merely a particular instance of her self-appointed task of teaching me, who had been trained in museology and was primarily interested in material culture, how to be an anthropologist. When she introduced me to the sponsor of the potlatch, I offered to film the event. He not only granted the request, but asked if I would tape record it also, on his machine. From this significantly collaborative beginning, the Provincial Museum now has an inventory of 100 contemporary potlatches recorded on film and tape and accompanied by detailed notes. This is an invaluable scientific and artistic collection, accessible to outsiders with the permission of the hosts of the potlatches. It has also been a vehicle through which the Museum has been able to train young Kwakwa̱ ka'wakw in the techniques of recording and analysing cultural events, a practice that has assumed greater importance as the people have taken on the task of cultural education in their own community and to the larger community.

One consequence of renewed potlatch activity by the Kwakwa̱ ka'wakw was a resurgence of public interest in traditional artifacts. Collectors and art dealers simply moved in and within a few years most of the regalia that had survived earlier events was gone. The Provincial Museum responded by commissioning the carving of masks at the Museum. Henry Hunt, Tony Hunt, and Richard Hunt were hired and built up a collection of nearly 200 items that could then be used in local communities when required. This aspect of our activity is currently being phased out because a new generation of carvers has arisen and individual Kwakwa̱ ka'wakw are increasingly commissioning them to carve the newly necessary ceremonial regalia.

In the early days I was frequently challenged by young men and women about my intentions; many thought that I was foolish to waste my time with old people and irrelevant lifeways. But as time passed the reality and validity of displaying one's mythic origins from a magic past and the logic of confirming these through an attendant potlatch were recognized by that younger generation. Perhaps one of my most treasured experiences came several years ago when I cruised through Blackfish Sound on the modern seine boat owned by a successful Kwakwa̱ ka'wakw fisherman. "You know," he said, "when I first met you I thought your interest in the old people was silly and I thought they were silly to spend so much time and effort in their old age to get money and gifts together to give away. But now that I have given a potlatch I can say that I felt much better giving away ten thousand dollars than ever I would have if I took that money and spent it on myself. The old people are right. . . ."

Certainly the past can never be entirely regained. Those privileged few of us can capture some sense of what it was all about through discussions with elders still living today. The sensitive reader can discover in printed passages left by such authors as Boas and Hunt some of the power of the oratory, of the richness of the language, of the incredible technical and artistic accomplishments of the Kwakwa ka'wakw. And that inquisitive student can discover the Kwakwa ka'wakw are becoming their own historians. Through language and cultural programs run by the Kwakwa ka'wakw in their own museums and in public and alternative schools, today's young Kwakwa ka'wakw are being offered an insight into a world that was in many ways denied their parents.

Recommended Readings

Barnett, H. G.
   1938   "The Nature of the Potlatch," *American Anthropologist*, 40: 349-58.
            This short article remains one of the most simply yet clearly stated
            definitions of the potlatch.
Boas, Franz
   1897   *The Social Organization and Secret Societies of the Kwakiutl Indians.* United
            States National Museum Report for 1895, Washington, D.C.
            Boas's first major descriptive work on Kwakwa ka'wakw society, the
            potlatch, and ceremonial dances. Many masks are illustrated and the use of
            these briefly described.
   1909   *The Kwakiutl of Vancouver Island.* Memoir of the American Museum of
            Natural History No. 8. New York.
            A comprehensive description of Kwakwa ka'wakw technology and
            industries such as weaving and woodworking.
   1910   *Kwakiutl Tales.* Columbia University Contributions to Anthropology, Vol. 2.
            New York.
            This and a later companion volume published in 1935 with the same title
            contain considerable information about Kwakwa ka'wakw mythological and
            traditional beliefs.
   1921   *Ethnology of the Kwakiutl.* 35th Annual Report of the Bureau of American
            Ethnology, Washington, D.C.
            A fascinating two-volume work containing descriptions of food-gathering
            and food-preparation techniques as well as lengthy descriptions of family
            histories that provide considerable insight into social customs.

1930 *The Religion of the Kwakiutl Indians*. Columbia University Contributions to Anthropology, Vol. 10, Part 2. New York.

Contains useful accounts of the mythological origins of the winter ceremonial, texts on shamanism, and insights into the Kwakwa̲ ka'wakw concept of prayer.

1935 *Kwakiutl Tales: New Series*. Columbia University Contributions to Anthropology, Vol. 26, New York.

1940 *Race, Language and Culture*. Helen Codere, ed. Chicago: University of Chicago Press.

A selection of essays written by Boas between the years 1891 and 1939 that provide a clear insight into the development of his thinking and contributions to the developing science of anthropology.

1966 *Kwakiutl Ethnography*. Helen Codere, ed. Chicago: University of Chicago Press.

Boas's most comprehensive statement on the Kwakwa̲ ka'wakw incorporating an incomplete manuscript and selections from published works, arranged and edited by one of Boas's foremost students.

Boas, F., and George Hunt

1902-05 *Kwakiutl Texts*. Memoir of the American Museum of Natural History, Vol. 5. New York.

George Hunt, Boas's Native ethnographer and associate, is given credit as co-author in this extensive work, which records much textual information in both Kwak'wala and English.

Codere, Helen

1950 *Fighting With Property*. Monograph of the American Ethnological Society, New York.

An interesting account of Kwakwa̲ ka'wakw potlatching, based on oral traditions, from pre-contact times to the early twentieth century in which potlatching and warfare are considered as related.

Curtis, E.S.

1915 *The Kwakiutl. The North American Indians*, Vol. 10. Norwood, Conn.

A well-organized work on the Kwakwa̲ ka'wakw including comprehensive descriptions of various winter ceremonials and their mythological basis.

Duff, W.

1964 *The Indian History of British Columbia*. Vol. 1, *The Impact of the White Man*. Anthropology in British Columbia Memoir No. 5, Victoria.

A sympathetic, sensitive account of Indian-white relationships in British Columbia, including lists of bands, population estimates, and other relevant data.

Ford, C.S.
1941 *Smoke From Their Fires*. New Haven: Yale University Press.
An amusing, insightful biography of Kwakwa ka'wakw Chief Charles Nowell, whose life spanned two eras and two cultures.

Hawthorn, Audrey
1979 *Kwakiutl Art*. Seattle: University of Washington Press.
A profusely illustrated work featuring many ceremonial items such as masks, rattles, whistles, blankets, painted screens, and the like. Descriptive texts provide an introduction to the use of ceremonial paraphernalia.

Holm, Bill
1983 *Smoky Top: The Art and Times of Willie Seaweed*. Seattle: University of Washington Press.
An excellent analysis of the personal artistic style of the greatest of twentieth-century Kwakwa ka'wakw artists, with insightful views into the man's role as singer, dancer, and leader at winter ceremonials and potlatches.

Spradley, James P.
1969 *Guests Never Hungry: The Autobiography of James Sewid, a Kwakiutl Indian*. New Haven: Yale University Press.
One Kwakwa ka'wakw chief's view of his own life and his people, with particular emphasis on the years 1930 through 1967. Particularly interesting is the insight into the emerging role of Indian fishermen and their dealings with a white bureaucracy.

PART IX
Conclusion

CHAPTER 26
Taking Stock: Legacies and Prospects

C. Roderick Wilson and R. Bruce Morrison

So where are we? As Canada approaches the end of the twentieth century, what can be said about the place of Inuit, Metis, and First Nations people? In answering the question, we will briefly review where we have been, consider the contours of current life, and give some thought to what lies ahead.

In the early decades of this century it was generally believed that Native people were dying, both literally and culturally. In earlier centuries disease had swept most populations on the continent, laying waste whole communities. By this century the worst killers, particularly smallpox, were abating, but Native populations generally continued to decline through the 1920s. In both Canada and the United States the so-called Indian wars were over. Indians and Metis, defeated militarily, seemed literally to be at "the end of the trail," as a popular painting of the period put it.

Reserves were established across southern Canada, and, under the authority of the Indian Act, agents decided which Natives were Indians and controlled where Indians could live and travel, what crops they could plant, to whom they could sell their produce, whether or not they could butcher their own animals for their own consumption, and a myriad of other details of daily life. The Act explicitly prohibited various activities, such as alcohol consumption and voting, taken for granted by ordinary Canadians. It also outlawed participation in ceremonies that were central to many Indians, the Sun Dance of the Plains and the potlatch of the Northwest Coast. This is analogous to passing a Catholic Act to regulate the lives of Canadian Catholics that prohibits them from attending mass, or passing a Baptist Act banning baptism.

To put it simply, Indians were now administered as a colonial people. The common assumption was that those who managed to survive physically would in time become members of Canadian society virtually indistinguishable from others. To that end the Act provided that any Indians acquiring an education, economic independence, or a non-Indian husband would automatically cease to be Indian. They obviously now had the means to participate in society as Canadians and, it was assumed, had already become separated from their natal communities.

The Metis, whether Red River Metis or simply Natives who for one reason or another did not have legal status as Indians, were generally left to whatever fate they might find. Various schemes designed to extinguish any Aboriginal claim were introduced; these usually took the form of scrip entitling the bearer to land. Many Metis did not receive scrip, and most who did were not in a position to take advantage of its potential (for a number of cultural, technological, and economic reasons). As a result, most Metis have had no special status; legally, many were seen as squatters on crown land. Until the Constitution Act was passed in 1982, Alberta was the exception, having passed in 1938 a Metis Betterment Act establishing "colonies" on the model of the federal reserves. Although the Act provides a significant opportunity for some Alberta Metis to find land that is legally secure, this protection entails a substantial loss of local control and subjection to an external bureaucratic structure. Other provinces have also developed programs specifically to alleviate social problems associated with the Metis. On the one hand these programs are mute testimony to the unrealistic nature of the federal government's assumptions about the circumstances under which it considers itself to have fulfilled its obligations to Canadian Indians. On the other hand, the provincial agencies administering these programs tend to put their clients into a limited version of the same kind of dependent, controlled status as the federal government has historically placed status Indians.

Although the Inuit have a long history of contact with outsiders, the harshness of their environment and the lack of resources that would bring significant numbers of Euro-Canadians to the Arctic have until very recently inhibited the development of a colonial administration. That changed in the early 1950s as the government felt it necessary for national security purposes to create a northern presence and because, on humanitarian grounds, it felt obligated to provide educational and health services. In the late 1950s the trend further accelerated when for many Inuit both the caribou and the fish failed and people starved. One consequence of increased services was an increased governmental presence that is colonial in character. The nature of this colonialism is illustrated by an event: in late 1984, as Inuit heard of widespread famine in Ethiopia, the people responded with great generosity – famine and sharing are things they know about. The town of Spences Bay, in addition to money collected from individuals, sent the entire surplus from the town budget, some $48,000; their gift was disallowed on the grounds that all expenditures by the town in excess of $200 need government approval. (One of the ironies of this case is that by 1984 the centre of colonial control for northern settlements was no longer Ottawa, but Yellowknife.)

As each chapter has indicated, however, Canada's Aboriginal peoples have, by and large, survived their colonial experiences. Admittedly, there have been substantial losses, both demographic and cultural, but Canadian Native societies have demonstrated the capacity and will to make major accommodative changes to their new circumstances, to attempt to change some of those circumstances, and to maintain their separate identities. Given the desperate conditions of many of these societies fifty or a hundred years ago and the strength of the social forces working for their assimilation, their continued presence as functioning societies is a considerable feat.

Some "Hard" Data

How many Natives have survived a century or more of colonialism and what are their characteristics? According to statistics collected by the Department of Indian Affairs and Northern Development (DIAND), as of 1991 there were 511,791 Indians in Canada. This apparently straightforward statistic, however, becomes amazingly complicated upon scrutiny. Like other statistics published by Indian Affairs, it refers only to those registered as Indian by the federal government. This population of status Indians may vary significantly, both in total numbers and in other ways, from populations defined by other criteria. In the Canadian census, for instance, people are allowed to self-designate themselves with regard to ethnicity. In the 1991 census only 460,680 people designated themselves as Indian, 10 per cent less than DIAND's count; in 1981 the census count was 13 per cent higher! While the DIAND count is based on precise criteria as to who exactly is legally an Indian, and that is a question of importance, the point is that there are other legitimate terms in which one can phrase the question of who is an Indian.

The term "non-status Indian" designates individuals who may think of themselves as Indian and so be regarded by others, but are excluded from government lists. In government statistics they are usually lumped together with Metis people, both being "unofficial" Indians (at one time both groups frequently were referred to as "half-breeds"; this may or may not have been appropriate in particular instances). In the 1991 census, some 135,000 people designated themselves as Metis, up significantly from 98,000 in 1981. This is nevertheless a very low number that probably indicates more about the unsatisfactory nature of the census question or about the current usefulness of the term than about how many people it could properly be applied to. By way of contrast it can be noted that the Metis and Non-status Indian Association in the single province of Ontario claims a membership of over 200,000. Depending on the criteria employed, estimates of the non-status and Metis population for the country as a whole range from a low of some 400,000 to over two million.

The Inuit have been administered, and counted, separately from Indians. Because their bureaucratic history has been briefer and less subject to efforts to exclude community members from official lists, there is less disagreement about how many there are. The 1991 census listed 36,215, up from 25,370 in 1981.

The federal government has kept careful count only of status Indians and Inuit. The constitution recognizes Indians (undefined), Inuit, and Metis as Aboriginal people. Accordingly, we can only state that they number somewhere between 700,000 and 3.5 million. It is no longer the case, however, that the only detailed statistical data on Canada's Aboriginal peoples are those collected by DIAND; the 1991 census process included a major survey of self-reported Aboriginal people. Both kinds of data are used in this brief interpretive review.

As the following table indicates, Ontario has the largest status Indian population in the country, followed by B.C. One thing the table does not show is what proportion of the provincial population is Indian. For Ontario and all provinces to the east, the proportion is low, no more than 1 per cent. The proportion in the four western provinces is high, up to almost 5 per cent, and very high in the North (up to about 20 per cent in

Table 26.1
Status Indian Residence by Region, 1991

Region or Prov.	Number of Bands	Population (% of Nat.)	On-Reserve (% of Prov.)	Off-Reserve (% of Prov.)
Atlantic	31	19,935 (3.9%)	13,633 (68.4%)	6,302 (31.6%)
Quebec	39	50,728 (9.9%)	35,953 (70.9%)	14,775 (29.1%)
Ontario	126	117,152 (22.9%)	61,882 (52.8%)	55,270 (47.2%)
Manitoba	60	76,793 (15.0%)	51,017 (66.4%)	25,776 (33.6%)
Sask.	68	78,573 (15.4%)	42,379 (53.9%)	36,194 (46.1%)
Alberta	41	60,303 (12.3%)	41,565 (65.8%)	21,604 (34.2%)
B.C.	196	87,135 (17.0%)	46,093 (52.9%)	41,042 (47.1%)
N.W.T.	17	11,856 (2.3%)	9,279 (78.4%)	2,559 (21.6%)
Yukon	14	6,450 (1.3%)	2,940 (45.6%)	3,510 (54.4%)
Totals	592	511,791	304,759 (59.5%)	207,032 (40.5%)

SOURCE: Compiled from DIAND statistics, 1992.

the Northwest Territories). If we were to look at the proportion of Aboriginal people instead of registered Indians, the relationships remain roughly constant, but the numbers change and the contrasts heighten: in the central and eastern provinces the proportion of the population considered Native rises to no more than 2 per cent, while in Manitoba (the highest province) it rises to 11 per cent, with the Yukon at 23 per cent and the NWT at 62 per cent!

B.C. stands out in the table for its high number of bands, and it does have (at 445), with the Yukon (at 460), the smallest average band size; Alberta (at 1,470) has the largest average band size. While the NWT has by far the fewest people living "off-reserve," it also has virtually no one actually living on reserves as almost none were ever established. While the category "off-reserve" is not quite the same as urban, the column is indicative of the extensive and ongoing urbanization of Canada's Indian population. The national average of 41 per cent living off-reserve is up dramatically from 29 per cent in only a decade. Even the NWT, at 22 per cent living off-reserve being the least urban region, exhibits a major shift from the 7 per cent figure of a decade ago.

A somewhat different perspective on residential patterns is provided by another set of DIAND statistics involving the characterization of communities as urban, rural, remote, or "special access." Using these criteria, the Atlantic region, Alberta, and Saskatchewan have their status Indian populations most concentrated in urban and rural areas (at over 90 per cent), while the most remote is Manitoba (at almost 50 per cent), followed by the Yukon and NWT. Census data indicate that "southern" cities having the highest proportion of Native people resident are Regina, Saskatoon, Winnipeg, and Edmonton, although Winnipeg has the largest Native population.

Canada's Native population is younger than the non-Native population and is growing at a faster rate. Among the general population, 21 per cent are under fifteen years old; the corresponding figure for Indians is 37 per cent, for Metis is 38 per cent, and for Inuit is 43 per cent. At the other end of the scale, those fifty-five and older comprise 20 per cent of the general population but only 7 per cent for Metis and Indians and 6 per cent for Inuit. Such differences have consequences. The present Indian population is characterized by an unusually large number of young, economically dependent people. This has created a high demand for educational and social services. In the coming decades, however, as this group matures, they will generate new demands for employment opportunities, frequently in regions now having few jobs. A second consequence is more internal to the Indian community. What kinds of pressures for change are created by a situation in which, quite suddenly, the majority of the population is very young but very few are elderly?

While a population that is growing instead of dying suggests a social turnaround of more than simply demographic consequence, it does not mean that all is well for Canadian Indians. Although mortality rates continue to drop, they are still high; for people under forty-five they are typically three times the national average. The death rate for children under one year of age declined dramatically in recent decades, but it is still twice the national average. Violent deaths generally are three times the national average and among the young may be ten times the national rate. Suicides among young Indian adults are very high; for fifteen- to twenty-four-year-olds the rate is six times the national average. Conversely, middle-aged and elderly Indians have suicide rates close to or below those of the general population. Further, non-Indians are about three times more likely to die from cancer or diseases of the circulatory system than are Indians. Indians are thus at higher risk in many, but not all, categories of mortality.

Such statistics could be multiplied almost endlessly, but it is necessary to ask questions about what they mean. Usually they are presented much as they have been here, with an explicit contrast between Indian and non-Indian. It seems obvious that Indians are in most respects severely disadvantaged in comparison to other Canadians. Unfortunately, the data frequently do not allow a meaningful comparison, because in critical ways the populations being compared are so different. To take a specific example where there has been little change in recent decades: nationally there are about four deaths by fire per 100,000 people each year, while the corresponding figure for Indians is about thirty. What weight, however, should be given the fact that most Indian communities are in rural or remote regions? As noted above, in some regions of the country a very large number of Natives live in areas of difficult access. Would the incidence of death by fire in correspondingly remote non-Native communities be any lower? Perhaps, but we do not know, so we are left comparing apples and oranges. Thus, although the data do not really provide a sound basis for social action, agencies must act on the available information. While presumably no one argues that there should be a fire hydrant next to each trapper's cabin, the argument is frequently made that all Canadians should have the same level of social services. This noble ideal, ostensibly redressing apparently scandalous social inequity but ignoring the diverse real-world conditions in which people live, in turn becomes a rationale either for moving Indians to places where there are fire hydrants or for bringing urban amenities, through industrial development, to rural and remote people. Neither solution is necessarily beneficial. That is, "comparative" statistics can buttress arguments for providing services that Native communities desire, or they can be used to justify programs that would undercut their social or economic basis (note the chapters by Asch and Feit for recent examples). In other words, the attempt to create equal living conditions for Indians, buttressed by non-comparable data, confuses general equality with specific identity and results in socially undesirable consequences.

There are other interpretive problems. Hospitalization rates for tuberculosis among Indians and Inuit have recently been two and three times the national average. Does this result from lack of reasonable health care? How relevant are the isolated living conditions of many of these people? What of the general antipathy toward treatment that isolates the victim from family, community, and even treatment that is culturally relevant? How significant is the Aboriginal genetic predisposition to tuberculosis? In spite of the high current rate, perhaps it is better considered as a prime example of something the government has done right: the Inuit rate is only about 8 per cent of what it was thirty years ago, and the Indian rate is less than 20 per cent of what it then was.

Indians are much less likely than other Canadians to have a legally sanctioned marriage. This in some part reflects the failure of the government to recognize traditional forms of marriage. More importantly, it indicates the impact of legislation on behaviour. Unmarried mothers receive much higher welfare payments than do separated or divorced mothers. Until 1985 the Indian Act, section 12(1)b, stripped Indian status from women, and the subsequent children of women, who married men who were not legally Indian. For decades many Indian women found it not in their interest to be formally married. This may well have implications for family stability and social attitudes, but the statistics cannot reasonably be interpreted as they might be for non-Indian populations.

As a last example, consider that five times as many Indian children as non-Indian are in the "care" of the government. While the Indian population has almost doubled in the last twenty-five years, the percentage of Indian children being taken into care has additionally doubled. In the same period, the number of adoptions of Indian children has grown by a factor of five, while the proportion being adopted by non-Indians has grown from about 50 per cent to about 80 per cent (put another way, eight times as many Indian children are now lost to the Indian community as formerly). This has been explained largely on the basis that these children are now living in better material and social conditions. That claim would of course be difficult to substantiate in many cases, but even if it were true, would the pattern be justified? By what standards does one judge – is the number of toilets per household an appropriate measure? Does a community have a right to its children where parental care has in fact broken down?

Finally, to return to an earlier point, however inadequate the DIAND statistics are as indicative of conditions for Aboriginal people generally, and however misleading they may be when interpreted out of their cultural and social context, the fact that these statistics have been generated

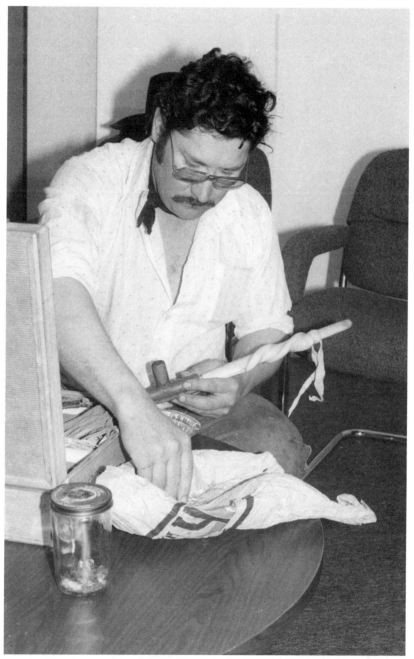

PLATE 26.1. Cree Shaman Russell Willier preparing for a pipe ceremony at a University of Alberta medical clinic. The shaman is working with anthropologists and medical practitioners to explore the healing dimensions of traditional Cree medicine. Courtesy of Provincial Museum of Alberta.

about one segment only of the Canadian population, in order to facilitate their administration, is in itself a dramatic statement about the nature of the relationship.

Renewal

Optimism is increasing in many Native communities today. That is not to say that all is well. Even the average non-Indian is aware of at least some aspects of the negative statistical profile as it is generally presented: inadequate housing, over-representation in prisons, high mortality rates, etc. Nevertheless, the negative picture is much less than the whole story. The main story has to do with the renewed vitality of Native society.

The reader will remember that reference has been made from time to time throughout this book to the impact of images and ideas on our thinking. A dominant image in Canadian thinking is that Native people are best considered as part of the past: their social structures and economies are antiquated; they may have a legitimate or even honoured place in history, but their traditions are a hindrance to them and the country; that they might have a viable future as Natives is almost unthinkable. This pervasive stereotype, when reinforced by the generally held negative statistical profile of contemporary Native people, has profoundly damaging consequences. These negative effects may be seen at work in the general population, in school textbooks, among planners, and at times among Native peoples themselves.

In attempting to counter the notion that Native society is moribund, we have adduced two approaches. Several chapters, particularly those dealing with people living in more remote parts of the country, have demonstrated that changes in the lifeways of Indian peoples have been substantially less than has commonly been supposed. A second approach has been to note that, although traditional behaviours may have been substantially modified, there are important continuities in meaning, purpose, and function (or, although social behaviour has changed, the cultural rules generating behaviour have not). Our approach here is to argue that the Native community, even in those areas where there is less continuity with the past, is experiencing renewal.

Renewal, as used here, takes many forms and includes all aspects of life – economic, social, political, educational, and religious. Most of all, it has to do with identity. For increasing numbers of Canada's Aboriginal people, to be Native (whether Inuit, Metis, or Indian) is to have pride. Symbolically, one of the most important areas of Native renewal is their growing success in controlling alcohol abuse. In part this relates to the dominance of the image of the drunken Indian in Euro-Canadian society. More importantly, it has to do with the fact that it is largely through their own efforts that this major social problem is being controlled. The point is best made by reviewing some specific cases.

Alkali Lake in central B.C. is home to about 400 people. Fifteen years ago the chief and his wife felt almost alone in being sober and were desperate to do something to alleviate the terrible problems they saw associated with drinking. They had no particular expertise or resources. Starting with one person, a band councillor in whom they saw potential, they worked on him, even to the extent of following him into the bar and just sitting there as he drank. In time he responded to their intensive attention (shaming is a powerful traditional technique of inducing socially approved behaviour), and they turned to others. After four years they had recruited only a handful of non-drinkers, but it was a start. The chief learned to exert other kinds of pressure also. People who committed alcohol-related offences on the reserve were presented with the option of choosing to enter treatment or of being dealt with by the law. He learned that bootleggers could be charged under the Indian Act, and went himself with the RCMP to collect evidence to convict the five bootleggers on the reserve, one of whom was his mother. Minimal fines were levied, but the point was clear that he meant business and that subsequent charges would be made under the Criminal Code. Welfare and family allowance checks were converted into groceries and clothing before people could drink them. As these efforts took hold, other areas of life changed. A number of families pooled their resources to start a grocery store. Several families bought a house in town for their high school students to use. A piggery and a co-operative farm were started. Seeing the positive changes, DIAND provided funds to start a sawmill. In short, the entire social and economic fabric of the community was revitalized. Although at this point in time the economic aspects of the case described, written in 1985, seem overly optimistic due to the cessation of short-term DIAND funding, this does nothing to diminish the almost miraculous social transformation that was accomplished.

An urban community in Ontario suffered economic hardship as local industries closed in 1982. Many turned to alcohol; suicide attempts rose to an astronomical seventeen per month. In this instance, there were trained personnel at a treatment centre for alcohol abuse, but they lacked sufficient staff to provide services to the community at large or directly to address the high suicide rate. The centre workers were able, however, to mobilize the community to draw on its own resources to effect a major turnaround, primarily through forming numerous small groups to provide mutual social support.

On a more formal level, the work of the Nechi Institute at Edmonton in training Native people to work in alcohol and drug-abuse centres is noteworthy. Central to their program is an affirmation of Nativeness. This is expressed in many ways, but particularly in learning to appreciate traditional culture (including encouraging trainees to draw on spiritual resources, however defined) and in learning to recognize and deal with the anger and denial they have acquired through their interaction with non-Native society. The program has been very successful. A study of the 1,300 trained in the first ten years indicates that 39 per cent have gone on to further education, 66 per cent report higher income, 68 per cent are working actively with service clubs or recreational organizations in their communities, there has been a 166 per cent increase in the number working with alcohol programs, and so on. A major thrust in recent years, and this is true nationally also, is to focus on youth programs and suicide prevention.

Conclusions to be drawn from these examples include: (1) although we can discuss alcoholism and its treatment as isolated matters, in the real world life for both the individual and the community demonstrates interconnectedness; (2) although Nechi and other organizations may work closely with non-Native organizations such as Alcoholics Anonymous, the active leadership of local Native people is imperative; (3) although professional expertise may be useful when available, it is probably more important that plans be locally devised and implemented; and (4) it may be that for many problems – particularly if they are chronic – technical answers are less important than social ones, for resolution will likely involve concepts such as respect, dignity, and control. To put these comments another way, the examples cited illustrate the attempts of Canadian Native people to create an appropriate Native milieu for themselves.

Given this analysis, the reader will not be surprised to learn that there are also increasing numbers of Native-run businesses. So much is this the case that some of the major banks now have Native financial services divisions. There are also Native-owned trust companies. These moves represent explicit, self-interested decisions to invest resources in Native communities and Native people because they are recognized as having profit-generating potential. As a banker noted when the trend started, "The thing that held native people back has been lack of capital and no structure for capital formation. . . . They're starting to hire the kind of talent that's necessary to do it. When you put together the people, resources, land and dollars, you get an explosive situation. I think this will be one of the big stories in finance and development" (O'Malley, 1980).

The Sawridge band near Slave Lake, Alberta, is a prime example of the trend. It opened the first Native-owned hotel in Canada in 1973. It has since enlarged the hotel, opened another in Jasper, and built a shopping centre in Slave Lake. The band is fortunate in having modest oil revenues to initiate these ventures and in the capable management of Chief Walter Twin. While traditional government development structures often discouraged responsible management, many contemporary leaders recognize it as a key to achieving their goals.

It is also clear that Native leaders recognize the importance of intersector linkages: economic development is not solely economic in its purposes or effects. In Saskatchewan the Meadow Lake District chiefs have pooled their resources to implement a broad range of development activities. They successfully took over a school system, partly to promote their long-range plans for developing local leadership. They have followed this up by contracting a consulting firm that specializes in training Third World businessmen. Not only are their own entrepreneurs being trained, but the chiefs obtained rights to sell the program both to other reserves and to non-Indians. They are now planning to take on the management of a forest reserve on the Scandinavian model; they would be responsible for the forest's total management, including silviculture, harvesting, wildlife, and recreation. In other words, it would be a modern version of traditional concerns for the total productivity of the land.

Such developments contrast sharply with the historic past in which reserve economies usually had little impact on regional economies except as a *raison d'être* for government services. A good example of the new potential has occurred on the Huron reserve near Quebec City. Under the leadership of Chief Max Gros Louis, fourteen businesses were organized. The band is now the largest employer in the area and sells its products to Canadian Tire, Eaton's, and foreign markets. When the companies were organized fifty-two families were on welfare. Now all able-bodied persons, as well as 125 Euro-Canadians, are employed.

Educational innovation was alluded to above in the context of economic change; it needs to be considered in its own right. One of the most significant changes of the past three decades is the growth of band-controlled schools and school systems. This is not an automatic panacea, but it has been of vital importance in restoring a sense of community and personal identity that goes far beyond learning the "three R's." That schools can teach both computer programming and traditional languages, that functionally monolingual students (and they still exist) learn to read

French or English better if they are first literate in their own language, that children have the inherent right to have at least some appropriate role models in their schools: these are ideas that need both to be accepted widely and to be pondered at length. The residential schools of the past may indeed not have been intentionally villainous, but we all, and especially Native people, are still paying for the psychological and social havoc they created.

That the number of Native students in the post-secondary educational systems has increased exponentially in recent years is in part an aspect of generalized Native renewal. That the growth is so impressive is also a function of the base being so low; in absolute terms the numbers are still small. That the first Native medical doctor in Canada was recently graduated is a matter of pride, but also of shame. Nevertheless, students in these and other programs are important. It is critical that Native communities have functioning in them educated people, including professionals (the current ratio of Native medical doctors to the total Native population in Canada is less than 1:30,000; for the general population it is about 1:500). It is also of importance to the national community that some of them enter mainstream Canadian society and there be seen to be competent.

There have always been Native intellectuals. There even have been Native academics, including anthropologists, but their numbers have been few. One also needs to remember that some of the early Native anthropologists were not called that, but rather were referred to as informants. That, hopefully, has changed. Among the changes is the number of Native people, trained in anthropology and other disciplines, who are using that training to analyse productively aspects of their own situations. As anthropologists we find this especially exciting because, while there are difficulties in studying one's own society and culture (partly because one of the universal features of culture is the creation of generally accepted fictions), the insights of an insider are nevertheless frequently of a nature virtually unaccessible to an outsider. *The Canadian Journal of Native Education* is a good source of some of this material, much of it done by graduate students.

We will in no way do it justice, but we must mention at this point not merely academic writing, important though it is, but writing of all sorts – life stories, poetry, plays, songs, novels, (even) an opera. Or perhaps, especially an opera. If Natives have accepted contemporary country music as part of their culture, why not opera? And for much of this material there is not only the writing, but also the performing. And there is also the performance of non-written art. It is all significant simply because it is there; Native people are alive and they are expressing their joys and sorrows through the arts as do other people who are alive.

A final point in this section is that economic development, operas, and alcohol treatment centres are important not only in their own right, and as examples of a general renewal, but are inextricably linked with renewal as spiritual phenomena. Anthropologists have analysed the series of Indian attempts early in the colonial era to regain control of their lives by religio-political means as a series of revitalization movements. The Longhouse Religion of the Iroquois, the Ghost Dance of the Sioux, the Native American Church, and the Shakers of the west coast are historic examples still current. Recent movements are more diffuse, so we have spoken only of renewal, but there are linkages. North American Natives have consistently responded to crises essentially as spiritual problems, the specific outworkings of which are linked by a core of meaning.

Traditional religious forms have long been repressed in much of Canada, but they often merely went underground. Increasingly, the meaning of these forms is being rediscovered or more openly acknowledged. Some of the momentum is legislative (the "Potlatch Law" was dropped in 1951; elders may now conduct services in federal prisons), but the larger factor is a resurgent nativism. Traditional ceremonies such as the sweat, pipe, fast, and Sun Dance are now widely practised. It is important to note that this is not merely the repetition of something that the grandfathers did, but a revival or even a reinvention of living traditions (for many Native people it is also true that Christianity has become at least part of their spiritual identity).

Today, as in the past, activities that are primarily ceremonial are an important part of Native calendars. Possibly the best example is the former Ecumenical Conference at Morley, Alberta, annually drawing thousands of participants from across the continent. On a smaller scale Native people attend personal or regional rites in growing numbers.

The outworkings of this renewed spiritual heritage are many. They include such diverse and related activities on the west coast as constructing longhouses, erecting totem poles, carving ceremonial regalia, making prints and paintings, taking potlatch names, and joining traditional societies. They include such varied "political" acts as Chief Robert Smallboy leading his band into the wilderness to escape contamination by Euro-Canadian society, the American Indian Movement occupying DIAND offices in the 1970s, and traditional chiefs lobbying the British House of Lords to prevent the patriation of the Canadian constitution.

They include economic acts as apparently separate as remote James Bay Cree hunters accepting the lives of moose and beaver and Metis architect Doug Cardinal successfully winning an international competition to design a new building for the National Museum of Civilization in Ottawa.

The formation of Canada constituted a massive, sustained shock to Aboriginal society. Contrary to Euro-Canadian expectations, Native people have survived. It is yet too early to say that they are everywhere flourishing, and they are still threatened, but the evidence of renewed vigour is there for those who will see it.

The Need for Structural Change

In spite of the positive signs of renewal in Canada's Native communities, for these developments to come to fruition there must be basic change in the structural arrangements whereby Aboriginal peoples are governed as part of Canadian society. The failures of the past and the present are not merely the result of such factors as inadequate health care services, inappropriate textbooks, or restricted access to capital, important though these matters are. While failures of health, education, and economic growth must be addressed in their own right, and while it is important to be aware that Native people are experiencing some success in resolving these social problems, it is essential to recognize that the subordinate legal status of Native peoples will continue to manifest itself in various forms of social malaise if the status quo is maintained. To a greater or lesser extent all Native problems are rooted in the fundamental fact of Canadian Native history and contemporary life, that they are subjugated peoples without control over the defining facts of their lives.

Native people are of course quite aware of their colonial status, although all might not put it in these terms. The various forms of renewal – artistic expression, religious rites, political activism, even Native businesses – have in common a strong sense of identity, in being Native as opposed to being Euro-Canadian. Given this, it is also to be expected that Native leaders have a long tradition of attempting to create conditions whereby Native communities can function as polities within Canada, or, in the current phrase, to achieve some form of self-government.

The facts of life on the reserves have changed considerably in recent decades, but the fundamental nature of the Indian-government relationship has changed not one whit. Indians have been granted the right to vote and to drink, agents no longer live on the reserves, and many bands have control over expenditures; many harsh and arbitrary features of the reserve system have been moderated. Consultation and development have become bywords of the new era. Unfortunately, a close examination of the changes reveals that nothing has been altered: assimilation (first officially repudiated in 1946) remains the overall goal, and Ottawa, however benign its intentions and practices, retains ultimate power. A few examples illustrate the point.

The Indian Act was last rewritten in 1951. Among other changes, the clause making the potlatch and Sun Dance illegal was dropped. While in a sense this was a victory for all Native people, it is more significant that the change was unilateral: there was no consultation, no apology, no compensation, and no return of confiscated property.

Indian Affairs was reorganized in 1964 to provide increased responsibility to personnel working at the community level. Much the same impetus that gave rise to this reorganization led to the commissioning of a landmark investigation by anthropologists to analyse data collected nationally on the educational, social, and economic conditions of Indians and on this basis to make policy recommendations. Commonly called the Hawthorn Report, its release in 1967 touched the national consciousness with its detailed inventory of the disadvantaged conditions of most Indians. Amid promises from Ottawa of increased consultation, the reserves were almost flooded with community and economic development workers. Two comments are relevant: (1) government action to correct long-standing problems resulted from studies by non-Indian academics, not as a result of the needs themselves or of the petitions of Native people; and (2) while DIAND sent many fine people to work on various projects, many failed because the local community did not have the power to make key decisions. Such failures may leave the community worse off than before.

Shortly thereafter, the now infamous 1969 White Paper on Indian Policy was released. At the stroke of a pen it proposed to abrogate federal responsibility for Indians. Appearances to the contrary, the White Paper was actually well intentioned, but it was based on assimilationist assumptions. Three characteristics of its chief promoters (Prime Minister Pierre Trudeau and Indian Affairs Minister Jean Chrétien) stand out as symptomatic of general problems in Indian-government relations: (1) they had no understanding of Indian culture or history; (2) their genuine concern for the rights of individuals left no place for the concept of group rights; and (3) as politicians they tended to judge questions of Indian rights from the perspective of their dominant concern, how alternative responses would affect the struggle to keep Quebec in Confederation. The proposals were totally and emphatically rejected by

Indians, primarily through the activity of provincial and national Indian associations. This in a sense marked their coming of age as bodies created by Indians in response to the necessity of acting corporately when attempting to negotiate with the government. Nevertheless, it took a sustained, national effort to block a government initiative that was disastrously ill-conceived.

In 1974 the government established the Office of Native Claims. Typical of its work was resolving a claim by Treaty No. 7 Indians that they had never received the annual funds for ammunition stipulated by the treaty. A simple contractual obligation a century old could be settled only after the creation of a special agency by the government.

When writing the first version of this chapter in 1985, we stated, "At this moment the government continues to propose, as it has for several years, immanent change in section 12(1)b of the Indian Act, which strips Indian status from women who marry non-status men. While the present legislation clearly produces inequity, whatever change is made in this clause merely changes the formula whereby winners and losers in the 'Indian game' are determined. It will not address the basic problem of Ottawa's defining who can be an Indian." There is in 1994 little reason to change that assessment. The legislation, commonly referred to as Bill C-31, was passed later that year. It has had enormous impact; as of 1993, 113,000 people had received status as Indians under the Act, with tens of thousands more to come. For many, being reinstated has been a profoundly significant event; for many others, it has meant that not much has changed. The legislation, for many Indians, continues to be very controversial, partly because of perceived continued inequities and a federal failure to provide funding, but primarily because, while the result may in the end be that bands will have control over their membership, the process itself was not negotiated but imposed unilaterally by Parliament.

The courts, while generally protecting treaty rights, have not held them sacrosanct. In a series of cases concerning hunting rights (starting with *Regina v. White and Bob*, two B.C. Indians accused of hunting deer on a reserve contrary to provincial game regulations), the courts have held that treaties take precedence over provincial law. However, in *Regina v. Sikyea* (where a Treaty No. 11 Indian shot a goose for subsistence purposes out of season), the court ruled that the federal Migratory Birds Convention Act unilaterally invalidated that aspect of the treaties. This is quite consistent with the nature of a parliamentary democracy, wherein any government "promise" is subject to change by a simple majority vote. The decision is, of course, contrary to the Indian view that a treaty can be changed only by mutual consent and that the necessity of mutual consent further implies that Indians exist and have rights independent of any act of Parliament.

Here again, however, recent events force some amendment of the argument. In a case involving the Musqueam of B.C., *R. v. Sparrow* (1990), the Supreme court decided that federal regulations on fishing did not apply to the Musqueam because their right to fish was, in the language of the Constitution Act, an "existing aboriginal right." This was the first time the court addressed the issue of what the language of section 35(1) of the Act actually meant. It was a significant and historic reversal of much of the trend noted above. However, as Asch and Macklem (1991) note, the judgement was made not on the basis of inherent Aboriginal rights but of contingent rights, of rights ultimately deriving from the action of the state.

A Basis for Change

George Manuel, Indian elder statesman, developed the concept of the Fourth World in a seminal book of that title. The idea refers to tribal peoples who have become incorporated into modern nation-states, but it rejects the notions associated with the Third World concept. An image that Manuel uses to express his central idea is the Two Row Wampum Belt, an Iroquois record of an early treaty in which two parallel rows run the whole length of the belt. It symbolizes the continued, undiminished existence of two independent yet intimately connected realities. It represents his vision of what Canada must become if Aboriginal peoples are to participate fully in the nation.

Manuel's vision is at odds with the picture of Indian-government relations elucidated above. Perhaps the clearest expression of the assimilationist-unilaterist position was articulated by then Prime Minister Trudeau: "we won't recognize aboriginal rights. . . . It's inconceivable . . . that in a given society one section of the society have a treaty with the other section of the society" (1969: 331). Fortunately for Canada's Native people, their own efforts, rulings by the courts, and public opinion have shifted the political realities.

Historically, intense lobbying by Native organizations, particularly in response to the 1969 White Paper and around the Constitution Act of 1982, has been central in stemming pressure for accelerated assimilation and in enlarging the non-Native constituency that believes new legislative alternatives for Native governance are possible.

Recent court decisions have had a profound effect on government policy. British colonial policy, most clearly enunciated in the Royal Proclamation of 1763, recognized Aboriginal rights; this eventually led to treaties and the reserve system. The government's theory was that treaties extinguished Aboriginal title; one consequence was the view that even reserves were owned by the crown and held "at the good will of the sovereign" in trust for her Indian wards. Court decisions involving Aboriginal rights tended to be incredibly ethnocentric by modern standards, reserving full rights to those Natives who, by European standards, were civilized.

The 1973 Supreme Court judgement in the Nisga'a case was a turning point. Since they had never signed a treaty, the Nisga'a claimed still to possess Aboriginal rights. They also used anthropological testimony to demonstrate that aboriginally they had exercised a sophisticated form of land tenure. Although the Nisga'a lost the case on a technicality, all six judges giving substantive decisions recognized that the Nisga'a had aboriginally possessed rights of a kind that the court could recognize; they split evenly on the question of whether these rights persisted. The Prime Minister was forced to acknowledge that perhaps Aboriginal peoples had more rights than he had thought.

Subsequent initial judgements in cases involving James Bay Cree and Dene claims reinforced the idea of continuing rights. In the Dene case the claimants were signatories to a treaty (No. 11), but the universal testimony of those then present was that it had not been presented as something that would lessen, let alone terminate, their rights. Court recognition, or near recognition, of persisting Aboriginal rights encouraged the government, and Native groups, to negotiate agreements rather than risk all in court, where neither side could be sure of winning. The court decisions allowed Natives negotiating "comprehensive" agreements (the Inuit, Dene, and James Bay Cree) to press for recognition of continuing decision-making rights, not mere public consultation.

The Mackenzie Valley Pipeline Inquiry and the 1977 report by Justice Berger are noteworthy not only because they showed that an eminent jurist thought the Dene had continuing social and political rights and because ordinary Dene successfully communicated their views to the court and to the public, but because the Inquiry demonstrated widespread public support for the notion of treating the Dene fairly, i.e., of recognizing continuing Aboriginal rights. This and similar cases also deeply involved anthropologists and other scientists in such support roles as gathering and analysing data and refuting the assimilationist arguments of the developers. In fact, the demands for solid evidence regarding such matters as historic and contemporary land-use patterns have led to the development of more sophisticated research techniques.

The 1982 decision of the Supreme Court in favour of the Musqueam band of Vancouver is another turning point. It recognized that: (1) Aboriginal title still exists; (2) bands own reserve land; (3) verbal promises by federal officials are legally binding; and (4) DIAND must transact Indian business only with the permission of the band council and in its best interest.

Finally, as noted above, the *Sparrow* case, while in several regards a significant step in recognizing the continuing nature of Aboriginal rights, makes those rights contingent on state action and hence lessens the likelihood of government or judicial recognition of inherent rights to self-government.

Toward Self-Government

What, then, are the practical prospects for Native self-government in Canada?

The Inuit of the eastern Northwest Territories will achieve self-governance in the near future. By virtue of geographic and historic vagaries, they remain a substantial majority in their region, and so Nunavut (Our Land) will become a reality in 1999, and perhaps eventually a province, without the necessity of special constitutional arrangements. Nunavut will be both an ordinary territory, or province, and an essentially Inuit domain. That there will be a parallel and unified Dene realm in the western NWT (Denendeh) seems much less likely. Negotiations that might have led to this have ceased. What is now being offered to the Dene communities is a form of legislated, municipal/administrative self-government. Some regions are working toward this within the framework of the comprehensive claims process, and others on the basis of treaty rights. In both cases the federal government insists, as it does elsewhere, that as a basis for settlement the Dene must agree to the extinguishment of all remaining Aboriginal rights, including the inherent right to self-government.

Inuit residing in northern Quebec have generally been treated as though they were status Indians. Although as geographically separate and locally dominant as the Inuit of the eastern NWT, by virtue of a political history extraneous to them they are part of an established province that, like all provinces, is not interested in diminishing its land base or powers. The James Bay Agreement, however, does grant them and the neighbouring Naskapi and Cree somewhat more autonomy than most status Indians.

The Inuit (and Indians) of Labrador (and Newfoundland) have been treated much as Metis, with no particular rights. Before Newfoundland joined Canada in 1949 they were considered to be ordinary citizens of the colony. Since Confederation the federal government has extended Aboriginal status to them only from the mid-1980s.

The Constitution Act, 1982, states that "The existing aboriginal and treaty rights of the aboriginal peoples of Canada are hereby recognized and affirmed," and "In this act, 'aboriginal peoples of Canada' includes the Indian, Inuit and Metis peoples of Canada." What these clauses will come to mean for Natives outside the NWT is not at all clear, although with the *Sparrow* case a beginning has been made. It is possible to read them in a way that would not, for instance, benefit Aboriginal people in Newfoundland. However, some forms of self-government may be developed without recourse to the constitution. Many Natives see the process of renewal as being, in a broad sense, a path to self-government. That is, through various means of self-help they are actively taking increased control over their own destinies, regardless of external support or opposition. For status Indians, however, despite the extent of internal renewal generated, there remain the formal, unilateral mechanisms of federal power. As previously noted, although renewal is requisite to dignity, sustained renewal requires an end to dependence.

For status Indians, the constitution presents a formidable obstacle to negotiating a new relationship with the federal government in that such a change would now require consent from a majority of provinces. Even if provincial agreement were forthcoming (and granting substantial power would likely be resisted), many treaty Indians quite correctly insist that the provinces can in principle have nothing to do with either their treaty or Aboriginal rights. The same impediments apply to Metis as well, with the additional hurdles that most have no collective land base (and the provinces have jurisdiction over crown land) and that their Aboriginality is less firmly established in the public mind. There are, however, potentially significant court cases in process involving Metis claims.

Nevertheless, the federal government has publicly committed itself to proceeding toward self-government and is working on a piecemeal basis to that end. Substantive negotiations have begun with only a handful of bands – at the present rate the process will take a century or more – and the government continues to resist the idea of inherent self-government, but it is a start. In the meantime, numerous bands are taking control of at least part of their system, on the basis that you do what you can.

In 1969, when the White Paper was presented, it would have seemed ludicrous to suggest that in twenty-five years some Canadian Native people would be well on their way to achieving meaningful self-government and that for others the possibility could seriously be discussed. The Two Row Wampum Belt may yet become a meaningful symbol of the Canadian experience.

Recommended Readings

Asch, Michael

1984 *Home and Native Land: Aboriginal Rights and the Canadian Constitution.* Toronto: Methuen.

An analysis of the political rights of Aboriginal peoples as they have been conceived and developed by Native groups, the Canadian courts, and the federal government.

Dosman, E.J.

1972 *Indians: The Urban Dilemma.* Toronto: McClelland and Stewart.

Delineates connections between reserve policy and urban life, the adaptive strategies of different social classes, and the impact of various social agencies.

Francis, Daniel

1992 *The Imaginary Indian: The Image of the Indian in Canadian Culture.* Vancouver: Arsenal Pulp Press.

An exploration of the roots of our images about Native people and the current realities flowing from those ideas.

Frideres, J.S.

1993 *Native People in Canada: Contemporary Conflicts*, 4th edition. Scarborough, Ont.: Prentice-Hall.

An historical and sociological analysis of the legal, demographic, and social status of Canadian Native people.

Goddard, John

1991 *Last Stand of the Lubicon Cree.* Vancouver: Douglas & McIntyre.

A detailed account of Canada's best-known case of failure to come to agreement on a land claims settlement.

Little Bear, Leroy, Menno Boldt, and J.A. Long, eds.

1984 *Pathways to Self-determination: Canadian Indians and the Canadian State.* Toronto: University of Toronto Press.

A collection of papers, the majority by Indians, concerning the political philosophy and practical problems of achieving self-determination.

Manuel, George, and Michael Posluns

1974 *The Fourth World: An Indian Reality.* Don Mills: Collier-Macmillan.
A profound, simple, and influential combination of political philosophy and personal narrative. Essential reading for the serious student and a marvellous starting point for the novice.

McFarlane, Peter

1993 *Brotherhood to Nationhood: George Manuel and the Making of the Modern Indian Movement.* Toronto: Between the Lines.
A study of the life of George Manuel and his impact on the Canadian Indian movement.

Morse, B.W., ed.

1985 *Aboriginal Peoples and the Law: Indian, Metis and Inuit Rights in Canada.* Ottawa: Carleton University Press.
This book has replaced Cumming and Mickenberg's now somewhat dated *Native Rights in Canada* as the standard work on the topic.

Perpetual, Jeanne, and Sylvia Vance

1993 *Writing the Circle: Native Women of Western Canada – An Anthology.* Edmonton: NeWest.
Over fifty Indian and Metis women write about their lives, to great effect.

Ponting, J.R., and R. Gibbins

1980 *Out of Irrelevance: A Sociopolitical Introduction to Indian Affairs in Canada.* Toronto: Butterworths.
A detailed examination of the history, structure, personnel, and interrelations of DIAND and the National Indian Brotherhood.

Tanner, Adrian, ed.

1983 *The Politics of Indianness: Case Studies of Native Ethnopolitics in Canada.* Social and Economic Papers No. 12, Institute of Social and Economic Research. St. John's: Memorial University of Newfoundland.
A review essay on the nature of political dependency followed by case studies on the Micmac, a Dene community, and a provincial Indian association.

Tennant, Paul

1990 *Aboriginal Peoples and Politics: The Indian Land Question in British Columbia, 1849-1989.* Vancouver: University of British Columbia Press.
A detailed political history of the treatment of Indian lands in a complex jurisdiction.

Tester, Frank James, and Peter Kulchyski

1994 *Tammarnit (Mistakes): Inuit Relocation in the Eastern Arctic, 1939-63.* Vancouver: University of British Columbia Press.
A broad examination of the evolution of Canadian Aboriginal policy in the North during the formative stage of the modern era.

Waldram, James B.

1988 *As Long as the Rivers Run: Hydroelectric Development and Native Communities in Western Canada.* Winnipeg: University of Manitoba Press.
Modern economic development projects are examined in the context of the historic relationship between the crown and the colonized.

Weaver, S.M.

1981 *Making Canadian Indian Policy: The Hidden Agenda 1968-1970.* Toronto: University of Toronto Press.
The definitive study of how the 1969 White Paper came to be; reveals the government's internal debate over policy formation.

Additional References Cited

Asch, Michael, and Patrick Macklem

1991 "Aboriginal rights and Canadian sovereignty: an essay on *R. v. Sparrow*," *Alberta Law Review*, 29: 498-517.

DIAND

1992 *Basic Departmental Data.* Ottawa: Ministry of Supply and Services.

O'Malley, Martin

1980 "Without reservation," *Canadian Business* (April): 37-41.

Trudeau, P.E.

1969 "Remarks on aboriginal and treaty rights," in P.A. Cumming and N.H. Mickenberg, eds., *Native Rights in Canada*, 2nd edition. Toronto: General Publishing, 1972.

GLOSSARY

affinal Related by marriage.

allotment in severalty A form of landholding in which single pieces of land are owned by individuals, as opposed to various forms of communal ownership.

autochthonous Aboriginal, indigenous.

babiche Thin, dehaired strips of rawhide used in the manufacture of various artifacts, such as snowshoes and fish nets.

bast The inner bark of trees, or fibre obtained therefrom.

bola A hunting instrument or weapon consisting of two or three stone or metal balls joined by thongs; when successfully hurled, it entangles the legs of its prey.

bilocal residence Post-marital residence with or near the family of either the wife or husband.

cognatic Descent rules and groups formed by the operation of such rules in which descent is reckoned through both male and female links, most commonly in the form either of bilateral descent (reckoned through equal affiliation with the relatives of one's father and mother) or of ambilineal descent (reckoned through either male or female links).

consanguine A "blood" relative.

ecotone A transitional zone between two environmental types.

endogamy Marriage within one's social group.

ethnography 1. The fieldwork method of cultural anthropology in which a specific group is intensively studied through participation in their daily lives. 2. A study reporting the results of such fieldwork.

ethnology The theoretical method of cultural anthropology; the study of human behaviour generally through cross-cultural comparisons.

exogamy Marriage outside of one's social group, typically a clan or lineage.

extended family A social group consisting of near relatives in addition to the central conjugal unit and their offspring.

factor A person who carries on business transactions for another; specifically, a senior field rank in the Hudson's Bay Company.

gentrian Pertaining to any of a number of colourful birds with limited ability to fly, particularly the turkey.

leister A barbed, three-pronged fish spear.

matrilineal Pertaining to descent traced through the female line (children of both sexes are assigned membership in the kin group of their mother).

matrilocal Post-marital residence being with the family of the wife's mother.

nuclear family A domestic group consisting of a wife, husband, and their children.

ossuary A place where bones of the dead are deposited.

patrilineal Descent through the male line; children belong to the father's kin group.

patrilocal A couple living with or near the husband's father.

polygyny That form of plural marriage (polygamy) in which one man marries two or more women.

primogeniture The pattern whereby the eldest child, or the eldest son, inherits particular rights.

totem Derived from an Ojibway word referring to relatives, the term has primary reference to animist notions linking contemporary kinship groups to animals, natural objects, or natural phenomena from whom various rights and obligations are derived through descent.

unilineal Pertaining to descent traced exclusively through either the father's or the mother's line.

usufruct Literally, to use the fruit; the right to make use of and to benefit from that which is not, strictly speaking, owned. Typically this might entail the right to hunt, fish, trap, or otherwise harvest the resources on a tract of land.

weir A fence-like structure placed across a stream or inlet; in conjunction with fish traps, it facilitates the efficient harvesting of fish.

INDEX